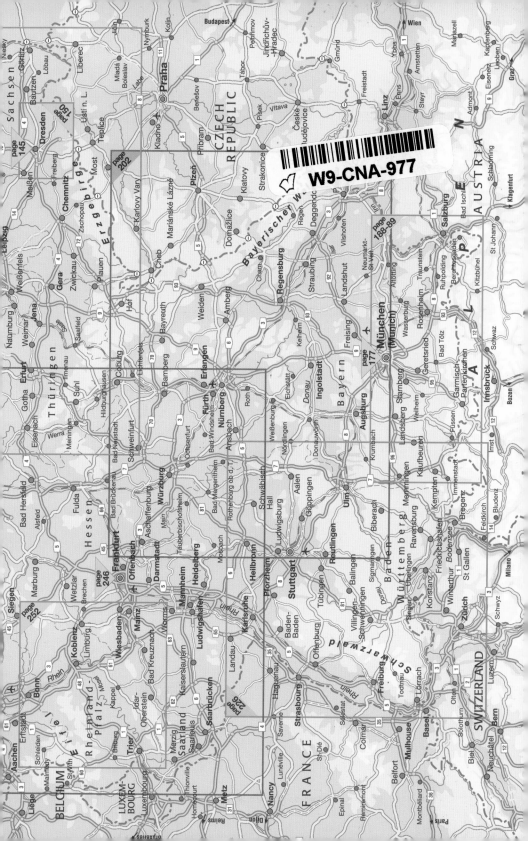

GERMANY

APA PUBLICATIONS L

Part of the Langenscheidt Publishing Group

INSIGHT GUIDE
GERMANY

ABOUT THIS BOOK

Editorial
Project Editors
Tony Halliday
Series Editor
Dorothy Stannard
Picture Manager
Steven Lawrence

Distribution

UK & Ireland
GeoCenter International Ltd
Meridian House, Churchill Way West
Basingstoke, Hampshire RG21 6YR
Fax: (44) 1256 817988

United States
Langenscheidt Publishers, Inc.
36–36 33rd Street, 4th Floor
Long Island City, NY 11106
Fax: 1 (718) 784 0640

Australia
Universal Publishers
1 Waterloo Road
Macquarie Park, NSW 2113
Fax: (61) 2 9888 9074

New Zealand
Hema Maps New Zealand Ltd (HNZ)
Unit D, 24 Ra ORA Drive
East Tamaki, Auckland
Fax: (64) 9 273 6479

Worldwide
Apa Publications GmbH & Co.
Verlag KG (Singapore branch)
38 Joo Koon Road, Singapore 628990
Tel: (65) 6865 1600. Fax: (65) 6861 6438

Printing

Insight Print Services (Pte) Ltd
38 Joo Koon Road, Singapore 628990
Tel: (65) 6865 1600. Fax: (65) 6861 6438

©2009 Apa Publications GmbH & Co.
Verlag KG (Singapore branch)
All Rights Reserved
First Edition 1990
Third Edition (updated) 2008

CONTACTING THE EDITORS
We would appreciate it if readers
would alert us to errors or out-
dated information by writing to:
Insight Guides, P.O. Box 7910,
London SE1 1WE, England.
Fax: (44) 20 7403 0290.
insight@apaguide.co.uk

www.insightguides.com

The first Insight Guide pioneered the use of creative full-colour photography in travel guides in 1970. Since then, we have expanded our range to cater for our readers' need not only for reliable information about their chosen destination but also for a real understanding of the culture and workings of that destination. Now, when the internet can supply inexhaustible (but not always reliable) facts, our books marry text and pictures to provide those much more elusive qualities: knowledge and discernment. To achieve this, they rely heavily on the authority of locally based writers and photographers.

How to use this book
The book is structured both to convey an understanding of the country and its culture and to guide readers through its sights:

◆ To understand Germany today, you need to know something of its past. The first section of this book covers the country's history and culture in lively, authoritative essays written by specialists.

◆ The central Places section provides a full rundown of all the attractions worth seeing. The main places of interest are coordinated by number with full-colour maps.

◆ The Travel Tips listings section provides a convenient point of reference for information on travel, hotels, restaurants, shops and festivals. Information may be located quickly by using the index printed on the back cover flap – and the flaps are designed to serve as bookmarks.

Neuschwanstein Castle.

The contributors

Edited by **Tony Halliday**, this new edition builds on past editions which have evolved to take account of the enormous changes that have taken place in Germany in recent years.

The history section, including articles by **Roger Jopp**, **Martin Clemens** and **Herbert Ammon**, was given a fresh focus by **Michael Ivory**, who also compiled the Decisive Dates and wrote "A Golden Age", based on original work by **Sven Hanuschek**, author of the feature on "German Film". The topical "Germany Today" was written by **Anne Midgette**, who also provided features on cuisine, modern art and the performing arts, as well as the "Festivals" and "Great Art Masters" picture stories and many of the smaller panels. **Stephen Brook** wrote about wine.

The chapters on Berlin and Potsdam were written by **Petra Dubilski** and revised by **Christiane Petri**, who also provided short pieces on the Babelsberg Film Studios, the Berlin Wall and the architect Karl Friedrich Schinkel. The articles describing the new federal states in the east (most originated by **Wieland Giebel**) have been updated by **Günther Wessel** who also revised several chapters on the old Federal Republic. The chapters on the Mecklenburg Lakes and the Baltic Coast were originally written by **Thomas Gebhardt**; **Bettina Schumann** wrote The North Sea Coast; and **Horst Kuhley** contributed the chapters on Hamburg and Lübeck to Flensburg.

Other areas of the country are described by **Joachim Beust** (Black Forest); **Carla Meyer** (Munich, Franconia and Heidelberg); **May Hoff** (The Alps and Lake Constance); **Maja Specht** (Romantic Road); **Dieter Vogel** (Rhine and Moselle); **Monika Römer** (Road to Cologne); **Walter Jakobs** (Ruhr) and **Reinhard Böhme** (Fairy-tale Road). **Michael Bienert** wrote the features on the VW Beetle and Goethe. **Trudie Trox** describes the Dinkelsbühl Kinderzeche; **Simon Holhäuser** writes about cuckoo clocks; **Christine Rettenmeier** provided features on Bavarian architecture, glassmaking and Graff Zeppelin; **Rita Henss** wrote about Frankfurt and the Seven States; and **Ortrun Egelkraut** compiled the Travel Tips.

This latest update was undertaken by **Trudie Trox**, who contributed The Best of Germany, and coordinated and edited by **Alexia Georgiou**.

Map Legend

— ·· —	International Boundary
— — —	State Boundary
⊖	Border Crossing
— · —	National Park/Reserve
— — —	Ferry Route
Ⓢ	S-Bahn
Ⓤ	U-Bahn
✈ ✈	Airport:International/Regional
🚌	Bus Station
P	Parking
❶	Tourist Information
✉	Post Office
† ⛪	Church / Ruins
†	Monastery
☾	Mosque
✡	Synagogue
🏰	Castle / Ruins
∴	Archaeological Site
∩	Cave
⚑	Statue/Monument
★	Place of Interest

The main places of interest in the Places section are coordinated by number with a full-colour map (e.g. ❶), and a symbol at the top of every right-hand page tells you where to find the map.

INSIGHT GUIDE
GERMANY

CONTENTS

Maps

A map of Germany is on the
front flap; a plan of the Berlin
subway is on the back flap

Introduction

History

Features

Places

Roland guards
the market place
in Bremen.

Travel Tips

THE BEST OF GERMANY

Romantic castles, medieval towns, electric and evolving Berlin, hearty fare and refreshing beers, the regained splendour of Dresden and the crystal-clear vistas of the Bavarian Alps... Here, at a glance, are our recommendations for your visit

TOP ATTRACTIONS

● **Cologne Cathedral.** Germany's most spectacular cathedral and a masterpiece of Gothic architecture, its treasures include the Shrine of the Magi. *See page 264.*

● **The Berlin Wall.** It divided Berlin for nearly 30 years, but parts can still be seen: at the East-Side Gallery in Friedrichshain, a 1.3-km stretch has been saved. *See page 100.*

● **Oktoberfest, Munich.** The world's largest fair, a 16-day event in September where revellers gather in huge tents to eat, drink beer and be merry. *See page 175.*

● **Jewish Museum, Berlin.** The spectacular building houses a unique presentation of Jewish culture and testimonies of Judeo-German history. *See page 110.*

● **Lake Constance.** One Lake, three states sharing its shores: Germany, Austria and Switzerland. Visit picturesque Konstanz and Lindau, the Zeppelin Museum in Friedrichshafen, or board one of the ferries that ply the lake. *See page 225.*

● **Schloss Sanssouci, Potsdam.** This small palace is a stunner thanks to its monumental flight of terraces, designed by Frederick the Great in 1744. *See page 117.*

● **Rhine Valley.** Flanked by gentle vineyards or dramatic outcrops and crowned by the odd castle, the stretch from Rüdesheim to Koblenz is the epitome of German Romanticism. *See page 253.*

● **Pinakotheken, Munich.** Baroque and Renaissance paintings in the Alte Pinakothek, 19th- and early 20th-century collections in the Neue Pinakothek, contemporary installations in the Pinakothek der Moderne. *See page 183.*

● **Heidelberg.** With the Romantic movement, the castle – which took 400 years to build but which the Thirty Years' War left in ruins – captured the public imagination. *See page 282.*

● **Sächsische Schweiz** (Little Switzerland of Saxony). Take a trip to the Bastei to experience this bizarre landscape of eroded sandstone along the Elbe. *See page 153.*

ABOVE: Glorious Sanssouci.
LEFT: Berlin Wall fragment.
BELOW: Cologne Cathedral.

BEST ART COLLECTIONS

- **Kunsthalle Tübingen.** Not one of your 'usual' showcases for invaluable collections, its exhibitions garner international praise. *See page 236.*
- **Museum Ludwig, Cologne.** Based on the private collection of the late Peter Ludwig, chocolate factory owner, this first-class museum traces the evolution of European and American art from the 19th to the 20th century. *See page 267.*
- **Staatsgalerie, Stuttgart.** A fantastic array of European Art from the 14th to the 20th century, exquisitely presented in a post-modern building. *See page 236.*
- **Römisch-Germanisches Museum,**

Cologne. Look back over 2000 years into the glorious past of the wealthy Roman settlement of Colonia. *See page 266.*
- **Wallraf-Richartz-Museum, Cologne.** Collections of old German masters from the 14th to the 16th century and the French impressionists too. *See page 268.*

SUPER-MUSEUMS

- **Deutsches Museum, Munich.** From a coal mine to microchips and the lightning experiment in the Faraday cage – 15,000 exhibits make this the biggest museum in the world. *See page 179.*
- **Museumsinsel, Berlin.** Not just one museum but a whole bunch, spanning oriental and Roman antiquities to 20th-century art. *See page 107.*

- **Museumsufer Frankfurt.** Cultures of the world, cinema, architecture, communication, applied arts, 19th and 20th century art – the Museumsufer has it all. *See page 248.*

NORTHERN GEMS

- **Greetsiel** is the image of a small, unpretentious harbour village on the North Sea coast, full of colour and bustling with life. *See page 321.*
- **Halligen Islands.** The most untouched and unusual islets in the Wattenmeer (tidal zone) of the North Frisian Islands: farmhouses on these 'molehills' sit just above the high-tide mark. *See page 326.*
- **Altes Land.** Driving from Hamburg to Stade in spring is like being swallowed up by a big cloud of blossom. The Altes Land is the biggest fruit-growing area in Germany, even prettier

for its half-timbered houses. *See page 317.*
- **Rügen.** Grand white cliffs, wide sandy beaches and tree-lined alleys of chestnut and lime have attracted many painters to Germany's largest island. *See page 343.*
- **Stade** prides itself on the typically northern German redbrick architecture of its lovely historic centre, contained within the Burggraben (old moat). *See page 318.*
- **Stralsund Oceanographic Museum.** In a futuristic shell of contemporary architecture visitors experience the secrets of marine life. *See page 342.*

ABOVE LEFT: Albrecht Durer's *Pfeifer und Trommler* (circa 1504), Wallraf-Richartz Museum. **ABOVE RIGHT:** Stade. **LEFT:** working steam engine (1862) at the Deutsches Museum.

8

MOST PICTURESQUE TOWNS

- **Alsfeld** brings to mind a fairytale, all carved corner-posts and half-timbered houses dating from the 14th to the 16th century. *See page 290.*
- **Arnstadt.** One of the most beautifully pre-served historic centres in Germany, with fine Renaissance architec-ture, and also one of the oldest – first cited in 704. *See page 166.*
- **Dinkelsbühl,** entered by one of its four main gates, is a charming ensemble of half-tim-bered houses and narrow lanes towered over by the parish church of St George. *See page 210.*
- **Dresden.** Once called 'Florence on the Elbe',

its baroque elegance has been revived by enormous renovation programmes. Visit the Semperoper, the Zwinger and the rebuilt Frauenkirche. *See page 144.*
- **Meersburg** on Lake Constance. Its elegant houses with Gothic and Baroque gables cluster around two castles, the oldest dating from Merovin-gian times. *See page 228.*
- **Rothenburg ob der Tauber,** on the Ro-mantic Road. The strong wall enclosing Gothic and Renais-sance buildings re-flects Rothenburg's medieval status as a wealthy imperial town. *See page 211.*

THE FOLLIES OF LUDWIG II

- **Linderhof,** a cosy palace far from the crowds of the Munich Residence. Here King Ludwig II could live his dreams in a setting worthy of Wagner's operas. *See page 195.*
- **Neuschwanstein.** Me-dieval in style but built in the 19th century, with an oriental inte-rior and a dramatic alpine backdrop: a fairytale castle for a fairytale king. *See page 196.*

- **Herrenchiemsee.** The Bavarian king had Versailles in mind when he had this castle built on a wooded is-land in Lake Chiem-see. *See page 187.*

TOP: the stunning interior of Dresden's reconstructed Frauenkirche. **ABOVE LEFT:** Neuschwanstein Castle, a fairytale come true. **ABOVE RIGHT:** Munich brew.

BEST FOOD AND DRINK

- **Bread and rolls** come in an overwhelming selection. Slow-baked, chocolate brown Pumpernickel origi-nates from Westphalia, while Bavaria is famous for its shiny Brezeln, studded with coarse salt.
- **Beer.** From pale draught lagers to quench the thirst and the fresh sparkle of yeasty Weissbier, to slightly sweetish, often stronger Dunkles Bier (dark beer) or extra strong Starkbier, originally brewed for Lent.
- **Sausages** are a staple on all menus and at festivals, markets and fairs. Frankfurters are the most common, but don't miss grilled Bratwürste.
- **Asparagus.** From May until 24th June

this vegetable is a spring delicacy, served with Hollandaise sauce, ham or gam-mon and new potatoes.
- *Schwarzwälder Kirschtorte* (**Black Forest Cherry Gâteau**) is the queen of cakes for the late-morning or afternoon tradition of *Kaffee und Kuchen* (coffee and cake).
- **Wine.** Forget all about Liebfrauenmilch and try the honest crus of the ambitious young winegrowers in Fran-conia, Saxonia, and the Rhine and Moselle.

GREAT LANDSCAPES

● **Donaudurchbruch.** Near the monastery of Weltenburg the river Danube channels its course through massive limestone, cutting an impressive gorge. *See page 201.*

● **Königssee.** This crystal-clear, deep alpine lake with its tiny chapel of St Barholomä is closed in by majestic mountains, foremost the ragged Watzmann. *See page 189.*

● **Mecklenburgische Seenplatte.** With the Müritz national park as its core, this lakeland area has become a incomparable home to wildlife such as sea eagles, opreys, black storks and even rare cranes. *See page 125.*

● **Spreewald.** Since 1991 a UNESCO biosphere reserve, this lowland area crisscrossed by a labyrinth of streams and canals is a wonderfully lush and shady landscape, ideally experienced by boat. *See page 142.*

● **Spessart.** Half-way between Frankfurt and Würzburg this region boasts extensive woods of oak and beech interspersed with idyllic meadows. *See page 287.*

ABOVE: the clear water and skies of the Alps at Königssee. **RIGHT:** at Charlottenburg Palace.

BEST CASTLES AND PALACES

● **Burg Eltz.** With the river Eltz surrounding it on three sides and protected by massive walls and towers, this is the embodiment of the ideal medieval castle. *See page 257.*

● **Schloss Charlottenburg, Berlin.** The former residence of the Prussian royal family, embedded in a magnificent park, contains

top-notch art collections. *See page 111.*

● **Schloss Güstrow.** A unique Renaissance ensemble of palace and park with rooms showing a precious collection of medieval and Renaissance art. *See page 340.*

● **Schloss Nymphenburg, Munich.** The late-baroque palace with its gardens and beautiful pavilions allows a glimpse of its 18th-century heyday. *See page 183.*

● **Wartburg.** Martin Luther found refuge in this medieval castle above the village of Eisenach; Goethe famously campaigned for its restoration. *See page 169.*

● **Würzburger Residenz.** The bishops of Würzburg had the financial clout to commision this masterpiece of baroque decor. *See page 215.*

MONEY-SAVING TIPS

Tourist cards The larger cities as well as certain regions offer cards which are valid for travel on public transport and give free or reduced admission to museums and attractions, and even discounts in certain restaurants. When you arrive at the airport, check whether the card is already valid for your journey into town. *See page 373.*

Public transport For hopping around town, day passes for buses, trams and the metro can make for big savings. For trains, enquire about low-price regional and weekend tickets. There are always reductions for families and mini-groups. *See page 349.*

Free admission Many museums and art galleries have free or reduced admission on a certain day of the week, often Sunday, or sometimes for the last hours on the late-closing day. *See page 373.*

Hotel weekend arrangements Many city hotels which mainly cater to business travellers offer attractive weekend rates for a 2- to 3-night stay, sometimes even including a tourist card or a city tour .

Tagesmenü A restaurant's daily changing menu, the *Tageskarte*, reflects what fruits and vegetables are in season. For lunch, even posh restaurants normally include a couple of low-price two- or three-course set meals, the *Tagesmenü*, or just a main course, the *Tagesgericht*.

Cinemas Many cinemas have reduced ticket prices at the beginning of the week.

THE CHANGING FACE OF GERMANY

Culture and landscape combine in Germany to provide a travel destination of exceptional variety

Germany, politically on Europe's centre stage, is one of the classic tourist destinations. A turbulent history, ever-changing landscapes, unspoilt nature reserves and a wealth of impressive cultural attractions provide a varied menu, and the ease with which English is spoken makes it a more accessible destination than many other European countries.

Its cosmopolitan cities throb with life, their boulevards lined with cafés, pubs, bars and discos inviting you to drop in and stay a while. Hamburg and Berlin are especially famous for their nightlife and "closing time" is an unknown phrase.

Some of the world's greatest art can be found in Germany's magnificent museums, which also organise regular exhibitions of historical and contemporary significance. During World War II the cities were badly bombed, but most of the architecturally important buildings have been reconstructed or – miraculously – survived undamaged. Those which largely escaped the bombing include Cologne Cathedral, which by the end of the war towered practically unscathed among the surrounding ruins (mirroring the survival of St Paul's Cathedral in London). Meanwhile, in the centre of the lovely baroque city of Augustus the Strong, Dresden's Church of Our Lady has regained much of its pre-war splendour. And Berlin has become one large building site as the city rediscovers its role as the German capital and embellishes itself with innovative architecture.

In the country's many castles and palaces – built on the choicest sites – the visitor can wander in the landscaped parks in which they're set and escape into the dreamlike world of knights and princes. Medieval towns beckon visitors into the past, and the open-air museums that are such a feature of the German countryside also offer a fascinating look into the life of bygone ages.

Leisure time is cherished by Germans, many of whom relish outdoor sports. The mountain terrain of the Alps is ideal for climbing, mountain biking, hang-gliding and skiing, while yachting enthusiasts, windsurfers and beach fans make for the seashores of the north and the banks of the country's lakes.

Not so well known are the tranquil but no less attractive landscapes of the Mecklenburger Seenplatte (Lake District), the Sächsische Schweiz (Saxony's "Little Switzerland"), or the heavily wooded upland tracts of the Spessart, Rhön and Odenwald. They can be explored by canoe or on foot, on excursions which end within the welcoming walls of a typical German country inn. ❏

PRECEDING PAGES: Augustus the Strong as Golden Horseman in Dresden (title page); Oktoberfest parade in Munich; low tide on the North Sea mud flats.
LEFT: an artist and his work, observed in Hamburg.

Decisive Dates

Circa **10,000 BC:** As climatic conditions become milder towards the end of the Ice Age, groups of Upper Palaeolithic hunter-gathers move northwards across Germany in pursuit of reindeer.

Circa **4,000 BC:** Areas of easily worked soil have been cleared of primeval forest and are cultivated by Neolithic people in Rhineland and elsewhere. These first farmers are succeeded by Bronze Age people and then, in the Iron Age, by Celts.

Circa **500 BC:** The Celts begin to suffer the depredations of Germanic tribespeople moving southwards from the Baltic coast and islands.

ROMAN AND HOLY ROMAN EMPIRES

58 BC: The attempt by Germans to move westwards into Roman-dominated Gaul is blocked by Julius Caesar, who drives them back across the Rhine.

AD 9: The Germans frustrate the Roman wish to extend their frontier eastward to the River Elbe in the Battle of the Teutoburger Wald, in which warriors led by Hermann destroy three legions commanded by Varus. The Romans stabilise their domain with the *limes*, a line of fortifications linking the Rhine and the Danube.

Late 5th–early 6th century: Clovis (or Chlodwig), the Merovingian king of the Franks, establishes a power-ful kingdom between the Rhine and the Seine and extends its territory far into present-day Germany.

800: The Frankish ruler Charlemagne (Karl der Grosse) is anointed Holy Roman Emperor by the Pope.

843: The Treaty of Verdun weakens Charlemagne's unified empire by dividing it into three realms. The eastern Franks are now a recognisably German nation.

MEDIEVAL GERMANY

955: Otto the Great is crowned emperor by the Pope, but the following centuries are marked by a struggle between Papacy and Empire, in which successive popes undermine the Emperor's power by supporting his enemies, among them princes and archbishops.

1152–90: Reign of Frederick Barbarossa of the Hohenstaufen dynasty, an enthusiastic Crusader who raises the power and prestige of the empire.

1241: The formation of the Hanseatic League linking ports and trading cities confirms German economic dominance of the North Sea and Baltic coasts.

1356: The constitutional means whereby the Emperor is chosen is established by the Golden Bull. The four princes and three archbishops who make up the electoral college see their power significantly enhanced.

1410: The Teutonic Knights, responsible for much of the German settlement of the Baltic, are defeated by Poles and Lithuanians at the Battle of Tannenberg.

REFORMATION AND WARS OF RELIGION

1517: Augustinian monk Martin Luther nails his 95 theses to the door of the church at Wittenberg, marking the beginning of the Reformation. Though Luther is subsequently excommunicated, he completes his translation of the Bible into German in the castle of Wartburg under the protection of the Duke of Saxony.

1555: The Peace of Augsburg brings religious wars to a temporary end and acknowledges the division of Germany into a multitude of Catholic or Protestant states.

1618–48: Thirty Years' War renews religious conflict. Although drawing in Denmark, Sweden and France, it is almost entirely fought in Germany. The land is left devastated and much of the Empire's borderland (Netherlands, Alsace) passes into the hands of foreign powers.

THE RISE OF PRUSSIA

1701: The granting of the title "King" to the Hohenzollern Elector of Prussia marks the rise to power of this hitherto minor state, based on a centralised administration and well-disciplined standing army.

Under Frederick the Great (1740–86) Prussia acquires Silesia and participates in the partition of Poland.

1806: Napoleon Bonaparte absorbs the Rhineland and establishes a chain of puppet states stretching from Bavaria in the south to Westphalia in the north.

1813: Germany is suffused with nationalistic feeling and Prussia leads a coalition to victory over the French army at the "Battle of Nations" near Leipzig.

1815: The Congress of Vienna confirms Prussia as the pre-eminent power in northern Germany and establishes the Germanic Confederation consisting of 35 states and four free cities.

THE MOVE TO UNITY

1834: A customs union, the Zollverein, removes barriers to commerce between the German states.

1848–49: The "Year of Revolutions" awakens hopes of a liberal, united Germany, but the National Assembly meeting in Frankfurt proves indecisive and is eventually dissolved by the threat of military force.

1866: The Prussian Chancellor, Bismarck, provokes war with Austria. Following the defeat of the Austrian army at Königgrätz, Austria is excluded from German affairs, which from now on are dominated by Prussia.

1871: The French Emperor, Napoleon III, is lured into war by Bismarck. Victory over the French leads to the unification of Germany under Prussian leadership.

DISASTERS AND DIVISIONS

1914–18: The outbreak of World War I. Initial German successes quickly give way to the attrition of trench warfare. In October 1918, Germany requests an armistice and Emperor Wilhelm II goes into exile.

1918–33: The democratic Weimar Republic is undermined by the rise of nationalism and chauvinism, which finds its focus in the National Socialist Workers Party led by Austrian-born Adolf Hitler.

1933–45: The totalitarian Third Reich is led by Hitler into rearmament, territorial conquest and, in 1939, into war. A run of German military successes comes to an end at the battles of Stalingrad and Alamein and the war finishes with Hitler's suicide and Nazi Germany's unconditional surrender in May 1945. The surviving Nazi leaders are indicted and tried at the Nuremburg Trials.

1949: Germany divides into the Federal Republic of Germany in the west and the Communist German Democratic Republic (GDR) in the east.

PRECEDING PAGES: medieval Cologne. **LEFT:** Teutonic Knights at a tournament. **RIGHT:** Konrad Adenauer, first Chancellor of the Federal Republic of Germany.

1961: The GDR builds the Berlin Wall to stop the exodus of its population to the free and affluent West.

REUNIFICATION

1989–99: The Berlin Wall demolished and, in 1990, the two Germanys are reunited. In 1994, Russian, British and French forces withdraw from Berlin. In 1999 Germany adopts the euro. The German Parliament moves back to Berlin.

2000: Millennium Expo 2000; Hanover hosts 40 million guests from all over the world.

2002: Heavy rainfall causes destructive flooding.

2004: Horst Koehler is elected president.

2005: Parliament ratifies EU constitution. Dresden's iconic Frauenkirche church is reconsecrated 60 years after it was razed by Allied bombers in World War II. Angela Merkel, leader of the conservative Christian Democrats (CDU), takes over from Gerhard Schroeder to become Germany's first female chancellor. She heads a "grand coalition" between the CDU, CSU and SPD.

2006: Due to extreme snowfall, roof collapses at a Bavarian ice rink, resulting in over a dozen fatalities. Football World Cup held in Germany.

2007: *The Lives of Others* by German film director Florian Henckel von Donnersmarck wins the Oscar for Best Foreign Film.

2008: A new non-smoking law bans smoking in restaurants and pubs. ❑

CHURCH, EMPERORS AND KINGS

From the Dark Ages to the Enlightenment, Germany's turbulent history

mirrors the rise and fall of the continent's great dynasties

Parts of the territory of present-day Germany have been inhabited for a very long time indeed. Half a million years ago, *homo heidelbergensis* roamed near the Neckar Valley in the vicinity of today's Heidelberg, while the bones of famous Neanderthal Man from the countryside near Düsseldorf date from about 50,000 years ago. In the centuries before the Romans began to take an interest in the lands to the north of the Alps, the advanced Celtic *La Tène* culture dominated a vast area stretching from northern France to the Balkans.

The Celts built cities which the Romans called *oppida*; the largest oppidum south of the Danube was located near present-day Malching, a small town near Ingolstadt in Bavaria. North of the Celtic domain lived Germanic tribes, their origins obscure. To the Celts these Germans were a constant thorn in the flesh as they pushed south and attempted to subjugate Celtic territory. The Celts were also subject to pressure from the Romans, who completed their conquest of Celtic Gaul in 58 BC and then moved to secure their frontier against the Germanic tribes to the east and north.

In AD 60 the Roman historian Tacitus characterised the Germans thus: "They have blue eyes and red hair, and although they have an impressive build and are strong fighters, they are not given to hard graft." These German tribesmen must indeed have appeared unruly and uncultured to the sophisticated Romans. There were no cities and agriculture was not developed much beyond subsistence level.

The Romans under Emperor Augustus planned to annex troublesome Germania, but after the disastrous defeat of three of the Empire's finest legions at the Battle of the Teutoburger Wald in AD 9 by the Cheruscan leader Arminius (Hermann), the Romans opted to withdraw and accept the Rhine and the Danube as the frontier of the empire. They secured their territory by building

a 550-km (350-mile) line of fortifications, known as the *limes* (now a World Heritage Site), linking the two rivers. Along this distant frontier, cities such as Cologne (Colonia Agrippinensis), Mainz (Mogontiacum), Trier (Augusta Treverorum) and Augsburg (Augusta Vindelicorum), were built on the Roman pattern. The "Barbar-

ians" thus came face to face with unimaginable luxury: theatres, public baths, roads, bridges and villas were built in order to make life more bearable for the Romans in remote Germania.

From Clovis to Charlemagne

In the 5th century AD the Germanic tribes pushed westward from the Rhine and southward from the Danube. These movements, part of the great "Migration of the Peoples", helped bring about the collapse of the Roman Empire, though this had not been the intention of tribal leaders who had mostly acknowledged Roman authority and merely wished to enjoy the benefits of Roman prosperity. By the 10th century,

LEFT: the minstrel Walther von der Vogelweide.
RIGHT: Roman watchtowers like this one were strung out along the *limes*.

this westward and southward movement had ceased, and the linguistic boundary between Germanic dialects and the descendants of Latin such as French and Italian was more or less as it is today. The names of many of the tribal kingdoms of the period have persisted into modern times, giving us both France (the kingdom of the Franks) and the French name for Germany, Allemagne (the realm of the Alemanii), as well as Saxony, Swabia and Bavaria. The restlessness of the Germans was paralleled in the east by the westward movement of Slavonic peoples, who by the 6th century had reached the line of the River Elbe.

The most prominent of the early Germanic kingdoms was that of the Franks, who, having settled in what is now Belgium, emerged as a major power. Their success was due to their leader, Clovis, from the house of Merovingia. In the 30 years of his rule, he transformed his warriors into a mighty army and extended his realm eastwards as far as the Weser, westwards and southwards as far as the Atlantic and Spain. Wherever the Franks advanced, they found the country firmly in the control of bishops, because Christianity had been the official state religion of the Roman Empire ever since AD 380. Doing business with the bishops was of mutual advantage. After Clovis was baptised

IMPERIAL AACHEN

Charlemagne established his capital and principal court at Aachen, where he built a magnificent palace and founded an academy to which many of the greatest scholars of the age were invited. They included his trusted advisor, Alcuin of York.

in AD 496, he knew he could rely on the support of the bishops, and they, in return, could reinforce their position through the power and authority of the king.

From AD 768 onwards, it was Charlemagne who guided the fortunes of the largest empire in the western world. Like his predecessors, he maintained no fixed residence, preferring to travel through the country with his entourage and to live on his various estates. Through a long series of bloody and cruel campaigns, it took Charlemagne more than 30 years to bring the German tribes to heel, to Christianise them and to annex their territory. By the end of his reign only England, southern Spain and southern Italy remained outside his influence.

Charlemagne regarded himself as the legitimate heir of the Roman emperor, and sealed this position by having himself crowned emperor, in Rome by the pope, on Christmas Day AD 800. His most notable achievements were the organisation of the empire's administrative structures and the establishment of its cultural base. He standardised the laws of all the tribes within his realm and divided it into states to which he assigned loyal leaders. He established schools in the monasteries throughout his empire and, with the help of the clergy and the monastery-trained laymen, introduced Latin as the official language of the realm.

The monastery and palace schools taught the art of book illustrating, translated the classics and established libraries. We have these institutions to thank for translations of the writings of Caesar, Tacitus and Juvenal.

The beginnings of German history

Under Charlemagne's rule, the division of the empire into east and west would have been unthinkable. Yet, within 30 years of his death, it became reality. In 843 his grandsons divided the empire between them at the Treaty of Verdun and it is this year that marks the actual beginning of German history. The first king of the Eastern Empire, Ludwig the German

(843–76), ruled over a land which for the first time could be called "German". Forty years after his death his last male descendant died, thus ending the Carolingian dynasty in the eastern empire. The right of succession passed to the king of the Germanic tribe whom Charlemagne had so bitterly fought against, the Saxon Henry I (the Fowler).

It was Henry's son, Otto the Great, whom fate called upon to make one of the most important decisions for the west, namely to defend the realm against the Hungarians. In AD 955 Otto and his army defeated the invaders on the Lechfeld, south of Augsburg (Bavaria).

The other major threat was posed by over-ambitious princes who threatened the empire with disintegration from within. However, Otto mastered this problem through wise choice of associates and by the inclusion of the Catholic Church in the governing process. The bishops could often advance to important political posts, not only because they were educated and good administrators, but also because they had no heirs to threaten the power of the king.

Thus fortified, Otto, just like Charlemagne, succeeded in capturing the iron crown of the Langobard dynasty and intervened in the political chaos in Rome. He was also responsible for bringing the Western Slavs into the fold of the Catholic Church, thus securing the Empire's eastern borders.

Church and emperor

From AD 906 right up until the fall of the empire in 1806, the title of emperor was inseparably linked to that of the German king. The realm came to be called "The Holy Roman Empire of the German Nation", with the status of the emperor being defined as the ruler over "eternal" Rome.

The Carolingians and the Church had co-operated for mutual advantage: Charlemagne made his conquests in the name of the Church and the Church expanded its influence. However effective this partnership was, it carried with it a danger which came to the surface in the 11th and 12th centuries and rocked western Christendom. The Church had taken on an increasing amount of secular responsibility. The

emperor would intervene in the election of the bishop and make sure that only those who were interested in secular power got anywhere in the church. The bishops became prince-bishops, and this secularisation of the Church did not find favour with the Pope in Rome.

The struggle between the Pope and the emperor began with the Investiture Controversy of 1076, when Pope Gregory VII tried to revoke Henry IV's appointment of a new Archbishop of Milan. The Pope was dismissed but hit back by excommunicating the emperor and forbidding him to rule over the German and Italian kingdoms. Henry, whose position was

already weakened by opposition from the nobility, was compelled in 1077 to go down on his knees and beg the Pope for forgiveness.

He won back his position but his authority was severely shaken: the powerful princes no longer recognised the emperor to the extent that they had previously. The title of the king was no longer to be linked to birth but was to be decided by the nobility. Even the outstanding kings of the Hohenstaufen period, Frederick Barbarossa (1152–90), Heinrich VI and Frederick II (1212– 50), ruling in an era considered by many to be the high point of medieval Imperial rule, could not achieve a lasting return to the old order.

LEFT: the German Imperial sceptre.
RIGHT: bust of Charlemagne, founder of the Holy Roman Empire of the German Nation.

The days of chivalry

A dominant figure in the high Middle Ages was the knight. His power challenged by the rise of great dukedoms, the emperor encouraged the formation of a new landed nobility, whose ranks were swelled by inter-marriage with a rising merchant class and administrative officials. At the centre of this new social order, the knight became the bearer of an important new courtly culture that spread through palace, castle and country estate.

HONOUR THY MISTRESS

Greatest of all minstrels was Walther von der Vogelweide (1170–1230). His poems perfectly embodied the virtues of medieval chivalry; in 1204 he outshone all his rivals in the "Battle of the Poets" at Wartburg Castle.

guests to join him in Mainz for a great courtly festival. Similar festivals were held at the Wartburg. The German *Minnesang* was based on a social convention, the literary expression of what was called *Frauendienst*, a code expressing a lover's relation to his mistress. Writing in passionate language but showing the utmost respect and dignity, the *Minnesänger* paid homage to an idealised sweetheart, invariably someone of higher status than the poet himself and thus unattainable.

Courage, strength and dexterity were required of the knight, but so too were the virtues of inner harmony, self-discipline, honour, loyalty and compassion. The whole of Christian Europe subscribed to these ideals, not least because of the experience of the Crusades, which between the 11th and 13th centuries provided a common goal for all Europe's knights.

A literature emerged based on traditional myths and legends, on the songs of wandering minstrels and on Oriental tales picked up in the course of the Crusades. Influenced by the troubadours of France, the *Minnesang* or court lyric enjoyed great popularity. In 1184, for example, Emperor Frederick Barbarossa invited 70,000

Medieval towns and cities

Until the turn of the 1st millennium, the only cities were those that had been established in Roman times. After that time, cities emerged from monastic centres (Munich), castles (Nuremberg), river crossings (Frankfurt) or at the intersections of the few major European trade routes (Cologne). The princes soon came to recognise the advantages of these settlements. Here they could exact customs and taxes and obtain rare goods and excellent craftsmen.

Between 1100 and 1250 the number of towns in Germany increased tenfold. Many of these towns, Berlin, Leipzig and Dresden among them, were founded to the east of the old frontier dividing Germans and Slavs. For much of the Middle Ages, Central and Eastern Europe was the scene of an epic eastward expansion. Driven by population pressure and high land prices, German settlers migrated eastwards in search of cheaper farmland. Fired by religious zeal and anxious for new converts, German churchmen were instrumental in the Christianisation of the Slavs, while Slavonic rulers, impressed by German industriousness, encouraged tradespeople and craftsmen to settle in new towns where German customs prevailed and which were ruled by German law.

Between the Elbe and the Oder, the Slav presence virtually disappeared, leaving only the tiny remnant of the Lusatian Sorbs around Bautzen and Cottbus, who maintain their distinct identity today. Further east, beyond today's German frontier, Pomerania, East Prussia, Silesia and the

LEFT: medieval armour for a virtuous knight.
RIGHT: the Romanesque Maria Laach Monastery.
FAR RIGHT: officer cadet in the Thirty Years' War.

frontier uplands of Bohemia were largely Germanised, and further east still there were flourishing trading cities like Reval (today's Estonian capital of Tallinn) or Lemberg (today's Lvov).

Within towns, every citizen had a right to certain freedoms but inevitably, some were more equal than others. The most important class was that which the town had to thank most for its prosperity, namely the merchants. Initially only their associations were represented on the councils and thus they had all the power. Then, between the 13th and 15th centuries, the craftsmen, organised into guilds, succeeded in gaining their share of power in many town halls.

But many poorer urban dwellers, including maidservants, domestic servants, the illegitimate, beggars and outcasts, remained dependent on the goodwill of the church or charities established by wealthy citizens. Fortunately, the rich had been convinced that only those who gave something to the needy could expect God's mercy. As a result, they often financed hospitals, as well as old people's homes and sometimes housing for the poor.

Originally the Germans were a genuinely free people. However, this all changed in centuries of upheaval punctuated by countless wars. Many small farmers, who found it hard

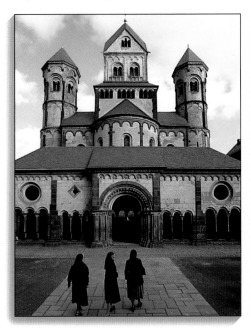

CHURCHES AND CATHEDRALS

Profiting from their country's location in the centre of Europe, Germany's church architects have often been exposed to influences from abroad. Completed in AD 792, Charlemagne's polygonal Palatine Chapel at Aachen owes much to Byzantine models such as the Church of San Vitale in Ravenna, while just over two centuries later, the great Church of St Michael in Hildesheim developed principles first used in French abbeys such as Cluny. The cathedrals at Worms and Speyer, however, together with the Maria Laach monastery in the Rhineland and the Church of the Apostles in Cologne, are all outstanding examples of a distinctly German version of the Romanesque style. In its

magnificent cathedral, Cologne also possesses one of the finest achievements of Gothic architecture. Other cathedrals that owe much to the influence of northern France are Freiburg and Regensburg, while along the Baltic coast the "Brick Gothic" churches of cities such as Lübeck and Stralsund have an identity all their own.

But perhaps the greatest glory of German church architecture was still to come; especially in southern Germany, the power of the Counter-Reformation was exuberantly expressed in any number of superb baroque churches, including the magnificent Vierzehnheiligen by Balthasar Neumann *(see page 219)*.

to make a living when they were continually being called up to fight, were forced to hand over their property to the landowners as a means of buying their way out of military service. They got their land back for cultivation but only in return for dues and services such as building and maintaining roads and helping with the harvest.

Religious devotion and Luther

With their economic and legal position drastically curtailed, many peasants found comfort in the Christian religion, which promised compensation in the next world for earthly

suffering. Their piety was manifest in the many chapels and pilgrimage churches, the worship of relics and the popular religious tracts of the time. This Christian zeal also had its dark side, however, in the persecution of "witches" that spread throughout Europe towards the end of the Middle Ages.

Against this background of religious devotion, the deplorable state of affairs within the church was keenly felt. The moral decline of the papacy, the insatiable greed of the church and the theological ignorance of the clergy were the main objects of criticism. The church exploited believers' fear of purgatory and damnation to obtain the money required for ambitious building projects and the maintenance of a luxurious lifestyle. For a specified sum, anyone could buy a pardon and shorten the time spent in purgatory.

During the 15th and 16th centuries, critical theologians constantly attacked these practices. From 1517 the German monk Martin Luther set about reforming the church through a series of damning theses. Luther denounced the authority of the Pope, renounced the special status of the clergy as mediators between God and man and instead formulated the idea of a general priesthood involving all believers.

Luther found support among all levels of society; among the lower nobility, the townsfolk and the impoverished peasant. His campaign for an end to discrimination against peasants and his battle against the authority of the church in the countryside led to an uprising against all authority. In the spring of 1525, the first monasteries and castles went up in flames in southwest Germany and the rebellion spread like wildfire throughout central Europe. But the peasants were poorly equipped and, in 1526, the revolt was brutally crushed by the superior forces of the nobility. More than 100,000 peasants either died in battle or were subsequently executed.

The unity of the church was now broken and western Christianity was split between the Catholics and the so-called Protestants. The teachings of Luther were a powerful weapon in the hands of those princes seeking independence from the emperor and the Pope, particularly in northern and central Germany. Religion became a territorial matter and the schism was an important factor in the fragmentation of Germany into sovereign states.

A NEW ERA BEGINS

Luther's successes would not have been possible without a changed world view and developments in science, technology and economics. The medieval view that life on earth served merely as a hard test for the eternal life to come changed in the 14th and 15th centuries. In 1445, Johannes Gutenberg invented the printing press, so enabling the population at large to have access to new ideas. Education expanded and in the 15th century a number of universities were founded in Germany (Leipzig 1409, Freiburg 1455), and their curriculum became increasingly devoted to secular subjects. In the cities, reading and writing rooms were established.

The Thirty Years' War

Despite all attempts on the part of the Catholic church to stem the spread of Lutheran Protestantism and to win back lost territory, by 1600 the new sect had become the most powerful religious-political force in Europe. The religious conflict was further exacerbated by the rivalry between the newly established sovereign states and the struggle between the emperor and his princes.

The war was sparked in 1618, when Protestant noblemen threw Catholic councillors from the windows of Prague Castle (the "Defenestration of Prague"). The conflict soon enveloped the whole of Europe. Both sides used mercenaries, who were not averse to swapping allegiances, and were fed and paid from the spoils of war. There was torture and rape, and towns were sacked and pillaged.

After 30 years of war, central Europe was so desolated and exhausted that peace negotiations finally led to agreement. The Treaty of Westphalia brought about recognition for both sides but Germany remained hopelessly divided, with only the emperor and the common language providing a last vestige of unity. The German population had been reduced by one-third. Epidemics were rife, hunger reigned and the Holy Roman Empire had become an empty shell.

Recovery

Germany gradually recovered from the wounds of war and living conditions soon began to improve, promoted by monarchist absolutism which, following the example set by the French king Louis XIV, found favour among many princes. They saw themselves as the centre of the state, appointed by and answerable only to God. Some of the finest achievements in German art and architecture date from this time.

Palaces and parks, such as Nymphenburg just outside Munich, were laid out on the model of Louis XIV's Versailles, generally on a more modest scale permitted within their means. The geometric planning of such palaces and their gardens gave physical expression to the power and new sense of order that such princes had attained.

By far the largest states within the empire were the Austrian Habsburg realm and the Prussian house of Brandenburg, which in the 17th and 18th centuries emerged as the two new great powers in central Europe. Austria expanded to the southeast at the expense of the Turks, repopulating the devastated lands by means of a planned programme of resettlement which attracted migrants from many parts of Germany, though collectively they came to be known as "Danube Swabians". In the north, Prussia amalgamated a number of fragmented states with the help of its mighty army. In the 18th century, much influenced by the new ideas

of the European Enlightenment, rulers emerged in both states who regarded themselves more as "servants of the state" than as absolute rulers. Under Frederick the Great (1740–86), the Prussians abolished torture, supported religious tolerance and secured the personal rights of the citizens. But at the same time the nobility maintained all its privileges and the peasants remained totally dependent on the lord of the manor. In Austria Joseph II went even further than Frederick, but most of his reforms were so rash that they had to be repealed by his successors. In both cases, however, the necessary steps had been taken to herald the emergence of the modern, centralised state. ❑

LEFT: Martin Luther, the great religious reformer.
RIGHT: Frederick the Great of Prussia, the great state reformer.

RENAISSANCE FACES: WINDOWS ON THE SOUL

The artists of 15th- and 16th-century Germany not only put their world in perspective, but also produced penetrating images of human beings.

The Renaissance, or "rebirth", of classical humanist principles saw a flowering of creative thought all over Europe. In painting and sculpture, the age's new ideals found illustration. In place of Gothic stylisation, painting discovered perspective, and gloried in the illusion of real human figures occupying real space. This led to a boom in portraiture as Albrecht Dürer, Lucas Cranach, Hans Holbein and others created breathtakingly realistic, exactingly detailed images of their fellow men and women. They carried this eye for realism over into their sacred images: Cranach, for example, is now better known for his paintings of Adam and Eve and other Biblical themes.

One other early master was Matthias Grünewald (1475–1528). In his great Isenheim Altar, in Colmar (Alsace), he combined precision with dramatic colour contrasts and contortions of the figure in the service of expressive illustration.

But the quintessential German Renaissance man was Albrecht Dürer (1471–1528). A goldsmith, draughtsman, engraver and painter, the Nuremberg-based Dürer travelled widely in Italy and the Low Countries. His work brilliantly incorporated the technical and human developments of the Italian Renaissance and the detail of early Netherlandish painting. Dürer was the first artist to extensively develop the genre of self-portrait.

Less well-known internationally are the sculptures of Tilman Riemenschneider (c 1460–1531) and Veit Stoss (c 1450–1533), whose saints and angels are no less alive and human than the two-dimensional figures of their painter contemporaries. In his Würzburg workshop Riemenschneider supplied the whole of Franconia with exquisite woodcarvings *(above)*. Having grown up in Nuremberg, woodcarver Veit Stoss did much work in eastern Europe.

◁ **FALL OF MAN**
Detail of Tilman Riemenschneider's *Last Supper* in the Holy Blood Altar, Rothenburg. The master woodcarver's career came to an abrupt end: after spending time in prison following an uprising in 1525, he lost his hands and never carved again.

◁ EYE TO DETAIL

In the quintessential self-portrait of the Renaissance (c 1500), a Christ-like Albrecht Dürer gazes directly out at the viewer.

▽ RELIGION AND POLITICS

Lucas Cranach the Elder (1472–1553) painted 35 images of Lucretia in between portraits of his patrons at the Saxon court.

HANS HOLBEIN THE YOUNGER

Like newspaper photos, the articulate images of Hans Holbein the Younger (1497–1543) bring a bygone era into sharp focus. Holbein followed Dürer both as master of portraiture and as a world traveller. He was one of the few German artists of international renown in his day. His portraits record the journeys of a man who moved from Augsburg to England where, as court painter to Henry VIII, he died of the plague.

Holbein's portraits are a gallery of contemporary personalities, from Erasmus to the wives of Henry VIII. *Portrait of the Merchant George Gisze (above)* shows how Holbein fused his father's naturalism and Flemish influence with his own inimitable style. In the northern tradition, each object has its own symbolism, from the Oriental rug to the vase of flowers. In other portraits, Holbein left the background matte, with letters across it both identifying the subject and emphasising the two-dimensionality of the picture plain in contrast to the plasticity of the face.

◁ THE BOTTOM LINE

A master draughtsman as well as painter, Dürer imbued every line of his mother's portrait with expressiveness and humanity.

△ THE FACE IN 3-D

With a human rather than idealised face, this statue of St Joseph (St. Mary's Altar, Krakow) is typical of the woodcarving of Veit Stoss.

A GOLDEN AGE

The big names of German culture span the complete range, from philosophy to literature to classical music, all suffused with Sturm und Drang

Despite, or perhaps because of, Germany's fragmentation into a bewildering array of kingdoms, dukedoms, bishoprics and other statelets, the 18th and early 19th century saw the emergence of some of German culture's most enduring achievements, in philosophy, literature and music.

With Descartes' pronouncement *"Cogito; ergo sum"* (I think; therefore I am), the Enlightenment saw the final release of thought from the constraints of religious tutelage, but it was Germany that subsequently became the heartland of philosophical thought. Gottfried Wilhelm Leibnitz (1646–1716) had prepared the way with his belief that a pre-ordained harmony formed the basis of the relationship between Man and God and between the body and the soul, but it was Immanuel Kant (1724–1804) who delved further into the possibilities and limits of human perception. Never venturing beyond his East Prussian home town of Königsberg (now part of the Russian Federation and renamed Kaliningrad), Kant became professor of logic and metaphysics at the city's university. In his *Critique of Pure Reason* (1781) he contended that, through a synthesis of empiricism and rationalism, the discerning individual could isolate the essence of an object among countless individual phenomena (the so-called Thing in Itself – *Ding an sich* – theory). His *Critique of Practical Reason* (1788) dealt with the relationship between the individual and society as a whole.

Weimar Classicism

Kant's view that all human beings should take responsibility for themselves and make the most of their intellect and potential was a decisive influence on the poets and philosophers of the Classical age in German literature, a period associated above all with the city of Weimar. The residence of the dukes of Thuringia,

Weimar had a reputation as a small but lively centre of the arts, but it was towards the end of the 18th century that it became the focal point of Germany's literary life. Many important writers of the period lived here, while others such as Jean Paul, Johann Peter Hebel and Heinrich von Kleist stayed for varying periods

of time. In 1772 Christoph Martin Wieland (1733–1813) was engaged by the liberal Countess Anna Amalia as a teacher. He was followed by Goethe, Herder and Schiller, all of whom were brought to Weimar by the Countess's son, Karl August. Little known outside Germany, Wieland wrote the first educational novel (*Geschichte des Agathon*, 1776), the first German-language opera libretto (*Alceste*, 1773), as well as the first German translation of Shakespeare. A personal friend of some of the most prominent figures of the day including Kant and Schlegel, he was for 20 years the editor of the *Teutscher Merkur*, a literary magazine written in a light, journalistic style.

LEFT: flute concert in Sanssouci by Adolf Menzel.
RIGHT: Friedrich Schiller, a leading figure in the Classical age of German literature.

Goethe

Born in Frankfurt-am-Main, Johann Wolfgang von Goethe (1749–1832) first arrived in the little royal town of Weimar on 7 November 1775, when he was 26 years old. The young author had already won fame at home and abroad with his novel *The Sorrows of Young Werther*.

But Goethe was much more than just a talented writer and it was Weimar that was to provide him with the stage on which to demonstrate what a universally gifted man he was. It wasn't long before he had risen from being the friend and tutor of the

20-year-old Duke Karl August to become a top civil servant with a seat on the Privy Council.

After spending a year in Italy in 1778, Goethe took up the posts of Education Minister and Director of Theatre. From now on he was to devote much of his energy to literature and also to a wide spectrum of scientific subjects, writing numerous valuable theses on botany, zoology and climatology, as well as his famous treatise on colours.

Although Goethe's output was huge, his incomparable place in the history of German culture is not only the result of his writings. Of the works which truly stood out above the rest, he once said: "they are but fragments of a greater confession". This was something more than a *Weltanschauung* or perception of the world. Goethe was an extremely perceptive and practical person, no great friend of philosophy and mere theoretical sciences. He became a universal thinker because he wanted to live universally, exploring every avenue that was presented to him. Goethe's greatest achievement, therefore, was life itself. Whether he viewed the world through the eyes of a lover, a natural scientist, a politician or a traveller, the profound effect that he was to have on later generations could only be compared to that of a classical work of art.

His compulsive hunger for knowledge and the pursuit of his own personal development is also the theme of his famous drama about Faust. His "main work", written in two parts, took him 60 years to complete. The scholar Faust, weary of all the stagnant knowledge contained in books, submitted himself to the Devil, for it was only Mephistopheles who had the key to open the door to every possible experience that the world could offer. Despite all his experiences and successes, in the end Faust is a broken man; cleverer but not wise, rich but not happy. The angels save his soul from the claws of the Devil, because: "whoever strives shall be redeemed".

Viewing his own life in the same tragic light, Goethe sought similar salvation for himself. "My conviction as to our continued being is based on the notion of constant application to the task; for when I work tirelessly right to the end, nature is duty-bound to assign me another form of existence, should my present one no longer be able to endure my spirit."

Nature was Goethe's god, his guiding light, and the study of nature was his form of worship. The young Goethe became renowned as the greatest "original genius" of his time, as the prototype of that creative individuality, which, as far as it was manifested in his own emotions, gave birth to a new language.

When Goethe was old, he looked upon himself as a "collective being", for whom the wisdom of old age and all life's works were a loose synthesis of thousands of influences. He refused to be merely a representative of a Germany heading towards a nation state; as a translator and critic and the writer of *East-West Divan*, he strove for the creation of a "world literature" in the hope that the embattled peoples of Europe "should become aware of one another, should understand one another, and if they cannot love one another, then they should at least learn to be tolerant." ❑

LEFT: Goethe, the universal genius.

Wieland's arrival in Weimar was followed by that of the great duo of Goethe and Schiller, and of Johann Gottfried Herder (1744–1803). Herder became an authority on folksong; his *Stimmen der Völker in Liedern* (Voices of the Peoples in Song) of 1779 was suffused with his appreciation of traditional popular culture.

At the beginning of their careers, both Johann Wolfgang von Goethe (1749–1832) and Friedrich von Schiller (1759–1805) were associated with the movement known as *Sturm und Drang* (Storm and Stress) which, inspired by the teachings of Jean-Jacques Rousseau, advocated the breaking of literary conventions in favour of a celebration of emotion and a return to Nature. But the talents of both men were far too great and too diverse to be contained within any one literary category.

Schiller's greatest and most enduring successes were the blank-verse drama *Don Carlos*; the historical tragedies *Wallenstein* and *Maria Stuart*; and his final work, *William Tell*; all of which grappled with problems of personal or political responsibility. In 1799, together with Goethe, he founded the Society of Weimar Friends of the Arts (Gesellschaft der Weimarer Kunstfreunde). They proclaimed their new concept of Classicism, rooted in the ancients, in the publications *Horen* and *Propyläen*.

Posterity has recognised Goethe as the nearest the age produced to a universal genius. His best-known work is the drama *Faust*, but he was also an outstanding lyric poet and novelist, and immersed himself in philosophical, art-historical and scientific studies *(see opposite)*.

In Weimar, the great thinkers lived cheek by jowl, intrigued against one another and didn't consider themselves too sophisticated for the ways of provincial society. At the same time, both Goethe and Schiller took a lively part in the literary gatherings at the homes of Countess Anna Amalia and Johanna Schopenhauer, but during this period popular taste tended towards lighter works and people were avidly reading the ironical fantasies of novelist Jean Paul and picaresque tales such as *Rinaldo Rinaldini* (1798) written by the librarian Christian August Vulpius, the brother of Goethe's Christiane, the artificial flower-maker whom he eventually married in 1806.

Right: Johann Sebastian Bach, whose music has inspired countless interpretations.

Music masters

From the mid-18th century, a great period of German classical music began, with many composers encouraged and sustained by enlightened patrons. One of a dynasty of composers and musicians, Johann Sebastian Bach (1685–1750) served as Kapellmeister and organist at Weimar and Cöthen, as well as filling the post of cantor at the Thomaner School in Leipzig. Perhaps his best-loved works are the six *Brandenburg Concertos*, written at Cöthen but dedicated to the Margrave of Brandenburg who had commissioned them. In 1747 he played before Frederick the Great and his improvisations on a

theme proposed by the king took shape as *The Musical Offering*. Bach is celebrated as the master of pure form. His religious works have an enduring appeal, among them the Cantatas, the *St John* and *St Matthew Passions*, the *Mass in B Minor* and the *Christmas Oratorio*. His compositions for piano also have an enduring popularity. His works are pure and spiritual in form and often – as in the *Art of Fugue* – not even related to particular instruments. Neither a tuba quartet nor a jazz combo can destroy his music; scarcely any other composer's work has inspired so many different interpretations.

Born in Halle, George Frederick Händel (1685–1759) made his debut in the orchestra of the Hamburg opera, then earned himself the epithet "*Il divino Sassone*" (the divine Saxon) during tours of Italy where he played the organ as well as working on compositions. In 1710 he was appointed director of music at the court of the Elector of Hanover, but took frequent leaves of absence to try his fortune in London, where he presented his opera *Rinaldo* in 1711. Permanent residence in London followed when his master became King George I of England.

ENGLISH HERO

When George Frederick Händel was buried in Poets' Corner in London's Westminster Abbey, more than 3,000 people attended the service, mourning the loss not only of a great composer, but of a much-loved national figure.

Artistically, Händel employed rigorous methods; he is said to have hung the tyrannical prima donna Francesca Cuzzoni out of a window, threatening to drop her until she agreed to follow his musical instructions. In London he introduced the Italian style of baroque opera, but after his work was subjected to a musical caricature in *The Beggar's Opera* by John Gay and Johann Christian Pepusch, his response was to concentrate on oratorios. He wrote *Belshazzar*, *Jephta*, *Judas Maccabaeus* and, greatest of them all, the *Messiah*. His orchestral works – organ concertos, concerti grossi and his famous *Water Music* – were frequently performed.

Move to Vienna

Later in the 18th century the centre of gravity of German musical creativity shifted southeastwards, from Germany proper to the Austrian capital of Vienna, with its immortal triumvirate of Haydn, Mozart and Beethoven.

The musical abilities of Joseph Haydn (1732–1809) were first discovered by the master of the Vienna Boys' Choir. He was brought from his home in the Lower Austrian countryside and it was in the capital that he learnt the art of composing. For 20 years he was employed by Hungarian Prince Esterhazy as choirmaster, working at the Prince's palaces at Eisenstadt in Austria and Fertöd in Hungary. Here he had the security he needed in order to devote his energies to completing countless compositions. His works range from pre-Classical compositions to music suffused with the spirit of *Sturm und Drang*, and embrace all the musical styles of his time. Some of his music was intended to entertain high society, whose darling he was, while other works bear the marks of intensive soul-searching. Among his greatest compositions are *The Creation* (1789) and *The Seasons* (1804). Haydn was also responsible for the music of Germany's national anthem.

Haydn was quick to recognise the child genius from Salzburg, Wolfgang Amadeus Mozart (1756–91), who performed his first concert at the age of six. Mozart spent his childhood and youth on musical tours throughout Europe, playing before some of the most important personages of the time. He was then employed as choirmaster by Archbishop Colloredo of Salzburg, who failed to recognise his talent. As the very first freelance composer, Mozart's financial situation was always precarious; he spent the last 10 years of his life in Vienna, without a fixed income and beset by hunger and illness, a fact which makes his musical achievements all the more remarkable. His greatest success was the premiere of his opera *Don Giovanni*, performed in Prague in 1787. Mozart was the most important operatic

---

LEFT: Haydn, one of a triumvirate of great Vienna-based composers.

RIGHT: the other two were Mozart and Beethoven.

composer of the period, committed to the ideas of the Enlightenment. The political dynamite to be found in *Il Seraglio*, *The Marriage of Figaro*, *Cosi fan Tutte* or *The Magic Flute* may not be as relevant today, but the psychological and dramatic power remains intact. There is hardly another composer whose work remains so totally alive; one just has to think of the 25 piano concertos, some 40 symphonies, the *Requiem* and the chamber music.

Like Mozart, Ludwig van Beethoven (1770–1827) worked as a freelance composer. He was born in Bonn, the Rhineland city which remains intensely proud of its most famous son, and was first employed as a musician in the local Elector's orchestra. But, still a young man, he was drawn to Vienna, where Haydn had agreed to give him lessons, and it was here that he made his home. Beethoven created a musical language of an unmatched power of expression.

His revolt against musical norms makes itself clear in his love of dissonance. Best known of his works are the five piano concertos, the opera *Fidelio*, the piano sonatas, the string quartets and above all the nine symphonies. The music of the Romantic movement further developed his subjectivity, replacing rigidity of form with emotion and expression. ❏

THE ROMANTICS

The subjectivity of *Sturm und Drang* was carried on into the early years of the 19th century by a group of writers who saw themselves as the disciples of Goethe, though none of them was able to match their master's transcendence of all categories. Their Romanticism expressed itself in a fascination with the Middle Ages, a continuing absorption in emotion and in a preoccupation with "inwardness", a cultivation of the mysterious, innermost self. Their principal symbol was the "*Blaue Blume*", the blue flower symbolising infinity and the unattainable. Some of their number lived the typically truncated lives of the Romantic hero; Wilhelm Heinrich Wackenroder (1773–98), whose main work *Herzensergiessungen eines kunstliebenden Klosterbruders* (Outpourings of an Art-obsessed Monk) was a collaborative effort with his friend Ludwig Tieck, died at the age of 25. Friedrich von Hardenberg (1772–1801), better known as Novalis, explored strange realms of blood, darkness and death, before he too perished of exhaustion at a tragically early age.

Some of the most compelling images of the German Romantic movement are in paintings. No artist has more vividly portrayed the individual at one, yet separate from, luminous landscapes of forest, heath, mountain and seashore than Caspar David Friedrich (1774–1840).

RESTORATION

Metternich may have redrawn the map of Europe following the Napoleonic Wars,
but the Industrial Revolution changed the face of Germany forever

Germany at the end of the 18th century was neither an empire nor a united country. Instead, it was a patchwork quilt of 350 principalities and more than 1,000 small states where kings, electors, dukes, counts and knights, monasteries and cities jealously guarded their sovereignty and where bishops governed as secular rulers. The only two powers of any distinction were Prussia and Austria. The loose union of states with the grandiose title "Holy Roman Empire of the German Nation" had no common system of taxation and no common army. After 200 years of strife, Germany had reverted to the Middle Ages.

Four-fifths of this curious empire's 23 million inhabitants were tied to the land. In the west the peasants paid their lords in money and in kind, providing services for little or no remuneration, while the Church demanded its tithe from the yearly harvest. In the extensive Prussian lowlands east of the Elbe, the peasants and their families were subjects of the lords of the manor, obliged to perform compulsory labour on his estate. They were not allowed to marry freely and could not leave the estate without permission of the landowner. Prussian peasants were soldiers of the king, carried off periodically to take part in wars waged by the nobility.

Nor was the structure of hundreds of small states conducive to the development of business and industry. Each state and town had its own trading conditions and its own coinage, weights and measures. Restrictions imposed on the guilds and customs barriers made free competition impossible. Strict local legislation prevented the free movement of people.

Enter Napoleon

In 1803, under the auspices of Napoleonic France, a radical clean-up in fragmented Germany began. Many of the small states lost their independence. Napoleon declared Bavaria and

LEFT: *Walker above the Mist* by the Romantic painter Caspar David Friedrich.
RIGHT: Patriots rally at the Hambach Festival of 1832.

Baden-Württemberg to be kingdoms and the Confederation of the Rhine was founded under his protection.

The 900-year-old Holy Roman Empire of the German Nation now ceased to exist. After Prussia had declared war against France, its army's heavy defeat near Jena and Auerstedt

in 1806 exposed the extent of its internal weakness. The army dispersed, the king fled and, when Napoleon marched into Berlin, there was no resistance. Europe's mightiest military state, with its 200,000 soldiers, had collapsed like a house of cards.

Defeated armies learn quickly and the Prussians learnt too. Reformers came into the fold: men like Baron von Stein and Graf Hardenberg, officers of the calibre of Scharnhorst, Gneisenau and Clausewitz. The peasants were granted their liberty, the guild order was lifted for some trades, the civic administration was restructured and the army was completely reorganised. A national liberation movement grew in Germany. Gneisenau demanded mobilisation and a national uprising against the French, and after Napoleon's crushing defeat in Russia in 1812, the time was ripe. The hesitant Prussian king was faced with a *fait accompli* by patriots when, in the spring of 1813, anti-French revolts broke out all over Germany. With the support of Russia, Great Britain and Austria, Prussia finally declared war again on France.

The Battle of Nations near Leipzig on 17 October 1813

NAPOLEON'S LEGACY

Many Germans welcomed Napoleon's reforms, such as the abolition of serfdom. But support vanished when the extent of France's territorial ambitions became clear. Beethoven, a former fan of Napoleon's, declared him "architect of a new tyranny".

was a turning point in European history. Napoleon's army was surrounded and defeated and France was forced to withdraw to the west of the Rhine. After Napoleon's final defeat at Waterloo, Germany's fate was to be decided at a congress of the victors in 1815 in Vienna.

Triumph of the restoration

At the Congress of Vienna it was the powerful Prince von Metternich of Austria who tied together the threads of the new European order. Germany and Italy were once again divided into small states, Poland was made part of Russia and Hungary remained firmly under Austria's thumb. In a triumph for the forces of reaction, the old feudal order and the Catholic Church were re-installed in their traditional positions. Outside Germany proper, Austria's centre of gravity shifted east, while within, Prussia expanded west and became the dominant power. At its feet lay 34 principalities and four free imperial cities, combined into a loose confederation without a leader. The intention of the Congress of Vienna was for Germany to remain divided and powerless while the monarchs of Russia, Prussia and Austria founded a "Holy Alliance" of the eastern powers, bound together by the ideals of monarchical absolutism.

Reaction and Nationalism

In the universities, students organised rallies against the princes' confederation. Their symbol was a black, red and gold flag. When in 1819 the pro-Russian writer Kotzebue was murdered by a student, Metternich reacted with the Carlsbad Decrees. All opposition was suppressed, the students' societies proscribed and the universities placed under police control.

The overthrow of King Charles X in Paris in July 1830 was the signal for a general outbreak of unrest throughout Europe. There was an uprising in Leipzig, the destruction of a palace in Brunswick and the sacking of the police headquarters in Dresden, followed by open revolt in Brussels and, at the end of the year, revolution in Poland. Although the protests were crushed by Holy Alliance troops, the bourgeois-democratic movement could not be extinguished. In May 1832, 30,000 people came together at Hambach Castle to demand a free and united Germany. The so-called Hambach Festival was attended by townsfolk, peasants, craftsmen, academics and students whose leaders gave passionate speeches expressing bitterness at their wretched living conditions. Metternich's police arrested the ringleaders and the colours black, red and gold were banned.

In the south German states, the monarchs preserved their constitutions, but allowed the citizens a certain amount of participation in government by introducing so-called "second chambers". In Prussia, Austria and many other states, however, absolutism – the single-handed rule of the monarchs – continued to dominate the body and the soul of the people. "When I think of Germany at night, then I am robbed of sleep," wrote the poet Heinrich Heine.

Railways and poverty

Meanwhile, the Industrial Revolution was knocking ever louder on Germany's doors. The age of the train had arrived and in 1835 the first German steam locomotive chugged its way along the 6-km (4-mile) stretch between Nuremberg and Fürth. It was with railways, canals and new wide roads, with money and steam, that the up-and-coming citizenry started to undermine the old feudal order. A portent of future national unity was the creation in 1834 of the Zollverein, a customs union of 18 of the German states.

The other side of the economic boom manifested itself in the increasing poverty of the lower classes. There was no more room for all the craftsmen and many ended up working long hours for little pay in the factories. In 1844 in Silesia the weavers revolted and smashed all the machinery. The appalling social conditions forced many to emigrate, primarily to the USA. Karl Marx and Friedrich Engels worked on their theories of revolutionary socialism in Paris, Brussels, London and Manchester. The air was thick with the smell of radical change.

Germany at the barricades

The year 1847 saw a general economic crisis in Europe: failed harvests, rising inflation, mass starvation, bank collapses, falls in production and serious unemployment. To make things worse, the winter of 1847–8 was unusually hard. The first unrest was seen in the cities and once again the struggle began in Paris, though the revolution quickly spread to Germany. The peasants set palaces on fire and withheld taxes and other dues. Public meetings demanded reforms and a parliament. The rulers were put on the defensive and in order to avoid the worst they were forced to make certain concessions. Common citizens were granted ministerial posts, and the bourgeoisie was allowed to share in government and to form armed militias.

On 18 March the revolt reached Berlin and barricades were erected in the streets. After

---

Left: Berlin 1848: Germany to the barricades.
Right: the first German National Assembly convened in St Paul's Church in Frankfurt.

being forced to order the retreat of his forces, the Prussian king appointed a liberal government. Parliaments were voted in the member states of the German Confederation and on 18 May 1848 an elected German National Assembly finally came together in the church of St Paul in Frankfurt.

It was hoped that the National Assembly would become a permanent body that would proclaim the nation's sovereignty and institute democratic reforms. But the Assembly failed to challenge the established centres of power. No powerful people's army was created under its auspices and a governing body without the

backing of an armed force could not be taken seriously. The liberal majority was afraid of the demands of the radical left, which wanted a republic, and refused to sanction the lifting of feudal dues that the peasantry was still required to pay. And when the liberals, shocked by the bloody fights in Paris that June, joined the nobility, the train of revolution ground to a halt. The absolutist overlords knew how to use their power. In Vienna the rebels were shot down by Field Marshal Windischgrätz and in Berlin the revolution had to contend with Prussian General Wrangel. In Frankfurt, the St Paul's Assembly, which had resisted resorting to arms, was dispersed at sword-point. ❏

EMPIRE TO DICTATORSHIP

Bismarck unified Germany under Prussian rule, but this
achievement was squandered by Nazi dictatorship and two World Wars

aw and order returned to the land. But although the revolution had been crushed, the problems that had caused it remained. The national state had to be created: if not revolutionary or liberal-democratic, then reactionary; if not as a pan-German state with Austria, then as a single state (under the leadership of Prussia). What actually happened will forever be linked with the name of Bismarck.

Bismarck and unification

Born in 1815, Otto von Bismarck learnt the art of diplomatic intrigue during the eight years he spent as a Prussian delegate at the Frankfurt Assembly. He recognised that Prussia could prosper only if Austria became weak. In October 1862 he was summoned by King Wilhelm I to head the Prussian government. His first task was to bring the liberals in parliament into line – which he did, thoroughly. Then, without much regard for parliament or the constitution, he pushed through the modernisation of the Prussian army. His first master stroke, however, came a year later when he obtained the support of Austria in winning back from Denmark the states of Schleswig and Holstein. Then, against the will of the small German states, he started a deliberately calculated war against the Habsburg monarchy. The decisive battle was near Königgrätz in 1866, where superior Prussian technology – including breech-loading guns – overwhelmed the Austrian army.

Bismarck's revolution from the top transformed the map of Germany. Prussia annexed large areas, including Schleswig-Holstein, and France and Austria were forced to agree to this territorial expansion. Prussia succeeded in forcing Austria out of Germany and in the newly established North German Federation it achieved unchallenged hegemony.

After the defeat of Austria, for the Prussians there was now only one major competitor in

Europe: France. Bismarck provoked Napoleon III by decreeing that a Hohenzollern prince should take over the vacant Spanish throne, knowing that this would be unacceptable to the French emperor. Napoleon III demanded that Prussia renounce its claims. Wilhelm I rejected the demand and, with encouragement from

Bismarck, the desired war broke out. The superior German forces triumphed at Sedan on 1 September 1870 and Napoleon III was taken prisoner. After a terrible siege, German troops marched into Paris, where in March 1871 the working population had hoisted the red flag of social revolution. France was forced to accept a harsh peace settlement, handing Germany the province of Alsace-Lorraine and 5,000 million francs in war reparations.

The new, united German Empire was proclaimed not in Germany, but in France, in the Hall of Mirrors in the Palace of Versailles. It was not born out of any national democratic movement, but out of diplomatic agreements

---

LEFT: the proclamation of the Second German Empire in Versailles.
RIGHT: Otto von Bismarck, the "Iron Chancellor".

between German kings and princes. It was not the result of a victory of the citizens over the nobility, but of the monarchy and nobles over the citizens. The empire was to last for 47 years until its disintegration at the end of World War I in 1918. It was home not only to Germans but, against their will, to large numbers of Alsatians, Poles and Danes.

Industrial awakening

While the empire's authoritarian political system was marked by paralysis, its economy was the most dynamic in Europe. At the beginning of the 19th century, four-fifths of the

product soared past that of France and by 1900 it had drawn level with that of Great Britain. Despite being banned from 1878 to 1890, the Social Democratic Party secured many benefits for the new industrial working class and, by 1912, it had become the strongest political force in the Reichstag (Parliament).

War looms

In South West Africa, East Africa, Togo, Cameroon and in the Tsingtau enclave in China, the black, white and red flag of the Emperor was raised. Great Britain, the main competitor, was challenged on the seas by a massive pro-

population had been tied economically to the land, but by the end of the century this figure had been whittled down to barely one-fifth. Germany was transformed from a country of farmers into an industrial nation.

The 5,000 million francs of war reparation helped the German economy achieve an unparalleled boom. In the so-called "*Gründerjahre*" (years of industrial and economic expansion) between 1871–4 joint stock companies sprang up like mushrooms. The Ruhr industrial area developed into the most important industrial centre in Europe, with the Essen-based armaments manufacturer Krupp alone employing 50,000 people. In the 1870s, the gross national

gramme of warship construction, part of the *Weltpolitik* espoused by Admiral Tirpitz and backed by Kaiser Wilhelm II. Good relations were cultivated with Turkey and in 1902 the Sultan approved the construction of a railway that was intended to link Berlin to Baghdad. To wrest Morocco (rich in iron ore) from France, the gunboat *Panther* was ordered to Agadir, but to no avail; Morocco remained French.

All the great European powers were now arming themselves in preparation for the big show-down, which was to be fought over the redistribution of colonies and markets. After the assassination of Austrian Archduke Franz Ferdinand in Sarajevo by Serbian nationalists, the Berlin government forced its ally into a war with Serbia, thereby throwing down the gauntlet to Russia and France.

"I am no longer aware of any parties, I only recognise Germans," announced Kaiser Wilhelm at the outset of hostilities. Applause came from all factions, including the Social Democrats, who voted for the massive credits required for war. Germany's war aims had been outlined in a secret memorandum: annexation of the mining region of Briey in Lorraine, the wearing down of France, the subjugation of Belgium, Luxembourg and much of Eastern Europe, as well as the establishment of a European customs and economic union under German leadership. In the end, none of these plans came to fruition. As the war raged on, the military and economic inferiority of the Austro-German camp became clear. The switch to unrestricted submarine warfare marked the beginning of the end, since it forced the United States to enter the war against Germany.

KAISER WILHELM II

German imperial might was the theme of Kaiser Wilhelm's speeches, but during World War I he was just a figurehead, far removed from the great warlord of popular imagination. Subsequently exiled to Holland, he lived a quiet life with his family.

Defeat and revolution

In the course of the war, Germany had transformed itself into a military dictatorship. A state of siege, censorship and forced labour became part of everyday life, as did a diet of cabbage stalks. People were starving while gold was swapped for steel. The increasingly detested war was financed by loans. The Russian Revolution in October 1917 brought hostilities to an end in the east, and enabled Germany to transfer forces to the Western Front. But a final German offensive in the west was soon brought to a halt and the Allies, reinforced by US troops, began a steady advance.

At the end of September 1918 Germany's ally Bulgaria capitulated, cutting off oil supplies from the Balkans. General Ludendorff convinced the Kaiser that an immediate ceasefire was needed and that a parliamentary government be formed to "pick up the pieces".

In November 1918 Germany was transformed from a military dictatorship into a

republic of workers' and soldiers' councils which took over local control. The hour of social democracy and that of its leader, Friedrich Ebert, had arrived.

The "council of people's representatives" – as the six-member social democratic government called itself – was intended to steer the country towards a socialist republic. But Friedrich Ebert had no intention of letting this happen and secretly secured the support of the army. The first Congress of

German Councils met in Berlin in 1918, with the vast majority of the 489 representatives coming from the ranks of the Social Democratic Party. It was decided to hold elections for a national assembly and all political power was entrusted to Ebert's council.

A brief and bitter civil war broke out in Berlin, in the course of which the leaders of the Communist Party, Rosa Luxemburg and Karl Liebknecht, were assassinated by a group of soldiers. Meanwhile, the representatives of the national assembly gathered in Weimar to elect Ebert as president of the first German democratic republic, which came to be known as the Weimar Republic.

LEFT: the dawn of the railways: the stretch from Berlin to Potsdam around 1850. **RIGHT:** Friedrich Ebert, the first president of the German Republic.

After the revolution

Germany was now a republic with a constitution based on adult suffrage, an eight-hour working day and recognised trade unions. But into the ranks of the conservatives came incorrigible monarchists, old generals, discharged soldiers, reactionary Junker aristocrats, anti-Semites, bankers and influential press barons. These forces created the legend of the "Stab in the Back", the pernicious notion that war had been lost from within.

> **FAILED ARTIST**
>
> Hitler saw himself as a great artist. Undeterred by rejection from the Vienna Academy, he eked out a living by selling his anaemic watercolours of street scenes.

And then there was Versailles, where in July 1919 Germany had to sign a humiliating treaty. The country lost all its colonies, while Alsace and Lorraine were returned to France, Danzig (Gdansk) put under the control of the League of Nations and much of eastern Germany including the so-called "Polish Corridor" given to Poland. The west bank of the Rhine was occupied by Allied troops. The Saar industrial area was administered by the League of Nations and its coal fields were given to France. There were huge sums to be paid in the form of reparations. Paragraph 231 of the Treaty burdened Germany with exclusive guilt for the war. A union of Germany and Austria was expressly forbidden.

These measures, far milder than the settlement Germany would have imposed had she won the war, were interpreted as revenge, and provided the stimulus for a new wave of German chauvinism and revanchism.

The Weimar years

Despite its many foes, and a series of crises, the democratic Weimar Republic survived, even flourished, albeit briefly. In Munich, in 1923, an obscure nationalist orator of Austrian origin named Adolf Hitler attempted to overthrow it in a farcical uprising that became known as the "Beer Hall Putsch". The would-be revolutionaries were easily dispersed by the police. Arrested and given a lenient sentence by a sympathetic judge, Hitler used his time in jail to write his unreadable political testament *Mein Kampf* ("My Struggle").

In the same year, Germany defaulted on reparations payments, and the Ruhr industrial region was occupied by the French army, unleashing run-away inflation. The cost of everyday items rose to billions of marks, and employees rushed to spend their wages before they became worthless. The thrifty middle classes saw their savings vanish, while unscrupulous speculators made fortunes. The hyper-inflation was eventually brought under control, but it left a legacy of bitterness and cleared the way for political extremism.

For a few years in the mid-to-late 1920s, modest prosperity returned, the arts thrived, and there was a degree of social peace, at least on the surface. Then came the Wall Street Crash of 1929. Unemployment rose from just over a million to 3 million in 1930 and 6 million in 1933. Extremist solutions to the country's problems gained credibility; Hitler's Nazis re-emerged, many of them in the brown uniform of the stormtroopers of the SA, eager to battle it out on the streets with their deadly enemies, the Communists. In a series of elections, the Nazi vote rose, though they never formed a majority in parliament and by 1933 their popularity had begun to diminish. But behind the scenes, reactionary circles were plotting, hoping to make

LEFT: Joseph Goebbels, head of the Nazi ministry of public enlightenment and propaganda. **RIGHT:** the masses salute the Führer at a rally in Nuremberg.

use of Hitler; and on 30 January 1933 President von Hindenburg appointed Adolf Hitler as Chancellor of the German Reich.

The Nazis in power

The curtain went up on the barbarous stage of the Third Reich – a terror that was to last for 12 years. First of all the Communist Party was banned and its leaders forced into exile or thrown into concentration camps. After elections in which the Nazis acquired 44 percent of the vote, all the parties with the exception of the Social Democrats accepted the Enabling Act which gave the government virtually unrestricted powers. The Nazis thus came to power quite legally. The trade unions were broken up and all other political parties abolished. The one-party dictatorship functioned under the "leadership principle". Factories, offices, schools, universities, radio and the press were regimented and forced into step.

There were the Sturmabteilungen (SA), the Schutzstaffeln (SS), the storm and defence brigades, the German Work Front, the National Socialist Women's Movement, the German Girls' Association, the Hitler Youth, Strength Through Joy, and Beauty Through Work. The Nazis aimed to exercise complete control over

GERMAN RESISTANCE

Hitler's popularity combined with Gestapo terror crippled all German attempts at resistance to his regime. But centres of opposition existed all through the Nazi period, chiefly in the upper echelons of the army, suffused with aristocratic disdain for the criminality and vulgarity of the Führer and his followers. A shadow regime stood in waiting, ready to take over the government of the country should an army coup d'état succeed. In July 1944 it nearly did. A bomb placed by much-decorated officer Claus von Stauffenberg exploded in the conference room at Hitler's East Prussian HQ. But the Führer, miraculously, was only slightly injured, and the planned military uprising was swiftly crushed.

Hitler's luck had saved him on a previous occasion. In 1939, working entirely on his own, a humble cabinet-maker called Georg Elser set a bomb to explode at a Munich beer-hall reunion. The bomb went off, killing eight people, but Hitler had left early and so escaped. Munich also saw the activities of the "White Rose" group of fearless young people led by brother and sister Hans and Sophie Scholl, who were eventually caught in 1943 distributing anti-Nazi leaflets around the university.

Most opponents of the regime met a horrible end by torture and execution, an inestimable loss of human talent for the momentous task of postwar reconstruction.

the body and soul of the people. Mass gatherings, torchlight processions and spectacular party congresses fanned the patriotic flames. The Nazis made noises about the chosen Nordic race and began the grisly business of excising all "inferior life". The Jews were declared second-class citizens, were targeted in the ruthless *Kristallnacht* attacks of 9 November 1938 and, from 1941, were led to the "Final Solution". Millions of European Jews died a gruesome death in the extermination camps of Auschwitz-Birkenau, Treblinka, Majdanek and Buchenwald. The word holocaust was added to the vocabulary of war.

World war and capitulation

After coming to power, Hitler had explained the essence of Germany's foreign policy to army and navy commanders: "acquisition by force of new export markets", "acquisition and Germanisation of new land in the east". The Nazis embarked on a four-year plan of war preparations and soon tanks were rolling on the new motorways that had been built specially for them. Within five years Hitler had recouped just about everything that Germany had lost at Versailles. In 1935 the Saar was returned to its "German mother", and one year later the Wehrmacht marched into the Rhineland. In March 1938 came the annexation of Austria and after

the Munich Conference the Sudetenland in Czechoslovakia became part of the Reich. The British and French policy of appeasement at the Munich Conference failed miserably. After the Soviet-German non-aggression pact of 23 August 1939, Hitler and Stalin decided how they would carve up Europe between them. In September, German troops invaded Poland, triggering the start of a massive conflict.

With a death toll of more than 50 million, it was to be the most terrible war ever known. For the first two years, as German forces, supported by their allies, marched determinedly from one victory to another, it seemed entirely possible that Hitler would win. By early 1941 the Nazis controlled most of continental Europe and now, in league with Italy, sought to bring Africa under their yoke.

But fortunes began to change when Hitler, looking for "living space" to the east, sent three million troops to invade the Soviet Union in June 1941. No more successful than Napoleon had been, his advance came to a halt before Moscow. When the USA entered the war in December 1941 after the Japanese attack on Pearl Harbor, the final outcome of the war was no longer in doubt. Britain, the United States and the Soviet Union presented a militarily superior alliance and, fighting on so many fronts, sapped the Nazis' strength. The defeat of the 6th Army at Stalingrad in 1943 and the Allied landings in Normandy in 1944 signalled the end of Germany's aspirations.

Area bombardment by Allied air forces was reducing German cities to rubble. The bombing campaign reached a climax in February 1945, when Dresden – filled with refugees from the advancing Red Army – was attacked. An unquenchable firestorm was unleashed, in which as many may have perished as in the attack on Hiroshima.

On the morning of 29 April the Russians launched a massive attack on Berlin's inner defences. The next day Hitler and his mistress, Eva Braun, committed suicide in their bunker. It was the end of the Third Reich. The Nazis surrendered unconditionally. Their dream had been to conquer new territory for Germany and to make the nation an invincible world power; now the country lay in ruins, occupied and divided. The dream had turned to nightmare. ❑

LEFT: Hitler arrives in the Sudetenland.

Weimar Culture: Rise and Fall

The cultural life of the Weimar Republic with its innovatory spirit and its sheer productivity has led many commentators to look back on it as a Golden Age, not least because of the Nazi repression which followed and which drove most of its creative spirits into emigration or "inner exile".

After the terrible experience of the Great War, many artists devoted themselves to what were seen as progressive causes. Much architectural talent was deployed in the field of social architecture. Between 1924 and the advent of the Great Depression, more working-class housing was built in Germany than any other country in the world. Schemes included the famous Weissenhof Estate in Stuttgart with its array of white-walled, flat-roofed houses and flats designed by some of the century's most renowned architects, among them Walter Gropius, Ludwig Mies van der Rohe and Bruno Taut.

The savage caricaturist George Grosz was joined by other artists such as Otto Dix and Max Beckmann in portraying not only the horrors of war but in attempting to reveal the ugly realities of the peace – a seemingly democratic republic being steadily undermined by the forces of violence and reaction. A similarly grim and forbidding picture – relieved by wit and sharp melody – emerges from the *Dreigroschenoper (Threepenny Opera)* and *Aufstieg und Fall der Stadt Mahagonny (Rise and Fall of the City of Mahagonny)*, the musical *tours de force* put together by playwright Bertolt Brecht and composer Kurt Weill in 1928 and 1929.

In literature, perhaps the most influential anti-war novel was Erich Maria Remarque's *Im Westen nichts Neues (All Quiet on the Western Front)* of 1929. Other writers anatomised the blinkered acceptance of authority that had helped propel Germany into disaster and were shortly to do so again. Heinrich Mann's *Der Untertan (The Patrioteer)* of 1918 is a masterly evocation of a "Man of Straw" (its alternative title in English). While it was Hollywood that turned *All Quiet on the Western Front* into a successful movie (in 1930), the seminal film of the Weimar period was *The Blue Angel* (1930), starring a sultry Marlene Dietrich and based on the 1905 novel *Professor Unrat (Small Town Tyrant)* by Heinrich Mann.

Throughout the Weimar period, conservative and reactionary forces had vigorously resisted all forms of modernism in the arts. With the Nazi seizure of power in 1933, this resistance became outright oppression. Cultural institutions of all kinds were purged of progressives and Jews, unsuitable art was removed from gallery walls and creative people of all kinds were driven to emigrate. The Western world, particularly the USA, benefited enormously from the outflow of talent. The evolution of modern architecture in the United States is hard to imagine without the presence there in the 1930s and later of such luminaries as Walter Gropius and Mies van der Rohe. Many outstanding scientists, including

the great Albert Einstein, were also driven into exile by the Nazis.

The Nazis didn't only burn books: in 1939 the Berlin fire brigade made a funeral pyre of some 4,000 pictures. But what the Nazis intended to be a coup de grâce to modern art backfired on them; the massive Exhibition of Degenerate Art they staged in Munich in 1937 featured what are now recognised as some of the century's masterpieces, works by Emil Nolde, Oskar Kokoschka, Ernst Kirchner and Franz Marc, Dix and Beckmann. Two million visitors crowded into the gallery, five times more than turned up to the insipid offerings of officially approved Nazi art housed in the adjacent building, nicknamed Palazzo Kitschi by Munich wits. ❑

RIGHT: Albert Einstein, one of many forced into exile.

DIVISION AND REUNIFICATION

*In the aftermath of World War II, Germany remained a
divided country until the fall of the Berlin Wall*

The end of the Third Reich came with the battle for Berlin. On 30 April 1945 Adolf Hitler committed suicide in the bunker of his chancellery and on 1 May the Red Army hoisted the Soviet flag on the ruins of the Reichstag (Parliament).

The country was divided into four zones of occupation. The Soviets obtained the east, the Americans the south, the British the northwest and the French the southwest. Deep within the Soviet sector, Berlin was divided too.

At the Potsdam Conference, from July to August 1945, the "Big Three" – Joseph Stalin, US President Harry Truman and Winston Churchill (succeeded after the British election by Clement Attlee) – agreed on the aims of the combined occupying regime: demilitarisation, deNazification, democratisation and decentralisation of the economy and the state.

Germany starts again

The Third Reich had reduced Germany to a heap of ruins. Cities such as Hamburg, Cologne, Magdeburg, Nuremberg, Würzburg and Dresden had been devastated by bombs. Berlin and many other cities that had seen heavy ground fighting were little more than rubble. The war had destroyed one-fifth of Germany's manufacturing capacity and production sank to one-third of its 1936 level. Not a single major bridge across the Rhine remained intact.

Between 1945 and 1948 a total of 12 million extra Germans flooded into this destroyed country, whose size had been reduced by a quarter. More than two million people lost their lives during this period of exodus and forced expulsions from the German-settled areas in the east. Much of the population suffered from starvation and illness, particularly during the "hunger winter" of 1946–7. In order to survive, they bartered, hoarded, dealt on the black market and stole. City dwellers headed for the

LEFT: most German cities were reduced to rubble by the end of the war: picking up the pieces in Berlin.
RIGHT: Hamburg fared no better.

country to swap pianos, carpets and jewellery for eggs, ham and potatoes. US or British cigarettes became the principal unit of currency.

The Nuremberg trials

On 24 November 1945 the surviving leaders of the Nazi regime were put on trial at Nuremberg.

Twenty-four politicians, ideologists, military men and industrialists, including Hermann Goering, Alfred Rosenberg, Albert Speer and Gustav Krupp were charged with crimes against the peace and crimes against humanity. Twelve of the accused (including the absent Martin Bormann) were sentenced to death; three were sentenced to life imprisonment and two to between 10 and 20 years.

The German people as a whole were confronted with the realities of the Nazi regime. A process of "deNazification" affected the whole population, though it was discontinued after 1948 in the western zones. In the east, the anti-fascist purge bore the mark of Stalinist terror from the moment it began, as concentration camps such as Sachsenhausen and Buchenwald were brought into use once again, not only to punish the functionaries and supporters of the Nazi regime but tens of thousands of other randomly arrested people who had been denounced to the authorities.

The policies of occupation

Regardless of the Allied Control Council, the occupation authorities under their respective military governors pretty much did as they pleased. In the Soviet zone, under the catch-phrase "anti-fascistic-democratic reform", a

West, and on the Americans in particular. The private relief campaigns and the "care parcels" sent by the American people contributed to this pro-American stance, which was then further reinforced by the events that were being witnessed in the east.

The different policies in the occupied zones reflected the differences in the political systems as well as the conflicts of interest between the two superpowers. In Eastern Europe – the huge area that had been handed to Stalin at Yalta in February 1945 – the Communists installed dictatorships in their "peoples' democracies". The Marshall Plan, intended primarily to rebuild the

revolution took place from the top aimed at eradicating the "roots of fascism, militarism and war". This included a comprehensive land reform, the nationalisation of the banks, the expropriation of all "those interested in war", extensive dismantling of industrial plants and the establishment of the "Soviet joint-stock company", which took over more than 30 per-cent of industrial capacity. Many people fled the Soviet zone, an exodus that was to continue until the building of the Berlin Wall in 1961.

In the western zones, too, the dismantling of industry continued right up until 1949, resulting in soaring unemployment. Nevertheless, many Germans continued to pin their hopes on the

economies of war-shattered Europe, was also seen as a means of halting Soviet expansion. As the Iron Curtain descended in Europe, it was clear to all where the political-strategic centre of the Cold War conflict would lie: in defeated and occupied Germany.

The division of Germany

Agreement with the USSR on the future of Germany seemed impossible and the decision was made by the Western powers to divide the country. Christian Democrat chairman, Kon-rad Adenauer, supported the integration of the west zones into the western family of nations. And the leader of the German Socialists (SPD),

Kurt Schumacher, who had suffered for 10 years in Nazi concentration camps, also turned down any deal with the Communists.

At the London conference on 7 June 1948 it was agreed that western Germany should be involved in the rebuilding of Europe (OEEC), that the Ruhr industrial area be subject to international control and that a new West German Federal Republic be created. The Soviet representative left the Allied Control Council in Berlin in protest.

DIPLOMATIC ADENAUER

A native of Cologne, Konrad Adenauer was Federal Chancellor from 1949–63. His greatest achievement was his work in reconciling Germany with its former enemies, especially France.

Berlin was officially divided in September 1948. Elections were held in the western zones and in September 1949 the Federal Parliament held its first session. Theodor Heuss was elected the first president and Christian Democrat chairman Konrad Adenauer became Bundeskanzler (Federal Chancellor). The new Bundesrepublik Deutschland (Federal Republic of Germany) was a parliamentary democracy made up of a number of states including Bavaria, North-Rhine Westphalia and Lower

On 20 June 1948 a new unit of currency was introduced, which proved to be one of the most important foundations of West German prosperity – the Deutschmark.

Confrontation with the USSR came to a dramatic head when the Soviets imposed a complete blockade of the western sector of Berlin. The Allies organised a massive airlift, which supplied the West Berlin population with food and coal until the blockade was lifted on 12 May 1949.

LEFT: Nazi war criminals stand accused at the Nuremberg Trials, which opened in November 1945.
ABOVE: marching to Stalin's tune in East Berlin.

Saxony. But the Western powers made quite sure that they retained control of Berlin, with all the symbolism which that city held for a "united Germany".

The other German state

The Communist-dominated SED (Socialist Unity Party of Germany) attacked the West Germans' "politics of division" but then set about founding an East German state. On 29 May 1949 the elected People's Congress approved a constitution for the German Democratic Republic (GDR), which occupied about a third of the area of pre-war Germany (the states now known as Berlin, Brandenburg,

Mecklenburg-Western Pomerania, Saxony, Saxony-Anhalt and Thuringia). Wilhelm Pieck became the president of the GDR and Otto Grotewohl, formerly a Social Democrat, became prime minister of the SED government. Social Democrats were systematically purged from its leadership ranks. By 1952 the Communist Party Chairman Walter Ulbricht had swung the policy firmly behind the "development of socialism" and better relations with other Communist states. A one-party state had been created.

During this critical period, rebellion broke out on 17 June 1953. Construction workers in

East Berlin reacted to an increase in work quotas by strike action and mass demonstrations, and these quickly developed into an insurgent movement throughout the GDR. The strike slogans developed into outright demands for free elections and the reunification of Germany. The government reacted sternly, claiming the strike was stirred up by supporters of the West, and used Russian tanks against the protesters. The crushing of the uprising not only succeeded in securing the political survival of Walter Ulbricht, but it also helped the West German Chancellor Konrad Adenauer to election victory in 1953 and reinforced his policy of integration with the West.

The "economic miracle"

In West Germany the currency reform of 1948 began to have its desired effect on economic stability. Consumer goods appeared once again in shop windows and industrial production increased correspondingly, helped by the billions of dollars of cash and credits provided by the Marshall Plan. In the 1950s the world began to talk of the German "economic miracle" – the *Wirtschaftswunder*: high growth rates of around 8 percent, a marked reduction in unemployment and a steady increase in the standard of living. The economic recovery went hand-in-hand with the development of a socially orientated market economy.

The system could only be as successful as it was through the restrained wage policy practised by the West German trade unions. Under their parent organisation, the DGB (German Trades Union Council), the strong unions limited their class struggle to rhetoric and acted as upholders of the economic system – as "social partners". The West German Social Democrats also differentiated between Marxist theory and practice and made Keynesian redistribution concepts the theme of their Godesberg Manifesto in 1959.

By the end of the 1950s the West German economy accounted for no less than half the industrial production of the European Economic Community, which had been founded in 1957 as the basis for further economic and political integration within Europe.

As the economic gap between the two Germanys became a chasm, the GDR leadership erected the infamous Berlin Wall in August 1961 to help prevent any further exodus of refugees from East Germany. Now the Federal Republic became a magnet for unskilled workers from Italy and Southern Europe, followed in the late 1960s by hundreds of thousands of further "guest workers" from Turkey.

Military integration

After the Korean War (1950–53), the Western powers insisted on the rearmament of the West German state. Chancellor Adenauer exploited this military interest in exchange for the acquisition of a higher degree of sovereignty for the

LEFT: riots on the streets of Berlin in June 1953.
RIGHT: "Cookie Bombers" relieve blockaded Berlin in the 1948 airlift.

Federal Republic. A conservative Catholic, Adenauer was less concerned with the question of the country's eventual reunification than with gaining an equal say for the Federal Republic in the chambers of the new European Economic Community (EEC).

As far as the Soviets were concerned, a rearmed West Germany as part of a western alliance represented a provocation of incalculable proportions. In 1952, in an attempt to prevent Germany's integration with the West, Stalin offered a peace treaty for a united, neutral Germany. The Soviet Union was prepared to sacrifice the East German state for a political price, and its offers were repeated several times before the Federal Republic's entry into NATO in 1955. The chance for a reunification of Germany had been presented but it was a chance that Adenauer, who rejected neutrality, chose to ignore.

Realising that US forces would not be withdrawn from Germany, the Soviet Union now proceeded with the consolidation and expansion of the area under its control. In 1955 the GDR acquired its own armed forces, the Volksarmee (Peoples' Army,) and entered the Eastern Bloc's new military alliance, the Warsaw Pact.

ESPIONAGE IN THE COLD WAR

At the epicentre of Cold War tension between East and West, divided Germany underwent endless trauma, particularly in the field of espionage, where one German's patriotic duty would be another's treachery. West Germany's automatic granting of citizenship to anyone defecting from the East made it relatively easy for the GDR's Ministry of State Security to plant its agents in useful positions in the government and security apparatus of the Federal Republic.

Masterminding these operations was the charismatic figure of Markus Wolf, the longest-serving of the Soviet Bloc's intelligence chiefs. One of his most productive strategies was the dispatch of personable male agents with the task of seducing lonely middle-aged female secretaries with access to classified information; some of these "Red Casanovas" even went as far as marrying their victims in order to remain above suspicion.

But Wolf's greatest coup was probably the deployment of Günther Guillaume against the West German Chancellor, Willy Brandt. Guillaume used personal connections to worm his way into Brandt's confidence, eventually in 1969 becoming his personal secretary. For five years he supplied his East German master (and thus the KGB) with invaluable information on western policy. His exposure in 1974 shook West Germany and led directly to Brandt's resignation.

The new Ostpolitik

After the Cuba crisis in 1962, when America challenged the USSR's right to base missiles on the Caribbean island, it seemed as though the superpowers had arrived at détente. In West Germany, Willy Brandt, heading a social democrat-liberal coalition, geared his new Ostpolitik towards the preservation of the unity of the German nation under the prevailing conditions of division. On the international level, this policy was aimed at forcing a "recognition of reality" – the reality of the postwar borders.

With Brandt's election as Federal Chancellor in 1969 there emerged a leader who was,

largely for tactical reasons, reviled by various political opponents both for his anti-Nazi stance during the war, when he had fled to Norway, and for now acknowledging the reality of the "other Germany", something that was anathema to most politicians in the conservative CDU. As for the ordinary East Germans, many pinned their hopes on Brandt. In March 1970 they gave him an enthusiastic reception when he arrived in Erfurt for the first negotiations with the GDR Prime Minister Willi Stoph.

The road to reunification

The long-term perspective of the liberal Ostpolitik towards a reunification of the country became rather lost in the 1970s and 1980s. The preservation of two German states came to be defended, especially in German intellectual circles. The two states had gone their separate ways for so long that many felt that reunification had no longer any place on the political agenda. Only occasionally – as, for example, in 1976 when the GDR expelled the poet and singer Wolf Biermann whose songs had attacked the East German leader Erich Honecker – were doubts cast on this ideology of division.

German unity came about very suddenly, when nobody really expected it would happen at all. In 1987, Erich Honecker had been received in West Germany with great ceremony, thereby seeming to confirm the existence of two equal-ranking German states. Two years later, in October 1989, East Germany celebrated its 40th birthday with the leaden slogan: "The development of the German Democratic Republic will continue to be the work of all the people." This motto would prove to be true – but in a very different way to that which the GDR regime had envisaged.

When Mikhail Gorbachev came to power in the USSR in 1985, the GDR leadership made it clear that it would continue on its dogmatic course, if necessary against the will of the reformer in the Kremlin. But in 1989 the reform-minded Communist government of Hungary opened its border with Austria, refusing to obstruct the flight of "holiday-making" East Germans to the west. Every evening, Western television beamed pictures of the apparently inexhaustible stream of refugees into East German living rooms, but the government refused to be deflected from its rigid course.

1968 AND ALL THAT

The late 1960s marked a turning point in the development of the Federal Republic. Following the economic recession of 1966–7 the country was rocked by student revolts. The protests were directed primarily at the Vietnam War, but they also discovered the revolutionary theme of global emancipation. As their idols, the students chose Ho Chi Minh, Mao Tse-Tung and Che Guevara.

More important in the long run was the revolution that took place within society itself through the "1968 generation". In a roundabout way, the "68" philosophy of life led to the emergence of the powerful German ecological movement that was later known as "the Greens".

Now was the moment for the East German opposition to act. A group of 100 people published an "Appeal 1989" for the founding of a "New Forum", calling for a broad dialogue on problems and a common search for solutions. Within a few weeks, some hundred thousand citizens had joined the New Forum.

The Wall collapses

Before that fateful Monday demonstration in Leipzig on 9 October 1989 – these demonstrations had already been occurring each week for months – the situation became critical. Task forces were placed on the alert and local

neutralised the hard-line stance of the regime, and in the event the state held back.

On 18 October, Honecker resigned, his closest confidantes with him. But the party leadership in Berlin had not begun to recognise the changing times. Instead of entering into negotiations with opposition groups, it attempted to save itself with non-committal announcements of reform once things had quietened down. But this wasn't good enough. On 4 November, a million people took to the streets in Berlin demanding a pluralist democracy for the GDR. On 9 November, almost the entire Politburo resigned and, at the end of a press conference,

hospitals prepared blood supplies. The press announced that "counter-revolutionary activities" would be stopped for good, if necessary "with weapons in hand". But on that evening, 70,000 people gathered and Leipzig experienced the largest demonstration since the uprising on 17 June 1953. The demonstration could well have been smashed by force had not Kurt Masur, director of the Gewandhaus orchestra, gone on radio together with two local SED secretaries to appeal for calm. This effectively

LEFT: Mikhail Gorbachev's reforms led to the ultimate collapse of the Berlin Wall.
ABOVE: east meets west at the Brandenburg Gate.

it was announced, almost casually, that the travel laws were no longer in place. A few hours later, TV stations broadcast astonishing scenes of joy as hundreds of thousands crossed the Wall from East to West Berlin, watched by the guards who would once have shot to kill anyone approaching the border.

Some thought that the two German states might continue to exist side by side, but the people's verdict was made clear in East Germany's first – and last – free elections; they would only be satisfied with reunification. On 3 October 1990, ecstatic celebrations marked the merging of East and West Germany. The postwar period was over. ❑

GERMANY TODAY

Reunification first brought joy, then consternation. Germans increasingly began to question their social values and their role within Europe

German reunification is now history. Both within and outside the country, everyone has got used to the new silhouette that sprawls across central Europe on the nightly TV news maps, occupying the space where two countries used to be. Germans themselves have stopped making quite such a firm distinction between the "old states", the *Alte Länder* of West Germany, and the "new states", the five *Neue Länder* of the former German Democratic Republic (GDR). Today, Germany's 16 states form a patchwork as varied and decentralised as the country has known virtually since it first became a sovereign nation in 1871.

But exactly what is the identity of this country, which is on the one hand Europe's economic powerhouse, yet which on the other hand is still torn by questions of its past history and its future role in the world? There's no single answer. But there are a few definite elements to help orientate the observer.

United yet divided

The biggest event in the history of postwar Germany was the fall of the Berlin Wall. On the morning of 9 November 1989, the sound of chisels hacking at the graffiti-spattered concrete divide between East and West Berlin was broadcast around the world, and the world happily joined in the heady celebrations that followed the destruction of what had symbolised both the country's division and the cold war in general.

But for all the joy of a divided country coming together again, anticipation quickly turned to trepidation. The West German government had never officially recognised East Germany, so its only option politically was to absorb the other country as soon as possible. But many East Germans, while eager to profit from the benefits of the Western lifestyle, weren't as uniformly thrilled as Westerners had expected

at the prospect of abandoning, lock, stock and barrel the only country they had ever known: to them, the West seemed all too ready to dismiss the GDR out of hand. Yet, on 3 October 1990, East Germany ceased to exist; and on that day, the growing pains officially began.

Reunification has clearly brought many tan-

gible benefits to the former East Germany. Much has changed physically in the east. Buildings have been repaired and sport the latest in artificial cladding and ready-made ornamentation from the new do-it-yourself markets that stand cheek by jowl with Western-style supermarkets; roads have been resurfaced for the new western cars that speed past the few Trabants and Wartburgs that have managed to survive.

But beneath this improved surface, there's still not only a profound sense of otherness, but also an awareness that the "new states" may take far longer than anyone expected to reach western levels of prosperity. Indeed, some fear that the decades of dictatorship may leave a

PRECEDING PAGES: German reunification celebrations outside Berlin's Reichstag on 3 October 1990.
LEFT: children at Augsburg's Christmas market.
RIGHT: in party mood by Berlin's Brandenburg Gate.

mark forever. For a long time many *Wessis* (West Germans) regarded *Ossis* (East Germans) as backward, slow, lacking in initiative and enterprise. In their turn, Easterners thought of their western fellow-citizens as arrogant, pushy, superficial, and lacking any sense of social solidarity. There is some truth in the stereotypes; Westerners reared in the "capitalist jungle" seem more independent than those whose individuality and initiative were suppressed by the Communist system.

But as well as the persistence of differences in attitude, there are real and sometimes unsettling differences in the way the East has

evolved since reunification. Despite huge subsidies and financial transfers from West to East, paid for by special taxes, the eastern economy has hardly produced the "blossoming landscapes" promised by Chancellor Kohl in the heady early days of reunification.

The sclerotic heavy industries favoured by the Communist regime have almost all gone, wiping out hundreds of thousands of jobs, which have been only partly replaced by a slowly expanding service sector and modern plants like VW's spectacular glass-walled production line in Dresden. Wholesale depopulation threatens, as people of working age migrate westward in search of jobs, leaving their communities with an unbalanced age structure. This has particularly affected the countryside, but towns like Görlitz on the border with Poland have lost significant numbers of their inhabitants, and even Dresden, with its thriving tourist industry and regained role as state capital of Saxony, has only recently managed to regain its pre-1989 population level.

Economic realities

Germany as a whole nevertheless remains the economic powerhouse of Europe, and the high quality products of its industries continue to enjoy worldwide admiration. In the late 1990s, few were really surprised when Daimler-Benz bought the Chrysler Corporation and Volkswagen acquired Rolls-Royce. BMW may have burnt its fingers with its purchase – and subsequent sale – of Britain's ailing Rover, but its successful update of the Mini was a tribute to the supremacy of German automobile engineering. But like other mature European economies, Germany's growth rate is sluggish. It could be said

OSTALGIE

Despite the Wall, the shortages, the omnipresence of the Stasi secret police and state interference in all areas of their lives, many citizens of the old GDR look back on the rather grey Communist times with a warmth neatly summarised as "Ostalgie" ("nostalgia for the East"). There is no denying that as long as you played by the rules, the state did provide everything a model subject might need: from crèches and summer camps for adolescents to jobs for life, trade union holiday homes and old age pensions (though the elderly were more than welcome to clear off West and become a burden on the capitalists). Living standards might not have been high, but a sense of social solidarity prevailed.

No wonder then that "Ostalgie" has flourished, homing in on some of the key products of the not-very-efficient East German consumer industry – such as Vita-Cola or gherkins from the Spreewald. The Trabant enjoys a vigorous after-life, with restored cars taking visitors on a "Trabi-Safari" round East Berlin. *Ostalgie-Partys* pack in the crowds, with dancing to *Ost-Rock* oldies, appearances by Erich Honecker doubles, and free entry for anyone dressed up in the uniforms of the People's Army or the Free German Youth organisation.

And it is not only Easterners who are gripped by Ostalgie: the 2002 film "Goodbye Lenin", an evocation of the East German idyll, was the work of Westerner Wolfgang Becker!

that the country's strong trade unions have painted themselves into a corner, with a 36-hour working week and a generous minimum wage. Certainly Germans pay for their benefits; with income taxes of up to 54 percent, life here isn't the "free ride" some foreigners imagine.

All the same, a German car worker regards six weeks of annual leave, full health benefits and a comfortable home not as luxuries but as a matter of course. And the short working week allows plenty of time to relax in a beer garden with friends and family in the long summer evenings. There's stiff and widespread opposition to any attempt by companies to downsize and by gov-

emerging globalised era, the nettle will have to be grasped, by a government of whatever colour.

Green concerns

Foreigners commonly stereotype Germany as a place that's clean and where the trains run on time. And indeed, its order and tidiness are part of what make this country such a pleasant place to live in or to visit. Clean white farmhouses sit in well-tended fields; the cities are dotted with expanses of green park, and some of the underground rail systems are as clean as office buildings. Other prominent features of these German cities include bike lanes with their own traffic

ernment to tamper with what is one of the world's most generous and far-reaching social networks. In the early years of the new millennium the task of shifting some of the responsibility for welfare back from the state to the individual fell to the left-wing Red-Green coalition, provoking furious debate and angry demonstrations, and threatening to undermine the government's electoral base. But few doubt that with an ageing population – it's reckoned that by 2035 Germany will be the "oldest" country in the world – and in the

LEFT: dressing up to show nostalgia for the old East.
ABOVE: market stalls such as this one near Berlin's Brandenburg Gate provide the props for dressing up.

lights and recycling containers in every square.

Tidiness doesn't happen by itself and it's no accident that Germany is one of the most ecologically minded countries in the world. One of the first priorities after German reunification was to clean up some of the soured, polluted land spoiled by heedless industrial development in the GDR; and indeed, places like Bitterfeld, once a particularly malodorous corner of the world, are actually being given new life. On a day-to-day level, quality-of-life concerns led to the implementation of catalytic converters in cars early on. Citizens regularly form protest groups against new stretches of motorway through their neighbourhoods. Political parties devote themselves to such noble but quixotic goals as banning cars from cities altogether. A plethora of animal-rights activists protest against vivisection and the fur trade with petitions in the pedestrian zones and posters in metro stations.

The public transport network, with its high-speed intercity trains, its immaculate S-Bahn and Metro systems, and its smooth-gliding trams, might be the envy of other countries, but the car, preferably a high-powered Mercedes, Audi or BMW, remains king. At its disposal is the close-knit mesh of *Autobahnen*, the motorways planned in Weimar days, begun by the Third Reich, and extended by every govern-

persuading his pacifically minded colleagues that sending German forces to keep the peace in former Yugoslavia was morally acceptable. Nevertheless, like the vast majority of Germans, Fischer opposed the invasion of Iraq and refused to join the US-led coalition which ousted Saddam Hussein in 2003.

Literate society

Political involvement is another hallmark of this highly literate society. Indeed, visitors often think that the Germans are better informed about events in their home countries than they are themselves. Take a look at a German news-

ment since. There's still no general speed limit on the *Autobahn*, and the freedom to drive as fast as they like is a prerogative that most Germans still insist on, despite the frightening accident statistics.

With its roots in the student unrest of 1968, the protest culture came of age in the late 1990s, when the ecologically minded Green Party, despite the objections of its more radical members, entered government as the junior partner in a coalition with the Social Democrats. Its journey from street protest to parliamentary responsibility was embodied in the figure of one of its leading "Realos" (Realists), Joska Fischer; as Foreign Minister, Fischer was instrumental in

paper and you'll see why: there's enough text in the weekly paper *Die Zeit* to keep a reader busy for several weeks. There are tabloids, but not on the British or US scale; and the leading daily papers run more to long, thoughtful – even verbose – articles. The country's news magazines have been equally influential, including *Der Spiegel*, which, since its founding in the period immediately after World War II, has shaped public opinion through its editorial posture of the sceptical non-aligned observer and guardian of the public conscience.

Publishing in Germany has a long history, dating back to Gutenberg's invention of the first printing press with moveable letters in the

1430s. Germany has traditionally been the land of the small- and medium-sized publishing house, though with its acquisition of Random House in 1998, the giant Bertelsmann group became the largest publisher in the world.

Considering the comparatively limited market of the German language, it is astounding how large the industry has become – a fact reflected every year in October at the International Book Fair in Frankfurt, where the German contingent packs the main hall. Many of the deals struck here are for co-publisher's agreements, an indication of the fact that Germans tend to read more foreign than home-produced literature: the bestseller lists, especially for fiction, are dominated by US, British and other foreign authors, and in 2004 Tolkien's *Lord of the Rings* was voted the country's favourite read.

Education

Whatever they read in their spare time, Germans still study Goethe and Schiller at school *(see page 33)*. Regulated by the individual states, the country has a strong educational system. Strong, but segregated: by the age of 10, a child has been slated either for vocational training in a Realschule or Hauptschule or for the university track in a Gymnasium, in which 12 or 13 years of schooling culminates in the *Abitur* (comparable to England's A-levels, or France's *Baccalauréat*).

In fact, Germany's educational system is built on essentially medieval foundations. Vocational training still moves young workers and artisans through the traditional progression of apprentice-journeyman-master, just as it was practised in the medieval guilds. It is a system that has worked well, producing the highly trained workforce that has been the bedrock of Germany's industrial success.

In contrast, university students pursue their academic studies in a loose, rather unsupervised programme that can extend over five, six, even seven or more years. And, because German universities are available to everyone with an *Abitur* certificate, they are becoming increasingly overcrowded. In 1997, students protested against these conditions; but, although they were very vocal about what they didn't like, they seemed rather unclear about exactly what they wanted.

LEFT: the ICE trains, here in Berlin Hauptbahnhof, just one symbol of the modern, efficient Germany.
RIGHT: magazine readers are spoiled for choice.

German identity

The issue of whether being German can be a source of pride was earnestly debated in the first years of the new millennium, on the whole inconclusively. Images of the country's clouded past still inhibit many from expressing anything that might be thought of as patriotism or nationalism (always excepting excitable football fans). The younger generation, despite having had nothing at all to do with the crimes of the Nazis, can feel uncomfortable, almost apologetic, about being German. Indeed, there is often a tendency for people to bend over too far in the opposite direction – as, for example,

CHANGING TIMES

The process of transition to a service economy in Germany has been a gradual one. Until the 1980s, shops were legally obliged to close at 6 or 6.30pm on weekdays, and all day Sundays, meaning that office workers had to rush if they wanted to buy groceries. After much debate, store hours were extended to 8 or 8.30pm. This giant step for German shoppers has paved the way for shopping centres open until 10pm, 24-hour service stations-cum-mini marts, and Sunday opening for bakeries as well as shops in tourist areas. "The customer is always right" has also emerged as an approach, its absence heretofore not due to deliberate rudeness but simply the result of a different system.

in the aversion some might have to the operas of Richard Wagner, grimacing with distaste at their evocation of a Nazi past rather than looking beyond the Nazi misappropriation of Wagner's music to see in these works one of the glories of German culture.

It's important to keep this in mind when considering, the persistence of neo-Nazi "incidents", like the harassment – sometimes violent – of asylum-seekers and other obvious foreigners, or the noisy pilgrimage to the home town of Rudolf Hess, Hitler's deputy. Demonstrations of German nationalism can quickly grow ugly, like any effusion of feelings that

only by the SS. For all their controversy, these debates allowed feelings to be aired and represented – a step in the long process of healing.

But the German identity is not just about a relationship to one period of the past, nor is it simply a question of nationality. Far more important for many Germans is their regional identity which, partly because of the country's short history as a unified nation, remains very strong. Beyond the rather crude distinction often made between Prussians (northerners) and Bavarians (southerners), most people like to define themselves first and foremost in terms of the specific regions from which they come, whether it be

have been repressed too long. But rather than these radical (and indefensible) outbursts by a tiny minority, a better indication of the general population's efforts to come to terms with both negative and positive aspects of German identity were the nationwide debates sparked by works dealing with the Holocaust or World War II.

Emotional discussions were prompted by the film *Schindler's List*; by the book *Hitler's Willing Executioners*, about the culpability of average German citizens in the Holocaust; and by the exhibition *Crimes of the Wehrmacht*, which showed images of Wehrmacht soldiers committing wartime crimes on civilians that many Germans thought had been perpetrated

Lower Franconia or Upper Bavaria. They will be equally keen to class themselves as European.

Germany in Europe

It is, above all else, the European project that has enabled Germany to put much of its past behind it. The spirit of cooperation which is supposed to characterise the European Union was espoused by Konrad Adenauer, the first Chancellor of the Federal Republic. Since then the torch has been carried by successive chancellors, notably by Helmut Kohl, who earned his place in history not only as the longest-serving head of government and the architect of German reunification but as a passionate advocate of

European integration. Nevertheless, in 1994, Kohl still felt that it was not appropriate for the leader of Germany to attend the 50th anniversary of the D-Day landings in Normandy; 10 years later, it was significant that his successor, the Social Democrat Gerhard Schröder, not only attended the ceremony, but was able to declare openly that the landings had heralded the liberation of Germany itself from Nazism.

In the same year, 2004, Germany moved centre stage in Europe as the EU welcomed 10 new member states, most of them former satellites of the old Soviet Union. In 2005, new chancellor Angela Merkel, emerging as a unifying force in European politics, was quick to demonstrate her special concern for these latest member states while calling for tough economic reforms if Europe's precious welfare systems were to be saved. The country now had open borders with Poland and the Czech Republic, nations with whom relations remained prickly though polite. Germans worry about the potential loss of jobs to low-waged Poles, while many Poles still feel Germany has not done enough to make good its wartime devastation of their country. Less numerous than Poles, the Czechs nevertheless embody a source of competitive, highly skilled labour, and in addition are adamant in their refusal to reconsider the justice of their postwar expulsion of the German population of the Sudetenland.

Citizens and foreigners

A much-vexed issue of German identity has been the way the country treats its foreigners. German policy on immigration was in the past governed by a law dating back to 1913 based on the principle that only those with "German blood" have automatic right of citizenship. This has been of considerable benefit to ethnic Germans whose ancestors settled over the centuries in many regions of the former Eastern Bloc; after the collapse of this alliance around 1990, many of them flocked back to "their" country, where they were entitled to the pensions, benefits and other perks of a normal German citizen.

The 7.2 million-plus *Ausländer*, or foreigners, living in the country were long denied the same privilege. While Germany has been remarkably generous in taking in both asylum-seekers and

foreign guest workers, these foreign residents have generally remained "foreigners", not Germans. This has become especially apparent in the case of the huge population of Turks (now about 2 million) who first arrived in the 1950s and 1960s and continue to form a major part of the blue-collar labour force, either in industry or doing minor jobs like sweeping streets, cleaning buildings and collecting rubbish.

Their children, of course, have grown up in Germany, speaking fluent German and attending German schools and universities. These children have formed a nebulous caste not quite at home in either country, with many feeling that they

have little or no stake in German society. The issue is given extra edge through the vexed question of Turkey's entry into the EU, a move most Germans oppose. The "foreigner debate" has run for years. Many foreigners were granted automatic right of citizenship for the first time with a law passed in 1999 entitling people to German citizenship through birth rather than bloodline.

Official recognition of the fact that Germany is a country of immigrants reflects an increasingly multicultural society. While conservative forces may bemoan the dilution of German nationhood, most Germans are content to live in an ethnically diverse society – and to them race simply isn't an issue. ❏

LEFT: immigrant shipyard workers in Bremerhaven.
RIGHT: Chancellor Angela Merkel, leader of Germany's coalition government, enjoys a cabinet meeting.

FOOD AND DRINK

From Bavaria to Schleswig-Holstein, Germany's cuisine is surprisingly varied, mirroring the country's climate, landscape and lifestyle

The story of food in Germany begins, as one might expect, with beer. Medieval monasteries housed some of Germany's first kitchens. The monks cultivated gardens and livestock, ran dairies, gathered fruit, herbs and wildflowers to distill distinctive brandies, or schnapps, and grew hops to brew the country's first beer. The oldest brewery in Germany, Weihenstephan in Freising, in Bavaria, is documented as early as AD 1040.

Beer and bread

For over 500 years Germany was proud of the fact that its 1,400-odd breweries were still bound by the "purity laws" *(Reinheitsgebot)* of 1516, which stipulate that only hops, malt, yeast and water may be used. But the lobby of beer drinkers and breweries could not prevent the abolition of the old laws to allow free movement of goods within a single European market. Germans claim their country's beers – *Helles*, or blond beer; *Dunkles*, dark beer; *Pils*, thinner and slightly bitter; *Weissbier*, a yeasty, cloudy brew; and legion other local variants – are especially flavoursome. Beer was truly a food in the Middle Ages, particularly during Lent, when monks could drink but were limited as to their food intake. As a result, they brewed their beer with an extra kick; this *Starkbier* (strong beer) is still a Bavarian tradition.

The other staff of life in Germany is bread. Few countries offer such a range and selection of this staple food. The rolls *(Brötchen or Semmel)* served with hotel breakfasts are well and good, but to understand the appeal of German bread you have to go into a traditional bakery and examine the array of sourdough and rye loaves: big flour-dusted wheels of *Bauernbrot* (farmer's bread); the firm compact bodies of *Vollkorn-* and *Sonnenblumenbrot* (wholewheat or sunflower-seed bread), filled with grains that crunch between your teeth; *Pumpernickel*, dark

chocolate brown in colour or thick, chewy *Brezeln* (pretzels), warm out of the oven, studded with chunks of salt.

Like bread and beer, most of the signature elements of German cuisine have developed out of basic ingredients and bear traces of a peasant origin. People ate what they could cul-

tivate themselves and the relatively cold climate didn't allow for many green vegetables: potatoes *(Kartoffeln)* and cabbage *(Kohl* or *Kraut)* dominated. Principal crops now include barley, wheat, oats and rye. Apart from various kinds of game *(Wild)* – for example *Reh* (venison), *Wildschwein* (wild boar) or *Hase* (rabbit), or fowl such as *Fasan* (pheasant) – beef *(Rind)* and pork *(Schwein)* dominate, not forgetting the numerous offal dishes which are very popular in the south.

This does not mean that dining out in Germany is monotonous. For one thing, the country's restaurants today reflect Germany's growing internationalism and large resident immigrant population. The presence of Italian and Turkish "guest workers" is demonstrated in a plethora of Italian restaurants and döner kebab stands. Compounding these offerings are a wide array of Asian eateries: Chinese, Vietnamese, Thai, Indian and Japanese sushi bars. And, at the high end of the price scale, there are a few bastions of French *haute cuisine*.

Then there are legion restaurants, large and small, which are devoted to serving up local specialities in

land's *Sauerbraten*, a kind of pot roast of marinated beef. As for the dumplings, called *Knödel* in the south and *Klösse* in the north, the choice tends to be between *Kartoffelknödel* (potato dumpling), a rather rubbery globe; and the Bavarian *Semmelknödel*, a bread dumpling that more readily absorbs the meat's sauce. *Knödel* are also the centrepieces of local braised dishes: *Rahmpilze* or *Rahmschwammerl*, fresh mushrooms in a thick cream sauce, might have greater

> **EATING WEISSWURST**
>
> The best way to eat *Weisswurst* is to slit the sausage along the middle and separate the edible inside from the skin. Some people prefer to open one end and suck out the contents. *Weisswurst* is normally eaten before midday.

new, creative incarnations, demonstrating a growing awareness of the virtues of other cuisines and of how to work those into the best of German cooking.

Some local specialities

A "typical" German dining experience remains roast pork, red cabbage and a dumpling: *Schweinebraten*, *Blaukraut* and *Knödel*. Local specialities along these lines include Bavaria's *Schweinshax'n*, a roasted pork knuckle served encased in a crispy layer of bubbling fat; Berlin's *Eisbein*, the same portion of the pig's anatomy, but pickled; or *Spanferkel* (suckling pig). More generally appealing is the Rhine-

appeal than similar concoctions of *Lüngerl* (lung), which are eaten only in southern Bavaria. Then there are *Leberknödel*, liver dumplings, presented in plain beef broth as a first course of *Leberknödelsuppe*.

Sausages, or *Wurst*, one of the best-known features of German cuisine, are more often a snack or light lunch than a proper dinner. Each German region has its own and its own way of eating them. The Frankfurter needs no introduction; try the thinner, tasty *Rheinische* or, in the Rhineland Palatinate, *Pfälzer*. You can make a good meal of *Nürnberger Bratwürste*, finger-sized delicacies served in groups of six or eight on a bed of sauerkraut. Würzburg's

Blaue Zipfel are pickled in brine. And in Munich, between ten and eleven in the morning, when people in other countries take a coffee break, is the time for *Weisswurst*. Borne to your table in a tureen of hot water, these fat veal sausages, white as their name implies and flecked inside with parsley, are simmered – never boiled – and eaten with a sweet, grainy mustard and a tall glass of yeasty *Weissbier*.

Other kinds of preserved pork include numerous varieties of ham *(Schinken)* and bacon *(Speck)*. In the middle of the country you find *Kasseler Rippchen*, a kind of smoked porkchop. And Bavaria's *Leberkäs*, another snack

For all the prevalence of pork, Germany is not without its seafood – or lakefood. In the southern part of the country, fresh *Forellen* (trout) are caught in the rivers and lakes. In Lake Constance, there are 35 kinds of fish, including pike-perch *(Zander)*. And the northern part of the country, of course, is home turf for fishermen; specialities here include *Matjes*, young herring, often served in a sauce of sour cream, onion and apple.

Chicken, too, is a staple, especially in beer gardens and at Oktoberfest, where the standard order is *ein halbes Hendl* – half a chicken spitroasted to a satisfyingly crispy brown.

bar standby, is a kind of meatloaf served in hot slices in a roll slathered with mustard *(Senf)*.

Many local specialities are variants on the basic ingredients of meat, potato and onion. In the Rhineland, there's *Himmel und Erde*, "heaven and earth", a combination of potatoes, onions and apples; or *Hunsrücker Festessen*, sauerkraut with potatoes and ham. In Leipzig, however, the signature meal is *Leipziger Allerlei*, a combination of various young vegetables garnished with dumplings.

LEFT: more than 300 different varieties of bread are baked in Germany.
ABOVE: sampling the local flavours in Passau.

Vegetarians stick to *Obazda*, a cheese spread of Camembert, egg yolk and butter, served with thinly sliced raw onions and *Brezeln*. Similar to this is the Rhineland's *Handkäs' mit Musik*, a curd cheese served with onions: the latter provide the "music" of the dish's name. Vegetarians should also try to come in May, asparagus season. Schwetzingen and Schrobenhausen in the west, as well as Beelitz in the east are the epicentres of this *Spargelzeit*: the fat white asparagus is served with everything from smoked salmon to ham to plain melted butter.

Apart from dumplings, potatoes are the most common German *Beilage* (side dish): *Pellkartoffeln* (boiled and salted potatoes), *Bratkartof-*

feln (thick wedges roasted to a crispy brown), or *Kartoffelbrei* (mashed potatoes). *Reiber-datschi* or *Kartoffelpuffer* (thin, crispy potato pancakes) are eaten as a main dish together with stewed fruit. Noodles are common too, especially in Swabia and Baden-Württemberg, which is home to one of Germany's happiest culinary inventions, *Spätzle*. These "little sparrows" are chewy, twisted homemade noodles and form the basis for the ultimate variation on macaroni and cheese, *Käsespätzle*. Other noodle specialities from this region are *Schupfnudeln*, a thicker, ovoid noodle made with potatoes (and similar to Italian gnocchi) served mixed with sauerkraut

and bits of *Speck*, a type of bacon, and *Maultaschen*, the German answer to ravioli.

Baden-Württemberg has one of the best cuisines in all of Germany. A roadside inn in the Black Forest may prove to sport a Michelin star and a French-trained chef (Wehlauer in Baden-Baden is one such). Apart from the old standby Black Forest Cherry Gâteau (*Schwarzwälder Kirschtorte*), one autumn tradition is *Zwiebelkuchen*, onion tart, served with *Federweisser*, the youngest white wine, which goes down like fizzy grape juice: the combination produces both inebriation and flatulence in short order. Black Forest ham (*Schwarz-wälder Schinken*) is the best in the country.

Sweet delights

In Bavaria, where the culinary influence is from neighbouring Austria, you find *Mehlspeisen*, or "flour dishes": *Dampfnudel*, a steamed dumpling swimming in custard, sprinkled with cinnamon or poppy-seeds; *Kaiserschmarrn*, a thick pancake sliced in strips, sprinkled with raisins and powdered sugar and served with plum compote or apple sauce; or *Ausgezogene*, a type of deep-fried doughnut. Another confection is the jelly doughnut known as *Krapfen* which, though available year-round, is particularly associated with Carnival.

Christmas, of course, is the season with the greatest number of baked treats. Nürnberg's signature is *Lebkuchen*, or gingerbread: these thickish discs, baked on a circle of papery, edible wafer *(Oblaten)* and glazed with sugar or chocolate, are packed for export all over the world. More like British gingerbread men are the spicy *Spekulatius* biscuits: the dough is pressed into moulds shaped like people or animals. Aachen's version is known as *Printen*. In Dresden, Christmas is the high season for *Stollen*, the famous local yeast coffee cake, often with a marzipan centre.

In Germany, such baked goods represent a kind of afternoon tea: four o'clock is the hour for *Kaffee und Kuchen*, when ladies flock to elegant cafés. Cakes include *Baumkuchen*, a dryish sponge cake baked in compact rings, sometimes coated in chocolate; *Bienenstich* (bee sting), a yeasty sweet bread surrounding a thick layer of butter cream; or, in the south, *Zwetschg'ndatschi*, a rectangular plum tart. After dinner, people are more likely to eat more liquid desserts: *Rote Grütze*, a compote of red fruits, is served with thick cream, ice cream or vanilla sauce *(Vanillesauce)*.

Spearheading the growth of Germany's culinary culture is the southern part of the country, perhaps because leading chefs prefer to open up shop in some picturesque Alpine village than in a busy city. Michelin stars are clustered in Munich but twinkle also in Düsseldorf and, increasingly, in Berlin. But whether the meal is in a gourmet temple or a simple inn, the best way to round it off is with a shot of schnapps – from *Enzian* to *Kirschwasser* – to settle the stomach and make a gesture to the monks who launched the adventure of German cooking. ❑

LEFT: Austrian-influenced apple strudel.

German Wine

Eighty years ago the top wines of Germany were priced at the same level as a great Bordeaux such as Lafite. By the 1970s the overall reputation of German wines had slumped to a dismal level. The German wine industry itself was largely to blame, having bent over backwards to produce vast quantities of cheap sugary wines to please an undemanding market.

Yet Germany has picked up its reputation and remains the source of some of the greatest white wines in the world. Its secret weapon has always been the Riesling grape. This astonishingly versatile grape variety is capable of producing rich dry wines or gloriously honeyed sweet wines. Those grown in northern regions such as the Moselle have the additional benefit of being very low in alcohol – with half the level you would encounter in a burly red from southern Europe – yet amazingly long-lived. Good Riesling can age in the bottle for at least 20 years, becoming more rich and complex as time goes by. Although bone-dry Rieslings are produced in the Moselle, they can taste tart to those unaccustomed to the style, and most visitors prefer slightly sweet wines such as a classic Kabinett or Spätlese, where a hint of sweetness is perfectly balanced by the wine's refreshing acidity. The ultra-sweet wines made from Riesling, such as *Beerenauslese* or ice wine are, unfortunately, both rare and very expensive.

Riesling is never aged in large barrels that would mask the complex flavours that arise from the soil on which it is grown. Travel along the Moselle river and you will see the vineyards planted on steep slate soils that give a wonderfully racy mineral tang to the wines. In the Rheingau, where the vines are planted on a series of slopes facing due south across the Rhine, the varied and often rocky soils give different nuances and complexity to the wines. Unlike the Moselle, the Rheingau is a region of largely princely and monastic estates, many of which are open to visitors. Rheinhessen is an often overlooked region, as its plains are the source of Germany's least distinguished wines, but along the Rhine, above villages such as Nierstein and Nackenheim, are red-soiled vineyards that produce wonderfully zesty Rieslings, both sweet and dry.

Riesling thrives in regions where natural acidity is best preserved. Elsewhere in Germany you will find considerable diversity. In Franconia, especially around Würzburg, Silvaner as well as Riesling produce bone-dry whites of power and concentration. Further east in the Saxony region around Dresden, the Müller-Thurgau grape gives robust whites for everyday drinking.

Baden is a particularly enticing region, stretching for a couple of hundred kilometres south along the Rhine on the opposite bank to Alsace. This too is a dry wine region, and one of the few areas where good red wine can be made. Gutedel (Chasselas) is a local white speciality, but the Burgundian varieties such as Pinot Blanc and Pinot Noir deliver far more interesting wines. They also offer a perfect match to the fine regional cuisine.

The Rhineland Palatinate lies midway between the Riesling zone and the southern zones, and its wines reflect this. Villages like Forst and Deidesheim are the source of fine, sometimes dry Rieslings, but you can also find rich whites and sometimes reds from the Burgundian varieties, as well as thrilling sweet wines from varieties such as Rieslaner.

The problem for the wine-loving visitor to Germany is that one is spoilt for choice. If anything, wines are made in too many styles – in Baden and Württemberg you can even find smooth red wines produced to appeal to local tastes. Fortunately, most estates and cooperatives welcome visitors and allow you to taste extensively before you buy. ❑

RIGHT: Rheingau grapes.

THE PERFORMING ARTS

Generous state subsidies and long-standing cultural traditions have helped
Germany to develop a theatre and music scene all of its own

A ïda as a cleaning woman? *Il Trovatore*'s Manrico as the head of a motorcycle gang? Nazis marching through *Boris Godunov*? These improbable scenes are everyday happenings in German theatres.

Theatre and opera

Germany's largely state-supported arts scene is virtually unparalleled the world over, and nowhere is this clearer than in the country's theatres. There's no Federal Ministry of Culture in Germany, but the 16 states and individual communities support more than 150 theatres. Most sizeable towns have their own, usually producing spoken drama and opera, musicals and dance. Many of their employees, from administration to the *corps de ballet*, prompters to percussionists in the orchestra pit, are technically state officials, with year-round salaries, full benefits and paid holidays.

Classical pieces from Goethe and Schiller, Mozart and Wagner, and "foreigners" such as Shakespeare and Verdi form the staple diet of Germany's theatregoers. The fact that the theatre scene is dominated by a staple of classics has led to the development of *Regietheater* or "director's theatre": the creative emphasis has gradually shifted from the author of a play or the composer of an opera to the stage director, whose job it is to cast in a new light works which many people in the audience know almost by heart.

Regietheater was born in postwar East Berlin, where the director Walter Felsenstein took over the Komische Oper and began producing radical re-interpretations of opera. For Felsenstein, musical values were weighed against the importance of dramatic effect: he wanted to present operas that were viable works of theatre, with three-dimensional characters and the power to move, even to shake up, the audience. Gone were the old clichés of over-

weight singers performing stock, empty gestures; rather, Felsenstein based his readings on psychological interpretations of a work's characters, situations and settings. Sometimes, he even set an opera in a modern context rather than the historic one the composer had intended; this practice, radical when it came on

the scene, has become virtually routine today. Not everyone liked Felsenstein's stagings at the time; but they managed to transform the views of a whole generation.

Another major 1950s influence on contemporary German stage direction was Wieland Wagner, Richard's grandson, who ran the festival at Bayreuth from 1951 to 1966. In his productions, he stripped sets down to a bare minimum, leaving simply clad singers in the sparsest of settings. In the tetralogy of the *Ring* cycle, for instance, he relied almost exclusively on coloured light for effect.

Both Felsenstein and Wieland Wagner have had a profound influence on the way theatre is

LEFT: a performance of *Hamlet Machine* in the Deutsche Theater, Berlin. **RIGHT:** a comic portrayal of Brünnhilde in Wagner's opera *Die Walküre*.

presented today in the German-speaking world. Felsenstein's students carried their teacher's torch all over Germany: plenty of theatres still mount productions by the late Ruth Berghaus, Harry Kupfer or Joachim Herz. Other notable directors include Claus Peymann, Johannes Schaaf, Herbert Wernicke, Peter Konwitschny, Hansgünther Heyme, Frank Baumbauer, Dieter Dorn and Friedrich Schirmer.

Of course, directors don't only re-interpret classic works of the past; some also create pieces that are wholly new. East German-born Einar Schleef veers from re-interpreting the ancients to trying to introduce their theatrical

values – such as the Greek chorus – into contemporary, enigmatic and very long works of avant-garde theatre. John Kresnik has developed a kind of provocative dance-theatre hybrid. Swiss director Christoph Marthaler specialises in wryly humorous examinations of the human condition: in Murx, a railway station waiting room becomes a metaphor for the stagnation of reunified Germany. An overview of the year's hottest productions of spoken theatre, selected by an international jury, is presented at the annual Theatertreffen in Berlin.

Classical ballet to Tanztheater

Opera and spoken theatre aren't the only beneficiaries of Germany's generosity to the arts: dance, too, is subsidised, and this fact has drawn expats aplenty. In the 1960s and 1970s, the ballet companies of Stuttgart and Hamburg attracted international attention: Hamburg for the classical, elegant works of US-born John Neumeier (still active there); Stuttgart for the perhaps more innovative interpretations of the late John Cranko (whose *Romeo and Juliet* and *Onegin* have attained the status of modern classics).

In 1984, the American William Forsythe took over Frankfurt's ballet company and proceeded to take modern ballet in a whole new direction, developing balletic movement in unprecedented ways and interpolating a mixture of German *Tanztheater*.

This latter genre demonstrates that Germany has a vital dance tradition of its own. Before the war, Essen's Folkwang School was a centre for Expressionist dance with such figures as dance theorist Rudolf Laban and choreographer Kurt Jooss. The latter's ballet *Der Grüne Tisch (The Green Table)* has become a modern classic: the table of the title is a negotiating table, around which elderly politicos wrangle until war breaks out with all its attendant horrors.

While expressionist dance, like expressionist painting, was effectively curtailed by the Nazis, the blend of dramatic narrative and dance in works like *The Green Table* influenced the development of "dance theatre" decades later. The most widely recognised figure in this genre is Pina Bausch, whose company in Wuppertal explores interpersonal relations and the human condition, as well as choreographic movement, in works such as *Carnations* or *1990*.

COSMOPOLITAN INFLUENCES

Regietheater's influence has spread all over the Western world. Wieland Wagner's abstractions influenced the US *Theatermacher* Robert Wilson; Felsenstein's precepts inspired a whole school of stage direction at the English National Opera. But partly because of Germany's generous system, many foreign artists are drawn here, giving audiences a chance to see Wilson's latest works at Hamburg's Thalia Theatre or the Berliner Ensemble. At Munich's National Theatre Englishman Sir Peter Jonas brought a touch of subversion to the city's once staid opera climate. His successor, Austrian-born Nikolaus Bachler, started his international career in Vienna.

"Classical" spaces, classical music

German art isn't all about exploring the new. The architecture of its theatres and concert halls perfectly reflects its identity: on the one hand, a healthy dose of the modern, with the many theatres and halls that were built after the war (such as the philharmonic halls in Berlin and Munich); on the other, a glorious past reflected in faithful restorations of the Semperoper in Dresden, the National and Cuvilliés theatres in Munich, the Staatsoper in Stuttgart and Unter den Linden in Berlin.

Quintessential artistic expression of that glorious past is the symphony orchestra, which

But of course, even symphony orchestras undergo a certain degree of change. Flagship of the country's orchestras, the Berlin Philharmonic lost a piece of its history with the death of Herbert von Karajan. Sir Simon Rattle succeeded Claudio Abbado in summer 2002. Leipzig's Gewandhaus, which at 300-plus years of age is the oldest orchestra in the country, played a key role in the mass demonstrations of 1989 that led to the fall of the Wall; it was shaken when its long-time conductor Kurt Masur, who restored the orchestra to its position of musical excellence after long years of neglect under the Socialist regime, departed

basically took on its present form in 19th-century Germany and still performs a predominantly 19th-century repertoire. Listening to some of the country's leading ensembles, such as the Dresdener Staatskapelle or the Bamberg Symphony Orchestra, you're transported back in time. It was long maintained of Leipzig's Gewandhaus that one reason the ensemble was able to preserve its signature rich, mellow string tone was that most of its players were trained at the same conservatory, where this tradition was kept alive.

for the New York Philharmonic. Masur wasn't the only beneficiary of the traditional American regard for German conductors; Philadelphia was able to claim Wolfgang Sawallisch.

For years Munich has deserved the title "city of conductors", demonstrating that conductors can travel in both directions across the Atlantic. Lorin Maazel led its best orchestra, the Bavarian Radio Orchestra (Bayerischer Rundfunk); Zubin Mehta took over at the Bavarian State Opera and handed over to Californian Kent Najano in 2006; while James Levine, formerly artistic director at the Metropolitan Opera in New York, acted as chief conductor of the Munich Philharmonic before Christian Thielemann's succession in 2004. ❑

LEFT: *Frida Kahlo* by John Kresnik.
ABOVE: James Levine, taking control in Munich.

CONTEMPORARY ART

From the "Bridge" and the "Blauer Reiter" to the Bauhaus and Beuys,
Germany is home to a vibrant modern art scene

While art lovers today tend to think of the late 19th century as the period of the development of French Impressionism, the new nation of Germany was also taking its place on the international arts scene.

The works of Caspar David Friedrich had already given visual expression to the dramatic principles of the Romantic movement, depicting Man alone in communion with Nature, set amid wild natural beauties by storm or moonlight. Innovation remained a byword for Germany's artists, producing eccentrics on the one hand, major creators on the other. Franz von Stuck, the Klimt of Munich, created smoky Jugendstil portraits in his fantastic villa around the turn of the 20th century; Arnold Böcklin painted nymphs and other classical deities. But new developments were already brewing that were to leave such creatures of the imagination in the dust of dramatic artistic advances. Artistic expression moved into the foreground.

Expressionist masters

In 1905 in Dresden, a group of artists formed an alliance known as *Die Brücke* ("the Bridge"). Emil Nolde, Ernst Ludwig Kirchner, Karl Schmidt-Rottluff and their colleagues helped create and define the Expressionist movement with their colourful, direct canvases. At the same time, Russian émigré painter and teacher Wassily Kandinsky was already at work in Munich on increasingly colourful and increasingly abstract landscapes; in around 1912, he and his colleagues Franz Marc, August Macke, Alexej Jawlensky and Gabriele Münter, his wife and student, became known as the *Blaue Reiter* ("Blue Rider") school, working with bright, colourful forms and simple shapes. Within a decade, Kandinsky was to plunge into an altogether different world, that of the Bauhaus, as was another member of the Blue Rider circle, Paul Klee *(see page 81)*.

LEFT: self-portrait by the great Expressionist Max Beckmann (1926).
RIGHT: *Deer in the Forest* by Franz Marc (1911).

Parallel developments were taking place in the north of the country. Born in Dresden, Paula Modersohn-Becker spent two years at an artists' colony in the village of Worpswede near Bremen *(see page 318)*. Later influenced by the likes of Gauguin and Cézanne, she worked against a background of the traditional land-

scapes and genre paintings that had so characterised 19th-century German artistic production; like them, she broke free of tradition by translating "genre" images of still lives, landscapes and portraits into a vibrant, colourful oeuvre curtailed by her early death at 30.

More radical principles soon came into play. Shaken by the devastation of World War I, the Dada movement, born in Switzerland, extolled nonsense and principles of chance in the construction of art. Kurt Schwitters, a poet and graphic designer as well as a visual artist, began creating his *Merz* constructions and beautiful little collages; Max Ernst also produced collages and poems in Cologne. Berlin hosted the first major Dada show in 1920, but the movement was very much international rather than German: the use of found objects became most famous in the sculptures of Marcel Duchamp (1887–1968).

Figurative art "returned" with a vengeance in the 1930s, although, of course, in some instances it had never left. The sculptors Käthe Kollwitz and Ernst Barlach produced strong, moving figures throughout their careers, images of common people extolling the human condition and, often, speaking out eloquently against

MAX BECKMANN

Beckmann's highly individual, distorted, expressive style derived from the suffering he experienced at first hand while working as a hospital orderly in World War I.

complex images and masterful use of paint combine to create strong impressions that linger in the mind, from self-portraits to his monumental triptychs.

But this didn't matter much to the Nazis, who proscribed as "degenerate" almost all of Germany's artistic talent (see page 47). As a result, many of Germany's greatest artists carried the creative spark abroad to light new flames in other countries. The USA benefited particularly: Beckmann, Hans Hofmann and Josef Albers settled there to work

war (both artists, not surprisingly, were proscribed by the Nazi party). And the cartoon-like, bitingly ironic and sometimes grotesque images of Otto Dix (1891–1969) or former Dadaist George Grosz (1853–1959), leading proponents of the "New Realism", became a quintessential expression of the kind of outré degeneracy that characterised life in the Weimar Republic.

A brilliant synthesis of the painterly skills of the Expressionists and the subject matter of the New Realist came in the works of Max Beckmann (1884–1950), arguably the greatest painter of 20th-century Germany. Beckmann is in a sense his own school: his powerful though

and teach, becoming leading lights for a new generation of US painters, many of them emigrants themselves – Arshile Gorky, Willem de Kooning, Mark Rothko – who were to become known as the "New York School".

Postwar developments

After the war, Germany's artistic life, like the rest of the country, had to rebuild on the remains of what was left of its pre-war glories. In the abstract-dominated miasma, the feature that emerged most particularly was the -

ABOVE: *Der Blaue Reiter* by Wassily Kandinsky.
RIGHT: *Tisch mit Aggregat 1958–87* by Joseph Beuys.

Documenta, a contemporary art show launched in Kassel in 1955 and still held at intervals of five years *(see page 292)*. Its founder, Arnold Bode, a painter and professor, had as his goal the reestablishment of Germany within the global forum on art. Documenta became known for an eclectic mélange of what was going on not only in Germany, but around the world, as German art reflected international trends: the abstraction of the 1950s or the "capitalist realism" of the 1960s, with Pop Art on the one hand and outré assemblages of consumer goods, as made famous by the Fluxus movement, on the other. Now in its twelfth incarnation, Documenta continues to steer international discourse down new paths.

Among Germany's leading postwar artists are Gerhard Richter (his ongoing "Atlas" displays highlights of the artist's physical and personal world in assemblages of Polaroids and magazine photos), Sigmar Polke and Blinky Palermo; but all of these are eclipsed by Joseph Beuys (1921–86). Beuys, first a student and then a lecturer at the Düsseldorf Academy, was a leader in the international movement away from conventional artistic media towards the kind of "happenings" and installations that have today become a cornerstone of the art world.

These days, Beuys's sculptures made of fat seem veritably passé; and one has lost track of how many artists have staged a "happening" involving the destruction of a piano. More socially minded, or enduring, projects included a weekend event which involved people sweeping up Berlin's Alexanderplatz – the dirt and litter are enclosed in a perspex container and exhibited as a relic of the work – or his rows of

stones and trees, the "1,000 Oaks" project that has taken root, literally, in Kassel, New York and other places around the world.

Cologne has long been the epicentre of Germany's postwar art world, filled with galleries and museums. But in the past 15 years, Munich has been moving up to compete with Cologne with a host of new galleries showing cutting-edge work and important shows of contemporary art at the museums Haus der Kunst, Pinakothek der Moderne and Lenbachhaus. In both these cities, as in burgeoning Berlin, visitors can admire works by leading contemporary artists such as Rebecca Horn or Rosemarie Trockel. ❏

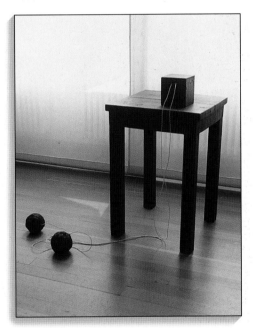

THE BAUHAUS MOVEMENT

"The Bauhaus seeks to unify the individual components of artistic creation, to reunite the disciplines of sculpture, painting, applied art and handicraft as indivisible elements of a new style", stated architect Walter Gropius (1883–1969), who founded the Bauhaus School in Weimar in 1919. Although short-lived – it was shut down by the Nazis in 1933 – the Bauhaus represents one of the major influences on modern architecture and on the entire discipline of industrial design. The original Bauhaus was a school where Gropius and other "masters" – Klee and Kandinsky, Laszlo Moholy-Nagy and Marcel Breuer – taught "apprentices" to practise not only art, but skilled craftsmanship as well. In its definition of "craft" or "skill" the Bauhaus also embraced the technology of the modern age, operating on the precept that aesthetic form should go hand-in-hand with practical function. Ornament was stripped away and buildings or furniture were pared down to the bare bones, be they concrete blocks (such as Gropius's 1926 Bauhaus school building in Dessau) or skyscrapers of metal and glass.

After the Nazis closed the school, many of the Bauhaus artists travelled to the United States, where as teachers and active artists they had a profound and lasting effect on American architecture and continued to shape the field of industrial design.

GERMAN CINEMA

Rising out of the postwar doldrums, Germany's film scene
today harks back to the heyday of Babelsberg

As guest of honour at the Babelsberg gala film evening in February 1993, Billy Wilder made a prophetic speech: "I'm convinced that Babelsberg will once again be among the world's best studios." A few months earlier DEFA, the former state-owned GDR film factory, had been sold to a French investor.

picture industry that was still very much in its infancy. Robert Wiene directed the first expressionistic silent film, *The Cabinet of Dr Caligari*. Fritz Lang made a series of crime films around the figure of *Dr Mabuse* and his - *Metropolis* (1926) is regarded as the first - science fiction film, setting new standards of

Since then, a considerable sum of money has been invested and the Babelsberg Film Studios really have become a major player in the international film and media world. The latest boost has come from media giant Sony, which in 1998 announced a massive investment programme destined to make Berlin the film capital of Europe.

Film pioneers

The German film industry experienced its heyday in the era of Babelsberg's UFA studios. It was here in the 1920s and early '30s that both German and Austrian directors invented a variety of new stylistic methods in a motion

animation technique. Friedrich Wilhelm Murnau established with his *Nosferatu – A Symphony of Horrors* (1922) the genre of the vampire film. For *The Last Laugh* he also invented the "freed" camera. Previously the camera had stood firmly fixed in one place but now it was moveable, lifted by crane, looking at people and buildings from new perspectives.

All these pioneers have something in common with many of their colleagues – comedy directors Max Ophuls and Ernst Lubitsch, the early psycho-thriller experts Otto Preminger and Robert Siodmak, the scriptwriter-turned-director Billy Wilder, Josef von Sternberg and Marlene Dietrich, who had become famous with *The Blue Angel* (1930), Peter Lorre and Fred Zinnemann: they all emigrated around 1933 to Paris or Hollywood because they were Jewish or because they saw their work endangered by the rise of the Third Reich.

A few, especially younger artists such as Billy Wilder *(The Lost Weekend, Sunset Boulevard, The Apartment, Some Like it Hot)* and Fred Zinnemann *(High Noon, From Here to Eternity)*, first achieved fame in Hollywood and some, such as Lang and Lubitsch, managed to continue their success in the US; the majority, however, went under, both artistically and financially. Marlene Dietrich was one of the exceptions among the actors: she was forgiven her first, poor Hollywood films. Her acting and singing ability were enough reason for producers to keep their faith in her.

Decline and revival

With the loss of its greatest talent, the German film industry sank into obscurity. The Nazi propaganda films were followed in the 1950s by the so-called *Heimat* films, ingenuous comedies and superficial period pieces. Their plots were often exciting and their casts were not without their star quality (Romy Schneider, Heinz Rühmann), but German film-making only regained its international esteem at the end of the 1960s, through the work of young authors involved in the so-called *Junger Autorenfilm*. Artistically, it was influenced by France's *nouvelle vague*, in which Jean-Luc Godard and François Truffaut were among the most prominent names. Politically, it rejected the continued suppression of the German past and found support from the student movement of 1968. Alexander Kluge, Rainer Werner Fassbinder, Volker Schlöndorff, Werner Herzog, Reinhard Hauff and Wim Wenders directed their first films in those years; they were followed by Margaretha von Trotta, Helma Sanders, Herbert Achternbusch and Hark Bohm. Yet soon after great successes like Schlöndorff's version of *The Tin Drum* (Golden Palm at Cannes), the German film industry drifted to a fringe position in its own country. At the same time, there was a process of internationalisation, even Americanisation.

LEFT: Marlene Dietrich soared to fame in *The Blue Angel*. RIGHT: a scene from Murnau's *Nosferatu*, which established the genre of the vampire film.

International themes

The chief reason for this is most likely to be found in the production conditions in Germany. The only large studios, Munich and Berlin, could not be compared to Hollywood or Rome and money was short. German directors faced the choice of either making films for the avant-garde cinema and a small public or changing countries. Trotta went to Italy, Schlöndorff and Wenders filmed in the US and Wolfgang Petersen *(The Boat)* also went to work in Hollywood. But this situation was not without its positive side: German films, which no longer clung exclusively to domestic issues.

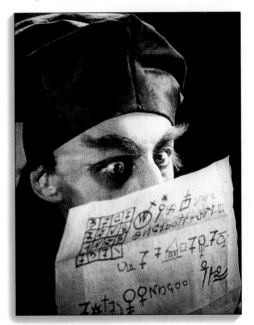

New possibilities

The late 1990s saw a revival of the domestic industry, fuelled largely by a remarkable comedy boom; home-produced films now take some 20 percent of the box office in Europe's biggest market. The fact that German film is still highly regarded abroad is demonstrated by the rapturous reception granted Oliver Hirschbiegels' impressive work *Der Untergang*, with Bruno Ganz depicting Adolf Hitler during his last days in the Berlin "Führerbunker", not to mention the success of Florian Henckel von Donnersmarck's Stasi-drama *The Lives of Others*, which won the Oscar for Best Foreign Film in 2007. ❑

FESTIVE TRADITIONS, LOCAL COLOUR

Germany's old traditions live on in a range of colourful festivals, from the parades of Carnival and the Oktoberfest to town and village celebrations.

Düsseldorf, with its glittering boutiques and skyscrapers, is a modern urban centre. But visit it or the other big cities along the Rhine, Cologne, Bonn and Mainz, during Carnival and this world is turned on its head, with parades and revelry and a complete suspension of everyday rules. Even in these cosmopolitan cities, the originally pagan tradition of Carnival lives on.

Germany works hard and plays hard. Moreover, local festivals underline the different characters and customs of the individual German states, which weren't confederated until 1871. It's a long way from the showy parades of the Carnival to the grim masks of a *Fastnet* in the Black Forest.

Some festivals commemorate specific historic events, such as the Dinkelsbühl *Kinderzeche* in which the town's children march out and plead with the Swedish army to spare their homes *(see page 210)*. The world-famous Oktoberfest in Munich dates back to the celebration of Ludwig I and Princess Therese's wedding in 1810. There are many more beer – and wine – festivals all over the country. Strong on tradition, too, are the *Schützen-feste (above)*, the celebrations of the local shooting associations.

▷ IN A WHIRL
More than just a beer-drinker's extravaganza, Munich's Oktoberfest is also a fair with amusement park rides – great fun for kids

△ HERITAGE PRESERVED
Dating back to the Middle Ages, the ubiquitous *Schützenfeste* have become festivals of local costumes and mores.

△ STREET PARTY
In most of Southern Germany, Carnival time is known as *Fasching*. The colourful proceedings in Munich constitute a massive street party.

▷ FASTNET FACE
In the Black Forest area, the heathen Alemannic origins of Carnival, here called *Fastnet*, are evident in the carved wooden masks.

▷ WEDDING GROUP
In 1475, some 10,000 people attended the wedding in Landshut of Duke Ludwig the Rich's son, George, to the Polish princess Jadwiga.

CHRISTMAS MARKETS

The smell of *Glühwein* wafts around stalls selling *Lebkuchen* (gingerbread) and Christmas ornaments, while carol singers make joyful sounds from the balcony of the town hall. Christmas markets are one of the highlights of the year.

The *Christkindlmarkt* has its roots in the Reformation, when Catholic saints' days were abolished and children were left without presents on 6 December, St Nicholas' Day. To compensate, it was said that the Christ Child *(Christkind)* brought gifts on the night of his birth. The markets sprang up to meet the demand for gifts, and became a popular tradition. Having flourished during the early 19th century they were almost forgotten until their rediscovery in the 1930s. The most famous *Christkindlmarkt* is the one at Nuremberg *(above)* with a local schoolchild appearing as the market's namesake.

◁ **FEAST OF FOOLS**
At Carnival time, the *Rosenmontag* parades in Mainz and Cologne, the day before Shrove Tuesday, are televised nationally. Carnival kings and queens reign over the festivities.

▷ **SUN, MOON AND STARS**
On 11 November children commemorate St Martin's Day by parading through the streets bearing homemade candlelit lanterns and singing traditional songs about the charitable saint.

◁ **CELEBRATIONS**
Five centuries on, the Landshut Wedding is re-enacted every four years in a pageant.

▷ **BLAST OFF**
Culminating on Shrove Tuesday, Carnival officially begins on 11 November at 11am.

PLACES

A detailed guide to the entire country, with principal sites clearly cross-referenced by number to the maps

I t is hard to find a single image that fairly conjures up Germany, in the way that a beret-wearing wine drinker would suggest France or a cuckoo clock would identify Switzerland. One reason is that Germany is less homogeneous than most European countries and any familiar image – such as that of the *lederhosen*-clad beer imbiber – represents only one distinct part of the staunchly federal nation, not all of it. In that respect, perhaps Germany is Europe's equivalent to the United States. It offers a variety of landscapes, all packed into a country that stretches around 1,000 km (620 miles) between the north coast and the Alps and about 700 km (435 miles) at its widest point from west to east. There is much to discover, whether in the unchanging delights of the countryside or the vibrant culture of the cities.

Lots of lines run through the colourful mosaic on the map. The north and east are mainly Protestant, but in the south and west Catholics are in the majority. Nowadays Bavaria and Baden-Württemberg are among the most prosperous states of the republic, whereas during the Middle Ages the Hanseatic League and the north – despite its structural weakness – were richer. Even today, recent history notwithstanding, the east-west divide is not simply a matter of rich and poor.

The Bavarians jokingly describe the *Weisswurst-Äquator* ("veal sausage equator") that runs along the River Main as the border between them and the Prussians, who seem to include everyone who isn't Bavarian. In reality, the border of the Roman empire ran along the Main and the Rhine and left its mark on both culture and lifestyle. That the Romans didn't succeed in moving this border further north had its compensations, as they didn't have to do without their customary wine – the only place in Germany where wine is grown on the other side of the Rhine–Main line is near Dresden on the Elbe. Baden is excellent wine country but in the north they prefer beer and *Klaren* (clear schnapps). The enjoyment of beer is something the Prussians and the Bavarians do have in common.

Because of its federal structure, Germany does not have just one dominant political and cultural centre, such as you find in France or the United Kingdom, but several. For this reason, we chose four cities as the starting points on our voyages of discovery: the three largest state metropolises – Berlin, Hamburg and Munich – as well as the financial centre, Frankfurt-am-Main. ❑

PRECEDING PAGES: the bold shapes of the Wallraf-Richartz Museum in front of Cologne Cathedral; the Museum für Moderne Kunst, Frankfurt; Norman Foster's dome adds modernity to the Reichstag in Berlin.
LEFT: Bavarians wear their traditional costumes at the Oktoberfest.

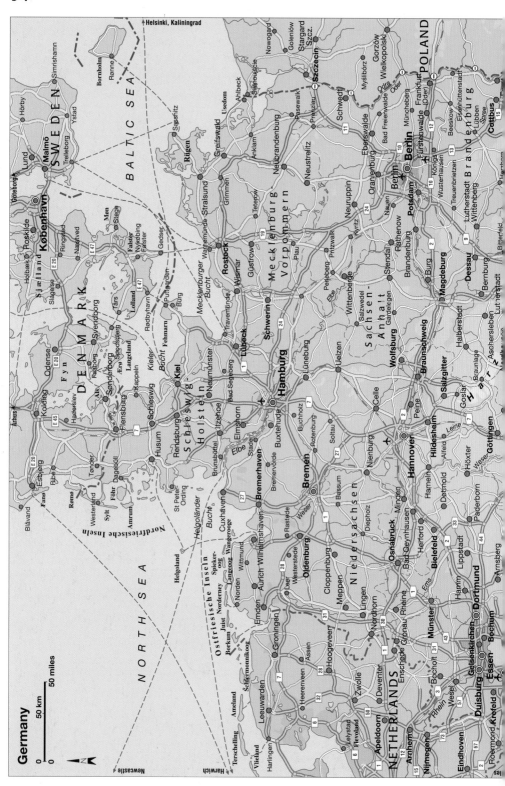

Germany

50 km

50 miles

N

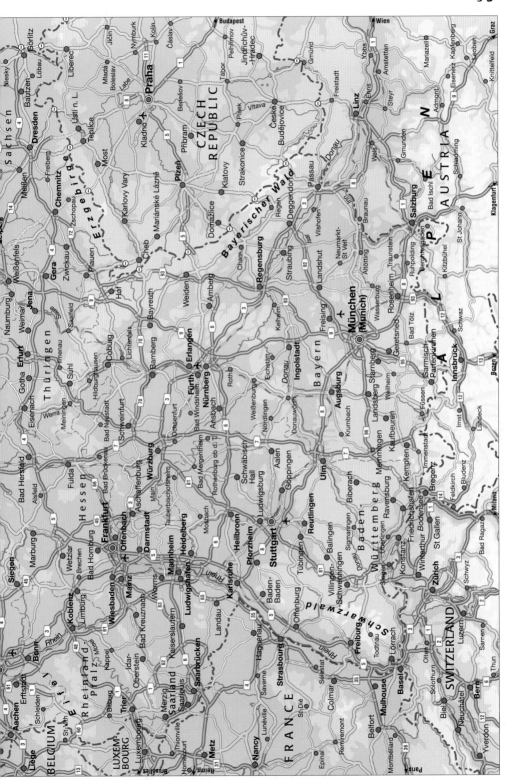

BERLIN AND THE EASTERN STATES

*In addition to Germany's capital, the five eastern states
embrace the area covered by the former GDR*

The eastern part of the country has become a favourite destination for West Germans, who like to explore this somewhat unknown territory where villages and cities are rapidly catching up with the western states.

In Berlin, at least, there is hardly a trace of the old border crossings, yet nowhere else are the consequences of reunification felt so strongly. Berlin is frenetic about its old/new role as the capital of Germany. Will it be the same as it was in the legendary 1920s? In 1995, the artists Christo and Jeanne-Claude dealt in their own inimitable way with the past and the future by wrapping up the Reichstag: for two weeks the city centre watched the transformation of the building with awe; pictures also shape history, even if it is only fleetingly. The festival atmosphere is spreading and there is a new feeling of kinship, a feeling reinforced in 2004 when the borders of the European Union shifted eastwards, entrenching Berlin firmly in the centre of Europe.

Visitors will relive the classic Berlin, the Kurfürstendamm and the historic centre in the throes of change. They can also look forward to the reliable old mainstays: the Berlin museum landscape is richer than ever; the theatre, even after budget cuts, is still lively; the green oases still attractive – in terms of the variety of species of birds and plants, the parks and forests are some of the richest areas in Germany.

Berlin is no longer an island; it stretches out towards the countryside. Lying in the middle of eastern Germany, it is surrounded by the five new federal states. Mecklenburg-Vorpommern, Brandenburg, Thüringen (Thuringia), Sachsen (Saxony) and Sachsen-Anhalt make up these five. While these areas possess countless attractions, many Germans from the south and west are much less familiar with them than they are with neighbouring European countries. The infrastructure has changed dramatically in the past few years to meet the requirements of the growing numbers of increasingly sophisticated and demanding visitors.

A journey through this new Germany throws up countless high points: around the Mecklenburg Lakes are large areas of beautiful, unspoilt nature; the largest fleet of paddle steamers in Germany operates on the River Elbe between the wild, romantic sandstone mountains on the Czech border and the vine-covered terraces near Dresden; Weimar, not far from the Thuringian Forest, is the birthplace of the German classical era, so it is hard to avoid the large crowds of visitors to the Goethe House in Frauenplan; in Harz, Otto the Great left untouched countless Romanesque buildings among the small, half-timbered houses. As a famous old saying puts it: "Chemnitz works, Leipzig trades, Dresden lives." All have their attractions. ❑

LEFT: the TV tower on Berlin's Alexanderplatz marks the city's historic centre.

BERLIN

Map on page 102

The club and theatre scene in Mitte and Prenzlauer Berg is just as much part of the German capital's culture as its fine buildings, Philharmonic concerts and richly endowed museums.

A fter the fall of the Wall, Berlin took advantage of a unique chance to redesign its city centre and make the metropolis a worthy seat of government of the entire republic and once again a focal point for the whole country. In recent years, the old-but-new capital has expanded at a rapid pace, as it did after 1871, during the *Gründerzeit* (time of foundation of the German Reich). The new developments around Potsdamer Platz, which for more than five years was the biggest building site in Europe, are now among Berlin's most popular attractions. But the Berliners have never been too fazed by the things going on around them. Great and often notorious historical events have been absorbed with endearing matter-of-factness into the Berliners' everyday life.

Berlin is an exciting place to live, work and visit. Existentialist artists and innovative young entrepreneurs alike feel themselves drawn by the same Berlin atmosphere. But it is also possible to escape the chaotic bustle very quickly, for example by visiting the Nikolskoe beer garden high above the River Havel when the evening sun spreads its warm light, or by leisurely dipping oars into the river's maze-like backwaters. No other city in Germany has such a fine recreational zone right on its doorstep.

LEFT:
the Sony Centre,
Potsdamer Platz.
BELOW:
Kaiser Wilhelm
Memorial Church
seen through the
Berlin sculpture.

Great historical importance

Berlin's history goes back further than many people realise. Two Slav settlements on opposite sides of the Spree river developed into the trading towns Cölln and Berlin, which united in 1307 and joined the Hanseatic League in 1359. The event that sealed the city's future importance came in 1415, when King Sigismund named Friedrich von Nürnberg, a member of the Hohenzollern dynasty, as Prince of Brandenburg.

From that point on, the Hohenzollerns dictated the course of the city's history. In 1486 Berlin became the royal seat and, from 1642 on, it was developed by one Hohenzollern prince after another. Under their rule, Prussia grew to become the greatest state of the German Empire, alongside Habsburg Austria.

The Great Elector, Friedrich Wilhelm, invited foreign artists to Berlin, welcomed the industrious French Huguenots and established trading companies and small industries. The coronation of his son Friedrich III as King of Prussia in 1701 was a further step on the road to prosperity and power. The rivalry between the young kingdom and Austria reached its climax during the reign of Frederick the Great (1740–86), under whom Berlin acquired the splendour of a European capital; the population of the city doubled, and cotton and silk manufacturing made the city the centre of the German textile industry.

After the Seven Years' War (1756–63) Prussia was officially recognised as a European power. It was not until 1806 that Prussia suffered its first defeat, when Napoleon's forces occupied Berlin for two years. This challenge to Prussian power created an atmosphere conducive to reformist activity, inspired by the French Revolution and the ideas inherent in the British economic system. With the foundation of Berlin University by Wilhelm von Humboldt in 1810 the centre of reformist ideas moved from Königsberg to the royal seat of residence. Freiherr vom Stein and Prince von Hardenberg were among the most important figures who worked for Prussia's political and economic revival, which ended in 1819 with the resignations of the reformist ministers Boyen and Humboldt.

In 1848 Berlin was the centre of Germany's March Revolution, in which conservative forces again retained the upper hand. After the foundation of the German Empire in 1871 the Prussian King also ruled as German Emperor, Wilhelm I, and Berlin became the imperial capital.

With the coming of the industrial revolution the populations of Germany's big cities grew at an explosive rate, and workers' settlements sprang up around the large factories. At the close of World War I the last German Emperor, Wilhelm II, had to abdicate and Karl Liebknecht proclaimed the Free Socialist Republic from the balcony of Berlin's Stadtschloss.

After the short-lived Weimar Republic Adolf Hitler chose Berlin as his political power base from 1933. World War II led to the unconditional surrender of Germany and, of course, of Berlin, which was almost completely destroyed. The city had four-power status (United States, Great Britain, France, the Soviet Union) until 1990. The Soviet-ruled sector was cut off from the rest of the city in 1961 in the dramatic overnight construction of the Berlin Wall.

BELOW: remnants of the Berlin Wall.

THE BERLIN WALL

Visitors who want to see what remains of the Wall today must seek out the former Prussian provincial parliament building in Niederkirchnerstrasse in Berlin-Mitte or the East-Side-Gallery in Mühlenstrasse in Friedrichshain, where artists work away on bits of the demolished Wall. Its old line can hardly be recognised in present-day Berlin. The former "death strip" has long since been swamped by development – it had, after all, cut right through some of the best land in the city.

The scenes of 13 August 1961, the day Berlin was cut in two, are still vivid in many people's minds. Literally overnight, not only were capitalism and Communism divided, but families too. The Wall was 161 km (100 miles) long, 4 metres (13 ft) high and studded with watchtowers. To Erich Honecker's East German regime, it was an "anti-Fascist protective wall". To the rest of the world, it was a symbol of repression and the place where more than 70 people died. The opening of the Hungarian border for fleeing East Germans on 9 November 1989 led inevitably to the Wall's fall: masses of people flooded out of East Berlin, welcomed by jubilant West Berliners.

Today, the Wall and its victims are remembered by the Mauerpark memorial complex on Bernauer Strasse.

The Wall, which was the symbol of the city for 28 years, now belongs to history. Now that it has gone, perhaps the most striking thing about Berlin is that it has two city centres. On the one side, on Alexanderplatz, the TV tower, built as the unmistakeable emblem of the "capital of the GDR", marks the historical centre of Berlin, Berlin-Mitte. On the other, the blue Mercedes Star affixed to the Europa-Center marks the location of the Kurfürstendamm, the bustling centre of the western part of the city.

Map on page 102

The Kurfürstendamm

The **"Ku'damm"** was once *the* street for taking a stroll in West Berlin. Despite competition from the east side of town since the collapse of the wall, the Ku'-damm has not yet lost its powers of attraction. "I so long for my Kurfürsten-damm," once sang Berlin's very own inimitable singer and actress Hildegard Knef. There's not much left, though, of the proud and beautiful late 19th-century mansions which once lined the noble boulevard and which suffered severe bombing in World War II. For centuries the Ku'damm had played an important role in Berlin after Prince Elector Joachim II had it laid out in the 16th century as a bridle path leading out to the hunting grounds. Kurfürstendamm means "The Electors' Road".

Only with Germany's industrial expansion from 1871 onwards did the street begin to take shape. Inspired by the Champs Elysées in Paris, Bismarck decided that he wanted just such a boulevard for the new capital of the *Reich*. Building work proceeded in "Wilhelminian" style: generous, ornate and even florid; truly representative of the age. The Kurfürstendamm subsequently became the place where Berlin was youthful, where the wildest entertainment could be had and where everything considered Bohemian was on offer. That was particularly the case during the "Roaring Twenties". The most famous meeting-place in those days was the Romanische Café, situated where the Kurfürstendamm meets Joachims Ahaler Strasse.

After the ravages of World War II and the division of the city into east and west, the Kurfürstendamm recast itself as the cultural centre of West Berlin. But the old splendour of the Ku'damm could never be recreated. Ugly new buildings replaced the fine old ones lost in the war. The more exclusive businesses, such as chic boutiques and antiques shops, are now found between Adenauerplatz and Fasanenstrasse, while Tauentzienstrasse and Wittenbergplatz became the home of fast-food chains and downmarket stores.

But Wittenbergplatz (at its corner with Tauentzien-strasse) is also the address of the stylish Kaufhaus des Westens (the Department Store of the West), known as **KaDeWe**, a huge shop with a floor to please every taste. The building was the only one of Berlin's great department stores to withstand the bombing during World War II.

The first place on the Ku'damm most people head for is **Breitscheidplatz** with the ruins of the **Kaiser Wilhelm Gedächtniskirche ❶** (Memorial Church), together with its blue-glazed rebuilt version. The towering church was built in 1895 in memory of the well-loved Emperor Wilhelm I. It was left in its ruined state

 TIP

If you want to do some shopping and also want to get away from the Ku'damm's large international chain stores, try the little side roads. Bleibtreu, Knesebeck- and Schlüterstrasse in particular offer a large choice of colourful boutiques.

BELOW: the iconic KaDeWe department store.

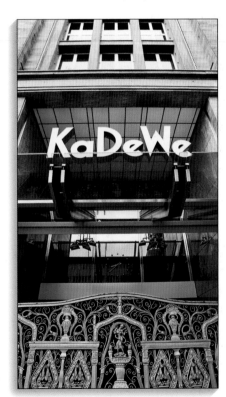

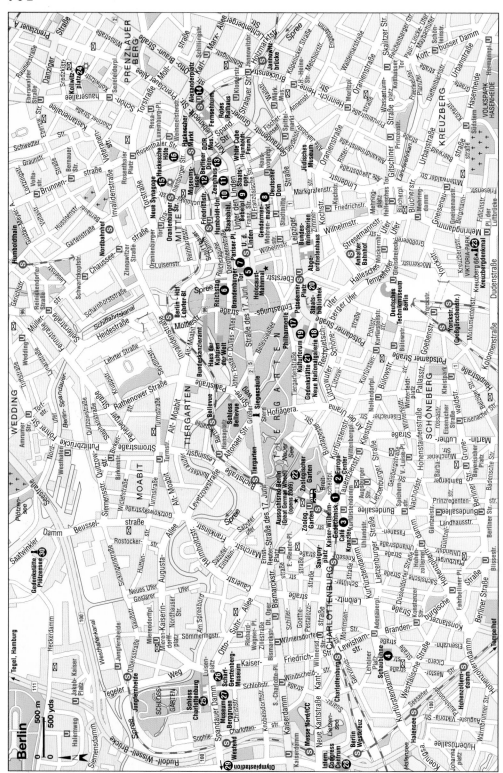

after the war and a slender belltower with a low church assembly hall was built beside it, a structure the Berliners refer to as their "lipstick and powder compact". In the summer, all sorts of people adopt as their meeting place the so-called **Wasserklops**, a huge fountain created by the sculptor Schmettau which stands next to the **Europa-Center ❷**. The building remains one of the tallest in Berlin, crowned by that highly symbolic Mercedes Star and housing a huge range of shops, restaurants, bars and a cabaret.

A few steps away is the famous **Café Kranzler ❸**, nowadays reduced to a small café in the traditional rotunda. Next to it is the new Kranzlereck, a Helmut Jahn highrise, with offices and stores and a wide plaza which houses an aviary. On the opposite corner, the quarter-circle facade of the Swissôtel is another new landmark, while behind the Bahnhof Zoo train station on Jebensstrasse No. 2 is the newly installed **Museum für Fotografie**, which houses the Helmut Newton Collection, legacy of the world-famous photographer who died in 2004. Close by, on Lehniner Platz, stands the avant-garde **Schaubühne ❹**, a theatre building in the expressive style of the 1920s.

The historical centre

Things are a lot more leisurely over in **Berlin-Mitte**, where Berlin was really born. Here one is endlessly confronted by Berlin and Prussian history, reminders of the city's beginnings as two small settlements, Berlin and Cölln. Of course, most of the historical buildings to be seen here are not the originals and much – the City Palace of the Hohenzollern Emperors, for example – has been lost forever. Although severely damaged during the war, it was the Stalinist authorities of the former GDR who actually finished the building off in the 1950s. The copper-coloured Palace of the Republic, seat of parliament and popular amusement during SED rule, stood in its stead before being demolished in 2008. Until 2010, when construction is to commence on the **Humbolt-Forum** – incorporating the historical facade of the old City Palace – the new **White Cube** will serve as temporary art forum and exhibition hall.

The gateway to Berlin-Mitte is the famous **Brandenburg Gate ❺**. Since its inauguration in 1791, this structure has been a symbol of the fate first of Prussia and then of Germany. Napoleon marched triumphantly through it on his way to Russia, and sent back to Paris as war booty the gate's crowning ensemble, the Quadriga (the Goddess of Victory on her horse-drawn chariot). In 1814, the Quadriga was brought back in triumph by Marshal Blücher.

Barricades were erected at the Brandenburg Gate during the revolution of 1848; kings and emperors paraded here; the revolutionaries of 1918 streamed through it to proclaim the republic; and the Nazis staged their victory parades here.

Following the construction of the Berlin Wall, the entire area around the monument was cordoned off. During and after the collapse of the Wall, the gate became a central symbol of the hopes and expectations of a united Germany. Finally reopened to pedestrians at the end of 1989, the Brandenburg Gate is now – after a splendid restoration – the favoured setting for public

Map on page 102

No other city in Germany has a wider choice of entertainment than Berlin.

BELOW: the Brandenburg Gate.

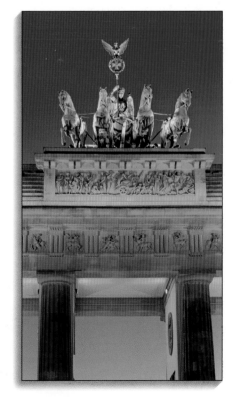

events, such as the New Year's Eve party and the Berlin Marathon. In summer 2005, New York architect Peter Eisenman's enormous **Holocaust Memorial**, the "Field of Stelae", opened just to the south of the Brandenburg Gate. The field of 2,700-odd tilting stone slabs, 17 years in the making, is accessible night and day.

To the north of the Brandenburg Gate, on Platz der Republik, is the **Reichstag ❻**, which has now reawoken to new life after decades of slumber. The English architect Norman Foster has redesigned it as the home of the German Parliament, the Bundestag. The Reichstag is one of Berlin's most historic buildings. With the foundation of the German Reich in 1871, a parliament building was required and it was duly completed by Paul Wallot in 1894 in the Italian Renaissance style. It was badly damaged by fire in 1933 and then in 1945 it was totally destroyed by Allied bombs. Between 1957 and 1971 it was rebuilt but without its dome, until Sir Norman Foster returned it to its former glory. Inside the new glass dome, based on the original, is a broad spiral ramp which enables visitors to watch parliamentary proceedings from above, while the roof garden (with a café-restaurant) provides unique views across the cityscape.

At the other side of the Brandenburg Gate is **Pariser Platz ❼**. World War II obliterated the houses that used to surround the square, once the abode of important personalities such as the Prussian Prime Minister Friedrich Karl von Savigny, the composer Giacomo Meyerbeer, the dramatist August von Kotzebue and the painter Max Liebermann. The Prussian Academy of Arts was also based here. Recent years have seen the square rebuilt to its original design, with modern architectural touches by the likes of American architect Frank Gehry. The **Hotel Adlon**, the city's top hotel during the days of the German Empire, was also rebuilt and in 1997 once more opened its elegant rooms and suites to guests.

The circumstances surrounding the Reichstag fire on 27 February 1933 are still open to debate, but whether the event was contrived by the Nazis or whether it was an independent act, it provided the excuse for the Nazi regime to assume emergency powers and crack down on all opponents.

BELOW: exploring and reflecting in the Field of Stelae.

Unter den Linden

Map on page 102

The square marks the beginning of **Unter den Linden**, undoubtedly the most Prussian of Berlin's streets, planned by the Great Elector, Friedrich Wilhelm, in 1647. The Classical structures conceived by the 19th-century architect Karl Friedrich Schinkel, which transformed the city into "Athens on the Spree", testify to the fact that Berlin once ranked among the most magnificent European cities. Here, too, much was annihilated during the war and ruined by socialist misplanning in the postwar years. However, strolling down this elegant boulevard today, the ambience of the old metropolis seems almost tangible.

It is open to debate which of Schinkel's buildings is the most beautiful. Some maintain that it is the **Schauspielhaus** (theatre), known as the Konzerthaus, on **Gendarmenmarkt ❽**. Framed by the German Cathedral and the French Cathedral, the entire square is an aesthetically perfect ensemble. In front of the Schauspielhaus stands Begas' **Schillerdenkmal** (Schiller Memorial) dating from 1868.

The old Opernplatz, now renamed **Bebelplatz ❾**, is where the Nazis burnt more than 20,000 books in 1933. At its centre, the Equestrian Statue of Frederick the Great is one of the most important works of Berlin's sculptor Christian Daniel Rauch. (Horse and rider head in the direction to Schlossplatz, the historical centre of the old city.) The square was planned by Frederick the Great as the "Forum Fridericianum". The **Staatsoper Unter den Linden** (Opera House), the **Alte Königliche Bibliothek** (Old Library) and **St Hedwig's Cathedral** combine to create a masterpiece of urban architecture. Enrico Caruso once sang at the Opera House and Richard Strauss conducted there. At present it is directed by internationally renowned conductor and pianist Daniel Barenboim. St Hedwig's Cathedral, modelled after the Roman Pantheon, was built in 1747.

The German Cathedral on Gendarmenmarkt.

BELOW: statue by Schinkel on the Schlossbrücke.

KARL FRIEDRICH SCHINKEL

Much of the splendour that Berlin acquired during the post-Napoleonic era is thanks to the genius of one architect, Karl Friedrich Schinkel. Born in 1781 in the town of Neuruppin to the north of Berlin, by the time of his death in 1841, he had endowed his native Prussia with two true "Schinkel towns": Berlin and Potsdam.

State architect of Prussia from 1815 and professor at the Berlin Royal Academy from 1820, Schinkel eventually presided over all major building projects in Prussia. The plan of every project, if not designed by himself, at least went across his desk. Many of his schemes were far too ambitious for Friedrich Wilhelm III, but his successor, Friedrich Wilhelm IV, shared Schinkel's enthusiasm for the Classical structures of Italy and Greece and consented to almost every scheme Schinkel proposed. Buildings such as the Old Museum, the Neue Wache, the Bauakademie (destroyed in World War II) and the Schauspielhaus were thus created, alongside numerous statues.

Schinkel's work represents the high point of German and indeed European Classicism but he was also fascinated by the neo-Gothic style, as can be seen from his memorial on Berlin's Kreuzberg *(see page 110)*. Furthermore, he attained distinction as a painter and illustrator.

BELOW: Zeughaus with Schlüter's death masks.

On the opposite side of Unter den Linden are two more bastions of German culture, the **Staatsbibliothek zu Berlin** (Library for Prussian Cultural Heritage) and the adjacent **Humboldt University** . The latter was erected between 1748 and 1766 by Johann Boumann the Elder as a palace for Prince Heinrich, the brother of Frederick the Great. In 1810, on the initiative of the eminent philologist Wilhelm von Humboldt, the building was converted to a seat of learning. Among the renowned academics to work and study here were Albert Einstein and the brothers Grimm.

The **Neue Wache** is Schinkel's most complete work. It was his first building in Berlin and it possesses all the harmony of the Classical age. In GDR days, People's Army soldiers goose-stepped in front of the Neue Wache, which served as a memorial to the victims of Fascism and militarism. After much debate, the temple-like building was re-inaugurated as the **Central Memorial** of the Federal Republic of Germany in 1993. The bronze *pietà*, *Mother and Son* by Käthe Kollwitz is dedicated to "all victims of war and violence".

Located further towards the river, the **Zeughaus** ⓫ (the former Arsenal) is Berlin's largest baroque building and one of Germany's finest. Schlüter's 22 warriors' death masks in the courtyard are well worth closer inspection. The building now houses the **Deutsches Historisches Museum** (German Historical Museum; open daily 10am–6pm). Following its extensive renovation, the old Zeughaus building houses a permanent exhibition leading visitors through the whole of German history from earliest times up to the present day. At the back of the museum buildings the Sino-American architect Ieoh Ming Pei has added a spectacular glass building, which displays a changing cycle of exhibitions.

The Museum Island

The **Museumsinsel** ⓬ (Museum Island) and its collections rank as one of the world's finest museum complexes. In 2000 it was declared a world heritage site by UNESCO (all museums open Tues–Sun 10am–6pm, Thur until 10pm). This cluster of museums came about as a result of a decree by Friedrich Wilhelm III to the effect that the royal art collections were to be made accessible to the public. The stunning diversity of displays includes everything from ancient archaeological artefacts to early 20th-century German and European art. The Museum Island is undergoing enormous restoration work in the hands of British architect David Chipperfield. Until work is completed in 2015, visitors might find the occasional door closed. Be that as it may, it requires more than an afternoon to visit all the museums of Museum Island.

The first to be opened, in 1830, was the **Altes Museum** (Old Museum; also open Mon), regarded as one of Schinkel's most impressive buildings. Inside and out it was specifically designed to serve its purpose, namely to display works of art. Following substantial wartime damage, it was reconstructed and reopened in 1966. The beautiful neoclassical rooms house internationally renowned exhibitions, as well as parts of the Antikensammlung (Collection of Classical Antiquities). The **Ägyptisches Museum** (Egyptian Museum; open daily 10am–6pm), with its impressive collection of antiquities, is also temporarily to be found here. It will relocate to the reconstructed Neues Museum when that opens in 2009.

The **Pergamon Museum** contains Berlin's most highly regarded artistic treasure, a section of the Pergamon Altar (180–159 BC). It was taken from the ancient Hellenic city in western Turkey after excavations in 1878 and today forms part of the Collection of Classical Antiquities. The frieze describes the battle of the Gods against the Titans. In the same collection is the Market Gate from Miletus which is on two floors and dates from the time of Emperor Marcus Aurelius. Under the same roof is the exquisite **Islamic Museum** (also open Mon) and the **Vorderasiatisches Museum** (Near East Museum), well known for its architectural monuments, which include the Processional Way and the Ishtar Gate.

The **Bode Museum**, a splendid building next to the Spree, was initiated in 1897 by art historian Wilhelm von Bode who became known here and abroad as the longstanding chief curator of Berlin's museums. Its 60-metre-long strongroom, which houses the world-renowned collection of the Münzkabinett (Numismatic Museum), is a spectacular place.

The **Alte Nationalgalerie** (Old National Gallery) is the first building on the Museum Island which has been reopened after extensive renovation and it is now one of the most beautiful and most visited museums in Berlin. The gallery houses important paintings and sculptures from the 18th to the 20th centuries. Amongst others, you can see the marble statue of Queen Louise and her sister Friederike by Johann Gottfried Schadow.

Parts of the gallery's colonnaded perimeter reach to the river bank. The equestrian statue of the museum's donor Friedrich Wilhelm IV is situated in front of the Corinthian temple-style building. There is also a little park with statues by the sculptors August Gaul, Louis Tuaillon and Reinhold Begas to explore.

Map on page 102

Detail of the Ishtar Gate in the Near East Museum, a section of the Pergamon Museum.

BELOW: "Viktoria" by Rauch in the Old National Gallery.

TIP

Opposite the Cathedral
the vividly interactive
DDR Museum (Karl-
Liebknecht-Str. 1,
Mon–Sun 10am–8pm,
Sat 10am–10pm),
loved by visitors since
it opened in 2006,
shows life as it was in
the GDR. Here you can
look, touch, listen,
rummage through
drawers… even the
kitchen and the Trabi
smell authentic.

BELOW:
the synagogue in
Oranienburger
Strasse.

Alexanderplatz and beyond

Berlin Cathedral  is a monument to the Wilhelminian expression of splendour. The Cathedral was built in 1894, as the "chief church of Protestantism". It served as the family church of the Hohenzollerns, where the imperial children were baptised, confirmed, later married and where family members were buried.

From here it's not far to **Alexanderplatz** ⓮. This vast, often windswept space is dominated by the **Fernsehturm** (Television Tower), which was completed in 1969. Rising to 365 metres (1,100 ft), it is Berlin's highest structure. There is a fine view of the city from the observation platform, which is in the lower half of the steel sphere at a height of 203 metres (650 ft). The Tele Café above it revolves twice every hour. In the future, however, a high-rise ensemble of offices, shops and flats is to thrust its way skywards.

Oranienburger Strasse to the north of Museum Island offers an attractive, young and lively milieu. Here a variety of interesting pubs, little restaurants and eccentric clothes shops are situated side by side. Oranienburger Strasse and the surrounding streets form the old Jewish quarter of Berlin. In the 1920s, it was in this district that many east European Jews, fleeing from persecution, found a new home. Before the Nazis arrived on the scene it was a bustling area awash with cultural vitality. Above the rooftops you can see the shiny golden dome of the **Neue Synagoge** ⓯. Built in 1866 by Friedrich August Stüler, it was destroyed not by the Nazis but by the Allied bombs of World War II. The modern Moorish Alhambra style building has since been reconstructed. Since 1995 the **Centrum Judaicum** has been housed here, a museum documenting the history of Jewish life in Berlin and Brandenburg. A fine sample of meticulous restoration is the **Hackesche Höfe** ⓰, a lovely labyrinth of often interconnected yards typical of Berlin, built in Art Nouveau style and now thronged with extravagant ashion and accessories boutiques

A forum for culture

The name of the **Tiergarten** district may justifiably be associated with the well-loved park of the same name, but Tiergarten is much more than that. Its **Kulturforum**, planned as a postwar equivalent of the Museum Island, is dominated by architect Hans Scharoun's **Philharmonie** ⓱ (Concert Hall). This is where the Berlin Philharmonic shone under the direction of Herbert von Karajan; now the orchestra is conducted in different but still masterly style by Simon Rattle. Next door is the **Kammermusiksaal** for chamber music recitals. There is a show almost every night in either of these venues. Most museums in the Kulturforum are open Tuesday to Friday 10am–6pm, and weekends 11am–6pm, with late openings on Thursdays. The **Musikinstrumenten-museum** (Museum of Musical Instruments) on Tiergartenstrasse contains an impressive collection of more than 2,500 instruments. In the airy **Kunstgewerbe-museum** (Museum of Arts and Crafts; Thur no late opening), which was built in 1985 by Rolf Gutbrod, there are textiles, furniture, glassware, fashion and goldsmiths' work from the Middle Ages to the present day.

The **Neue Nationalgalerie** ⓲ (New National Gallery) was conceived as a modern building by Ludwig Mies van der Rohe but is basically a Classical tem-

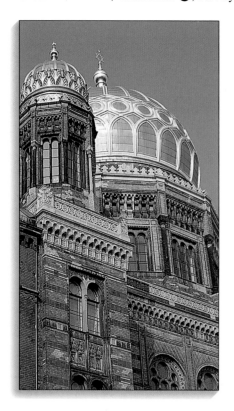

ple. Apart from well-known artists from the former GDR, the works of Oskar Kokoschka, Otto Dix and many other 20th-century masters are exhibited. The **Kupferstichkabinett** ⑲ (Prints and Drawings Collection) has 80,000 drawings, watercolours, gouache works and 520,000 graphic pages by artists from all over the world, including 27 of Botticelli's 85 illustrations for Dante's *Divine Comedy*. The **Gemäldegalerie** (Painting Gallery), set in a remarkable piece of modern architecture by Heinz Hilmer and Christoph Sattler, possesses one of the world's finest collections of European art from the Middle Ages to the late 18th century.

Not far from here is **Potsdamer Platz** ⑳. Numerous shops, restaurants, bars, cinemas, a casino, hotels and the Musical Theatre attract Berliners and tourists alike. The spectacular buildings are the work of famous architects like Renzo Piano, Helmut Jahn and Hans Kollhoff. The 22-storey **debis-Haus** contains in its huge atrium Jean Tinguely's machine sculpture *Meta-Maxi*. Next to this is the popular mall **Potsdamer Platz Arkaden**. The **Sony Center** across Potsdamer Strasse, built as Sony's European headquarters, is a popular spot as well. Seven buildings surround the forum, which is conceived as a light-flooded arena with a tented roof. The futuristic building also houses cafés and restaurants, apartments, the **Filmhaus** with cinemas and the **Filmmuseum Berlin** (open Tues–Sun 10am–6pm, Thur until 8pm), which exhibits among others the Marlene Dietrich Collection. In the red clinker-clad **Kollhoff** building, the express elevator leads to a panorama platform with breathtaking views.

About five minutes' walk from the Nationalgalerie in Stauffenbergstrasse is the **Gedenkstätte für die Opfer des 20. Juli 1944** ㉑ (Memorial to German Resistance). It was in this building, the Supreme Army Command, that the unsuccessful attempt on Hitler's life was planned in July 1944. Several senior

Map on page 102

Soaring architecture in Potsdamer Platz.

BELOW: the Neue Nationalgalerie.

TIP

In Invalidenstrasse in
Berlin-Mitte, the
Hamburger Bahnhof, a
former station, is well
worth a visit. It houses
the first Berlin
museum of European
and American
contemporary art, with
works by Beuys,
Warhol and
Lichtenstein. Open
Tues–Fri 10am–6pm,
Sat 11am–8pm, Sun
11am–6pm.

BELOW: the
Jüdisches Museum.

army officers, including Graf von Stauffenberg, were court-martialled and shot immediately after the assassination attempt.

Nearby is the **Tiergarten**. This splendid park was once the royal hunting ground and enclosure for wild animals. A century ago, the famous landscape gardener Peter Joseph Lenné (1789–1866) turned this area into a beautiful park. A stroll across the shaded avenues, past the lakes and watercourses with their small bridges, leads to the **Zoologischer Garten** ㉒ (open daily 9am–dusk). Initially Friedrich Wilhelm IV presented the Berliners with his own royal animal collection in 1842. The zoo was almost destroyed during the bombardment of World War II when only 93 animals survived. Now there are 1,500 different species and about 14,000 mammals and birds, making it the most extensive collection of animals in the world. The Aquarium is a good tip for rainy days. Adjacent to the zoo and dwarfing its surroundings is the **Great Berlin Wheel**, at 185 metres (607 ft) the tallest ferris wheel in Europe, set to open at the end of 2009.

Lively districts

Since the fall of the Wall, **Kreuzberg** has developed into a showpiece of "multicultural life", with Turks, Greeks and citizens of former Yugoslavia making up 30 percent of its residents. And Kreuzberg is no longer on the edge of west Berlin but back in the centre, just to the south of Berlin-Mitte.

Kreuzberg took its name from the eponymous hill, which is one of the highest points in Berlin at 66 metres (216 ft). The **Kreuzberg Memorial** ㉓ at its summit was designed by Karl Friedrich Schinkel in 1821 in memory of the victories of the wars of liberation. Around the Kreuzberg is the **Viktoria Park**, an oasis of relaxation for local residents. Kreuzberg's main attraction is the **Jüdisches**

Museum Berlin (Jewish Museum) in Lindenstrasse (open daily 10am–8pm, Mon until 10pm) with more than 2 million visitors in its first three years. The spectacular building by Daniel Libeskind is a richly symbolic construction. The permanent exhibition offers a journey through German-Jewish history and culture, from its earliest testimonies, through the Middle Ages to the present.

Map on page 102

These days the **Prenzlauer Berg** district, to the northeast of Berlin-Mitte, has become a trendy place for young people. During the industrialisation and land speculation of the 19th century this district arose as a housing area for low-paid workers and the poor. Wartime bombing and the demolition which followed left airy backyards where children today play and their parents hold barbecue and beer parties. The heart of Prenzlauer Berg is the area around **Kollwitzplatz ㉔**. The statue of the artist Käthe Kollwitz has graced the square since 1958. She lived at 25 Kollwitzstrasse for 50 years from 1891 onwards, together with her husband, the doctor Karl Kollwitz, who went to work in the poor quarter of the city.

When the evening sun glows on the faded street facades and the restaurants and cafés have opened their doors and the gates to their beer gardens, the area throbs with life. One street, **Husemannstrasse**, was spruced up in the GDR days as a showpiece of "Old Berlin" urban style and today it has the atmosphere of an open-air museum. In nearby Rykestrasse is the Berlin synagogue that escaped total destruction.

Charlottenburg

Before its incorporation by Berlin, **Charlottenburg** was the richest town of the Brandenburg Marches. Imposing villas around central **Savignyplatz** still give an idea of its past wealth. Its central attraction now is the **Charlottenburg**

BELOW:
Charlottenburg
Palace.

Palace (open Tues–Fri 9am–5pm, Sat–Sun 10am–5pm), named after Queen Sophie Charlotte, grandmother of Frederick the Great. The palace itself contains several collections. There are the historical rooms which used to be the living rooms of Friedrich I and later of Frederick the Great. Apart from its many famous collections, its magnificent park is also worth a visit. In the Ehrenhof is the impressive statue of the Great Elector by Andreas Schlüter. It was cast in bronze in 1700 and is one of the finest works of German baroque.

Opposite the entrance to the palace is the **Scharf-Gerstenberg-Museum**  (open daily 10am–6pm) with an impressive collection of surrealist art, including graphic cycles by Goya, Piranesi and Klinger. Across the way, the **Berggruen Collection** (open Tues–Fri 10am–6pm, Sat–Sun 11am–6pm) displays about 100 paintings, sculptures and drawings from eight artists: Picasso, Klee, Matisse, Cézanne, Van Gogh, Braque, Laurens and Giacometti. Opened in 1996, the gallery provided Berlin with a much-needed forum for classical modern art, something that had been missing from the city since the days of the Reich.

A less elegant contrast is provided by the aluminium-clad **International - Congress Centre**, beside which the **Funkturm** television tower (with viewing platform) and the **Fairgrounds** of the 1920s and 1930s seem positively old-fashioned (S-Bahn Messe Nord).

The **Olympic Stadium** at the Reichssportfeld was built for the 1936 summer Olympics; after a massive overhaul, the stadium hosted some of the 2006 FIFA World Cup matches. The grounds also contain the **Swimming Stadium**, the **German Sport Forum**, the **Maifeld** festival site and the **Waldbühne**, one of Europe's finest open-air stages and a mecca for rock fans.

Athletes in stone at the Olympic Stadium.

BELOW: the cupola of the Scharf-Gerstenberg-Museum.

The Nazi reign of terror is commemorated at the **Gedenkstätte Plötzensee ㉚** in Hüttigpfad, to the northeast of Charlottenburg. Hundreds of political prisoners and freedom fighters of many nations were murdered in the infamous execution centre (S-Bahn Beusselstrasse).

Maps:
City 102
Area 113

Forests and lakes

Away from the centre of Berlin there are numerous attractive places where you can escape the bustle of big-city life. But first some more culture: situated to the southwest of the centre, **Dahlem ㉛** is the site of the main buildings of the **Freie Universität**, with their nearby **Museen Dahlem** (open Tues–Fri 10am–6pm, Sat–Sun 11am–6pm), whose exotic and colourful exhibits make a visit to this part of the city very worthwhile. The complex combines three impressive museums under one roof: the **Museum für Indische Kunst** (Museum of Indian Art), the **Museum für Ostasiatische Kunst** (Museum of East Asian Art) and one of the most popular, the **Ethnologisches Museum** (Ethnological Museum). The latter collection, on which the museum was originally based, was established as long ago as the 17th century by Friedrich Wilhelm, the Great Elector. Today, with its huge variety of sculptures, paintings, cult objects and masks, it is fascinating for all those interested in different cultures. The highlight is a large hall exhibiting boats, in particular a reproduction from a drawing by James Cook of a catamaran from the Isle of Tonga.

The Ethnological Museum has a wealth of treasures from many lands.

Nearby, the **Botanical Garden** (open daily, summer 9am–7 or 8pm, winter 9am–4 or 5pm), with its numerous plants from all over the world, invites visitors to a stroll. On rainy days you might seek protection in the world's highest tropical greenhouse, which contains a large collection of exotic plants.

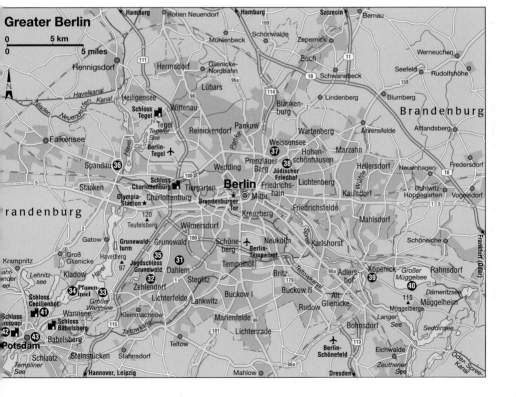

TIP

From Easter until the end of October there is a boat service on Wannsee. You can use it to make trips of varying length between Berlin and Potsdam (1–5 Kronprinzessinnenweg, S-Bahnhof Wannsee; tel: 803-8753).

The charm exuded by the suburb of **Zehlendorf** ㉜, to the southwest, is defined by its successful combination of wealthy mansions, forests and stretches of water. The **Grosser Wannsee** ㉝, a lake with a famous beach – the **Strandbad** – comes to life as early as Easter, when the local watersports clubs sail into the new season. Unfortunately, there is no promenade along the lakeside. Nonetheless, you can happily absorb the atmosphere from the **Wannseeterrassen**, from where you can watch the yachts and excursion vessels, or hop on a boat yourself to take a "Haveltour". There is also a children's playground on the terrace.

The pearl of the Havel river and lakes is **Pfaueninsel** ㉞ (Peacock Island). Reachable only by ferry, its gardens take hours to explore. As well as peacocks and magnificent flora, the island is dotted with several buildings of historical interest, which originate mainly from two periods: the peacock pen, flats for the servants and the small white castle go back to King Friedrich Wilhelm II and his lover Wilhelmine Encke, while the gigantic aviary in the wood and the exotic dairy date back to King Friedrich Wilhelm III and his wife Queen Louise. The interiors of the castle can be visited (open Apr–Oct Tues–Sun 10am–5pm).

Stretching between the Havelchaussee to the west and the Königsallee to the east, the vast **Grunewald Forest** is accessible to walkers in all directions. A footpath leads down to the beautiful Grunewaldsee and the **Jagdschloss Grunewald** ㉟ (Grunewald Hunting Lodge; closed for renovation; reopening scheduled for 2009), whose Renaissance-style rooms contain an extensive collection of German and Dutch paintings. Close by, there is also the **Waldmuseum** (Forest Museum; open Tues–Fri 10am–3pm, Sun and holidays noon–5pm).

BELOW: permanent resident of Peacock Island.

Map on page 113

Located astride important trade routes, the suburb of **Spandau** ㊱, which received its town charter in 1232, is actually older than Berlin. The **Citadel** won strategic importance in medieval times. Under the rule of Prussia's "Soldier King" it became, along with Potsdam, Prussia's arms factory. In more recent times, Spandau became known for the prison in which Rudolf Hess, Adolf Hitler's deputy, was detained for many years. When he committed suicide there in 1987 the prison was torn down and a shopping centre built in its place.

One peripheral area with typically Berlin suburban ambience is **Weissensee** ㊲, named after the lake of the same name, around which the village was founded in about 1230. Today the lake, with its **Park** and **Open-Air Theatre**, is one of the chief attractions. The **Jüdischer Friedhof** ㊳ (Jewish Cemetery) on Herbert-Baum-Strasse is one of the most important in Germany. Here lie such prominent Berlin figures as the architect Walter Gropius, the sculptor Hugo Lederer, the hotelier Berthold Kempinski and the publisher Rudolf Mosse.

Köpenick ㊴ hit the headlines in 1906 when the cobbler Voigt took over the city treasury, disguised in a captain's uniform. The Kaiser is said to have been so amused by the ruse that Voigt was pardoned. In 1931, Carl Zuckmayer based his play *Der Hauptmann von Köpenick (The Captain of Köpenick)* on the incident. Köpenick has the loveliest area of water in Berlin, the **Grosser Müggelsee** ㊵. Fed by the River Spree, this is the largest of Berlin's lakes. A walk along the 6-km (3½-mile) shore of the lake between the Spree tunnel to the west and the landing stage at Müggelhort to the south is especially recommended.

South of the lake, the Köpenick Forest covers a vast area, including the **Müggelberg** hills, which on a clear day provide wonderful views of up to 50 km (30 miles) across Berlin. ❑

The story of Voigt the cobbler, the "Captain of Köpenick", was often quoted abroad as a striking example of the Prussian propensity to follow without question anyone in uniform.

BELOW: Wannsee.

Map on page 113

POTSDAM

Potsdam has played a major role in German and European history. It was here that Frederick the Great held court and that the Allies decided the destiny of Europe after World War II

Potsdam (pop. 150,000) was first mentioned in the record books in AD 993, and was known as *Poztupimi*, literally "under the oak tree". For hundreds of years this small Slavic fishing town on the Havel was a provincial backwater of absolutely no importance. But things began to change when Friedrich Wilhelm, the Great Elector, lost his heart to this sleepy town. Some say he liked the hunting here, for hunting indeed was one of his passions. He made it his second home after Berlin and had the castle built in 1662. Potsdam became an important part of the history of Prussia due to the Tolerance Edict of 1685 through which the Elector introduced asylum for people who were expelled from France, the principal benefactors being the Huguenots.

The Great Elector's son, Friedrich I, held an extravagant court at Potsdam in imitation of Versailles, but his son Friedrich Wilhelm I, who was later known as the Soldier King, had no time for such frivolity. He was the first European monarch to wear uniform, and his motto concerning his subjects was "the soul is for God, the rest is for me". He drummed into his subjects the virtues of prayer, duty, hard work and thriftiness. These are all traits that have become identified with the Prussian character. Friedrich Wilhelm I expanded Potsdam into a garrison city to house his élite troops.

BELOW: Sanssouci in all its splendour.

The city's present glory is mainly thanks to Friedrich II. The Sanssouci Palace was the result of one of his own designs. Having come here to escape government business in the capital, he went on to bequeath numerous rococo buildings to Potsdam, which became known as the "Pearl of the Havel".

His great-nephew Friedrich Wilhelm IV continued in this great tradition. The Prussian chief architect, Karl Friedrich Schinkel, made a classical impression on the face of Potsdam. The sprawling gardens were laid out by the landscape designer Peter Joseph Lenné. A unique and harmonious symbiosis between buildings and nature emerged, a heritage which still characterises Potsdam (in 1990 large areas of Potsdam were granted UNESCO World Heritage status).

The popularity of the city flourished and, just before World War I, Crown Prince Wilhelm had **Cecilienhof Palace ❹** built in the English manorial style. As soldiers were dying in the trenches, the prince allowed himself the luxury of this summer retreat. In the summer of 1945, the Cecilienhof was chosen as the conference venue for the three victorious powers who decided on the future of the defeated Germany. The inside of the palace was swiftly reconstructed to enable it to be used as a workplace for the delegates. The conference room with the famous round table and the studies of Churchill, Stalin and Truman have been preserved in their original state and are open to the public (open Tues–Sun, Apr–Oct 9am–5.30pm, Nov–Mar 9am–4.30pm). The Cecilienhof is also the home of a first-class hotel and restaurant.

Sanssouci

Whenever anyone speaks about a visit to Potsdam they are usually referring to **Sanssouci ❷** (open Tues–Sun, Apr–Oct 10am–5.30pm, Nov–Mar 10am–4.30pm).

TIP

Interested in hearing music from Frederick the Great's period? There are concerts held in some of the most beautiful of Potsdam's palaces and churches (Potsdamer Hofkonzerte, May–Sept; tel: 0331-245609).

BELOW: Britain's Clement Attlee, the USA's Harry Truman and the USSR's Joseph Stalin at the Potsdam Conference.

The New Palace at Sanssouci was built according to Frederick the Great's designs.

BELOW: equestrian statue of Frederick the Great in front of the Orangery.

Frederick the Great had this small palace designed in 1744 according to his own plans and had it built in an old vineyard despite objections from his architect, Wenzeslaus von Knobelsdorff. It is here that Frederick patronised the fine arts and gave his renowned flute concerts. He also entertained French philosopher Voltaire here, in order to debate literature and philosophy with him. Today, tourists flock to Sanssouci, with its 12 gloriously decorated rooms. Outside is the impressive 97-metre (300-ft) parterre with its 35 huge caryatids and dome with the name Sanssouci inscribed in gold letters.

The Prussian Palace and Berlin-Brandenburg Parks Foundation not only sponsors the palace but also the expansive, 290-hectare (717-acre) park which contains numerous architecturally interesting objects that are well worth seeking out. Situated south of the main alley, behind the precisely planned and planted groups of trees, the gold of the **Chinese Tea House**, with the figure of a rotund mandarin on the roof, dazzlingly reflects the sunlight. The clover leaf-shaped house represents the fashion for exotic Chinese styles prevalent in the 18th century. At the end of the long main path, the **Neues Palais** (New Palace), a typical example of royal architecture, was the home of Frederick the Great's household and guests towards the end of his reign. Nearby is the impressive **Charlottenhof Palace**, which was designed and built in a Classical style by Schinkel for Friedrich Wilhelm IV, as were the atmospheric **Roman Baths**.

On the other side of the park you will find the **Orangery**, which was constructed in the Italian Renaissance style. The orange trees were not the only guests to spend their winters in these halls. The crowned heads of friendly nations also regularly stayed here.

There are more palaces and gardens nearby as part of the World Heritage Site: Babelsberg, Neuer Garten, Pfingstberg and Sacrow, as well as Glienicke and Peacock Island *(see page 114)* on the Berlin side of the Havel.

The city centre

Potsdam ➍ was once one of Germany's most beautiful cities, next to Dresden and Würzburg, but today one would have to look very closely in order to find evidence as to how this reputation came about. In the postwar years much of the beauty of the town centre was destroyed by the construction of high-rise blocks of flats next to historically important buildings.

Be that as it may, the town is well worth exploring. The Broadway of Potsdam is Brandenburger Strasse, a pedestrian zone which stretches between the bright yellow **Brandenburg Gate** on the one side to the Catholic **Church of Saints Peter and Paul** on the other. A commercial area is now thriving, with plenty of antiques, leather goods and small bars. The streets around the Nauen Gate are especially popular.

The **Holländisches Viertel** (Dutch Quarter) is a big attraction. Friedrich Wilhelm I was inspired by the red brick gables of Dutch houses when he ordered the building of these four blocks. The Soldier King even tried to lure Dutch craftsmen and artists to settle the area, but few came. He therefore moved Prussian craftsmen and his infantry into some of the buildings. The majority of the buildings in the Dutch Quarter

have been beautifully restored. If you wander down Mittelstrasse or Benkert-strasse you will find contemporary craftsmen at work alongside street cafés.

There is a rather surprising building in the old market place (Am Alten Markt) opposite the **Church of St Nicholas** (yet another example of Schinkel's work). Known locally as the "Tin Can", it is in fact a modern theatre which the city fathers decided to construct soon after reunification on what had been, up until 1960, the site of the imposing Potsdam Palace. This metal monstrosity was built in response to the lack of suitable space for the **Hans-Otto Theatre**. The Potsdam Palace is going to be reconstructed; the majestic Fortunaportal, crowned by the deity of fortune, appears already in its old splendour.

Anyone interested in the history of film and cinema should visit the **Film Museum** in Potsdam's Breite Strasse (open daily 10am–6pm; English guide available at the entrance). The building that was once the Royal Stables is now home to an exhibition of well displayed cinema posters and other relics of the past. It also houses film props of the Babelsberg Film Studios, such as costumes once worn by Marlene Dietrich and Zarah Leander. One of the most popular displays is the "Welte-Kinoorgel", an organ dating back to cinema's early days, when silent movies were accompanied by live music.

The postwar authorities also decided to tear down the **Garnisonkirche** (Garrison Church), once a symbol of Prussian militarism and God-fearing morality, which used to stand on the land at the corner of Dortustrasse and Breite Strasse. In 1945, shortly before the end of World War II, this church was burnt out, when Potsdam was subjected to intensive bombing, but the walls were left standing. It was the demolition experts who finally brought these walls down in 1968. The Data Centre now stands on the site. ❑

Map on page 113

Potsdam's Church of St Nicholas (Nikolaikirche) was designed by Karl Friedrich Schinkel.

BELOW: welcome to Cinefantastic at Babelsberg.

BABELSBERG FILM STUDIOS

The internationally known Babelsberg Film Studios have lost none of their magic. The silent film *Der Totentanz (The Dance of Death)* starring Asta Nielsen and, later, Paul Wegener's *Golem* are still remembered today, as is Fritz Lang's science-fiction epic *Metropolis*. One famous film after another was shot here.

In 1992 the studios, previously operated by the UFA and DEFA organisations, were transformed into an ultra-modern media- and film-centre. Now international productions are shot here with actors such as Gérard Dépardieu, Jeanne Moreau and Omar Sharif. In 2001, Jude Law and Joseph Fiennes took starring roles in *Duel – Enemy at the Gates*, then the most expensive film ever to be shot in Europe.

There is a "Studio Tour" where you can see how films are made from behind glass screens. The favourite attraction is the Stuntmen Show. Actors play out an adventure story set against scenery resembling Bryce Canyon and Yellowstone National Park in the USA. Another is the Showscan-Action cinema, where you sit on moveable chairs and see a film with 60 pictures per second accompanied by sound effects – a taste of cinema technology of the future. (Grossbeerenstrasse, Potsdam-Babelsberg; open mid-Mar–Oct 10am–6pm, closed Mon and Fri June and Sept; tel: 0331-7212738.)

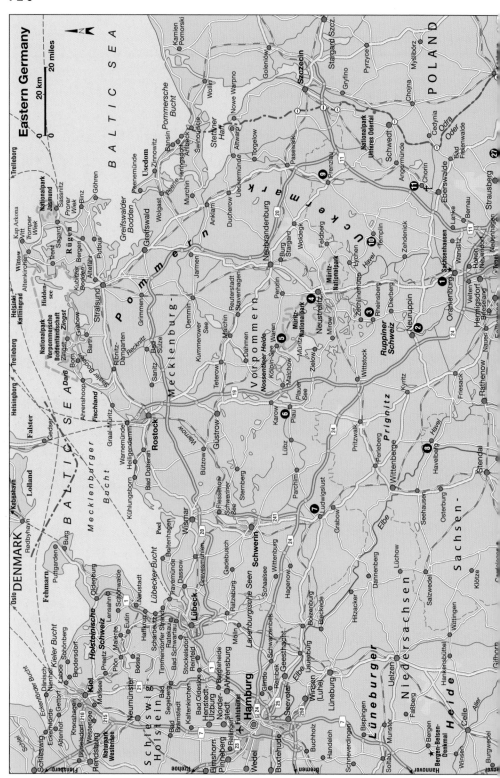

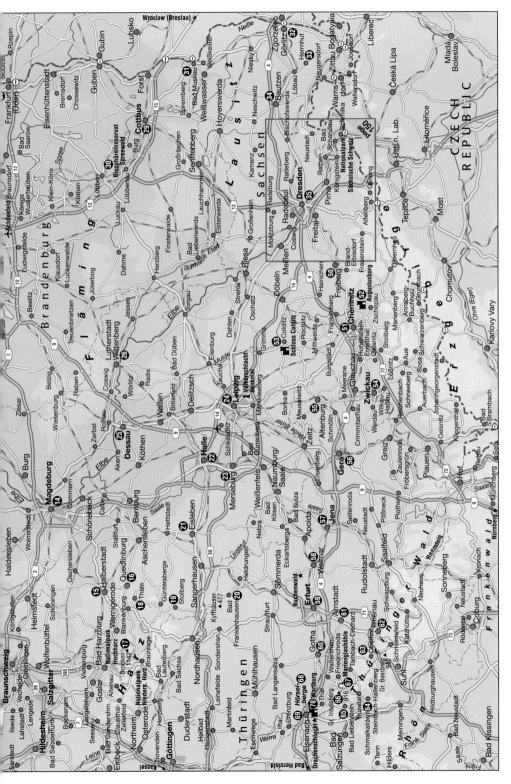

BRANDENBURG AND THE MECKLENBURG LAKES

A trip through Brandenburg reveals some fascinating local history, while the Mecklenburg Lakes offer fine scenery, plenty of solitude and some delightful unspoiled towns

The Brandenburg countryside is pleasantly varied. On the one hand you have the sandy earth with its dusty fields and dark pine woods. On the other, you can enjoy the soft meadows, which virtually drip with water and always end up in a lake. Many of the towns and villages of Brandenburg were named after old noble families; Bredow and Ribbeck are two examples. The writer Theodor Fontane (1819–98) hailed from these parts. A trained chemist, he turned his hand to writing and journalism after the failure of the German Revolution in 1848, and spent much of his time travelling. An Anglophile, Fontane translated Shakespeare into German and in the years he spent in Britain (1855–59), he wrote about Scotland *(Beyond the Tweed)*. It was this journey that inspired him once more to return and write about his homeland in *Strolls through the Brandenburg Marches*, in which he describes the history, legends and anecdotes of the region. He regarded the relationship between England and Scotland as very similar to that between Prussia and its border regions.

Some 25 km (15 miles) north of Berlin on the B96 is **Oranienburg ❶**. The town, originally named Bötzow, was founded around 1200. When Friedrich-Wilhelm of Brandenburg, the Great Elector, built a new Dutch-style residence here in 1651, he named it for his wife, Louise Henriette of Orange, and the name came to be applied to the town as well. In 1814, a sulphuric acid factory moved to the palace and it was here that the chemist Friedlieb Ferdinand Runge first succeeded in separating aniline and carbolic acid, two of the most important raw materials for the chemical industry, from coal tar. Fontane commented that the sulphur fumes eroded the last vestiges of Oranienburg's splendour. However, the palace and its park, laid out as an English-style garden in 1879, have been partially restored to their former glory (open Apr–Oct Tues–Sun 10am–5.30pm, Nov–Mar Sat–Sun 10am–4.30pm).

There is a darker side to local history. The village of **Sachsenhausen**, just to the north of Oranienburg, was the site of the first concentration camp to be constructed by the Nazis on German soil, in 1936. Of a total of some 200,000 who went through Sachsenhausen, more than 100,000 died, principally from disease, starvation, execution and overwork in the local armaments factories. Only in 1990 was it discovered that after the war, Stalin's secret police had murdered political opponents on the very same site and had buried them in mass graves in the nearby forest (open mid-Mar–mid-Oct daily 8.30am–6pm, otherwise until 4.30pm).

LEFT: Rheinsberg Palace, a literary setting.
BELOW: memorial at Sachsenhausen.

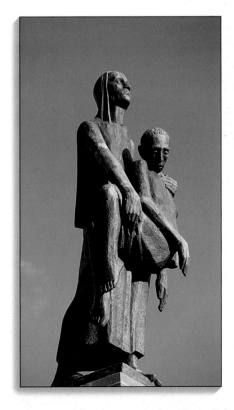

Theodor Fontane,
writer and
anglophile, at home
in Neuruppin.

BELOW: detail from
a Neuruppin
broadsheet
showing riots in
Berlin in 1848.

On the trail of writers

Theodor Fontane was born in **Neuruppin** ❷, which was rebuilt in an early Classical style with a chessboard street pattern following a disastrous fire that engulfed almost the entire original town in 1787. In the **Museum Neuruppin** (Local Museum) in August-Bebel-Strasse 14/15 (open Apr–Oct Tues–Fri noon–5pm, Sat–Sun 11am–5pm, Nov–Mar Tues, Fri and Sun 11am–4pm), there is numerous Fontane memorabilia as well as exhibits on the life of Karl Friedrich Schinkel (1781–1841), the town's second famous son, who made his career in Berlin as the state architect of Prussia *(see page 105)* but was also active in his home town. While most of the reconstruction after the fire was the work of Bernhard Matthias Brasch, it was Schinkel who later rebuilt the 13th-century **Dominikanerkloster** (Dominican Monastery). The town also became famous through the *Neuruppiner Bilderbogen*, pictorial broadsheets published by Gustav Kühn: the Bilderbogen Gallery in the Museum Neuruppin contains the world's largest broadsheet collection *(see below)*.

A visit to **Rheinsberg** ❸ is another literary must. Rheinsberg is the setting of *Rheinsberg: a Book for Lovers* by Kurt Tucholsky (1890–1935). With a gentle romantic touch, the revered satirist and poet managed to change this small town into a place of pilgrimage for people in love who wished to enjoy a "series of dazzling days" as Tucholsky's characters Claire and Wölfchen did. Above all, there is a **Palace** (open Tues–Sun, Apr–Oct 10am–5.30pm, Nov–Mar 10am–4.30pm), a small Sanssouci surrounded by a fairytale park and an old town laid out like a chessboard. There are round towers, a colonnade of pillars which stretch down to the Rheinsberg lake and plenty of northern German rococo, which all go back to the time of Wenzeslaus von Knobelsdorff (1699–1753), a companion and favourite

NEURUPPIN BROADSHEETS

Scandals, news, personalities – just like the tabloid papers of today, the Neuruppin broadsheets *(Neuruppiner Bilderbogen)* would report on anything and anybody in the limelight of society or of public interest, and regularly covered world events. While the aim of the publisher, Gustav Kühn, was to provide a continuous flow of up-to-date information on topical matters, many of the reports were to be taken with a pinch of salt; more often than not what seemed to be reality actually originated in the rich fantasy of the broadsheet illustrators. As Theodor Fontane observed, even the most detailed information on faraway lands only just discovered by Livingstone and other explorers was somehow known to the illustrators, even before the arrival of any Westerners. But as far as reputation was concerned, *The Times* couldn't hold a candle to the Neuruppin broadsheets. As Fontane himself wrote: "*The Times* is like a bishop, while the broadsheets are like missionaries going everywhere."

Between 1810–37 no less than 22,000 broadsheets were published with a total print run of around 100 million. They were produced much like comic strips, with 12-colour or black and white drawings, each with a caption describing the event.

architect of Frederick the Great, who enjoyed living here as Crown Prince. After his accession to the throne, Frederick gave the palace to his brother Prince Heinrich in 1744, who lived there for 50 years.

Lakeland

It would take a lifetime to get to know the meandering rivers and lakes which belong to the Mecklenburg Lake District north of Rheinsberg. If the mathematical facts are correct, there are about 1,800 lakes in the Mecklenburg-Vorpommern area. Wildlife has flourished in this region following the creation of three nature reserves in 1990: the Feldberg-Lychener Lake District (1,120 sq. km/432 sq. miles), the Müritz-Nationalpark (313 sq. km/121 sq. miles) and the Nossentiner-Schwinzer Heath (320 sq. km/124 sq. miles). Müritz and the other lakes have become home to wildlife such as kites, falcons, sea eagles, ospreys, black storks and numerous species of duck.

Densely forested hills, sandy plains with moors and pine woods, inland dunes and broad reed belts form the landscape of the countryside that was created by the last Ice Age. It is best to experience the idyll by canoe or inflatable dinghy with the right maps and a tent in your luggage. Even if you are conducting a spur-of-the-moment tour of the area you can still arrange a canoe for one or more day trips on short-term hire from local clubs.

Past large and small stretches of water, the country road takes you to **Neustrelitz ❹**, a baroque town planned and built in 1733 as a residence for one of the dukes of Mecklenburg-Strelitz. Many of the baroque buildings are lost, but there are still some beautiful neoclassical monuments, such as the Town Hall, dating from 1841. You will search in vain for the baroque palace, which was destroyed by fire in 1945 and whose ruins were subsequently dismantled. The **Palace Park**, laid out in the style of an English country garden remains, however, and holds many small gems, such as the raised temple, the Neo-Gothic palace church and an avenue lined with sandstone statues of ancient divinities.

The **Müritz**, which is Germany's second-biggest lake after Lake Constance, is only 1½ hours' drive away from the 3.5 million-strong conurbation of Berlin. It's the beginning of the Mecklenburg Lake District. Those who visit the lake cannot miss **Waren ❺**, which has been a health resort since 1845. Fontane knew that "in the whole of God's world there is no better place in which to take a cure". Nowadays there are also facilities for sailing, diving and windsurfing, but the town itself, more than 700 years old, is also worth exploring. There are some beautiful half-timbered buildings such as the Löwenapotheke (apothecary) dating from 1623. The **Müritz Museum** near the lake will tell you all about the history and nature of the countryside and also has the biggest **Freshwater Aquarium** in Germany (open Tues–Sun, summer 10am–6pm, winter 10am–4pm). A beautiful view of the town, which is built up in terraces, can be enjoyed from the water aboard one of the pleasure steamers that go to Röbel on the southwest shore or steam across Kölpin, Fleesen, Malchower and Plauer Lakes to reach the town of Plau.

 Map on pages 120–21

 TIP

From June to August each year, the Schloss Rheinsberg Chamber Opera presents an array of young talent from across the world, staging old favourites as well as lesser-known operatic works (tel: 033931-39296; www.kammeroper-schloss-rheinsberg.de).

BELOW: blustery day at the Müritz.

"Make the most of your time" is written on the facade of the Town Hall in **Plau** . Those who follow that advice will find many treasures here. Apart from the abundance of water, there is the **Town Church** (13th century) with a late Gothic, richly decorated altarpiece; an old **Castle Tower** with an 11-metre (36-ft) deep dungeon; and an ingenious lift bridge over the Elde, which was built in 1916. An exhibition near the church displays the work of Wilhelm Wandschneider (1866–1944) whose sculptures are scattered all around Mecklenburg (open June–Sept Mon–Fri 10am–noon, 1–3pm, Sat 10am–noon, Oct–May Mon–Fri 10am–noon).

Little Versailles

Some names are full of music, at times elegiac and heavy, at others dainty and light, but they all played their part in history. In **Ludwigslust** ❼ (pop. 12,000) there once stood a hunting lodge where Duke Christian Ludwig II resided, one presumes in not altogether unhappy circumstances. From 1756 to 1837 the area rose to become a Residenz (or royal seat) and was planned and developed as the "Little Versailles" of Mecklenburg, with lots of baroque and even more Classicism, a **palace** (open summer daily 10am–6pm, winter Tues–Sun 10am–5pm) well worth seeing and an enormous **park** in which you can easily lose yourself. For a truly magnificent display of splendour the duke's purse was too small – so most of the palace interior decoration is made out of paper-mâché.

Before returning to the city, you pass through more unspoiled landscape. Between Ludwigslust and Berlin, around the little towns of Perleberg, Pritzwalk and Kyritz lies the **Prignitz** – a flat, forested region dotted with sleepy villages. There is the occasional lake to bathe in and the roads are mostly narrow.

TIP

In the Ludwigslust castle park, the beautiful half-timbered Schweizehaus is a popular restaurant with a garden terrace.

BELOW: picturesque Plau.

There is little dramatic landscape, just forest and fields in this remote, almost forgotten part of the country. It's an idyllic place for cyclists.

During the first weekend of September especially (Thursday to Sunday) it's worth taking a detour through the little town of **Havelberg** ❽ (pop. 7,200) which rises up out of the agricultural plain on the B107. Every year a **Horse Market** is held here on Havel Meadow – along with the flea market traders and carousel owners in tow. Transactions require little formality. A simple handshake, an exchange of notes, and the horse has a new owner.

Nearby is the confluence of the Havel and the Elbe, the river which once formed the border between the Germans and the Slavs, which explains why the **Cathedral** (1170) has some of the characteristics of a castle.

Border country

An alternative excursion from Berlin, and an area you pass through if you're heading for the Baltic Sea Coast, leads northeast through the **Uckermark**, the historical borderland between Pomerania and Mecklenburg. This area, characterised by lakes and peaceful waterways, forests and clearings, is excellent walking country. It's a swan's paradise and ever since King Wilhelm I of Prussia came swan hunting here, a swan has been on Prenzlau's coat of arms.

But history has not always been kind to **Prenzlau** ❾ (pop. 20,500). The town suffered badly during the Thirty Years' War and in 1945 it was almost reduced to ashes. However, three city gates, the Schwedtertor, Blindowertor and Mitteltor survived. In the **Kulturhistorische Museum**, located in the beautiful cloisters and enclosures of a 13th- and 14th-century Dominican monastery, you can learn more about the history of Uckermark and life in medieval times (open Tues–Sun 10am–5pm). Not far from the museum is the **Church of St Nicholas** with its carved Renaissance altar dating back to 1609.

Following the route southwest and then south from Prenzlau back towards Berlin, you will reach **Templin** ❿ (pop. 14,000). This little town with its narrow half-timbered houses is surrounded by a 1,700-metre (1-mile) long town wall, 50 towers and three impressive gates and is considered to be Brandenburg's best-preserved fortified town. One of the gates, the **Prenzlauer Tor**, houses the **Volkskunde Museum** (Folklore Museum; open Tues–Fri 9am–noon, 1–5pm, Sat–Sun 1–5pm, Oct–Apr until 4pm) where traditional tools used by craftsmen are on display. Walking through the centre you reach the market square with its baroque **Town Hall** and if you carry on walking along Rühlstrasse you finally arrive at the **Eulenturm**, a tower with a peculiar entrance 6 metres (19 ft) above the ground. Once imprisoned here, captives had no hope of escape.

A bit further to the east near Federal Highway 2 lies **Kloster Chorin** ⓫ (Chorin Monastery), one of the finest examples of local Gothic brick architecture from the 13th century. It was founded by Cistercian monks and after the Reformation was used as a cattle shed. You can see the ruin of the church, the cloisters and the famous west facade (open daily Apr–Oct 9am–7pm, Nov–Mar 9am–4pm). ❏

Map on pages 120–21

Map on pages 120–21

TIP

Open-air classical music concerts are regularly performed in Chorin Monastery. Book well in advance as the concerts are usually very popular (tel: 03334-657310).

BELOW: Chorin Monastery.

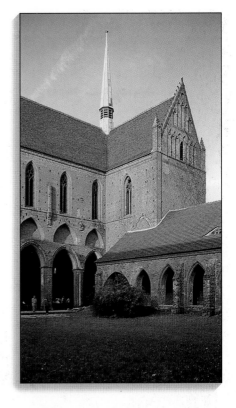

THROUGH THE HARZ TO LEIPZIG

Map on pages 120–21

With its legends of ghosts and witches, the Harz holds an important place in German folklore. But history, too, is everywhere on this tour to the city Goethe called "Little Paris"

The journey from Berlin through Saxony-Anhalt to Leipzig and back past Dessau and Lutherstadt Wittenberg is a series of contrasts. In the Harz, the picture-book landscape is one of half-timbered houses and fine Romanesque buildings. There is also the fantasy world of the witches of the Brocken. The industrial present takes over in Halle, while Leipzig is clearly a busy city currently being rebuilt after decades of neglect. Dessau and the Lutheran town of Wittenberg are both associated with some important names in German history and culture.

Just beyond Potsdam to the west of the Grosser Zernsee lies the island town of **Werder** ⓬ (pop. 22,000). Many Berliners come here at the end of April for the Baumblütenfest (Blossom Festival) and return later in the year for the fruit harvests. Relaxing in one of the cafés overlooking the Havel and treating yourself to home-made fruit cake or fruit wine is a year-round pleasure.

Brandenburg

Follow the road beneath a canopy of oak, linden, chestnut and maple trees to the town of **Brandenburg** ⓭ (pop. 78,000), passing the flat, watery and wooded Havelland. Straddling the River Havel, the town, originally called Brennabor, was once the main fortress of the West Slavic Hevelli tribe. In AD 928 Emperor Heinrich I tried to capture it, but it wasn't until 1157 that the fortifications were finally taken by Albrecht the Bear. The town only really established itself when it became a bishopric. In the 14th and 15th centuries the area flourished as a centre for trade and the manufacture of cloth, but Brandenburg's importance declined following the rise of Berlin as the residence of the Elector. Prosperity returned in 1690 when Huguenots, expelled from France, arrived in the area, bringing with them new tanning techniques.

Today, the townscape is dominated by the steel industry yet there are still some gems. The **Cathedral** (open Mon–Sat 10am–4pm, Sun 11am–5pm), which dates back to the Middle Ages, is the oldest surviving building in the Brandenburg Marches. First built in Romanesque style, the church was transformed at the end of the 14th century into a Gothic basilica. Among its art treasures are 13th-century stained-glass windows and the bishops' tombstones. The **Dommuseum** (Cathedral Museum) contains calligraphy and textiles from the Middle Ages.

In the old town it is worth taking a look at the **Old Town Hall** (1470) and, in what used to be called the new town, the parish church of **St Catherine**, completed in 1401, is also of interest.

LEFT: not your usual shop welcome.
BELOW: Quedlinburg.

Romanesque roots

Magdeburg (pop. 234,000), the capital of Saxony-Anhalt, lies at an important intersection of road, rail, river and canal routes and is easily the biggest inland port in eastern Germany. First impressions of this city tend to be rather disappointing due to the extent of the damage suffered during World War II. At an earlier time, Magdeburg did attain considerable historical significance. Under Otto I the city developed into a centre for Slavic missionary work. He elevated the status of the city by building a castle and installing an archbishop.

Many of the Romanesque buildings that were constructed during this period have survived. The **Kloster Unserer Lieben Frauen** (Monastery of Our Lady, 1064–1160) is one of the most important Romanesque buildings in Germany. The church, which now serves as a concert hall, is dedicated to the composer Georg Friedrich Telemann, who was born in Magdeburg in 1681. A festival is held in his honour every second year. After renovation work, the **Museum of Cultural History** has reopened with an exhibition commemorating 1200 years of cultural history in Madgeburg. The collection includes the "Magdeburger Reiter" (*c.* 1240), said to be the oldest free-standing **Equestrian Statue** in Germany. A replica of the statue stands in the **Alter Markt** (Old Market Place) in front of the Baroque **Town Hall**. The city's **Cathedral** towers above the other buildings and is visible from afar. Dating from 955, the cathedral was rebuilt in Gothic style in 1209 after it had been destroyed by fire. The opulent furnishings include 14th-century choir stalls, 15th-century alabaster statues, a late 16th-century pulpit and numerous tombstones. A monument by Ernst Barlach pays tribute to those Germans who fell during World War I.

The name of **Otto von Guericke** (1602–86) will be familiar to students of physics. He was born in Magdeburg and became the city's mayor for a short time. In 1656 he pumped the air out of two hemispheres to create a vacuum. As the two halves remained firmly together, his experiment proved the existence of atmospheric pressure.

The fertile soil of the surrounding countryside lies close to the city boundaries and the vast fields are of North American prairie proportions. **Halberstadt** , formerly an episcopal residence, was almost completely destroyed during World War II, though the **Cathedral** and the **Liebfrauenkirche** (Church of Our Lady), a 12th-century Romanesque basilica, have been carefully restored. After 250 years of building work, the cathedral was consecrated in 1491. The most impressive of its treasures are on display in the cloisters: Romanesque tapestries, crystal crosses and liturgical vestments. Nearby, the **Heineanum** displays some 16,000 stuffed birds and 10,000 eggs (open Tues–Fri 9am–5pm, Sat–Sun 10am–5pm).

The half-timbered wonder

At the foot of the Harz mountains lies **Quedlinburg** , famous for its old town. With no fewer than 1,200 half-timbered houses, most of which date from the 15th and 16th centuries, the inner quarter resembles an old-fashioned picture postcard and UNESCO has listed the town as a World Heritage Site. The highly recommended **Fachwerkmuseum** (Museum of Half-

TIP

At 60 metres in height, the Millennium Tower in Madgeburg's Elbauenpark is the tallest wooden tower in the world. Housed within is a unique exhibition devoted to 6,000 years of technological development (open Apr–Oct Tues–Sun 10am–6pm).

BELOW: half-timbered Quedlinburg.

timbered Houses; open Apr–Oct Fri–Wed 10am–5pm, Nov–Mar 10am–4pm) at Wordgasse 3, in the oldest half-timbered house in Germany (built around 1300), documents the development of this building style.

On the castle hill stands the late Romanesque **St Servatius Stiftskirche** (Collegiate Church, 1070–1129). In the crypt lies the tombstone of King Heinrich I. The church treasures, seemingly lost after 1945, miraculously appeared in Texas in 1991 and returned to Quedlinburg in 1993. On display in the treasury (open May–Oct Tues–Sat 10am–5.30pm, Sun noon–5.30pm, closes 1–2 hours earlier other months) are delicate reliquaries of rock crystal and gold, an elaborately carved ivory comb and two manuscripts in jewelled covers. Nearby lies the **Klopstockhaus** where an exhibition (open Sun–Wed 10am–5pm, Nov–Mar until 4pm) documents the life and work of the great religious poet Friedrich Klopstock, who wrote *The Messiah*. He was born in Quedlinburg in 1724. Another museum worth stopping at is the **Feininger-Galerie** (Schlossberg 11), which holds a splendid collection of graphic works by German-American painter Lyonel Feininger (1871–1956).

The Hochharz National Park

At the heart of the Hochharz National Park is the **Brocken Mountain ⏶**, which reaches a height of 1,140 metres (3,740 ft) above sea level. In good weather, the panoramic view from the summit is quite stunning. Many people make the journey to the top aboard the **Harzquerbahn** steam railway from Wernigerode, a trip which takes about 1½ hours. As an alternative you can take a wonderful drive through dark, dense spruce forests along the winding, picturesque country roads to Nordhausen, but that is a good 3-hour trip. From the Brocken the waters of the

Map on pages 120–21

Scared of ghosts? On some late afternoons you might meet the awesome Spectre of the Brocken. However, it is perfectly harmless, produced by the giant shadows of visitors cast on the clouds welling around the summit.

BELOW: high up in the Harz.

Witches are a constant hazard in the Harz.

River Ilse roar along an attractive valley and down a series of rapids, the **Ilse Waterfalls**. From **Thale ⑱**, set between the wild and rugged **Teufelsmauer** – the Devil's Wall, which makes a marvellous ridge walk – and the impressive **Bode** valley, a cable car crosses to the **Hexentanzplatz** or "Witches' Dance Square" between the villages of Schierke and Elend, the place where the *Walpurgisnacht* scene in Goethe's *Faust* is said to have taken place. The mountains, lakes and rivers of the Harz have a unique range of flora and fauna and the area ranks as one of the most remarkable nature reserves between Scandinavia and the Alps.

Reformers of the Middle Ages

Stolberg **⑲** is the birthplace of the reformer and revolutionary **Thomas Müntzer** (*c.* 1490–1525) and one of the most romantic towns in the Harz. Although he was influenced in the beginning by Martin Luther, Müntzer soon realised that Luther's views were not radical enough. His goal was the creation of a system in which all men are equal and land is shared for the common good. He established a liaison with rebellious farmers and, in contrast to Luther, preached a militarist philosophy. Around a third of Germany was opposed to feudal law and the church was in turmoil. However, in 1525 the feudal lords joined together and 5,000 farmers were slaughtered in Frankenhausen at the foot of the Kyffhäuser hills. Müntzer himself was beheaded.

To commemorate those peasant uprisings, the construction of the **Panorama Museum** in **Bad Frankenhausen ⑳** was commissioned during the 1980s. Here the enormous panoramic painting by Werner Tübke, entitled *Frühbürgerliche Revolution in Deutschland* (Early Civil Revolt in Germany) can be seen (open Tues–Sun Apr–Oct 10am–6pm, Nov–Mar 10am–5pm). Close

BELOW: Martin Luther's statue in Eisleben.

by lies the largest karst cave in the southern Harz foothills, the Barbarossa Cave. It may be viewed as part of a guided tour.

Martin Luther (1483–1546) was born in **Eisleben** ㉑ and a statue in the market reminds the townsfolk of their most famous son. The house where he died has been converted into the **Luthermuseum** (open Apr–Oct daily 9am–6pm, Nov–Mar Tues–Sun 10am–5pm). For over 4,000 years, copper mining has been of great importance in the region. The exhibits in the town's **Heimatmuseum** (Local History Museum; open daily 9am–5pm) – some over 2,000 years old – testify to this longstanding tradition.

Industrial centres and more

Eisleben is the last of the romantic Harz towns. From here, the scenery becomes less attractive. Although Halle and Merseburg occupy nice locations on the banks of the Saale, they lie at the heart of eastern Germany's industrial centre.

After a short stroll through the town centre, which was spared during the war, it will become apparent that **Halle** ㉒ (pop. 232,000) is not just a dull, industrial town. In 968 Halle came under the jurisdiction of the bishops of Magdeburg and from the 11th century onwards the saltwater springs provided the foundation for the prosperity of the people. Around 400 years later a bitter struggle between the people and their episcopal masters ended with defeat for the rebellious middle classes.

In the 17th and 18th centuries, the university, founded in 1694, developed into a stronghold of enlightenment and pietism. At the end of the 19th century the ban on the existence of socialist parties was lifted and Halle was the venue in 1890 for the first conference of the SPD (German Socialist Party).

The spacious **Market Square** in the centre has retained its unique combination

Map on pages 120–21

TIP

In Eisleben the new annex to the house where Luther was born is a fabulous example of progressive contemporary architecture in a historical context. It has been deemed worthy of an architectural award.

BELOW: the Market Square in Halle.

BELOW:
Romanesque carving in Naumburg Cathedral.

of churches and historic buildings. The **Council Chambers** and **Town Hall** are overlooked by the four towers of the market's **Frauenkirche** (Church of Our Lady, 1529–55). Martin Luther preached here, and George Frederick Händel, the town's best-known son, was at one time the organist. More about the composer's life can be discovered in the **Händel-Haus** in his birthplace, (Grosse Nikolai-strasse 5; open Apr–Oct Tues–Sun 10am–6pm, other months until 5pm). There is also a statue of him opposite the church on the market place and the city holds a Händel festival. Immediately adjacent, the freestanding **Rote Turm** (Red Tower) with 76 bells soars to a height of 84 metres (275 ft). Near the **Cathedral**, which contains some fine examples of late-Gothic sculpture, stands the former **Residence** of Cardinal Albrecht II (16th-century). This houses the **Geiseltal Museum** (open Mon–Thur 9am–noon, 1–5pm, Fri until 3pm, Sat–Sun 9am–1pm) with a display of notable fossils. One of the most important art collections in eastern Germany is in the **Moritzburg** (1484–1503) on the Schlossberg, or Castle Hill. This contains exhibits of German painting and sculpture from the 19th and 20th centuries, including works by Lovis Corinth, Max Liebermann, Wilhelm Lehm-bruck and Ernst Barlach (open Tues 11am–8.30pm, Wed–Sun 10am–6pm).

Also worth visiting is the historic orphanage of the **Franckesche Stiftungen**, which conserve a complex of half-timbered houses, including the reconstructed "Wunderkammer" (curiosity cabinet) from 1741 and a library from 1728. While in the north of town, not only the Sky Disc of Nebra (*see margin tip*) but also well presented exhibitions on the Bronze and Stone Ages beg a detour to the **Museum für Vorgeschichte** (Museum of Prehistory; Richard-Wagnerstrasse 9; open Tues–Fri 9am–5pm, Tues until 7.30pm, Sat–Sun 10am–6pm).

Merseburg ㉓ is the home of one of the earliest chapters of German history.

THE ROMANESQUE ROAD

Nowhere else in Germany, perhaps with the exception of the Rhineland, can you find as many historic buildings dating back to Romanesque times as in Saxony-Anhalt. Forbidding walls, tiny windows and wonderfully atmospheric cloisters bear impressive testimony to the days when this region was regarded as the centre of Germany. After all, the first German emperors came from here. Carolingians, Ottonians and Salians didn't have stationary capitals, but moved with all their royal household from one stronghold to the next, leaving behind them a trail of palaces, churches and castles.

The Romanesque Road connects about 70 of the most impressive buildings dating back to the period between 950 and 1250. The best starting point is Magdeburg, from where two different routes start – one to the north, the other to the south. The southern route, more or less parallel to the route described from Magdeburg to Halle, is the prettier part of the tour. It is essential to plan extra trips, for the Harz area also contains such jewels as the Collegiate Church in Gernrode (10th-century) and Burg Falkenstein (11th-century); and from Merseburg it is only a stone's throw to Naumburg's cathedral (13th-century) and Castle Neuenburg in Freyburg (11th-century).

On the Stadthügel, originally the raised site of a fortified palace built by Heinrich I in the 10th century, the **Cathedral** and **Schloss** (15th–17th centuries) are close neighbours. In the days of the German Empire, more than 20 Imperial Diets convened here between 933 and 1212. The complex of buildings has its focus in the beautifully tended **Schlossgarten**, a park filled with delightful treasures, which provides the setting for the Assembly House, the Palace, the Orangery and a café. Of greater cultural significance, however, is the Cathedral. The building we see today was started in 1015 and took on its present form, characterised by its four towers, in the 16th century. Showpieces of the luxurious interior include the bronze memorial (1080), the font (*c.* 1150) and the richly decorated choir stalls. The famous **Cathedral Collegiate Archive**, founded in 1004 by Bishop Wigbert, contains a collection of medieval manuscripts which are among the earliest extant examples of German literature. They include the priceless **Merseburger Zaubersprüche**, an ancient charm to protect fighting men and their horses from harm. Dating back to the 9th–10th centuries, they lay undiscovered in the cathedral library until 1841.

Maps:
Area 120
City 136

The pavements of Leipzig have returned to their former elegance.

Leipzig

Two centuries ago, Goethe named **Leipzig ㉔** "Little Paris" and, with a population of just over 500,000, it was the second-largest city of the former GDR. In 1930 the population was around 700,000, but the division of Germany hit this established centre for publishing and exhibitions particularly hard. The publishing industry in Leipzig started way back in 1481 and grew to monopolise the German book trade in the 19th century. In 1842, a central ordering and delivery centre was established, so that nearly all publishing houses in Germany had to distribute their books via Leipzig. This practice continued until 1945, when many publishing houses relocated to the west and Leipzig surrendered to Frankfurt-am-Main its status as the prime city for book fairs. With the annual Leipzig bookfair at the Lewf fairgrounds however, the town has won back its reputation for international publishing.

BELOW: acrobatics at the university.

The earliest signs of habitation date back to the 6th and 7th centuries, when the Slavic Serbs settled here and named it "Lipzi" ("under the lime trees"). As foreign trade grew, two important routes crossed the lowlands around Leipzig, and where they met, merchants and craftsmen began to make their home in the 10th–11th centuries. In 1268 the Margrave of Meissen gave it special trading privileges and it was granted a market in 1497 by Kaiser Maximilian I. Thus the town flourished as a trading centre.

With the founding of the **university** in 1409, Leipzig also became a cultural centre, which attracted many influential students over the centuries, among them the historian Leopold von Ranke, the philosophers Gottfried Wilhelm Freiherr von Leibnitz and Friedrich Nietzsche, and the poets Friedrich Gottlieb Klopstock, Gotthold Ephraim Lessing, Johann Wolfgang von Goethe and Jean Paul.

The **Leipziger Congress** took place in 1863, initiated by German workers' unions. The political programme was the brainchild of Ferdinand Lassalle, who was elected President of the General German

Workers' Union at the congress. The influential socialists Clara Zetkin, Rosa Luxemburg and Franz Mehring were employed on the left-wing newspaper, the *Leipziger Volkszeitung*, founded in 1894.

Leipzig's contemporary history also shows a dynamic tendency towards change. The city became well known for its Monday Demonstrations, which were a forerunner of the peaceful revolution in 1989. Today's Leipzig is known as the "Boomtown of the East". Among the recent additions to Leipzig's cultural line-up are two new museums that opened their doors at Sachsenplatz in late 2004: the relocated **Museum der Bildenden Künste** (Museum of Fine Arts) and adjacent to it, a new branch of the Stadtgeschichtliches Museum (Local History Museum).

On first sight of the **Hauptbahnhof Ⓐ**, or Main Station, constructed in 1915 and the largest terminal station in Europe, the visitor may be surprised by the unusual symmetrical layout of the building. The reason for this lies not with any aesthetic concept, but in the fact that two completely independent railway companies used to share the building; the eastern side was owned by Saxony, the western by Prussia. Two open-air staircases lead from the main concourse which is around 300 metres (980 ft) long, 33 metres (108 ft) wide and 27 metres (89 ft) high. The city centre, with its market square, is 10 minutes' walk from here.

In **Katharinenstrasse Ⓑ**, two buildings bear testimony to its former magnificence. Apart from the Romanushaus, richly decorated with putti and garlands, and the Fregehaus with its marvellous gable and 16 dormer windows, all other buildings were destroyed during World War II. Past the **Alte Waage** (Old Scales) dating from 1555, where goods were once weighed, you reach the **Old Town Hall Ⓒ** on the **Market Square**. It was built in 1556 on the foundations of the previous Gothic Town Hall and the former Wool Weavers' Guild House. The arcades

BELOW: the clock-tower of the Old Town Hall.

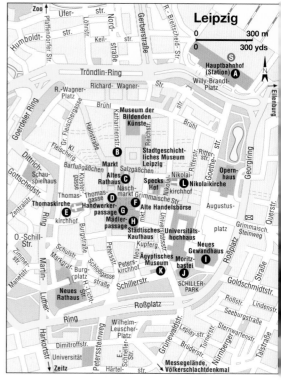

were added in 1907 and today it houses the **Stadtgeschichtliches Museum** (City History Museum; open Tues–Sun 10am–6pm). Directly opposite, the **Hand-werkerpassage**  was reopened in 1989, recreating the lives of medieval crafts-men. At the end of the alley, over the entrance to the "Coffe Baum", the oldest coffee house in the town incorporating a small museum (open daily 11am–7pm), there is a carving showing a Cupid offering a bowl of coffee to a Turk.

The Thomasgasse leads to the **Church of St Thomas** **E**, home of the **Thomaner Choir**. The church was founded in around 1212 by Margrave Dietrich the Distressed as the Augustinian collegiate church, and assumed its current late-Gothic form in the 15th century at the hands of Claus Roder. When the opening of the university was celebrated in 1409, the choir had already been in existence for nearly 200 years. Johann Sebastian Bach (1685–1750), who became choirmaster and organist in 1723, wrote the majority of his motets for this choir. The Thomaner, one of the best choirs in the world, can often be heard in this, their home church. More can be learnt about Bach's life in the **Bach Museum** (open daily 11am–6pm).

Returning to the Town Hall, to the rear can be found the idyllic **Naschmarkt** (food market) and the **Alte Handelsbörse** **F**, the Baroque exchange building con-structed along Italian and Dutch lines. Once a meeting place for merchants during the fairs, it now hosts cultural events. Continue past the statue of the young Goethe that stands in front of this building and you will come to **Auerbachs Keller** in the **Mädlerpassage** **G**. This old student pub was the setting for the famous scene in *Faust*. Pictures from the legend already adorned the walls in Goethe's day.

At the same exit, to the right, is the Zeitgeschichtliche Forum Leipzig (Forum of Contemporary History), which documents the resistance movement in East Germany. To the south is the **Städtisches Kaufhaus** **H**. This store was for-

Johann Sebastian Bach was appointed cantor of Leipzig's Thomas School in 1723.

BELOW: the Mädlerpassage.

Studying hard at the students' club.

merly the site of the old Gewandhaus (Cloth Hall), which accommodated not only the cloth trade but also the city's orchestra. The **Gewandhaus** ❶ is on the Augustusplatz. The orchestra was founded in 1781, and among its most famous conductors were Felix Mendelssohn-Bartholdy, Bruno Walter, Wilhelm Furtwängler and, latterly before his departure for New York, Kurt Masur.

Next to the Gewandhaus, Leipzig's highest building, the former **Universitätshochhaus** (142 metres/473 ft), soars heavenward. The building has the shape of an open book and after its completion locals nicknamed it "Wisdom Tooth". From here it is only a short distance to the remnants of the old town fortifications, the **Moritzbastei** ❷. The former Studentenklub (students'club), is now the most popular cultural centre for young people at Leipzig with jazz clubs, bars and cafés.

The **Ägyptisches Museum** (Egyptian Museum) ❸ is situated to the southwest of Augustusplatz (open Tues–Sat 1–5pm, Sun 10am–1pm). From here it is a short walk west to the **New Town Hall**, built on the foundations of the 13th-century Peissenburg. The **Church of St Nicholas** ❹, to the north of the square was begun in the 12th century in the Romanesque style. The Gothic chancel dates from two centuries earlier and the late Gothic triple nave was consecrated in 1523. Decorative plasterwork on pillars and vaults and the Classical interior are evidence of the city's former wealth. In 1989 the weekly services in this church led to the famous Monday Demonstrations.

South of the city, the **Völkerschlachtdenkmal** commemorates the military victory over Napoleon in 1813. A 91-metre (300-ft) monument erected on a mound was dedicated by Kaiser Wilhelm II to mark the battle's centenary. Visitors can climb 500 steps to the cupola for magnificent views of the city.

BELOW: original Bauhaus in Dessau.

Bauhaus in Dessau

The route from Leipzig to Berlin passes **Dessau** ㉕. In 1919, Walter Gropius founded the Bauhaus school in Weimar which became one of the most important art schools of the 20th century *(see page 81)*. In 1925 it was moved to Dessau. The group of budding artists, architects, designers and photographers lasted until 1933, but the movement was then closed by the Nazis. It was not until 1977 that the town decided to reopen the **Bauhaus Building** as a museum, though since 1996 it also functions as a centre for design (open daily 10am–6pm). Further examples of Bauhaus architecture include the old labour exchange on August-Bebel-Platz designed by Gropius, the Bauhaus housing estate with the Co-operative Building in the Törten district and the Meisterhäuser in Ebert-Allee (open Tues–Sun 10am–6pm, winter until 5pm). A British bombing raid on Dessau on 7 March 1945 destroyed over 80 per cent of the town. All that remained of the Royal Palace (1530) was a ruined wing, which has subsequently been restored. **St Mary's Church** (1712–17) has also been rebuilt. Near the town centre, **Schloss Georgium**, houses an art collection with works from the 16th–20th centuries.

Dessau's heyday was in the time of Prince Leopold Friedrich Franz von Anhalt-Dessau (1740–1817), who surrounded himself with artists, poets and architects. He established the Dessau Wörlitz Garden Realm, one of the finest English-style country parks (1764–1800) in Germany at the **Schloss Wörlitz** (1769–73), an English country house which houses an art collection with works by Averkamp, Rubens and Canaletto. A boat trip through the canals and artificial lakes takes about an hour. Over 800 varieties of trees and innumerable exotic plant species are planted among hills, winding paths and antique sculptures. The grounds are dotted with various buildings, including an Italian farmstead, a Greek temple, a Gothic folly and a palm house.

The world-famous Bauhaus, along with the Masters' Houses, have formed part of the UNESCO world heritage sites since 1996, as does the nearby Dessau Wörlitz Garden Realm. The whole natural area is under UNESCO protection by the Middle Elbe Biosphere Reserve.

BELOW: in the grounds of Schloss Wörlitz.

Wittenberg – Luther's town

Approaching **Lutherstadt Wittenberg** ㉖ (pop. 46,000) from the west the first impression is of the tower of the **Schlosskirche**, whose dome resembles a crown. It was to the door of this church, on 31 October 1517, that Martin Luther posted his 95 Theses against the Catholic practice of indulgences, following peasant uprisings in Hungary, Transylvania, Slovakia, Switzerland and southern Germany. News of this quickly spread throughout Europe and the Reformation began. Three years later, Luther, excommunicated by the Pope, broke away from the church authorities. By the **Luther Oak** to the east of the town he burned the Papal Bull and the Canon, the basis of medieval law. Close to the oak is the Lutherhaus, where the **Luther Hall** is the largest museum in the world dedicated to the Reformation (open Apr–Oct daily 9am–6pm, Nov–Mar Tues–Sun 10am–5pm). Luther and his colleague Melanchthon are buried in the Schlosskirche.

There are many other places of interest in Wittenberg: the Gothic **Parish Church of St Mary** (where Luther preached), the **Melanchthonhaus**, the electoral **Castle** and the **Cranachhöfe** (Markt 4, Schlossstrass 1), where the painter Lucas Cranach the Elder (1472–1553) lived from 1505–50. Exhibitions are held in the old courtyards amid artisans' quarters. ❏

BERLIN TO DRESDEN

Heading south via the fascinating Spreewald, you arrive at the splendid city of Dresden and beyond it the natural beauty of the sandstone mountains straddling the Czech border

Map on pages 120–21

When Berliners take a trip out into the countryside, the **Märkische Schweiz** (Little Switzerland of the Brandenburg Marches), is one of their favourite destinations, with its beeches and oaks, lakes and heaths, villages where time seems to stand still and houses which have more the character of lowly cottages than opulent farmsteads. The little town of **Buckow ㉗** is the quiet capital of the region and is not entirely unjustified in claiming the title "Pearl of Little Switzerland". By the 1920s it had become a resort well known for its healthy air. Bertolt Brecht (1898–1956) and his wife, the actress Helene Weigel, stayed here from 1952 for three summers in the **Eiserne Villa**, where he wrote his poetry cycle *The Elegies of Buckow*. Now the **Brecht-Weigel-Haus** (open Apr–Oct Wed–Fri 1–5pm, Sat–Sun 1–6pm, Nov–Mar Wed–Fri 10am–noon, 1–4pm, Sat–Sun 11am–4pm) is a museum where you can see items of furniture as well as costumes and props used in the première of *Mother Courage*.

Trade on the Oder and Neisse

The Germans and the Poles are endeavouring to foster a close relationship, a fact which is clearly evident in the border town of **Frankfurt Oder ㉘** (pop. 65,000). It was here, in 1991, that the **University of Viadrina** was created in order to establish a spiritual bridge; of the 5,000 students enrolled here, one-third come from Poland. The college is carrying on its tradition as the first university of the state of Brandenburg; it was founded here in 1506 but moved to Breslau in 1811.

In 1430, Frankfurt Oder joined the Hanseatic League and developed into a prosperous trading city. It was during this time that three important buildings were constructed in the North German, red-brick, Gothic style: the **Town Hall**, **St Mary's Church** and the **Franciscan Monastery**. The latter, situated in Lebuser Mauerstrasse in the north part of the city, is now used as a concert hall bearing the name of Carl Philip Emanuel Bach (1714–88), son of Johann Sebastian (also known as the "Berlin" Bach), who worked as the choirmaster from 1734–8. Another of the prominent sons of the city is the dramatist and poet Heinrich von Kleist (1777–1811). A museum devoted to his life and works is situated in Faberstrasse 7 (open Tues–Sun 10am–6pm).

Until reunification, the textile industry and brown coal mining provided **Cottbus ㉙** (pop. 100,000) with an economic basis. Over the years a number of radical changes have taken place. In 1991 the Technical University was inaugurated, leading to financial investment in the surrounding area. The success of the National Garden Exhibition in 1995 enhanced the image of the "little metropolis" and drew parallels

LEFT: Art Nouveau department store in Görlitz.
BELOW: Sorb woman in the Spreewald.

with the city's masterpiece of landscape gardening, **Branitz Park**, designed in 1846–71 by Prince Hermann von Pückler-Muskau. The stables, palace and Smithy park blend harmoniously with the gardens.

In the centre of the town lies the **Old Market**, bordered by fine baroque townhouses and the Lion Pharmacy containing the **Brandenburgische Apothekenmuseum** (Pharmacy Museum; guided tours Tues–Fri 11am and 2pm, Sat–Sun 2pm and 3pm; shop for teas and herbs Tues–Fri 10am–5pm), which includes an old laboratory and collections of herb remedies. By contrast, the **Brandenburgische Kunstsammlung** (art collection; open Tues–Sun 10am–6pm, Thur until 8pm), in an old power station, is devoted to 20th-century collages, photographs, posters and design. The **State Theatre** is a first-class example of Art Nouveau architecture; it was built by Bernhard Sehring in 1908. The **Wendish Museum** (open Tues–Fri 8.30am–6pm, Sat–Sun 2–6pm) describes the history of the Sorbian minority which originated in Niederlausitz.

To the northwest of Cottbus lies the **Spreewald** , a large area of marshy lowlands criss-crossed by a labyrinth of streams, all tributaries of the River Spree. The flora here is unique, hence this nature park being recognised by UNESCO as a biosphere reserve since 1991. One way of enjoying the enchanting waterscape is to join other tourists for a ride on one of the traditional flat punts, but for a more intimate commune with nature you can also hire a rowing boat. The best starting point for a trip around the area is **Lübbenau**. The small town, where tourist trips around the Spreewald were started as early as 1882, is also well worth a visit in itself. Stroll around the old centre or the **Schlosspark**. The neoclassical mansion itself has been turned into a hotel.

Only 47 km (29 miles) southeast of Cottbus towards the Polish border lies **Bad Muskau** ③. Prince Pückler-Muskau was born here in 1785. Here, too, in the aristocratic-rural idyll of the Old Castle (16th-century), he created a 600-hectare (1,480-acre) park which spans the Polish border and is a masterpiece of garden design. In 2004, the garden was awarded UNESCO heritage status.

Görlitz ② (pop. 57,000), the most easterly town in Germany, experienced its economic heyday in the 15th century. Its citizens mainly traded in cloth, especially in woad, a plant used in the production of blue dye. Two major trade routes met here at the most important crossing over the River Neisse: the road from Stettin and Prague via Frankfurt-an-der-Oder and the one linking Leipzig and Breslau.

The most important Renaissance buildings around the **Town Hall** originate from this era. These include the **Schönhof**, which is the oldest Renaissance house in Germany. There are also numerous late-Gothic churches. Visible from afar are the towering spires of the 15th-century parish church of **Saints Peter and Paul**. With its main altar (1695), pulpit (1693) and the late-Gothic St George's Chapel, it is well worth visiting. The double-winged altarpiece in the **Dreifaltigkeitskirche** (Trinity Church) dates back to 1510 and looms over a Gothic pulpit (14th-century). The grave of the mystic philosopher Jakob Böhme (1575–1624) is to be found in the cemetery of the **Church of St Nicholas** (15th-century). The **Kaisertrutz** and the neighbouring tower are

TIP

From Lübbenau you can visit one of the many restaurants and beer gardens in the Spreewald, accessible only by boat. Delicious fish dishes are among the specialities of the region.

BELOW:
the Spreewald has numerous channels to explore.

today home to the town's art collection (open Tues–Sun 10am–5pm; restoration works in progress). An example of the town's later prosperity is the magnificent **Art Nouveau Department Store** (Kaufhaus Hertie/Karstadt) on Demianiplatz.

Map on pages 120–21

Minority interests

To the south of Löbau, between Bautzen and Görlitz, lies **Herrnhut** ❸, the home of the religious community of the Moravians (or Herrnhuter). The brotherhood was founded in 1722 by the pious Count Nikolaus von Zinzendorf and his Bohemian-Moravian fellow-believers. The **Völkerkundemuseum** (Museum of Anthropology; open Tues–Fri 9am–5pm, Sat–Sun 9am–noon, 1.30–5pm) has a display of objects collected from their missionary work.

There are still approximately 100,000 Sorbs living around Bautzen, Cottbus and the Spree Forest. As ancestors of a western Slavic people, who settled the Lausitz even before the first millennium, the Sorbs have maintained their own language and culture. Sorbian is a Slavic language which uses Latin script as well as special letters. Since 1948 the Sorbs have been given autonomy with schools of their own. Their parent organisation, the "Domowina" based in **Bautzen** ❸ (pop. 40,000), was founded in 1912. It is here that the **Sorb Museum** provides an introduction to their culture and history (open Apr–Oct Mon–Fri 10am–5pm, Sat–Sun 10am–6pm, Nov–Mar Mon–Fri 10am–4pm, Sat–Sun 10am–5pm).

Bautzen was also a flourishing trading centre, a fact reflected today in the core of the old town, with the **Town Hall** (1729–32), **St Michael's Church** (1498), the ruins of **St Nicholas Church** and some fine baroque houses. **St Peter's Cathedral** (1293–1303) has been used by both Catholics and Protestants since the Reformation (1524), when it was agreed that the Protestants take the nave

ABOVE: the town hall is one of many fine buildings in Bautzen.
BELOW: stained glass window at the Sorb Museum.

and the Catholics the choir. Standing on a granite outcrop, **Ortenburg Castle** was built as a border outpost during the eastwards expansion of the Germans. It first belonged to Bohemia and after 1635 to Saxony. The most notorious building in Bautzen is the prison (1903), where political prisoners of the GDR served out their sentences.

Florence on the Elbe

It is only another 50 km (30 miles) to the high point of this tour, **Dresden** ㉟ (pop. 480,000). Millions of visitors each year flock to the "Florence on the Elbe", which in 1990 took up its role once again as the capital of Saxony. Apart from the city itself, the surrounding countryside, dotted with old towns and palaces, is well worth exploring.

Dresden will forever be associated with the devastating bombing raid that took place on the night of 14 February 1945, when almost the entire city centre was completely destroyed by a series of firestorms. At least 35,000 people, including many refugees, lost their lives in the inferno. A great deal of restoration was done during the days of the GDR, a process that has continued apace since reunification. The **Frauenkirche** (Church of Our Lady), whose ruins long stood as a reminder of the senselessness of war, has been rebuilt as a precise copy of its former self.

It was on the site of this church that the foundations of Dresden were laid, in the middle of the 11th century, when a Christian missionary centre was established by monks out to convert the heathen Slavic Sorbs. Merchants settled here at a crossing point over the Elbe. In 1485, the Albertine succession, the Saxon line of the ruling Wettin family, elevated Dresden to a royal city.

Dresden's most resplendent era came after the Thirty Years' War with the

Having returned to Dresden after the bombardment, children's writer Erich Kästner noted in his diary that while it was not uncommon to stand in front of your house without a key, it was most unusual to stand there with a key and no house.

BELOW: "Goldener Reiter" – Augustus the Strong on horseback.

arrival of the king of Poland and future elector of Saxony, Augustus the Strong (1670–1733). Most of the the city's baroque masterpieces are due to this one man, a leader with a boyish soul who not only enjoyed life to the full but, as a man of great vision, was responsible for the planning of this, *his* city.

The 100-metre (330-ft) high **Town Hall tower A** is the tallest structure in Dresden, and will remain so by law. The 13th-century **Kreuzkirche B**, meanwhile, is the city's oldest place of worship, said to contain a fragment of the Holy Cross. After it was destroyed in the Seven Years' War, it was rebuilt between 1764 and 1792 and remains a beautiful example of the baroque style. Vespers take place every Saturday in the company of the church's famous choir, the **Kreuzchor**. The historic centre of Dresden is now a UNESCO site, but its status remains endangered while the city council favours the building of a new bridge across the Elbe. The UNESCO committee has suggested a tunnel, which would leave Dresden's characteristic river panorama unaffected.

Around Theaterplatz

No visitor to Dresden should miss the **Zwinger Palace C**, a masterpiece of German baroque. Commissioned by Augustus the Strong and completed between 1710 and 1732 by the court architect Matthäus Daniel Pöppelmann and sculptor Balthasar Permoser, the original design was based on the orangery at Versailles. But with its mighty gateways, its pavilions, galleries and gardens, the complex grew to take up an enormous area. By 1719 enough of the palace had been completed for it to host the marriage of Prince Friedrich August II (1696–1763) to the Archduchess Maria Josepha (1699–1757), a daughter of Austria's Habsburg empress Maria Theresia.

Maps:
Area 120
City 145

The name Dresden is derived from the Sorbian "dreszdany" – place of the swamp forest people. Many towns in eastern Germany have names of Slavonic origin.

BELOW: one of the pavilions of the Zwinger Palace.

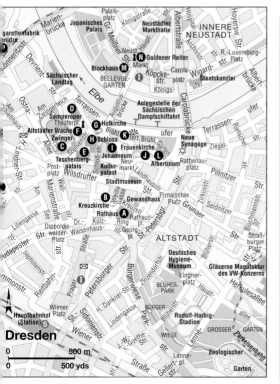

The Zwinger houses a number of galleries and collections (all open Tues–Sun 10am–6pm), of which the **Gemäldegalerie Alte Meister** (Old Masters' Art Gallery) is the most important. It was designed by Gottfried Semper (1803–79) and completed in 1854. There are more than 2,000 works of art to be admired here, including the *Sistine Madonna* by Raphael, Rembrandt's *Self Portrait with Saskia*, and Dürer's *The Seven Pains of Maria,* as well as a temporary exhibition from the **Galerie Neuer Meister**.

The **Rüstkammer**, located in the east wing of the palace, contains a superb weapons collection (15th–18th centuries) and court costumes (16th–18th centuries; due to move to the castle). Scientific instruments (the earliest of which date from the 13th century) are exhibited in the **Salon of Mathematics and Physics** (closed until 2009). Meissen porcelain, in addition to early Chinese ceramics, is displayed in the **Porcelain Collection** in the long gallery, the second-largest such collection in the world after the Serail collection in Istanbul.

Architecturally and musically, the **Semperoper ◗** (1870–8) is of equal prominence. Standing next to the Zwinger in the grandly proportioned Theaterplatz, the opera house was designed and built by Gottfried Semper in the Italian high baroque style on the site of an earlier theatre which, prior to burning down, had staged the premieres of Richard Wagner's operas, *Rienzi* (1842), *The Flying Dutchman* (1845) and *Tannhäuser* (1845). In 1905 and 1908 respectively, the premieres of *Salome* and *Elektra* by Richard Strauss were performed in the new building. In front stand the equestrian statue of King Johann and the memorial to the composer Carl Maria von Weber, who was the musical director in Dresden from 1817 to 1826. The building, which was destroyed by bombs in 1945, re-opened in 1985 with a production of Weber's opera *Der Freischütz*.

One of numerous scientific instruments in the Salon of Mathematics and Physics in the Dresden Zwinger.

BELOW: the baroque Hofkirche.

The restoration of the **Taschenberg Palace** was completed in 1995 and today it serves as a luxury hotel (www.kempinski-dresden.de). Inside, it is possible to view the stairwell, built in 1707–11 according to the design of Pöppelmann. The neoclassical **Altstädter Wache** ❻ (Old Town Guard House) with its temple-like facade, was built between 1830 and 1832 according to the design of Karl Friedrich Schinkel. Theaterplatz is dominated by the baroque **Hofkirche** ❼ (Court Church, 1739–55). The exterior niches contain 78 statues, while highlights of the interior include Permoser's beautifully carved wooden pulpit (1712–22) as well as the Silbermann organ (1753).

The restoration of the **Castle** ❽ (Residenzschloss, 1547), which was totally destroyed during World War II, was begun in the 1960s and scheduled to be completed by 2006 in time for the city's 800th anniversary. The four-winged Renaissance building now acts as the cultural centrepiece of this great Saxon city. First to return to its original home was the Collection of Prints, Drawings and Photography. The spectacular Green Vault, which followed suit, is stacked full of the treasures of the Saxon princes – precious stones, jewellery, ivory, pearls, corals, crystal and more. From here the **Langer Gang** (Long Passage) leads to the **Johanneum** ❾, the erstwhile royal stables on the Neumarkt, which now houses the **Verkehrsmuseum** (Transport Museum; open Tues–Sun 10am–5pm). Along the wall of the passage, 35 Wettin rulers are depicted in a royal parade. In 1876, the mural was rendered in scratchwork, but in 1906 this was overlaid by 24,000 ceramic tiles from Meissen.

Rising from the rubble

The **Frauenkirche** ❿ (1726–43), potent symbol of Dresden's destruction, stands almost in the middle of the square. In front of this church Martin Luther looks sagely at his Bible. The 95-metre (312-ft) high dome of the Frauenkirche caved in after a bombing attack in 1945. An anti-war monument during the GDR period, Germany's most important Protestant church has been rebuilt as a symbol of conciliation, largely with donations from German and international foundations, British ones especially. After the monumental 10-year reconstruction effort, the official consecration took place in October 2005. Its characteristic dome, called the "stone bell" owing to its shape, once more dominates the Dresden skyline. The Neumarkt quarter around the church is to regain its status as the historical heart of the city.

Passing the Dresden Hilton Hotel you come to the **Sekundogenitur** – once the library of every second-born prince and now a café and wine bar – and on to the **Brühlsche Terrace** ⓚ. The latter was originally part of the old city's 16th-century fortifications until Heinrich Graf von Brühl had it converted into a landscape garden in 1738.

Initially built as the Armoury, the **Albertinum** ⓛ behind the Frauenkirche is home to the **Galerie Neuer Meister**, which houses 19th-century masterpieces such as Caspar David Friedrich's *Cross in the Hills* and Paul Gauguin's *Two Women from Tahiti* (closed for renovation until 2010; exhibition in the Hietwinger).

Map on page 145

TIP

Take a trip on the Elbe in one of the excursion boats (Sächsische Dampfschiffahrts-gesellschaft, Hertha-Lindner-Strasse 10, tel: 0351-866090; www.saechsische-dampfschiffahrt.de).

BELOW: risen from the ashes, the Frauenkirche.

From Schlossplatz cross the **Augustusbrücke**, the oldest and most attractive bridge in the city, to reach the **Neustädter Ufer** on the other side of the river. There you pass the **Blockhaus** , a fortification from the middle of the 18th century, and the **Memorial of Joseph Fröhlich**, court jester of Augustus the Strong. An equestrian statue of the famous king himself, the **Goldener Reiter** , stands at the Neustädter Markt, cast out of copper in the 18th century. Sadly, only a few of the baroque houses he constructed in this part of the city have survived the war, but the Hauptstrasse, connecting the centre with Albertplatz, is still one of the city's most beautiful avenues. North of Albertplatz, you will find Dresden's trendy area with lots of fashionable pubs, cafés and galleries.

At the edge of the centre

To the west of the city centre the **World Trade Centre** reflects Dresden's development into a modern commercial metropolis. This ultra-modern trade-and-office complex with its 120-metre (393-ft) long, glass-covered shopping arcade was completed in 1996.

Follow Könneritzstrasse to the north and you'll reach a building resembling a large mosque at the point where Magdeburgerstrasse branches off to the left. But not everything is what it seems. Cigarette manufacturer Hugo Zietz had his new factory, the **Zigarettenfabrik Yenidze** , built in the shape of a mosque between 1909 and 1912. There is a large Oriental dome made of colourful glass with chimneys camouflaged as minarets. The reason behind all this was not only to advertise his Oriental cigarettes, but also to bypass the law that banned factory buildings with high chimneys within the city boundaries. After all, Dresden was supposed to be a centre of the arts and a royal residence. Today the dome soaring high above the

The huge floods of the River Elbe in the summer of 2002 brought immense damage to the infrastructure of many towns and buildings, including the Semper Opera House and the Old Masters' Art Gallery in Dresden. Rebuilding began almost immediately, and most tourist attractions reopened soon after.

BELOW: river traffic.

offices is a fitting setting for romantic literature evenings no less (www.1001 maerchen.de). On a more banal note, visitors may want to stop by at the **Deutsches Hygiene-Museum** near the Grosser Garten Park (open Tues–Sun 10am–5.30pm).

Dresden's environs

The most popular weekend excursion for the people of Dresden, elegant **Loschwitz 36** was once a haven of peace for the nobility and educated élite of the city. You can reach it by crossing the Elbe via the unusual "Blaues Wunder" bridge on the road to Pillnitz and then taking the world's oldest suspension railway that leads directly up to Loschwitz Heights. From here there is an impressive view over the Elbe Valley and the city. There is a good restaurant in the Luisenhof Hotel. Nearby is the wooded area of **Dresdner Heide 37** (Dresden Heath). In devising an organised system of paths through the woods, Heinrich Cotta (1763–1844) was an early pioneer of nature walks.

The museum at **Graupa 38** is dedicated to the life and works of Richard Wagner (open Tues–Sun 10am–4pm), who was director of music in Dresden from 1843–49. The museum displays photographs, posters and letters relating to the composer, as well as a collection of old musical instruments.

A visit to the Carl Maria von Weber Museum in **Klein-Hosterwitz** is best carried out in conjunction with a trip to **Pillnitz Palace 39** (park open May–Oct daily; palaces open end Mar–Oct Tues–Sun 10am–5pm, Nov–Mar Sat–Sun only 11am–2pm), the opulent riverside summer residence of Augustus the Strong, who would come here by Venetian gondola to visit his various mistresses. Conforming to the exotic tastes of the courtly late baroque, this pleasure palace was designed by the architect responsible for the Zwinger, Matthäus

Maps:
City 145
Area 150

TIP

You get the best view of Pillnitz Palace when you approach it from the river, as Augustus the Strong used to do.

BELOW: Pillnitz Palace, summer residence of Augustus the Strong.

The glorious setting of Moritzburg Castle has attracted numerous artists – and photographers.

Daniel Pöppelmann. With its sweeping pagoda-like roofs, it is an important example of the Chinese style fashionable at the time. In the extensive grounds the large camellia imported from Japan in 1770 immediately draws your attention. It is a riot of blossom in the spring.

Downstream on the Elbe

Following the river downstream, **Radebeul** ❹ can be reached by tram. Passing the old wine-growing estates, you arrive at the yellow **Spitzhaus**, built around 1650, and today a popular restaurant where you can enjoy a magnificent view. Beneath the flight of steps (designed by Pöppelmann) leading up to the building stands **Haus Hoflössnitz**, which contains the Weinbaumuseum (Viticulture Museum; open Tues–Fri 10am–1pm, 2–6pm, Sat–Sun 10am–6pm). This was originally Augustus the Strong's "summer-house" and he would come here during the grape harvest to join in the wine festivals and vintner parades. The state vineyard of Saxony, **Schloss Wackerbarth**, offers entertaining guided tours (daily at 2pm and 5pm, Sat–Sun hourly tours starting noon; wine tasting included; tel: 0351-89 550).

With his gripping tales of lands he had never even visited, Karl May (1842–1912) was Germany's answer to Sir Henry Rider Haggard. The **Karl May Museum** (open Tues–Sun 9am–6pm, Nov–Feb 10am–4pm) is located in Villa Shatterhand, where the writer lived out his final years. The museum exhibits material relating to the author as well as to the culture of Native Americans in Villa Bärenfett ("Villa Bear Grease", built in 1926), the wooden house of Patty Frank who donated his large ethnological collection to the Karl May Foundation. Karl May is buried in the Wasastrasse cemetery.

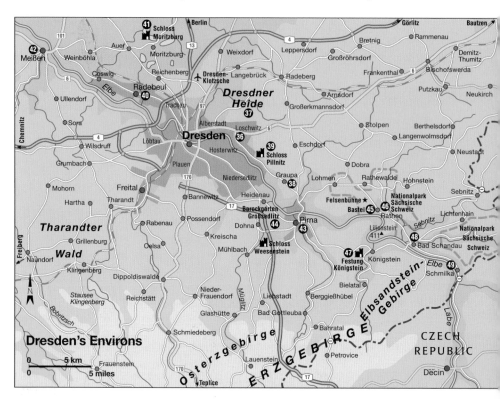

Dresden's Environs

Moritzburg Palace ❹, 15 km (9 miles) from Dresden, is accessible by a narrow-gauge railway that spookily howls its way through the forest. The palace, originally a Renaissance hunting lodge (1542–46), was converted and expanded for Augustus the Strong by Matthäus Daniel Pöppelmann from 1723 to 1736 in baroque style. The landscaping included adding pools around the palace to create a truly magnificent setting. Within the building, the **Baroque Museum** (open summer daily 10am–5pm, winter Tues–Sun 10am–4pm) houses an excellent collection of crafts and other treasures (including porcelain, furniture and portraits). The beautiful countryside around Moritzburg attracted many artists. In 1995, on the 50th anniversary of the death of the artist **Käthe Kollwitz**, a **museum** dedicated to the life and work of this revered Expressionist artist was opened in the house where she died (open Apr–Oct Mon–Fri 11am–5pm, Sat–Sun 10am–5pm, Nov–Mar Tues–Fri noon–4pm, Sat–Sun 11am–4pm).

The wine-producing town of **Meissen** ❷ became a diocesan town back in AD 968 and used to be the hub of Saxony. The **Albrechtsburg**, completed in 1525, was the first of the Wettin family's residential castles. In 1710, Augustus the Strong had moved the production of porcelain here in order to keep the formula a secret. Augustus had apprehended the runaway apprentice chemist Friedrich Böttger, so that he might employ his alchemy skills in the production of gold and thereby rescue the shattered finances of the state. However, Böttger's experiments only resulted in porcelain. Today, the castle houses an art collection with a variety of exhibits including a Saxon sacred statue collection from the 15th and 16th centuries and, of course, a collection of early Meissen porcelain (open daily Mar–Oct 10am–6pm, Nov–Feb 10am–5pm). Porcelain is still produced in Meissen today and a workshop open to the public has been set up

Map
on page
150

TIP

After visiting the Albrechtsburg, treat yourself to a cup of coffee and some homemade *Meissner Fummel*, a local pastry speciality, in the Café Zieger at the bottom of the steps to the hill.

BELOW: a distinctive brand of porcelain.

MEISSEN PORCELAIN

Baron Utz, hero of Bruce Chatwin's novella *Utz*, refused to flee to West Germany with his friend Dr Orlik. He just couldn't bring himself to leave his Meissen porcelain collection behind; nothing – not even the chance to escape the political oppression of the GDR – could ever mean as much to him as the "white gold" of Meissen.

Meissen Porcelain, also called Dresden Porcelain, was the first successfully produced true porcelain in Europe. The secret of true porcelain, similar to that produced in China, was discovered in 1709 by the alchemist Johann Friedrich Böttger and a year later the Meissen Porcelain Factory was opened. The factory's zenith was reached after 1731 in the modelling of the sculptor Johann Joachim Kändler and an underglaze blue decoration called *Zwiebelmuster* (onion pattern) was introduced in about 1740. Marked with crossed blue swords, the porcelain became world-famous. The name Meissen stood for artistic porcelain creations, for wealth and style; enthusiasts all over the world still pay top prices for unique 18th- and 19th-century pieces.

Even today, every item leaving the workshops is handmade. An exhibition hall displays the range of Meissen porcelain (open daily 9am–6pm, Nov–Apr 9am–5pm).

in the **Meissen Porzellan Manufaktur** (Porcelain Factory) in the town (open daily 9am–6pm, Nov–Apr until 5pm).

Meissen Cathedral (which was started around 1260) possesses sacred paintings and a number of important sarcophagi. The **St Afra Church** (13th century), part of the former Augustinian seminary, is also well worth a visit – as is the **Church of St Nicholas**, which preserves large figures of Meissen porcelain. There is a fine view of the town from the tower of the Church of our Lady.

Sächsische Schweiz National Park

The "Little Switzerland" of Saxony encompasses the Saxon part of the Elbsandstein Mountains, the sandstone uplands straddling the Czech border to the southeast of Dresden. The gateway to the region is the beautiful town of **Pirna** ❸, a major trading centre in the Middle Ages. As restoration work progresses, a stroll through the narrow streets provides an insight in to the prosperity of the citizens of the time. The **Town Hall**, which stands alone in the centre, displays architectural influences spanning five centuries, starting with the ground floor, which dates back to 1485. The portals and gables are of Gothic origin and the tower was added in 1718.

The **town houses** surrounding the marketplace are graced with fine arcades and oriel windows. Those particularly worth inspection are **No. 3**, with its five canopied niches (1500) and **No. 7**, the **Canalettohaus** (1520), with its steep and richly decorated gable. Remarkably, it is still possible to appreciate fully the "Canaletto view" that presented itself to the master as he painted scenes of this marketplace. The tower of the **Church of St Mary**, to the east of the town centre, is a good vantage point from which to view the town, the rolling foothills

ABOVE: statuary at Grossedlitz Baroque Gardens.
BELOW: the rugged crags of the Bastei.

of the Erzgebirge (Ore Mountains) and the Sächsische Schweiz. The single-naved church with its ribbed vaulting was built between 1504 and 1546.

Five km (3 miles) outside Pirna are the romantic **Grossedlitz Baroque Gardens** ㊽. Originally designed for Graf Wackerbarth, the property was acquired by Augustus the Strong in 1723. He completely redesigned the place to provide a suitable setting for his extravagant parties, commissioning the addition of statues, flights of steps and an array of fountains from his specialist, Matthäus Daniel Pöppelmann.

The **Sächsische Schweiz** was declared a national park in 1991. A popular area for climbing and hiking, the name was actually coined by two Swiss artists who studied in Leipzig. The paintings of Adrian Zingg (1734–1816) and Anton Graff (1736–1813) can still be seen in the galleries of Dresden. But with the Grosser Winterberg topping out at only 552 metres (1,810 ft), the mountains here are just molehills when compared to the mighty Alps. The biggest lure of the region is the fascinating topography, with cliff faces carved in a multitude of forms, free-standing pillars of rock and deep ravines running between them.

Over the centuries, the region has drawn numerous artists, including the painter Caspar David Friedrich and the composer Richard Wagner, whose *Lohengrin* is supposed to have been inspired here. Before the railway was completed in 1850 and steamships first started sailing in 1875, the wealthy were carried by litter through these rugged hills.

River trip

One of the best ways to appreciate the countryside is by taking the steamer from Dresden to the border town of Schmilka. The first stunning feature is the rugged cliffs of the **Bastei** ㊺, from the top of which there are superb views. At the Rockfall, one of the most popular crags, a 70-metre (250-ft) long stone bridge crosses the impressive **Mardertelle Gorge**.

The ship soon pulls in at the health spa of **Rathen** ㊻, a town closed to vehicles. In summer, the amphitheatre of cliffs provides a natural backdrop for the open-air theatre. **Königstein Fortress** ㊼ (open Apr–Sept daily 9am–7pm, Oct until 5pm, Nov–Mar 9am–4pm) stands sentinel 360 metres (1,180 ft) above the river. You can visit the living quarters and atelier of the inventor of the "white gold", Friedrich Böttger (*see page 151*), who was imprisoned here from 1706–7. The views are stunning from the **Lilienstein** (415 metres/1,360 ft), which is only reachable on foot.

Bad Schandau ㊽ stretches along the river for some distance. Built in 1704, the local parish church is a great attraction. Both the pulpit and the altar are carved from local sandstone and the altar is set with precious stones. Hikers can take the **Karnitztal Railway**, incorporating the very best technology that the 1920s could provide (latterly augmented by solar power), to the Lichtenheimer Waterfalls. This is the starting point for the climb to the **Kuhstall** (Cow Shed), a deep cave in which the local farmers hid their cattle during the Thirty Years' War. Finally, you will arrive at the Czech border near **Schmilka** ㊾; the river itself marks the border for several miles. ❑

Map on page 150

BELOW: Pirna.

DRESDEN TO JENA

This stretch between Saxony and Thuringia examines some interesting facets of German culture, from mining to Trabant motor cars to precision glass. There is a detour to the famous Colditz Castle

Map on pages 120–21

O ne of Saxony's oldest industries is mining – indeed the whole mountain range bordering the Czech Republic to the southwest of Dresden is known as the Erzgebirge (Ore Mountains), where minerals (lead, tin, silver and iron ores) have been extracted since the 12th century.

Until the local mines were closed in 1969, **Freiberg** ⑤⓪ (pop. 50,000) was Saxony's most important mining town. The first silver mine was discovered in 1168, causing a silver rush. Miners poured in from everywhere, hoping to make their fortune. Until the 15th century it remained the richest town in Saxony, even dwarfing Dresden and Leipzig. Some of the town's buildings still display this former wealth. There is the early 15th-century **Town Hall**, the early Renaissance **Haus Obermarkt** and the **Dom Unser Lieben Frauen** (Cathedral of Our Lady, 1484–1512), with its magnificent interior. During the summer months the cathedral is the venue for concerts: the organ is a masterpiece built in 1711 by the famous organ builder Silbermann. There is also a **Stadt- und Bergbaumuseum** (Mining Museum; open Tues–Sun 10am–5pm), as well as an empty shaft of the "Reiche Zeche" (where silver was mined), now open to visitors during a daily guided tour. Visitors to Freiberg in June should look out for the Bergparade, a colourful procession of members of the local miners' associations, following an old tradition common to all Saxony's old mining towns.

Chemnitz ⑤① (pop. 240,000) was once the region's most important industrial centre, thanks mainly to its heavy engineering, locomotive factories and textile industry. One of the city's main attractions is the huge statue of Karl Marx's head, known as the **Marxkopf** (Lew Kerbel, 1971), which has since become an accepted symbol for Chemnitz. From 1953, until it was renamed in 1990, the city was known as Karl-Marx-Stadt.

Almost the whole of the inner city was destroyed during World War II. The **Rote Turm** or Red Tower, dating from the 12th century, is the last remaining section of the city's fortifications and now houses an exhibition documenting the city's growth. Over the centuries, this tower has served as the law courts, as a prison and as a residence for the local governor. The complex of buildings in the **Theaterplatz** consisting of the **Opera House** (1906–9), a neo-Romanesque church and the **König Albert Museum** (open Tues–Sun noon–7pm) have also survived. The museum is perhaps the most interesting of the three, not least for its Jugendstil (Art Nouveau) interior. It houses the **Kunstsammlungen Chemnitz** which, *inter alia*, displays important examples of Impressionist and Expressionist paintings. In Moritzstrasse 20 the former shopping centre DAStietz, built in 1912, now houses the **Museum für Naturkunde** (open Mon, Tues, Thur, Fri 10am–8pm, Sat–Sun 10am–6pm) and is worth

LEFT: the university tower in Jena.
BELOW: inside Freiberg's cathedral.

seeking out as it is one of the few places in the world where it is possible to see a petrified forest. The **Schlossbergmuseum**, originally a Benedictine monastery (1136) and later the Elector's Palace, is now used for exhibitions on local history (open Tues–Fri 1–7pm, Sat noon–9pm, Sun 10am–6pm). Concerts are often held in the delightful Renaissance Hall and Kreuzhof. Some areas of the city, such as Kassberg, with its Art Nouveau houses, Sonnenberg and the area around the castle, illustrate the city's architectural developments. The **Sächsische Industriemuseum**, in the huge hall of a former foundry, is dedicated to the industrial heritage of the region.

Augustusburg 🏵, Saxony's largest castle, is situated about 10 km (6 miles) to the east of Chemnitz. Elector August I had it built in 1725 on the site of a medieval castle, and it is listed by UNESCO as the earliest example of rococo architecture in 18th-century Germany. Linked to the castle are the **Museum für Jagdtiere und Vogelkunde** (Hunting and Ornithology Museum), as well as the **Motorradmuseum** (motorcycle museum) with its enormous collection of vintage motorbikes and a carriage exhibition (open daily Apr–Oct 9.30am–5.30pm, Nov–Mar 10am–4.30pm). In the castle chapel is an altarpiece by Lucas Cranach the Younger (only on view as part of a guided tour).

Thirty km (18 miles) north of Chemnitz is Colditz 🏵, a small town located in the valley of the Mulde dominated by its famous castle *(see below)*.

ABOVE: motorcycle history at the Augustusburg.
BELOW: these days visitors to Colditz come voluntarily.

Home of the Trabi

It seems almost as if the citizens of **Zwickau** 🏵 (pop. 100,000) had wanted to ensure that their town would always be the last entry in a gazetteer. In the first document relating to the town (1118), the place was recorded as "ZZwickaw".

COLDITZ

It has housed princes and paupers, served as a lunatic asylum, a hospital and an old people's home. Fascists tortured their political foes and German Communists imprisoned their enemies here. But above all it is prisoners of war who made sinister Colditz Castle world famous. Between 1940 and 1945, 1,500 Allied officers were held captive here and their daring attempts to escape have been immortalised in films, books, television series and documentaries. Very few of the attempts succeeded, but the prisoners carried on plotting their escapes, trying the impossible. There were the British officers who constructed a glider from bed timber and linen, hoping to launch it from the castle's attic (the war ended before they got a chance to put their contraption to the test). Or those who dug a 50-metre (164-ft) long tunnel, only to be discovered days before its completion.

Colditz was built on the remains of a 12th-century castle that had been destroyed by fire. Restoration work has brought the Renaissance castle back to its former glory. Part of the castle is used for events, while a historic museum is open to the public (open daily Apr–Oct 10am–5pm, Nov–Mar 10am–4pm; guided tours at 10.30am, 1pm and 3pm).

It initially grew up around a tollbooth on the Prague to Halle trading route, but the town flourished in the 15th and 16th centuries thanks to its cloth-making industry and silver mining in the surrounding hills. Zwickau was the GDR's centre for bituminous coal mining until 1977. The Trabant car was manufactured at the old-fashioned Sachsenring works. The first cars to be produced in the area – at Mosel near Zwickau – rolled off the production line in 1904. After German unification, Volkswagen agreed to invest in the plant. The history of the Trabant is displayed in the **August Horch Museum** (open Tues–Sun 9.30am–4.30pm) and a rally is held here in June.

All the most interesting sights are grouped around the **Hauptmarkt**, the main marketplace. These include the recently renovated neo-Gothic **Town Hall**; the **Gewandhaus** or Cloth Market (1525), converted into a theatre in 1823; as well as a number of grand patrician houses, one of which was the birthplace of the composer **Robert Schumann** (1810–56). The **museum** is dedicated to his life and work (open Tues–Fri 10am–5pm, Sat–Sun 1–5pm).

The late-Gothic parish **Church of St Mary** (1206) has undergone numerous alterations and extensions – mostly during the 15th and 16th centuries – as a result of fires. Among its treasures are an early Renaissance pulpit, a late-Gothic altar cross, many tombs and a mobile Sacred Tomb, which reaches a height of at least 5 metres (16 ft). Also of particular interest is the late-Gothic high altar made by the Nuremberg Wohlgemut workshop.

Altenburg ⑤ is the first Thuringian town along this route. The town is associated with skat, one of the most popular card games in the German-speaking world. The three-handed game using 32 cards was developed in the early 19th century from older games and it is here in Altenburg that the "Skat Board of

Map on pages 120–21

Between 1953 and 1991, when production was discontinued, more than three million Trabis were produced in Zwickau. It is quite a sight every June when Trabant owners from all over the country gather here and vote for the "Trabi of the Year".

BELOW: the chapel at Altenburg Palace.

Control" is based. Surrounding the marketplace or the **Brühl** are the **Seckendorfsche Palais** (1725), former government buildings, a number of impressive townhouses – and the **Skatbrunnen**, the only memorial dedicated to a card game. The **Schloss**, dating originally from the 10th century, but rebuilt in the 18th, is the home of the **Spielkartenmuseum** (Playing Cards Museum; open Tues–Sun 10am–5pm), which confirms Altenburg's claim as the home of skat and which boasts a large collection of playing cards and a playing card manufacturing studio dating from 1600. The **Lindenau-Museum**, built in the Italian Renaissance style between 1873 and 1875, houses several valuable art collections. On display here are Italian paintings from the pre- and early Renaissance periods as well as sculptures and paintings from the 19th and 20th centuries (open Tues–Fri noon–6pm, Sat–Sun 10am–6pm).

Gera ⑤⑥, first mentioned in official records in 1237, lies picturesquely on the middle reaches of the Elster. Its population of about 125,000 makes it the second-largest town in Thuringia. Gera's history stretches back over more than 750 years and traces its growth via its heyday as the principal city and residence of the princes of Reuss to its revival as an important industrial centre. Since reunification, it has become the focal point of East Thuringia.

The market square is very pretty. It is dominated by the Renaissance **Town Hall** (1573–5), noted for its richly decorated six-storey staircase and tower (57 metres/187 ft). It is surrounded by a number of beautifully restored buildings, most notably the Renaissance **Stadtapotheke** (chemist), with an elaborately carved oriel window, and a three-storey baroque **Government Building** (1722).

Of particular interest are the Gera Vaults, constructed at the beginning of the 18th century as underground cellars for the brewery. In Vault No. 188 there is

TIP

Worth a short detour from Gera or Jena is the site, near Nebra, where the Nebra Sky Disc – a bronze disc bearing the oldest extant depiction of the heavens – was discovered in 1999 *(see page 134)*. Stop by Naumburg on the way.

BELOW: inside Otto Dix's house in Gera.

an exhibition illustrating "Minerals and Mining in East Thuringia". The largest private housing complex in Gera is in the Ferbersches House, which contains the **Museum für Angewandte Kunst** (Museum of Applied Arts). The baroque Orangery is home to the city **Kunstsammlung** with paintings by Lucas Cranach the Elder, Rembrandt and Liebermann, among others. The great realist painter **Otto Dix**, best known for his etchings and paintings of World War I casualties, was born in Gera in 1891 and his birthplace is now a **Museum** (all museums open Tues 1–8pm, Wed–Fri 10am–5pm, Sat–Sun 10am–6pm).

Three churches in the town are worth a visit: the **Church of St Mary**, a late-Gothic, single-nave church (15th century); the triple-nave, baroque **St Salvatorkirche** (St Saviour's, 1720) with early 20th-century Jugendstil paintings; and the **Dreifaltigkeitskirche** (Trinity Church, 14th century).

Carl Zeiss (1816–88) was one of Jena's philanthropists, organising his business so that the workers had a share in the profits.

Jena

Jena ❺⑦ (pop. 103,000) is the last stop before Weimar. But unlike its more illustrious neighbour, Jena is known mainly for its technical prowess. Carl Zeiss (1816–88) recognised early on that industrial progress depended on co-operation between the world of science and business. He opened his first optics workshop in 1846. When he was joined by the physicist Ernst Abbe in 1866, he achieved commercial success. Abbe built the first microscope, while the precision optical lenses needed were developed by the chemist Otto Schott. Schott was responsible for the invention of heatproof Jena glass. The **Optical Museum** (open Tues–Fri 10am–4.30pm, Sat 11am–5pm) in Carl-Zeiss-Platz documents the achievements of the two main glass producers and has a display of 13,000 instruments. The **Zeiss Planetarium** (1926) in the **Botanical Gardens** offers presentations and laser shows.

BELOW: the Optical Museum in Jena.

Other famous names have also been associated with Jena. In 1789 Friedrich Schiller presented his inaugural lecture on the ideals of the French Revolution at the university (founded in 1558). A **Memorial** to the dramatist is in the summer house where he wrote *The Maid of Orleans* between 1797 and 1802 (open Apr–Oct Tues–Sun 11am–5pm, Nov–Mar Tues–Sat). Philosopher Johann Gottlieb Fichte encountered problems with the university authorities in 1799, when he was accused of being an atheist. He responded with a letter asking that "it be read before it is confiscated". The irony was lost on his superiors and Fichte was suspended. Two other famous philosophers, Schelling (from 1798) and Hegel (from 1805) also studied here.

Collegium Jenense, originally a 13th-century Dominican monastery and the oldest university building, stands on the marketplace, where its founder, Prince Johann Friedrich, is remembered by a memorial. Stop at the Gothic **Town Hall** (1377) with its "Schnapphans". On the hour, a figure in a jester's cap opens his toothless mouth and snaps after a ball held out to him by a pilgrim, whereupon an agonising scream rings out. The **Romantikerhaus** nearby is dedicated to Tieck, Novalis, Brentano and the Schlegel brothers, heroes of German Romantic literature (open Tues–Sun 10am–5pm). ❑

WEIMAR AND THE THURINGIAN FOREST

Map on pages 120–21

After a tour of Weimar, visitors can follow in the footsteps of Goethe through the beautiful Thuringian Forest, where legends surrounding the Wartburg open a window onto another world

The natural starting point for any journey across the Thuringian forest is the city of **Weimar** ⑤ (pop. 65,000). From the mid-18th century Weimar was the hub of German cultural life and when the city was nominated as one of the European Cities of Culture in 1999 to coincide with the 250th anniversary of the birth of Goethe, it strongly asserted its traditional role as a crucible for the arts.

It is above all Goethe and Schiller who are associated with Weimar and the great literary epoque known as Weimar Classicism *(see page 31)*. But nothing here would have got off the ground had it not been for the influence of one lady, the cultured Duchess Anna Amalia, daughter of Duke Karl I and niece of Frederick the Great. The government of the duchy of Saxony-Weimar-Eisenach was left in her hands after her husband died in 1758. She made sure her sons, Karl August and Konstantin, had the best education and to this end summoned as tutors the poet and professor of philosophy, Christoph Martin Wieland and the Prussian officer Karl Ludwig von Knebel. The latter soon introduced Karl August to Goethe, who had already become famous through his work *The Sorrows of Young Werther*.

Karl August took over the affairs of state from his mother in 1775 and it was not long before he summoned Goethe to an elevated office in the duchy. Goethe's position as privy councillor enabled him to initiate a series of reforms. In 1786, after around 10 years of state affairs, Goethe left for his sojourn in Italy. On his return to Weimar in 1788, he assumed new responsibility as education minister and director of the Weimar theatre. This period saw the growth of a special relationship, founded on their mutual passion for the theatre, between Goethe and Schiller, who had come to live in Weimar from 1799. For example, Goethe was actively involved in the preparation and rehearsals for the first performance in 1799 of Schiller's drama *Wallenstein's Camp*.

The early years of the 19th century saw the death of several leading literary figures. The theologian and philosopher Johann Gottfried Herder, who came to Weimar in 1776, died in 1803, Schiller in 1805, Anna Amalia in 1807 and Wieland in 1813. Goethe outlived them all, dying on 22 March 1832.

The **Schlossmuseum** (castle) houses the **Kunstsammlungen zu Weimar** (Weimar Art Collections; open Tues–Sun summer 10am–6pm, winter 10am–4pm), including masterpieces by Lucas Cranach the Elder, Tintoretto, Rubens and Caspar David Friedrich. Nearby, the Grünes Schloss (Green Castle) is the repository of the **Herzogin-Anna-Amalia-Bibliothek**

LEFT: Goethe and Schiller.
BELOW: the Kavalierhaus of Belvedere Castle, Weimar.

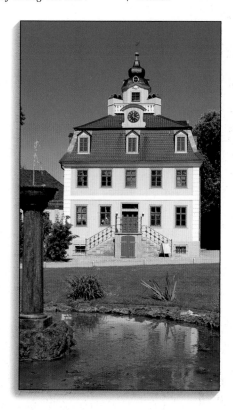

Welcome to Weimar.

(Library). A fire in 2004 destroyed the extraordinarily beautiful rococo hall, and an estimated 30,000 books (of the 120,000-volume collection) were lost to the flames, but in October 2007 the hall was reopened. A further 600,000 volumes are to be found in the "Goethe and Schiller Archives" (1896) on the opposite bank of the River Ilm. **Goethe's Gartenhaus** (Summer House; open daily summer 10am–6pm, winter 10am–4pm) is also located on the eastern side of the river. It still looks as if the great poet has just popped out and will be back any minute. It was here that he and his future wife Christiane Vulpius spent some of their happiest days.

Goethe's House (open Tues–Sun summer 9am–6pm, Sat until 7pm, winter 9am–4pm) is on the Frauenplan, not far from the market. Here, too, everything is just as he left it. Only his living and working quarters at the back of the house are preserved from close public scrutiny. The library is protected by a screen, and the 6,500 volumes contained within are still arranged according to Goethe's system. The permanent exhibition in the building next door is dedicated to the principal personalities of the "Weimarer Klassik" – Goethe, Schiller, Wieland and Herder. The **Schillerhaus** (open Wed–Mon summer 9am–6pm, winter 9am–4pm) is also not far away. Schiller lived here until his death, and the rooms have been recreated with historical accuracy.

Anna Amalia spent a good 30 years of her life in the baroque **Wittumspalais** (1767), at that time Weimar's intellectual and cultural centre. Today it is used to display furnishings from Goethe's era, together with the **Wieland Museum** (open Tues–Sun summer 10am–6pm, winter 10am–4pm). The **Goethe and Schiller Memorial** stands in front of the **Deutsches Nationaltheater**, where the Weimar Constitution was passed in 1919. The baroque **Kirms-Kraokow-Haus** (open

BELOW: the Rococosaal in the Anna Amalia Library.

Apr–Oct Tues–Sun 10am–6pm) provides an example of the wealthy lifestyles of the Classic epoch. The church of **St Peter and St Paul**, diagonally opposite, is well worth a visit, both for its architecture, originally late-Gothic and rebuilt in the baroque style, and for its winged altarpiece by Lucas Cranach the Younger.

Another of the many famous inhabitants of Weimar was Johann Sebastian Bach, who was court organist here from 1708 to 1717. Franz Liszt, Richard Strauss and Friedrich Nietzsche also lived here. Having spent most of his life in Wittenberg, Lucas Cranach the Elder came here in 1552 as court painter and established his studio in the **Cranachhaus** on the marketplace, the oldest surviving house in the city. He died in Weimar a year later, at the age of 80. It was in Weimar, too, that Walter Gropius founded the Bauhaus School, which later moved to Dessau. The **Bauhaus Museum** chronicles the founding of this school (open daily 10am–6pm). Also worth visiting is the Neues Museum with an annex in a former power station and a spectacular collection of contemporary art.

Apart from the historical sites, the traditional culinary venues of the city have also been preserved. These include the "White Swan", the "Black Bear", the "Elephant Hotel" that served as the location for Thomas Mann's novel *Lotte in Weimar*, and "Goethe's Café".

However glorious a past Weimar might have had, the image of the city remains tarnished by the fact that it was the site of the **Buchenwald** concentration camp, established in 1937. More than 60,000 people from some 35 countries were murdered in the camp, which was especially notorious for medical experiments on living human beings. The camp was liberated by the Americans on 11 April 1945. The memorial, whose 50-metre (164-ft) high clock tower is visible for miles around, is situated on the **Grosser Ettersberg**, about 1 km (½ mile) from the camp. A museum depicts the camp's history (open Tues–Sun Apr–Oct 10am–5.30pm, Nov–Mar 10am–3.30pm).

BELOW: the Statue of Roland in Erfurt's market square.

The capital of Thuringia

Following the political changes of the early 1990s, **Erfurt ⑨**, with a population of 200,000, has become the largest town in Thuringia and also its state capital. Once restoration work has been completed, Erfurt will be a truly splendid city, including such historic buildings as **Das goldene Rad**, the **Krone**, the **Fruchtbasar** and the **Andreasviertel**.

It was from Erfurt that the Anglo-Saxon missionary St Boniface set out to convert the heathen Germans to Christianity. In the Middle Ages Erfurt derived a great deal of wealth from the export of woad, the raw material for rich blue dyes. Market gardening developed into an important source of revenue from the 17th century onwards, giving rise to the permanent garden exhibition at the EGA park, where there is also a museum set in a former castle (open daily Mar–Oct 9am–6pm, May–Sept until 8pm, Nov–Feb 10am–4pm).

In 1891, Erfurt saw the Party Conference of the SPD (Social Democratic Party), whose resolutions (the Erfurt Programme) replaced the Gotha Programme. A meeting between Willy Brandt and Willi Stoph in 1970 heralded the new *Ostpolitik* of the Federal Republic, relieving the tension between the Eastern bloc and the West.

Of particular interest in the **Cathedral**, founded in 742, are the Gloriosa, one of the largest church bells in the world, and the Wolfram, a candelabra dating from the 12th century. Other treasures include stained-glass windows some 15 metres (50 ft) high, the choir stalls and the baroque altar. The **Church of St Severin** (12th-century) houses the tomb of St Severin who died around 1365.

The city's skyline is punctuated by the towers of around 20 further churches and monasteries of the various holy orders who settled here, including Dominicans, Augustinians, Benedictines and many others. The visitor can get an idea of the former wealth of the city by taking a stroll through the **Fish Market**, fronted by the neo-Gothic **Town Hall** (1869–71) that stands near the **Statue of Roland** (1591) and two fine Renaissance houses – one of which, the "Zum Roten Ochsen", is home to the Kunsthalle Erfurt (art gallery).

The medieval **Krämerbrücke** is the only covered bridge to be found north of the Alps. This once formed part of the old east-west trade route and today houses artists' studios and antique shops. Visitors can find out more about the history of the bridge in the **Brückenhaus** (open daily 10am–6pm, winter Tues–Sun).

Former royal seat

The town of **Gotha** ⑥ (pop. 47,000) can be recognised from afar by the distinctive Schloss Friedenstein standing out above the town's skyline. The town is one of the oldest in Thuringia and was once a royal seat. In the Middle Ages its economic prosperity reached its peak through trade in cereals, timber products and woad for blue dyes. **Friedenstein Castle** was built after the Thirty Years' War, between 1643 and 1657. The earliest example of a baroque castle in Germany, its rooms are magnificently furnished. The **Schlossmuseum** with its precious Kunstsammlung

Erfurt was known as the German Rome or "the town abundant in towers" (die Turmreiche) because it once had 43 churches and 36 monasteries.

BELOW: St Severin's Church in Erfurt.

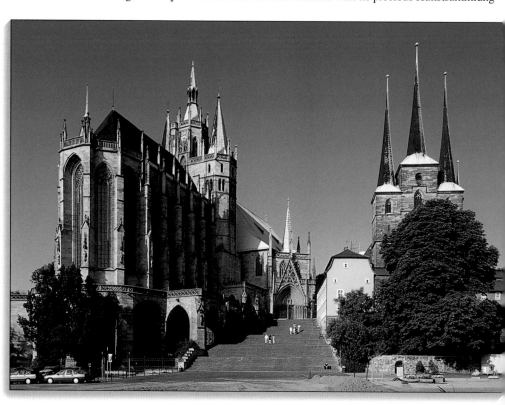

(Painting Collection) includes works by Lucas Cranach the Elder, Rubens and Frans Hals. Additional attractions include a small **Copperplate Exhibition** and an **Art Room**. In 1774, the **Ekhof Theatre** housed in the castle was the first in Germany to offer its actors fixed engagements. The stage accoutrements are preserved in their original condition. All eyes are once more turned to the stage for the annual Ekhof Theatre Festival (July), while the costumed Baroque Festival (end August) breathes life into the castle and park. The **Regionalmuseum** presents a lovingly arranged collection of historic artefacts as well as rural domestic items.

If all this has still not satisfied your thirst for knowledge, you can visit the **Museum der Natur** (Natural History Museum), if only to see a rare example of very early baroque museum architecture. This can be followed by a relaxing stroll in the castle grounds or a refreshing drink in the Pagenhaus-Restaurant (all museums open Tues–Sun summer 10am–5pm, winter 10am–4pm).

All the medieval buildings are clustered together around the delightful **Marketplace**, with the red **Renaissance Town Hall** (1567–77) forming the centrepiece. A little further on is the **Augustinian Monastery**, with its beautiful cloister and Gothic church (of particular note are the chancel, royal box and the 16th- and 17th-century graves and memorial stones).

Gotha also supplies an important date in the struggle for workers' rights. In May 1875, the German Social Democratic Workers' Party united with the General German Workers' Union to become the forerunner of today's SPD.

Towns of the Thuringian Forest

To the south of Weimar, Erfurt and Gotha lie the undulating hills of the Thuringian Forest. A deceptive amount of history and culture is hidden in these

Map on pages 120–21

TIP

In Gotha, look out for the Cranachhaus at the corner of the market square. You will recognise it by the family's emblem – a winged snake.

BELOW: the Town Hall in Gotha, city of cartography.

beautiful surroundings. From 1620, the Bach family made their contribution to the musical world in the attractive town of **Arnstadt** ⑥. Johann Sebastian was the organist in the church which today bears his name from 1703–7. A memorial museum is to be found in the **Haus zum Palmbaum** (open Tues–Sun 9.30am–4.30pm).

With its beautifully preserved Old Town, Arnstadt is one of the most ancient towns in Germany (first cited in 704). In the baroque **Castle** of 1728 (open Tues–Sun 9.30am–4pm), the unique **Mon Plaisir Puppenstadt** (Dolls' Town), containing over 400 dolls from the period 1690 to 1750, collected by Princess Auguste Dorothea, is on display – it is the largest historical doll collection in the world. There are further collections of valuable exhibits including 16th-century Brussels tapestries, a display of porcelain, *Dorotheenthaler* faïence pottery, paintings from the 16th to 20th centuries and rococo carvings. There is an interesting steam locomotive collection at the **Museum im Lokschuppen** (Engine Shed; open Fri–Sun 10am–5pm).

Goethe often spent time in **Ilmenau** ⑥, simply relaxing or else on official business, as he was inspector of the silver and copper mines here. The poet's apartment on the Marketplace has been opened as a **Goethe Memorial Museum** (open daily 9am–noon, 1–4pm). Ilmenau marks the beginning of the **Goethe Way**, which ends in Stützerbach (waymarked G, 18 km/11 miles). From Ilmenau a winding road leads to **Oberhof** ⑥ at 830 metres (2,720 ft). Most of its 100,000 annual visitors come for the winter sports, attracted by the ski-jump complex, the biathlon stadium and the speed-skating rink.

The small town of **Schmalkalden** ⑥ made history with the *Schmalkaldischen Bund* (League of Schmalkalden), formed in 1531: the Protestant clergy united to confront the power of the central Catholic Imperial regime. In the 1546–47 War of Schmalkalden, Charles V finally overpowered the League's army, but the Imperial force was waning. The first historical mention of the town came about 700 years earlier, in 874. At that time Schmalkalden was in the hands of the House of Thuringia. It was later controlled by the counts of Henneberg, and finally the counts of Hessen (Kassel). Wilhelm IV von Hessen had **Schloss Wilhelmsburg** (1585–90) built as his hunting lodge and summer retreat. The ornamental walls of the rooms display fine examples of plaster work and frescoes. The castle's **museum** houses an interesting display on the development of the iron and steel industries from the 15th century onwards (open Tues–Sun, summer 9am–5pm, winter 10am–4pm).

The **Neue Hütte Monument to Technology** commemorates the iron smelting industry of the 19th century. From 1745, Schmalkalden was a centre for gun-making and in World War II hand grenades and anti-tank guns were manufactured here. Two bombing raids destroyed houses and factories, but a small part of the medieval town was left undamaged, including a section of fine, half-timbered houses, churches and the Town Hall.

The narrow winding road now leads across the narrow **Trusetal** with its waterfall to **Bad Liebenstein** ⑥ where cottage industry goes hand in hand with the

BELOW: memorial to a young Bach at Arnstadt.

area's natural resource of healing waters. Since 1610, this spa town has prided itself on cures for heart disease. The landscape garden of Schloss Altenberg, 2 km (1 mile) to the north, is well worth a visit.

Map on pages 120–21

Nature in the Thuringian Forest

Undulating, thickly forested hills, narrow river valleys and rounded mountain tops all combine to form the unique quality of the Thuringian Forest. Goethe himself enjoyed the natural surroundings of this region and today's hiker will be in good company if he follows the **Rennsteig** – the famous, 168-km (105-mile) long-distance ridge path that crosses the whole area, from Höschel, past Eisenach, to Blankenstein (five days). The route also passes by the **Grosser Inselsberg** (916 metres/3,000 ft) ⑥⑥. Although this is only the fourth-highest mountain in the region, its summit offers the best views.

The Rennsteig has been used since prehistoric times. During the Middle Ages it became a popular trade and messenger route. The word "rennen" means to run.

Not far from Eisenach is the impressive **Drachenschlucht** (Dragon's Gorge), with 10-metre (33-ft) high sheer cliff walls which lean towards each other leaving only a 73-cm (30-inch) gap. A 3-km (2-mile) path leads from Sophienaue through the mossy gorge.

A visit to the glittering **Marienglashöhle** ⑥⑦ near Friedrichroda, one of the largest crystal caves in Europe, is a very popular excursion. Its walls are covered in patterns formed by gypsum crystals up to 60 cm (24 inches) long. A natural geological window reveals the rock strata (open daily Apr–Oct 9am–5pm, Nov–Mar 9am–4pm).

On the northern edge of the forest, near Sattelstadt (on the B7 in the direction of Gotha), lie the **Hörselberge** ⑥⑧, a 7-km (4-mile) long limestone feature steeped in legend. This is supposedly the home of Frau Holle, who is reputed to

BELOW: Thuringian sausages are sold at stalls such as this one all over the region.

Lutherhaus detail in Eisenach.

keep a stern watch over both the hard-working and the lazy. Here also is the cave of Venus, who is said to have ensnared the knight Tannhäuser for seven long years. Wagner used this story in the plot of his opera of the same name.

At the northern tip of the forest is **Eisenach** ⑥, whose biggest attraction is the mighty Wartburg. Before embarking on an ascent to the castle, however, it is well worth taking time out for a stroll around Eisenach's idyllic streets. On the market square you will find the **Town Hall**, which dates back to the late Middle Ages. Next to it stands the **Stadtschloss** (castle), created in the 18th century for Duke Ernst August von Sachsen-Weimar, and opposite the castle the church of **St George**. The oldest parts of this church were built in Romanesque style in 1180. In 1515 it was enlarged in late-Gothic style, only to be badly damaged a few years later during the Peasants' Revolt. In the churchyard is the gravestone of Ludwig der Springer, the legendary founder of the Wartburg.

One of the oldest townhouses in Eisenach was the home of Martin Luther, who lived here between 1498 and 1501. The **Lutherhaus** is mainly dedicated to Luther himself, and his translation of the Bible, but it also contains an interesting collection of religious publications from the 16th century (open daily 10am–5pm).

Johann Sebastian Bach is another famous name associated with the town. The **Bachhaus**, which also houses a display of ancient musical instruments, was set up at Am Frauenplan 21, believed to be where the great composer and musician was born in 1685 (open daily 10am–6pm).

BELOW: exhibits from a more glorious age at the Thuringia Toy Museum in Sonneberg.

As in Erfurt and Gotha, the fight for workers' rights is also represented here. The Eisenach party conference in 1869 led to the foundation of the Social Democratic Workers' Party. Since 1896, the town has developed as an important

THURINGIAN TOYS

Rocking horses, animals, carts, spinning tops, pull-along toys, swords, but above all dolls – that's what made the southern Thuringian town of Sonneberg world famous.

Ever since the Middle Ages, people from this region had traded in carved and painted wooden toys and dolls. However, toy-making on a larger scale only began to flourish around 1700, possibly inspired by emigrants from Berchtesgaden. By 1729, there were 30 companies in Sonneberg exporting huge quantities of wooden toys and by 1913 a fifth of the world's toy production originated from this town and its environs. Production declined after World War I, and today only a few companies still produce toy trains, dolls and cuddly toys.

During the 18th century, much of the wood used for dolls and other toys was replaced by a mixture of flour and gum. Then in 1806 came papier mâché, which until the introduction of plastic dolls, remained the predominant material of Sonneberg's dolls, produced mainly in little cottage industries. For the wealthier children there were also dolls with exquisite china heads. Sonneberg's toys were popular among children all over the world. However, not all the children were allowed to play: child labour used to be very common in Thuringia.

centre of the motor industry, and under the GDR, the Wartburg was manufac-tured here. In 1989, Opel took over and invested a billion marks in the factory.

Map on pages 120–21

The mists of time

On a rocky plateau 400 metres (1,300 ft) above the town is the historic **Wartburg Castle ❼⓿** (open daily Mar–Oct 8.30am–8pm, Nov–Feb 9am–5pm). It is so well protected that in all its 900 years it has been besieged just once, and never captured. Legend has it that it was founded in 1067 by Ludwig der Spring-er. By the 19th century the castle had fallen into decay, and a restoration pro-gramme, for which Goethe had long campaigned, was carried out under the sponsorship of Karl Alexander of the house of Saxe-Weimar-Eisenach.

The Wartburg's reputation as the most quintessentially German of all German castles and all the legends that surround it are due in no small degree to the special interest devoted to it by the Romantic artists of the early 19th century. Their search for the origins of German culture led to a reverence for all things medieval. Thus the theme of the legendary *Sängerkrieg* (War of the Trouba-dours) which took place at the Wartburg reappears in several works of the Romantic era: in E.T.A. Hoffman's *Die Serapionsbrüder* (1812), Ludwig Tieck's *Phantasus* (1816) and Richard Wagner's opera *Tannhäuser* (1845). The *Sängerkrieg*, a Middle High German literary piece, describes a meeting between the most famous *Minnesänger* (troubadours) – Walther von der Vogelweide, Wolfram von Eschenbach and Heinrich von Ofterdingen – at the Wartburg dur-ing the time of Prince Hermann I (1190–1217).

Another story connected with the Wartburg tells of the life of the pious Elisabeth (1207–31), canonised in 1235. At the age of 14 the Hungarian king's daughter married the Earl of Thuringia, Ludwig IV. Deeply influenced by the conviction of the Franciscan friars that poverty saves the eternal soul, Elisabeth founded churches and several hospitals. The legend of the Miracle of the Roses tells of how she hid bread and meat under her coat to take to the poor. When she was stopped and searched by her husband's men, the food turned to roses. The walls of Elisabeth's Bower are decorated with a glass mosaic showing scenes from the legend.

BELOW: the Wartburg, a castle steeped in history.

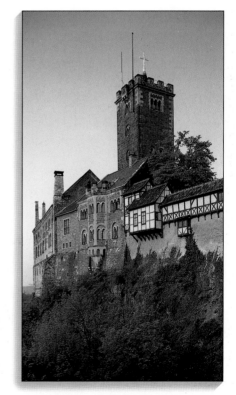

The link with Luther

The most famous connection with the Wartburg is that of Martin Luther. He was excommunicated by the Pope in 1521 and brought before the Reichstag in Worms to recant his thesis. Luther refused and was placed under the ban of the Empire. His overlord, the Elector Friedrich III of Saxony, brought him in secret to the Wartburg, where he began his German translation of the original Greek New Testament.

The second storey of the castle is taken up by the magnificent banqueting hall supported by 12th-century columns. Here are hung the banners of the nationalist Protestant German students who took part in the re-nowned **Wartburgfest** in 1817 celebrating the Luther tercentenary. They proposed the unification of Germa-ny into one empire, contrary to the interests of the con-servative princes and rulers of small states. ❑

MUNICH AND THE DEEP SOUTH

Southern Germany entices the visitor not only with its historic cities but also with its scenic mountains, lakes and forests

Some call it the "world metropolis with a heart", others refer to it as "the village of a million people". Munich, capital of the Free State of Bavaria, is certainly a city of world status, not only because of its size but also because it is the headquarters of international companies such as Siemens and BMW. In addition, with its Pinakothek art galleries, it possesses three of the world's greatest museums, as well as several top orchestras. Munich has remained a "village" because it exudes that atmosphere the world now describes as *Gemütlichkeit*, even though at times this has something to do with the influence of beer. Whenever opinion polls go looking for Germany's favourite city, Munich always takes first place. The Nymphenburg Palace, the River Isar, the Deutsches Museum, the Oktoberfest, the Olympic Stadium – Munich has a lot to offer.

A Bavarian king became one of the most colourful of Europe's rulers: Ludwig II. The palaces and castles of the "Fairytale King", whether Neuschwanstein, Herrenchiemsee or Linderhof, put all other tourist attractions, far and wide, entirely in the shade; an excursion to his Herrenchiemsee Palace should be included in every itinerary.

Mention Munich, too, and the Alps come to mind. In Bavaria they might be slightly lower than elsewhere, but they are no less impressive. The foothills, too, form a picture-postcard landscape, in which baroque churches thrust their onion-domed towers heavenwards. Only some 56 km (36 miles) from Munich, the 2,000-year-old city of Augsburg offers magnificent art treasures and historic old buildings such as the Fuggerei. A visit to this hospitable trading city, one of the biggest in Germany back in 1500, is a rewarding excursion. A journey north along the Romantic Road takes the traveller back to the 16th and 17th centuries in places such as Nördlingen, Dinkelsbühl and Rothenburg. These towns, which have survived the centuries virtually intact and present well-preserved little worlds of their own, appeal to the romantic in any visitor.

Further afield, southern Germany opens up great expanses of rich landscape and offers a wealth of sights to enjoy: from the baroque Residenz of Würzburg, which has been described as one of the finest palaces in all Europe – see for yourself when you visit the town, Franconia's wine centre; to the shores of Lake Constance, where palm trees and banana trees are quite at home; or again to the Black Forest, a paradise for those who enjoy the great outdoors as is the Bavarian Forest, which straddles the Czech border in the east. ❏

PRECEDING PAGES: traditional Bavarian concert during Munich's Oktoberfest.
LEFT: Neuschwanstein Castle.

MUNICH

Lying on the River Isar, with the majestic Alps and several Bavarian lakes a short drive away, Munich has many recreational activities and cultural attractions

Map on page 177

With a population of about 1.4 million, the Bavarian capital is Germany's third-largest city after Berlin and Hamburg. The large number of museums and art collections and the variety of music and theatre events make Munich a cultural metropolis of international rank. Here, too, is located Germany's largest university, with almost 100,000 students. More publishers have their headquarters in Munich than in any other German city. In recent decades, the city has also developed into a high-tech centre.

Despite copious amounts of international seasoning, Munich has managed to retain an almost provincial flavour. The true natives, having found a way to ignore all the hustle and bustle around them, continue to take pride in their Bavarian customs and traditions, thus ensuring their continuation in this otherwise cosmopolitan city. The city works hard and plays hard. Its carnival season, Fasching, is as well known as its beer "temple", the imposing Hofbräuhaus. No sooner is Fasching over than it's strong beer time at the Starkbier festival. Munich has more than 100 beer gardens, the largest of which – the Hirschgarten – accommodates more than 8,000 people under its spreading chestnut trees.

At the end of September it's time for the 14-day Munich beer festival, the Oktoberfest (affectionately termed *Wies'n* by the locals), which draws more than six million visitors every year to the vast Theresienwiese grounds. The festival began in 1810, when a horse race and other events were held here to celebrate the marriage between Crown Prince Ludwig (later King Ludwig I) and Princess Therese of Sachsen-Hildburghausen. Until well into the 19th century, horse races and shooting contests remained the highlights. Now, in addition to the fairground attractions, the main attraction is the beer tents, each accommodating more than 6,000 people.

Opera and ballet festivals, a Film Festival and a Biennale pack Munich's cultural calendar, with open-air concerts and ballet performances at the palaces of Nymphenbürg and Schleissheim and in the courtyard of theResidenz among the highlights.

The city's origins

A monastery known as *Munichen* (meaning monks in High German) is known to have existed here from the 8th century. In 1158, Duke Henry the Lion had a vital bridge over the Isar moved south to Munich, diverting the salt trade route between Bad Reichenhall and Augsburg and enabling Munich to prosper from the taxes levied on this valuable commodity.

Emperor Frederick I Barbarossa legalised Henry's action and the rapidly growing settlement soon won the right to hold markets and to mint coins. In 1180 Barbarossa awarded Duke Otto von Wittelsbach, the ruler of the Palatinate, the imperial state of

LEFT: the Glockenspiel draws the crowds on Marienplatz.
BELOW: Oktoberfest parade.

King Ludwig I transformed Munich into a city of truly European standing.

BELOW: the Maximilianeum, seat of the Bavarian parliament.

Bavaria. His dynasty guided Bavaria's fate for almost 750 years, until 1918

Duke Wilhelm IV (1493–1550) chose Munich as his residence and the capital of Bavaria. He and his successor, Albrecht V, enforced Catholicism to the exclusion of other religions throughout Bavaria. During the reign of Maximilian I (1597–1651), the city suffered the ravages of the Thirty Years' War (1618–48). The column outside the Town Hall, the Mariensäule, was erected at the end of the war and marked a period of recovery. Under the Elector Max II Emanuel (1679–1726) Munich attained the rank of a European city.

In the 18th century, the city once more became involved in the tumults of war and occupation. Famine and poverty struck. After the alliance with Napoleon in 1806, which made Bavaria a kingdom, the city entered a new period of prosperity as a royal capital and seat of residence. Napoleon dissolved the monasteries and had their estates nationalised. In 1819 the first Bavarian parliament assembled in Munich. King Ludwig I (1825–48) continued with monumental architectural works and secured Munich's standing as a European city. He was an enthusiastic patron of the arts and collected works that formed the nucleus of Munich's two best-known museums, the Glyptothek and the Alte Pinakothek. His large-scale re-planning of Munich created the city's present layout and classical style, notably with the magnificent Ludwigstrasse.

After the death of the "Fairytale King" Ludwig II, Munich developed into a large modern city under the regentship of Prince Luitpold (1886–1912), and by the turn of the 20th century had a population of about half a million. But Munich again suffered heavily under war – this time World War I. Popular revolutionary pressure brought about the abdication of Ludwig III, the last king of Bavaria, in November 1918. A council of workers, soldiers and peasants was

formed, with the leader of the revolution, Kurt Eisner, at its head. Eisner became Bavaria's first Prime Minister but was assassinated shortly afterwards.

The end of the revolutionary "Räterepublik" ushered in a new and unhappy chapter of German history. It was in Munich that Adolf Hitler rapidly rose to the leadership of the NSDAP, the Nazis. On 8 November 1923, he staged an abortive coup against the national government. The putsch was put down and Hitler was imprisoned. With the 1938 Munich Agreement in which Hitler, Mussolini, Chamberlain and Daladier sealed the fate of Czechoslovakia, the "capital of the [Nazi] movement" won further questionable significance. Hitler's expansionism was to bring Munich great wartime misery: 70 bombing raids reduced the city to little more than a pile of rubble. Eventually Munich was occupied by US troops, with the people offering no resistance.

The city centre

Munich's true centre, its extensive pedestrian shopping area, begins near the **Hauptbahnhof** or main railway station at busy **Karlsplatz Ⓐ**, which is known by the locals as Stachus. At the end of the 18th century, the square and its imposing gate, the 14th-century **Karlstor**, were part of the city walls. Passing through the gate you step into the pedestrian zone, passing the **Richard Strauss Fountain**, the **Deutsches Jagd-und Fischereimuseum** (German Hunting Museum; open daily 9.30am–5pm, Thur until 9pm) and the **Church of St Michael Ⓑ**, one of the most famous Renaissance churches in Germany where Ludwig II, the doomed "Fairytale King" of Bavaria, is buried, along with other members of the Wittelsbach dynasty. Munich's landmark cathedral, the **Frauenkirche Ⓒ** (Church of Our Lady) is a late-Gothic edifice of red brick,

Map on page 177

TIP

In the Hunting Museum check out the Wolpertinger, Bavaria's fabulous winged and horned creature. However, it is just the taxidermist's fantasy running wild: the Wolpertinger only exists in fairytales and legends.

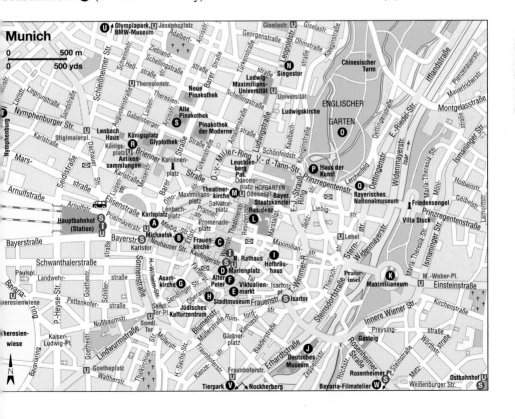

The Virgin Mary, Munich's patron, surveys Marienplatz.

consecrated in 1494. The soaring building, with its two distinctive onion-domed towers, represents the pride and the prosperity of the city's population in the late Middle Ages. The church is among the largest hall churches in southern Germany. Of particular note in the interior are the three Gothic stained-glass windows in the choir gallery. The crypt contains the tombs of 46 Wittelsbach princes and several cardinals of the Munich-Freising diocese. From the south tower there's a fine view over the city and the Alps, which look deceptively near when the warm dry wind known as the *Föhn* is wafting in from the south.

Central **Marienplatz** ❼ throbs with life throughout the year – in spring and summer, when the street entertainers are doing their thing and in deepest winter when the Christmas Market takes over, the stalls clustering around the statue of Munich's patron, the Virgin Mary, who looks down on the scene from her place atop a marble column.

One entire side of the square is taken up by the neo-Gothic **Rathaus** or Town Hall (1867–1908), with a world-famous **Glockenspiel** in its 85-metre (278-ft) tower. The carillon and its mechanical figures depict two episodes from Munich's history: a tournament held in Marienplatz in 1568 and the *Schäfflertanz* (dance of the coopers) commemorating the end of the plague in Munich in 1517. There are performances three times a day from March to October (11am, noon and 5pm) and every day at 11am and noon in winter. The Tourist Information Office is situated under the arches at the base of the town hall. The **Old Town Hall** (1470–74) sits rather forlornly amid all this attention on the eastern side of Marienplatz, although its modest exterior contains one of Germany's finest Gothic halls. It also houses a small but interesting **Toy Museum** (open daily 10am–5.30pm).

Across the road from the Old Town Hall is the **Church of the Holy Ghost**,

BELOW: the towers of the Frauenkirche and the Rathaus (from left to right).

originally built in the 14th century but fully restored in florid rococo style (18th century). Behind the church is the **Viktualienmarkt** , Munich's colourful open-air food market (*Viktualien* means victuals), with its enormous variety of produce, ranging from rosy Bavarian apples to tropical fruits, simple sausages to expensive venison. There are friendly bars and a couple of beer gardens to recover from the rigours of shopping. A food court and a range of craft boutiques are also to be found at the restored covered market, the **Schrannenhalle**, which doubles as a cultural forum.

From the tower of the nearby **Alter Peter** ⑦, as the locals call the venerable Church of St Peter, Munich's oldest parish church, there's a fine view as far as the Alps. The **Rindermarkt** (the former cattle market) leads to Sendlinger Strasse, with its richly stocked shops and the remarkable **Asamkirche** ⑧. The Church of St John Nepomuk is known by the name of the famous Asam brothers who built it between 1733 and 1746, giving it a magnificent rococo interior.

The **Münchner Stadtmuseum** ⑨ (Munich City Museum; open Tues–Sun 10am–6pm), a short walk from Sendlinger Strasse, was built as an arsenal and livery stable in the 15th century and now has regular showings of art and design and a permanent exhibition devoted to the history of the city. Its **Puppet Museum** holds regular performances. Opposite, the new **Jüdisches Museum** (Jewish Museum; open Tues–Sun 10am–6pm) offers a rich panorama of Jewish life and culture in Munich over the centuries.

Return to Marienplatz via Viktualienmarkt and turn right into Tal, whose most famous attraction is the Weisses Brauhaus which serves cuisine that's as authentically Bavarian as the surroundings. True locals come here at 11am to eat *Weisswurst*, a speciality of the city. If you go up Sparkassenstrasse, a right turn followed by a left will bring you to the famous **Hofbräuhaus** ⑩, offering similar food and ambience on a larger scale but catering more to a tourist crowd.

The Tal leads out to **Isartor**, another of the old city gates, which contains a museum devoted to the popular Munich comedian Karl Valentin. Beyond lies the world's largest science and technology museum, the **Deutsches Museum** ⑪ (open daily 9am–5pm), situated on an island in the River Isar. It contains more than 15,000 exhibits, from sailing boats to aeroplanes and from steam engines to microchips. Replicas of coal and salt mines record the development of the mining industry. To see everything would take days.

Opposite, on the right bank of the Isar, is the **Müllersche Volksbad** (Müller's Public Baths). This magnificent swimming pool, built in Art Nouveau style between 1897–1901, is well worth a visit if you feel like a swim. From here it's a short stroll along the river to the **Maximilianeum** ⑫ (1857–74), seat of the Bavarian Parliament. It stands proudly at the end of **Maximilianstrasse**, laid out as an avenue of regal magnificence. The street has retained much of its elegant character, attracting some of the city's chicest shops, boutiques, bars, cafés and art galleries. Here, too, is the **Museum für Völkerkunde** (Museum of Anthropology; open Tues–Sun 9.30am–5.30pm), with its ethnology collection, and the **Munich Kammerspiele**, one of Germany's best theatres.

Map on page 177

As well as the famous "Morisken" Dancers (above) the City Museum houses a Film Museum and cinema which shows rare foreign-language films.

BELOW: the rococo interior of the Asamkirche.

Wittelsbach residence

Maximilianstrasse opens out into **Max-Joseph-Platz**, dominated by the columned facade of the **National Theatre**; the theatre is in striking contrast with the modern Residence Theatre next door, named after the neighbouring royal palace, or **Residenz** ❶ (open daily Apr–mid-Oct 9am–6pm, mid-Oct–Mar 10am–4pm, last admission one hour before closing), home of the Wittelsbach rulers for 600 years. Before the Residenz was built, the Bavarian dukes' power base had been the Alter Hof between Max-Joseph-Platz and Marienplatz. The palace's south facade, modelled on Florence's Pitti Palace, was built by the architect Leo von Klenze for Ludwig I in 1835.

Highlights of the Residenz include former royal theatre the **Cuvilliés Theatre**, a red and gold rococo jewel that is still in use, and the **Antiquarium**, a grand hall built by Duke Albrecht V in 1571 to house the Electoral Library. The largest secular Renaissance interior north of the Alps, the Antiquarium is now used for state receptions. Albrecht also founded the **Schatzkammer**, or Treasury, where priceless Wittelsbach treasures, including coronation crowns and accoutrements, are on view.

A visit to Schwabing

From Max-Joseph-Platz, Residenzstrasse leads to Odeonsplatz, dominated by the **Feldherrnhalle** and the 17th-century **Theatinerkirche** ⓜ. Erected in 1841–42 by Gärtner, the Feldherrnhalle (Field Marshals' Hall) is modelled on the Loggia dei Lanzi in Florence and contains a memorial commemorating the victory of the Bavarian army in the war of 1870–71. It was in front of the Feldherrnhalle that Hitler's march through Munich during his attempted putsch of

TIP

Take a look inside Dallmayrs food halls in nearby Dienerstrasse. The range of produce is mouth-watering.

BELOW:
Antiquarium at the Residenz.

1923 was brought to a halt. With its twin towers, imposing 71-metre (236-ft) high dome and yellow facade, the Theatinerkirche (Theatine Church), otherwise known as St Cajetan's, was the first piece of Bavarian baroque, commissioned from Italian builders by the Elector's Italian wife Henriette Adelaide. Its interior has a magnificent high altar and more Wittelsbach tombs.

Map on page 177

From Odeonsplatz, elegant **Ludwigstrasse** leads north towards Schwabing. Ludwig I commissioned architects Friedrich von Gärtner and Leo von Klenze to design it as another regal Munich thoroughfare. They lined the street with impressive neoclassical buildings, including the **Bayerische Staatsbibliothek**, one of the largest German libraries, and the **Ludwig-Maximilians-Universität**. Situated at one end is the **Siegestor ❶** (Victory Gate), which was erected in 1850 to commemorate the Bavarian soldiers who were killed during the Napoleonic wars.

At this point, Ludwigstrasse gives way to **Leopoldstrasse**, once the bustling heart of the legendary artists' district of Schwabing and still a pulsating nightlife centre, with cafés, bars and nightclubs. Munich's famous park, the **English Garden ❷**, east of Leopoldstrasse, was laid out in 1785. It acquired its name because of its informal, so-called English style and is one of Europe's biggest parks, providing a wonderful recreation area right in the heart of the city and extending literally for miles to the north.

A fine view of Munich's distinctive silhouette can be enjoyed from the park's **Monopteros** (a Grecian temple), which shares a corner of the park with the famous beer garden by the **Chinesischer Turm** (Chinese Tower). Completed in 1791, it was modelled on the outlook tower in Kew Gardens, London. It did not survive World War II but was rebuilt in 1952. Nearby runs the Eisbach, a channel of the River Isar that attracts bathers in the summer. To the north of the

ABOVE: the Monopteros in the English Garden.
BELOW: the famous beer gardens at the Chinese Tower.

BEER GARDENS

By five o'clock on a hot summer's afternoon, you can find most of Munich's population sitting out under the chestnut trees in one of the city's beer gardens, hoisting a *Mass* (a litre mug) of beer, polishing off a *Hendl* (roast chicken) and lingering until late into the night, when lights festooned in the branches light up the area like a stage set.

Class barriers are unknown here. A group of rowdy youths may be seated between a group of middle-aged men in *Tracht* and three elegantly coiffed ladies in Jil Sander outfits, at a single table. Self-service is the rule and standing in line is part of the beer garden experience. Not that you have to buy all of your food: many a family comes with a picnic basket loaded with radishes, cheese, cold cuts, bread, even a chequered tablecloth, and picks up beer to accompany the meal.

In Munich, beer gardens come in all shapes and sizes. While the classic brass band still oom-pahs away from the Chinese Tower in the English Garden, jazz sets the tone at the popular Waldwirtschaft in Grosshesselohe, south of Munich. However little Max Emmanuel Brauerei as well as the Osterwaldgarten in Schwabing still concentrate on traditional specialities such as *Knödel* (roast pork with dumplings) or a filling *Bratzeit* (white bread, cheese and cold meats).

Chinese Tower, a pleasant stroll leads to the Kleinhesseloher See, a boating lake with another popular beer garden.

At the southern end of the park is one of Munich's few remaining Hitler-era buildings, the **Haus der Kunst**  (Museum of Modern Art; open daily 10am–8pm, Thur until 10pm), now home to 20th-century masterpieces including works by Picasso, Matisse, Dali, Klee and Warhol. The **Bayerisches National-museum** ◒ (open Tues–Sun 10am–5pm, Thur until 8pm), further along Prinzregentenstrasse, provides a comprehensive insight into the history of Bavarian art and culture from the Middle Ages to the present day.

An art eldorado

The densest concentration of the city's art treasures is to be found to the west of the city centre in the so-called Maxvorstadt. **Königsplatz** ◒, probably the most impressive square in Munich, is lined on all sides by neoclassical buildings. Commissioned by Ludwig I, they earned Munich the sobriquet "Athens on the Isar", though the square saw a less glorious period when it was paved over and used by the Nazis as a parade ground in the 1930s.

The **Antikensammlung** (open Tues–Sun 10am–5pm, Wed until 8pm) contains collections of world-famous Greek vases, Roman and Etruscan statues and artefacts made of glass and terracotta, while the **Glyptothek** (open Tues–Sun 10am–5pm, Thur until 8pm) is devoted to Greek and Roman sculpture. Around the corner on Luisenstrasse is the **Lenbach Villa**, built in 1890 in Tuscan style for the Munich painter Franz von Lenbach. Today it houses one of Munich's most attractive galleries, the **Städtische Galerie im Lenbachhaus** (Municipal Art Gallery; open Tues–Sun 10am–6pm) and displays works by many Munich artists from the

ABOVE:
the Lenbach Villa.
BELOW:
exhibits in the
Neue Pinakothek.

15th to the 20th century, with the *Blauer Reiter* group featuring prominently.

Nearby Karolinenplatz has an **obelisk** erected in 1812 as a memorial to Bavarians killed in Napoleon's Russian campaign. On the left, Barerstrasse leads to the **Alte Pinakothek** ❺ (open Tues–Sun 10am–5pm, Thur until 8pm), one of the most important art galleries in Europe. Here the works of European masters from the 14th to the 18th century are exhibited, with an emphasis on the Dutch and Flemish schools (the collection of Rubens' is perhaps the finest in the world). The adjacent **Neue Pinakothek** has about 400 paintings and sculptures covering modern periods, from Impressionism to Art Nouveau and symbolism (open Wed–Mon 10am–5pm, Wed until 8pm). Adjacent to these museums, the **Pinakothek der Moderne** (open Tues–Sun 10am–5pm, Thur–Fri until 8pm) houses a number of modern, avant garde and graphic art collections.

Map on page 177

A royal garden house

The summer residence of the Bavarian princes and kings, **Nymphenburg Palace** ❼ (open daily Apr–mid-Oct 9am–6pm, mid-Oct–Mar 10am–4pm) was built at the start of the 18th century by the Italian master Agostino Barelli. It is one of the most famous late-baroque palace estates in Germany, complete with gardens, pavilions, galleries and the building in which Nymphenburg porcelain has been produced since 1761. There is a fascinating **Schönheitsgalerie** (Gallery of Beauties), commissioned by Ludwig I and including a painting of the dancer Lola Montez, whose affair with Ludwig was one of the reasons for his abdication in 1848. The **Marstallmuseum** (Stables Museum) contains a collection of royal coaches, sleighs and ceremonial vehicles. Children will enjoy the **Museum Mensch und Natur** (Natural History Museum; open Tues–Fri 9am–5pm, Thur until 8pm, Sat–Sun 10am–6pm) in the north wing. The park contains a number of smaller buildings, including the **Badenburg**, a lodge with baroque baths built in 1721; the octagonal **Pagodenburg** from 1719; the **Magdalenenklause**, which Max Emanuel had built as a hermitage for himself in 1725, and the **Amalienburg**, a hunting lodge completed in 1739 by Franz Cuvilliés the Elder and now regarded as a masterpiece of European rococo.

The dancer Lola Montez originally hailed from Limerick in Ireland. She was the favourite in Ludwig I's "Gallery of Beauties".

BELOW: the Olympic Tower.

Olympic stadium

Munich's ring road (or the U3 underground) brings you to the **Olympiapark** ⓤ, built for the Olympic Games in 1972. The **Olympic Stadium** has a tent roof which spans the whole site in a series of giant "spider webs". Designed by Behnisch and Partners, it can accommodate 78,000 people. The same architects were responsible for the **Olympia Hall**, which is now a concert venue, and the swimming pool. The revolving restaurant at the top of the 290-metre (960-ft) **Olympic Tower** affords some magnificent views of Munich and the Alps, but these can also be seen from the Olympiaberg, a small hill created from the rubble of houses destroyed during World War II. The stadium setting is completed by an artificial lake, where in summer a floating stage provides a venue for concerts and theatre performances.

To the north of the ring road is another symbol of modern Munich, namely the administrative tower of the **Bavarian Motor Works** (BMW), which bears an

The tent-style roof of the Olympic Stadium.

BELOW: inside the futuristic space of BMW Welt.

uncanny likeness to an engine. Next to it is the bowl-shaped BMW **Museum**, which is devoted to technical developments and a collection of classic motorcars, motorcycles and aircraft engines (open Tues–Fri 9am–6pm, Sat–Sun and holidays 10am–8pm). Next door the BMW **Welt**, or the BMW delivery centre by Wolf D. Prix and the Viennese architecture firm Coop Himmelb(l)au, strikes an equally extravagant tone with a roof envisioned as a floating cloud. It offers a world of shops and restaurants (guided tours Mon–Fri 9am–4pm, Sat–Sun 10am–4pm).

Soccer fans are catered for in the UFO-like shape of the **Allianz Arena** stadium, home to the Bayern Munich football team. Acccording to what teams happen to be playing, the stadium's outer shell can be lit up to glow red, blue or white (tours daily 1pm in English, except on match days; pre-booked general tours 9.30am–5.30pm).

Another Munich attraction worth a visit is the **Tierpark** ⓥ (Zoo; open daily Apr–Sept 8am–6pm, Oct–Mar 9am–5pm). Situated at Hellabrunn in the south of the city by the River Isar, this is one of the finest zoos in Europe, notable for its spacious enclosures. It was also the first zoo in the world to be organised along geographical lines. One of the most popular attractions is the children's section, where kids can feed, touch and stroke the animals. Apart from visiting the enclosures, take a stroll through the enormous aviary at the centre of the zoo.

However Munich's principal natural attraction is the **River Isar**, and you need hardly cross a single road to pedal along its cycle tracks from the zoo to the north.

Further south, at Geiselgasteig, is the **Bavaria Filmstadt** ⓦ (open daily Mar–Oct 9am–4pm, Nov–Feb 10am–3pm). These film studios have been responsible for a number of acclaimed international productions, including *The Never-ending Story* (1984) and *Enemy Mine* (1985). The submarine used in *Das Boot*, the epic story of a submarine crew in World War II, is the centrepiece of the studio tour.

Easy trips from Munich

One of the most appealing aspects of Munich is the splendid countryside right on the city's doorstep, especially on the banks of the **River Isar**. There are some interesting old towns, too, all of which are easily reached by the S-Bahn (suburban) trains that link up with the underground system in the centre of the city.

One highly recommended trip is to Freising, 33 km (20 miles) north of the city. **Freising** was once a powerful episcopal centre: as long ago as the 8th century the bishops St Corbinian, St Boniface and Arbeo lived here. The monastery had its golden age under Bishop Otto of Freising, uncle of Emperor Frederick Barbarossa. On the hill stands the originally Romanesque Basilica of St Mary and St Corbinian. The crypt of the church, which contains the shrine of St Corbinian, has undergone considerable alterations, notably through the stucco and painting work of the Asam brothers. In 1146 the world's first brewery was founded in Freising's Benedictine abbey of **Weihenstephan**. The abbey now forms part of Munich's Technical University, but the beer is still produced and there is a pleasant beer garden in which to sample it.

On the way to Freising, you might want to stop off at **Schleissheim** to visit the magnificent New Palace (open Tues–Sun Apr–Sept 9am–6pm, Oct–Mar 10am–4pm), commissioned by Elector Maximilian II Emanuel and completed in the early 19th century. The Baroque Gallery is part of the **Bavarian State Picture Collection** and contains works from leading European schools of painting; there are also some fine *Gobelin* tapestries. The neighbouring **Gartenschloss Lustheim**, given as a wedding present by the Elector to his wife Maria Antonia, contains a fine collection of Meissen pottery. Nearby is the **Historische Flugwerft Schleissheim**, an aircraft hangar that forms a branch of the Deutsches Museum. Historic aeroplanes and exhibitions of aviation history and technology can be viewed.

To the west of Munich is the town of **Dachau**, a name that will always be associated with one of the Third Reich's most barbarous concentration camps. The camp, on the eastern edge of town, has been preserved as a place of remembrance and the museum documents the horrors of the Holocaust (open Tues–Sun and public holidays 9am–5pm).

The Bavarian Lakes

There are other easy S-Bahn connections to the south of Munich, notably to the Starnbergersee and Ammersee lakes. **Lake Starnberg** (on the S6 suburban railway) is criss-crossed by steamers. In Starnberg is the church of St Joseph, a charming late-rococo building with a superb high altar by Ignaz Günther. One popular stop is **Berg** on the remoter, eastern shore of the lake, where a cross in the lake marks the spot where King Ludwig II was drowned.

Ammersee, 35 km (22 miles) from Munich and also accessible on the S-Bahn railway, is not as crowded as Lake Starnberg, although its main town, **Herrsching**, is a good starting point for walks into the hills and to **Kloster Andechs**. The reputation of this famous Bavarian monastery is largely based on the quality of its beer. There are fine views of the Bavarian countryside from the beer garden terrace. ❑

Map on page 177

TIP

Andechs hasn't only got beer to offer. The cheese aficionado should try the delicious, strongly flavoured local cheese in the Klosterbräustüberl, or the O'bazda – mashed camembert with onions and paprika.

BELOW: Andechs, a monastery made famous by its beer.

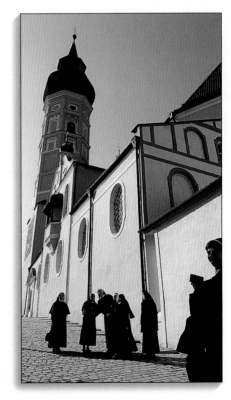

ALONG THE ALPS

*Defiant precipices, green meadows, bubbling rivers and villages
bright with paintings and flowers – the Bavarian Alps form
an ever-changing vista of stunning scenery*

Map
on pages
188–89

T here are numerous ways of reaching the Alps and whichever way you head south of Munich, you'll always end up in magnificent countryside. The following itinerary follows the mountains from east to west, along the German Alpine Road.

From Munich, the A8 motorway to Salzburg leads past **Chiemsee** ❶, Bavaria's largest lake, situated at the foot of the beautiful Alpine Chiemgau foothills. Turn off at the Bernau exit and follow the signs to Prien, from where it is only 2 km (1 mile) to the lakeside settlement of **Stock** with its landing stages for passenger boats out to the islands in the lake. (Stock can also be reached aboard the little green steam train that has run between Prien and the lake ever since 1887.) The main island on the lake is known as **Herrenchiemsee**. Here, in the middle of the woods, stands Ludwig II's glorious imitation of the palace of Versailles, completed in 1878 (open Apr–Sept 9am–6pm, Oct 10am–5.45pm, Nov–Mar 9.40am–4pm). Though only the central tract was ever completed, Ludwig conceived the palace as the highest expression of the princely splendour and regal might of the Bavarian throne. In summer, concerts are held in the stately Spiegelsaal (Hall of Mirrors). The King Ludwig Museum offers a fascinating insight into the King's life and his love of music and theatre. Also well worth visiting on the island is the Old Palace, which hosts temporary exhibits in its baroque library. It was here, in 1948, that the German constitution was formulated.

Ferries also run to the smaller island of **Frauenchiemsee**, where Duke Tassilo III founded a convent for Benedictine nuns in 782. The convent itself is now a college and not open to visitors, but the church – a beautiful combination of Romanesque, Gothic and baroque architectural styles – is. Take time to walk around the island past gardens brimming with flowers and enjoy a drink or a meal in the lovely Gasthaus Inselwirt. There is a small fishing community and the speciality *Räucherfisch* (smoked fish) is sold locally.

Continue southeast on the A8, and just before the Austrian border take the exit on the B20 for **Bad Reichenhall** ❷. The old centre of the town with its spa resort is well worth a visit. Inhaling and drinking the saline spa waters offers visitors relief from respiratory disorders. In the old salt refinery, 400,000 litres of this spa water drip over a brushwood grating. Some of the water evaporates, thereby increasing the salt content of the air and imparting a curative effect.

The section of the German Alpine Road between Bad Reichenhall and Berchtesgaden (B20) is without doubt one of the most panoramic routes in the entire Alps. Views of the spectacular mountain scenery of the **Berchtesgadener Land** lurk behind every bend, with the 2,710-metre (8,900-ft) **Watzmann**, Germany's

LEFT: St Bartholomä on Königssee is accessible only by boat or on foot.
BELOW: another Bavarian beauty.

The slide is one of the highlights of the Berchtesgaden salt mine tour – particularly for the kids.

second-highest mountain, dominating the scene. According to legend, the area was once ruled over by a king who was such a tyrant that all his subjects lived in perpetual fear. Finally, when he yet again vented his cruelty on a local shepherd family while out on one of his hunting expeditions, higher powers intervened and he and his family were immediately turned to stone. And there they remain today, the Watzmann, his wife and five children.

The basis for the wealth of the present mountain spa of **Berchtesgaden** ❸ was established by Emperor Frederick Barbarossa when he granted the local Augustinian monks prospecting rights for salt and ore. The **Salzbergwerk** (salt mine, just outside town in Bräuhausstrasse) is still in operation and a visit is highly recommended (open daily May–Oct 9am–5pm, Nov–15 Mar and Apr 11.30am–3pm). Having donned traditional mining garments, visitors descend about 500 metres (1,640 ft) into the depths; a boat ride across a subterranean lake forms part of the tour.

On walking through the old town centre, the most striking sights are the typical Upper Bavarian buildings in the Weihnachtsschützenstrasse and its side streets, featuring pastel-coloured facades decorated with fine stucco. In the Metzgerstrasse, the outdoor wall paintings on the former hotel *Zum Hirschen* (now a bank) depict the sumptuous pleasures of Bavarian cuisine.

Well worth visiting is the secluded **Schlossplatz**, with the castle of the prince-priors and the abbey church of Saints Peter and John the Baptist. In the 19th century the castle, with its pink and white stucco facade, was taken over by the Wittelsbachs as a hunting lodge and summer residence. The **Schlossmuseum** (guided tours only, Sun–Fri mid-May–mid-Oct 10am–noon, 2–4pm, mid-Oct–mid-May 11am–2pm) has a fine collection of weapons, furniture and paintings.

BELOW: the glorious Ramsau Valley.

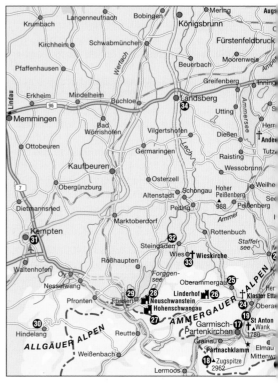

Eagle's Nest

Most people associate Berchtesgaden with the name of Adolf Hitler. In 1935, Hitler had the famous "Eagle's Nest" built on the **Obersalzberg** to the south-east of the town, where he would receive party luminaries and important visitors from abroad. Hitler's residence, the Berghof, and most ancillary buildings were dynamited in 1952, but a new **Document Centre** gives an insight into the history of National Socialism and especially this place, including a visit to an original bunker (open Tues–Sun, Apr–Oct 9am–4pm, Nov–Mar 10am–2pm). Higher up, the **Kehlsteinhaus**, the former "tea house" – a present from the Party to the Führer – still stands. Since 1951, it has belonged to the German Alpine Club; there are magnificent views from the restaurant terrace.

South of Berchtesgaden, deep in the Berchtesgaden National Park, is the crystal-clear, 8-km (5-mile) long **Königssee** ❹ lake. At its southern end is the Maler-winkel (painters' corner), with its stunning views. Halfway along the western shore is the tiny chapel of **St Bartholomä**, its round domes outlined against one of the most beautiful backdrops you could hope to find. The giant east face of the Watzmann directly above is one of the biggest mountaineering challenges of the eastern Alps. For the less energetic, the best way of admiring the dramatic scenery is from one of the electrically powered boats which tour the lake.

From Königssee, cut through the village of Schönau to reach the B305, the German Alpine Road (Deutsche Alpenstrasse). The road gives access to the glorious **Ramsau Valley**. At the entrance to the village of **Ramsau** ❺ stands the clinker-roofed church of Saints Fabian and Sebastian, while on a wooded slope beyond the village is the baroque pilgrimage church of St Mary. Idyllic though the setting may be, it was from here in the 18th century that 1,000 Protestant

Map on pages 188–89

TIP

An alternative way of exploring Königssee is to hire a rowing boat at the jetty. If you're fit enough you can make it all the way to St Bartholomä and back.

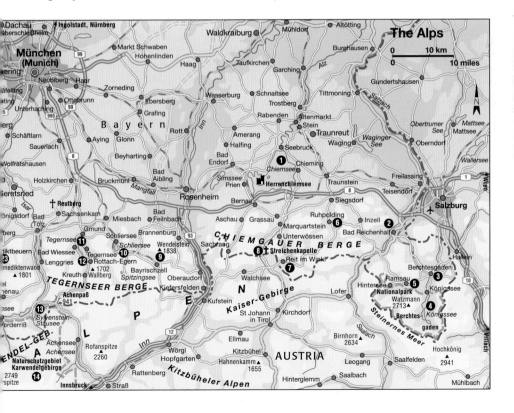

"heretics" were driven out of their parish into exile. At the head of the valley is delightful **Hintersee**, where rowing boats are available for hire.

The German Alpine Road (B305) continues through Inzell, passing inviting country inns with beer gardens shaded by chestnut trees. The stretch between Inzell and Reit im Winkel is one of the most beautiful of the entire route, leading as it does through the **Chiemgau Alps Nature Reserve**, with limestone summits giving way to forested slopes and Alpine meadows. At the heart of it all lies **Ruhpolding ❻**, with its numerous sport and recreation facilities. The **Holzknechtmuseum** (open Tues–Sun 10am–5pm) recalls the bygone days when the locals lived mainly from timber, which they cut for use in the salt mines.

Situated in a broad valley, **Reit im Winkl ❼** is a famous winter sports resort with guaranteed snow on the Winklmoosalm (1,160 metres/3,800 ft). In the warmer months the area is also superb for walking; to the south are fine views of the Wilder Kaiser mountains, just over the border in Austria. To the north of Reit im Winkl at **Unterwössen**, an 8-km (5-mile) detour leads along the Achen Valley to the **Streichen Chapel ❽**, situated high above the mountain stream. From the beer garden of the inn there are fine views over the Chiemgau Alps.

The route continues north through Grassau to rejoin the A8 *autobahn* near Chiemsee, before heading south on the A93 towards Innsbruck. Here take the Brannenburg exit and follow the toll road through the dramatic **Tatzelwurm Gorge**. According to legend, access to the gorge was once barred by a dragon.

The road emerges at the Sudelfeld ski resort (1,100–1,450 metres/3,610–4,760 ft), and continues through hilly pastureland to Bayrischzell, from where a cable car leads to the summit of the **Wendelstein ❾** (1,838 metres/6,030 ft; also reached via the rack railway from Brannenburg). An ascent of the

ONIONS AND FLOWERS

Just a look at the houses and churches provides indication enough of the prosperity of Upper Bavaria: carved timbers, painted facades, balconies brimming with geraniums and onion-domed churches. Most of these buildings were erected from the late 17th century when, after the depredations of the Thirty Years' War, the Catholic Church and the bourgeoisie could afford to rebuild their properties as monuments of pride, power and triumph over the defeated Protestantism. The churches' rich stucco work and colourful frescoes – mostly by Italian artists – taught the illiterate congregation of God's glory; some of the style elements were repeated on secular mansions in the towns, decorated with sgrafitto and the distinctive *Lüftlmalerei (see page 195).*

Out in the country, farmers renovated their properties by replacing wooden walls with stone, adding a second floor with a higher ceiling, furnishing the structure with a broad wooden balcony and finishing it off with an overhanging roof to protect it from snow. A number of open-air museums provide an excellent insight into the rural architecture of Upper Bavaria. They include the Gleutleiten Museum near Kochel, the Amerang Museum at Chiemsee and the museum at Sonthofen in the Allgäu.

Map on pages 188–89

Wendelstein is very worthwhile, not only for the superb views from the summit, but for several other attractions, including the **Geo Park**, which takes you back 250 million years to the time when the mountain was still a coral reef under the ocean, and a show cave that leads into the mountain. Germany's highest church is also here (the Bergkircherl was built in 1718 and continues to attract a steady stream of pilgrims), as well as the country's most modern observatory.

On towards **Schliersee** ⑩, a village oasis at the edge of the small lake of the same name and centred around the Parish Church of St Sixtus, whose frescoes and stucco are the early work of Johann Baptist Zimmermann (1680–1758).

In the midst of a picture-postcard landscape of gently sloping meadows lies **Tegernsee** ⑪. First to arrive at this lake were the monks; then came the Wittelsbachs, the Bavarian royal family, followed by a host of famous artists. After the war, Tegernsee became a haven for politicians and wealthy businessmen, who secured expensive plots of land by the lake shore.

In the picturesque town of **Tegernsee**, the **Monastery Church of St Quirin** has a baroque doorway which opens on to a triple-naved basilica with a ceiling fresco by Johann Georg Asam. Those who enjoy more raucous entertainment should call in at the **Herzogliche Bräustüberl** to sample the beer. Examples of Upper Bavarian domestic architecture can be found in the Rosengasse.

At the southern end of the lake is the twin community of **Rottach-Egern** ⑫. A sign at the far end of the town indicates the station for the cable car to the summit of the **Wallberg** (1,702 metres/5,583 ft). This mountain is a starting point for some moderately tough hikes; colourful hang-gliders hover around its summit. On bright winter days, lazy sun-worshippers take it easy on their chalet terraces while keen Alpine skiers make the most of the slopes.

TIP

In winter at weekends there are long queues at the Wallberg cable car as it is great fun to race downhill on sledges (rental at the cable car).

LEFT: windsurfing on Tegernsee.
BELOW: young and old in traditional Bavarian costume.

Tranquillity on the Sylvensteinsee.

BELOW: the craft of violin-making has a long tradition in Mittenwald.

The German Alpine Road continues along the B307 to **Kreuth** – another popular winter sports venue – and the **Achen-Pass** (941 metres/3,087 ft). Just beyond, the River Isar was dammed in 1959 to create the **Sylvensteinsee Reservoir** , which engulfed the old village of Fall. In **Vorderriss**, beyond the western end of the lake, the Gasthof zur Post restaurant marks the start of a 15-km (9-mile) long, narrow forest toll road through the **Karwendel Mountain Nature Reserve** ⑭. With its narrow valleys and towering summits, the Karwendel range, most of which lies in Austria, is a paradise for climbers and hikers.

Huddled against the western buttresses of the Karwendel, **Mittenwald** ⑮ enjoys one of the most spectacular locations of any town or village in the Alps. Its outstanding landmark is the baroque tower of the **Church of Saints Peter and Paul**, one of the finest church towers in Upper Bavaria. Mittenwald, once an important centre of trans-Alpine commerce, is world-famous for its violin-making. In front of the church is a monument to Matthias Klotz, who learned the trade in Italy from Antonio Stradivari (1644–1737), before returning to his home village. Local violin-makers still produce the instruments today, and visitors can learn more at the **Geigenbaumuseum** (Violin Making Museum; open Tues–Sun 10am–5pm, off-season 11am–4pm). For more fine views, visitors can take the cable car ride to the top of the Karwendelspitze.

To the west lies the Wetterstein range, the main bastion of the Bavarian Alps. A good way into the heart of the range is to take the long valley road from Klais to the village of **Elmau** ⑯. Three hours' walk from Elmau, perched on a spur 1,860 metres (6,100 ft) above sea level and dominated by the massive bulk of the Dreitorspitze peak, is Ludwig II's little "Persian" palace of **Schachen**. Built of wood and carved with intricate Persian designs, this building is perhaps

as great a testimony as any to Ludwig's infatuation with the bizarre. Surely nobody but the "Fairytale King" could have dreamed of building an edifice so exotic and substantial in such a remote place as this.

Germany's highest mountain

At the foot of the Wetterstein range lies Bavaria's most famous resort, **Garmisch-Partenkirchen** ⓱. When the Olympic Games were held here in 1936, the two towns of Garmisch and Partenkirchen were merged to form a twin community. The Olympic ice-skating and skiing stadia are located in Partenkirchen. In Garmisch, the central Marienplatz is surrounded by a number of especially attractive buildings, including the Old Apothecary with its black and white scratchwork facade.

The summit of Germany's highest mountain, the **Zugspitze** ⓲ (2,962 metres/ 9,717 ft) can be reached either by taking the rack railway from Partenkirchen or the even faster cable car from nearby Eibsee. On a clear day, visitors are greeted by a spellbinding panoramic view extending from the Grossglockner to the ridge-line of the Bohemian Forest. The high corrie of the **Zugspitzplatt** to the southwest of *Schneefernerhaus* is the highest-altitude ski resort in the country. The summit can also, of course, be reached on foot, but for a more relaxing walk, visitors are recommended to take the track through the dramatic mountain gorge of **Partnachklamm**, which again penetrates the inner sanctums of the Wetterstein range.

Off the beaten track, a flight of steps on the western slopes of the **Wank** mountain leads to the late-baroque 18th-century votive Chapel of **St Anton** ⓳. The dome fresco by the Tyrolean painter Johannes Holzer is a masterpiece.

For an insight into the local history, folklore and crafts of the region, visit the Werdenfelser Heimatmuseum (Partenkirchen, Ludwigstrasse 47; open Tues–Fri 10am– 1pm, 2–6pm, Sat–Sun 10am–1pm).

LEFT: the mountains from below at Riesersee. **BELOW:** the summit of the Zugspitze is Germany's highest.

Along the Kesselberg Road

To the north of Mittenwald, an attractive excursion follows the B11, the line of the old Kesselbergstrasse, which even in medieval times was used by merchants from Venice to transport their goods to the north. Heading back through Wallgau, you soon arrive at the **Walchensee** , the highest mountain lake in Germany (802 metres/2,630 ft). In clear weather, the Herzogstand (1,730 metres/5,680 ft; accessible by cable-car) offers superb views of the high Bavarian Alps as well as numerous ranges in Austria, including the Grossglockner. After Urfeld, the road rises to a pass before descending in a series of hairpin bends to the **Kochelsee** ㉑. Shortly before the end of the mountain route, a sign indicates the cul-de-sac road to the **Power Station** (tours available), which since 1924 has utilised the water piped down from Walchensee above.

The painter **Franz Marc**, an important representative of German Expressionism, lived in **Kochel**, where a newly extended **museum** in Herzogstandweg now commemorates his work (open Tues–Sun and holidays, Apr–Oct 10am–6pm, Nov–Mar 10am–5pm).

In **Murnau** ㉒ on the **Staffelsee Lake**, the "Russian House", where the painters Gabriele Münter and Vasili Kandinsky lived from 1909–14, will also be of interest to art lovers (open Tues–Sun 2–5pm). The **Schlossmuseum** (castle museum) also has exhibits relating to the Blauer Reiter group of artists, Austrian writer Ödön von Horváth (1901–38), and life in the Murnau Moors (open Tues–Sun 10am–5pm).

Benediktbeuern ㉓, dating back to the 17th century, was formerly a powerful Benedictine monastery. It has recently been restored to its former glory by the Salesian Don Bosco order. The **Anastasia Chapel** (1751–53) by Johann Michael Fischer is a rococo masterpiece.

Opened in 1924, the power station at Kochelsee, utilising the 200-metre (656-ft) drop between Walchensee and Kochelsee, was the brainchild of Oskar von Miller, founder of the Deutsches Museum in Munich.

BELOW: the Passion Plays at Oberammergau are staged once every 10 years.

After joining the B2 back towards Garmisch, turn right in Oberau to arrive at **Kloster Ettal ㉔**, a baroque Benedictine abbey. The dome fresco depicts 431 figures on a total painted area of 1,300 sq. metres (3,993 sq. ft).

The Passion Plays of **Oberammergau ㉕** have brought fame to this little town. After an epidemic of the plague in 1633, to which one in every 10 inhabitants succumbed, the survivors vowed to perform Christ's Passion every 10 years thereafter as thanksgiving for their deliverance. The first performance was staged in 1634; the year 2000 celebrated the 40th season. A commercial enterprise operated according to stringent rules under the supervision of the parish council has also been set up. The auditorium of the Passion Play theatre has a seating capacity of 4,800 and overlooks the world's largest open-air stage.

Oberammergau is also famous for the fine frescoes on the facades of its typical Upper Bavarian houses, which is not surprising when one considers that Franz Zwinck, the "inventor" of the Italian-influenced fresco technique known as *Lüftlmalerei*, lived and worked in the town during the 18th century.

The King's castles and the Allgäu

Not far away, in the secluded Graswang valley, is one of Ludwig II's three famous castles, **Linderhof ㉖** (open daily Apr–Sept 9am–6pm, Oct–Mar 10am–4pm). Designed by Georg Dollmann, the castle embodies stylistic elements from the baroque and rococo although it was built between 1870 and 1879. Its 10 rooms are adorned with almost stifling pomp. In the dining room, the table was designed as a "Magic Table" straight from *Grimms' Fairy Tales*, and appears through a trap door in the floor. There are also artificial caves in the park, a Moorish Pavilion and the *Hundinghaus*, a type of hunting lodge which Ludwig mod-

Map on pages 188–89

Religious motifs adorn many of the houses in Oberammergau and other Upper Bavarian villages.

BELOW: Ludwig II's Linderhof Palace.

Map on pages 188–89

The Neuschwanstein Musical Theater was built near Füssen to stage a musical about the Fairytale King.

BELOW:
stucco work on a Landsberg facade

elled on the stage set of Wagner's opera, the *Valkyrie*. The gardens are beautiful. French formality near the castle gives way to an Italian-style, terraced garden, and this in turn merges with an English-style landscaped garden.

Hohenschwangau Castle ㉗ near Füssen (open daily April–Sept 9am–6pm, Oct–Mar 10am–4pm) was originally a medieval castle, which Crown Prince Maximilian of Bavaria had had restored in neo-Gothic style in 1833. King Ludwig II spent much of his youth here. Inside it preserves relics from the past, ranging from cannonballs to one of composer Richard Wagner's pianos.

To realise his dream world, Ludwig chose a secluded eyrie high above the Pöllat Gorge at the other side of the valley. **Neuschwanstein Castle ㉘** (open daily Apr–Sept 9am–6pm, Oct–Mar 10am–4pm) was a total anachronism even at the time it was built (1869–86). Only inhabited for a matter of days, its sole *raison d'être* during its existence was that of a glorified stage set. In the **Sängersaal** ("Minstrels' Hall") that forms the centrepiece of the fairytale castle, Ludwig II staged performances of scenes from the opera *Tannhäuser*.

From Neuschwanstein, a wide view opens out over the Forggensee, the Allgäu Alps and **Füssen ㉙**, above which rises the 16th-century **Hohes Schloss**, a former summer residence of the Bishops of Augsburg. Füssen is a popular resort and an ideal base for excursions into the Allgäu Alps: to the delightful settlement of **Hindelang ㉚**, for example, with its impressive mountain backdrop, or further, via Sonthofen, to the **Breitnachklamm Gorge**.

Rococo masterpiece

As well as claiming to be the oldest city in Germany (founded by the Romans in AD 18), **Kempten ㉛**, 30 km (18 miles) northwest of Füssen, has a number of noteworthy sights, including the Residenz, the Church of St Lorenz and the late-Gothic Town Hall.

North of Füssen, at **Steingaden ㉜**, is the Romanesque **Steingaden Monastery**, where the master architect of the famous School of Wessobrunn, Dominikus Zimmermann (1685–1766) is buried. In the church at nearby **Wies ㉝**, he was able to realise his plans for a synthesis of rococo artistic forms, embodying perfect harmony between architecture and decoration. In 1745, he was commissioned by the Steingaden monastery to plan a pilgrimage church to accommodate a statue of the *Flagellation of Christ*, on whose face a farmer's wife had discovered tears in 1739. From this date onwards, the chapel was the destination for countless pilgrims. The magnificent ceiling painting, which creates the illusion of vaulting on a flat surface, is by Johann Baptist Zimmermann.

Further north still, **Landsberg ㉞** grew rich on revenue from bridge tolls and the salt trade, subsequently investing its wealth in the obsessive decoration characteristic of the rococo. Dominikus Zimmermann planned the Rathaus (Town Hall) in the main square and worked on the Dominican Church and St John's Church, encouraging other rococo artists to visit. A further point of historical interest is that, after his failed putsch in Munich in 1923, Adolf Hitler was imprisoned in the jail in Landsberg, where he also wrote *Mein Kampf*. ❏

The Fairytale King

After his first meeting with Ludwig II, who was just 18 years old when he came to the throne in 1864, Richard Wagner wrote: "He is unfortunately so handsome and sophisticated, so soulful and sincere that I am afraid his life will just fade away like some divine dream". The young Bavarian king greatly admired Wagner and one of his first official acts was to summon the composer to Munich and settle his debts.

Ludwig was appreciative of the fine arts, and he loved music and the theatre. Tall, handsome and with a bearing which commanded respect, he was in his youth the very picture of a fairytale prince. For the first year after his coronation he eagerly involved himself with ruling his kingdom. But it was a job for which he was neither suited nor equipped: he had little idea of how to respond to his subjects' affections and he preferred to leave the affairs of state to his ministers.

By Ludwig's day, the decline of the monarchy had long since set in. Bavaria already had a parliament and the business of government lay in the hands of professional politicians. The Industrial Revolution was rapidly changing the face of the country and the small degree of sovereignty that Ludwig had was further reduced by the founding of the German Reich in 1871. For Ludwig, there was only one way to go in order to secure for himself some kind of immortality. Revolted by the real world, disappointed by people and tormented by a homophile disposition he could not suppress, he fled into a world of dreams and aesthetic illusion. Convinced that he was the successor and equal to the Sun King, Louis XIV of France, he designed Herrenchiemsee as a replica of Versailles.

His favourite residences were Berg Castle and Hohenschwangau, both of which he had inherited from his father. From these retreats, he organised the building of Linderhof and Neuschwanstein, the latter his romanticised version of the medieval world. None of Ludwig's creations had any function; they were just petrified realisations of his dreams.

Initially Ludwig's castle mania was harmless enough because he funded it from his own pocket. But when his projects started to place heavy burdens on the state coffers, ministers became concerned. In 1886, the government had the King declared insane by four psychiatrists who had never even seen him. Ludwig was deposed and forcibly taken to Berg Castle on Lake Starnberg. And there, on the evening of 13 June 1886, he and his physician were found drowned in the lake.

The exact circumstances of the tragedy have never been entirely clarified. The official version, that the King committed suicide and dragged his doctor down with him, has been the subject of much dispute. Many maintain that he was murdered. Whatever happened, Ludwig is revered by many Bavarians to this day. And millions of visitors annually come to his castles, to wander through the state rooms and marvel at the work of this unhappy king, who while hiding himself away from the world created the last great monument to the myth of royalty as embodied in age-old legends and fairytales. ❑

RIGHT: Ludwig II, portrayed as the very picture of a fairytale king.

MOUNTAINS, LAKES AND BIG SKIES

Bavaria is much more than a playground for climbers and hikers. The magnificent scenery provides recreational pursuits for all seasons

With its dramatic mountain scenery and gentle hills, bubbling streams, meandering rivers and glorious lakes, it is no surprise that Bavaria is the most popular holiday destination in Germany. Tourists and locals alike are drawn by the region's magic.

Skiing is the number one winter pastime and local children begin learning it as soon as they can walk. Only an hour's drive from Munich, the alpine ski resorts of Reit im Winkel, Spitzingsee, Garmisch and, further to the west, the Allgäu, offer pistes of all grades of difficulty. Cross-country ski tracks that are almost guaranteed snow in winter snake along the foot of the Alps or through the Bavarian Forest. Among the most attractive cross-country skiing areas are the Ramsau Valley near Berchtesgaden *(above)* as well as the Jachenau and the Ammertal near Linderhof Palace.

CYCLIST'S DELIGHT

In the summer, hiking, of course, is very popular, but so too is cycling. Road bikes and mountain bikes, together with biking maps, can be hired from tourist offices and private firms in the most popular areas – and not just in the mountains. In Franconia, pedal your way along the River Main and explore the wine country; discover the Middle Ages along the Romantic Road to the south of Würzburg; or cycle among the meadows by the Isar and Danube in eastern Bavaria. It's even possible to go "cycling without luggage" *(Radeln ohne Gepäck)* between Starnberg and Füssen – you enjoy the landscape with its castles and beer gardens while a bus transports all your luggage.

▷ **ABOVE THE CLOUDS**
Parasailers and hang-gliders have taken over the sprawling tops of the Bavarian Forest, as well as many lesser Alpine summits.

△ **GO WITH THE FLOW**
Slowly canoeing along the Altmühl, the Danube or other rivers north of the Alps is the ideal way to enjoy nature at close quarters.

▽ **COOL'S THE RULE**
For the young in particular, snowboarding is the trendy thing to do. If you don't want to make a fool of yourself, however, make sure you have the right technique when negotiating the halfpipe.

△ **ON TOP OF THE WORLD**
Skiers can always take a break in the warm spring sunshine and enjoy the view, like here at the Fellhorn in the Allgäu.

A HIKER'S PARADISE

People used to say that you shouldn't go off hiking in the Alps before Whitsuntide. These days, improvements in equipment enable the hiking aficionado to venture off before the snow has even begun to melt, and the number of winter hikers is growing.

Summer or winter, there is a huge choice of detailed hiking maps and books available from specialist outlets and tourist offices. While "wild" camping is not allowed in the Alps, mountain huts, run either privately or by the German Alpine Club (Deutscher Alpenverein) allow you to plan extended hikes, for example in the Karwendel range. Other popular routes include the challenging 60-km (40-mile) "Allgäu high-level" route between Oberstdorf and the Oberjoch. Less tiring is the Prälatenweg between Marktoberdorf and Kochel. Whichever route you choose, book your huts well in advance.

◁ **WHITE WATER**
The Alpine rivers present a wide variety of challenges to kayakers. The best stretches are on the Loisach, Inn and Salzach.

▽ **TAKING THE PLUNGE**
Lake Starnberg and other Upper Bavarian lakes are ideal for all kinds of watersports, from swimming to surfing and sailing.

▽ **ON LINE**
The fast-flowing rivers of the Alpine foothills are rich in trout, while the lakes further north attract anglers for their carp and other species.

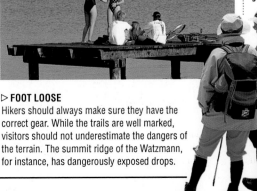

▷ **FOOT LOOSE**
Hikers should always make sure they have the correct gear. While the trails are well marked, visitors should not underestimate the dangers of the terrain. The summit ridge of the Watzmann, for instance, has dangerously exposed drops.

EASTERN BAVARIA

*As well as the historic towns of Regensburg, Passau and Landshut,
Eastern Bavaria has vast expanses of rolling countryside and
the Bavarian Forest runs along the Czech border*

Map on page 202

Heading north from Munich, bypass the town of Freising *(see page 185)* on the B11 and head northeast for another 30 km (19 miles) to arrive in the old ducal city of **Landshut** ❶ (pop. 58,000). Situated on the River Isar, Landshut is well worth seeing on account of its beautifully preserved old town and the bustle of its streets, which have retained the same essential character as they had back in 1475. That was the year in which the Archbishop of Salzburg officiated at the marriage of Princess Jadwiga of Poland to George, the son of Duke Ludwig the Rich, in St Martin's Minster. The ducal event is celebrated to this day: the *Landshuter Hochzeit* (Landshut Wedding) is Germany's most famous historical pageant and is performed every four years (2009, 2013). Apart from its role in the wedding, the minster is famous for its tower – it is the tallest brick church tower in the world at 131 metres (430 ft).

Landshut is dominated by **Burg Trausnitz** (Trausnitz Castle), an occasional residence of the Wittelsbach dukes since its foundation in 1204. It was expanded and reworked over the years, including some Renaissance additions in the 16th century. You can still see St George's Chapel and the Narrentreppe ("Fools' Staircase"), frescoed in 1578 with huge *Commedia dell'Arte* figures. In addition to the shady gardens there is a large café terrace offering excellent views over the city.

LEFT: full of myth and legend: the Bavarian Forest.
BELOW: brown bears near Grafenau.

From the Isar to the Danube

Neustadt is 45 km (28 miles) along the B299 from Landshut, and from here it is only another 18 km (11 miles) along the Danube to **Kelheim** ❷, a town at the confluence of the Danube and the Rhine-Main-Danube Canal. The monument perched high above the river is the Befreiungshalle (Liberation Hall), which was built by Ludwig I to commemorate the wars of liberation from Napoleon (1813–15). One of the biggest attractions in the town itself is the **Archaeological Museum** (open Apr–Oct Tues–Sun 10am–5pm). Some of its most important exhibits were uncovered during the building of the Rhine-Main-Danube Canal in the 1980s, when scientists discovered that the area around Kelheim was settled during the Neanderthal age about 80,000 years ago.

From Kelheim, you can stroll along the right bank of the Danube past the deepest and narrowest stretch of the river, the **Donaudurchbruch** (Danube Gap), and on to the famous **Kloster Weltenburg** ❸. Built in 1715–34, the monastery church is a south German baroque masterpiece of the Asam brothers. Most visitors, however, take the boat (every 45 minutes). The trip along this stretch, where the river cuts through the Jurassic limestone, is one of the highlights of a tour through Eastern Bavaria.

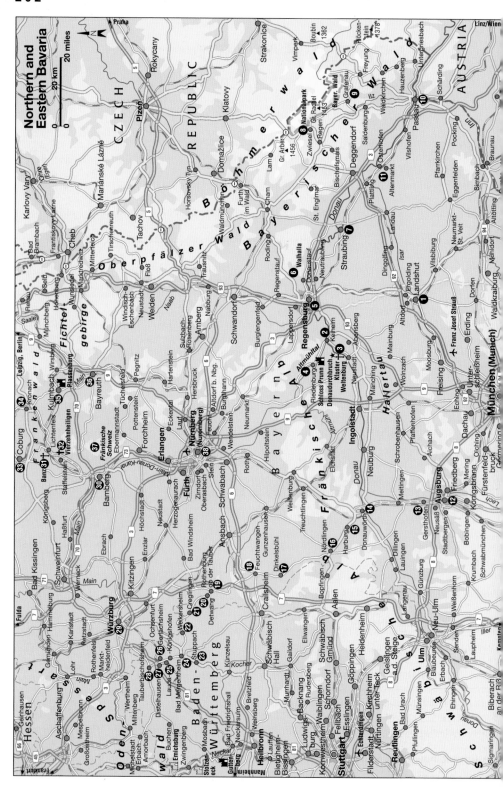

Northern and
Eastern Bavaria

N

20 miles

20 km

0

CZECH REPUBLIC

AUSTRIA

München (Munich)

It is also possible to make a detour along the **Altmühltal ❹**, still a very pleasant valley even since the completion of the Rhine-Main-Danube Canal. In Essing the Danube is spanned by the longest wooden bridge in Europe. A further highlight, 8 km (5 miles) upstream, is **Schloss Prunn** (open Apr–Oct daily 9am–6pm, Nov–March Tues–Sun 10am–4pm), perched on a high cliff 100 metres (330 ft) above the canal near Riedenburg. With its sturdy keep, it is said to be a perfect example of a medieval knights' castle. One of the original manuscripts of the *Nibelungenlied* was discovered here in 1575.

Map on page 202

A cross-section through time

After a 15-km (9-mile) drive along the B16, the 2,000-year-old city of **Regensburg ❺** (pop. 130,000), founded as *Castra Regina* by the Emperor Marcus Aurelius in AD 179, comes into view. The Anglo-Saxon Irish missionary St Boniface made the city a bishopric in 739. Five hundred years later, in 1245, it became a free imperial city and developed into an important medieval centre and a hub of European commerce. It was the regular seat of the Reichstag from 1663 until the disintegration of the old empire in 1806.

The Danube valley at Regensburg was inhabited long before the arrival of the Romans. A Celtic settlement on the same spot where the Romans founded their city was called Radabona.

Regensburg lies at the northernmost point of the Danube, which is navigable as far as the Black Sea. World War II left the city largely undamaged. A fine view can be enjoyed from the 12th-century **Steinerne Brücke** (Stone Bridge), a masterpiece of medieval engineering, 310 metres (1,017 ft) in length. The river is lined by stately mansions, over whose roofs tower the 105-metre (345-ft) spires of **St Peter's Cathedral**, the most impressive gothic structure in Bavaria (1250–1525). Its treasury contains exquisite reliquaries, crosses, chalices and vestments. The cathedral is also home of the famous boys' choir, the Domspatzen ("Cathedral Sparrows").

BELOW: painting in Regensburg.

Near the Cathedral is the *porta praetoria,* the northern gate of the former Roman citadel. Pass the bishop's palace and then turn right at the Niedermünster church where there are some interesting Roman excavations. Beyond lies the picturesque Alter Kornmarkt (Old Corn Market) and the **Herzogshof** (Ducal Palace), the residence of the Bavarian dukes from AD 988. The Ducal Hall has a magnificent ceiling.

The Gothic hall in the **Old Town Hall** (1350) was once the meeting place for the Reichstag. Down in the cellars of the Reichstagmuseum is a grisly medieval torture chamber. German law in those days specified that if an accused criminal survived three days of torture without confessing he could go free, even if he had been convicted by a court. Bachgasse leads to **St Emmeran's church**, once part of a Benedictine monastery founded in the 8th century, and the adjacent palace of the Princes of Thurn and Taxis.

A culinary note: Regensburg is noted for *wels*, a fleshy Danube fish, and fried sausages. Try them at the riverside **Wurstküche** near the Stone Bridge.

The Bavarian Forest

On the river bank, 11 km (7 miles) east of Regensburg, just outside Donaustauf, stands the Bavarian **Walhalla ❻**, a copy of the Parthenon temple on the Acropolis in Athens. It was designed by royal architect Leo von Klenze and built between 1830 and 1842 for King Ludwig I as a hall of fame for illustrious figures from the German-speaking world.

South of the Danube, the landscape flattens out into the Gäuboden plain, Bavaria's grain belt. In August, there's an annual Gäuboden Festival in **Straubing ❼** that attracts more than one million visitors, making it Bavaria's biggest folk festival after Munich's Oktoberfest.

TIP

If you're in Grafenau on the first weekend in August don't miss the "Salzsäumerfest", when the locals celebrate the town's salt-trading past.

Away to the north of the Danube, the landscape looks very different: the upland, heavily wooded **Bavarian Forest** extends as far as the Czech border, where it joins the Bohemian Forest to form the largest uninterrupted stretch of forest in central Europe. This is a great place to come for those wishing to get away from it all and enjoy the wide open spaces. The area has some moderately high peaks, including the Lusen (1,375 metres/4,510 ft), Dreisessel (1,330 metres/4,360 ft), Rachel (1,450 metres/4,755 ft) and the Grosser Arber (1,455 metres/4,770 ft), with its idyllic lake. The mountains are criss-crossed with trails and paths for hikers, and in the winter they are popular skiing venues. Numerous resorts offer comfortable accommodation, sporting and recreational facilities and the Czech Republic is never very far away.

The small town of **Zwiesel ❽**, reached from the A3 *autobahn* via Deggendorf and Regen, is a centre of the region's famous glass-making industry *(see below)*. A popular driving route heads south from Zwiesel through beautiful meadow and forest scenery to **Grafenau ❾**, the gateway to the **Bavarian Forest National Park**. The National Park Information Centre in nearby **Neuschönau** (open daily 9am–5pm) has fascinating exhibits and displays on all aspects of forest life. But the biggest attraction for visitors here is the **Tierfreigelände** (Animal Park) where, over an area of 200 hectares (500 acres), the primeval animals

BELOW: glassblower at work.

GLASSMAKING

The Bavarian Forest, together with the neighbouring Bohemian Forest, has long been a centre of fine glass production. Established from the 14th century onwards on the ready availability of the raw materials silicon and wood, workshops developed to specialise in products ranging from mirror glass and lenses to goblets, vases and other decorative household items. The strenuous skill of glassblowing in particular has occupied generations of families. For centuries, the finest glass in Europe came from Venice but then, in the 17th century, Bohemian artisans invented crystal glass. Often decorated with gold or tin, it conquered the world market.

Running for 250 km (150 miles) between Neustadt/Waldnaab and Passau, the Glasstrasse introduces visitors to world-famous factories like Schott (Zwiesel) or Joska (Bodenmais); to tiny designer workshops and their showrooms; and to museums. The Glasmuseum in Frauenau or the Museum Susice (Schütthofen) just across the Czech border boast an incredible variety of crystal and coloured glass, of unique snuff boxes and other decorative items from six centuries of glass production, including some very rare snuff boxes. The 100-plus workshops in the area offer top quality at reasonable prices.

Map on page 202

of the forest – such as wolves, lynx, otters and bison – roam in relative freedom. Neuschönau is also the starting point of numerous forest trails.

City on three rivers

The geographer and writer Alexander von Humboldt included **Passau ⑩** (pop. 51,000) on his list of "the world's seven most beautifully situated cities". Passau's location at the confluence of three rivers, the Danube, the Inn and the Ilz, is indeed spectacular, with the old town huddling on one narrow stretch of land between Danube and Inn.

The old streets and the riverside atmosphere give the town an almost Venetian feel and there is enough to keep the visitor happy for hours. Alongside its 600-year-old Apothecary, Residenzplatz is the site of the old and new Bishops' Palaces, as well as a number of fine houses rebuilt in the 17th century in the local baroque style. Nearby Domplatz (Cathedral Square) is dominated by **St Stephen's Cathedral**, which was founded in the 8th century, expanded in baroque style in the 17th century, subsequently destroyed but then rebuilt anew. Between May and September almost all visitors to Passau assemble here at noon to listen to the music resounding from the 17,300 pipes of the world's largest church organ.

Staying with the church theme, there is one final gem well worth seeing before leaving Eastern Bavaria. In **Altenmarkt ⑪**, close to the small farming community of **Osterhofen**, 35 km (20 miles) northwest of Passau on the B8, stands the **Church of St Margarethe** (follow the signs to "Asamkirche"). With its perfectly harmonised baroque gilding, stucco and frescoes, it is regarded as one of the Asam brothers' greatest masterpieces. ❏

Exposed to repeated flooding, many of the ground floors of Passau's old town houses are uninhabited. Inside there are high steps leading up to the first floor.

BELOW: Passau, the city on three rivers.

THE ROMANTIC ROAD

Idyllic medieval towns separated by wide open stretches of glorious countryside, the jewels of the Romantic Road are strung together like the pearls of an exquisite necklace

Map on page 202

The Romantische Strasse (Romantic Road) runs between Füssen in the Allgäu and the city of Würzburg. To travel along its entire length is to experience the panoply of a historical drama playing from Roman times right up to the present day. This section starts in Augsburg, which was founded by the Romans, and follows the B25 to Rothenburg before continuing along the Tauber Valley. The townscapes of Nördlingen, Dinkelsbühl and Rothenburg are a reflection of 16th- and 17th-century history and old German imperial glory. But it wasn't just emperors, kings and nobles who played a role here: the burghers and peasants also played their part, as did numerous wars and sieges.

Augsburg and the Fuggers

First-time visitors to **Augsburg** ⑫ are usually surprised at the wealth of artistic treasures in a city of only 265,000 inhabitants. But Augsburg looks back on more than 2,000 years of history rich in tradition: in 15 BC a Roman military camp was established and soon developed under the name of *Augusta Vindelicorum* into an influential town. The medieval trading city of the 11th century grew to a commercial centre and episcopal seat situated at the crossroads of the important routes linking Italy and the centre of Franconian-Carolingian power. By about 1500, Augsburg was among the largest cities in the German-speaking world. Emperor Maximilian I and Charles V raised money from the Fuggers, one of the wealthiest families in Europe, in exchange for trading and mining rights.

This wealthy banking and merchant family was responsible for an extraordinary social housing settlement, located in the old Jakobervorstadt artisan quarter, the **Fuggerei**, which dates from 1516. In accordance with the testament of its founder, Jakob Fugger, poor Catholic senior citizens can rent a small home here for a peppercorn rent (€0.88) per year. The **Fuggerei Museum** is located at Mittlere Gasse 13 (open daily Apr–Oct 8am–8pm, Nov–Mar 9am–6pm).

Ten minutes' walk west of the Fuggerei is the centre of the old city axis (Maximilianstrasse–Karolinenstrasse–Hoher Weg), with the imposing **Rathaus** (City Hall) and neighbouring **Perlachturm** (Perlach Tower), offering great views over the city. Designed by Elias Holl, the Renaissance City Hall (1615–20), with its onion-domed towers and a magnificent **Goldener Saal** (Golden Hall; open daily 10am–5.30pm), was intended to symbolise bourgeois wealth. The same purpose was assigned to the fountains that mark the route of broad Maximilianstrasse. Passing the **Moritzkirche** (Church of St Maurice), the visitor arrives at the former financial centre of the Western world, the 16th-century **Fuggerhaus** (Maximilianstrasse 36/38).

LEFT: sword dance in Dinkelsbühl.
BELOW: Jacob Fugger in his Augsburg office.

Further up the street at number 46 is the fine **Schaezlerpalais**, an ideal home for the Deutsche Barockgalerie (open Tues 10am–8pm, Wed–Sun 10am–5pm), which includes work by German masters of the 16th–18th century.

At the head of the street stands the **Minster of St Ulrich and St Afra**, a late-Gothic basilica with an interior decorated by Renaissance masters. From here, it's worth the walk to the old city walls at the **Rotes Tor** (Red Gate), where outdoor opera and operetta productions are staged in summer, and then along the streams back to the city centre, past the ancient homes of tanners and smiths. On the way, you can call in at the **Schwäbisches Handwerkermuseum** (Crafts Museum; open Mon–Fri 1–5pm, Mon–Tues also 9am–noon, Sun 10am–5pm) in the former Heilig-Geist-Spital, or visit the interesting **Römisches Museum** (open Tues 10am–8pm, Wed–Sun 10am–5pm) in a former baroque church.

The earliest signs of settlement in Augsburg are to be found in the area of the **Dom** (Cathedral). The Romanesque-Gothic cathedral is the home of precious works of art, including valuable altar pictures and the oldest known glass windows in Germany (dating from around 1130). The beautiful windows, showing the prophets Jonas, Daniel and Hosea as well as Moses and King David, are in the southern section of the central aisle. The south portal has magnificent 11th-century bronze doors, replete with Biblical motifs. On the section of so-called Roman wall south of the cathedral is a plaque commemorating the 1555 *Augsburger Religionsfrieden* (Peace of Augsburg), which brought the religious wars sparked by the Reformation to a temporary end.

The skills of the town's artists are displayed in other Augsburg churches, including the **Annakapelle** with its Fugger tombs. Further local creative genius is documented at the birthplace of dramatist Bertholt Brecht (1898–1956) at

Contemporary art fascinates in the H2 museum in the Glaspalast, one of Augsburg's former textile factories (Amagasakiallee; open Tues 10am–8pm, Wed–Sun 10am–5pm). While in a former spinning mill, the Augsburger Kammgarnspinnerei, a new textile museum, will open in 2009.

BELOW: the Golden Hall, Augsburg Town Hall.

Map on page 202

Auf dem Rain 7 (open Tues–Sun 10am–5pm); and the home of Mozart's father Leopold (Frauentorstrasse 30). At the MAN vehicle factory, there is another museum dedicated to Rudolf Diesel, inventor of the eponymous engine.

The little town of **Gersthofen** ⑬ just outside Augsburg is a centre for hot-air ballooning. It was from here in 1786 that the first German balloon journey was undertaken – a feat celebrated in Gersthofen's **Balloon Museum** in the old water-tower (open Wed and Fri 1–5pm, Thur 10am–7pm, Sat–Sun and holidays 10am–5pm).

The Wörnitz, the river that follows much of this itinerary, flows into the Danube. Shortly before it does so it embraces a small island known as Werth. In the shadow of the Schwäbische Alb uplands, the trading and free imperial city of **Donauwörth** ⑭ emerged during the Middle Ages from the island's fishing community. The city's principal sights lie along its main trading route, today's Reichstrasse: the **Fuggerhaus** (1536) on the west side; the 13th- to 18th-century **Rathaus** (Town Hall) on the east; and between them the parish church with the heaviest bell in all of Swabia, the 6.5-ton *Pummerin*. The **Käthe-Kruse-Puppenmuseum** (Doll Museum; open Apr and Oct Tues–Sun 2–5pm, May–Sept 11am–5pm, Nov–Mar Wed, Sat–Sun and holidays 2–5pm) has more than 200 dolls and figurines, carousels, dolls' houses and miniature theatre stages.

Just a few miles further north, the **Harburg** ⑮ is one of Germany's largest castles (12th–18th century). The fortress above the Wörnitz Valley watched for centuries over the important trade route between Augsburg and Nuremberg.

Käthe Kruse dolls, first manufactured in 1910 and now produced near Donauwörth, are still very popular with children.

BELOW: kids in Nördlingen.

A crater for astronauts

First recorded as *Nordlinga* in 898, **Nördlingen** ⑯ became a free imperial town in 1215 and flourished as a trading centre, its Whitsun fair drawing tradespeople from all over Europe. The city's 3.5-km (2-mile) long fortifying wall took shape between the 14th and 17th centuries, and a walk along it gives the visitor a view of ancient tanners' homes with their drying lofts and dwellings ranging from almshouses to patrician Renaissance mansions. The Rathaus (Town Hall) and Tanzhaus were also designed in noble, imposing style.

The **Stadtmuseum** in the former Heilig-Geist-Spital (infirmary) documents local and regional history, including the battle of Nördlingen (1634) when, during the Thirty Years' War, the imperial army finally defeated the Swedish forces (City Museum; open Mar–Oct Tues–Sun 1.30–4.30pm).

From the 90-metre (295-ft) tower of the late-Gothic St George's church, fondly known as the **Daniel**, there's a panoramic view of the 99 villages of the **Rieskrater**. This crater around Nördlingen was formed 15 million years ago when a giant meteorite struck the earth's surface at a speed of around 70,000 km (40,000 miles) an hour. The impact discharged enormous amounts of rock and earth, which came down in a wall-like formation about 13 km (8 miles) in diameter. In 1970, NASA sent its Apollo 14 astronauts to train in the Ries because its geology is so similar to the moon's. The modern **Rieskrater-museum** (open Tues–Sun 10am–4.30pm) has a fascinating multimedia show that explains the very specific geological history of the crater.

Romantic Dinkelsbühl and Rothenburg

A fine view of **Dinkelsbühl** ⓲ is to be enjoyed from the banks of the Wörnitz. The architecture and layout of the town indicate a close relationship between the rulers and the ruled. The houses here are small and the streets narrow, with a good deal of space given over to vegetable plots and orchards. Beyond the remains of the old moat there are fish ponds and fields. A statue of the Dinkel-bauer (*Dinkel* farmer) in the park recalls the cultivation of *dinkel*, or spelt, an early form of wheat, which was once cultivated widely in the Tauber Valley and is enjoying new popularity among ecologically-minded farmers.

Dinkelsbühl can only be entered through one of its four main gates; the steeple of the parish church of St George points the way to the centre. The market square was for centuries the traditional trading centre, while horse-drawn carts were parked on the nearby Weinmarkt (wine market). Half-timbered **Deutsches Haus** (German House; now a fine hotel and restaurant) and the Schranne, the town's former granary, are two particularly fine buildings. Every year in July the historical play known as the **Kinderzeche** and a colourful parade commemorate the Thirty Years' War (1618–48), when Dinkelsbühl was under siege by Swedish forces (*see box below*).

Back on the Romantic Road (the B25), **Feuchtwangen** ⓳ is the next stop. In summer the Romanesque cloisters of the Stiftskirche, the collegiate church, serve as a stage for excellent open-air theatre. The church's altar is the work of Michael Wolgemut, Albrecht Dürer's teacher. The Romanesque Church of St John, the 16th-century **Zehentstadel** (tithe barn) and the **Fränkische Museum** with its beautiful furniture and porcelain (open May–Sept Wed–Sun 11am–5pm, Mar, Apr and Oct–Dec 2–5pm), all grouped around the market square, are also worth visiting.

BELOW: keeping in step with the Dinkelsbühl tradition.

DINKELSBÜHL'S KINDERZECHE

In 1632, when the Thirty Years' War was raging and the situation seemed hopeless, the watchman's daughter, Lore and other children of Dinkelsbühl appealed to the Swedish commander to spare the town – a famous and dramatic story re-enacted each year by local inhabitants, yet one of pure myth. The name of the colourful costume festival actually derives from the springtime school holidays, when, in a tradition dating back to the 16th century, Latin teachers and pupils were allowed to run up a bill (*Zeche*) in local pubs which would then be settled by the town council.

Over the centuries the children developed the custom of musical parades in historical costume. When, by the end of the 19th century, Romanticism was booming, Dinkelsbühl desperately needed a historical play to compete with Rothenburg. They could not have foreseen the success of their venture: Dinkelsbühl in July is just one big stage. More than 2,000 locals set about building Swedish camps, cook "medieval" style in front of the church and parade their superb horses. The high point is always the appearance of the "Young Commander" – once the best Latin pupil – in a red and white rococo uniform, and his speech praising the courage of the young children followed by a concert of the Dinkelsbühler Knabenkapelle (Youth Band).

Rothenburg ob der Tauber 🔟 has become the embodiment of Germany's romantic past. The number of visitors who descend on Rothenburg every year (1.3 million) speaks for itself. Yet an overnight stay in Rothenburg can be thoroughly recommended, coupled with an evening stroll through the quiet lanes, a meal of Franconian specialities in one of the atmospheric restaurants, such as the famous Baumeisterhaus (1596), and perhaps a visit to the Figurentheater (a puppet show at the Burgtor).

Rothenburg's streets converge like the spokes of a wheel from the city gates and walls to the central marketplace, with its **Rathaus** (Town Hall), a combination of Renaissance front and Gothic rear. From its 55-metre (180-ft) high tower the historic town centre and the course of the old defence wall can be made out. To the south it's marked by the Johanniskirche (St John's Church) and to the east by the archway of the **Markusturm** and the **Weisser Turm**.

The special status of early Rothenburg (a free imperial city as early as 1274) provided the town with the basis for its prosperity. Its citizens traded in wine, livestock and wool and very soon a new city wall had to be built. That second wall is very well preserved and the one-hour stroll along its walkway is well worth the effort. The walk could begin at the Klingenbastei bastion in the northern part of the wall, following a visit to the 14th–15th century **St-Jakobs-Kirche** (Church of St James). This houses a *Heilig-Blut-Altar* (Altar of the Holy Blood) containing a masterful representation of Christ's Passion, executed from 1501–5 by the great woodcarver and sculptor Tilman Riemenschneider *(see page 28)*. Follow the wall eastwards and then south and you come to the **Spitalbastion** (Infirmary Bastion). Returning towards the centre of town along Spitalgasse you'll find yourself in **Plönlein**, the prettiest part of Rothenburg and one much favoured by

Map on page 202

BELOW: the Plönlein in Rothenburg.

Mayor Nusch saved Rothenburg from the Swedes by downing this enormous tankard of wine.

photographers. The **Mittelalterliche Kriminalmuseum** (Museum of Medieval Crime; open daily Apr–Oct 9.30am–5.15pm, shorter hours in winter) next to the Johanniskirche has exhibits recalling the horrors of the Thirty Years' War, which did not spare Rothenburg. One of the central events of the war, a wager that saved the town from destruction in 1631, is marked by a scene on the astronomical clock which adorns the former Ratstrinkstube (town hall tavern), next to the town hall, and by regular theatrical performances. The fabled wager pitted an elder of the town, former Mayor Nusch, against an enormous *Humpen*, or tankard of wine. Tilly, commander of the besieging troops, offered to spare the town if anyone could down the 3.25 litres (7 pints) of wine in one go. Nusch accepted the challenge, accomplished the feat and saved the town.

Nusch's feat is not the only thing celebrated on stage: the Pfingstfestspiel (Whitsun Festival) and the Reichsstadtspiele in September include programmes of Hans Sachs plays featuring the wit, slyness and simplicity of the local peasants, and performances of the traditional *Schäfertänze* (Shepherd's Dances).

Woodcarvings and other works of art

Just to the north of Rothenburg is **Detwang** ㉒, where the church of St Peter and Paul contains the **Passionsaltar**, one of Tilman Riemenschneider's last works. What many regard to be Riemenschneider's greatest achievement can be admired in **Creglingen** ㉑, whose Herrgottskirche (Church of Our Lord) has been a pilgrimage church since the 14th century when a farmer is said to have ploughed up some eucharistic bread. In 1500 the princes of Hohenlohe had a church built on the site and Riemenschneider was commissioned to carve an altar dedicated to the Virgin. The **Fingerhutmuseum** (Thimble Museum) here contains some 2,000 examples of the seamstress' tool.

BELOW: detail of Riemenschneider's Altar of the Virgin Mary in Creglingen.

In **Weikersheim** ㉒, the seat of the princes of Hohenlohe, the former servants' quarters by the square mark the entrance to the **Schloss**, an archetypal courtly residence in miniature. The belfry dates from the 12th century, but its baroque cap was added in the 17th century. The coffered ceiling in the palace's south wing is a masterpiece of the period while the garden with its orangery and statues of scenes from ancient mythology is pure baroque.

It is worth making a detour to **Stuppach** ㉓ to see Matthias Grünewald's *Madonna* (1519). A priest named Blumhofer acquired the painting from the estate of the Order of Teutonic Knights in 1812 and until 1908 it was thought to be to Rubens. The complex symbolism and the brilliance of the paintwork are the main points of interest.

In 1826, a shepherd rediscovered the lost salt spring of **Bad Mergentheim** ㉔. A hotel was opened up a few years later when the water was found to be helpful in the treatment of kidney and bladder complaints and since then the town has never looked back. The settlement was founded by the Franks but the Order of Teutonic Knights first put Mergentheim on the map when they moved their headquarters here in 1525. With the help of generous donations from grand masters, kings and dukes, the 13th-century moated castle was lavishly converted into a palace for the knights in around 1600.

baroque church was completed in 1736. The palace now houses the **Deutschor-densmuseum** (Knights' Museum; open Apr–Oct Tues–Sun 10.30am–5pm, shorter hours in winter). The market place is surrounded by ornate half-timbered and plasterwork buildings. Near the 16th-century Town Hall, a statue of Wilhelm Schutzbar, also called Milchling, adorns the Milchlingbrunnen (fountain). He was the man responsible for bringing the knights' order to the town.

For centuries, **Lauda-Königshofen** ㉕ has been the hub of a wine-producing region. A 16th-century house at Rathausstrasse 25 used to belong to a grower and now houses a small wine museum and Heimatmuseum (Local History Museum; Apr–Oct Sun and holidays 3–5pm). The half-timbering and baroque ornamentation demonstrate clearly that Lauda's citizens have profited from the noble grape. **Gerlachsheim** ㉖ and **Distelhausen** ㉗ both have impressive baroque churches. Motorists will notice the occasional roadside shrine; these explain why the -locality is sometimes described as the "Land of God" or "Madonna country".

The highlight of the lower Tauber Valley is **Tauberbischofsheim** ㉘. Take a stroll from the bridge through the pedestrian zone. The house of the wine merchant Bögner, a baroque mansion dating from 1744, and a pharmacy form the gateway to the market square with its neo-Gothic Town Hall (1866). The baroque church on the south side of the square is dedicated to St Lioba. St Boniface founded a convent here around 725, hence the name of the town, which means "home of the bishop". Lioba, probably related to St Boniface, was the convent's first abbess. Both the wheel in the town's coat-of-arms and the **Castle** (14th–16th century) serve as reminders that the Mainz prince-bishops held sway here from the 13th–19th century. There is a fine view over the town and the Tauber Valley from the watchtower. ❑

Map on page 202

BELOW: the castle square in Tauberbischofsheim.

S. KILIANUS

FRANCONIA

*Although part of Bavaria, Franconia is a distinctive region.
In addition to its cities, numerous attractions are tucked away in its
lovely countryside, including some fine artistic treasures*

Map
on page
202

The journey through Franconia starts in the city of **Würzburg** (pop. 130,000). Established as a bishopric during the 8th century, the city's long history of rule by successive prince-bishops has dictated the majestic appearance it presents today. This is all the more remarkable because the city was practically annihilated by a massive Allied bombing raid just before the end of World War II, on 16 March 1945. During that fateful night the populace sought refuge in the old Marienberg Fortress. Towering over the city on the opposite side of the River Main (pronounced "mine"), it was a safe distance from all the destruction. This detachment had served the fortress well over the centuries: as the residence of the prince-bishops from the 13th century, the populace was also kept at arm's length.

The city experienced its heyday in the 18th century under the rule of the House of Schönborn, but it was a flourishing place long before that. In 1575, Prince-Bishop Julius Echter of Mespelbrunn founded the Juliusspital for the poor and, in 1582, the old university. It was here some 300 years later that Wilhelm Conrad Röntgen discovered the X-ray.

One of the statues on the old Main Bridge that links the city with the fortress is that of St Kilian, the patron saint of wine. Wine-making in Franconia goes back more than 1,200 years and Würzburg has always been the centre of its production and marketing. There are many places where one can sample the predominantly white wine from the distinctive *bocksbeutel* bottles, including the wine cellar of the above-mentioned Juliusspital in the Juliuspromenade, and the Bürgerspitalweinstuben in Theaterstrasse. October, the month of the wine harvest, is the best time to explore the villages of the Franconian wine district, most of which lie to the south of the city. Every weekend a wine festival is held in one of the villages – in Volkach, Frickenhausen and Eisenheim.

A magnificent residence

A good place to start a tour of the city is the **Residenz** (open daily Apr–Oct 9am–6pm, Nov–Mar 10am–5pm), built from 1720–44 by Balthasar Neumann and ranked as one of the finest baroque palaces in Europe. When Johann Philipp Franz of Schönborn became prince-bishop in 1719, he decided to move his residence from the Marienberg to the city in order to be more at the centre of things. He commissioned Neumann to build the "palace of all palaces" and Neumann duly obliged.

Neumann, the master builder of the German baroque, created his own memorial within the palace by designing what is undoubtedly one of the most beautiful staircases of the baroque-rococo era. The

LEFT: St Kilian
on the Old Main
Bridge.
BELOW: view across
the Main of
Würzburg's Festung
Marienberg.

Statuary in the Hofgarten.

stairwell extends right up the two-storey building and is crowned by a single concave vault 30 metres (100 ft) long by 18 metres (60 ft) wide. More renowned than the vault itself is the **ceiling fresco** painted by the Italian artist Giambattista Tiepolo, who was summoned to Würzburg in 1750 to create the largest painting in the world. Tiepolo depicted the Gods of Olympus and allegories of the four continents known at the time. The Tiepolo paintings in the Kaisersaal allude to the marriage between Emperor Frederick Barbarossa and Beatrix of Burgundy in 1156. Miraculously, the frescos survived the Allied bombing of 1945 unscathed. After a tour of the interior, take time to stroll in the **Hofgarten** behind the Residenz, with its fine wrought-iron gates and beautiful baroque group of figures.

From the Residenz follow Hofstrasse to Kiliansplatz and the Romanesque cathedral. Dedicated to St Kilian, the apostle of the Franks and the patron saint of the city who was murdered in AD 689, the cathedral had to be rebuilt after its destruction in 1945. The **Schönborn Chapel**, one of Balthasar Neumann's most important works, is built onto the cathedral transept and contains the shrine of the prince-bishops of Schönborn. St Kilian lies in the crypt of the adjacent **Neumünsterkirche** (New Cathedral). There is another significant grave behind the church in the peaceful **Lusam Garden**: that of the medieval poet and troubadour Walther von der Vogelweide. His surname means "bird meadow" and the lid of his tomb features four hollows which collect rainwater for the birds.

Kürschnerhof to the right leads through to the yellow **Falcon House**, whose stuccoed baroque facade is a precise reconstruction of the 1751 original. Ahead on Marktplatz is the 15th-century **Marienkapelle** (Chapel of the Virgin). Over its south door are copies of Tilman Riemenschneider's *Adam and Eve*, while the north door features an even more unusual work of art: faced with the challenge

of depicting the Immaculate Conception, the sculptor showed God impregnating the Virgin by means of a tube running into her ear.

Further towards the Main, the **Old Town Hall**, called Grafeneckart, has Romanesque origins. The building was acquired by the city in 1316 and extended many times. One of the additions is the imposing Renaissance tower, another the Roter Bau (Red House) erected in 1659. The nearby **Karmelitenkloster** (Carmelite Monastery) has been part of the town hall since the 19th century.

Cross the **Alte Mainbrücke** (Old Main Bridge), with its statue of St Kilian, and follow the steep path up to the **Festung Marienberg**. Founded in 1201, the massive rectangular fortress encloses a courtyard and the 13th-century keep as well as the Renaissance fountain and the Church of St Mary. Between 1253 and 1719, the prince-bishops used it as a stronghold to keep the ever more powerful townsfolk at bay. During the Peasants' Revolt of 1525, the lower classes attempted to take the fortress by burying explosives under its walls. After 1631, when the city was taken by Gustav Adolf of Sweden during the Thirty Years' War, the fortress was extended and began to take the form of the building seen today, with its baroque facades and the Fürstengarten (Princes' Garden).

One of the main attractions of the fortress is the **Mainfränkisches Museum** (open Tues–Sun Apr–Oct 10am–5pm, Nov–Mar 10am–4pm), whose exhibits include a remarkable collection of statuary by the woodcarver and sculptor Tilman Riemenschneider (1460–1531), who came to Würzburg from his home in the Harz Mountains in 1483 and rapidly rose to fame in Franconia. Such was his popularity that he was elected Würzburg's mayor in 1520. However, during the Peasants' Revolt he supported the peasants against the prince-bishop Konrad von Thingen. When they were ultimately defeated at the Marienberg

Map on page 202

TIP

Take a steamer along the Main to Veitshöchheim (7 km/ 4 miles), where you can visit the baroque palace with its rococo gardens, once the summer residence of the Würzburg bishops. The steamers leave Würzburg at the landing stage by the Alten Kranen. There are also romantic evening trips.

BELOW: you'll enjoy the local wine.

fortress, he was imprisoned and tortured. He died a broken man in 1531. On a hill to the south of the fortress is the **Käppele** (little chapel), which was designed by Balthasar Neumann as a pilgrimage church in 1748.

The puzzling statue

The journey continues towards the delightful medieval jewel of **Bamberg** ③⓪ (pop. 71,000), an old imperial and episcopal city first mentioned in AD 902. The **cathedral** contains the tomb of its founder Emperor Heinrich II, who elevated Bamberg to a bishopric in 1007, and of Pope Clement II, the only Papal tomb north of the Alps. It was consecrated in 1012, but it burned down twice and was finally rebuilt in 1237. Particularly impressive is the **Fürstenportal** (Prince's Door). The cathedral is the home of an unsolved riddle, namely the **Bamberger Reiter** (Bamberg Horseman), a medieval equestrian statue of unknown origin. Thought by some to represent the ideal of Christian knights in the Middle Ages, the unknown horseman and his mount occupy a niche at the rear of the cathedral. On the left of the cathedral, in the former chapter house erected by Balthasar Neumann in 1730, is the Diocesan Museum with its cathedral treasury of unique exhibits, including the cloak of Heinrich II.

A narrow street separates the cathedral from the **Alte Hofhaltung** (Old Residence). This magnificent Renaissance building, completed in 1569, was once the imperial and episcopal palace. It is now the **Historisches Museum** (Museum of Local History; open May–Oct Tues–Sun 9am–5pm).

Aufsessstrasse leads to the 290-metre (951-ft) heights of the Michaelsberg, surmounted by the **Church of St Michael**, part of a former Benedictine Abbey founded by Heinrich II in 1015. The famous facade above the broad stair-

In 1993 Bamberg's well-preserved medieval city centre was nominated by UNESCO as a World Heritage Site.

BELOW: Bamberg's old Town Hall on the River Regnitz.

case leading up to the entrance (1677) is the work of the renowned Dientzenhofer brothers. Suttestrasse, or Maternstrasse, leads up to the 12th-century -
Karmelitenkloster (Carmelite Monastery), whose Romanesque cloisters are
the largest in Germany.

The **Old Town Hall** stands picturesquely on an island in the River Pegnitz,
linked to the banks by a bridge. It also houses the **Sammlung Ludwig** collection of baroque porcelain and glazed earthenware. There is also an excellent
view of Bamberg's **Little Venice**, with fishermen's old houses on the right bank
of the river. From here you can wend your way back to the cathedral square
through a maze of narrow alleys, passing the former **Dominican Church** with
its attractive 14th-century cloisters. Until recently it was the home of the famous
Bamberg Symphony Orchestra, which now performs in a modern concert hall,
the **Sinfonie an der Regnitz**. At the top of the picturesque steps of the Katzen-
berg is the **Schlenkerla**, one of the best *Rauchbier* inns *(see margin note)*.

The Main Valley

Between Staffelstein and Lichtenfels are two rare jewels of baroque architecture.
On a 421-metre (1,380-ft) hill stands the fortress-like **Banz Abbey** ③. Founded
in 1069, it served as a Benedictine abbey until 1803 and later as a palace belonging to the ruling Wittelsbach family. It is one of the greatest achievements of German baroque. On the opposite side of the valley, 3 km (2 miles) from Lichtenfels
off the B173 road, is the absolute zenith of the era – the **Vierzehnheiligen** ② (Pilgrimage Church of the Fourteen Saints) by Balthasar Neumann. It was built
between 1743–51 and named after 14 saints whom a pious shepherd in the 15th
century claimed to have seen several times.

Map
on page
202

TIP

While in Bamberg,
don't forget to call in
at one of the
Rauchbier inns.
Rauchbier (smoked
beer) is a speciality
of the town, though
it is not to
everybody's taste.

BELOW: inside the
Vierzehnheiligen.

BALTHASAR NEUMANN

Tiepolo's ceiling fresco of the four continents in Würzburg's Residenz was meant to depict everything under
the sun. So it's not surprising that the fresco includes portraits of people who loomed large in Tiepolo's world: the
painter himself with his son; the Prince-Bishop von Greif-
fenclau, who commissioned the work; and the building's
architect, Balthasar Neumann (1687–1753).

Born in Eger, Neumann moved to Würzburg in 1709,
starting his career in the artillery force of the Prince-
Bishop where he showed a keen interest in defence engineering. Having singled him out for architectural work,
the Prince-Bishop sent Neumann to Paris and Vienna to
discuss plans for his new palace. The resulting Residenz,
begun when he was only 25, is a perfect example of the
way Neumann's work combines the lightness of the Italian and Austrian baroque with the formal organisation of
French architecture. In smaller buildings, animation is even
more pronounced: the rococo church of Vierzehnheiligen
is an explosion of light, colour and movement. The fact
that most of its walls are curved accentuates the dramatic
effect of this church's intricate architecture – and demonstrates the kind of intellectual complexity that singles out
Neumann as *the* master of German baroque.

Grilled sausages and other delicacies

The marketplace in **Coburg** ❸ is a fine place to linger, though exactly how long you remain may depend on how hungry you are. One reason for being here must be to savour the legendary Coburg sausages, relatives of the more common Thuringian variety. The air is redolent with the aroma of the glowing pine cones over which the sausages are grilled 365 days a year. From the town hall the statue of Coburg's patron saint, St Maurice, dubbed *Bratwurstmännle* (Sausage Man), observes the scene. The opulent facade of this rococo building (1580), with its decorated high gables, is typical of Coburg.

Coburg isn't only famous for its sausages. In 1840, Albert, the younger son of the Duke of Saxe-Coburg-Gotha and his wife Louisa, married his first cousin, Queen Victoria. A memorial to the Prince Consort stands in the marketplace. Adjacent is **Schloss Ehrenburg** (open Tues–Sun Apr–Sept 9am–5pm, Oct–Mar 10am–3pm), which from 1547 until 1918 was the city residence of the Dukes of Coburg. The adjacent **Puppenmuseum** (Dolls' Museum; open daily 9am–5pm, Nov–Mar Tues–Sun 10am–5pm) houses some 600 antique dolls.

Another reason for visiting Coburg is the **Veste Coburg** (open Easter–Oct 9.30am–5pm, Nov–Mar Tues–Sun 1–4pm), the fortress on the hill above the town which, with its triple ring of fortifications, is one of the largest and most impregnable of all German castles. Built in 1200, it provided a refuge for Martin Luther during the Augsburg Imperial Diet in 1530. The fortress houses a large collection of paintings and copperplate engravings by Luther's artist friend Lucas Cranach the Elder (1472–1553), as well as a fine display of hunting weapons.

Cranach was born in the town of **Kronach** ❹ on the B303. The town, dominated by the 12th-century Rosenberg Fortress, is an idyllic place, with narrow

BELOW: gala evening at the Bayreuth Festival Theatre.

alleys, attractive houses and a preserved medieval town wall with towers and gates. In the fortress the **Franconian Gallery** contains masterpieces of Franconian art from the 13th–16th centuries (open Tues–Sun Mar–Oct 10am–5.30pm, Nov–Feb 10am–4pm).

More beer is drunk in Germany than in any other country in the world, and the citizens of **Kulmbach** ❸, 20 km (13 miles) southeast of Coburg on the B85, claim that their town is the "world capital of beer", and that there is no beer stronger than the *Kulminator* special brew. The breweries use the water from the nearby Fichtel Mountains and Franconian Forest. Well worth seeing in Kulmbach is the Renaissance castle **Plassenburg** that towers over the town. It contains the **Deutsche Zinnfigurenmuseum** (open Apr–Oct daily 10am–6pm, Nov–Mar Tues–Sun 10am–4pm) with an amazing collection of 300,000 tin figures re-enacting historic scenes and battles.

The Wagnerians' Mecca

The town of **Bayreuth** ❻ (pop. 75,000) is associated above all with the composer Richard Wagner, who built an opera house here in 1876. Every year it is the setting for the Wagner Festival, which runs from 25 July to 28 August. The city's operatic tradition, however, was begun by the cultured Margravine Wilhelmina, Frederick the Great's favourite sister, who commissioned the architect Saint-Pierre to design the **Bayreuth Opera House**. It is now regarded as one of Germany's best-preserved baroque theatres.

Saint-Pierre was also responsible for the **Neues Schloss** (New Palace), now the home of a beautiful faïence collection, with some attractive fountains outside. Richard Wagner and his wife Cosima, Liszt's daughter, lie buried in the park close to Franz Liszt himself in **Villa Wahnfried**. The **Eremitage** (Hermitage Palace) is another famous building in the east of Bayreuth, as is the baroque **Altes Schloss** (Old Palace), with an interior grotto and fountains to rival the splendour of its historic rooms.

Further on towards Nuremberg is the region known as the **Fränkische Schweiz** ❼, Franconia's "Little Switzerland", on account of its striking upland scenery. There are indeed some impressive crags, such as those that tower above the romantic hill village of **Tüchersfeld**. The high point of a tour through this beautiful national park is the 1-km (½-mile) long limestone cave, the **Teufelshöhle** (Devil's Cave) near **Pottenstein**, a fascinating underground world of caverns and grottoes.

Nuremberg

To the south you will reach the old, free imperial city of **Nuremberg** ❽ (pop. 500,000), the second-largest city in Bavaria and an important industrial and commercial centre. Devastated by bombs in World War II, it has been faithfully restored and much of its old charm remains. Nuremberg was founded in the 11th century by Emperor Heinrich III as a base for his campaigns in Bohemia, and the settlement rapidly developed into an important trading centre. Elevated to a free imperial city by Emperor Friedrich II in 1219, it retained this status until 1806 when it was annexed by the Kingdom of Bavaria. From the 12th–16th

Map on page 202

TIP

A destination for every Wagner fan is Villa Wahnfried, where Richard Wagner and his wife Cosima lived. It now houses the Richard Wagner Museum (open daily 9am–5pm, Tues and Thur until 8pm, Nov–Mar daily 10am–5pm).

BELOW: outward-bound in Franconia's "Little Switzerland".

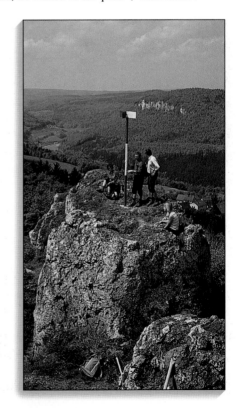

BELOW: Nuremberg
is dominated by the
Imperial Castle.

centuries nearly all the emperors maintained their residence in the Kaiserburg (castle), and held their imperial diets here. At that time, Nuremberg was regarded as the unofficial capital of the Holy Roman Empire of German Nations.

Between the 15th and 17th centuries, the city attracted artists and scientists. Names such as Albrecht Dürer, and Veit Stoss are testimony to this age of artistic achievement. From 1600 onwards, the political and economic importance of the city declined and real prosperity only returned when the first German railway between Nuremberg and Fürth was inaugurated in 1835.

One hundred years later a less celebrated chapter in Germany's history was written in Nuremberg. The Nazis wanted to revive the city's tradition as the old capital of the Reich and so they built a massive stadium in which, between 1933 and 1938, the notorious rallies were held. The Reichsparteitagsgelände (rally ground) now contains a permanent exhibition entitled "Faszination und Gewalt" (Fascination and Terror) in the **Zeppelintribüne** (open Mon–Fri 9am–6pm, Sat–Sun 10am–6pm). From 1945 to 1949, Nuremberg again became the focus of world attention when Nazi war criminals were put on trial by the Allies.

Back to the Middle Ages

The River Pegnitz divided Nuremberg's **Old City** into the Sebalderstadt in the north and the Lorenzerstadt in the south, both surrounded by a sturdy 13th-century defensive wall with 46 fortified towers – the landmarks of the city – and five main gates: the Spittlertor, the Königstor, the Frauentor, the Laufertor and the Neutor. The enormous **Kaiserburg** (imperial castle), built on sandstone crags high above the old city, consists of three architectural components, each from a different historical period. The western crags provide the foundations for

the Kaiserburg, which was erected in the 12th century during the reign of the Hohenstaufen Emperor Frederick Barbarossa. Then there is the **Burggrafenburg**, the first royal castle built by the Salians in the 11th century. The **Kaiserstallungen** (imperial stables), built as a granary in 1485, is now a youth hostel.

Map on page 202

Near the castle, the Tiergärtnertor leads to **Albrecht Dürer House**. This 15th-century building, where the famous artist lived from 1509 until his death in 1528, is now a museum (open Tues–Sun 10am–5pm, Thur until 8pm, July–Sept also open Mon).

On the Town Hall Square stands the protestant **Church of St Sebald**, a late Romanesque columned basilica from 1256. St Sebald's tomb is a masterpiece of the German iron foundryman's art and was cast by Vischer in the 16th century. The moving Crucifixion group by Veit Stoss dates from the same period.

Next is the **Hauptmarkt** (main market), the site of Nuremberg's famous annual **Christkindlesmarkt** (Christmas Market). The richly carved **Schöner Brunnen**, a beautiful 19-metre (62-ft) high fountain, stands before the **Frauenkirche** (Church of Our Lady, 1349). The church has an interesting facade with the famous **Männleinlaufen**, a clock which at noon every day re-enacts the homage of the Seven Electors to Emperor Charles IV. The interior contains the **Tucher Altar** (1440). The **Town Hall**, whose oldest part is the hall with stepped gables, dates from 1340. In the basement are medieval dungeons with gruesome torture chambers. Nearby is the well-known **Gänsemännchen** fountain (1555), incorporating a figure of a peasant with two geese spouting water.

Situated on an island of the River Pegnitz, the **Heilig-Geist-Spital** (Holy Ghost Hospital) was founded in the 14th century for old and needy citizens. The German emperor's imperial insignia were kept here until 1796. In the courtyard lies an impressive Crucifixion group by Adam Krafft and the 14th-century Hansel Fountain.

Beyond this is the **Church of St Laurence**, built between the 13th and 15th centuries. Particularly impressive is the chancel with its fine star vaulting, suspended from which is the beautifully carved Annunciation created by Veit Stoss in 1517. Another work by the same artist is the crucifix, which can be seen at the high altar together with Adam Krafft's world-famous *Tabernacle*.

Königstrasse, the main shopping street, extends from St Laurence's past the **Mauthalle**, which was built as a granary around 1500 and is now a restaurant with a beautiful old vaulted cellar. Situated at the Kornmarkt, the **Germanisches Nationalmuseum** (open Tues–Sun 10am–6pm, Wed until 9pm) is one of the most important museums devoted to German arts and culture, with artefacts dating back to pre- and early history. There are also works by Albrecht Dürer. The **Neues Museum Nürnberg** displays interesting objects from its unique contemporary art and design collection in a spectacular new building.

Past the early-Gothic church of St Clare stands the Old Nuremberg **Handwerkerhof**. Formerly a craftsmen's yard, it is now a living museum displaying medieval handicrafts and pieces in gold and other precious metals. It also covers the manufacture of the famous Nuremberg gingerbread. ❑

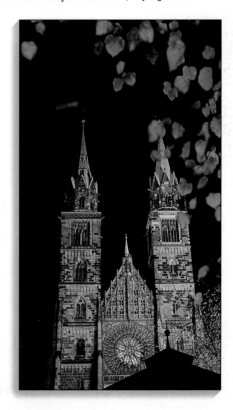

BELOW: Nuremberg by night.

LAKE CONSTANCE

With its warm climate and picturesque scenery, together with some beautiful towns on or near the lakeshore, Germany's largest lake has long been a popular holiday destination

Map on page 226

Backed by the panorama of the Alps, Lake Constance (Bodensee) is more the size of an inland sea. More than half of its 538 sq. km (208 sq. miles) belongs to Germany; the rest is shared by Switzerland and Austria. The climate is mild enough for orchards of apples, pears and plums to flourish. The long hours of sunshine ensure that the grapes in the vineyards ripen at the same time as those in Mediterranean countries.

The silent lion

A tour can commence in **Lindau ❶** (pop. 24,500), an island town on German soil connected to the mainland by a road and rail causeway. In 15 BC the Romans established a military base on the island and fishermen subsequently came to settle in the area. At the end of the 13th century, Lindau became a free imperial city, whose economic prosperity was closely linked to the Lindau Messengers. This courier service – at that time a complete novelty – operated routes between Italy and northern Europe. The climax of the town's importance came in 1496 when the Imperial Diet assembled in the town hall. In 1803, Lindau lost its free imperial city status and in 1806 became integrated with Bavaria.

With its broad promenade, the **Seehafen** (harbour) is flanked by a number of hotels and inviting cafés. The harbour entrance is guarded on one side by a 33-metre (108-ft) high lighthouse and on the other by the symbol of Bavaria, a stone lion. The lion has never been able to roar because the sculptor forgot its tongue. The **Mangturm** tower, which is all that remains of the old fortifications, stands in the middle of the promenade. From here it isn't far to the **Reichsplatz**, the main square, dominated by the **Lindavia Fountain** and the Gothic **Old Town Hall**. Both the back and the front of the building are richly decorated with frescoes depicting events from the Imperial Diet. The **Diebesturm** (Brigand's Tower) is situated in Zeppelinstrasse, adjacent to the Romanesque **Church of St Peter**, in which frescoes depicting the Passion are attributed to Hans Holbein the Elder.

Another interesting sight on the **Marketplace** is the baroque painting on the facade of the **Haus zum Cavazzen** (No. 6). It houses a museum with the largest art exhibition in the Lake Constance region, as well as exhibits on local history and culture (open Apr–Oct, Tues–Fri and Sun 11am–5pm, Sat 2–5pm).

Austrian foray

From Lindau it is only 10 km (6 miles) to **Bregenz ❷**, the capital of the Austrian province of Vorarlberg. The town comes to life during July and August when the Bregenz Opera Festival is performed on the largest

LEFT: the church of St Mary at Birnau on the shores of the lake.
BELOW: the harbour entrance at Lindau.

floating stage in the world. The lakeside promenade draws thousands at week-ends, although better views of the lake itself can be enjoyed from the top of the **Pfänder** mountain (1,065 metres/3,495 ft), which can be reached by cable car.

In and out of Switzerland

Switzerland is just a few minutes away from Bregenz. The former prosperity of **Rorschach ❸** (from the corn market and weaving mill) is reflected in the fine facades of the patrician houses on the Marienberg and the high street. The local history museum in the baroque former **Kornhaus** (corn exchange) has some interesting exhibits (tel: 071 841 7034).

Some 15 km (9 miles) to the west, **Romanshorn ❹** is the terminus for ferries to Friedrichshafen on the German side of the lake. On the way it is well worth making a detour south to **St Gallen ❺** (pop. 75,000). Founded in 612, the Benedictine abbey was one of the first education centres in Christian Europe and contains a magnificent baroque library.

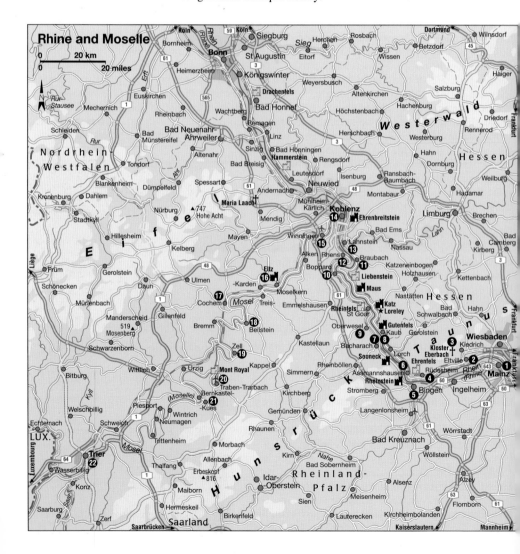

Konstanz (pop. 81,000) is the largest town on the lake, situated between the main "Obersee" and the much smaller "Untersee" to the west. The Romans erected a camp here and named it after the emperor Constantinus Chlorus. Konstanz became a bishopric in 540. The most important event in the town's history was the Reform Council of 1414–18, during which the only election of a pope (Martin V) on German soil took place. The prince-bishops also sentenced the reformer John Hus to death here. He was burned at the stake in 1415. The council met in the **Council Building** (old town), built in 1388 as a corn and wine warehouse.

Other buildings worth inspection are the Romanesque-Gothic **Minster** (11th–16th century) and the town hall. An early-Gothic replica of the Holy Sepulchre is to be found in the **Mauritius Rotund**, which has a viewing platform offering a panorama of the town and the lake. Historians come to the Kunkel Haus to view the fine **Weber Frescoes** (late 13th century), which depict the individual stages in the manufacture of silk and linen (guided tours only, check with the tourist office).

Strongly recommended is a detour along the Rhine to Switzerland. With its well-preserved walls and townhouses, **Stein am Rhein** ❼ is known as the "Swiss Rothenburg" and on fine summer days it is just as crowded. Most of the houses date from the 15th and 16th centuries, though the facade decoration is mainly from the early 20th century. You can escape the bustle by visiting the former Benedictine abbey, with its Romanesque cloisters and attached museum. During the Reformation, much of the abbey was transformed into a Protestant church. The detour continues to the **Rheinfall** ❽ (Rhine Falls) near Schaffhausen. The impressive spectacle of the Rhine plunging 21 metres (69 ft) along a length of 150 metres (450 ft) is best enjoyed from below. One of the boats even takes visitors right underneath the falls. With its 16th-century Munot Tower and its Benedictine monastery, **Schaffhausen** itself is also worth a visit.

Also to the west of Konstanz, on the Untersee, the island of **Reichenau** ❾ is linked to the mainland by a causeway. It is the most important centre of market gardening in Germany (Munich's central market is one of the main outlets for its quality produce), with 15 percent of the 5-km (3-mile) long and 2-km (1-mile) wide island being taken up by glasshouses. The **Benediktinerkloster** (Benedictine abbey) on Reichenau was a major spiritual centre of western European culture for 300 years (724–1000). Charlemagne's sons were educated here.

Situated on a small peninsula at the western end of the Untersee is the town of **Radolfzell** ❿, which gets its name from the monastery of Cella Ratoldi, founded here in 826 by Bishop Radolf of Verona. The monastery's successor, the **Minster**, houses the relics of the town's three patron saints, Senesius, Theopont and Zeno. The **Hausherrenfest** is held in their honour on the third Sunday in July and on the following Monday is the *Mooser Wasserprozession*, when a procession of flower-bedecked boats takes to the water. The town's main square is surrounded by fine baroque buildings.

On the other side of the Bodanrück peninsula in Überlinger See lies the famous flower island of **Mainau** ⓫. This subtropical paradise is in full bloom

Map on page 226

TIP

In mid-August many visitors come to Konstanz and the neighbouring Swiss Kreuzlingen to celebrate the "Seenachtfest" (Night on the Lake Festival) with a fireworks display.

BELOW: Schaffhausen and the Rhine Falls.

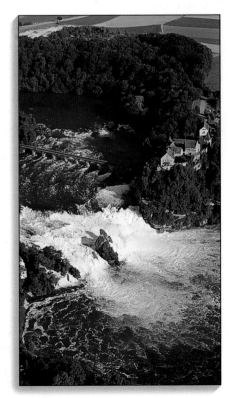

The stilt houses at Unteruhldingen testify to the ingenuity of the lakeshore dwellers.

between March and October and can be reached by ferry from the mainland, as well as by bus and car.

Opposite Mainau on the northern lakeshore lies **Überlingen** ⓬, a picturesque little town with much of its medieval fortifications still intact. In the 13th century, Überlingen was made a free imperial city and derived much of its former wealth through trade from the hinterland. The best view of the town is either from the lake itself or from the tower of the Gothic **St Nicholas Minster**, the largest church in the Lake Constance region. From its long harbour promenade steep streets lead up to the old town centre. The town hall contains the splendid **Council Chamber** created by Jacob Russ in 1490, with its wonderful wood-carved frieze of statuettes representing the 41 medieval trades.

Five km (3 miles) from Überlingen on the road to Meersburg, the lake is dominated by the pilgrimage church of **Birnau** ⓭ with its magnificent rococo decor. Its main attraction is a lifesize, roguish putto, *The Honey Sucker*. At **Unteruhldingen** ⓮ near Uhldingen-Mühlhofen is a reconstruction of a Stone Age village, built on stilts in the lake. The **Pfahlbau Freilichtmuseum** (Stilt House Open-air Museum; open Apr–Sep daily 8am–6pm, Oct 9am–5pm, Mar and Nov Sat–Sun 9am–5pm) was created in the 1920s and clearly shows how the fishermen and hunters of the Stone and Bronze ages lived and worked, building their houses on stilts in order to protect themselves from their enemies.

Magic of the Middle Ages

BELOW: the rooftops of medieval Meersburg.

Meersburg ⓯ is considered to be one of the best-preserved medieval and baroque towns in Germany. The magic of the place, which has never been destroyed, is best appreciated in the evening after most of the tourists have

gone. Those who remain have time to admire the half-timbered houses in peace, accompanied by the melody of bubbling fountains and church bells. The historical centre is marked by the **Altes Schloss** (Old Castle), one of the oldest in Germany, which dates from Merovingian times (AD 481–737). In the **Neues Schloss** (New Castle), the old summer residence of the prince-bishops of Konstanz, classical concerts are now performed. The imposing staircases, designed by Balthasar Neumann, are the showpiece of the fabulous Baroque building. The **Fürstenhäusle** formerly belonged to Annette von Droste-Hülshoff (1797–1848), one of Germany's leading poets, whose crime novel *Judenbuche* is on the reading lists of many German schools. Her statue stands before the bridge to the Old Castle.

Map on page 226

Friedrichshafen ⓰ (pop. 58,000), the second-largest town on Lake Constance, rose to fame at the end of the 19th century when shiny silver airships were built here. Airships will forever be associated with their inventor, Graf Ferdinand von Zeppelin *(see below)*. One of the principal attractions of the town is the **Zeppelin Museum** (open July–Sept daily 10am–5pm, Oct–June Tues–Sun 10am–5pm), a fine piece of modern architecture that forms an extension to the equally impressive railway station. The latter is the region's most important example of the Bauhaus style. The focal point of the museum is the full-scale replica of a section of the Airship *LZ 129*, known as the *Hindenburg*, which flew across the Atlantic several times before being destroyed by fire in 1937. The museum also has an art section, with exhibits from the Middle Ages to the present day, including the world's largest collection of works by the realist painter Otto Dix. In summer 2009 the new **Dornier Museum** for aeronautics will open at the Friedrichshafen airfield (www.dorniermuseum.de). ❏

BELOW: a Zeppelin hovers above Friedrichshafen.

GRAF ZEPPELIN

Thursday, 6 May 1937. It was a miserable evening in Lakehurst, New Jersey, as the *Hindenburg* approached its anchorage after a 77-hour flight from Frankfurt. Suddenly the ground crew heard a "bang" and seconds later the stern of the airship was engulfed in flames. Thirteen passengers, 22 crew and one German Shepherd dog died in the disaster; and with it the Nazi regime lost a symbol of its industrial and technological might.

At that moment, only the name reminded the world of the genius behind those giant "flying cigars": Graf Ferdinand von Zeppelin (1838–1917), who was born in Konstanz. In 1895, the noble engineer received his first patent for his invention of a "steerable aircraft with suspended cabins". On 2 July 1900, an airship, the *LZ I*, rose over Lake Constance for the first time, having been constructed at Friedrichshafen. Over the next 20 years more airships emerged from the hangar: the *Bodensee* carried passengers from Friedrichshafen to Berlin; in 1924 the *ZR III* (later *Los Angeles*) became the first German aircraft to cross the Atlantic; the *Graf Zeppelin* made it as far as the Antarctic and South America; and finally, the *Hindenburg* offered first-class transatlantic comfort – until that fateful evening in New Jersey.

THE BLACK FOREST

*The Black Forest has more than clocks and cherry gâteau. It is an
attractive landscape dotted with picturesque architecture and
has a culinary repertoire unmatched in Germany*

Map
on page
226

The Romans described the Black Forest as an impenetrable wilderness inhabited only by wild beasts and barbarians. Much has changed since their day
and there is little danger now of being set upon by a wild boar. The region
has been made accessible by road, rail and an extended network of walking
trails. There is little left of the dense pine forest as it existed in ancient times.

Like their predecessors the Celts, the Romans never dared venture into the
depths of the forest. The Alemanni, too, who came after them, preferred to plant
their crops along the periphery. It was only around the turn of the first millennium
that the occasional clearing was made by Christians for the establishment of
monastic settlements and the forest, steeped in myth and legend, began to reveal
its secrets. From the 16th century onwards, the woodland was cleared from the
navigable river valleys and agriculture was established. Small industries arose,
notably glass- and watch-making, and together with forestry, tourism and certain
high-tech industries, these remain the backbone of the Black Forest economy.

Tourists have been drawn to the Black Forest ever since the 18th century,
attracted by the contrast of the Rhine Plain and the mountains rising some 1,200
metres (4,000 ft) above it. In the lowlands the summer days are hot and a
favourite pastime is sitting outside to enjoy a meal and a glass of good wine. The

LEFT:
uninterrupted view
towards the Alps.
BELOW: "Zum Roten
Bären" in Freiburg
is the oldest inn
in Germany.

forested slopes rising above the picture-postcard
valleys provide extensive possibilities for walking.
Grouse and pheasant, buzzards and hawks, deer, foxes
and badgers populate the more remote areas, where
the locals still cling to their traditions, wearing their
beautifully embroidered costumes on public holidays.

University city

The development of **Freiburg** ⓱ (pop. 220,000) has
always been closely linked to the Catholic Church.
Immediately after its founding in 1457, the **University**
became famous throughout Europe as a centre of liberal humanism. In the middle of the 16th century it
enjoyed a reputation as a Jesuit bastion of the Counter-
Reformation. It remained true to this strict Catholic
tradition right up until the 1920s. Nowadays its students are responsible for the *joie de vivre* of the city,
whose unique character is also due to its spectacular
location between the Black Forest and the vineyards
of the Rhine.

The city centre is characterised by narrow cobbled
streets and the fast-flowing rivulets called *Bächle,*
which are perfectly clean now but in medieval times
acted as sluices for carrying away sewage. This area
centres on the bustling Münsterplatz, which provides
the setting for the Gothic **Freiburg Münster** (1202–
1513). Only 82 years after the granting of the city
charter in 1120 the people began construction of a

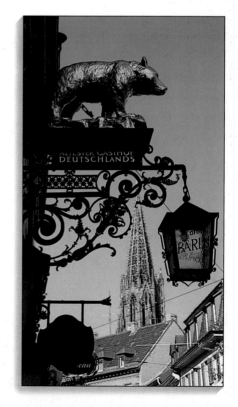

Woodcarvings such as this one at Titisee are typical of the Black Forest.

parish church, which soon grew into one of the most magnificent minsters of medieval Germany. Many consider its 116-metre (380-ft) high tower to be the finest in Christendom. Excellent classical concerts are often staged here. An ascent of the tower can prove a memorable experience when the mighty bells ring, causing the tower to vibrate. The southern side of the square is bordered by three beautiful buildings, including the **Kaufhaus**, dating back to 1520.

Around the minster is one of the most picturesque open-air markets in Germany. On a bright Saturday morning in summer the minster seems to float like a giant ship in a sea of stalls, vendors, housewives, musicians, tourists, preachers, flowers, bread, vegetables, fruit and grilled sausages.

Begin exploring the old city by walking eastwards from Münsterplatz to the **Schwabentor** (Swabian Gate), the gate tower to the old city walls. The **Zum Roten Bären** (The Red Bear Inn), which claims to be the oldest inn in Germany, is not far away. To the south the **Gewerbebach Canal** was once the main artery of the city's medieval economy and to the west is the Rathausplatz featuring Freiburg's early Renaissance **Rathaus** (Town Hall). An example of late-Gothic architecture is the **Haus zum Walfisch** on the corner of Franziskanerstrasse. Only five minutes from Münsterplatz, the **Schlossberg** is an area of parkland ideal for a stroll.

Excursions from Freiburg

A trip to the top of the nearby mountain, the 1,284-metre (4,200-ft) high **Schauinsland** ⓲, promises a fine panorama over the surrounding landscape. The cable car to the top can be reached by taking the No. 2 tram and then the No. 21 bus to Horben. On clear days there is a magnificent view, from the Black Forest across the Rhine Plain to the Vosges beyond.

Just a 10-minute drive to the north of Freiburg on the B3/B294 is one of the most beautiful valleys in the Black Forest, the idyllic, if busy, **Glottertal** ⓳. The road climbs until the towers of the Benedictine **Abbey of St Peter**, founded in 1093, come into view. On All Saints' Day and Good Friday there are processions to its opulent baroque church.

The journey onwards towards **St Märgen** ⓴ is accompanied at every turn by wonderful views of the hills and valleys. Here the Black Forest still retains its original character, with dense woodland, wild streams and peaceful valleys, where the roofs of the typical Black Forest farmhouses almost touch the ground. St Märgen offers a perfect compromise between remoteness and the comforts of modern-day tourism. The focus of this idyllic centre is the 12th-century Augustinian monastery.

When venturing east of Freiburg to **Titisee** ㉑, forget your car and take the train. The half-hour journey from Freiburg, along tracks that were laid in 1887, is an unforgettable experience. The stretch runs from the station at **Himmelsreich** (Realm of Heaven) to **Höllsteig** (Hell's Rise) station, climbing about 625 metres (2,050 ft) as it does so – a record for German railways. The journey up the gorge can be broken at the hill resort of **Hinterzarten**, where Queen Marie-Antoinette once dined. At weekends the road leading down to the picturesque Titisee is choc-a-bloc with visitors. It is a popular retreat, where people like to stroll around the lake (approx. 1½ hours' walk) or opt for the more strenuous ascent of the **Feldberg** (1,490 metres/4,900 ft), the highest mountain in the Black Forest at the head of the scenic Bärental. Beyond the lake, the road follows the bank of the more peaceful Schluchsee to **Bonndorf ㉒**, with its tempting culinary speciality, the Black Forest Ham. To the north lies the **Wutachschlucht** (gorge) nature reserve.

The Tuscany of Germany

The maritime winds blowing through the Rhine Valley are responsible for the mild climate that has made the western part of the Black Forest an important region for the cultivation of fruit. The vineyards among the foothills of the **Markgräflerland**, dropping gently down to the plain to the south of Freiburg, are reminiscent of more southern climes. The little town of **Staufen ㉓**, 20 km (12 miles) to the southwest of Freiburg, became famous in 1539 when the alchemist Dr Faustus was murdered in the Gasthaus zum Löwen (Lion Inn) by one of the higher-ranking devils. Faustus, who probably blew himself up while making gold for the local baron, was later immortalised by Goethe's famous drama. Today, the "devil" waits in the form of Markgräfler wine.

Situated on a rounded hill, **Badenweiler ㉔** has been a health resort ever since AD 100. Peace and quiet are guaranteed here, as cars are barred from the town. The spa gardens contain the remains of an old Roman Baths.

Rising from the plain west of Freiburg, the **Kaiserstuhl ㉕** (Emperor's Seat) has the perfect climate for the cultivation of fruit and vines. The rock is of volcanic origin and during periods of intense sun the ground can heat up to temperatures of 70°C (158°F). This creates a unique micro-climate where wild

Map on page 226

TIP

The Wutachschlucht nature reserve is an ideal hiking area. The best place to start is Bad Boll to the north of Bonningen. The Ludwig-Neumann-Weg, partly cut into the rock, guides you through the most romantic part of the gorge. Good footwear is essential.

BELOW: harvest time in the Markgräflerland.

The Alemanic carnival goes back to pre-Christian times, when people tried chasing the winter away with frightening masks. Later those celebrations were taken over by converted Christians to mark the last days before Ash Wednesday, the start of six weeks of fasting until Easter.

orchids and unusual butterflies abound. Small wine-producing villages such as **Oberbergen** have retained their traditional character. The visitor can sample the full-bodied *Sylvaner* in **Achkarren**, the aromatic *Gewürztraminer* in **Bickensohl** and the velvet-red *Spätburgunder* in **Oberrotweil**.

The town of **Breisach** ㉖, perched on basalt cliffs above the Rhine, is dominated by the **Minster**, which was built between the 12th and 14th centuries and contains a huge wooden carved altar by the unknown master "H.L.". It is rated as one of the most beautiful examples of German woodcarving. The town is a very lively place in summer with art festivals and, in July, one of the best-known wine festivals – the "Hock".

Idyllic road to Stuttgart

The whole length of the road from Freiburg to Stuttgart winds along small river valleys through an area of outstandingly beautiful landscape, where the traveller is constantly tempted to stop to admire the views.

Along the route, mechanical intricacies can be admired in the **Uhren-museum** (Clock Museum) in **Furtwangen** ㉗ (open daily, Apr–Oct 9am–6pm, Nov–Mar 10am–5pm, guided tours 11am). Clocks of all shapes and sizes are on display. A particularly fine piece is the one with the tailor who, every hour on the hour, has a shoe banged on his head by his wife. In **Schonach** ㉘, further north, is the largest cuckoo clock in the world. Its cuckoo alone measures nearly 1 metre (3 ft) from beak to tail.

The nearby **Triberger Wasserfälle** ㉙, which rise to a height of 103 metres (338 ft), are the highest waterfalls in Germany. From Triberg or St Georgen, the Black Forest Railway runs to **Hausach** ㉚ and provides one of the most scenic

Below: clocks come in all shapes and sizes.

BLACK FOREST CLOCKS

A ll over the world the Black Forest is often known by three symbols: the tasty *Schwarzwälder Kirschtorte* (Black Forest cherry gâteau), the albeit lesser known red-bobbled *Bollenhut* (hat) for unmarried women, and the cuckoo clock.

During cold winter days the Black Forest peasants were always looking for ways to supplement their meagre income. The first simple carved wooden clocks were produced in the 17th century and sold to customers all over Europe. The story goes that in 1738, Franz Anton Ketterer brought back the first "cuckoo clock" from Bohemia, even though this had no cuckoo, not even the small house where the cuckoo pops out. The latter was the brainchild of the architect Eisenlohr, who in 1850 designed a house in the shape of a railway station for the front of the clocks. Nobody knows who put the cuckoo in there later – but that was the day the "real" cuckoo clock was born.

Nowadays, not only cuckoo clocks are produced in the Black Forest, but modern clocks and wristwatches as well. The clock-making tradition can be seen on the 320-km (200-mile) long Deutsche Uhrenstrasse (German Clocks Road), which starts in Villingen-Schwenningen, and on its way through delightful countryside passes more than 30 places where clocks are made.

Map on page 226

railway journeys in the land. Three km (2 miles) to the south of Hausach on the B33, the **Freilichtmuseum Vogtsbauernhof** is well worth a visit (open Mar–Oct 9am–5pm). It is an open-air museum consisting of houses and farm buildings from the different regions of the Black Forest, complete with old furniture and agricultural implements. It gives a vivid impression of what life used to be like here and also traces the development of agriculture and forestry in the region.

Another popular destination for the Black Forest visitor lies 20 km (12 miles) to the northeast of Hausach in the Kinzig Valley. The former Benedictine Monastery Church in **Alpirsbach** ❹ is one of the most beautiful Romanesque basilicas in Germany and has hardly been altered since it was built in 1095–9.

Turning east from Freudenstadt, the road leads to **Nagold** ❹, a town beautifully situated on the river of the same name where four valleys meet. Alongside old, half-timbered houses, the 1,000-year-old **Church of St Remigius** contains some beautiful frescoes and an unusual statue of the Virgin.

"Calw is the most beautiful place I know on earth," declared Hermann Hesse (1877–1962), who was born here. **Calw** ❹ still exudes that feeling of youthfulness and vivacity that the author so masterfully captured in his novels. After a visit to the **Hesse Museum** (open Tues–Sun 11am–5pm), a stroll through the town with its delightful half-timbered houses will confirm this opinion.

Freiburg's Swabian counterpart is **Tübingen** ❹ (pop. 87,000), Germany's smallest university town where students outnumber locals by a ratio of more than three to one. It has attracted poets and philosophers since the 16th century. There was Johannes Kepler (1571–1630), the first man to calculate the orbit of the planets; and Wilhelm Schickhardt who, in 1623, invented the world's first mechanical calculator. The philosophers Hegel and Schelling lived here, as did

The strict lifestyle of Hirsau's monks became a role model for many other medieval monasteries. The brothers were forbidden to talk and were only allowed to eat broad beans, eggs, cheese, vegetables and fish.

BELOW: a glimpse into the past at the Vogtsbauernhof.

such writers as Hölderlin and Hauff. All were students at the Evangelischer Stift (Tübingen Foundation), a theological seminary established in 1536.

Tübingen is built at the foot of two hills overlooking the Neckar and Ammer rivers. Its medieval attractions survived World War II intact. Particularly worth seeing are the 15th-century Gothic **Stiftskirche** (Collegiate Church), and behind it the oldest parts of the **University** founded in 1477, where the reformer Philipp Melanchthon lectured from 1514 to 1518. Down on the Neckar among weeping willows is the **Hölderlin Tower** where the poet Hölderlin, who had become insane, lived from 1807 until his death in 1843. From there the Bursagasse leads past the church to the **Town Hall**, a half-timbered building dating from 1435. On the old Marketplace, farmers still come, in rural costume, to sell their wares. Above, the **Burgsteige** path climbs to the 16th-century **Hohentübingen Castle**, which offers splendid views over the rooftops down to the Neckar.

City of the luxury limousine

Capital of the federal state of Baden-Württemberg, **Stuttgart** ❸ (pop. 595,000), has the highest per capita income of any city in Germany. This is due in part to its having been chosen in 1926 as the location for the manufacture of Germany's luxury Mercedes cars. Opulence was displayed differently by the rich and powerful in earlier times, as evidenced by the 16th-century **Altes Schloss** (Old Palace) on Schillerplatz. Opposite is the **Neues Schloss** (New Palace, 1746–1807), which currently houses the ministries of Culture and Finance. The Schlossplatz, or Palace Square, is popular for shopping and has a new attraction for art lovers – the extravagant **Kunstmüseum**. The **Staatstheater** stands opposite the palace gardens, and occupying a postmodern building behind the thea-

TIP

The Kunsthalle in Tübingen is internationally renowned for outstanding exhibitions of art (open Tues 11am–7pm, Wed–Sun 11am–6pm).

BELOW: downtown Tübingen.

tre, the **Staatsgalerie** (State Art Gallery; open Tues–Sun 10am–6pm, Thur until 9pm) contains one of southern Germany's leading art collections. Situated close to the main station, the **Linden Museum** (open Tues–Sun 10am–5pm, Wed until 8pm) has an interesting ethnological collection.

In the district of Untertürkheim automobile fans will find the fascinating new **Mercedes-Benz-Museum** (open Tues–Sun 9am–5pm). On the right bank of the Neckar, in the district of Bad Cannstatt, Gottfried Daimler demonstrated the world's first petrol-driven car in 1886. This is also where the Cannstatter Was'nfest, Stuttgart's answer to the Munich Oktoberfest, is held every autumn. Also well worth a visit is the **Porsche Museum** in Stuttgart-Zuffenhausen, which has about 50 cars of the famous manufacturer on display (open Mon–Fri 9am–4pm, Sat–Sun 9am–5pm). Great fun for visitors with children is the **Wilhelma Zoo** in Stuttgart-Cannstadt (open daily summer 8.15am–6pm, winter 8.15am–4pm). One of Europe's most beautiful combined zoological and botanical gardens, it was laid out between 1843–53 in Moorish style and is home to more than 8,000 animals as well as numerous rare plants.

Jewellers, lawyers, gamblers and genius

Those who admire jewellery should make a point of stopping in **Pforzheim 36**. The reputation of Pforzheim's goldsmiths can be compared with that of the diamond cutters of Amsterdam and their history is told in the **Schmuckmuseum** in the Reuchlinhaus (open Tues–Sun 10am–5pm).

Northeast of Pforzheim in **Maulbronn**, the 12th-century **Cistercian Monastery** is the best-preserved medieval building of its kind in Germany.

The existence of **Karlsruhe 37** (Karl's Rest; pop. 286,000) is entirely due to the palace that Margrave Karl Wilhelm of Baden-Durlach built around 1715. Most of its attractions are found around the palace, which today houses the **Badisches Landesmuseum** (Baden State Museum; open Tues–Sun 10am–5pm, Thur until 8pm). The **State Majolica Manufactory** (open Tues–Sun 10am–1pm, 2–5pm), with a fine display of faïence pottery; the **Staatliche Kunsthalle** (open Tues–Fri 10am–5pm, Sat–Sun 10am–6pm) containing one of the best displays of European painting in southern Germany, and the **Botanical Gardens** (open Mon–Fri 8am–3.30pm) are all nearby.

The town is also the seat of the **Federal Constitutional Court**, guardian of the Basic Constitutional Law, and the **Federal High Court**, responsible for protecting the rights of the individual.

Although the spa tradition of **Baden-Baden 38** goes back to Roman times, it was not revived until 1838 when Jacques Benazet opened his **Casino**, a luxurious fun palace, in the Kurhaus. It suddenly became fashionable to visit Baden-Baden. The **Grosse Badener Rennwoche** at Iffezheim on the outskirts of the town, is the highlight of the German horse-racing calendar.

The lively centre of **Ulm 39** (pop. 120,000), birthplace of Albert Einstein (1879–1955), is well worth a detour. The skyline is dominated by the **Münsterturm**, which at 162 metres (530 ft) is the tallest steeple in Christendom. After the exhausting climb up the steeple, the Fischer Bastei beckons, with its old houses and welcoming bars set on the banks of the Danube. ❑

Map on page 226

TIP

For a scenic dining experience, try Stuttgart's landmark, the Fernsehturm (Television Tower), built in 1956 and once a technical sensation; on clear days you can even see the Alps. Another beautiful city panorama is offered by Cube restaurant, downtown in the new Kunstmüseum.

BELOW: cooling off in Baden-Baden.

FRANKFURT AND THE SEVEN STATES

Germany's western states constitute the heartland of the country's romance – and its industry

Situated at the heart of Germany, Frankfurt-am-Main is the hub of all national road, rail and air traffic. Having tried extremely hard to be at the forefront of high-rise building too, it has been given the nickname "Mainhattan". Although the city is the undisputed banking metropolis of Germany, it is not, as many people assume, the capital city of the federal state of Hessen. The state capital is Wiesbaden, which lies opposite Mainz on the Rhine.

Every year during Carnival one can see how Mainz really lets its hair down. One wonders whether the all-important archbishops enjoyed watching these heathen practices in the past as much as people do today. Be that as it may, the people in authority were then, and are now, the target of the buffoonery.

The various regions within easy reach of Frankfurt are full of contrasts, from the romantic castles strung out along Germany's river of destiny, Old Father Rhine, to the country's largest industrial area, the Ruhrgebiet, further downstream, where new clean industries are moving in to replace the old, providing new opportunities for employment as the traditional coal and steel industries have become less profitable.

But before the Rhine even reaches the Ruhrgebiet, there are two neighbouring cities competing against each other. There is Düsseldorf, a city symbolised by art and fashion, and there is the cathedral city and media centre of Cologne. Beer, ice-hockey and football are all important here and so is the unforgettable Carnival season. The Romans also once settled in this region – at least to the left of the Rhine – and the most impressive examples of Roman architecture are to be found on the banks of the Moselle, in Trier.

Nearby unfolds the beautiful countryside of the Eifel. Romanticism, including the sort represented by bands of robbers, is guaranteed in Heidelberg and the surrounding forests of the Spessart and Odenwald, where there are also many castles to be explored.

Hardly a German state is left untouched by a trip around Frankfurt, except for the five new states in the east and those in the extreme north. By following the Rhine you pass through Hessen, Rhineland Palatinate and North Rhine Westphalia (the largest of the federal states). The River Neckar flows through Heidelberg in Baden-Württemberg, and the Odenwald even stretches as far as Bavaria. The Fairytale Road of the Brothers Grimm leads through Hessen, Lower Saxony and up to Bremen in the north. ❑

PRECEDING PAGES: among Frankfurt's shining facades.
LEFT: a panoramic view of the Rhine with Bacharach in the foreground.

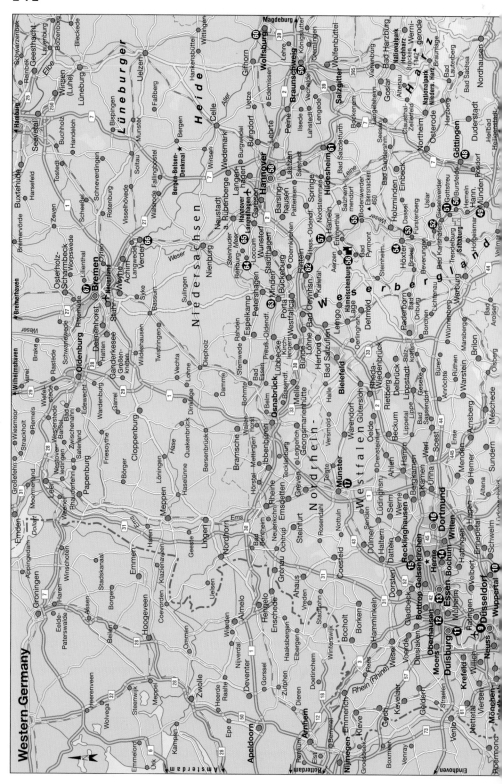

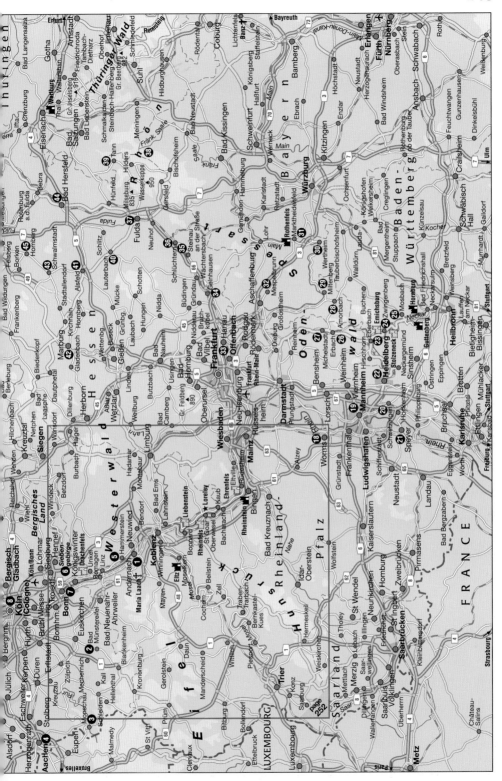

FRANKFURT

Frankfurt plays a key role in today's world of international finance. But the city is of historic importance too, for it was here that many German emperors were elected and crowned

Map on page 246

Frankfurt has developed into a pulsating metropolis. Thanks to its location at the intersection of important road, rail and air traffic routes, the heart of this vast conurbation has become the conduit for fast bucks and rapid careers. The new cathedrals of the world of finance – the spires of the skyscrapers that house the international banks and financial corporations – create a dramatic skyline which epitomises the power of this bustling city: the Bundesbank, the German Stock Exchange, plus many of the leading financial institutions of Germany and Europe, are concentrated within a very small area at the heart of the city. They include the new European Central Bank.

Frankfurt's infrastructure was not really ready for the spectacular growth that has occurred: the old shops and the resident population were forced out into other parts of the city or into the surrounding countryside as the tenants could no longer afford to pay the astronomical rents. It was the wish of the city fathers that the area around the main station be designated as a showcase – a vision that was emphatically fulfilled by the **Messeturm** (Trade Fair Tower), built in 1989 and at that time the highest office building in Europe, rising to 265.5 metres (870 ft). It has acquired two neighbours recently: the Castor and Pollux towers.

But Frankfurt may well pay a heavy price for progress and prosperity, as it is in danger of losing its past and everyday charm: the corner kiosk, or *Wasserhäuschen*, the friendly pub with garden and the *Lädsche*, that little store that sells practically everything and where people meet for a chat in the old Frankfurt dialect. Nevertheless, if you take a little time, it is still possible to discover the remnants of old Frankfurt. This city on the Main is also an important seat of learning. There are students everywhere and that means lively bars and a cultural paradise.

Paradoxically, in a spiritual sense Frankfurt stands for anything but the might of capitalism. In 1923, the Institute for Social Research was established here under the leadership of philosopher Max Horkheimer and sociologist Theodor Adorno. This was the "Frankfurt School", which acquired a worldwide reputation. Although the institute that revised the theories of Marx, Freud and other great thinkers had to move to Geneva in 1933 and then on to New York, Horkheimer and Adorno returned to Frankfurt in 1950.

Imperial centre

There is evidence of Celtic and Germanic settlements by the banks of the River Main dating from the 1st century BC, as well as Roman remains from the 1st and 2nd centuries AD. The name Frankfurt ("Ford of the Franks") arose about AD 500, when the Franks drove the Alemanni south, but the first written mention of *Franconofurd* appeared in documents in

LEFT: Frankfurt's Messeturm.
BELOW: street sculpture fun.

794 when an imperial gathering was held under Charlemagne. In the 12th cen-tury, the Hohenstaufens built a new castle here and the greatest of their ruler Frederick Barbarossa, became the first German emperor to be elected by prince and bishops in Frankfurt. For the next 650 years Frankfurt played out its role a the election city of the Holy Roman Empire of German Nations; after 1562, th German emperor was also crowned here, in the cathedral.

In 1810, Frankfurt became capital of the Grand Duchy of Frankfurt create by Napoleon. While a French protectorate, Frankfurt boomed as never befor the Jewish community was given equal rights and the Rothschilds rose become Europe's leading banking family.

After the Congress of Vienna in 1815, Frankfurt was again a free imperial ci and from 1816–66 the capital of the patchwork quilt of German states known the German Confederation. When, from 1830, German liberals and nationalis battled to establish a united and democratic Germany, Frankfurt was at th centre of the revolutionary fervour. But the German National Assembly c 1848–49, held in the Paulskirche, was only a shortlived affair. In 1866, Fran furt was annexed by Prussia, ending once and for all its free-city status.

When the Frankfurt Book Fair was re-established in 1949, the aim was simply to create a centrepiece for the German book trade. Nowadays it is primarily concerned with selling world-wide translation rights.

A stroll about town

Much of the Old City was destroyed during World War II, but a great deal ha been restored. The **Römerberg** Ⓐ with the **Gerechtigkeitsbrunnen** (Fou tain of Justice) at its centre is a good place to start and finish a tour of the city historic sites. The Kaisersaal or Emperor's Room in the **Römer** (open dai 10am–1pm, 2–5pm), Frankfurt's town hall, serves to remind visitors of th great moments in the country's distant past; it was here that the magnificer

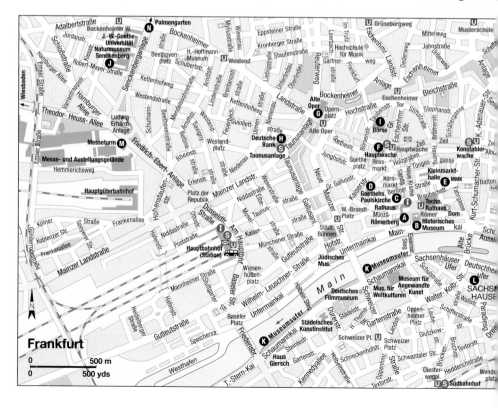

Frankfurt

0   500 m
0   500 yds

Map
on page
246

ronations took place. The next point of interest is the **Historische Ostzeile**, row of rebuilt, medieval half-timbered houses opposite the Römer. If a little stenance is required, then **Haus Wertheym**, the only original 16th-century, lf-timbered building provides a friendly atmosphere.

The Protestant **Nikolaikirche** (1290), originally the royal chapel, and the **Kaiser-** ɔm, the Emperor's Cathedral (foundations date from 852, rebuilt several times, e latest in 1953) are situated immediately adjacent. Among the many art treasures the cathedral, the most notable are the sculptures to the side of the chancel and ans Backofen's *Crucifixion* (1509) in the tower hall. At Römerberg, modern art touring exhibitions as well as action art shows are the specialities of the **Schirn-** unsthalle (Art Gallery; open Tues–Sun 10am–7pm, Wed–Thur until 10pm), hich also has an ambient, post-modern café-bar-restaurant to recommend it.

The **Historisches Museum** at Saalgasse 19 (open Tues–Sun 10am–6pm, 'ed until 9pm) is an amalgam of modern architecture and ancient buildings om the Hohenstaufen period – the Saalhof chapel dates from around 1170. On isplay here are exhibitions documenting the history of Frankfurt.

Just to the northwest of Römerplatz is the **Paulskirche** ❻ (1789–1833), here the German National Assembly, the first all-German parliament, con- ɛned. After suffering considerable damage in World War II, it was converted ito a concert hall in 1948. The Goethe prize and the Peace Prize offered by the erman publishing industry are awarded here every year.

Connoisseurs of German literature will find the **Goethehaus** ❼ at Grosser irschgraben 23–25 of interest. The house where Johann Wolfgang von Goethe, ermany's most famous playwright, was born and raised is now a museum (open lon–Sat 10am–6pm, Sun 10am–5.30pm; guided tours in German at 2 and 4pm).

TIP

Between the main railway station and the old centre around the Römer, Norman Foster's building of the Commerzbank and the Main Tower are the architectural highlights.

BELOW: the Historische Ostzeile.

*Inside the
Architekturmuseum.*

BELOW:
the Alte Oper.

A mix of museums

An impressive modern art collection is on show at the **Museum für Modern**
Kunst E (Domstrasse 10; open Tue–Sun 10am–4.30pm, Wed until 7.30pm
Built to fit a triangular site, it is nicknamed "the slice of cake" and its 40 room
are surprisingly varied in layout. Artists range from Roy Lichtenstein and And
Warhol to Joseph Beuys and Reiner Ruthenbeck. A Children's Room moun
exhibitions designed to stimulate young imaginations.

Shoppers should head for the **Hauptwache F** (1730), a former police static
that's now a café. The **Zeil**, Germany's longest shopping street, starts her
Opposite is a pedestrian zone known as the **Fressgass** ("Glutton's Lane"), s
called because of its many delicatessens and restaurants.

Situated at the end of the Fressgass, on Opernplatz, is the beautifully rebui
Alte Oper G. The old opera house is now both a concert hall and a congres
centre. Around the corner is the **Jazzkeller**, an important venue for jazz enthu
siasts. Nearby, opposite the Taunusanlage gardens, you can't miss the gleamin
twin towers of the **Deutsche Bank H**, while further east on Börsenplatz, the o
Börse I (Stock Exchange) occupies an elegant neoclassical building.

As well as its lively theatre scene, Frankfurt has a number of superb museum
Perhaps the most interesting one is the **Naturmuseum Senckenberg J** with i
excellent collection of fossils and dinosaur skeletons (Senckenberganlage 25
open daily 9am–5pm, Wed until 8pm, Sat–Sun until 6pm).

Nine museums line the south bank of the Main, a district known as th
Museumsufer K (most open Tues–Sun 10am–5pm, Wed until 8pm). Th
Städelsche Kunstinstitut displays paintings dating from the 14th century to th
present day, whereas the **Liebighaus** exhibits sculptures from antiquity to th

baroque period. The **Deutsche Filmmuseum** documents the German film industry and film performances are also staged here. On or near the Schaumainkai you'll find the **Deutsches Architekturmuseum**, the **Museum für Angwandte Kunst** (Museum of Applied Arts), **Museum der Weltkulturen** (Ethnological Museum), the **Deutsches Museum für Kommunikation** (Communication Museum; open Tues–Fri 9am–6pm, Sat–Sun 11am–7pm) and the **Ikonen-Museum** (Icon Museum) at Brückenstrasse 3–7.

Map on page 246

To the southeast of the museum quarter, the district of **Sachsenhausen ❶** has a wide range of restaurants, pubs, beer gardens and jazz bars. In the cafés around the Klappergass, the favourite tipple of the locals is a drink called *Ebbelwoi*, which is a kind of cider, often mixed with mineral water.

The **Messeturm ⓜ**, the gigantic, multi-storey tower (265.5 metres/870 ft) with its pointed roof, is the landmark of the Frankfurt fairground. Every October, thousands of publishers arrive to do deals at the **Internationale Buchmesse**, the world's biggest book fair. The **Internationale Automobilausstellung** (motor show) is another important event. If now is the time for a little relaxation, then try the **Palmengarten ⓝ**, one of Europe's most beautiful botanical gardens.

Tapping Ebbelwoi in Sachsenhausen.

Excursions

Frankfurt lies within easy reach of the Taunus mountains and many Frankfurters wishing to escape from the stresses and strains of city life seek refuge here at weekends. **Bad Homburg vor der Höhe** (pop. 52,000), only 17 km (10 miles) from Frankfurt in the foothills of the Taunus range, is a favourite destination. Even in Roman times the healing power of the local waters was well known. Later, celebrated guests included emperors, tsars and kings. English visitors marked out the first tennis court on continental Europe and later Germany's first golf course.

BELOW: a day out at the Opel Zoo.

There are some interesting sights in the large Kurpark, such as a **Siamese Temple**, a **Russian Chapel** and a casino. The baroque **Landgrafenschloss** (1680) overlooking the town was built by Friedrich II. From Bad Homburg it is only a short bus ride to **Saalburg**, a rebuilt Roman fort (AD 83–260) that once guarded the *limes*, the border of the Roman Empire. The **Saalburgmuseum** displays a collection of artefacts from this period (open daily 9am–6pm, winter 9am–4pm).

Line S4 of Frankfurt's S-Bahn takes 25 minutes to cover the distance to **Kronberg** (pop. 18,000), whose skyline is dominated by a castle of the same name (1230). Edible chestnuts, once of significant commercial value, can still be collected in the **Hardtwald**. First take a stroll through the delightful medieval town centre and then give the children a break by visiting the **Opelzoo**.

Oberursel is the gateway to the Taunus. The U3 underground line from Frankfurt will take you there in only 25 minutes. Footpaths up into the hills start at the Hohenmark station, but the highest peak in the range, the **Grosser Feldberg** (880 metres/2,886 ft), can be reached by car or bus. On a clear day the view extends across the Upper Rhine plain as far as Alsace. Opposite stands the more peaceful **Altkönig** (798 metres/2,617 ft). There is no road to the top – the footpath starts in Falkenstein. ❑

THE RHINE AND MOSELLE

Thanks to its brooding castles and steep-sided valley, the Rhine has long been the epitome of German Romanticism. The theme continues along the Moselle, also famous for its fine wines

Map on page 252

The Rhine has been Germany's "river of destiny" since time immemorial. Before AD 55, when Julius Caesar had the first bridge built across the river near Andernach, north of Koblenz, the Rhine formed the last frontier between the Roman Empire and the Germanic tribes. But when the Romans crossed this river the Germans were irrevocably drawn into the process of world history.

Countless vineyards and castles, idyllic towns and sombre legends have for centuries symbolised the conflicting traits that are said to mark the German national character: a zest for living and sentimentality on the one hand, brooding and haughtiness on the other. The belligerent and the romantic, the bustling and the idyllic exist side by side in the landscape of this river.

With a total length of 1,320 km (820 miles, of which 539 flow in Germany), the Rhine is the third-longest river in Europe, after the Volga and the Danube. It has its source at the base of the Gotthard Massif in the Swiss Alps and flows into the North Sea near Rotterdam. For the last 883 km (552 miles), from Rheinfelden near Basle to its estuary, the Rhine is the busiest waterway in Europe. Nearly 10,000 barges and freighters ply its waters every month with all kinds of cargo, while the water itself also carries seawards much of the waste that is created in the manufacture of those goods.

Despite pollution, which has been reduced considerably, the Rhine appears to have lost none of its romantic appeal, and for the millions of tourists from all over the world who come here every year it remains a symbol of both German history and the German spirit. The symbolism of the Rhine was reinforced by the German and also the English, Romantic poets.

LEFT: quality control on the Moselle.
BELOW: Burg Katz, near the famous Lorelei.

Gutenberg's city

Not far from the confluence of the River Main and the Rhine lies the ancient city of **Mainz** ❶ (pop. 195,000), which was founded as Magontiacum in 38 BC. After several hundred years of decline, the former capital of the Roman province *Germania superior* embarked on a long period of prosperity in AD 747 when St Boniface, the "German Apostle", made it the seat of an archbishop. The city thereby became the centre of Germanic Christendom.

The archbishops of Mainz were not only spiritual shepherds, but in simultaneously performing the role of chancellors to the Reich and electors of the emperor, they became one of the strongest secular powers in the Roman Empire of German Nations. In 1254 Mainz joined with Worms in founding the Rhenish League of Cities, which grew to become a group of 70 cities. Together they succeeded in releasing the Rhine from the grip of the robber knights, who during the vacuum of the Great Interregnum (1250–73) had gained a hold on most of Germany. Mainz's most famous son is undoubtedly Johannes Gutenberg (c.1397–1468), who was the inventor of the printing press. It was while living in Strasbourg, from about 1434 onwards, that he developed the revolutionary system of printing with moveable letters. After returning to his home town in 1448, he won the patronage of the Mainz tradesman Johann Fust, who advanced the necessary capital to print the 42-line Latin Gutenberg Bibles, of which 48 copies are known to exist today. The **Gutenberg Museum** contains a replica of the master's workshop (open Tues–Sat 9am–5pm, Sun 11am–3pm). Along with the old printing apparatus, the most valuable objects on display are two of the 48 extant Bibles, testimony to the amazing revolution that Gutenberg began. In 1477 a university bearing Gutenberg's name was founded in Mainz.

The mighty Romanesque **Cathedral** (AD 975) stands opposite the museum and, with its six red sandstone towers, remains the dominant feature of a city that practically had to be rebuilt after the devastation of successive bombing raids.

Once a centre of printed media, Mainz is now the home of some major German TV stations (ZDF, SAT1, 3SAT, SWR).

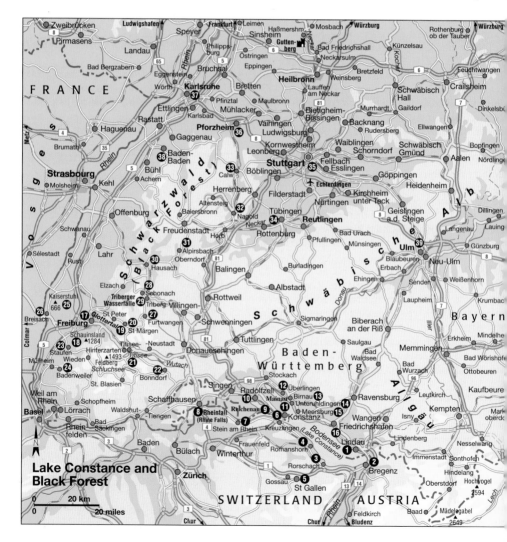

during World War II. Only about 20 original buildings remain. Mainz is the capital of the federal state of Rhineland-Palatinate, founded in 1949.

Near the cathedral stands the 14th-century Stephanskirche, where the artist Marc Chagall worked on painting the window until shortly before his death in 1985. The **Kurfürstliches Schloss** (Electoral Palace), a late-Renaissance building, houses the **Römisch-Germanisches Zentralmuseum** (Roman–Germanic Museum; open Tues–Sun 10am–6pm), as well as the banqueting halls in which the famous annual carnival performances are held.

A glass of wine in Rüdesheim

From Mainz the Rhine begins to meander its way through the steep valley separating the Taunus and the Hunsrück mountains. In addition to the barges, there are countless pleasure steamers plying up and down this romantic stretch of the river, which is accompanied by ever-changing vistas of quaint villages with pointed church spires and golden weather cocks, narrow gorges and steeply sloping vineyards.

Following the river downstream towards Koblenz, the traveller soon arrives in **Eltville ❷**, the *alta villa* of Roman days, seat of the electors of Mainz for 150 years. The tower of the **Kurfürstliche Burg** (Electoral Castle) recalls the days when the archbishops of Mainz sought refuge here in times of war and rebellion. Many 16th- and 17th-century townhouses and former residences of the landed gentry are worth seeing in the town centre, as indeed is the **Parish Church of Saints Peter and Paul** (built from 1350). The historic Rhine promenade, which at one time was scheduled to make way for a road and railway, has been saved by the efforts of a local pressure group.

In the north of Eltville, a narrow road branches off to the wine village of **Kiedrich** with the ruins of **Scharfenstein Castle** and **Kloster Eberbach ❸**. Here, in 1116, Augustinian monks first started cultivating their Rheingau vines, pressing specially cellared communion wine from their grapes.

Rüdesheim ❹, with its famous **Drosselgasse**, has somehow managed to market itself to millions of visitors as a typical, quaint wine "village". Despite the **Brömser Burg** (the oldest castle on the Rhine, built in the 9th century), there is very little to distinguish Rüdesheim from other settlements along this stretch of the river. All have typical half-timbered houses and all have narrow back alleys and *Weinstuben* (wine bars). The visitor would be well advised to steer clear of the crowds on the Drosselgasse itself and head for less busy pubs and restaurants, where the atmosphere can still be enjoyed – and at remarkably low prices.

From Rüdesheim a cable lift makes the journey to the 37-metre (121-ft) high **Niederwald Monument**, whose scale and position high above the Rhine are breathtaking. Created as an expression of Wilhelminian aspirations of power after the Franco-German war (1870–1), the statue they call **Germania**, symbolically depicted as a sword-brandishing Valkyrie, gazes defiantly westwards.

There is a ferry from Rüdesheim to **Bingen ❺** at the confluence of the Rhine and Nahe rivers. Together

Map on page 252

TIP

While in Rüdesheim, visit the Rheingau- and Weinmuseum, housed in the Brömser Burg, where you can learn more about the region and its wine production.

BELOW: Rüdesheim's famous Drosselgasse.

with the **Mäuseturm**, perched on a rock in the middle of the river, **Castle Klopp** controlled the Rhine at this point for Bishop Hatto of Mainz, who was thus able to derive considerable income from taxation of the commercial traffic both beside and on the river. The Mäuseturm later served as a signal tower to warn the passing traffic of **Bingen Hole** and its treacherous reef.

A string of castles

The next 16 km (10 miles) after Bingen Hole will make any visitor appreciate why the Rhine has played such a central role in so many fairytales and fables, legends and songs. The majestic Rhine, with its steep valley sides, forested slopes, vineyards and castles, holds not just those of a romantic disposition in its spell. Train passengers have a panoramic view from the comfort of their seats, for the railway line follows the river's course for the entire dramatic stretch between Bingen and Bonn. The castles recall the days when the robber knights, having rendered the land routes impassable, blocked the river with chains in order to demand tolls from the traders.

Just before Bingen the **Ehrenfels Fortress** stands sentinel above the right bank of the river. Nearby is the riverside town of **Assmannshausen ❻**, famous for its fine red wine. A ferry takes you to the left bank, where castle after castle – Rheinstein, Reichenstein, Sooneck, Hohneck, Fürstenberg and Stahleck – mark the riverside all the way to **Bacharach ❼**, with its lovely Old Town.

A few kilometres beyond Bacharach, the middle of the river is dominated by the picturesque **Pfalzgrafenstein Island** and its castle, a customs post built here in a watery location in the 14th century. It was at this point that Marshal Blücher crossed the Rhine on New Year's Eve 1813–14 with the help of a

All-weather cuckoo clock in Rüdesheim.

BELOW: Burg Pfalzgrafenstein, near Kaub.

pontoon bridge. He was in pursuit of Napoleon's forces who had just suffered a heavy defeat at the Battle of Nations near Leipzig. Opposite stands the small town of **Kaub** ❽ and **Gutenfels Fortress**, which was built in the 13th century. A little further on, the ruins of **Schönburg** come into view above the left bank of the river near **Oberwesel** ❾, a medieval town well worth visiting. Immediately beyond Oberwesel the smooth flow of the Rhine is disturbed by seven underwater rocks, the **Seven Maidens**. According to legend seven girls were turned to stone because they were so prudish. At least that's what the local lads would tell their girlfriends if they resisted their advances. By contrast, the **Lorelei** sealed the fate of many hapless boatmen *(see below)*.

A few minutes' drive further on, three castles appear simultaneously: **Katz Castle** and **Maus Castle** above the right bank and **Rheinfels Castle** on the left bank near **St Goar**. This is the location of an annual September firework display on the river, the **"Rhine in Flames"**. Not far away, **Sterrenberg** and **Liebenstein** castles, known as the two "hostile brothers", are separated from each other by a high wall.

Endless vineyards

The white towers of the Church of St Severin indicate the approach of **Boppard** ❿. Boppard, with its Rhine promenade, more than a mile in length, is the centre of the largest wine-producing region on the Middle Rhine. On the **Bopparder Hang** alone there are one million vines. A cable lift climbs to **Gedeons Eck** (302 metres/991 ft), where a magnificent view of the meandering Rhine divides the river into what look like four separate lakes – hence the name of this spot, the **Vier-Seen-Blick** (Four Lakes View).

Map on page 252

TIP

From July to September the vine-growing villages along the Rhine lay on magnificent fireworks displays illuminating the vineyards. and the river. The "Rhine in Flames" is a beautiful sight from a riverboat cruise (www.rhein-in-flammen.com; ww.rheinfeuerwerk.de).

BELOW: the Lorelei of legend.

THE LORELEI

Ich weiss nicht, was soll es bedeuten, dass ich so traurig bin, ein Märchen aus alten Zeiten, das kommt mir nicht aus dem Sinn. So begins the famous Lorelei poem, written by Heinrich Heine in 1824. It tells the story of a beautiful siren, the Lorelei, who would sit on the clifftop high above the river, combing her hair and singing seductively to passing boatmen. Thus distracted from the lurking dangers of the river, the boatmen would be lured to their watery grave. "I cannot divine what it meaneth..." is the beginning of Mark Twain's translation.

The poem, set to music by Friedrich Silcher in 1832, is famous the world over, the epitome of Rhine Romanticism. But Heine, who made it famous, was not the creator of Lorelei: the idea was dreamed up by the German Romantic poet, Clemens Brentano, who in 1801 included the ballad of Lore Lay in his novel, *Godwi*.

The story isn't just a figment of the imagination. Many boatmen did indeed perish in the treacherous currents of the narrows where the Rhine rounds the Lorelei cliffs, which rise 132 metres (433 ft) above the water. Parts of this stretch of the river have been dredged to create safe channels for barges and other boats, and signal masts have been erected so that the boatmen keep on course.

Die Loreley.

Die schönste Jungfrau sitzet / Dort oben wunderbar, / Ihr goldnes Geschmeide blitzet, / Sie kämmt ihr goldenes Haar.

Sie kämmt es mit goldenem Kamme / Und singt ein Lied dabei / Das hat eine wundersame, / Gewaltige Melodei.

TIP

In Koblenz visit the Plan (just around the corner from the Frauenkirche). This market square has been the meeting place for acrobats and musicians for centuries, and you may still see them performing here today. Lovers of contemporary art will be enchanted by the exhibitions of the Ludwigmuseum, in the Deutschherrenhaus.

BELOW:
Boppard by night.

Rivalling Bacharach for the sheer number of its half-timbered buildings is the little town of **Braubach** ⓫. The 13th-century **Marksburg Castle** above the town houses the fascinating **Museum of Castles**. A medieval festival is held here every two years. Diagonally opposite lies the small town of **Rhens** ⓬, in medieval times one of the main centres of power of the German realm. It was here, at the **Kings' Chair**, that the seven electors assembled to choose their kings and emperors. Downstream near **Lahnstein** ⓭, at the confluence of the Lahn, stands the **Wirtshaus an der Lahn**. Goethe used to come to this inn and he mentioned it in his writings. A summer theatre festival is held in the **Lahneck Castle**. Across the river stands **Stolzenfels Castle**.

Where the Rhine and Moselle meet

At the confluence of the Rhine and Moselle rivers stands **Koblenz** ⓮ (pop 110,000), the largest city on the Rhine after Mainz. The **Landesmuseum** (open Mar–Nov daily 9.30am–5pm) has an interesting selection of cultural, technical and historical exhibitions. From the fortress of **Ehrenbreitstein** above the right bank, there are excellent views of the city with the towers of the **Liebfrauenkirche** (Church of Our Lady, 12th–13th century) and the **St Kastorkirche** (Church of St Castor, 13th century). The **Mittelrhein Museum** on Florinsmarkt (Middle Rhine Museum; open Tues–Sat 10.30am–5pm, Sun 11am–6pm) contains works of art from the past five centuries. The origins of the city lie on the other side of the river (reached via the Pfaffendorfer Bridge), at the magnificent **Kurfürstliches Schloss** (Electoral Palace, 1777–86). The last Elector of Trier had it built on the site of the ancient *castrum ad confluence,* the Roman encampment that was established here in 9 BC.

On a promontory at the confluence of the Rhine and Moselle is a hallowed piece of ground known as the *Deutsches Eck* (German Corner), so named because it was here in 1216 that the Teutonic Knights established their first base. Between 1953 and 1990 the Deutsches Eck was also called the **Denkmal der Deutschen Einheit** (Monument to German Unity). In 1993, the controversial equestrian statue of Kaiser Wilhelm I was re-erected on the site; it had been blown up by US troops in the last days of World War II.

Above the Pfaffendorfer Bridge, with the Moselle on the left and the Rhine on the right, is the famous **Wine Village**. The Weindorf was built in 1925 as a replica of a wine-producing village complete with authentic vineyards and typical half-timbered houses from the most celebrated German wine-growing regions. Here you can take a breather and enjoy a refreshing glass of Moselle wine in preparation for the journey through that lovely valley of vineyards.

Along the Moselle

The idyllic Moselle Valley is the best known of all Germany's wine-producing areas and here enjoyment of good wine is inseparable from the lovely landscape and the region's 2,000-year history. The Romans knew how to sweeten life so far away from home and they bequeathed the Alemanni their Elbling grape, although the typical grape is now the Riesling.

To the left and right of the Moselle rise the uplands of the Eifel and Hunsrück. The steep, slatey southern slopes produce the best wine, although they are very difficult to work. In earlier times many of the vineyards were cultivated part-time, with as many as 12,000 vintners sharing an equivalent number of hectares (about 30,000 acres). Nowadays there are 9,000, mostly larger concerns, their land worked in a more productive and effective way – a necessary development in view of increased competition from other countries of the European Union. The wine of the Moselle Valley wasn't discovered by visitors to the region, but it certainly figures at the centre of most tourist itineraries; visits to wine cellars, vineyard tours, tastings and seminars all offer the opportunity to get to know everything about the noble grape. Every vineyard has its "open day", when visitors are invited to drop in and enjoy a free glass or two of its vintage.

Winningen ⓑ is the first of many typical Moselle villages, with its narrow streets and market squares, hemmed in by half-timbered houses, old wine vaults and new wine cellars. Take a look into the back courtyards and try some delicious cake in one of the charming cafés. And for more information on the wine and history of the Moselle Valley it's worth calling in at Winningen's **Wein- und Heimatmuseum** (Wine and Local History Museum; open mid-May–Nov Wed and Sat 3–4.30pm or by request, tel: 02606-2214 or 2126).

One of Germany's most beautiful castles, 6 km (4 miles) from the railway station at Moselkern, **Eltz Castle** ⓰ (open Apr–Oct daily 9.30am–5.30pm) is surrounded on three sides by the Eltz River. The castle was first mentioned in documents in 1150, and since then has belonged to the family of the Count of

Map on page 252

In Winningen, look out for the Weinhexe (wine witch) in the Weinhof, a sad reminder of the town's history. From 1630–60 there was a witchhunt in this area and 21 women were executed, having confessed to cooperating with the devil.

BELOW: dramatic Eltz Castle.

Elce. The castle was spared during the wars of the Middle Ages and also escaped destruction by the French, who destroyed almost all the castles in this area nearly 300 years ago. Thousands of visitors have been inspired by its towers, high gables and beautiful ornamentation. The treasures that the counts collected in the course of centuries can be admired in the weapons hall, the painting collection and the luxurious rooms.

Inside Beilstein's baroque church stands a black Madonna. This statue is older than the church itself and is said to have been brought here by Spanish soldiers during the Thirty Years' War.

Thirteen kilometres (8 miles) upstream from Eltz Castle, the little town of **Cochem** ⓱ is situated near the **Cochemer Krampen**, the first and biggest of many idyllic bends in the river. Cochem is dominated by its **Reichsburg** (Imperial Castle), built in 1027. From the castle walls, a fine view of the Moselle Valley and of the town's maze of little streets can be enjoyed. The **Kapuzinerkloster** (Capuchin Monastery, 1635) is also worth a visit. The **Moselle Promenade**, with its wine bars, cafés and restaurants, entices the visitor to take a stroll. Near Cochem's Moselle bridge is the entrance to Germany's longest railway tunnel, the 4,203-metre (4,596-yard) **Kaiser-Wilhelm-Tunnel** (1877), which cuts through the Cochemer Krampen.

Right on the bend is romantic **Beilstein** ⓲, whose historic houses, town hall and church snuggle up to each other between the river and the bordering slopes, crowned by a monastery and castle ruins. The route continues to the dreamy little wine-town of **Zell** ⓳, famous for its "Schwarze-Katz" vineyard.

Some 37 km (23 miles) from Cochem lies **Traben-Trarbach** ⓴, a spa and wine centre. You can take an excursion to **Mont Royal**, one of the largest European fortresses built under the French King Louis XI, and to the ruins of **Grevenburg** (14th century), from where there is a fine view of the Moselle Valley. Another 22 km (14 miles), brings you to pretty **Bernkastel-Kues** ㉑, in the heart of the central Moselle, one of the region's main wine areas. Some 65 million litres (14 million gallons) of wine, the product of more than 5,000 wine growers, are stored in the central wine cellars. The traditional Moselle wine festival in September attracts more than 200,000 visitors. Bernkastel's marketplace, with the ruined castle of Landshut rising over it, has become a symbol of the Moselle. The town is famous for its half-timbered houses, the filigree fountain railing in the market square and the weather vanes on the houses' gables. The **Cusanusstift**, for over 500 years a hospital, was a foundation established by cleric and philosopher Nikolaus von Kues (in Latin, Cusanus, 1401–64). Kues was an important supporter of German humanism who spoke out for religious tolerance. In the cellars of St Nicholas-Hospital is the **Moselweinmuseum** (Wine Museum; open daily mid-Apr–Oct 10am–6pm, winter 2–5pm), where for a small fee you can taste over 100 regional wines.

The trip continues along the winding course of the Moselle to Trier, past vineyards and through idyllic wine villages such as **Piesport** and **Neumagen**.

Germany's oldest city

Founded in 16 BC by the Emperor Augustus, **Trier** ㉒ (pop. 105,000) is considered to be Germany's oldest city. Trier was the residence of Diocletian, Constantine the Great and other Roman emperors. After it became a bishopric in the 4th century, the town was a centre of Christianity north of the Alps.

The **Porta Nigra** (2nd-century), which was once the gate of a Roman fortress and is 36 metres (118 ft) wide and 30 metres (98 ft) high, is considered the best-preserved structure of its kind north of the Alps. The Porta Nigra gets its name from the dark patina that has built up on the limestone blocks. The **Aula Palatina**, a basilica built in the 4th century as Constantine the Great's coronation chamber, and the **Kaiserthermen** (Imperial Baths), begun but not completed under Constantine, also date back to Roman times, as does the **Roman Bridge**.

It is only a short distance from the baths to the ruins of the antique amphitheatre, where 25,000 spectators once attended theatre presentations and bloody gladiatorial battles. The **Rheinisches Landesmuseum** houses a wealth of Roman treasures, including mosaics, sculptures, glass and coins. There are also exhibits from the region's history before the arrival of the Romans and after their departure (open Tues–Sun 9.30am–5.30pm).

The fortress-like **St Peter's Cathedral**, one of Germany's oldest churches in the Romanesque style (11th–12th century), bears witness to the Christian Middle Ages. The foundations date from the 4th century. Its treasures include many precious works including the 10th-century gold Portable Altar of St Andrew. From the church it is only a few steps to the **Hauptmarkt** (Main Market), a picturesque square surrounded by gothic, Renaissance and rococo buildings – a living art-history textbook. And from here, it is not far to Brückenstrasse 10, the house where **Karl Marx** was born in 1818. The house is now a **Museum** and attracts visitors from all over the world (open Nov–March Mon 2–5pm, Tues–Sun 10am–1pm, 2–5pm, Apr–Oct Mon 1–6pm, Tues–Sun 10am–6pm). ❏

Map on page 252

The Neumagner Weinschiff, a Roman wine barge in the Rheinisches Landesmuseum.

BELOW: the Porta Nigra in Trier is one of Germany's best preserved Roman structures.

THE ROUTE TO COLOGNE

After a detour through the hills and villages of the Eifel, the highlight of this continued journey down the Rhine is the city of Cologne with its mighty Gothic cathedral

Map on pages 242–43

I n the extensive region between Koblenz's "German Corner" and the western frontier of Germany lies the bleak but beautiful upland range of the Eifel. For those who followed the meanderings of the Moselle River all the way to Trier, there's a direct route back to the Rhine across these Eifel hills. For those who remain at the Rhine the riverside town of Andernach, near Koblenz, is the best starting point for a tour of the Eifel.

The Eifel

The Eifel is an area of great contrasts. This glorious highland area between Trier, Aachen, Bonn and Koblenz is dotted with picturesque half-timbered towns, old castles and monasteries. Broad plateaux as well as narrow gorges are typical of the landscape, as are the so-called *Maare*, round crater lakes that testify to the volcanic origins of the region.

Andernach ❶ itself is a former Roman settlement, *Antunnacum*. Parts of the medieval wall still surround the town, in the middle of which stands the splendid **Mariendom Cathedral**. On the shores of a crater lake near Andernach stands the Benedictine monastery and church of **Maria Laach Abbey**, whose abbey church (built 1093–1220) is among the most important Romanesque buildings in Germany. The entire abbey complex, whose monks have long since become experienced tour guides, marks the very apogee of Romanesque architecture.

To the north it is well worth taking a detour along the **River Ahr** (excellent red wines), through the picturesque villages of Bad Neuenahr/Ahrweiler and Altenahr and then up into the hills to **Bad Münstereifel ❷**. This small town in the Erft Valley is still surrounded by its perfectly preserved 13th-century town wall. Having entered through one of the four town gates, take a walk along the cobbled streets lined with half-timbered houses and visit the Romanesque House (1167), the 12th-century Romanesque church and the 14th-century town hall.

Monschau ❸ is delightfully situated in the Rur Valley. In the 17th and 18th centuries the little town became rich from the production of cloth, the manufacturers building stylish houses for themselves, including the **Rotes Haus** (Red House) of the clothmaker Johann Heinrich Scheibler. Today it houses a **Museum** (admittance Good Friday–Nov Tues–Sun at 10 and 11am, 2, 3 and 4pm), which includes a fascinating painting collection: all the pictures, together with frames, are painted directly onto the wallpaper. The town is dominated by its castle which today houses a youth hostel.

Aachen ❹ (pop. 260,000) is one of the oldest cities in Germany. It was a Roman spa, called *Aquisgranum*,

LEFT: Cologne's Wallraf-Richartz Museum and Cathedral.
BELOW: the Palace Chapel in Aachen.

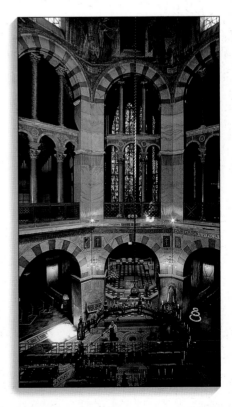

Charlemagne's throne in Aachen.

and rose to prominence in the 8th century as the favourite residence of Charlemagne, who made it the second city of his empire and a centre of Western culture and learning. When the ruler of the Franks died in 814 he was buried in the **Münster** (minster). The minster took centuries to build. Modelled on the church of Saint Vitale in Ravenna, its central part, the Palace Chapel, was completed during Charlemagne's reign in 768. His throne still stands on the upper floor at the western side: made of plain marble slabs, six steps lead up to it, just like the throne of Solomon.

To the north of the minster, where Charlemagne's palace once stood, is the city's enormous Gothic **Town Hall**, erected by the burghers in 1349. The facade is embellished with 50 emperor statues as well as images of the guilds and sciences. The main entrance is up a broad flight of steps, and on the top floor is the enormous **Reichssaal** (Imperial Hall), where numerous rulers were crowned. The **Karlsbrunnen** (fountain) in the marketplace is a favourite meeting point for students – Aachen is home to one of the most important technical colleges in Germany. No visitor to Aachen should come away without some *Printen*, a hard gingerbread-like biscuit.

Back to the Rhine

Back on the right bank of the Rhine, the road leads through Leutesdorf to the small village of **Hammerstein ❺**, watched over by the ruins of the 10th-century **Ley Castle**, where Count Otto von Hammerstein managed to defend himself and his wife Irmgard for three months against the emperor Henry II.

The prime attractions of **Linz** are the city gate towers, the late-Gothic town hall and the excellent local wine. From the **Kaiserberg** (Imperial Castle) there

BELOW: the Rhine from Drachenfels viewpoint.

are wonderful views across the river to the Eifel massif and the valley of the River Ahr. From Linz it is possible to take a ferry to the bridge at **Remagen**. At the end of the war, German forces blew up the bridges across the Rhine in order to slow down the Allied advance. Miraculously though, while 43 other bridges were destroyed, the one at Remagen remained standing long enough for the Americans to cross it, thus shortening the war by several days. The dramatic events are recalled by the **Friedensmuseum** (Peace Museum; open Mar–mid-Nov daily 10am–5pm), which is located in the only surviving tower of the railway bridge.

From the town of **Unkel** it is possible to make a detour to **Arenfels** and **Ockenfels** castles. The road leads through the picturesque hills of the **Siebenge-birge (Seven Mountains)** ❻, said to have been created by seven giants who dug a channel for the Rhine and left seven mounds of earth. Atop the Drachen-fels (Dragon Rock) stand the ruins of the 12th-century **Drachenfels Castle**. It was named after Siegfried, hero of the *Nibelungen Saga*, who slew the dragon and bathed in its blood to make himself invulnerable to attack.

Provisional capital

Before 1949, the major claim to fame of the sleepy electoral residence city and university town of **Bonn** ❼ (pop. 315,000) was as the birthplace of composer Ludwig van Beethoven (1770–1827). But it was then chosen as the provisional seat of the new Federal Government and transformed into a modern capital, with thousands of officials moving into the stately old buildings and new high-rise blocks built to house the various ministries and administrative bodies. When the Berlin Wall collapsed, the authorities were in the process of investing billions in more governmental construction projects, including a new parliamentary chamber. But under the terms of the reunification treaty of 1990, Bonn returned the function of German capital city to Berlin. Heated debates broke out about the future division of responsibilities between Bonn and Berlin. In June 1991, the German Parliament voted for a motion ruling that Berlin should assume its full role as the seat of parliament and government. But Bonn is growing accustomed to its new title of "Federal City" and is turning its attention increasingly to science and culture.

Thanks to its "Museum Mile" it already has quite a lot to offer, including the **Kunst- und Ausstellungs-halle** (Art and Exhibition Hall; open Tues–Wed 10am–9pm, Thur–Sun 10am–7pm) with exhibitions of art, technology, history and architecture. The **Kunstmu-seum** (Museum of Art; open Tues–Sun 11am–6pm, Wed until 9pm) houses works by August Macke, the Expressionists, Max Ernst and Joseph Beuys. The **Haus der Geschichte** (House of History; open Tues–Sun 9am–7pm) displays exhibits describing the history of the Federal Republic, whilst zoology is the theme of the **Forschungsmuseum Alexander Koenig** (open Tues–Sun 10am–6pm, Wed until 9pm).

The history of Bonn goes back to the *Ubii*, a Germanic tribe who were driven out by the Romans, and who called the place Bonna. Remains of the medieval city walls can be seen in the **Sternentor** (Star Gate) and the **Altes Zollhaus** (Old Customs House).

Map on pages 242–43

The Siebengebirge has been famous for its quarries since Roman times. Trachyte, andesite, latite and basalt are still quarried here.

BELOW: Beethoven in Bonn.

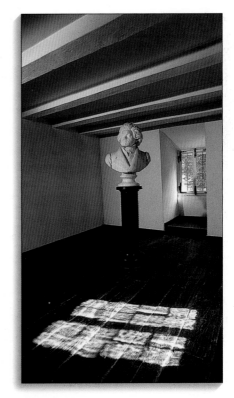

The farmers north of Bonn are called "Kappesboore", the "cabbage growers". The sheltered landscape and fertile soil provide rich farmland, where fruit and vegetables, including lots of cabbages, are grown.

Northeast of the marketplace, at Bonngasse 20, is the **Beethovenhaus** (open Apr–Oct Mon–Sat 10am–6pm, Sun 11am–6pm, Nov–Mar Mon–Sat 10am–5pm, Sun 11am–5pm), where the great composer was born in 1770 and grew up. Since 1889, the 16th-century building has housed the world's most important Beethoven museum, whose exhibits include the piano made specially for Beethoven in Vienna. Nearby, the **Beethovenhalle** on the Rhine promenade is today the setting for concerts and festivals. To the southwest on **Münsterplatz** stands the venerable Romanesque **Minster** with its 12th-century cloister.

In the wealthy suburb of **Bad Godesberg** stands the **Godesberger Redoute**, a fine rococo palace built in 1791–92, where Beethoven once performed concerts.

The cathedral city

The most rewarding and certainly most comfortable way to enter **Cologne** ❽ (Köln in German) is by train. Looking out of the window as the train clatters over the Hohenzollernbrücke, you can enjoy one of Europe's most spectacular city panoramas: the Rhine embankment with its colourful facades and pointed gabled roofs, above which tower the mighty spires of the **Cathedral Ⓐ**.

From the railway station a broad flight of steps leads up to the **Domplatte**, a windy open space where buskers and pavement artists perform before the great backdrop of the cathedral. With its awesome dimensions – 142 metres (472 ft) long by 43 metres (143 ft) high – the cathedral is the unmistakable landmark of this city of one million inhabitants. When it was complete the cathedral's 157-metre (515-ft) towers were the highest in the world. A winding staircase of 509 steps leads to a viewing platform 95 metres (312 ft) up in the south tower, where the view amply rewards the effort of getting there. On the

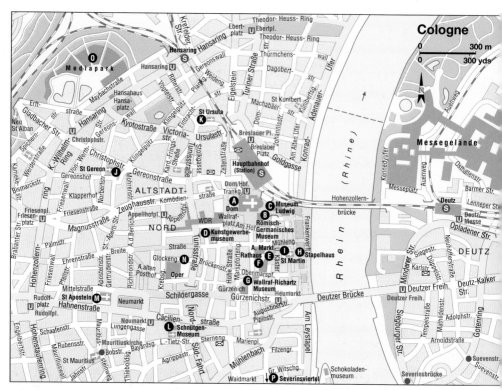

opposite side of the Rhine, in Deutz, you can pick out the tower of the city's exhibition halls, crowned at night by a shining "Köln" sign. The exhibition complex was erected in the 1920s by the lord mayor of the day, Konrad Adenauer, who in the 1950s was Chancellor of the Federal Republic. The other side of the tower offers views of the inner city, including the roof of the Museum Ludwig, in the shadow of the cathedral, and the Westdeutsche Rundfunk building. The pedestrian-zone shopping streets **Hohe Strasse** and **Schildergasse** cut their way through the area.

Back down at street level, it's useful to know the history of the cathedral. It was built as a new repository for the **Dreikönigsschrein** (Shrine of the Magi), which had been housed in the old cathedral since 1164. When in 1248 the Archbishop Konrad von Hochstaden gave his blessing to the commencement of construction work, Cologne was one of the world's wealthiest cities, Germany's largest city and the third largest in Europe after Paris and Constantinople. After the university was founded in 1388, the city became, from a religious, intellectual and artistic point of view, the enlightened focal point of the Rhine Valley.

In 1322, the cathedral's choir, the work of masters Gerard, Arnold and Johannes, was completed and eight years later the construction of the towers began. In 1560, however, work ceased and the cathedral remained just a torso with a choir but no transept or nave and uncompleted towers.

The building would never have been completed if the spirit of historicism and a wave of enthusiasm for the Middle Ages had not spread across Europe in the 19th century and fuelled the revival of the Gothic style. In 1842, the Prussian King Friedrich Wilhelm IV laid the foundation stone for the resumption of work and by 1880 the cathedral was completed, one of the most perfect examples of

Maps:
Area 242
City 264

In spring 1945 there was so little left of the original city that the Allies suggested it might be easier to rebuild Cologne somewhere else. Only the cathedral still stood proudly above the ruins.

BELOW: bridge over the Rhine.

"French" high-Gothic architecture. Although Allied air raids devastated almost all of the old town, the cathedral miraculously escaped heavy damage.

Cologne Cathedral leaves a deep impression on the visitor on account of the unmatched harmony of its individual elements. The interior reaches to the heavens with uplifting Gothic clarity. The centrepiece of the choir is the Shrine of the Three Magi, made in 1225 and the largest gold sarcophagus in the Western world. It was constructed to hold the relics of the Magi. The **Schatzkammer** (Treasury), which contains gold, precious stones and ivory work as well as liturgical robes and documents from many centuries, testifies to the extraordinary wealth of the Catholic Church. The **Cross of Gero** (*c.* 971) is the oldest wood-carved crucifixion work north of the Alps.

The heart of Cologne can be explored on foot and the visitor will constantly be reminded of the city's Roman past. Ancient cobbled streets and an intact thermal bath have been excavated and the **Römisch-Germanisches Museum** ❸ (Roman-Germanic Museum; open Tues–Sun 10am–5pm) contains priceless treasures and offers a fascinating glimpse of life as it was some 2,000 years ago, after the Romans had established their camp of *Colonia* here on the Rhine. The museum was built over the world-famous **Dionysos Mosaic**, which was discovered during construction work on an air-raid shelter. This 2nd-century masterpiece covers an area of 70 sq. metres (84 sq. yards) and consists of more than one million ceramic and glass components. It once covered the dining room floor of a Roman villa.

Next door is the museum complex, whose controversial roof construction stands out very clearly when the city is viewed from the cathedral tower. Within the modern complex is the Philharmonie – a well-known concert hall with wonderful acoustics – and the **Ludwig Museum** ❹ (open Tues–Sun 10am–6pm, first Fri of

BELOW: the Romans left an enduring legacy in Cologne.

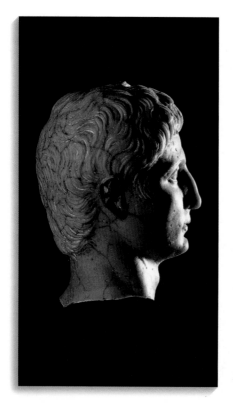

THE ROMANS IN COLOGNE

The first chapter in the history of Cologne was written by the Romans. The frontier of the Roman Empire was the Rhine, and along its western bank they founded their cities, leaving the east bank, which remained largely enemy territory, well alone.

In 38 BC the Roman commander Agrippa founded a fortified settlement, *Oppidum Ubiorum*, in order to help secure the Rhine frontier. This was the birthplace of Agrippina the Younger, who was the wife of Emperor Claudius, and it was at her request that the title of Roman colony was conferred upon the town in AD 50. It was named *Colonia Claudia Ara Agrippinensium*, shortened to Colonia; it later became the capital of Lower Germania.

There are traces of the Romans all over Cologne. The layout of the Roman streets is still recognisable. Excavations beneath and around several churches have revealed the remains of Roman temples, and under the town hall square lie the foundations of the *Praetorium* (governor's residence). The Römerturm (Roman Tower), to the west of the cathedral, was part of the original town wall, as was the Nordtor (North Gate), whose arch is now on display in the Roman-Germanic Museum, together with the Dionysos Mosaic and many other finds.

month until 10pm). The museum is named after the well-known German art collector and chocolate factory owner Peter Ludwig (1925–96), who bequeathed the city his collection of 20th-century art. Among its treasures are works by Schwitters, Ernst, Dalí and Magritte, the Blauer Reiter group (Marc and Macke), the Brücke (Kirchner, Schmidt-Rottluff, Nolde), the Bauhaus (Klee, Schlemmer), paintings by Picasso and Braque and sculptures by Barlach and Kollwitz. Nouveau Realisme and Pop Art are also represented (Warhol, Rauschenberg, Lichtenstein).

To the west of the cathedral, opposite the WDR building, the **Museum für Angewandte Kunst D** (Museum of Applied Arts; open Tues–Sun 11am–5pm) is also well worth a visit. It is one of the most important museums of its type in Germany and displays a wide spectrum of textiles, glass, furniture, ceramics and jewellery, from medieval times to the 20th century.

The Old City

Just a few hundred yards to the south of the cathedral is Cologne's other hub, the medieval **Old City**, at the centre of which is the lively **Alter Markt E** (Old Marketplace), one of the most attractive squares in the city. Like most other areas of central Cologne, the square was all but destroyed during World War II, but some of the townhouses, with their pointed gables, have been rebuilt. Just to the west is the **Town Hall F**, whose various sections take up most of Rathausplatz. Of particular interest here, in the basement of the newer "Spanish Building", are the excavated remains of the **Praetorium**, the seat of the Roman governor. It is possible to go in and even walk along an old Roman sewage conduit. The highlight of the old section of the town hall is the Hansasaal (1330), whose wooden ceiling looks like the upturned hull of a ship. Visible

Map on page 264

TIP

Should you be in Cologne at carnival time don't miss the colourful processions. The official start of Carnival is rung in on the Alter Markt on 11 November at 11.11am precisely.

BELOW: the Olivandhof shopping centre.

from far and wide, the Town Hall Tower (1407–14) was built in the style of a Gothic church tower. The chamber inside, with its seating and intarsia work by Melchior von Reidt, is one of the artistic masterpieces of the Rhineland.

The glass pyramid on the Rathausplatz marks the site of an ancient ritual bath known as the **Mikvah**, which still has a staircase leading down into it. It dates from the late 12th century and is testimony to the fact that this area was once Cologne's Jewish Quarter. Before it was mercilessly destroyed in 1424 and the Jews were driven out, this was one of the main Jewish centres in northern Europe.

South of the Mikvah you find the **Wallraf-Richartz Museum and Fondation Corboud ⑥** (open Tues–Fri 10am–6pm, Thur until 10pm, Sat–Sun 11am–6pm), which is considered to be one of Germany's leading art collections, incorporating medieval painters from Cologne such as Stefan Lochner, panel artists of the 14th–16th centuries (Cranach, Dürer and others), Dutch and Flemish works of the 16th–18th centuries (Rembrandt and Rubens), as well as French painters of the 19th century (Renoir, Monet, Degas, Manet and Cézanne).

Adjacent to the river is the city's old harbour area, whose most important warehouse building, the **Stapelhaus ⓗ**, was built anew after the war and today testifies to the former importance of the medieval trading centre of Cologne. Cologne's prosperity in the Middle Ages resulted not just in the creation of fine houses. Churches were also built in abundance and particularly in evidence are the city's Romanesque churches.

One of the best examples is the **Church of St Martin ①**. Dating from around 1170, the triple-naved columned basilica with its beautiful trefoil-formed choir was razed to the ground in the wartime bombing, but since being rebuilt in 1963 it has resumed its role as the outstanding landmark of the Old City.

BELOW: facades on Cologne's Alter Markt; St Martin's in the background.

The other faces of Cologne

A second Romanesque church of note, **St Gereon's** , stands at the other end of the pedestrian zone, near Appellhofplatz. The 11th-century church, built on a decagonal, oval floor plan, is worth visiting for its interior frescoes, the dome of its nave, its baptistry and sacristy. Closer to the cathedral is **St Ursula's** with its distinctive crowned cupola. St Ursula, the patron saint of Cologne, is said to have been slain here together with her following of 11,000 virgins by a horde of Huns whilst on her journey home from a pilgrimage to Rome. Visitors should also make a point of visiting **St Cecilia's**: dating from the mid-12th century, since 1956 it has been the home of the **Schnütgen Museum** (open Tues–Fri 10am–5pm, Sat–Sun 11am–5pm). It is named after the art-loving cathedral capitulary Alexander Schnütgen, who built up a large collection of religious art, specialising in sculptures, notably crucifixes and Madonnas. Further to the west, on the Neumarkt, is **St Aposteln** (Church of the Apostles), regarded by some as the finest of all Cologne's Romanesque churches.

Cologne isn't just a city of churches and museums, however. Its most famous international legacy is, of course, Eau de Cologne, production of which was established in the city in 1709 by the Italian chemist Giovanni-Maria Farina. Cologne's most famous house number, **4711**, is writ large in gold on the facade of the old Mühlens factory in the **Glockengasse**. Every hour on the hour between 9am and 9pm, you can hardly hear yourself speak as the carillon plays.

Within Germany, Cologne is a well-known media centre, the home of more state-owned and private TV stations than any other city in Germany. The headquarters of the Westdeutscher Rundfunk (WDR) are within a stone's throw of the cathedral. Visitors might like to visit the **Mediapark**, with its modern Cinedom cinema complex and numerous other facilities.

The city is also the undisputed capital of the art trade in Germany. Apart from large exhibitions in the trade fair halls, many small galleries with a good sense of the newest trends have set up business here.

Finally, Cologne has rightly earned a reputation as a city whose inhabitants "live and let live". The people of Cologne are proud of their past without living in awe of it; they are truly attached to their roots and that's their first principle of life. The best way to meet the locals is away from the crowds, in areas like the **Severinsviertel**. In a *Kölschen Weetschaff*, as the pubs are called, you will be served a glass of *Kölsch* (the local beer) by a *Köbes*, as the waiters are known. The people of Cologne are a good-humoured lot and there's no better proof of that than at Carnival – the famous, riotous Cologne Carnival – with its *Rosenmontag* (Monday before Ash Wednesday) procession, when virtually the entire population pours out onto the streets. Up goes the cry "*Kölle alaaf*" – "Long Live Cologne", and live it certainly does.

Düsseldorf, the Rhineland Paris

Lying 40 km (25 miles) to the north of Cologne, not far from the industrial Ruhr, the city of **Düsseldorf** (pop. 585,000) is the capital of Germany's most populated federal state of North Rhine Westphalia. It sits conveniently at the centre of a network of good

BELOW:
Düsseldorf's Rhine Promenade.

Memorial to the writer Heinrich Heine, who was born in Düsseldorf.

BELOW: Henry Moore's *Reclining Figure in Two Parts* (1969) in Düsseldorf's Hofgarten.

communications, served by motorways and at the junction of important north-south and east-west rail routes. Its airport is number two after Frankfurt-am-Main in numbers of charter flights.

The city lies on the right bank of the Rhine – in contrast to the Rhineland cities of Roman origin – and is connected by five bridges with the other bank and its considerably older neighbour, Neuss. The city rose to importance from being a *Dorf* (village) on the River Düssel (a tributary of the Rhine) because of its elevation to the seat of the local Dukes of Berg back in the 14th century. Although it was never as important as Cologne, Düsseldorf's royal patronage nevertheless resulted in it becoming a centre that attracted artists and writers. The Art Academy, founded in 1777, developed into one of the most respected such institutions in the country, a reputation reinforced by the artists Peter von Cornelius and Wilhelm von Schadow, among others. But the academy never rested on its laurels, and important modern impulses were released there, thanks to the work of Paul Klee, who was an academy professor from 1931–33, and the sculptor and "action" artist Joseph Beuys (1961–72). The German writer and francophile Heinrich Heine (1797–1856) was born in Düsseldorf. He was an admirer of Napoleon whom he celebrated in his book *Le Grand*. Napoleon always referred to Düsseldorf as "*mon petit Paris*". The **Heinrich-Heine Institute** (open Tues–Fri and Sun 11am–5pm, Sat 1–5pm) on Bilkerstrasse is home to the country's largest collection of documents illustrating the life and work of the great poet.

Düsseldorf's trademarks, the **Schlossturm** tower and the **Church of St Lambert**, with its characteristic slightly crooked spire, stand directly by the Rhine. The former thoroughfare that ran alongside the river, separating it from the old town, has now been banished underground, giving Düsseldorf an addi-

tional riverside open space, the Uferpromenade. It is now possible to walk unhindered by traffic from the river bank to the bustling old town, a square mile packed so solidly with pubs and restaurants that it has come to be known as the "longest bar in the world".

Another name that has stuck is "the office desk of the Ruhr", earned by Düsseldorf in postwar years when banks, courts, multinational firms, organisations of all kinds, state government departments, service industries and the state stock exchange all established themselves there. Düsseldorf is also a very important centre of trade and industry (iron, steel and chemicals), and it is significant that Japanese firms are much more strongly represented here than in Frankfurt. The city's importance for trade is reflected in the numerous trade fairs held here.

Düsseldorf maintains its reputation as a centre of the arts and it has many good museums: for instance, the **Museum Kunst Palast** (Museum of Art; open Tues–Sun 10am–8pm) in the Ehrenhof, with a collection of French, Italian and Dutch works from the 15th to the 20th century. The municipal **Kunsthalle** on Grabbeplatz 4 (open Tues–Sat noon–7pm, Sun 11am–6pm) stages regular exhibitions of modern art. Opposite, behind a highly polished marble facade, is the **Kunstsammlung Nordrhein-Westfalen K20**, and in the Ständehaus is **K21**, which together comprise the state art collections (K20 closed until autumn 2009; K21 open Tues–Fri 10am–6pm, Sat–Sun 11am–6pm). They show 20th-century works by artists ranging from Picasso to Lichtenstein and a comprehensive collection of works by Paul Klee.

Düsseldorf also cultivates art in the guise of decoration for the body. The international **Modemessen** (fashion fairs) in March and September have reinforced Düsseldorf's fame as a fashion centre. However, you can follow sartorial trends almost as well from a café on the celebrated **Königsallee** ("Kö" for short) as from front row seats at a catwalk show.

Gothic masterpiece

To the east of the Rhine, just a short drive from Cologne and Düsseldorf, lies the upland area known as the **Bergisches Land**. Extensive fir forests beckon hikers and walkers, while the region's reservoirs offer secure habitats for endangered species.

The region is named not after its hills (*Berg* means hill or mountain), but after the counts of Berg who were responsible for the rise of Düsseldorf. Their original seat was Altenberg in the secluded valley of the River Dhünn, but there is nothing to be seen of their castle here because in 1259 Cistercian monks used its stones to create the first **Altenberg Cathedral**, whose successor is regarded as one the finest examples of Gothic architecture in Germany. The simple interior is flooded by light penetrating the enormous West Window – the largest Gothic church window in northern Europe. Ten km (6 miles) to the north, on the River Wupper, lies the restored **Schloss Berg**, the main residence of the counts of Berg from 1118 to 1380, before they moved to Düsseldorf.

The centre of the area is **Wuppertal ⑩**, a city famous for its remarkable **Schwebebahn** (suspension railway), which was constructed along the Wupper in 1901. ❑

BELOW: Altenberg Cathedral.

Map on pages 242–43

THE RUHR

To the northeast of Cologne lies Germany's largest industrial region, the Ruhrgebiet. Every city here has its own special mix of industry, culture and reclaimed countryside

Map on pages 242–43

A ccording to UNESCO the Ruhr belongs, alongside cities like Paris and New York, to the greatest of the world's cultural landscapes. High acclaim indeed, particularly when one considers the problems caused by the coal and steel crises of recent years. But many Ruhr communities have managed to take at least the first steps out of the dead-end street in which, back in the 1970s and 1980s, they had found themselves, and considerable structural changes have taken place. Through the development of new industrial and service sectors they have tried to get to grips with unemployment. Examples of creative solutions are provided by the closed collieries that have been converted into places of cultural activity.

The people of the Ruhr, because of their tradition of living alongside people of the most varied backgrounds, are more tolerant than anywhere else in Germany. And, above all, the tough labour struggles have strengthened the traditional feeling of solidarity.

LEFT: barge traffic on the Ruhr.
BELOW: the *Kneeling Girl* by Wilhelm Lehmbruck in Duisburg.

The world's largest river port

Duisburg ⑪ (pop. 495,000), located north of Düsseldorf and on the western edge of the Ruhr, has been a trading post ever since the 12th century. Many people have come and worked in Duisburg, but the town's most famous son was undoubtedly Gerhard Mercator (1512–94), the cartographer who devised a way of projecting the surface of the globe so as to fit it inside a cylinder and produce the enduring Mercator Projection, still used in atlases today. Duisburg's real economic upswing began in 1831 with the construction of the world's largest river port. A tour by boat of Duisburg harbour, in which primarily iron ore, coal, slag and oil are loaded for shipping on the Rhine, is a fascinating experience. The **Museum der Deutschen Binnenschifffahrt** (Inland Shipping Museum; open Tues–Sun 10am–5pm) further elaborates on Duisburg's past.

But Duisburg also has its cultural side: together with Düsseldorf, it is the home city of the **German Opera on the Rhine** as well as the **Wilhelm Lehmbruck Museum** (open Tues–Sat 11am–5pm, Sun 10am–6pm) in which the works of the famous German sculptor (1881–1919) are displayed.

Oberhausen ⑫ (pop. 220,000) is Duisburg's neighbour, and is the birthplace of Ruhr industry, for the first iron foundry was built here at the end of the 18th century. Each year, it holds one of the world's longest-running film festivals, the International Kurzfilmtage, which has been running for more than 50 years. A visit to nearby **Bottrop** is worthwhile to see the **Quadrat Bottrop**, the city's museum block at Im Stadtgarten 20; and the **Josef-Albers Museum** (open Tues–Sat 11am–5pm, Sun

10am–5pm), featuring the work of this local-born artist who taught at the Bauhaus

Once known as the "armourer of the nation", **Essen ⓭** (pop. 585,000) no longer produces any steel: none of the original 22 collieries now operates. But it was in Essen that the industrialisation of the Ruhrgebiet actually began back in 1837, largely thanks to the innovative ability of the industrial pioneer Franz Haniel, who developed a way of getting the miners to the previously inaccessible bituminous coal, thus enabling the furnaces to produce pig iron very competitively. The steel boom began in earnest. When the mines went into decline Essen gained importance as a centre of service industries. Today, many an international industrial combine has its headquarters in Essen, such as Ruhrkohle AG, the largest German producer of coal, and RWE, the biggest power company in Europe, and Ruhrgas AG. The city is also an episcopal seat, has a university and is the shopping eldorado of the Ruhr.

With its extensive **Stadtwald** woodlands, the **Baldeneysee** lake recreation area and the **Grugapark**, Essen exemplifies perfectly the "green Ruhr" image. The city's Gruga Hall stages six-day cycle races, orchestral concerts and rock spectaculars, as well as exhibitions and trade fairs. The **Zeche Carl** arts and music centre is, like so many independent and officially subsidised complexes in other German cities, an integral part of the Essen cultural scene. The city's **Folkwangschule** has won international fame in the areas of music, dance, theatre and design and the exhibitions in the **Folkwang Museum** (open Tues–Sun 10am–6pm extended hours for special exhibitions) are renowned far beyond the state borders Another interesting feature of the city is the **Design Zentrum Nordrhein Westfalen**, housed in the old Bauhaus building modified in 1997 by British architect Sir Norman Foster. The centre lays on regular international design exhibitions.

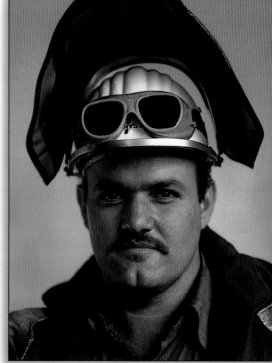

The last mine in **Bochum** ⑭ (pop. 400,000) closed in 1973, but the city is home to other branches of industry including Opel Cars, a subsidiary of General Motors. The Ruhr University, founded in 1965, was the first in the region. The city theatre, the Schauspielhaus, is among the country's best, while the **Deutsches Bergbaumuseum** (Museum of Mines; open Tues–Fri 8.30am–5pm, Sat–Sun 10am–5pm) is one of the most popular technical museums in Germany and the most important of its kind in the world. With replicas of mining villages, mines and real machinery, the museum guides the visitor through the history of industrialisation in Germany. The climax of the visit – great fun for children – is a trip down the demonstration mine.

To the northwest lies **Wanne-Eickel**, where one of the largest popular fairs in Germany, the *Cranger Kirmes*, takes place over 11 days in August. **Recklinghausen** ⑮ (pop. 128,000), on the northern edge of the region, is best known for the *Ruhrfestspiele*, an international theatre festival founded in 1946.

Brewing metropolis

Dortmund ⑯ (pop. 595,000), the modern city on the eastern edge of the Ruhr, is actually very old. It was granted the right to hold a market back in 880 and, more important, in 1293 it was given leave to start brewing beer. While its coal and steel industries have declined, Dortmund remains at the top of the German brewing league – more brewing goes on in Dortmund than in any other city in Europe, including its rival to the south, Munich. All is explained in a **Brauerei Museum** (Brewery Museum; open Tues–Fri 10am–5pm, Thur until 8pm, Sat–Sun noon–5pm) on the grounds of the Actienbrauerei.

Dortmund's revival began in the 19th century with the growth of the coal

Map on pages 242–43

According to a UN report, the Ruhr is one of the most culturally interesting regions of Europe. This fact is probably less due to the excellent established theatres than to the many smaller creative groups that receive little or no state subsidy.

BELOW: the Brewery Museum.

Map
on pages
242–43

and steel industries. The city was heavily bombed in World War II and was rebuilt in its present form, with a number of its historic buildings restored. It suffered again with the decline of mining in the region and in the mid-1980s unemployment rose to 15 percent. Today steel is a thing of the past. The **Westfälisches Industriemuseum** at the Zeche Zollern (open Tues–Sun 10am–5.30pm) has an impressive series of exhibitions portraying working and living conditions during the 20th century on the site of the former coal mine Zollern II/IV. The surface equipment and machinery rooms can be visited.

Dortmund's harbour, connected with the Ems River by the Dortmund-Ems Canal and with the Rhine by the Lippe-Seiten Canal, is the largest canal port in the whole of Europe. Dortmund's **Westfalenhalle**, with the capacity to hold 16,500 spectators, is the scene of mass popular events such as six-day cycle races, equestrian events, ice-skating revues and rock concerts. In the large **Soccer Stadium** Borussia Dortmund has won the highest honours, while athletics and swimming events are held in the stadium's neighbouring competition halls.

Moated castles

The northern fringes of the Ruhrgebiet give way to the Münsterland, the so-called "green belt of Germany". Between large isolated farms and flat fields surrounded by streams and canals, hundreds of moated castles, many of which are open to the public, lie hidden in the clearings in the woods. One of the best ways of discovering them is by bicycle and these are for hire in many of the towns and villages. The region is well-equipped with cycling paths.

The geographical and commercial centre of the Münsterland, **Münster ⑰** (pop. 272,000), was granted its city charter in the 12th century and it soon became a member of the Hanseatic League. The Treaty of Westphalia, which marked the end of the Thirty Years' War in 1648, was signed in Münster. The ceremony took place in the Gothic **Town Hall** (14th-century) on the large market square. The wonderfully restored square is dominated by the **Cathedral** (13th–14th-century), the largest church building in Westphalia. From the tower of **St Lambert's** (15th-century) hang the three iron cages in which the corpses of the leaders of the reformist Anabaptists, executed in 1536, were displayed.

Much of the splendid baroque architecture is the work of the Westphalian architect Johann Conrad Schlaun, including the **Castle**, now part of the university. The **Westfälisches Landesmuseum für Kunst und Kulturgeschichte** (Fine Arts Museum; open Tues–Sun 10am–6pm, Thur until 9pm), with fine altarpieces and Lucas Cranach paintings of Luther and his wife, should also be visited.

The quality of life in Münster has been enhanced by the banning of motorised traffic from the **Promenade**, which runs around the city along the course of the old fortification wall. Other sights that are well worth a visit in Münster include the **Planetarium**, **Zoo** and **Geologisch-Paläontologisches Museum** (Natural History Museum; closed for renovation until beginning of 2009).

BELOW: the Münsterland is famous for its moated castles, such as Vischering Castle.

Reviving the Ruhr

The River Ruhr, a tributary of the Rhine, has given its name to one of the world's largest industrial regions. Although coal mining here dates back to the Middle Ages, the Ruhr's industrial importance dates from the early 19th century when the Krupp and Thyssen firms started large-scale coal mining and steel production.

At that time the population of the region was 270,000. Originally, the Irish, Silesians and East Europeans came to work and settle here and, from the 1960s, they were followed by migrant workers from Italy, Turkey, Greece, Portugal and Spain. This cosmopolitan community transformed the area into a unique melting pot of European nationalities. The population of the Ruhrgebiet today numbers more than 5.5 million.

In the course of the region's development, many of the small towns grew and merged into one another. From the air, the Ruhrgebiet now looks like one massive conurbation, with dozens of sub-centres.

Right up until the 1980s the perception of the Ruhrgebiet was characterised by toil and sweat: men in protective clothing standing before the furnaces, silhouetted by the bright glow of molten iron; miners, their faces blackened by the coal dust, appearing at the surface after a day underground. This "romantic" vision of the Ruhr no longer holds: widespread and far-reaching structural changes have occurred, brought about by innovations in the area of research and technology and the growing awareness of the impact of heavy industry on the environment, as well as recent economic conditions.

The employment figures speak for themselves: at the end of the 1960s the coal mines employed around 266,000 people, but by 2007 the figure had dropped dramatically to a mere 34,000, with the end of the coal mines in sight. The numbers of people employed in the steel industry have also shrunk from 170,000 to 57,000 in the past 35 years. One of the leading roles in structural changes has been played by the sciences.

Until the 1950s the policy towards culture and education was governed by the maxim "we need workers, not intellectuals". The first university was founded in Bochum in 1965. Now, the universities of the Ruhrgebiet employ around 8,500 lecturers and 170,000 students are currently enrolled. Culturally speaking, there is no other region in Germany with such a rich concentration of museums, theatres and concert halls.

Preconceived ideas about the industrial landscape of the Ruhrgebiet usually contradict the reality of the situation. Admittedly, it is difficult to imagine that more than 60 percent of the 4,432 sq. km (2,754 sq. miles) is actually made up of farmland, forests and meadows. There are the scenic river landscapes of the River Ruhr itself, whose artificial lakes provide excellent recreation possibilities, as do the five major parks in Dortmund, Duisburg, Herne, Gelsenkirchen and Oberhausen. In some of the towns where the land has been abandoned by the mines and industry, it is being reclaimed for agriculture. This is a process that seems set to continue in the future. ❏

RIGHT: Essen's Zollverein Schacht XII (Pit XII) is an important industrial monument.

HEIDELBERG AND THE BERGSTRASSE

Map on pages 242–43

With millions visiting its castle each year, Heidelberg is one of the top destinations in Germany. There are more castles in the Neckar Valley and on the wooded heights overlooking the Bergstrasse

D riving south from Frankfurt, Heidelberg is not the first ancient city you'll come to with a glittering history. The A5 and then the A67 lead (via the Lorsch exit) to the old imperial city of **Worms** ⑱ (pop. 83,000), whose history goes back some 5,000 years to the Celts. During the time of the Migration of Peoples, Worms was the capital of the Burgundian realm that was destroyed by the Huns in AD 437, an event which provided the basis for the *Nibelungen Saga* with its hero Siegfried and grim villain Hagen *(see page 286)* and which is documented in the modern **Nibelungenmuseum**.

Numerous imperial diets were held in Worms. In 1521, Martin Luther defended his theses here against Rome and the emperor. The visitor can learn more about the city's past in the extensive **Stadtmuseum** (Municipal Museum; open Tues–Sun 10am–5pm), in the Andreasstift. In the city centre stands the **Cathedral** (12th–13th century). Particularly fine is the Gothic south door, with 700-year-old "pictorial Bible" reliefs. The interior contains a number of Romanesque and Gothic statues and the east choir is dominated by the baroque **High Altar** (1741). The red sandstone church is regarded as a fine example of late-Romanesque ecclesiastical architecture, the heaviness of its walls reduced by the use of glass – such as in the magnificent rose window.

To the west of the cathedral (at the junction of Andreasstrasse and Andreasring) is the **Jüdischer Friedhof** (Jewish Cemetery), Europe's oldest (11th-century) and, with 2,000 graves, the largest. The partly rebuilt **Judengasse** (Jewish Quarter) is on the other side of town. Also of interest are the **Town Hall**, the **Dreifaltigkeitskirche** (Church of the Holy Trinity, 1709–25) and the **Rotes Haus** (Red House), a fine 1624 Renaissance building on Römerstrasse.

Revisiting the Rhine

The region around Mannheim, together with its sister-city Ludwigshafen, is one of Germany's leading industrial centres. Nevertheless, **Mannheim** ⑲ (pop. 310,000) has much to offer the visitor in the way of art and culture. The city is marked by the sharp contrast between the busy river harbour and the stylish and elegant baroque architecture in the centre.

Mannheim was founded by the counts of the Palatinate, on the foundations of an 8th-century settlement. In 1606, the Elector Friedrich IV ordered the town to be fortified, However, this did not prevent it from being destroyed twice in war, in 1622 and 1689. It was subsequently rebuilt on a grid pattern that still characterises the city centre and in which the streets are named only by letters and numbers.

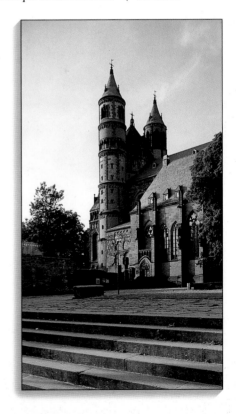

LEFT: Heidelberg and its castle.
BELOW: Worms Cathedral.

The city flourished from 1720 onwards after the Elector Carl Philipp moved his residence here from Heidelberg, but its period of glory ended when Karl Theodor chose Munich as his electoral seat. In the 19th century the Rhine became a major industrial waterway, and Mannheim developed into an important river port. In World War II the city was almost completely destroyed and now Mannheim has a modern character, but with many of the contemporary buildings incorporating attractive historical features.

Mannheim's major sight, the **Kurfürstliches Schloss** (Electors' Palace), built between 1720 and 1760, is one of the largest baroque palace complexes in all Europe. After suffering severe damage in the war, the main stairway, the palace church and the Knights' Hall were all rebuilt. Today, the palace is part of the university. Opposite the palace stands the **Jesuit Church**, completely rebuilt after 1945. The splendid interior decoration is true to the original. A few blocks towards the centre is the **Reiss-Engelhorn Museum**, housed in the former arsenal (open Tues–Sun 11am–6pm). It provides a comprehensive insight into the history of the city and has a number of collections, including some exquisite porcelain. Here also is the first bicycle, made by Baron von Drais in 1817 and a replica of the world's first car, invented by Carl Benz in 1886.

Art-lovers make for the **Städtische Kunsthalle** (Municipal Art Gallery; open Tues–Sun 11am–6pm), which has a collection of wonderful works from the 19th and 20th centuries. A boat trip around the huge harbour completes a visit to Mannheim. The boats depart from near the **Museum Ship** (replete with models of ships) at the Kurpfalz bridge from June to September.

After a detour to the **Schwetzingen Palace** ⑳, a royal summer residence surrounded by one of the most beautiful baroque gardens in Germany, sample the exquisite locally grown asparagus if in season (May–June). A stop is also recommended on the road to Speyer, on the bridge over the Rhine, for a fine panoramic view dominated by the city's imposing Romanesque cathedral.

Speyer ㉑ was founded in Roman times around AD 50 and was first mentioned as a bishopric in AD 343. A century and a half later it was taken by the Franks. Between 1294 and 1797, it was one of the seven Free Imperial Cities of the Holy Roman Empire of German Nations. More than 50 imperial diets were held within its walls. While Speyer survived the Thirty Years' War unscathed, in 1689, during the Palatine War of Succession, it was practically destroyed, its medieval heritage annihilated. As a result, only a few historical buildings remain to recall the glorious past.

The Romanesque **Cathedral**, with six spires, rises majestically over the city. The basilica, built during the Salian period between 1030 and 1125, set new standards for scale and design. At a first glance the exterior seems plain and austere; only after close inspection do the open dwarf galleries and their numerous columns and beautifully carved capitals catch the eye. Nor do the large decorative windows in the transept do very much to alter first impressions. This severity corresponds perfectly with the solemn mood within the building. The whole structure is supported by relatively slim columns with heavy

TIP

While in Mannheim, take a look at the fine Art Nouveau buildings clustered around Friedrichsplatz in a rare unity of style.

BELOW:
Speyer Cathedral.

Corinthian capitals and pilasters carved with geometric designs. In the impressive nave are the statues of eight German emperors who all found their final resting place here. Their tombs and those of their wives are located in the **Crypt**, the largest and, some say, the most beautiful in Germany.

Just south of the cathedral is the **Historisches Museum der Pfalz** (Museum of Palatinate History; open Tues–Sun 10am–6pm), containing a number of interesting collections as well as a section devoted to the history of wine. Other sights include the 12th-century **Jewish Baths**, formerly part of a synagogue; the **Altpörtel**, a 13th-century city gate from where there is a fine view of the city; and the Protestant **Dreifaltigkeitskirche** (Church of the Holy Trinity, 1701–17), with imposing ceiling frescoes.

Homage to Heidelberg

For many people **Heidelberg** ㉒ (pop. 145,000), like the River Rhine, is the embodiment of German Romanticism and its location alone certainly reinforces that impression. Situated on the edge of the Odenwald Forest, where the River Neckar reaches the Rhine Plain, the city nestles against the riverside slopes dominated by its famous castle. With several million people visiting the castle each year, Heidelberg is one of the most popular destinations in Germany.

Human settlers must have been attracted to this place 600,000 years ago, for that is the age of the jaw bone of *homo heidelbergiensis* – the oldest human bone ever discovered in Europe – found at nearby Mauer. Much later, the Celts came and settled here and the Romans constructed a fort. The city was first officially mentioned in 1196 as "Heidelberch" and from 1214 it came to be ruled by the powerful counts of the Palatinate. For almost 500 years the Electoral

Heidelberg is not only famous for its castle and university but also for the printing machines of the same name that are exported all over the world.

BELOW: custodians of Heidelberg's treasures.

College, the body responsible for electing the German kings, was controlled by these counts. And the city bears their unmistakeable mark to this day. Its major landmarks are the castle, the university (founded in 1386) and the Church of the Holy Ghost.

The city suffered greatly during the Thirty Years' War. It was occupied and plundered by the troops of the Catholic General Tilly. The Bibliotheca Palatina, the library built up by the counts, did not escape the pillage. Its priceless books were sent as spoils of war to the Vatican and only the German-language volumes were ever returned. During the War of Succession (1688–97) which, due to the unacceptable claims of the French King Louis XIV, involved half of Europe, Heidelberg was devastated by French troops, first in 1689 and again in 1693. The castle was in ruins for many years until the town's populace decided it was safe enough to commence reconstruction. But even then, in 1764, fate stepped in with a disastrous fire sparked by lightning. Down in the centre of the town, impressive new houses in 18th-century baroque style were built on the medieval foundations.

Mark Twain once described Heidelberg Castle as "the Lear of inanimate nature" in his A Tramp Abroad, 1880.

Heidelberg Castle

The main thoroughfare of the old city centre is the High Street, which today, together with the surrounding lanes, is a pedestrian precinct linking Bismarck-platz and Market Square in the west with the Kornmarkt (Corn Market) in the east. Here begins the 15-minute climb up Burgweg and the Kurzer Buckel to the **Castle** (open daily 8am–5.30pm, guided tours). Alternatively, take the funicular from Kornmarkt; it stops at the castle before continuing to the Königstuhl Heights (558 metres/1,860 ft).

BELOW: the Heidelberg tun, one of the world's largest wine vats.

It took 400 years before the whole complex, with its fortifications, domestic quarters and palaces, was complete, so the building styles evolved all the way from 14th-century Gothic to baroque. The castle is a testimony in stone not only to the power but also to the artistic taste of its creators. Some of the buildings remain in ruins, while others have been restored and are used for banquets, concerts and theatrical performances.

To the left of the massive gate tower (the Ruprechtsbau), the simple **Gothic House** is the oldest part of the complex. Here lived the Elector Ruprecht III, who was also responsible for the Church of the Holy Ghost in the city. The northern side of the courtyard is occupied by the **Friedrich Wing** (1601–7) with its impressive Renaissance facade bearing statues of the German kings. In the cellar is the famous **Heidelberg Tun**, one of the largest wine vats in the world with a capacity of 250,000 litres (55,000 gallons). It was guarded by Perkeo, the court jester, who was known for his thirst. It is said that he died after being persuaded to drink a cup of water after the wine to which he was accustomed. The adjacent **Castle Terrace** has fine views over the city.

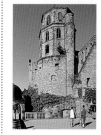

The Castle Terrace has fine views over the city.

The most interesting part of the castle is the **Otto-Heinrich Wing** at the east side of the courtyard, which combines elements of the Italian, Dutch and German Renaissance. The portal's composition of statues and ornamentation is very harmonious. As well as Christian saints, Roman gods are also depicted: Jupiter and Mars and the five virtues – strength, faith, love, hope and justice. The richly decorated doorway resembles a classical triumphal arch and above it stands Count Ottheinrich who had the building constructed from 1556–66. Today it houses the **Deutsches Apothekenmuseum** (German Apothecary Museum; open Apr–Oct 10.15am–5.45pm, Nov–Mar 10am–5.10pm), which has a collection of books, medical instruments and medicine bottles.

BELOW: *al fresco* in the old city of Heidelberg.

The old city

The tour through the old city begins at the **University**. This world-famous institution was founded in 1386 by Ruprecht I and is the oldest university in Germany. During the wars of the 17th century it lost much of its importance, regaining it only after it was reinaugurated by Karl Friedrich of Baden in 1805.

Today, the university has around 28,000 students (about one-fifth of the town's population). In 1930–32, to cope with the increasing numbers of students, a new university complex was built behind Universitätsplatz with the help of donations from the USA. The establishment later expanded to the other side of the Neckar. Student life today doesn't quite compare with the student days of yore. A reminder of the riotous past is the former **Studentenkarzer** (student lock-up) in Augustinerstrasse which, until 1914, served as a jail for students who were guilty of particularly bad 1or "indecorous" behaviour in public. The walls of the cells are covered with humorous drawings and graffiti.

Merianstrasse and Ingrimmstrasse lead back to the Kornmarkt and the market square, where two of the most famous of Heidelberg's student taverns, **Zum Sepp'l** (Joseph's Place) and **Roter Ochsen** (The Red Ox), are to be found. Traditional pubs such as these

remain the haunts of various student fraternities, whose customs are not only perpetuated by hard-drinking contests, but also by the "duels" where the aim is, as in the 19th century, to have a facial scar inflicted by an opponent.

The **Heiliggeistkirche** (Church of the Holy Ghost) stands to the north of the Kornmarkt. The mighty late-Gothic edifice (*c*.1450) is the largest church in the Palatinate. Its founder, Ruprecht III of the Palatinate, who later became King of Germany, lies buried here and the church also once housed the ill-fated Palatinate Library. Opposite (at Hauptstrasse 178) is the **Hotel Ritter**, with one of the finest Renaissance facades in Germany. The building survived the depredations of 1693 because it was the French commander's headquarters. Equally worth seeing is the adjacent former **Hofapotheke** (Court Apothecary, Hauptstrasse 190), a splendid baroque building.

From the church, Steingasse leads down to the river. The **Old Bridge**, which crosses the Neckar at this point, is another of the city's symbols. Goethe thought the bridge one of the wonders of the world, an opinion based not on its technical qualities but on the wonderful view it affords. Upstream looms the **Benedictine Monastery of Neuburg** and downstream the river gradually widens out into the Rhine Plain. Looking back, the city is perfectly framed by the archway of the bridge tower.

Across the river, a steep path winds its way up the Heiligenberg. In the tranquillity of the **Philosophenweg** (Philosophers' Path), one soon leaves the hustle and bustle of the city far behind. Barges chug slowly up and down the river below. The path leads to Bergstrasse, which runs down to the modern **Theodor Heuss Bridge**. Back on the other side of the river, the visitor arrives at **Bismarckplatz**, at the western end of the pedestrian precinct.

BELOW: plenty for all the family to enjoy.

Along the Neckar

Heidelberg's river, the Neckar, has its source in the Black Forest and runs for nearly 400 km (250 miles) before joining the Rhine. A good way of admiring its steeply wooded valley is from the deck of one of the white cruise ships that ply the winding river. Alternatively, you can follow the B37 from Heidelberg via Neckargemünd and Hirschhorn to reach the charming health resort of **Eberbach ㉓**. Standing sentinel above the town is the ruined Emichsburg Castle (11th–13th century), once the largest of the Hohenstaufen forts.

Before continuing north from Eberbach through the Odenwald, you could take a detour further along the Neckar to the south. Beyond the ruins of **Stolzeneck Castle**, high above the left bank of the river, lies **Zwingenberg ㉔**, a health resort with a beautiful castle dating from the 13th century.

The picturesque little town of **Mosbach ㉕**, with its many half-timbered buildings, dates back to the 8th century, when a Benedictine monastery was founded here. There are two noteworthy fortresses in the vicinity of the town. **Hornberg Castle** dates from 1148 and remains one of the most interesting castles on the Neckar. For 45 years it was in the possession of Götz von Berlichingen (1480–1562), the intrepid knight who is immortalised in Goethe's drama of the same name. The castle is now a hotel, but the museum installed in the tower and dedicated to the heroic deeds of this leading figure of the Peasants' Revolt is open to the public, as are the dungeon and knight's armoury.

A little further to the south near Hassmersheim, **Guttenberg Castle** is one of the oldest Neckar castles and among the best preserved. It is a splendid example of medieval castle design and clearly demonstrates the development from castles constructed purely for defence to those built for residential purposes.

Map on pages 242–43

Götz von Berlichingen was an intrepid knight, romanticised in legend as a German Robin Hood. When not engaged as a soldier, he kidnapped nobles for ransom and attacked convoys of merchants for booty, activities that twice put him under the ban of the empire.

BELOW: treasures of Guttenberg Castle.

Through the Odenwald to the Spessart

From Eberbach, the B45 cuts right through the heart of the Odenwald Forest, ancient hunting ground of the Burgundians (Nibelungen) and backdrop for the *Nibelungenlied (see below)*, to the picturesque towns of Erbach and Michelstadt. **Erbach** , a health resort and erstwhile residence of the counts of Erbach, has a well-preserved old town dissected by narrow alleys. The church dating from 1748 and the town hall, a 16th-century half-timbered building, are worth visiting, as is the **Deutsches Elfenbeinmuseum** (Ivory Museum; open daily Mar–Oct 10am–5pm, Nov–Feb Tue–Sun).

Not far away is **Michelstadt** ㉗, with half-timbered houses and romantic nooks. Its perfectly intact **Marketplace**, complete with town hall, is a jewel of medieval civic architecture, planned in 1484. Behind it is the parish church of St Michael and St Kilian (1461–1537) with Glockenspiel and the tombs of the Erbach nobility. Also worth inspection is the **Odenwald- und Spielzeugmuseum** (open daily 10am–5pm) with artefacts from Celtic and Roman times as well as a lovely doll collection from the 19th century.

Focal point of the old Franconian baroque town of **Amorbach** ㉘ is its abbey. The abbey church, with a Romanesque west tower, was reconstructed in baroque style between 1742 and 1747. Its interior, with gilding and frescoes, is a stunning example of pure rococo. Of special beauty is the iron gate to the choir, which once separated monks from the congregation. The huge baroque organ, in keeping with the mighty high altar, has 3,000 pipes and 63 registers and is the second-largest such instrument in Germany.

Ten km (6 miles) to the north lies **Miltenberg** ㉙, which is dominated by the castle of the same name built in 1210. Lying in the shadow of the old castle, the

TIP

If you walk up to Miltenberg Castle you'll be rewarded with a beautiful view of the town below and the meandering River Main.

BELOW: Siegfried slays the dragon.

THE NIBELUNG

What the *Iliad* and the *Odyssey* are to Greece and the Arthurian legends are to Britain, the *Nibelungen Saga* is to Germany: a statement of an archetypal myth that has remained an enduring element of the national identity.

The Nibelung legends are a blend of fact and fiction, recounting the history of the Burgundian (Nibelung) court, whose capital was at Worms, until its downfall at the hands of Attila the Hun (or "Etzel"). There are records of Attila defeating a Burgundian tribe in 437, and also documentation of Queen Brunhild, although no evidence has been found of an invincible Siegfried brought down by intrigue and betrayal.

One main source of the legends is the *Nibelungenlied*, penned by anonymous authors around 1200, probably drawing on the tales of wandering bards. The first half deals with the life and death of Siegfried, the second with the Nibelungs' total defeat by Attila. Another villain is the scheming courtier Hagen, who at one point throws the Nibelung treasure into the Rhine: there's a statue of him caught in the act by today's Nibelungen Bridge in Worms.

Richard Wagner used the concept of "Rheingold" in his opera cycle *Der Ring des Nibelungen*. Fritz Lang's masterful silent film adaptation is a more literal rendering of the saga.

architectural composition of the buildings has made the town world-famous. The fountain and the old timber-framed houses, as well as the former wine cellars from 1541, the 17th-century wine tavern **Zur gülden Cron** and the **Weinhaus am alten Markt** are world-renowned.

A pretty road along a bend of the River Main brings you to its confluence with the River Tauber at **Wertheim ⑩**, dominated by the ruins of its old castle. Narrow streets and high-eaved buildings give this old Franconian town its character. From Wertheim, the route continues northwards along the Main to **Marktheidenfeld ⑪**, whose half-timbered buildings lining the market square are still in good order. Just to the north stands **Rothenfels Castle**, towering 224 metres (735 ft) over the Main. Its stout defence walls and keep were built in the 12th and 13th centuries.

From Marktheidenfeld, the Franconian city of Würzburg *(see page 215)* is only a short drive away. In the other direction, the journey back towards Frankfurt takes you through the very heart of the **Spessart Forest**. The Spessart, which encloses the River Main in almost a square, is one of Europe's finest nature parks, with extensive oak woods and idyllic meadows. The author Wilhelm Hauff (1802–27) was inspired by the region to write his picaresque tale *Das Wirtshaus im Spessart*, which in turn gave filmmakers ideas for locally-shot scenarios featuring bands of robbers and ghosts.

Set in the middle of the forest is the small town of **Mespelbrunn ⑫**, location of one of Franconia's most popular attractions, the moated **Schloss Mespelbrunn** (open Mar–Nov Mon–Sat 9am–noon, 1–5pm, Sun 9am–5pm). The seat of the Echter von Mespelbrunn family, the castle, which seems to float on the water in its idyllic forest setting, was built in 1564 in Renaissance style and completed in the 19th century. It contains a valuable art collection. ❑

Map on pages 242–43

TIP

Don't forget to visit the pilgrimage church in Mespelbrunn. There you can see works of art by Tilman Riemenschneider and Hans Backoffen, including a crucifixion group.

LEFT: the moated castle of Mespelbrunn. **BELOW:** Michelstadt market square.

THE FAIRYTALE ROAD

A trip along the Märchenstrasse follows in the footsteps of the Brothers Grimm. The Weser Valley is picturesque and detours take in Hamelin, Hanover and Bremen

Map on pages 242–43

rom the Grimm Memorial on Hanau's market square, the German Fairytale Road runs north 595 km (370 miles) to Bremen, cutting right through the region where the brothers Jacob and Wilhelm Grimm (1785–1863, 1786–1856 respectively) collected and wrote up the traditional stories that are known today as *Grimms' Fairytales*. The story-telling talent of Wilhelm Grimm is to be credited for the rapid spread of the stories and their translation into more than 140 languages. The Grimm brothers also developed the basics of German grammar and published the first volumes of the German Dictionary.

The journey along the Fairytale Road begins just to the east of Frankfurt in the town where the two brothers were born, **Hanau am Main** ❸ (pop. 88,000). An atmospheric start to the journey is a presentation of Grimm fairytales on the summer open-air stage of the **Schloss Philippsruhe**. Within the palace, the **Hanau Museum** (open Mon–Thur 8.30am–4.30pm, Fri until 12.30pm) has local history exhibits as well as a collection of regional and Dutch art. Hanau has been a centre of the jewellery trade since the 16th century and on the old marketplace stands the **Deutsches Goldschmiedhaus** (German Goldsmiths' House, 1538–50), a fine, half-timbered building. Further skills were imparted by Protestant Dutch and Walloon refugees who arrived in the 17th century. The spa of **Wilhelmsbad** has a lovely park, and the **Hessisches Puppenmuseum** (Hessian Dolls Museum; open Tues–Sun 10am–noon, 2–5pm) is popular with families.

Gelnhausen ❸, 20 km (12 miles) from Hanau, prospered at the junction of important trading routes and was made an imperial free city in 1170. In that same year Frederick Barbarossa built a castle there, the **Kaiserpfalz** (1170–80), which developed into the centre of the Staufer dynasty. The first imperial assembly, or Reichstag, took place here in 1180.

The route across the **Kinzigtal** valley goes through **Wächtersbach**, which has retained the magic of a small residential town, as well as the attractive health resorts of **Bad Orb** and **Bad Soden**.

Grimm associations

The Grimm brothers spent their childhood in the **Amtshaus** (now a museum; open daily noon–5pm) in the little town of **Steinau an der Strasse** ❸, in the heart of one of Germany's most beautiful stretches of countryside, the **Bergwinkel**. Set among the rolling hills is the old monastery town of **Schlüchtern** ❸, where the **Bergwinkel Museum im Lauter'schen Schlösschen** (open Apr–Sept Tues–Sat 2–4pm, Sun 10am–noon, Oct–Mar Wed and Sun only) exhibits Grimm memorabilia as well as items recalling Ulrich von Hutten (1488–1523), a knight and poet who took on Luther's cause and fought for a German Empire free from foreign and priestly domination.

LEFT: Göttingen's "little goose girl" has been kissed by thousands of newly graduated students. **BELOW:** the Grimm Brothers in Hanau.

Where Boniface lies buried

An excursion to **Fulda** (pop. 64,000) ③ is recommended. The history of the episcopal city, set between uplands of the Rhön and Vogelsberg, goes back to 744 when St Boniface built a monastery on the ruins of a Merovingian castle. The monastery grew into the major centre of religion and science of the Frankish empire. Boniface was martyred in 745 in Friesland. His tomb, then still in the monastery's Church of the Redeemer, became a place of pilgrimage.

Fulda's baroque quarter is unique in its unity. Johann Dientzenhofer, working for the prince-abbots, reconstructed the Renaissance palace between 1706 and 1721, into today's **Stadtschloss** (City Palace). He was also responsible for the plans for the **Cathedral**, where the remains of St Boniface lie in the crypt. A baroque alabaster relief, framed by black marble, depicts his martyrdom.

The **Fulda Vonderau Museum** (open Tues–Sun 10am–5pm) has interesting cultural and natural history exhibitions, as well as paintings and sculptures. Children can enjoy the touch-sensitive displays and experiments in the **Kinder-Akademie Fulda**. Outside Fulda is the **Fasanerie**, a small baroque palace.

Between Fulda and Bad Kissingen lies the barren upland landscape of the **Rhön** ③, the remains of a volcanic massif. A mixture of high moorland and windy plains, the area is partly a nature reserve. Its highest point is the **Wasserkuppe** (950 metres/3,135 ft), whose name – meaning "water dome" – derives from the many springs to be found there. It was on the Wasserkuppe that gliding in Germany was born. After World War I, Germany was forbidden to develop its own air force, so the Germans took to the air in gliders. There's a **Deutsches Segelflugmuseum** (Museum of Gliding; open Apr–Oct 9am–5pm, Nov–Mar 10am–4.30pm), and trips are organised by the gliding school. To the northwest rises the summit of the **Milseberg** (835 metres/2,755 ft), where a pilgrimage chapel and the remains of a Celtic camp are found. In the **Rhöner Museumsdorf** (open April–Oct Tues–Sun 10am–noon, 2–5pm) in **Tann** ③, visitors are introduced to the traditional customs of the mountain peasants of the Rhön.

At **Lauterbach** ④ one is back on the Fairytale Road. Hundreds of thousands of garden gnomes are produced annually here and dispatched all over the world. The half-timbered houses around the **Ankerturm** give a foretaste of the next town, as **Alsfeld** ④ is well-known for its historic style of architecture. Its market square has an impressive **Town Hall** (1512–16), **Weinhaus** (1538) and **Hochzeitshaus** (Wedding House, 1564–71). Other fine stone and half-timbered houses (mostly 14th-century) line the streets of the Old Town. *Oak beams, carved corner-posts and transoms with inscriptions bear testimony to a high standard of medieval craftsmanship.

Forty km (24 miles) west of Alsfeld is the university city of **Marburg** ④ (pop. 80,000), the cradle of the German Romantic movement. It was here that the Grimm brothers began their research work into German fables. The old town centre, with its narrow streets and beautiful market square, extends from the banks of the Lahn up to the slopes of the Schlossberg. **St Elizabeth's Church** (1235–83) is an early-Gothic masterpiece, with aisles of equal height and impressive

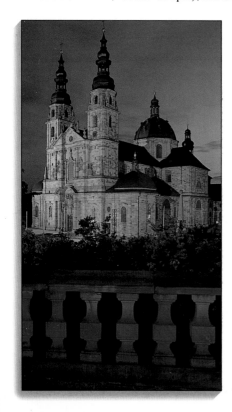

stained glass in the three middle windows of the choir. In the **Landgraves' Castle** (open Tues–Sun, Apr–Oct 10am–6pm, Nov–Mar 11am–4pm), with its great Gothic Knights' Hall, Luther and Zwingli held their famous "Marburger Religionsgespräche" in 1529. The **University**, founded in 1527, was the world's first Protestant university and it has a strong hold on Marburg life.

Map on pages 242–43

Little Red Riding Hood Country

The story of Red Riding Hood and the Wolf originates in the Schwälmerland area east of Marburg. Red Riding Hood's characteristic head-covering is part of the traditional costume still worn on local holidays in the processions that are part of such festivities as the **Salatkirmes** in **Ziegenhain** and **Hutzelkirmes** in **Treysa**. Examples of the costume can be seen in the **Schwalm Museum** (open Tues–Fri 10am–noon, 3–5pm, Sat 3–5pm, Sun 2–5pm) in **Schwalmstadt ㊸**.

Back on the Fairytale Road, the route leads through the health spas of **Neukirchen** and **Oberaula** on the southern slopes of the **Knüllgebirge** to **Bad Hersfeld ㊹**. This upland health resort is well known for its annual theatre festival in the **Stiftsruine**, the most extensive Romanesque church ruins north of the Alps. The **Lullus** and **Vitalis** springs are valued for their health-giving waters, while every October the town's founder is commemorated with a festival known as the Lullusfest.

The administrative centre of the region, **Homberg ㊺**, has many half-timbered buildings to admire, particularly on the market square, where old patrician houses stand alongside the large Gothic church of St Mary's, the **Marienkirche**. The **Krone** tavern, which was built in 1480, is said to be the oldest hostelry in Germany still functioning.

Bad Hersfeld's monastery was founded by Lullus, a follower of St Boniface in 769. Sadly it was burnt down by French troops in 1761.

BELOW: historic Marburg.

TIP

Highlights of Kassel's
Wallpaper Museum
include baroque gilded
leather wall coverings,
19th-century French
panoramas (with an
1814 depiction of the
Battle of Austerlitz),
and the "Tapas" – a
wall decoration from
the south seas.

BELOW:
Documenta mascot.

In **Fritzlar** ⑯, Boniface destroyed a sacred shrine of the heathen Germans: he felled the oak tree of the god of thunder and lightning, Donar, and founded a Benedictine monastery in its place in the year 724. An imperial city developed, whose importance can be judged today by the impressive medieval centre with defence walls and half-timbered houses around the market square. The **Cathedral** (11th–14th century) is the symbol of the city, which belonged to the prince-bishops of Mainz for centuries.

The once sleepy Residence city of **Kassel** ⑰ (pop. 200,000) has become the most modern centre of this region. After its almost complete destruction by Allied bombing in 1943, reconstruction changed the original city plan and only a few historical buildings were restored.

The city's symbol is the enormous **Hercules** statue that looks down on Kassel from the heights of the **Wilhelmshöhe Palace Park**, laid out in the 18th and 19th centuries. With a soaring fountain, the **Grosse Fontäne**, numerous waterfalls and artificial ruins, it can claim to be one of Europe's most grandiose parks. Built in 1786–1802, the **Palace** itself (open Tues–Sun 10am–5pm*) has a fine interior and collections of paintings by Dutch and Flemish masters as well as antiques. The **Deutsches Tapetenmuseum** (Wallpaper Museum*), housed in the **Hessisches Landesmuseum** (closed for restructuring in 2009), has a fascinating collection of wallpapers from many parts of the world (see adjacent Tip). The **Brüder-Grimm-Museum** (open daily 10am–5pm, Wed until 8pm) recalls the 30 years the Grimm brothers worked in Kassel.

Since 1955, the city has been a mecca for artists and art-lovers from all over the world: the **Documenta**, Kassel's presentation of contemporary art, is held every five years (next in 2012). For 100 days the world's best is on show

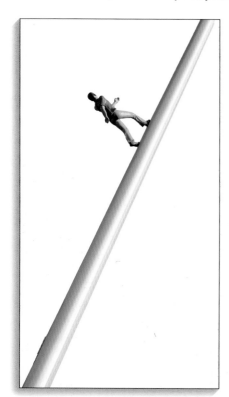

KASSEL DOCUMENTA

Travellers coming out of Kassel station are greeted by the figure of a man walking diagonally up a tall blue pole. For those who didn't know, this is the first sign that Kassel is a town known for its art.

Every five years, it hosts a show billed as the world's largest exhibition of contemporary art. And every five years, people flock here to examine, to criticise, to enthuse, to shake their heads and revel in their own perplexedness or incomprehension. Love it or hate it, Documenta always gives you something to talk about.

Documenta was founded in 1955 as a way of drawing more attention – and visitors – to a town that had been hard hit in World War II. Initially, the show was held at irregular intervals, but Documenta could regularly be counted on to create controversy, particularly when artists such as Joseph Beuys got in on the act.

The summer exhibition, which lasts for 100 days, is spread through a number of venues all over the city. Originally, it centred in the Fredericianum Museum, Europe's oldest museum building; now it not only extends to other buildings, but spills out into the city. Of late, works of art have been placed in pedestrian subways, on pavements, and even in the train station.

in a series of exhibitions, held in such venues as the **Museum Fridericianum** (open Wed–Sun 10am–6pm; Wed free entry), continental Europe's oldest museum building, and the Orangerie in the Karlsaue baroque park.

The Grimm brothers also worked in the university city of **Göttingen** ㊽. From 1351 until 1572 the city (pop. 135,000) belonged to the Hanseatic League. Its initial prosperity came to an end, however, in 1547 with the defeat of the Lutheran Schmalkadian Federation. The founding of the **University** by Prince Georg August von Hannover in 1734 gave Göttingen fresh impetus. By 1777, with no less than 30,000 students, Göttingen University had become the largest centre of learning in Germany and in the meantime more than 30 Nobel Prize-winners have studied or taught here. The city retains a special flair, and many fine buildings testify to its former prosperity, among them the Gothic **Church of St John** and the Old Town Hall, the **Altes Rathaus** (1369–1443). Centrepiece of the market square is the bronze **Gänseliesel**, a statue of the Little Goose Girl, who is traditionally kissed by every graduating student.

Map on pages 242–43

Along the Weser Valley

The Werra and Fulda rivers join together in Hannoversch Münden to form the River Weser. From here the river snakes along, twisting around countless bends on its 440-km (273-mile) journey to Bremen. Riverside meadows, spruced up towns and villages, castle ruins and Renaissance palaces lead one to believe that, just as in the fairytale of *Sleeping Beauty*, time actually could stand still here. At the end of the 16th century the Weser valley served as one of central Europe's granaries. The wealth of the area's rulers and residents can still be seen. Green rolling hills, some reaching a height of 500 metres (1,600 ft), stretch

BELOW: the Weser Valley near Münchhausen's Castle.

Visit the zoo near the Sababurg and come face to face with numerous native species.

along both sides of the river. The Wesertalstrasse runs along the right side. From here the panoramic views of the fishermen and rowing boats, freighters and excursion boats are just as lovely as those from the Fairytale Road along the left bank. Boat trips along the Weser are operated from the Bad Karlshafen area and from Bodenwerder to Hameln.

The picturesque town of **Münden** was founded in 1170 by the Thuringian landgraves. Münden has more than 700 well-preserved half-timbered houses, built over six centuries. The **Town Hall**, an early Weser-Renaissance structure, is worth a visit, as is the **Welfen Palace**. This dates from the 16th and 17th centuries and is a local history museum. The **Ägidien Church** contains the grave of the notorious Dr Eisenbarth (1663–1727). During the summer, a play about his radical methods of healing is performed every second Sunday from May to August. His house still stands in Langen Strasse.

Some 10 km (6 miles) to the north, a passenger ferry driven by the river current crosses the river to Hameln. **Bursfelde** , further downstream, is noted for its 12th-century Benedictine monastery, which has some medieval frescoes and a bell dating from the 14th century.

Huguenots and members of the Protestant *Waldenser* sect who had been subjected to persecution in their homeland were granted asylum in **Gottstreu** by the landgrave Karl von Hessen-Kassel (1677–1730). After the devastation of the Thirty Years' War, these immigrants were instrumental in rebuilding the area.

The hills on the left bank of the Weser are densely wooded. In the heart of the **Reinhardswald** forest and perched on a high plateau lies the **Sababurg**, where the Sleeping Beauty could well have been aroused from her slumbers. Although half of the castle is in ruins, the other half has been turned into a hotel with

BELOW: Weser Renaissance in Vlotho.

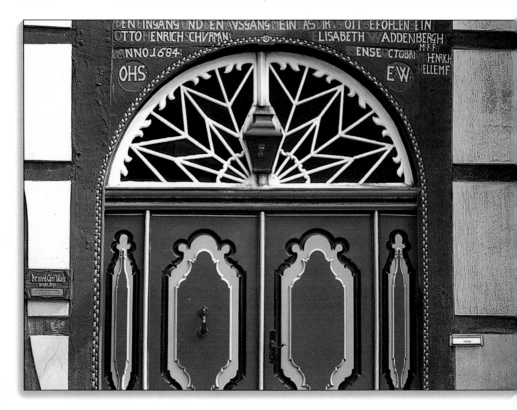

modern comforts. Nearby is a zoo that has specialised in the preservation of native species of animals. Towards Beberbeck lie 70 hectares (170 acres) of **Primeval Forest** where centuries-old beeches and oaks have survived. A bizarre geological phenomenon can be found between Friedrichsfeld and the **Trendelburg**. Known as the **Nasser Wolkenbruch** (Wet Cloudburst), it is a 12-metre (40-ft) deep crater lake that was formed when overlying strata collapsed.

Bad Karlshafen 52, the "white town", was founded in 1699 by Karl von Hessen-Kassel. To avoid paying customs duties, he drew up plans for a canal from the Diemel to Kassel, but only the harbour and 14 km (9 miles) of waterway were completed. Huguenots also settled here and the many well-preserved relics in the **Deutsches Hugenottenmuseum** (Huguenot Museum; open mid-Mar–Oct Tues–Sun 10am–5pm, Nov–Dec Sat–Sun 2–5pm) provide an insight into the history and culture that these refugees brought with them. The revenues from the town's era as a health spa, which began in 1730, made possible the construction of a multi-storey white baroque building that gave the town its nickname.

After Meissen, **Fürstenberg 53** is the oldest porcelain factory in Germany (founded 1747). A **Porcelain Museum** (open Apr–Oct Tues–Sun 10am–5pm, Nov–Mar Sat–Sun 10am–5pm) as well as the factory shop are housed in the **Renaissance Palace**. Nearby is **Höxter 54** with its ancient city walls, half-timbered houses and typical Weser-Renaissance **Town Hall**. To the northeast the former **Kloster Corvey** dates from 822. In medieval times this abbey was a cultural centre of European importance and in the 12th century the Imperial Diet often met here.

Baron von Münchhausen (1702–97), better known as the "Baron of Lies" (*Lügenbaron*), was born in **Bodenwerder 55**, a town of well-preserved city walls and half-timbered houses. A monument in front of the Town Hall was built in memory of the baron's "ride on half a horse". This building used to be the Münchhausen's family home and now houses the **Münchhausen Museum** (open Apr–Oct daily 10am–noon, 2–5pm). From the **Ebersnacken** hill (460 metres/1,508 ft) to the south of the town, a fine view extends across to the Harz mountains.

The castle of **Hämelschenburg 56** near **Emmern** is the best example of a Weser-Renaissance castle. Constructed between 1588 and 1599, the entire building, including the oriels and octagonal towers, is extremely well preserved.

Home of the Pied Piper

Hameln 57 (pop. 58,000), which grew out of a monastery in the 8th century, proudly and rightfully calls itself "the city of the Weser Renaissance". Just one among many beautiful buildings, the **Rattenfängerhaus** recalls the famous story of the *Pied Piper of Hamelin*. In 1284, the city was suffering a plague of rats. A fancifully dressed man named Bundtig who happened to be passing through the town promised to end the plague and was hired by the city fathers. He lured the rats out of the city by playing his flute, but the city fathers refused to pay him his reward. One Sunday, when all the adults were in church, he earned his revenge by once again playing his flute, this

Baron von Münchhausen became famous as a raconteur of extraordinary tales about his life as a soldier, hunter and sportsman. They became widely known and popular in many languages. The English-language edition (1793), The Adventures of Münchhausen, is still available.

BELOW: the Pied Piper of Hamelin.

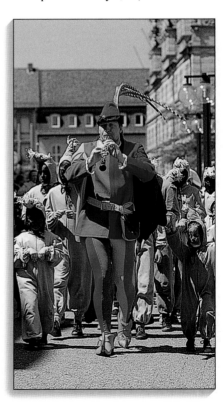

One theory about the Pied Piper of Hamelin is that he was actually recruiting young townsfolk to go to the new German colonies of eastern Europe. Once knights had conquered the area they needed settlers to populate their towns.

BELOW: Hanover's Town Hall is on the banks of a lake.

time luring away 130 children. Every Sunday from July to October, a play depicting this legend is performed in front of the **Hochzeitshaus** (Wedding House).

Detour to Hanover

Hanover ⑤⑧ (pop. 520,000), the capital of Lower Saxony* and the state's centre of trade and industry, is also well-known as the location of the **Hanover Messe**, the world's largest industrial fair, which is held annually in April, and as the host of Expo 2000. Founded in 1163, Hanover soon became a member of the Hanseatic League. From 1636 to 1866 the city was the seat of the dukes of Calenberg and for much of that time (1714–1837) Hanover and Great Britain were governed by the same ruler. In 1866 it came under Prussian control.

Because of the devastation suffered in World War II, this city has only a few remaining noteworthy structures. However, the 14th-century **Ägidien Church**, the old **Town Hall** and the **Marketplace** merit a visit. The grave of the philosopher Gottfried Wilhelm Leibnitz (1646–1716) is in the Neustädter Church, near the 17th-century **Leine Castle** (now the State Parliament). The **Kestner Museum** (open Tues–Sun 11am–6pm, Wed until 8pm) displays ancient Greek, Roman and Egyptian art. However, for many art-lovers, the collection of 20th-century art in the **Sprengel Museum** (open Wed–Sun 10am–6pm, Tues until 8pm) is the main highlight. The **Niedersächsisches Landesmuseum Hannover** (Lower Saxony State Museum; open Tues–Sun 10am–5pm, Thur until 7pm*) has an impressive collection of German impressionist paintings. West of Hanover along the Herrenhäuser Allee, the **Herrenhäuser Gardens** are worth visiting for their beautiful baroque layout, yet in a couple of years the castle destroyed in World War II will be rebuilt (as financed by the Volkswagen Foundation) to house new museums.

To the east of Hanover, **Braunschweig** (Brunswick in English; pop. 240,000) is Lower Saxony's second-largest city. Destroyed in World War II, it was quick to regain its position of economic significance. Henry the Lion, Duke of Bavaria and Saxony, lived here from 1166 onward. **Dankwarderode Castle** with its Brunswick lions, located in the centre of the old city, serves as his reminder. His gravestone, a fine example of Romanesque stone-masonry, lies in the nave of **St Blase Cathedral** (1173–95). A half hour's drive to the north is **Wolfsburg** ⑥ (pop. 120,000), home of Europe's largest car manufacturer, Volkswagen *(see page 299)*. The **Autostadt-Museum** with its huge, now accessible, car storage towers (open daily 9am–6pm, factory tours weekdays 9.15am) is worth a visit and can be combined with a boat trip on the Mittelland-Kanal.

North of Hanover on the N3 (16 km/10 miles north of Celle) is the site of the Nazi concentration camp of **Bergen-Belsen**, established in 1943 as a prisoner-of-war and Jewish transit camp. Among the 37,000 prisoners who died here from starvation, overwork and disease in unbelievably squalid conditions was Anne Frank, whose wartime diary later became world-famous.

South of Hanover is **Hildesheim** ⑥ (pop. 103,000). In this bishop's city (founded in AD 815), the Romanesque **Cathedral**, with its beautiful cloisters and superb art treasures, and **St Michael's Church** (1001–33) have been designated as World Cultural Heritage monuments. The Egyptian collection in the **Römer-and-Pelizäus Museum** (open Tues–Sun 10am–6pm) also justifies a visit to the city*.

Back to the Weser

North of **Rinteln** ⑥ on the Weser, **Schaumburg Castle** offers a delightful view of the valley. At **Porta Westfalica** the river has carved a 600-metre (1,968-ft)

BELOW: the Weser at Bad Karlshafen.

Map
on pages
242–43

wide gorge on its way from the Weserbergland region into the northern German plains. North of the gorge is the city of **Minden 63** (pop. 83,000) whose 13th-century **Town Hall** is one of Germany's oldest.

The well-preserved Cistercian monastery of **Loccum 64** (12th–13th century) lies to the north. The church is noted for its sumptuous interior. Cloisters, a hospital and other monastic buildings provide a vivid picture of life in a monastery. A side road leads from here to the expansive **Steinhuder Meer 65**. With a surface of 32 sq. km (12 sq. miles), this lake has a maximum depth of only 3 metres (10 ft). The southern and eastern shore are nature reserves: secure walkways bring visitors closer to the varied flora and fauna.

At the junction of the Aller and the Weser just outside Bremen lies **Verden 66**, a small town with a **Fairytale and Leisure Park**. An equestrian centre and museum will enthral horse-lovers. The **Cathedral** in the centre of the city, built in the year 786, is the oldest brick church in northern Germany.

Rome of the north

The old Hanseatic town of **Bremen 67** (pop. 548,000) together with the port of Bremerhaven, 57 km (35 miles) further to the north *(see page 322)*, comprises Germany's smallest state. The city was founded in the 8th century and was raised to the status of a bishop's city in 789 by Charlemagne. It was once known as the "Rome of the north" due to the fact that it was the departure point for the missionaries who converted the Scandinavians to Christianity. In 1358, Bremen joined the Hanseatic League and in 1646 became a Free Imperial City.

Today, Bremen is Germany's second-largest port after Hamburg, important for the shipment of motor vehicles, cereals, cotton, wool, coffee and tobacco. The

Look out for the "City Musicians" on Bremen's Town Hall.

BELOW: statue of Roland, Bremen.

Overseas Museum (Überseem; open Tues–Fri 9am–6pm, Sat–Sun 10am–6pm) has an ethnographic collection as well as replicas of Japanese and Chinese gardens and buildings. The **Focke Museum** (open Tues 10am–9pm, Wed–Sun 10am–5pm) also documents the region's maritime history. The **Kunsthalle Bremen** (Art Gallery; open Tues 10am–9pm, Wed–Sun 10am–5pm) displays numerous fine works including paintings from the 19th and 20th centuries.

Most of the attractions in the old part of the city are in or around the market square. The first building of interest is the 15th-century Gothic **Old Town Hall** with its ornate Renaissance facade. Its **Great Hall** is the venue for the annual **Schaffermahlzeit**, the world's oldest fraternal dinner. The **Ratskeller** in the cellar is famous for its Gothic vaults and five local specialities.

Close to the northwest tower is the statue of the *Bremer Stadtmusikanten* (Bremen Town Musicians). These four figures, a dog, a donkey, a cat and a rooster, are from a Grimm Brothers' fairytale.

The 10-metre (33-ft) high statue of **Roland** is located beside the Town Hall. Erected in 1404, it serves as a symbol of Bremen's independence. The **Cathedral** with its 98-metre (321-ft) high steeples embodies 1,200 years of history. Near the **Schütting**, the old merchants' house, is **Böttcherstrasse** with restored medieval buildings. From here it is only a few steps to **Schnoor**, the oldest part of Bremen. ❏

The VW Beetle

The customs officers at New York's LaGuardia airport could not believe their eyes. They had asked a businessman from Germany to open his baggage and were presented with blueprints and plans for a four-wheeled hunchbacked "thingumajig". The man insisted that the drawings were of a car, a car that he intended to sell in America. But the officials were not the slightest bit impressed and told him he wouldn't be able to pass his "thing" off as a car anywhere in the world. The documents were declared as "graphic art" on which the German had to pay $30 import duty.

The incident is supposed to have occurred around Easter time in 1949. The businessman was Heinrich Nordhoff, head of Volkswagen, Inc. His deft marketing skills turned this car into an overnight sensation and it became a German bestseller even in the heart of Chevrolet and Cadillac country. Of the 20 million "Käfer" (Beetles) ultimately produced, a world record that still stands, no fewer than five million were sold in the United States.

"Volkswagen" literally translates as the "people's car". In 1933, Adolf Hitler contracted the designer Rudolf Porsche to develop a car that the ordinary working man could afford. Despite opposition from the German automobile industry, the Nazis financed the building and testing of the first prototypes. In 1938, Hitler personally laid the foundation stone of the first Volkswagen factory. A whole town was built upon reclaimed swampland – present-day Wolfsburg. By the end of the war, the town's German population of 14,000 was outnumbered by more than 18,000 forced labourers from Russia and Poland. Today, 120,000 people live in Wolfsburg.

At the beginning of 1939, Germans were encouraged to open special savings plans to enable them to buy a VW. But the 270,000 people who did so never saw the "car for the common man", whose arrival had been hailed for years by the Ministry of Propaganda. During the war civilian projects were sacrificed to the requirements of the Wehrmacht and the projected VW was transformed into an all-purpose military vehicle that could be adapted to all terrains and climates. The Beetle's success after World War II, its reputation as the world's best-built small car, is largely thanks to the punishing trials that Porsche's military vehicles had to undergo during the war.

Immediately after the war in 1945, the British occupation authorities began the first limited production of the Beetle. Heinrich Nordhoff took over management in 1948. During his 20 years at the company the car became a hallmark of the German "economic miracle". VW engineers developed 36 new prototypes, but Nordhoff clung to the myth of the Beetle and would not let any of them go into production. Seen from the outside, there is hardly any difference between the 1948 and 1958 models, but in fact practically every single part was redesigned. VW went on improving the Beetle right into the 1970s and it was only in the 1980s that production of the old Beetle ceased.

But the Beetle story goes on: Volkswagen launched its New Beetle in 1998 – the year it bought the top people's car, Rolls-Royce. ❑

RIGHT: Rudolf Porsche's all-time bestseller.

HAMBURG AND THE COAST

*With Hamburg at its hub, Germany's coast extends
from the North Sea to the Baltic*

The beauty of the north and its coast always conquers the hearts of its guests. The spectacular drama of the landscape is matched by the drama played out in the skies, particularly when the winds blow, the heavens turn dark and the sun suddenly breaks through to drench the land and sea in a magical light.

Emil Nolde (1867–1956), the great northern Expressionist painter, never tired of bringing to life in his paintings the different moods and contrasts created by this light. He placed black peasant cottages next to violet-blue larkspur in front of blood-red skies. The tempestuous deep blue sea whips up a yellow-brown spray that foams under the poisonous yellow light. Foals stand teetering in the deep green marshland under skies of clouds torn by the winds. Nolde was a master of colour who opened many people's eyes.

Along the Baltic Sea coast, on the East Frisian islands, as well as on Amrum, Sylt and Föhr, you can encounter beautiful wide beaches of fine sand that are an open invitation for strollers and a paradise for water-sports fans. The Surf World Cup is competed for off the coast of Sylt, and Kiel is the home of the summer sailing regatta in what is known as the Kiel Week *(Kieler Woche)*.

Hamburg, the lively metropolis on the River Elbe, is situated between the three federal states of Schleswig-Holstein, Mecklenburg-Vorpommern and Niedersachsen (Lower Saxony). Hamburg lives off the sea: the North Sea to the west and the Baltic to the east. Apart from trade, the seas also bring the storm tides – Hamburg's last major floods in 1962 killed 308 people. The city's long tradition of trade is based on its own ethos and pride. Search as one may for magnificent buildings and beautiful examples of architecture, it becomes clear through the cityscape that Hamburg was always a city of the people rather than of the rulers.

East and west are combined in this capital. Millions of West Germans now visit the Mecklenburg-Vorpommern Baltic Sea coast. Until reunification, most people only knew the chalk cliffs of Rügen through the paintings of Caspar David Friedrich. Despite the modern influx, the region has managed to maintain its charm. It also has some great cities, including the Hanseatic towns of Rostock and Stralsund and the magnificent ducal city of Schwerin. ❑

PRECEDING PAGES: windjammers racing in Hamburg's harbour recall the city's maritime prowess.
LEFT: shielded against the elements in the traditional "Strandkörbe".

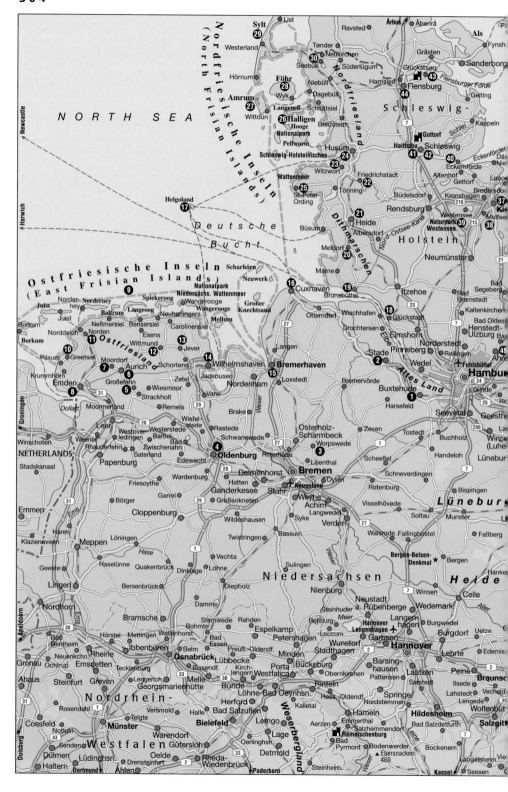

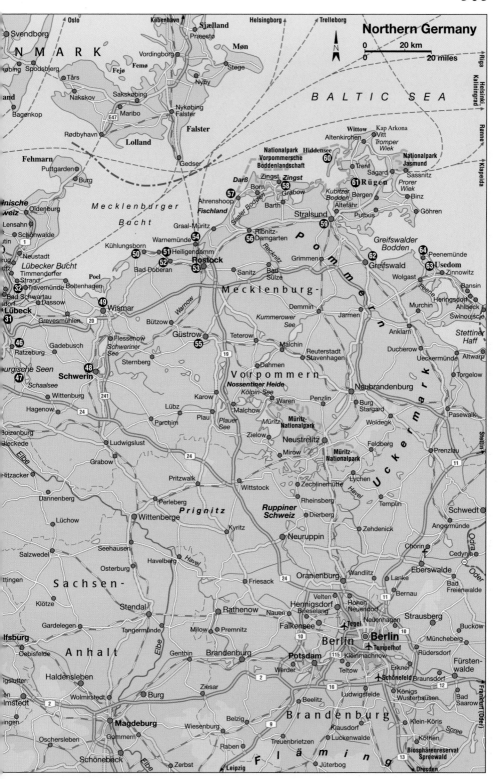

Svendborg

N M A R K

Oslo   København   Sjælland   Helsingborg   Trelleborg

Præstø

Vordingborg   Møn

øbing Spodsbjerg   Femø

Tårs   Fejø

Stege

Nakskov   Sakskøbing   Nyby

and

Bagenkop   Maribo   Nykøbing Falster

E47   Falster

Rødbyhavn   Gedser   Lolland

BALTIC SEA

Helsinki, Kaliningrad
Riga
Rønne
Klaipeda

Fehmarn   Wittow   Kap Arkona

Puttgarden   Altenkirchen   Vitt   Tromper Wiek

Burg   Nationalpark Hiddensee   Trent   Sagard   Nationalpark Jasmund

inische   Vorpommersche Boddenlandschaft   Sassnitz

weiz   Oldenburg   60   Prorer Wiek

Lensahn   Darß   57   Zingst   Zingst   61   Rügen   Bergen   Binz

Schönwalde   Ahrenshoop   Born   58   Grabow   Altefähr   Göhren

tin   1   Fischland   Barth   Kubitzer Bodden   Putbus

Neustadt   Graal-Müritz   Stralsund   Altefähr

Lübecker Bucht   Warnemünde   54   Ribnitz-Damgarten   56   59

Timmendorfer Strand   Kühlungsborn   50   51 Heiligendamm   Grimmen   62   Greifswalder Bodden   64 Peenemünde

32 Travemünde   Poel   52   Rostock   Sanitz   Greifswald   63 Usedom   Zinnowitz

Bad Schwartau   Boltenhagen   Bad Döberan   53   Bad Sülze   Wolgast   Peene   Bansin

dorf   Dassow   **Mecklenburg-**   Murchin   Heringsdorf

Lübeck   49   Wismar   Demmin   Jarmen   Ahlbeck

31   Grevesmühlen   20   Bützow   Kummerower See   Anklam   Swinoujście

46   Gadebusch   Flessenow   Güstrow   Teterow   Stettiner Haff

Ratzeburg   Schweriner See   55   Malchin   Ducherow   Altwarp

urgische Seen   48   Sternberg   19   Reuterstadt Stavenhagen   Ueckermünde

47   Schaalsee   Schwerin   Dahmen   Torgelow

Wittenburg   241   **Vorpommern**   Neubrandenburg

Hagenow   Karow   Kölpin-See   Penzlin   Burg Stargard   Pasewalk

Buizenburg   24   Lübz   Waren   Woldegk   Stettin

aleckede   Parchim   Malchow   Müritz   Müritz-Nationalpark   Feldberg   Prenzlau

Elbe   Plauer See   Zielow   Neustrelitz   11

Hitzacker   Ludwigslust   24   Mirow   Müritz-Nationalpark

Dannenberg   Grabow   Lychen   Schwedt

Lüchow   Pritzwalk   Wittstock   Zechlinerhütte   Havel   Templin   Angermünde

Prignitz   Rheinsberg   Schwedt

Salzwedel   Perleberg   **Ruppiner Schweiz**   Dierberg   Zehdenick   Oder

Seehausen   Wittenberge   Kyritz   Chorin   Cedynia

ttingen   Osterburg   Havelberg   Havel   Neuruppin   Eberswalde

Sachsen-   Friesack   24   Oranienburg   Wandlitz   Lanke   Bad Freienwalde

Klötze   Havel   Velten   11   Bernau   Buckow

Gardelegen   Stendal   Rathenow   Nauen   Hennigsdorf   Hohen Neuendorf   Neuenhagen   Strausberg

Ifsburg   Tangermünde   Milow   Premnitz   Falkensee   10   Tegel   Müncheberg

Oebisfelde   **Anhalt**   Genthin   Brandenburg   Werder   **Berlin   Berlin**   Tempelhof   Rüdersdorf

igslutter   Haldensleben   Ziesar   115   Kleinmachnow   Erkner   Fürsten-walde

en   2   Wolmirstedt   Burg   **Potsdam**   Teltow   Schönefeld   Braunsdorf   12

Imstedt   Belzig   10   Ludwigsfelde   Königs Wusterhausen   Bad Saarow

ingen   **Magdeburg**   Wiesenburg   Beelitz   **Brandenburg**   Klein-Köris

Gommern   9   Klausdorf   Luckenwalde   Spree

Oschersleben   Raben   Treuenbrietzen   Biosphärenreservat Spreewald

Schönebeck   **F l ä m i n g**   13

Zerbst   Leipzig   Jüterbog   Dresden

Elbe

Uckermark

HAMBURG

Maritime Hamburg has always been a cosmopolitan place, and its inhabitants are known for their liberal world view. Germany's principal trading city is also a cultural centre par excellence

Map on page 309

Hamburg is Northern Germany's leading city. With a population of 1.75 million, it is Germany's second-largest city after Berlin and its biggest port, one of the largest media and computer technology centres in the country, and in addition to this has a lively cultural scene.

Hamburgers have often influenced developments well beyond the national boundaries. Take the long-serving Federal Chancellor, Helmut Schmidt, who was known for his characteristic Hanseatic yachting cap and his sailor's pipe (without which European and world summits would simply not have been the same); or the humble hamburger itself (precise origins unknown), which was probably taken to the United States by 19th-century German emigrants and within a matter of decades established itself as an archetypal American food.

The city is also well-known for its colourful bars, providing a nightlife which knows no closing time, although those who prefer a quieter life will enjoy the many green corners and pleasant cafés to be found here too. Hamburg is threaded with waterways, and many an enjoyable day can be spent exploring canals and the port area by boat, discovering the city from the water before moving on to the the wonderful hinterland (including the regions of Mecklenburg-Vorpommern, Schleswig-Holstein and Niedersachsen in Lower Saxony). The open sea is always within reach, be it the quiet and charming Baltic coast or the strongly tidal North Sea – you can even try your hand at freshwater sailing on the Alster.

LEFT: the sound of flutes is a fitting scenario: Hamburg. **BELOW:** Hamburg's town hall, in the heart of the city.

From trading settlement to world city

Water has always been the lifeblood of the city. Ludwig the Pious, son of Charlemagne, was perhaps the first to realise that the location of the Hammaburg settlement, at the confluence of the Alster, Bille and Elbe rivers, had the potential to be extremely profitable and promoted it to an archbishopric in 831. His construction of a fortress here in the 9th century served the dual purpose of intimidating the inhabitants of the surrounding Saxon villages as well as providing a secure harbour from which to carry out commercial trade with the neighbours to the north and to the west. Around 100 years later the settlement was granted market status.

After years of power struggles, with the constant danger of raids from the neighbouring clan of Slavic Obotrites, the settlement at last entered a period of stability under the rule of Adolf von Schauenburg. A new town emerged, centred around the dwellings of sailors and merchants near the site of today's Nikolaifleet, with a harbour on the Alster river and facilities for the use of the Elbe. The evolution of Hamburg into a prosperous commercial city began in 1189 with the granting by Holy Roman Emperor Frederick Barbarossa of special trading rights, toll exemptions and navigation privileges.

TIP

Try some *Labskaus*, a traditional Hamburg dish. Potatoes, herring, corned beef, beetroot and onions used to be the staple of sailors. All mashed up with a fried egg on top, it made a hearty meal out on the ocean, as described by Herman Melville in *Moby Dick*.

From the 13th century, Hamburg served as the North Sea port for the wealthier city of Lübeck. The Hanseatic League developed out of this common trade bond. It became an autonomous free German city in 1510, and, with its conversion to Protestantism 19 years later, demonstrated its desire for independence from the German emperors. Owing to its well-constructed fortifications, Hamburg was able to withstand the ravages of the Thirty Years' War (1618–48) quite unscathed.

The transport of goods and people from Europe to the New World, starting in the 17th century, proved to be very profitable for Hamburg's merchants. It was during this growth period that the city made its major contributions to the development of German intellectual life. Among the best-known names of the Hamburg cultural scene were the composers Georg Friedrich Händel and Georg Philipp Telemann, both of them residents. Gotthold Ephraim Lessing, from 1767 the chief dramatist at the newly founded German National Theatre, wrote his *Hamburgische Dramaturgie*, and Matthias Claudius published the *Wandsbecker Boten* between 1771–76. The city's cultural life in the 19th century was further enriched by Felix Mendelssohn-Bartholdy, Heinrich Heine, Friedrich Hebbel and Johannes Brahms.

After Napoleon's downfall in 1814, Hamburg became a member state of the German Confederation, with the designation "Free and Hanseatic City of Hamburg" from 1819. The city's trade was extended to newly opened territories in Africa, Asia and the Americas. Even the great fire of May 1842, which devastated a quarter of the city, did not check the booming economy. The decision to join the German Customs League, vehemently opposed by many of the city's residents, actually brought immense trade advantages, as well as the development of new industry. By 1913 Hamburg was the world's third-largest seaport after New York and London. When Germany was forced to surrender almost its entire merchant

BELOW: the Speicherstadt.

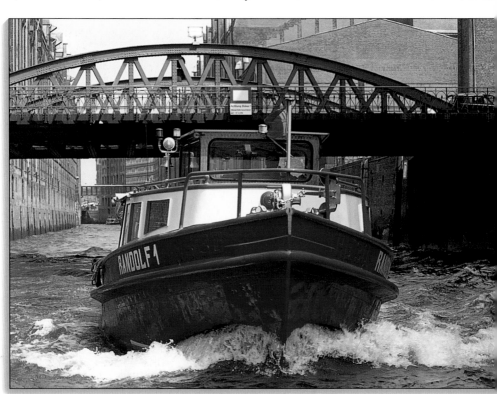

fleet to the victors of World War I in 1918, the port was naturally hit hard. It did not take too many years, however, for the losses to be recouped. The towns of Altona, Harburg and Wandsbeck were incorporated into Hamburg in 1937, bringing the city to its present size of 755 sq. km (290 sq. miles). Due to its strategic economic importance, Hamburg was the target for many bombing raids during World War II resulting not only in severe damage to the city but also in great losses to the civilian population, with a total of 45,000 dead and one million refugees. Even this blow was met with typical Hanseatic composure as the rubble was cleared and a new start made. In 1949, the city-state of Hamburg became a *Bundesland* (federal state).

The loss of its hinterland behind the East German border was a heavy blow, but the city sought successfully to compensate for this by attracting new industries. Hamburg is now the wealthiest community in Germany.

The port

For many visitors to Hamburg the first point of attraction is the **St Pauli Landungsbrücken** near the Old Elbe Tunnel. In former times, before the centre of commercial shipping activities was moved to the outskirts, steamers and sailing ships berthed at these piers. The **Rickmer Rickmers** (1896), a fine example of one of these windjammers and now a museum and restaurant, can be found close by. Today the landing stages serve as the departure point for boat tours of the harbour, an experience to be recommended. To venture further afield a 30-minute ferry ride on the Maritime Circle Line takes you to the southern harbour area and **Ballinstadt** (open Tues–Sun 10am–5pm), which documents the history of emigration – much like its immigration counterpart at New York's Ellis Island – mainly at the start of the 20th century, when mass barracks here housed the new arrivals.

Reminder of the days of sail: the Rickmer Rickmers.

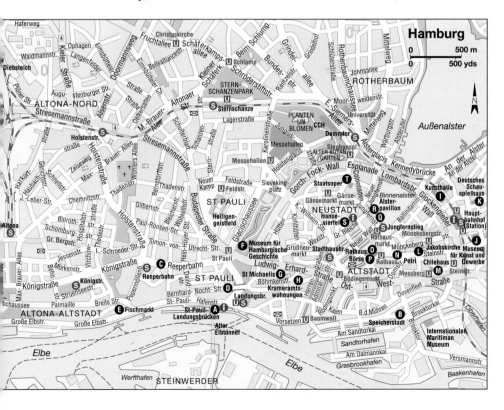

BELOW: exotic line-up at Harry's Harbour Bazaar.

A high point of the harbour tours is the world's largest warehouse complex, to be found in the **Speicherstadt** with its maze of wharves and canals The splendid baroque houses of a prosperous and densely populated merchant's quarter had to be demolished to make way for the Speicherstadt, which was built in 1884–88 by Franz Andreas Meyer to coincide with Hamburg's joining of the German Customs League. Coffee, tea, tobacco, spices and other produce are still stored in the Speicherstadt today in the typical neo-Gothic brick buildings, specially constructed to provide the perfect storage conditions. Trade goods stored in this **Free Port**, an enclosed area measuring 10 sq. km (4 sq. miles), are not subject to customs formalities. Visitors can learn more about this quarter's history by visiting the **Speicherstadtmuseum**, while an important aspect of trade is covered in **Spicy's Gewürzmuseum** (Am Sandtorkau 32; both open Tues–Sun 10am–5pm). **Miniatur Wunderland** (open Mon–Fri 9.30am–6pm, Tues until 9pm, Fri until 7pm, Sat 8am–9pm, Sun 8.30am–8pm; ticket booking recommended) is home to the biggest model railway in Europe, and the 10-storey **International Maritime Museum** (open Tues–Sun 10am–5pm last entry, Thur until 7pm) has an exhibition encompassing 3,000 years of seafaring history. Extending south from the Speicherstadt and so far a monster building site is the new **Hafen City**. Climb the orange watchtower for a bird's eye view of work in progress.

Most of the 12,000 ships that arrive annually in Germany's largest port are loaded and unloaded on the island of Steinwerder, reached via the **Old Elbe Tunnel** (1911) with its vehicle elevators and tiled walls (open to pedestrians). Further downstream the elegant **Köhlbrand Bridge** (1974) stretches above this swarm of ships and cranes, large and small barges, tugboats and motor launches. The bridge shares the traffic load with the *Autobahn* that goes through the **New Elbe Tunnel**.

In the 1980s, **Hafenstrasse**, with its "autonomous" squatters' houses, was the scene of violent confrontations between the government and a group of young drop-outs. Since then the situation has calmed down, with only a few brightly painted houses recalling the street's turbulent past, while on the opposite side of the Elbe a musical tent attracts hundreds of spectators every evening.

The nearby **Reeperbahn** ⓒ derives its name from the 17th-century ropemakers (*Reeper* in German) who worked in this area producing riggings for the sailing ships. Today this street and the immediately adjacent **Grosse Freiheit** and **Herbertstrasse** form the port's infamous "mile of sin", which developed out of sailors' entertainment needs; in amongst the sex shops, striptease joints and bars, the brick houses and the baroque facade of the church of St Joseph are the only reminders of its more historic past.

In **Harry's Harbour Bazaar** (open Tues–Sun noon–6pm) in **Balduinstrasse** ⓓ you can rummage to your heart's content and discover a wealth of curiosities. In the same street, the **Erotic Art Museum** makes its own contribution to the character of the area. The multitude of bars, cabarets and cheap entertainments in the red-light district have been known to distract many a Saturday-night visitor until the early hours of Sunday morning, when they head off to sample the unique atmosphere of the **Fischmarkt** ⓔ *(see below)*.

To the northeast, among the open spaces of the **Grosse Wallanlagen** is the informative **Museum für Hamburgische Geschichte** ⓕ (History Museum; open Tues–Sat 10am–5pm, Sun until 6pm), which has grown from a collection of local antiquities started in 1839 and contains a wide range of exhibits, from costumes to parts of old buildings and from architects' drawings to models of ships.

Follow Ludwig-Erhard-Strasse to the **Church of St Michael** ⓖ, whose

Map on page 309

The tower known locally as the "Michel".

BELOW: the Fischmarkt in full swing.

THE FISCHMARKT

Official market hours are over and what hasn't been sold by now will have to be thrown out. Hence some rapidly falling prices: "Add to that another bunch of bananas and a pound of cherries, as well as a bag full of apples! And all of that for only five euros!" Almost casually a bunch of bananas flies towards the astonished onlookers. Five euros change hands and large shopping bags are quickly filled up with fruit. The Fischmarkt in Hamburg, St Pauli, on a Sunday at 10am.

What originally began purely as a fish market in 1703 ranks nowadays as one of the sights every visitor to Hamburg must see: the colourful Sunday morning market held at the Fischmarkt, by the harbour, where items ranging from fish to secondhand household goods are available. The market attracts two types of casual visitor. There's the kind that strolls to the enormous fish auction hall for breakfast having spent a night in the city's pubs and clubs. There he can listen to another band or two and have a last dance before going home to sleep for the rest of the day. The other kind is more of an early bird, rising at the crack of dawn to breakfast on a cup of coffee and some bread rolls at the market, before starting off for a day trip into Hamburg's green environs.

132-metre (433-ft) baroque tower, known locally as the "Michel", is the symbol of Hamburg. Whether you take the 442 steps or the lift to the observation platform, it is well worth the ascent for the magnificent views of the city. On the way up you will also be able to admire the largest clock face in Germany. The church itself has been destroyed many times, but always rebuilt. It owes its present form to the design by Leonhard Prey and the renowned architect Ernst Georg Sonnin (1751–62).

In the vicinity are the **Krameramtswohnungen ⑭** (Shopkeepers' Flats), established by the shopkeepers' guild in 1676 and administered as an early form of widows' pension. This function was finally abandoned in 1969, but one of the widow's flats dating from 1850 is now an interesting **Museum** (open Tues–Sun 10am–5pm, closed in winter) with all the original furniture and features; the remainder have been taken over by craft shops, restaurants and bars.

The city centre

The more elegant side of Hamburg can be seen by strolling from the Main Railway Station into the city centre. But first a look at some fine works of art. Just to the north of the station, on Glockengiesserwall, is the **Kunsthalle ⑯** (Art Gallery; open Tues–Sun 10am–6pm, Thur until 9pm), which has one of the most magnificent collections of painting and sculpture in Germany. The Kunsthalle is divided into two parts: the **Old Building** contains works by artists from the 13th–20th century, including the German Romantic school spearheaded by Caspar David Friedrich; housed in the impressive cuboid structure designed by Oswald Mathias Ungers and opened in 1997, the **Galerie der Gegenwart** (Contemporary Gallery), is devoted to modern international art and contains works by Andy Warhol, Joseph Beuys, Bruce Naumann, Richard Serra and Georg Baselitz, among others.

To the south of the station, the **Museum für Kunst und Gewerbe ⑰** (Museum of Art and Crafts; open Tues–Sun 10am–6pm, Thur until 9pm) displays works of art of a variety of styles and epochs. Founded in 1877, it features one of the world's best Art Nouveau (Jugendstil) collections, including the completely furnished "Paris Room". The museum also contains a significant collection of ancient artefacts, as well as a section on the history of photography. Refreshments can be taken in the pleasantly designed historical restaurant on the first floor, the "Destille" (open Tues–Sun 11am–5pm).

The **Deutsches Schauspielhaus ⑱** (1900), immediately opposite the station, is the theatre where Gustaf Gründgens (1899–1963) used to direct, and later, Peter Zadek courted controversy with some stirring productions. Around the corner, the city's shopping district begins in **Mönckebergstrasse**, but be sure not to miss the **Jakobskirche ⑲** (Church of St James, 1340) with its Lucas altar (1499) and precious 17th-century organ built by Arp Schnitger.

The ancient settlement of Hammaburg once lay to the south of here. On the far side of the Burchardplatz is the enormous **Chilehaus ⑳**, built in 1922–4 by local merchant Henry Slomann, who had made a fortune importing saltpetre from Chile. The building is well known for its Expressionist architecture: the east corner is designed in the shape of the bow of a ship.

Back on the Mönckebergstrasse is the **Church of St**

TIP

Try to find the Thomas altar in the Kunsthalle. It was created by Master Francke in 1424 and depicts scenes from the life of St Thomas of Canterbury.

BELOW:
in the Museum of Art and Crafts.

Peter **Ⓝ**, Hamburg's oldest church (1050). It was destroyed by the Great Fire in 1842, after which it assumed its present form. Many valuable treasures from the church, including the Petri Altar by Meister Bertram (around 1420) are now on display in the Kunsthalle *(see opposite)*.

The **Market Square** provides an appropriate setting for the **Town Hall Ⓞ** (1886–87), the seat of Hamburg's Senate, *Bürgerschaft* (City Parliament) and Council, which reflects the prosperity of the Hamburg citizens of old. Many of the building's 647 rooms can be seen on a guided tour (in English every hour Mon–Thur 10.15am–3.15pm, Fri until 1.15pm, Sat until 5.15pm, Sun until 4.15pm). The facade is decorated in Renaissance style with figures depicting the German emperors. You can relax under the **Alster Arcades** over a cool beer and watch the swans glide by on the water. The atmosphere is a little hotter, however, in the financial world of the adjacent **Börse Ⓟ** (Stock Exchange), built in 1841.

Around the Alster

A few minutes away from the town hall is the **Binnenalster**, the inland lake. The **Jungfernstieg Ⓠ** was laid out as long ago as the 17th century; having been destroyed in the Great Fire of 1842, its shops and department stores are popular among locals and visitors alike. The **Alsterpavilion Ⓡ** facing the water is the point of departure for guided boat tours of the city.

Specialist shops, expensive department stores, glass arcades and first-class restaurants and cafés are located all around this lake. In wet weather, covered arcades such as the **Hanseviertel Ⓢ** are inviting places for a stroll. Nearby is the **Hamburgische Staatsoper Ⓣ** (Hamburg State Opera), which has gained world renown for its ballet performances under the leadership of the American dancer, John Neumeier.

Map on page 309

Watching Hamburg's streetlife.

BELOW: overlooking the Alster.

Map on page 309

When fish merchant Gottfried Clas Hagenbeck landed six seals at the fish market of St Pauli in 1848, he had no idea that this would be the beginnings of a famous zoo.

A short boat trip takes you from the Inland Alster to the Outer Alster or **Aussenalster**, where the Alster Park was laid out for the International Garden Show of 1953. To the north of the Aussenalster is the **Stadtpark**, a popular recreation area for residents of Hamburg's northern districts. It is also home to the **Planetarium**, whose observation terrace offers superb views over the city. In the summer the park's open-air stage hosts jazz and rock concerts.

There are various other parks where you can escape the bustle of the city, including the grounds of the **Wallanlagen**, the **Alter Botanischer Garten** and the **Planten un Blomen** with its greenhouses, playgrounds, fountains and Japanese Garden. **Hagenbecks Tierpark**, the world's first private zoo, has been in existence since 1907. The largest area of green in Hamburg lies to the north of the Stadtpark: with its 404 hectares (1,000 acres), the **Ohlsdorfer Friedhof** is the second-largest cemetery in the world after Chicago's.

Altona and beyond

Once an independent small town, **Altona** was incorporated into Hamburg in 1937. Founded in 1520, the village came under the rule of the Danes 100 years later. The **Altonaer Museum** (open Tues–Sun 10am–6pm, Thur until 9pm) provides a good insight into the eventful history of this area. Founded by means of a donation by the Hamburg cigarette manufacturer Hermann Reemtsma, the **Ernst Barlach House** (open Tues–Sun 11am–6pm) contains woodcuts, prints and sculptures by the great German Expressionist artist. The house is situated in **Jenisch Park** on the Elbchaussee, one of the most pleasant parks in the city.

BELOW: the villas of Blankenese.

The Elbchaussee, lined with luxurious villas, follows the north bank of the river. The village of **Övelgönne** with its many old houses, some dating back to the 18th century and once the homes of captains and pilots, is also the location of the **Harbour Museum**. The romantic houses in the former fishing village of **Blankenese** are now occupied by some of the city's richest inhabitants. At this point the **Bismarck Stone** affords a wonderful view across the water.

Downstream from here, near the **Schulau Ferry House** with its "ships in bottles" museum, is the **Willkommhöft** from where all ships entering or leaving Hamburg are greeted or bid farewell. The national flag of the ship's home port is hoisted and its national anthem is played over a loudspeaker.

Excursion to Lüneburg

South of Hamburg, near Undeloh, lies the **Lüneburg Heath National Park**. This was named after the old commercial city of Lüneburg whose meteoric rise was based on the mining of salt, which has been taking place here since 936. The monopoly on the salt trade, which Lüneburg gained when the neighbouring city of Bardowick was destroyed, brought immense wealth. The large number of Gothic brick homes is evidence of this affluence, and the magnificent **Town Hall** is a notable product of this period (1300–1706). The old warehouses, mills and harbour facilities can still be found in the Wasserviertel (Water Quarter), bearing a lasting testimony to the splendid era during which Lüneburg and Lübeck controlled the salt trade. ❑

Hanseatic League

What do the towns of Bruges and Novgorod, Lübeck and Bergen, Brunswick and Riga have in common? Between the 12th and 16th centuries they and a further 200 towns joined together to form the Hanseatic League. This association enjoyed greater economic and political influence than any German state before 1871. In addition, its military might exceeded that of many a kingdom of its time.

The League was originally created as an association of German traders abroad, as a means of providing mutual protection from attack. It also offered a more effective means of representation, and the advantages of shared office and warehouse space. The organisation expanded over the years to include more towns, especially in north Germany. From the mid-14th century, under the leadership of Lübeck, it controlled all trading on the North Sea and Baltic coasts.

The economic, military and political power of the Hanseatic League lay in the strict code of regulations with which all members had to comply. Council meetings were held at which decisions were taken on matters of common interest; these were then binding upon all members. Any trader who failed to abide by them was threatened with a total boycott by all members. No duties were levied on goods imported from member towns, which used a common system of weights and measures, and all paid in the same currency. The combined representation kept costs down and competitors at bay.

Over the years the Hanseatic League became so powerful that in 1370 it even dared to declare war on the King of Denmark in order to claim its rights in that country as well as access to the Baltic. The League was victorious, forcing the kingdom to accept another monarch and insisting that all their demands were met.

The League's market extended from Bruges and London in the west to Novgorod in the east. Its cavernous *Koggen*, high-sided freight ships with a capacity of 120–160 tons, brought raw materials such as furs, wax, salt, honey and amber from the Orient and transported metal goods, textiles, wine and beer from the West. It maintained transport routes to almost every sizeable town in northern and central Europe.

The heavily laden *Koggen* were also a popular prey for pirates looking to make a quick fortune. For a long time the League undertook a campaign against such incursions. Pirate raids were particularly bad between 1370 and 1402. One of the boldest pirates, Klaus Störtebeker, plundered every ship unable to escape his clutches, yelling as he did so, "God's friend – man's enemy!"

The Hanseatic League had passed its zenith by the end of the 15th century. Increasing numbers of princes gained control over the cities within their jurisdiction, and the rise of nation states such as Sweden, Russia and England placed further restrictions on the League's activities, thereby breaking its united front. In 1598, it abandoned the last of its overseas branch offices, in London. ❏

RIGHT: sailing ship from Lübeck, Queen of the Hanseatic League.

THE NORTH SEA COAST

Map
on pages
304–5

*With its islands and harbours, sandy beaches and mud flats,
and a hinterland of meadows and windmills, the North Sea Coast
offers a refreshing, if sometimes bracing change*

T he Hamburg director Hark Bohm described the North Sea as "the murderous sea" for his film *Nordsee ist Mordsee*, grimly reflecting the uneasy relationship between this unruly element and the fisherfolk, shipwrights, traders and pirates of Germany's northwest coast who, down the centuries, made it their livelihood. For all too often this was at the cost of their lives and all too often they were to see its waters carry away whole islands and sweep inland right up to their homes.

The North Sea has left its mark on an entire population. The inhabitants of Ostfriesland (East Friesland) are sometimes depicted as reserved and a bit stupid, making them the butt of "East Frisian" jokes. But these people have inhabited the region since 1000 BC. Forcibly Christianised by Charlemagne in the 8th century, the Frisians were long feared as potential rebels. These independently-minded peasants, with farmsteads surrounded by fertile farmland, formed their own republics, which remained in existence for centuries. Since then the Frisians have concentrated on commerce and maritime-related activities in which they have been just as successful as they were in farming.

Three types of landscape characterise this coastal region: the *Wattenmeer* (mud flats) with its unique life forms, an area flooded by the tide; the *Marschen*, the fertile flat meadowlands further inland that enabled the Frisians to become proud and independent farmers; and the *Geest*, the high and dry region of fields, moors and woods located between the Elbe and the Ems, worn smooth by the retreating glacier at the end of the last Ice Age. The Wattenmeer, which extends between the mainland and the East Frisian Islands for over 565,000 hectares (2,180 sq. miles), is protected as the **Wattenmeer National Park**, where over 250 life forms make up the specialised food chain created by the North Sea's shallow tidal waters.

The coastal resorts and islands have preserved much of their charm despite the summertime influx of tourists, while the meadowlands offer a taste of the original Frisian atmosphere. Thatched-roof farmhouses nestle in lush meadows with grazing Frisian cows, and the fields are surrounded by centuries-old hedges guarding against wind erosion in this landscape of quaint villages and windmills.

A sea of blossom

Every spring the countryside of the **Altes Land**, the area south of the Elbe between Hamburg and Stade, becomes a sea of blossom as the apple, cherry and plum orchards in Germany's largest fruit-growing area burst into flower. There have been fruit-growers here since the 14th century. Beautiful half-timbered houses lend added charm to the landscape.

LEFT: on the beach at Wangerooge.
BELOW: seasonal fruit in the Altes Land.

Guide in local costume.

In the heart of the Altes Land lies **Buxtehude** ❶, with its lovely Old Town, half-timbered houses, old market hall, **Town Hall, St Peter's Church** (1296, Gothic vaulted basilica), and, particularly worth seeing, the 13th-century **Canal Complex** on the Este. This served as a harbour until 1962. The town's **Regional Museum** (open Tues–Fri 1.30–5.30pm, Sat–Sun 10.30am–5.30pm), modelled on an old farmhouse, dates from 1913. A **Museum Train**, with a 1926 carriage, runs to neighbouring **Harsefeld** May to September on the second Sunday of the month.

The county town of **Stade** ❷ also has a fine old town centre. High above it looms the baroque tower of **St Cosmas' Church** (13th century), which has an organ by Arp Schnitger. For purposes of musical comparison there is also the Bielfeldt organ in **St Willehad's Church**. The streets are resplendent with half-timbered buildings such as the **Town Hall** (1667), the **Bürgermeister-Hintze House** (1621), the **Höker House** (1650) and the **Hahnentor** (Cock Gate, 1658). The pictures at the **Kunsthaus** (Art Gallery; open Tues–Fri 10am–5pm, Sat–Sun 10am–6pm) offer an early introduction to the work of the Worpswede School *(see below)*, while the **Heimatmuseum** (Local History Museum; open Tues–Fri 10am–1pm, 2–5pm, Sat–Sun 10am–1pm, 2–6pm) and **Freilichtmuseum** (Open Air Museum; same hours as the Heimatmuseum) record the life and times of this town. Stade first began to flourish as a trading port when it joined the Hanseatic League in 1267. Its port continues to be important but nowadays modern industry has firmly established itself alongside traditional shipbuilding.

Artists and their landscapes

The route now leads inland to the little village of **Worpswede** ❸. This owes its fame to the artists who chose to work here and who drew their inspiration from the primeval landscape of the **Teufelsmoor** (Devil's Moor). Among the first, in 1889, were Fritz Makens, Otto Modersohn and Hans am Ende, to be followed by others including Paula Modersohn-Becker. Their work can be seen in the **Haus im Schluh** and the **Grosse Kunstschau** (open daily 10am–6pm) but they also left their mark on the streetscape. Heinrich Vogeler was responsible for the **Station** and the Art Nouveau reworking of the **Barkenhoff** (Boatyard), while the **Logierhaus** (Guesthouse), Grosse Kunstschau and **Café Worpswede** – still a popular meeting place for painters and craftspeople – were all the work of Bernhard Hoetger.

The nearby Teufelsmoor, now a nature reserve, was at one time the largest unbroken stretch of moorland in Lower Saxony, although most of the moors have since been lost to peat digging and drainage. Worpswede's **Torfschiffswerftmuseum** (Peat Museum; open Mar–Oct Wed noon–3pm, Fri–Sat 3–6pm, Sun 10am–noon, 3–6pm) affords a glimpse of the life of those who worked on the moors. On the River Hamme at Worpswede there are berths for the cruise ships that ply the Lesum and Weser down to Bremen.

Further on to the west of Bremen *(see page 298)*, **Oldenburg** ❹ (pop. 160,000) became the seat of the Gottorfer Grand Dukes in 1785. Fine 17th-century townhouses, neoclassical buildings and lovely Art Nouveau villas testify to the wealth of the town. The

BELOW: facade decoration in Buxtehude.

period rooms in the **Schloss**, the Grand-Ducal Palace, are adorned with paintings by Johann Heinrich Wilhelm Tischbein and Ludwig Münstermann. Works by Old Masters can be seen in the impressive gallery of the **Landesmuseum**, the regional art and art history museum housed in the Schloss. The **Augusteum** (open Tues–Fri 9am–5pm, Thur until 8pm, Sat–Sun 10am–5pm) is the place to see paintings by the Worpswede School, Emil Nolde and Franz Radziwill. This bustling university town is the commercial and cultural capital of the region and has a packed programme of events, among them the annual **Oldenburg Kultursommer** (summer arts festival).

Map on pages 304–5

Peat moors and windmills

Heading northwest, past the moorland spa of Bad Zwischenahn and Westerstede, site of the Ammerland Wildlife Park, you come to **Grossefehn ❺**. Colonisation of the moors began with the first settlement here on the fen in 1633. The rich black peat was cut for fuel, an unhealthy job that was often forced labour for convicts, as can be seen in the **Fehnmuseum Eiland** (open Tues–Sun 10am–4pm) at **Westgrossefehn**. The peat was transported to the port at Emden, away from this landscape of canals, bridges, windmills and locks.

Aurich ❻ was at one time the seat of the Cirksena and subsequent ruling dynasties. The **Schloss** (1852) and many other neoclassical buildings, including churches and some townhouses, date from this period. The modern marketplace is very eye-catching. Its new **Market Hall** in white steel, and Aachen sculptor Albert Sous's **Tower** were initially controversial. The **Historical Museum** (open mid-Feb–Nov Tues–Sun 11am–5pm) is in the old **Chancery** and the Stiftsmühle (Pin Mill) holds the **Mill Museum** (open Apr–Oct Tues–Sat

BELOW: windmills are a part of the northern scenery.

11am–5pm, Sun 3–5pm). The town landmark is the 14th-century **Tower** of **St Lambert's Church** (1825). The most graphic of East Friesland's museums on the moorland colonists is the **Open Air Museum** (open Apr–Oct daily 10am–5pm) at **Moordorf** ❼ about 10 km (6 miles) from Aurich.

Emden ❽ (pop. 52,000) is the commercial hub of East Friesland. It has a port (one of the world's largest for car shipments) and a Volkswagen plant. To get a good impression of Emden's size, climb the tower of the **Old Town Hall**, a modern building incorporating parts of its forerunner, which was destroyed in 1944. The town hall also houses the **Ostfriesisches Landesmuseum** (East Frisian Museum; open Tues–Sun 10am–6pm) with an exhibition on Emden's history, including a collection of model ships. Harbour cruises leave from the Ratsdelft steps opposite. Another insight into the shipping world is to be found in the **Schifffahrtsmuseum** (Shipping Museum; open mid-Mar–Sept Mon–Fri 10.30am–1pm, 2.30–5pm, Sat–Sun 11am–1pm) aboard the *Amrumbank* lightship. Parts of the Old Town that still exist in the area of the Friedrich-Ebert-Strasse include the **New Church** (1648) and some fine rows of houses. The **Kunsthalle** (Art Gallery; open Tues 10am–8pm, Wed–Fri 10am–5pm, Sat–Sun 11am–5pm), together with the works displayed within by artists such as Emil Nolde, Paula Modersohn-Becker and August Macke, was bequeathed to the town by former *Stern* magazine publisher Henri Nannen.

Seven pearls in the sea

From Emden a car ferry sails to **Borkum**, the first of the seven **East Frisian Islands** ❾. Like the others, it grew from the sandbanks formed here in the seas on the edge of the Continental Shelf. Like them too, Borkum is very much at the mercy of the sea and the storm tides that used to flood ever-larger expanses of

The Frisian language, closely related to English, is now only spoken on the islands. The thriller The Riddle of the Sands *by Erskine Childers is a splendid evocation of life on the East Frisian Islands.*

BELOW: preparing to set sail.

land. People and livestock were drowned and whole villages would be washed right out to sea. But time and again the islands would be resettled, since there was no gainsaying that the North Sea, with its rich fish stocks, still constituted a plentiful supply of food. In the 18th century the men also used to work as merchant seamen and whalers.

The key to survival here nowadays is the concept of "gentle tourism": nature and countryside conservation are top of the agenda and every island includes guided nature walks among its attractions. Cars are only allowed onto the two largest and busiest islands, Borkum and **Norderney** (ferry from Norddeich). On the others it is a matter of light railway, horse-drawn transport and bikes only.

Baltrum is the smallest of the islands, with only 500 inhabitants, and **Spiekeroog** (ferry from Neuharlingersiel) is the greenest and most intact. **Langeoog** (ferry from Bensersiel) is the best for families, **Juist** (ferry from Norddeich) the most natural and **Wangerooge** (ferry from Carolinensiel), which for a time belonged to Czarist Russia, has the most chequered history.

Map on pages 304–5

Sanctuary for a seal in Norden.

Along the coast

The best place on the East Frisian coast for harking back to the past is **Greetsiel** ⑩, and the locals certainly know how to cash in on nostalgia. Despite this commercialisation, it is a real pleasure to stroll around the beautifully restored and pedestrianised streets in the centre. The hub of village life is the harbour with its crab boats; Greetsiel's chief feature, however, is its great windmills, the two **Galerieholländer**. One is still in working order and the other has a tea room and an art gallery. In fact this is just one gallery among many in the village – Greetsiel's **Kunstwochen** (art weeks) are well known throughout the country.

BELOW: angling is a popular pastime.

Norden ⑪, with its sandy beaches and green dunes at **Norddeich**, is East Friesland's largest coastal resort. Leisure facilities include the **Seawater Indoor Pool**, a small **Zoo** and a **Leisure Centre**. A particular favourite is the **Seal Sanctuary**, where orphaned seal pups are lovingly hand-reared. The **harbour** is a hive of activity with the comings and goings of ferries, fishing boats and yachts. At the heart of the town, around the large **Marktplatz**, there is a very fine cluster of buildings formed by the "Drei Schwestern" (Three Sisters) townhouses (dating from around 1600), next to the **Town Hall** (1884) and the **Mennonite Church** (1662–1835). The **St Ludger Church** (13th–15th century) is the largest church in the region and has a fine organ by Arp Schnitger. The **Old Town Hall** (open Tues–Sun 10am–4pm, Nov–Apr shorter hours) contains an interesting **tea museum** and a museum of local history, which vividly recreates scenes from domestic and working life.

Visiting **Wittmund** ⑫ is rather like taking a crash course in the East Frisian culture. Typical subjects include pottering about, drinking tea and milking the cows – and you can only qualify if you join in the fun. As he was inclined to do in so many churches in the region, organ-maker Arp Schnitger (1648–1719) also bestowed one of his many fine instruments on **St Nicholas Church**.

Jever ⑬ is another place to polish up your knowledge of East Frisian traditions when it comes to tea,

beer and fish. There are guided tours around the local **brewery** (enquiries, tel: 04461-13711), along with an opportunity to taste its famous Pilsener bitter. Jever's harbour enabled it to become an important entrepôt in the Middle Ages, but the most imposing reminder of its eventful past is the magnificent Renaissance **Schloss** (Palace), in which hangs a portrait of Csarina Catherine II, who ruled Jever between 1793 and 1818. The palace also contains a **Regional Museum**, which is worth a visit (open Tues–Sun 10am–6pm). A lot of green space and plenty of canals and fine buildings, some of them Art Nouveau, complete the townscape.

All this is in sharp contrast to **Wilhelmshaven** ❿ (pop. 85,000), whose brief history only dates back to 1854 when Wilhelm I of Prussia founded a naval port here. Life still revolves around the **port** which, thanks to oil, has since become highly commercial. The **Küstenmuseum** (open Apr–Oct daily 10am–6pm, Nov–Mar Tues–Sun 10am–5pm) on Rathausplatz tells the story of the area and its shipping, while the **Marinemuseum** (open daily Apr–Oct 10am–6pm, Nov–Mar 10am–5pm) covers Germany's naval history, including the courageous but ultimately disastrous experiences in both world wars. Children, meanwhile, will enjoy the underwater "research station" at **Oceanis** (open daily 10am–6pm).

Wilhelmshaven's opposite number, on the far side of the Weser estuary, is the town of **Bremerhaven** ⓯ (pop. 117,000), Europe's largest fishing port and container terminal. It was from its Columbus Pier, the "pier of tears", that more than 10 million Europeans embarked for the New World – an important fact in European history, documented in the award-winning **German Emigration Center** (open daily Mar-Oct 10am–6pm, Nov–Feb until 5pm). The Old Harbour also holds the **Deutsches Schifffahrtsmuseum** (German Shipping Museum; open daily 10am–6pm, Nov–Mar Tue–Sun) and its collection of historic ships

At the docks in Bremerhaven.

BELOW: the German Shipping Museum in Bremerhaven's Old Harbour.

including a Hanseatic merchant ship *(Hansekogge)*. A good place to take time out is the nearby **Columbus Centre** with its restaurants and shopping mall.

At the tip of the headland between the Elbe and Weser estuaries, the port of **Cuxhaven** ⑯ (pop. 52,000) squares up to the open sea. All the ocean-going giants pass by here on their way to Hamburg, making an imposing sight to behold from the **Alte Liebe** pier and nearby **lighthouse**. At low tide horse-drawn carriages cross the mudflats to the island of **Neuwerk**.

From Alte Liebe boats also depart for **Helgoland** ⑰, the small island of red sandstone that rises out of the sea 70 km (44 miles) off the mouth of the Elbe. Its exposed location explains why the island has changed hands so many times. It served as a pirate stronghold in the 13th century and was then owned by the Danes, followed by the British, who eventually handed it over to the Germans in 1890 in exchange for the island of Zanzibar. Helgoland served as a naval base in both world wars but the population eventually fled the bombing of World War II. A peaceful sit-in by young Germans led to the island being handed back to its former occupants in 1952.

It has since developed into a popular destination for visitors and can be reached from almost all North Sea ports. Its best-known landmark is **Lange Anna** (Big Anna), the free-standing rock stack at the north end of the island. The **Aquarium** (open Apr–Oct Mon–Fri 10am–4.30pm, Sat–Sun 1–3.30pm), recreates the underwater world of the North Sea.

Northwards through Dithmarschen

To pick up the second leg of this journey along the North Sea Coast, this time in Schleswig-Holstein, cross the River Elbe at **Wischhafen**. When the Danish

Map on pages 304–5

August Heinrich Hoffmann von Fallersleben created the German national anthem in 1841 while staying on Helgoland. His statue can be seen on the quayside.

BELOW: Library at the German Emigration Center.

Gothic brick churches, such as this one in Brunsbüttel, are typical of the north.

King Christian IV founded **Glückstadt** ⓲ in 1617 he was pursuing the ambitious aim of creating a flourishing centre for trade that would rival neighbouring Hamburg. To this end he attracted Jews, Mennonites and Dutch Protestants to live here by promising them freedom of religion and freedom from taxes. The face of Glückstadt reflects those lofty aims, especially in the old buildings around the marketplace and the harbour. These include the Dutch Renaissance **Town Hall** (1642) and the late-Gothic **Town Church** (1621). The **Detlefsen Museum** in the **Brockdorff-Palais** features interesting displays on whaling and history (open Wed and Sun 2–5pm, Thur–Sat 2–6pm).

The town of **Brunsbüttel** ⓳ owes its leading role in the petro-chemical and energy distribution industries to its position at the start of the **North Sea-Baltic Canal**, the world's busiest canal in terms of traffic. In the period between 1959, when its oil terminal came on stream, and 1995 – the centenary of the canal – Brunsbüttel handled 190 million tons of crude oil and mineral and chemical products. You can watch the huge canal locks in action from a viewing platform. For background information, visit the **Schleusenanlage Atrium** (Locks Museum; open mid-Mar–mid-Nov daily 10.30am–5pm). The focus is also on navigation in the **Heimatmuseum** (Local History Museum; open Tues, Thur and Sat–Sun 2–5pm, Wed 10am–noon), which includes a saloon from an Around-the-Horn sailing clipper. Something of the atmosphere of the old church parish still lingers on in the market square.

To the north of Brunsbüttel stretches the west coast of the Jütland Peninsula, a part of present-day Schleswig-Holstein that for centuries remained a bone of contention between Germany and Denmark. The southern part of the coast between the Elbe and Eider rivers is known as Dithmarschen, which for much of the

BELOW:
Dithmarschen is a major cabbage-growing area.

THE DITHMARSCHEN REPUBLIC

It was a collection of local parishes that formed the framework for the "Dithmarschen Republic", an association of wealthy farming families that held sway between 1070 and 1559 in the fertile marshland on the west coast of the Jütland Peninsula. These expert farmers sold their abundant harvests to the Hanseatic towns, becoming rich from the proceeds. They were shielded by the surrounding moors against any potential attack from the hinterland, but to protect their land from the sea they organised the building of a dyke. In 1434, they created their own central judiciary that developed into an administration known as the "Council of Forty-Eight" who arrived at all their important decisions "on the heath (Heide)".

In 1500 the Danish King Johann, who had been granted Dithmarschen in fief by Emperor Friedrich III, mobilised his 12,000-strong army against the republic. The situation seemed hopeless, but the wily farmers lured the Danes into a trap near Hemmingstedt and humiliated them by opening the dyke to flood them out. It was not until 1559 that Dithmarschen was finally forced to accept Danish rule, but it nevertheless remained a semi-independent territory right until 1866 when, together with Schleswig and Holstein, it became part of Prussia.

region's turbulent history managed to remain independent *(see below)*. Dithmarschen was first mentioned in the 9th century and the **Dithmarschen Cathedral** (9th–13th century) in **Meldorf** testifies to the peasants' early conversion to Christianity. The place where the Dithmarschen Council met developed into what is now the county town of **Heide** ㉑, with one of Germany's largest market squares. Heide is also the birthplace of Johannes Brahms (1833–97) and a museum devoted to the great composer has been established in the old family home, the **Brahmshaus** (open Apr–Oct Tues, Thur and Fri 2.30–4.30pm, Sat 10.30am–12.30pm, June–Sept also Tues–Thur and Fri 10.30am–12.30pm). The museum contains changing exhibitions. There is another museum to the Heide-born poet Klaus Groth, whose masterpiece, *Quickborn* (1852), is a series of poems in Low German *(Plattdeutsch)* dealing with life in Dithmarschen. Yet another interesting museum is the **Museum für Dithmarscher Vorgeschichte** (Museum of Prehistory; open Apr–mid-Oct Tues–Fri 9am–noon, 2–5pm, Sun 10am–5pm; shorter hours in winter) complete with a reconstructed farmhouse from the 1st century AD.

Dutch architecture

Lying on the Eider is the town of **Friedrichstadt** ㉒. Founded in 1621, it was largely built up by Dutch religious refugees. They modelled their second home entirely on their home towns, hence the little canals (boat tours available) and the lovely gabled houses. Particularly impressive is the market square, whose entire west side is lined with Dutch-style merchants' houses. Along the old cobbled streets too are fine townhouses, including the **Alte Münze** with its beautiful facade.

The Dutch were also responsible for the construction method of the *haubarge*, the large, handsome farmhouses characteristic of the **Eiderstedt** penin-

Map on pages 304–5

TIP

The best way to get around Friedrichstadt is by boat along the canals, but beware of the low bridges.

BELOW: Dutch settlers built these houses in Friedrichstadt.

The statue of Theodor Storm in Husum.

sula. They were built so that the wooden superstructure, anchored deep in the ground, would still be holding up the lofty central section even when a storm tide had ripped all the walls away. The most famous is the **Red Haubarg** at **Witzwort** ㉓ (now a pretty restaurant and a museum of rural life; open Tues–Sun 11am–10pm), which the poet Theodor Storm visited as a child.

It was Storm who christened his native town of **Husum** ㉔ that "grey town by the sea", and his novellas convey a vivid impression of life here and on the peninsula. Many of the places he described can still be visited. These include the **Schloss** (1582–1752) in the midst of its **park**, which is carpeted with purple crocuses in the spring; and the 19th-century **Merchants' Houses** by the old harbour. On the waterfront, look out for the **Stormhaus** (Storm House) and the **Tabak-Museum** (Tobacco Museum; open daily 10am–5pm). The **Nordfriesisches Museum** in the Nissenhaus (open Tues–Fri, Sun 10am–5pm) tells of sea dykes and storm tides. Paradoxically, it was a storm tide in 1362 that made the town's fortune: instead of being inland, Husum found itself on the coast and acquired a harbour. From here ferries sail to the Halligen and the North Frisian Islands.

At the end of the Eiderstedt peninsula is the pretty village of **St Peter-Ording** ㉕, with its extensive sands.

St Tropez of the North

BELOW:
the far north.

Off the coast of Husum lie **Nordstrand**, **Pellworm** and the **Halligen Islands** ㉖. The Halligen Islands used to be part of the mainland until the 1360s, when storm tides flooded over the marshes and only a few acres were left above sea level. Farmsteads are perched on earthbanks *(Warften)* for safety, for the flood warning is still sometimes sounded.

The Halligen and the tiny ports of Schlüttsiel and Dagebüll, situated to the north of Husum, are the departure points for ferries to the three biggest North Frisian Islands. On **Amrum** ㉗, the main bathing beach is a 17-km (11-mile) long sandspit (the Kniepsand), which gets pushed 50 metres (55 yards) further north each year, due to the effects of wind and waves. The island of **Föhr** ㉘, on the other hand, has relatively abundant vegetation. The **Friesenmuseum** on the island capital of **Wyk** (open Tues–Sun 10am–5pm, July–Aug also Mon, Nov–mid-Mar Tues–Sun 2–5pm) traces the history of the tribes who came and settled on these islands and coastal region in the 8th century. A windmill and the oldest house on the island dating from 1617 form part of the museum.

Germany's northernmost point is on the long island of **Sylt** ㉙. If you're travelling here from the mainland, take the train from Niebüll, which carries cars over the Hindenburg Causeway. The island owes its "St Tropez of the North" reputation to the jet-set crowd who love to hang out in places like **Westerland**, the capital, and **Kampen**, the smart beach resort known for its beautiful 30-metre (100-ft) high Red Cliffs. But Sylt also has plenty to offer for more ordinary mortals, such as families and young people. They prefer **List**, **Rantum** and **Hörnum**. Idyllic **Keitum**, that "loveliest of Frisian villages", complete with a 12th-century church, also manages to retain its charm far removed from the madding crowd. Evidence of the Neolithic presence on the island is provided by **Denghoog**, the megalithic tomb at **Wenningstedt**.

Back on the mainland in **Seebüll** ㉚, it is worth paying a visit to the **Nolde Museum** (open daily Mar–Nov 10am–6pm, Thur until 8pm), set in the studio and former home of the Expressionist painter, Emil Nolde. As well as the works of art on display, the garden and landscape leave a lasting impression. ❑

Map on pages 304–5

There are only 2,100 inhabitants left on Amrum. However, 100,000 tourists make their way there every year.

BELOW: living room in the Nolde Museum.

THE NORTH SEA: FRIEND AND FOE

The tides mould not only the landscape, but also the people. There is no way of escaping the constant struggle with the sea

The North Sea coastline, with its chains of small islands, hasn't always looked as it does today. Over the centuries, heavy storms and flooding have ravaged and shaped the landscape, taking land away at some places and depositing it elsewhere. Fertile land has disappeared under water, peninsulas have been turned into islands and islands have been totally submerged or broken apart.

Today the coastline is characterised by long sandy beaches, with tidal mud flats to one side and dunes and dykes, followed by marshland, to the other. This low-lying marshland – land reclaimed from the sea – is extremely fertile, but the farmers have a constant battle to keep the sea at bay. To make sure heavy storms don't flood their fields they continuously have to build new, higher dykes and maintain and control the old ones *(above)* – just as they have done since the 11th century.

LEISURE AND RECREATION

As hard as the struggle of the locals might be, this unique coastline attracts numerous tourists all year round. The unique Wattenmeer (tidal mud flats), the dunes and the beaches invite the visitor to explore the rich flora and fauna of the area; or for those who aren't interested in nature there are a wealth of other activities, such as sailing, surfing or cycling along the dykes on a hired bicycle. The North Sea certainly has something to offer everyone.

▷ **PROTECTION AND PRIVACY**
Typical of German beaches are the *Strandkörbe* (wicker chairs). They suc- ceeded the English- style mobile beach carts.

△ **A DAY AT THE SEASIDE**
By the end of the 19th century, North Sea resorts such as Westerland on Sylt had become fashionable.

▷ **COMMON CATCH**
Shrimps, landed in the ports of Friedrichskoog and Büsum, have always been part of the regional cuisine.

▽ **WIND POWER**
Windmills old and new are a common sight. The modern ones provide between 2 and 12 percent of energy needs.

LIFE ON THE ISLANDS

▽ **FACING THE ELEMENTS**
The coast is constantly battered by storms, often leaving a trail of destruction, as here on the promenade at Westerland on Sylt.

△ **GREAT FOR NOVICES**
The surfers who assemble on Sylt each September to compete for the Surf World Cup can expect windier conditions than these.

Few can understand why the inhabitants of the Halligen didn't give up their bleak existence long ago. The Halligen, tiny islands in the Wattenmeer, were once an area of fertile marshland, which over the centuries was submerged under water, leaving only a few specks of land remaining above sea level. Due to continued inundation from the sea, the fields are not suitable for arable farming. However, they are perfect for cattle grazing. The farms themselves are built on artificial mounds to protect them from the elements. Because of their ingenious construction, they can withstand the strongest storms: while the waves might wash away the walls, the roof remains intact to provide shelter.

Life on the larger North Sea islands isn't quite as harsh. Sheep and cattle rearing, as well as the farming of rye, oats and potatoes, were the mainstays of the economy. Farming and fishing are still important, but for most locals it is the tourist industry that now provides the primary income.

△ **HIGH AND DRY**
The *Wattenmeer*, the largest tidal mud flats in the world, form a unique habitat for more than 250 different species.

VIA LÜBECK TO FLENSBURG

The eastern part of Schleswig-Holstein offers a series of contrasts between the Baltic and its hinterland. Lübeck and Kiel have for centuries been the focus of the region's maritime prowess

Map on pages 304–5

Germany's northernmost state is strange but beautiful. The landscape of Schleswig-Holstein, sandwiched between the North Sea and the Baltic, is characterised by windswept trees, lovingly maintained brick houses, thatched cottages, grand farmsteads and hundreds of lakes set amid extensive deciduous forests. It is possible to cruise for miles through the lakes and rivers of the Holstein lowlands, just one of five nature reserves in the eastern part of the state. In the east, long *Förden* (fjords) cut inland wherever cliffs or sandy beaches have failed to check the Baltic Sea's advance. In most places, though, the scene around this tideless 55-metre (180-ft) deep sea is peaceful.

A lack of minerals has prevented the development of industry, thus earning the region a reputation as a "structurally weak area", living off agriculture and fishing. This was not always the case, however. For centuries trade between Scandinavia and the countries of eastern Europe flourished. During medieval times, Schleswig-Holstein's wealth came not only from agriculture but also from its strategic location. The people of this region controlled the land and sea routes that the other Baltic merchants had to use if they were to sell their goods. The most powerful force in this lucrative business was, of course, the Hanseatic League *(see page 315).*

LEFT: the Holsten Gate, symbol of Lübeck.
BELOW: making music in Lübeck.

Queen of the Hanseatic towns

For 250 years, **Lübeck** ❸ (pop. 213,000) was the undisputed commercial metropolis of the Holy Roman Empire. Founded in 1143 by Count Adolf II of Schauenburg on an island in the Trave River, the settlement was later acquired by Henry the Lion, who granted it a town charter. It was 1226 before Lübeck received the status of Free Imperial City. It grew into an important port for traders with partners around the Baltic Sea and in the west. Furs, tar, honey and amber were bartered for wool, copper and tin from England. At that time, salt was a valuable commodity, being used in food preservation. By 1356, Lübeck was the most powerful town in the Hanseatic League.

Lübeck is famous for its Gothic brick churches. Those arriving from the direction of Hamburg can spot the city's seven towers from a great distance. The **Church of St Mary** was built in the 13th century and served as a model for many of the brick churches around the Baltic. The foundation stone for the **Cathedral** was laid in 1173. This building, planned as a Romanesque basilica, was constructed in its present Gothic form in the 13th and 14th centuries.

The 14th-century churches of **St Ägidius**, **St Catherine** and **St Peter**, as well as the 13th-century **Church of St James** (St Jakobi), which houses one of Europe's oldest organs (15th century), are all grouped closely

together in the old part of the city, reached by crossing one of the many bridges. In former times, the rivers and canals provided protection for the inhabitants when the diplomatic skills of the merchants failed. There's a fine view from St Peter's tower, and the west front of St Catherine's displays terracotta sculptures by Ernst Barlach. The **St Annen Museum** (open Tues–Sun 10am–5pm), for medieval art, is nearby in the cloisters of a former monastery.

The **Holsten Gate** (1466), the most impressive of the few remaining sections of the city wall, formerly guarded the western entrance to the city and the 16th- and 17th-century **Salt Warehouses**, where Lüneburg salt was stored. Today it houses a **Museum** (open Tues–Sun 10am–5pm) with a large model of the city from the year 1650, as well as a collection of model ships.

In the centre of the city, just a short walk from the Holsten Gate, is the Gothic **Town Hall**. Dating from 1484 it is one of the oldest in Germany and a monument to the Swedish King Gustav Wasa can be found in the foyer. Until well into the 19th century, the unusual openings in the facade and arcades served as a protection against the weather for numerous market booths. Cafés on the market square sell the world-famous Lübeck marzipan.

A few steps further on is the 18th-century **Buddenbrook House** (open daily 10am–5pm, Jan–Mar 11am–5pm), former home of Thomas and Heinrich Mann. Thomas Mann's novel *Buddenbrooks* turned the house in Mengstrasse into an important literary shrine. The nearby **Schabbelhaus** is a good place to dine. Another restaurant is in the former **Haus der Schiffergesellschaft** (Shippers' Guild House) in Breite Strasse. The polished wooden furnishings, copper lamps and model ships anging from the ceiling serve as reminders of the many Hanseatic ship's captains who spent their last days here.

When Lübeck was occupied by enemy troops in 1407 there were only sugar and almonds left to feed the inhabitants. It is said that they were saved from starvation by a kind of loaf made from these ingredients. But this is only the legend of marzipan – it actually came to Europe from Syria.

BELOW:
Thomas Mann,
the family man.

THOMAS MANN

The book's subtitle was "Decay of a Family", but it could as easily have been "Rise". Thomas Mann's *Buddenbrooks*, published in 1901, was a historical novel tracing the decline of a bourgeois German family very like Mann's own, living in a town very much like Lübeck. But rather than representing the disgraceful end of the Mann line, Thomas was its acme. The success of *Buddenbrooks* launched one of Germany's most important literary careers.

Buddenbrooks is probably Mann's most accessible work. In the author's subsequent books, both his prose and his philosophy are more opaque. Mann was concerned with issues relating to the creative life: the relationship between creativity and neurosis or illness; the place of the artist in society. Many of his greatest works take up these themes: *Death in Venice* (1912), about an ageing composer's infatuation with a young boy, and *The Magic Mountain* (1924), set in a sanatorium.

Winner of the Nobel Prize for Literature in 1929, Mann was an outspoken opponent of the Nazis. He left Germany in 1933 and in 1936 moved to Los Angeles where he wrote his last great novel, *Dr Faustus*. He didn't set foot on German soil again until 1949 and died in Switzerland in 1955 at the age of 80.

The **Heilig-Geist-Hospital** (Holy Ghost Hospital; open daily 10am–5pm), with 13th-century frescoes in the cross vaults, was one of Germany's first old people's homes. Cross Glockengiesserstrasse to the **Füchtingshof**, an example of the quarters built by the rich merchants specifically to house the poor. Lübeck also has many **Wohngänge** settlements, built in the 16th century in gardens behind large middle-class homes to house the growing population.

Beaches and lakes

Located to the northeast in Lübeck Bay is **Travemünde** ㉜, which has been a part of Lübeck since the 14th century. From the beginning of the 19th century, the rich and the powerful, including many Scandinavians, have been enjoying this resort. Travemünde is a terminal for many ferry services linking Germany and Scandinavia. Stretching further to the north are the beaches and bathing areas of Lübeck Bay. Models in sand of original German castles are the trademarks of **Timmendorfer Strand**, **Scharbeutz** and **Haffkrug**, to name the most famous. One way to enjoy this scenic coastline is to take the Brodtener Steilufer clifftop walk, which follows a marked path between Travemünde and Niendorf. At Hemmeldorfsee, between Travemünde and Timmendorf, is Germany's lowest point – 44 metres (144 ft) below sea level.

A mere 10 km (6 miles) further to the north, the "mighty" heights of Schleswig-Holstein's "Little Switzerland" appear with their beech and oak forests surrounding approximately 200 lakes formed during the Ice Age. Forests cover the banks with *Knicks*, or earth mounds, guarded by hedges designed to protect the sandy soil from wind erosion.

The health resort of **Eutin** ㉝ is known as the "Weimar of the North". Here Johann Heinrich Voss (1751–1826) translated Homer's epics into German. Historic pictures painted by the 18th-century artist Tischbein during his stay are exhibited in the moated **Castle**. Summer concerts in honour of Eutin's most famous native son, Carl Maria von Weber (1786–1826) take place annually in the castle's park.

At the centre of the region, between the **Grosser** and **Kleiner Plöner See**, is the town of **Plön** ㉞. During the 18th century, the Renaissance-style moated castle by the lakeside was used by the Danish king as a summer residence. Having been used by the Nazis as a training centre, it is now a boarding school. The tower of the **Church of St Peter** in **Bosau** ㉟ provides a fine view across the entire region. This little church is just one of the venues for the **Schleswig-Holstein Music Festival** held in July and August.

North of Plön, the little town of **Preetz** ㊱ has a 13th-century Benedictine **Monastery** and a **Circus Museum** on pretty Mühlenstrasse. The **Seelenter See** north of Preetz provides a sanctuary for rare birds. Several manor houses and small castles are situated nearby, such as the **Bungsberg**, the highest point in the region (164 metres/538 ft).

Kiel, capital of Schleswig-Holstein

With its port and modern industrial area, **Kiel** ㊲ (pop. 235,000) is the dominant city in the state of Schleswig-Holstein. However, this has not always been

Map on pages 304–5

TIP

A homage to contemporary literature in Lübeck, the **Günter Grass-Haus** stands at Glockengiesserstrasse 21 (open Jan–Mar Tues–Sun 11am–5pm, Apr–Dec Mon–Sun 10am–5pm). Grass received the Nobel Prize in 1999 and is also a gifted artist.

BELOW: relaxation at Timmendorfer Strand.

the case. Since its foundation by Adolf IV of Schauenburg in 1233, the local economy has experienced many ups and downs. Kiel's role was not clearly established until 1865 when Prussia annexed Schleswig-Holstein. In 1871, the imperial naval harbour was founded and, in 1895, the Kaiser-Wilhelm Canal (Kiel Canal) was opened. In 1917, Kiel was named capital of the Prussian province of Schleswig-Holstein and in 1945 it became capital of the new federal state.

Because of its strategic importance, Kiel fell victim to heavy bombing during World War II. While no longer able to boast about the beauty of its historic buildings, Kiel nevertheless has considerable charm thanks to its location on the wide bay of the **Kieler Förde**. The railway station is only a few yards from the water's edge, from where passenger boats leave to zig-zag their way across the fjord, passing **Oslo Quay** where larger ferries lie at anchor, the **Hindenburg Quay** with its yachting marina, and the **Gorch Fock**. The lock gates of the great **Kiel Canal** (Nord-Ostsee-Kanal) can also be seen to the left. At the mouth of the estuary lies the resort of **Laboe**, where you can either squeeze into an old U-Boat or enjoy a wide panoramic view from the **German Naval War Memorial**.

Outside the **St Nicholas Church** (13th–15th century, rebuilt in 1951), stands one of Ernst Barlach's sculptures known as *Der Geistkämpfer*.

The modern **Castle** is now used as a concert hall, while the **Kunsthalle** (open Tues–Sun 10.30am–6pm, Wed until 8pm) exhibits works of art by local artists, including a section devoted to the Expressionist work of Emil Nolde.

Southwest of Kiel, the **Schleswig-Holstein Freilichtmuseum** in **Molfsee** ㊳ (Open-Air Museum; open Tues–Sun 9am–5pm, Nov–Mar only Sun 11am–4pm) is well worth a visit. Fishermen's huts, farm buildings, houses, workshops and mills from all over Schleswig-Holstein have been re-erected on the site. Visitors

BELOW: shipbuilding
in miniature in the
Kiel Museum.

can watch craftsmen at work, and try some ham from the smokehouse and fresh bread from the bakery. Not far from here is the **Westensee Naturpark ❸**, a nature reserve that is a popular place for a stroll, particularly at weekends.

Map on pages 304–5

Towards the Danish border

Travel north along the cliff-lined coast past the hamlets at Knoop, Dänisch Nienhof and Altenhof to reach the attractive seaside resort of **Eckernförde ❹**, which has been a thriving fishing port ever since it was founded in the 12th century. To the south of the Schlei estuary, you can still make out the earthworks of **Haithabu ❹**. Up until the 11th century, an important Viking trading centre was situated at this junction of the ancient north-south trade route and the waterway formed by the rivers Schlei, Eider and Treene. The **Viking Museum** at Haddebyer Noor (open daily 9am–5pm, May–Sept until 7pm, Nov–Mar Tues–Sun 10am–4pm) houses archaeological finds from the region. Among its number of valuable finds are the Nydam Ship, a 4th-century Viking long boat, and bodies that were discovered preserved in the bog.

Viking prow at Haddebyer Noor.

On the other side of the Schlei is **Schleswig ❷**, the oldest town in the state – it acquired its municipal charter in 1200. Close to the old town, which is well worth a visit, is the Renaissance castle of **Gottorf**, the largest princely residence in Schleswig-Holstein. This castle also houses the two most important museums in Schleswig-Holstein: the **Schleswig-Holstein Museum** (art collections from the Middle Ages to the 20th century) and the **Archaeological Museum** (both open Apr–Oct daily 10am–6pm, Nov–Mar daily 10am–4pm, Sat–Sun until 5pm), the largest museum of its kind in Germany.

The Bordesholm Altar by Hans Brüggemann can be seen in **St Peter's Cathedral** (12th–15th century), a Gothic brick church. The **Angeln** peninsula to the northeast of Schleswig also has distant historical connections: it was from here that the Angles, an ancient Germanic tribe, emigrated to England in the 5th and 6th centuries.

BELOW: interior decoration at Gottorf Castle, Schleswig.

For the remainder of the trip to Flensburg, take the coastal road from Kappeln, which passes through a richly varied landscape. The coast offers countless bathing beaches and many fine views of the sea open out along the way. Near **Glücksburg ❸** stands a beautiful moated castle of the same name (built 1587), once the summer residence of Danish kings. The gardens are used as a venue for cultural events.

From its early days as a fishing village during the 12th century, **Flensburg ❹** (pop. 87,000) emerged as an important trading centre at the head of the Flensburger Förde. In the 16th century, the town was Denmark's most important port, as illustrated in the **Schifffahrtsmuseum** (Maritime Museum; open Tues–Sun Apr–Oct 10am–5pm, Nov–Mar 10am–4pm). The narrow streets of Flensburg are lined with fine houses, medieval courtyards and modern warehouse conversions. The **Alt-Flensburger Haus**, which is set out like a merchant's house, is now one of the region's top restaurants. The **Nordertor** (16th-century), with its stepped gables, is the home of German rum making, a skill that arrived here in the 18th century from the West Indies. ❏

ALONG THE BALTIC COAST

Famous for its sandy beaches and chalk cliffs, the Baltic coast of Mecklenburg-Vorpommern offers a richly varied landscape, interspersed with old seafaring cities full of fine architecture

Map on pages 304–5

Bismarck used to quip that he would move north before the end of the world, as everything happens 100 years later up there – a saying as popular today as it was then. Travellers through Mecklenburg-Vorpommern may at first be inclined to agree and then be just as likely to find evidence to the contrary. It is true that the fruits of progress are not too apparent in this area, but neither could this sparsely populated federal *Land* be said to be behind the times. The whole area is more or less flat land, and everything seems to happen on the shores of one of the 1,800 lakes *(see also page 123)* or along the 340-km (210-mile) stretch of coast between the Bay of Lübeck and the Stettiner Haff.

This lovely coastline is deeply indented with many bays, alternating with a plethora of islands and peninsulas. There are four prosperous Hanseatic towns and numerous bathing resorts, which have succeeded in preserving their traditional seaside architecture. The steep coast can rise up to 120 metres (390 ft) above sea level and the never-ending beaches give way to marshy meadows and woodland. The *Bodden* landscape – inland expanses of water leading out into the open sea – often looks like the Baltic equivalent of the North Sea mud flats.

Castles, towns and lakes

Setting out from Hamburg, the first place encountered is **Ahrensburg** ❹, where there is a fine **Renaissance Palace**, constructed in 1595. Inside, there is an exhibition on the noble house of Schleswig-Holstein. The nearby 16th-century **Gottesbuden** (God's Huts) shows how the less well-off used to live. These two small brick houses were once a refuge for the poor and the sick.

To the east, the town of **Ratzeburg** ❹ lies in a beautiful setting between two lakes. Once an outpost for the conversion to Christianity of West Mecklenburg, it was elevated to the status of bishopric during the reign of Henry the Lion, and the romantic brick-built **Cathedral** was completed in the 12th century. The Cathedral Lodge of Ratzeburg was responsible for the construction of many churches in the area. Pillaging by the Danes in the 17th century accounts for the lack of medieval building, with the exception of the cathedral and the early-Gothic **Church of St George**. For this reason many of the townhouses date from the subsequent two centuries; along with the fact that it is enclosed by three lakes, this gives the town a harmonious feel.

The Expressionist sculptor, poet and playwright Ernst Barlach (1870–1938) spent his youth here. The **Barlach Museum** (open Tues–Sun 10am–1pm, 2–5pm) in his father's house can be found next door to the classicist **Parish Church** (1787–91). In the

LEFT: Ahrenshoop on Darss has a history as an artists' colony.
BELOW: Ahrensburg Palace.

Lilies at the Lauenberg Lakes.

Cathedral Close the Andreas Paul Weber House (open Tues–Sun 10am–1pm, 2–5pm) has an exhibition of fantastical and satirical pencil drawings.

The border between West and East Germany ran not far from here for several decades. For the local population this meant a severe restriction of freedom, but for the flora and fauna it was a time of prolific growth. The **Lauenburg Lakes** west of the former no-man's-land and the **Schaalsee** directly adjacent to the course of the former border, are a unique wooded water paradise whose rich inheritance includes orchids, sundew, cotton grass, marsh marigolds, cranes and storks. This lake area is now a nature reserve to ensure it remains undisturbed. It is best explored on foot or by bicycle, as the slower pace makes it easier to discover the hidden treasures of the lakes, pools and bogs and observe the freshwater ecosystems.

The region of Mecklenburg-Vorpommern begins just beyond **Mühlenmoor** on the B208. Among its population of two million, tourism has become the watchword, for many are pinning their hopes on new job opportunities in this service industry: the state may be rich in bright yellow rape fields and beautiful scenery, but unemployment is high.

The first to profit from the tourist trade were the larger towns and cities, rich in culture and history. Typical of these is the state capital **Schwerin** (pop. 102,000), the former ancestral seat of the Grand Dukes of Mecklenburg. The enormous **Palace** (open Apr–Oct Tues–Sun 10am–6pm, Nov–Mar until 5pm), built between 1843 and 1857 and much extended, is a popular destination. Situated on an island between the Burgsee and the Schweriner See, it is said to have 365 towers and turrets. The magnificent interior is quite remarkable: the dining room displays vases from St Petersburg and Berlin porcelain; the audience

BELOW: the state theatre and museum in Schwerin.

chamber is decorated with red silk wallpaper; and the throne room is crammed full of portraits. It is also worth taking a walk in the small **Burggarten** overlooking the lake, and then crossing the bridge to the baroque **Schlossgarten** with its canal and copies of sculptures by Balthasar Permoser.

On the town side of the palace is the delightful square, the **Alter Garten**, flanked by the magnificent **State Theatre** with its rococo auditorium and the **State Museum** (open Tues–Sun 10am–6pm), which contains an exquisite collection of the works of the Flemish and Dutch Masters. From the lofty heights of the nearby **Cathedral** tower (cathedral built 1270, tower added 1892), seven lakes can be seen, an amphibious world populated by swans and boats. The centre of town is worth visiting for its market square and the nearby **Schlachtermarkt**, which is occupied by stalls from Tuesday to Saturday. Visitors should also inspect the half-timbered frontages in the **Schelfstadt**, and the fine examples of neoclassical architecture on the Pfaffenteich lake.

The coast

The Hanseatic town of **Wismar** (pop. 48,000) is the first port we come to and our first glimpse of the sea. Its favourable location led to its swift expansion in the past. Ships sailed to Bergen and Bruges, and wagons travelled along the coast to Lübeck and the Baltic. It entered a rapid decline after the Thirty Years' War, and its fortunes did not improve again until industrialisation in the 19th century. Despite heavy losses in World War II, a number of historical buildings were saved from the ruins, including the churches of **St George** (15th century) and **St Nicholas** (14th–15th century) and the neoclassical **Town Hall** (1817–19), all cheek by jowl with numerous Gothic townhouses. Yet more variety is provided by the baroque buildings and Renaissance facades. Wismar's focal point is the cobbled **Markt**, with its handsome assemblage of architectural styles spanning a period of 500 years.

To the northeast of Wismar are the seaside resorts of **Kühlungsborn** 🄌 and **Heiligendamm** 🄍. The first of these is resplendent with a kilometre-long beach and new bridge, and the second, too, justifies its epithet "the white town by the sea" by its appearance. It was founded in 1793 and is thus the oldest resort in Germany. White neoclassical villas line the narrow strip of coast, reflecting the desire of noble and wealthy citizens to savour the beneficial effects of the salt waters in suitably opulent surroundings. A sea view was always *de rigueur*.

Some 10km (6 miles) north of Wismar, the scenic if windswept island of **Poel** is worth a diversion from the coastal road (use the causeway).

Bad Doberan 🄎 can be reached via the "green tunnel", the longest avenue of lime trees in Europe, or by leaving the car behind and taking the narrow-gauge railway on board *Molli*, chugging through the countryside at a leisurely 35 kph (20 mph). Doberan is best represented by its imposing 14th-century **Minster**, the Gothic church with a richly furnished interior, which was the centrepiece of a powerful Cistercian convent. From the 18th century, it was visited annually by the Mecklenburg court entourage. Europe's

Map on pages 304–5

TIP

Should you visit Schwerin in August, don't miss the pottery market on the Alter Markt. To find out exactly when, call Schwerin-Information, tel: 0385-5925212.

BELOW: the rolling hinterland.

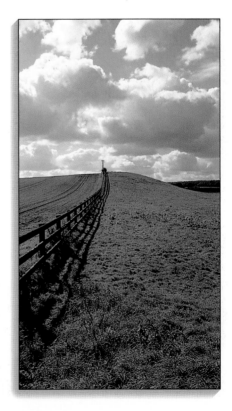

very first horse-racing course was opened in Doberan in 1807. The title "Bad" (spa) was added to its name in 1929 because of its iron-rich mud baths.

Where there are few openings, a gateway must be found. This purpose was served by **Rostock** (53) (pop. 103,000) in the difficult years of the GDR. Party leader Walter Ulbricht and his entourage created a "gateway to the world" from the ruins of the war, thereby bringing to the nearly 800-year-old Hanseatic town an international port, docks, and a population explosion. Its sense of civic pride and tradition, which were not diminished in the years following 1945, are amply illustrated by its stepped gables, rooftops, eaves and attics, three large churches, four magnificent city gates and one of the oldest universities in Europe.

A full tour of the town could take days. The **Kulturhistorisches Museum** in the Monastery of the Holy Cross (open Tues–Sun 10am–6pm) contains all manner of information on local history; the **Schiffahrtsmuseum** (Shipping Museum; open Tues–Sun 10am–6pm) tells amusing tales of sea voyages; and the **Church of St Mary** (13th–15th century) has an astronomical clock from 1472 whose calendar goes right up to the year 2017. To the north of Rostock, the 14th-century fishing village of **Warnemünde** (54) is perfect for a warm summer's day, with its thatched cottages and broad expanse of beach frequented by nudist swimmers.

Anyone who is staying in Rostock should also not miss an excursion to the old ducal seat of **Güstrow** (55) to the south. Here, there is a lot to see in a small area, including a brick **Cathedral** (1236), the **Parish Church**, the largest **Renaissance Palace** (16th century) in the north, and many traces of Ernst Barlach, who lived in the former provincial seat from 1910 onwards. Examples of his sculpture can be seen in the Cathedral, the Gertrude Chapel (1430) and in the **Atelierhaus**, the sculptor's former studio just outside the town.

BELOW: Rostock, historic bridgehead to the north.

The "amber coast" is actually in Poland, but in some years a few hundred-weight of amber can be found washed ashore on the German Baltic coast. If a stroll along the beach in search of this "northern gold" proves unsuccessful, results are guaranteed in **Ribnitz-Damgarten** 🐻, to the east of Rostock. The Recknitz, the river that forms the border between Mecklenburg and Vorpommern, flows through the town, and in the **Bernstein Museum** (open daily 9.30am–6pm) the fossilised resin glows in all its glory.

On the **Fischland-Darss-Zingst** peninsula a strong inshore wind always seems to be blowing, and human beings seem insignificant. It is a desolate wilderness of reeds, echoing to the continuous pounding of the waves. Small resorts try to attract holidaymakers to their vast expanses of beach, with camp sites and wicker beach chairs.

Ahrenshoop 🐻 has the usual sailors' and fishermen's houses, but also has a history as an artists' colony. More than a century ago, a painter discovered this remote spot, and brought a number of young artists to join him. Sand dunes, windswept cottages and shelters, and strangely twisted and storm-tossed trees were all committed to paper and canvas. Other popular subjects were the Darsser Forest, and the *Bodden*, the still lagoons sheltered from the wind by islands and peninsulas. Those who are familiar with the song "*Wo de Ostseewellen trecken an den Strand*" ("Where the Baltic waves wash on to the sand") can pay their respects to the local writer Martha Müller-Grahlert at **Zingst** 🐻.

Back on the mainland, **Stralsund** 🐻 (pop. 70,000) is a veritable showcase for brick, the typical building material of northern Germany. Red bricks give this town, Vorpommern's counterpart to Lübeck, its unmistakable appearance, which conservationists and visitors alike hold in high regard. The community, which

Map on pages 304–5

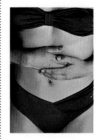

Bikini on the Baltic.

BELOW: Stralsund, Hanseatic town on the Baltic.

received its charter in 1234, has lived through and survived many conflicts over the centuries, including the Thirty Years' War, when the Swedes drove out Wallenstein and stayed themselves until 1815, and World War II, which made way for socialist influences.

Despite all the upheaval, Stralsund resembles a huge museum, and has won acclaim for its restoration projects. The Gothic **Town Hall** (facade from 1370–80) is an outstanding example of how filigree can be reproduced in brick. There is also the **Church of St Nicholas** (around 1366), with its *Nowgorodfahrer* pews; the **Church of St Mary** (15th century), with a baroque organ; and **St Catherine's Monastery** (13th–14th century), home of both the **Culture and History Museum** and the **Oceanographic Museum** (both open Tues–Sun 10am–5pm).

From Stralsund's harbour, and from the fishing village of Schaprode on the island of Rügen, boats set sail for the small Baltic island of **Hiddensee ⑥⓪**. Its name is reminiscent of a fairytale, recalling sun, wind and storms, mussels, amber and the unique northern quality of light, the cries of seagulls and the flight of cranes. People who allow themselves to be carried away by the magic of the name will not be disappointed by a visit to the "Söten Länneken" (sweet little place). There they will find no cars, four villages nestling in the landscape and, to the north of the island, 70-metre (230-ft) high cliffs with a lighthouse. This was the summer refuge of the poet Gerhart Hauptmann (1862–1946), but it did not remain his secret for long and in the first half of the 20th century the island became a meeting place for great minds. They included Thomas Mann, who liked to walk on the shore with his wife, Katja; Albert Einstein, who came here to ponder his next theory, and even the film-maker Billy Wilder.

TIP

Children will love the Oceanographic Museum in Stralsund. There are aquariums with colourful fish, turtles, seahorses, starfish, a 16-metre (52-ft) long whale skeleton, a coral reef and lots more.

BELOW:
aspects of Rügen.

Germany's largest island

If this region has a truly spiritual landscape, this has to be on **Rügen ⓺**, Germany's largest island. Caspar David Friedrich (1774–1840) immortalised its tall chalk cliffs in 1818. Today, the stream of traffic across the Rügendamm and the stream of visitors to the **Stubbenkammer** cliffs and the surrounding Jasmund National Park is never-ending. The island of the romantics has now become a holidaymakers' eldorado, and not without reason. The sea encroaches at various points on the 1,000 sq. km (386 sq. mile) island, producing a unique scenery composed of bays, gulfs and peninsulas, with wide beaches and steep cliffs. Inland it is characterised by avenues of limes and chestnuts, broad-leafed woods, fields and small villages. But Rügen does have other landmarks, including the two lighthouses at **Kap Arkona** and **Putbus**, the Baden-Baden of the north; the narrow-gauge railway "Rasender Roland" (Racing Roland); the conservation village of **Vitt**; and finally the **Granitz Hunting Seat** near Binz.

Returning to the mainland, Highway 96 leads to the venerable university town of **Greifswald ⓼** (pop. 67,000). At first sight it would appear that the town has not changed since the days when Caspar David Friedrich captured it in his paintings. The skyline punctuated by the towers of the churches of **St Mary** and **St Nicholas** (both 13th–14th century), the imposing townhouses on the Market Square, and the ruins of the **Eldena Monastery**, the foundation of this town, which was later to join the Hanseatic League, are all still there. However, a closer inspection will lead to the conclusion that the German *Realsozialisten* (realpolitik proponents) are not without reproach, having caused some irrevocable destruction of the town, which was given up without a struggle in World War II.

Since the 19th century, people have escaped from the capital to take the summer air at **Usedom ⓽**, hence the nickname "The Berliners' Bath". The second-largest island in Germany is now reviving these traditions, dusting down its guesthouses and hotels.

Resorts abound on Usedom: in the past, they reflected a social hierarchy; **Heringsdorf** attracted a different kind of visitor from **Bansin** or **Zinnowitz**. Some catered for the aristocracy and high financiers, while others accommodated officers and civil servants. Common to all are the picturesque beaches and the typical resort architecture with its promenades and villas seeking to outdo each other, with bay windows and turrets, large conservatories and ornate balconies. At the narrowest point of the island, at **Lüttenort**, there is an unusual museum, the refuge of the painter Otto Niemeyer-Holstein (1896–1984). This consists of a studio full of Baltic landscapes and portraits, a railway luggage van connecting two houses, and a garden abounding in sculptures.

V-bomb display

A museum of a completely different kind awaits the curious in **Peenemünde ⓾**. In the military research establishment here in the 1940s, Wernher von Braun developed the world's first liquid-fuel rockets. In the form of the V-bomb, these brought death and destruction to the south of England. After the war, Braun went to America, where he worked for NASA. ❑

Map
on pages
304–5

BELOW: wicker beach chairs by the pier at Rügen.

INSIGHT GUIDES

TRAVEL TIPS

GERMANY

TRAVEL TIPS

TRANSPORT

GETTING THERE
AND GETTING AROUND

GETTING THERE

By Air

Frankfurt am Main is the principal hub for international flights and offers good connections to other German cities. International services also operate from Berlin, Bremen, Düsseldorf, Hamburg, Hanover, Cologne/Bonn, Munich, Nuremberg, Saarbrücken, Leipzig, Münster/Osnabrück, Dresden and Stuttgart.

There are connections to 270 destinations worldwide from Frankfurt, many of them provided by the national airline Lufthansa (tel: 0871-945 9747 from UK, tel: 800-399 5838 from US; www.lufthansa.com), which offers a wide range of fare structures depending on season and on the age of the traveller. Air Berlin is Germany's second largest airline (tel: 0871-500 0737 from UK,

BELOW: entrance to the S-Bahn, Berlin.

tel: 866-266 5588 from US; www.airberlin.com). It is well worth making exhaustive enquiries if you want the best package for your travel needs.

Terminal 1 at Frankfurt Rhein Main airport can be reached by train, so the centre of Frankfurt (Hauptbahnhof) is only 15 minutes away. This is where you can join the main German inter-city rail network. A reliable public transport system, usually a shuttle service, links all German airports with the nearest city centre(s); there are always taxis.

Airlines flying from the UK and Ireland

Aer Lingus
Tel: 0870-876 5000 (from UK)
Tel: 0818-365 000 (from Ireland)
www.aerlingus.com
BMI
Tel: 0870-607 0555
www.flybmi.com
bmibaby
Tel: 0871-224 0224
www.bmibaby.com
British Airways
Tel: 0844-493 0787
www.britishairways.com
easyJet
Tel: 0871-244 2366
www.easyjet.co.uk
Flybe
Tel: 0871-700 2000
www.flybe.com
Jet2
Tel: 0871-226 1737
www.jet2.com
Ryanair
Tel: 0905-566 0000 (from UK)
Tel: 1570-224 499 (from Ireland)
www.ryanair.com

By Ferry

These shipping companies operate services from the UK to the continental mainland:

DFDS Seaways: Harwich–Hamburg; tel: 0871-522 9955; www.dfdsseaways.co.uk
Stena Line: Harwich–Hook of Holland; tel: 08705-707070; www.stenaline.co.uk
Seafrance: Dover–Calais; tel: 08705-711 711; www.seafrance.co.uk
P&O Ferries: Dover–Calais, Hull–Rotterdam, Hull–Zeebrugge; tel: 08716-645 645; www.poferries.com
Norfolkline: Dover–Dunkerque; tel: 0870-870 1020; www.norfolkline.com
Ferry connections also link Germany with Norway, Denmark, Sweden, Finland, the Russian Federation, Latvia and Lithuania.

By Train

You can travel on Eurostar (tel: 08705-186186; www.eurostar.com) from London Waterloo to Paris or Brussels, from where connections can be made with several German cities. Booking is not essential outside peak hours. For more details, contact the UK booking centre of:
Deutsche Bahn
Tel: 0870-243 5363; www.bahn.co.uk
For the various types of rail pass available for travel within Germany, *see page 349.*

By Coach

The extensive Germany motorway network *(Autobahnen)* covers the whole of the country and extends into all neighbouring countries.

There are regular coaches from the UK to Germany, connecting London with major cities such as Berlin, Cologne, Frankfurt-am-Main, Dortmund, Hanover and Munich.

For details and credit-card

bookings in the UK, contact **Eurolines**, tel: 08705-143 219; www.eurolines.com

GETTING AROUND

By Air

Lufthansa, with its main base in Frankfurt-am-Main, is the main provider of domestic air services. AirBerlin and Eurowings also operate regular services between the major cities and several regional airlines fly to smaller places. Although standard fares are quite expensive, if you book in advance (14 days minimum) and are not in possession of a rail pass, flying can be a cheaper option than travelling by rail.

By Coach or Bus

The so-called *Europabusse* are a cheap way of travelling between cities, many departing from main railway stations. Private bus companies operate services that link towns with smaller villages in the country. In remote parts this is usually the only form of public transport.

Among the different bus companies, Eurolines Germany, run by Deutsche Touring GmbH, offers some fascinating itineraries designed primarily for tourists, following scenic routes. **Deutsche Touring GmbH**, tel: +49(0)69-790 3501; www.touring.de.

The *BerLinienbus* links Berlin with many cities and popular tourist areas in both Germany and the rest of Europe (tel: +49(0)30-861 9331; www.berlinienbus.de).

By Train

Every day the Deutsche Bahn AG (DB) operates some 35,000 passenger trains over a 40,000-km (25,000-mile) domestic network, as well as many international through services. The high-speed network now covers about 3,500 km (2,000 miles) of track and is still being extended.

Travelling in Germany is not just about getting from A to B, but is a pleasurable experience, especially when following the course of the Rhine or heading south through the Black Forest or the Alps.

To avoid long hours behind the wheel and the stress of traffic jams on the motorways, travelling by rail is a very convenient and highly recommended alternative. The trains are fast, comfortable and you will reach your destination exactly on

time. But don't go straight to the station and just buy a regular ticket for the next train available. Think carefully about your route in advance and ask your travel agent or DB about the fare structure. You can save a lot of money by choosing the right option.

The Network

The German railway network is made up of three lines: ICE, EC/IC and IR. **ICE**: The ICE (Inter City Express) is a modern high-speed train that travels at 280 kph (175 mph) and links the major cities on an hourly or two-hourly basis. The carriages are air-conditioned, with office facilities, restaurants and snack bars available. You can choose your seat (reservation is recommended) in a compartment *(Abteil)* or in a saloon car *(Grossraumwagen)*.
IC/EC The IC (Inter City) and EC (Euro City) are similar in terms of comfort and on-train services to the ICE; they travel at high speed (200 kph/120 mph), at one or two-hourly intervals and connect about 80 important towns and cities.
Regional Other regional trains are called Regional Express (RE), Regional Bahn (RB) or Stadt Express (SE). Express trains *(D-Züge)*, traditional long-distance trains, still run on some lines. They are slower than the IC/EC services, but the fares are cheaper.
Motorail The German railway has a fully integrated motorail network, which connects with the rest of the European motorail network. Trains run mostly during the summer and at other holiday periods; most have sleeper, couchette and restaurant-buffet cars.
Overnight trains For night travel Deutsche Bahn offers the EC Night on a number of different routes, including international routes like Berlin–Paris–Brussels and onwards (after a change of trains) to London. There are three categories: cabins

ABOVE: a favourite form of transport.

(1 or 2 beds, shower and toilet), compartments with couchettes or reclining chairs. Breakfast is included, tel: 11861.
Bikes It is possible to take your own bicycle on many trains for a small extra fee, but because of limited space it is advisable to call the *Fahrrad-Hotline* in advance, tel: 01805-151 415.

Discounts and Passes

There are many different and often confusing reduced-fare schemes and passes. Some of these only apply to tickets purchased in Germany, others are for non-European citizens only.

For information on the above tickets, call **Deutsche Bahn**'s UK booking centre on 0870-243 5363 (lines are open Mon–Fri 9am–5pm), or log on to www.bahn.co.uk.

In addition, Rail Europe in the UK (www.raileurope.co.uk) and DER in the US (www.der.com) both offer a wide selection of rail passes.

City Transport

A widespread network of public transport systems exists in every large city. Those cities with a population of 100,000 and over provide a highly efficient bus network with frequent and generally very punctual services. You usually buy the bus ticket from the driver or at coin-operated machines on the bus or at the bus stop. In large cities, such as Berlin, Hamburg, Cologne, Munich, Frankfurt and Stuttgart, the bus routes are integrated with the underground (U-Bahn), the tram and the above-ground suburban railway (S-Bahn). The same ticket may be used on all four means of transport.

Booking Seats

It is generally advisable to make a seat reservation for trains. This service costs approximately an extra €2.50 (more for ICE/IC/EC trains). Children under 4 years of age travel free of charge, those aged 4 to 11 pay half fare. The information number for Deutsche Bahn is the same in all German cities: tel: 11861; train timetable (charge free): 0800 150 7090.

In many towns, reduced-rate tickets are sold for unlimited daily, weekly or monthly travel. There are also special tourist offers like the Welcome Card in Berlin, which includes 48 or 72 hours of free travelling on public transport, plus many discount coupons for sightseeing or cultural events (similar offers exist in other cities).

The Berlin Transport Company (**BVG**) operates a number of services specifically for tourists (Nos. 100 and 200 cover most of the major sites), as well as an express bus shuttle service between the airport and the city centre. Tel: 030-19449 for details (lines open 24 hours).

Passengers normally purchase their ticket from ticket machines. Inspections are frequent, and passengers travelling without valid tickets will be fined on the spot.

Cycling

Many book and bicycle shops, including the German Cycle Club (Allgemeiner Deutscher Fahrrad-Club), offer books and maps for cycling holidays. The Bund Deutscher Radfahrer (Association of German Cyclists) has guides for specific regions, whereas RV Verlag publishes cycling and walking maps entitled *Regio Concept*.

The alternative to taking your own bicycle is the *Fahrrad am Bahnhof* scheme, whereby cycles may be hired at railway stations. Prices are reasonable, with a reduction for rail ticket holders. Brochures available locally provide suggested tours to and from stations. This service is not available on all types of train.

Allgemeiner Deutscher Fahrrad-Club
Pf 107747, 28077 Bremen
Tel: 0421-346 290
Fax: 0421-346 2950
www.adfc.de; www.bettundbike.de
Bund Deutscher Radfahrer (BDR)
Otto-Fleck-Schneise 4,
60528 Frankfurt
Tel: 069-967 8000
Fax: 069-9678 0080

By Boat

It is always a good idea to get off the road and explore the country by boat. Regular boat services operate on rivers, lakes and coastal waters, including the Danube, Main, Moselle, Rhine, Neckar and Weser, the Ammersee, Chiemsee, Königsee and Lake Constance. Ferry services operate on Kiel Fjord and from Cuxhaven to Helgoland, to the East and North Frisian Islands, as well as to Scandinavian destinations.

Other boats just operate for pleasure trips and excursions. The Köln-Düsseldorf (KD) company runs pleasure cruises on the Rhine, Main and Moselle rivers every day from April to late October. In Dresden the Sächsische Dampfschiffahrts-GmbH offers cabin cruises on the Elbe between Dresden and Hamburg. The White Fleet in Potsdam and the Stern und Kreisschiffahrt in Berlin offer boat trips on the many waterways in and around these cities. Other navigable waterways include the Saale River and the lakes in Mecklenburg.

On Lake Constance in the far south of the country (Europe's third-largest inland lake), car ferries connect the German, Swiss and Austrian shores. Pleasure boats also operate on the lake.

The Euregio Tageskarte (day ticket), available for different zones, offers free travel on ferries and trains and reductions on entrance fees. Children up to 6 years of age travel free. Families with older children can ask for the additional Family Ticket for those between 6 and 15 years. www.euregiokarte.com.

Köln-Düsseldorfer Rheinschiffahrt AG (KD)
Frankenwerft 35, 50667 Cologne
Tel: 0221-208 8318
www.k-d.com
Sächsische Dampfschiffahrt
Hertha-Lindner-Strasse 10,
01067 Dresden
Tel: 0351-866 090
www.saechsische-dampfschiffahrt.de

Travelling on Foot

To explore Germany on foot, all you need is a good level of fitness, reliable walking shoes and a good set of maps, and you could walk from Flensburg to the Alps.

An intricate network of well kept and fully signposted local, regional and long-distance walking routes make walking one of the main pastimes in Germany. Footpaths in every region pass through beautiful landscapes or nature reserves. On longer sections

you will inevitably pass a restaurant or snack bar, and accommodation is usually easy to find.

Some long-distance walks are organised by clubs and the German youth hostel association, tourist offices and tour operators. Ask for details at the local tourist offices. Further information can be obtained from:
● Deutsches Jugendherbergswerk (German Youth Hostel Association) Bismarckstrasse 8, 32756 Detmold Tel: 05231-74010
Fax: 05231-740 149
www.djh.de
● The International Booking Network (a worldwide on-line booking service for youth hostel accommodation run by the International Youth Hostels Federation); www.hihostels.com
● Deutscher Alpenverein Von-Kahr-Strasse 2–4, 80997 Munich Tel: 089-140 030
www.alpenverein.de
● NaturFreunde Deutschlands e.V. Warschauer Strasse 58a, 10243 Berlin
Tel: 030-29 773 260
Fax: 030-29 773 280
www.naturfreunde.de

See page 385 for hiking firms operating in the UK.

Driving

The Road Network

Germany is covered by a modern network of motorways *(Autobahnen)* extending over 15,000 km (8,700 miles), making it one of the densest in the world. There are no toll-roads. Traffic drives on the right.

The *Autobahnen* are marked with an "A" on blue signs, while the regional roads are marked with a "B" on yellow signs. Motorway rest stops *(Raststätten)* every 30–50 km (20–30 miles) provide refreshments and toilet facilities. Often you will also find hotels and petrol at these

Travel Times

The following chart gives approximate journey times (in hours and minutes) from Berlin to other major cities in Germany.

	Air	Road	Rail
Hamburg	0.45	3.00	2.30
Cologne	1.05	7.00	4.35
Frankfurt	1.10	6.30	4.00
Munich	1.20	7.00	6.30
Dresden	—	2.30	2.15
Leipzig	—	2.30	2.10
Erfurt	—	4.30	3.30
Rostock	—	2.30	3.00

service stations. The petrol sold here is usually more expensive than in towns and along other roads.

The German tourist office publishes a booklet entitled *Autobahn-Service*, which provides information on all the facilities and services available on the motorways throughout the country.

For general road information, tel: ACE Stuttgart: 01802-336 677.

Regulations

Foreign travellers may drive their cars for up to one year if in possession of a national licence or international driving licence, car registration papers and proof of adequate insurance cover.

Traffic signs are international. At the junctions of two main or two minor roads, traffic coming from the right has priority unless otherwise indicated.

The general speed limit in Germany is 50 kph (30 mph) in towns and villages and 100 kph (60 mph) on open roads. Motorways *(Autobahnen)* and dual carriageways have a recommended speed limit of 130 kph (80 mph). But you will still find drivers speeding past at 180 kph (112 mph) or more in their Porsches, BMWs and Mercedes, which can be a little disconcerting if you are unused to it. Speed limits will vary according to road conditions. In certain residential areas the speed limit is 30 kph (20 mph). On streets with blue and white "Children Playing" road markings, the speed limit is walking pace only. Vehicles towing trailers are limited to 80 kph (50 mph) on all roads outside towns. There are on-the-spot fines for speeding and other infringements.

Children under 12 must travel in a special child seat in the back of the car and seat belts must be worn in both the front and the back of the car. The penalty for drivers and passengers who ignore this law is a hefty fine. The use of mobile phones is not allowed unless you use a headphone. All foreign cars must display a vehicle nationality plate. The legal alcohol limit is 50 mg per 100 ml.

Crash helmets are compulsory for motorcyclists (and pillion riders) riding vehicles that can attain a speed of more than 25 kph (15 mph).

Accidents

Before setting out on the road make sure you have a first-aid kit and a warning triangle in your car. Should you have an accident, switch on your hazard lights and put up the warning triangle at a safe distance from the scene of the accident.

Always ring the police when an accident results in personal injury.

Ask the other party for the name of their insurance company and their insurance policy number, and take the name and address of anyone who may have witnessed the accident. Do not forget to contact your own insurance company immediately.

Parking

Finding a free parking space in any city is still possible but very hard. There are specially marked parking zones where you have to buy a parking ticket in advance. Do not stay longer than your permit states – the traffic police are very efficient. Most cities have multi-storey car-parks, where you are charged on exit. Some shops return part of the parking fee if you show your ticket on paying for goods at the checkout. Car parking facilities exist near most tourist sights, but expect to pay for the privilege.

Disabled drivers should be warned that, although Germany is well-organised for the disabled traveller, an orange badge as used in the UK will not automatically entitle the disabled motorist to park freely in Germany.

Motor Organisations

The Allgemeiner Deutscher Automobil Club (ADAC) based in Munich and the Automobilclub von Deutschland (AvD) based in Frankfurt-am-Main have offices at all the main border-crossings and in the larger towns. They publish good-quality maps and guidebooks, and will assist foreign motorists, provided they belong to affiliated motoring organisations.

ADAC has rescue helicopters and operates an emergency service to relay radio messages to motorists. In both winter and summer radio stations use information provided by

BELOW: scenic train travel in Cologne.

Car Sharing

In every major city there are *Mitfahrerzentralen* (car sharing agencies, *see Yellow Pages*). These arrange lifts to all European cities, plus trips throughout Germany. Driver and passenger share costs (the agencies suggest reasonable amounts), the agency charges a small fee. A few agencies now operate for women only *(Frauenmitfahrzentralen)*.

the motoring organisations to keep road-users informed on traffic flow and roadworks.

Breakdown Services
ACE tel: 01802-343 536
ADAC tel: 01802-222 222
AvD tel: 0800-990 9909 (toll free)

Car Hire

Car hire *(Autovermietung)* is available practically everywhere. International companies with offices throughout Germany include Hertz, Avis and Europcar. For local car rentals enquire at your hotel's tourist information desk.

If you use the services of an international company and you come from an English-speaking country, probably all that is needed is your national driver's licence and a cash or credit card deposit. Smaller companies may insist on an international driver's licence.

Nationwide car reservations can be made under the following telephone numbers:
Avis tel: 01805-217 702
Hertz tel: 01805-333 535
Europcar tel: 01805-80000
Sixt tel: 01805-252 525

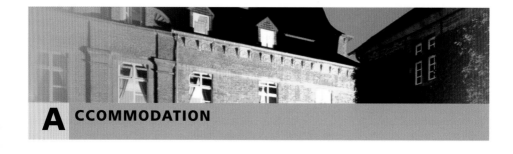

HOTELS, YOUTH HOSTELS, BED & BREAKFAST

Choosing a Hotel

Germany has a wide variety of hotels and guesthouses to choose from. Most international chains are represented and can easily be booked in advance.

Bed and breakfast hotels are often called *Hotel garni, Pension* or *Privatquartier.* Their addresses can be obtained from local tourist offices. Most are inexpensive and they provide contact with the locals, but do not expect luxury. Then there's the traditional *Gasthof,* normally located in the centre of a village or smaller town. They vary between old and simple, and old and fully renovated. You will also find modern hotels with all the comforts.

In rural areas, many castles and fortresses have been converted into luxurious hotels. Holidays on working farms are a good opportunity for city-based families to get a taste of day-to-day life in the country.

If you can, avoid large towns when there is a trade fair *(Messe)* going on. Accommodation, even in modest hotels, *pensions* and B&Bs, can be double the normal rate at these times, and rooms are seldom available at short notice.

B&Bs

Many people offer overnight accommodation in their houses, especially in the east (look out for *Fremdenzimmer, Gästezimmer* or

Zimmer frei signs). Private letting agencies *(Zimmervermittlung)* and tourist offices have listings and will help you find a room.

Farm Holidays

For farm holidays, ask for *Urlaub auf dem Bauernhof* brochures, available from tourist offices.

There is also an annual publication, in German, called *Ferien auf dem Lande.* It is available from Landschriften-Verlag/Zentrale für den Landurlaub, Maarstrasse 96; 53227 Bonn; tel: 0228-963 020; www.bauernhofurlaub.com

"Hay" or "Straw" Hotels

One unusual way of spending the night when travelling the Romantic Road – and in some other places – is in one of the "hay hotels" *(Heuhotels),* where beds are made from fresh hay covered with white linen (www.heuhotels.de; www.heuherbergen.de):
Weidenhof
Near Frauental, 7.5 km (4 miles) east of Creglingen
Tel: 07933-378
Fax: 07933-7515
www.ferienpension-heuhotel.de
Ferienbauernhof Ohr
Binzwangen 33, Colmberg, 13 km (8 miles) east of Rothenburg
Tel: 09803-289
Fax: 09803-233
www.ferienbauernhof-ohr.de
Next door, the Bauernhaus Gerda Ohr (tel: 09803-932 217) is a farm with lovely family apartments.

Youth Hostels

There are more than 600 youth hostels nationwide. Most of them have no age restrictions, although

Staying at a Spa Town

The Romans were the first to discover the healing effects of hot springs, and near today's towns of Baden-Baden, Trier, Aachen and other places they established thermal spas.

Later, in the 19th century, the spa culture was revived and emperors, kings and dukes from all over Europe met in the elegant *Kurorte* for relaxation, social events and private discussions about military alliances and royal marriages. It was during this period that richly decorated buildings and beautiful gardens were constructed in spa towns.

Germany has about 350 places that are recognised as a *Kurort* (health) or *Heilbad* (spa) town. Every possible medical treatment is available, with therapies based on natural resources, such as water, air or minerals.

Until recently, the German health service paid for a *Kururlaub,* a rest cure, for nearly anybody with a health complaint. Nowadays, because of the economic situation and welfare cuts, contributions are required, but it is still a very good deal.

Spas have acquired a reputation as haunts for the sick and elderly, but are now seeking to broaden their appeal to a younger clientele, which likes to opt for wellness holidays with a touch of luxury.

A special tax *(Kurtaxe)* is levied on hotel rooms on a per person per day basis, not just in genuine spa towns but also in some popular tourist spots.

For further information, contact: Deutscher Heilbäderverband Schumannstrasse 111, 53113 Bonn. Tel: 0228-201 200; fax: 201 2041; www.deutscher-heilbaederverband.de

you usually do have to pay more if you are over 27. As well as the traditional dormitories, many youth hostels now offer modern facilities, plus private bedrooms and family rooms. You will need an international YHA membership card. Book well in advance in summer and for weekend stays, as schools tend to block-book at popular times.

The directory of youth hostels (Deutsche Jugendherbergsverzeichnung) can be supplied by: **Deutsches Jugendherbergswerk**, Bismarckstasse 8, 32756 Detmold, tel: 05231-74010; www.djh.de.

In many cities there is a growing number of modern hostels which are a far cry from the traditional spartan youth hostel. They often have internet cafés, bars and comfortable lounges; there are no closing hours or age limits. Prices for a bed start at around €10.

Camping

Camping is very popular in Germany, and visitors will have no problem finding a camp site – there are around 2,000 dotted about the country, many in areas of outstanding natural beauty. Most are well equipped, with good bathrooms, power points and shops. Some are positively luxurious.

Recommended guidebooks are available from:
Deutscher Camping-Club e.V (DCC) Mandlstrasse 28, 80802 München. Tel: 089-380 1420, www.camping-club.de
ADAC, Referat Camping
Am Westpark 8, 81373 München. Tel: 089-7676 6202
Fax: 089-7676 2836.

Booking a Room

Tourist offices and agencies offer packages at prices that often seem to be more reasonable than if you pay directly at the hotel, especially if you choose a luxury hotel. Many tourist offices charge a small fee for the service, but it can be free.

Hotel Listings

Prices are usually for a double room, including taxes. In most

ABOVE: room service with a flourish.

cases, breakfast is included. Prices for smaller or basic hotels are per person in a double room, so they are not as cheap as you might initially think. It is always worth asking for a special weekend rate or a late-arrival discount.

ACCOMMODATION LISTINGS

BERLIN

Alameda-Berlin
Michaelkirchstrasse 15
Tel: 030-3086 8330
Fax: 030-3086 8359
www.hotel-alameda-berlin.de
Nice rooms in a friendly penthouse with a view. Between Kreuzberg and Mitte. **€€**

Albrechtshof
Albrechtstrasse 8
Tel: 030-308 860
Fax: 030-3088 6100
www.hotel-albrechtshof.de
A friendly, quiet place near the theatre quarter and Friedrichstrasse. **€€€**

A + O Hostel
Friedrichshain
Boxhagener Strasse 73
Tel: 030-297 7810
Fax: 030-2977 8120
Popular place for young travellers, with internet units and beer garden. **€**

Eastern Comfort
Mühlenstrasse 73–77
Tel: 030-6676 3806
Fax: 030-6676 3805
www.eastern-comfort.com
Youth hostel-type

accommodation on a boat on the River Spree, near the East-Side-Gallery – the longest remaining stretch of the Berlin Wall. Very clean, with a good atmosphere and a comfortable lounge on the upper deck. **€**

Estrel Hotel and
Convention Center
Sonnenallee 225
Tel: 030-6831 22522
Fax: 030-6831 2345
www.estrel.de
Berlin's largest hotel with more than a thousand rooms. Well away from the city centre in Neukölln, but with good travel connections (S-Bahn: 10 minutes to Alexanderplatz). Good level of comfort, not too pricey. **€€–€€€**

Frauenhotel Artemisia
Brandenburgische Strasse 18
Tel: 030-860 9320
Fax: 030-873 8905
www.frauenhotel-berlin.de
For women only. Friendly

rooms on the top floor of a residential building. Rooftop terrace. Close to the Kurfürstendamm. **€€**

Grand Hotel Esplanade
Lützowufer 15
Tel: 030-254 780
Fax: 030-2547 88222
www.esplanade.de
Luxury hotel by the Landwehrkanal in the Tiergarten district with own yacht for excursions and dinner cruises. The modern interior design provides a stylish touch. **€€€€**

Grand Hyatt Berlin
Marlene-Dietrich-Platz 2
Tel: 030-2553 1234
Fax: 030-2553 1235
www.berlin.grand.hyatt.de
The breathtaking interior architecture combines high-tech with an elegant modern design. Located right on lively Potsdamer Platz. **€€€€**

Honigmond Hotel
Tieckstrasse 12, corner of Borsigstrasse 28
Tel: 030-284 4550

www.honigmond-berlin.de
Cosy hotel-restaurant which stylishly combines modern design and antiques.

Honigmond Garden Hotel
Invalidenstrasse 122
Tel: 030-2844 5577
Fax: 030-2844 5588
Small hotel in a building dating from 1845, with a charming garden. Under the same management and with the same attentive service as the Honigmond Hotel. **€€€**

Hotel Adlon Kempinski
Unter den Linden 77
Tel: 030-2261 1111
Fax: 030-2261 2222

PRICE CATEGORIES

Prices are for a double room, including taxes and breakfast. Hostels and some smaller/more basic hotels are priced per person.
€ = less than €50
€€ = €50–110
€€€ = €110–180
€€€€ = more than €180

ABOVE: get your art fix at the Künstlerheim Luise.

www.hotel-adlon.de
Modern amenities and opulent luxury in the grand tradition of the original Adlon, where emperors and movie stars stayed. Close to the Brandenburg Gate. €€€€

Hotel Bleibtreu Berlin
Bleibtreustrasse 31
Tel: 030-884 740
Fax: 030-8847 4444
www.bleibtreu.com
Small but well designed rooms. Attractive courtyard. Good cuisine. €€€

Hotel Brandenburger Hof
Eislebener Strasse 14
Tel: 030-214 050
Fax: 030-2140 5100
www.brandenburger-hof.com
In this lively shopping quarter you'll find luxury in an historical building with a beautiful winter garden. Easy walk to the Europa-Center. €€€€

Hotel Palace Berlin
Budapester Strasse 45
Tel: 030-25020
Fax: 030-2502 1119
www.palace.de
Private luxury hotel with individually decorated rooms at the Europa-Center. The First Floor restaurant is renowned for its gourmet cuisine. €€€€

Jugendhotel Berlincity
Crellestrasse 22
Tel: 030-7870 2130
Fax: 030-7870 2132
http://jugendhotel-berlincity.com
Comfortably refurbished factory floors. Ideal for groups and families. €

Kempinski Hotel Bristol Berlin
Kurfürstendamm 27
Tel: 030-884 340
Fax: 030-883 6075
www.kempinski-berlin.de
Famous traditional luxury

hotel with elegant rooms. €€€

Künstlerheim Luise
Luisenstrasse 19
Tel: 030-284 480
Fax: 030-2844 8448
www.luise-berlin.com
Each room here has been created by a different artist (but no en suite facilities for the cheaper rooms). Close to the Spree and the Reichstag. €€–€€€

Motel One Berlin Mitte
Prinzenstrasse 40
Tel: 030-7007 9800
Fax: 030-7007 9801
www.motel-one.de
Everything is simple but perfect. One of four Motel One hotels in Berlin, of which the one in Dreilinden has been recently renovated. €€

The Regent
Charlottenstrasse 49
Tel: 030-20338
Fax: 030-2033 6166
www.theregentberlin.com
Most rooms overlook the Gendarmenmarkt, all are decorated and furnished in opulent traditional style. Renowned for its service. €€€€

The Schlosshotel
Brahmsstrasse 6–10
Tel: 030-895 840
Fax: 030-8958 4800
This exclusive hotel in the quiet residential area of Grunewald owes its decor to design supremo, Karl Lagerfeld. The former palace, surrounded by beautiful grounds, has a smart indoor pool and fitness area. Vivaldi gourmet restaurant. €€€€

Sofitel Berlin Gendarmenmarkt
Charlottenstrasse 50–52
Tel: 030-203 750
Fax: 030-2037 5100
www.accorhotels.com
A unique and luxurious hotel right in the traditional centre; only a short stroll to Freidmichstrasse and the Brandenburger Tor. €€€€

Swissôtel
Augsburger Strasse 44
Tel: 030-220 100
Fax: 030-2201 02222
www.swissotel.com
Luxury hotel with interesting architecture right on the Kurfürsten-damm. The restaurant serves delicious, light regional food. €€€€

The Westin Grand Berlin
Friedrichstrasse 158–164
Tel: 030-20270
Fax: 030-2027 3362
http://aktuelles.westin.de/berlin/
At the corner of the famous Unter den Linden. Luxury hotel in the old style with indoor pool and fitness club. Garden courtyard. Several restaurants. €€€–€€€€

Winter's Hotel Berlin
Rudolfstädter Strasse 42
Tel: 030-897 830
Fax: 030-8978 3100
www.winters.de/hotel-berlin
Friendly hotel with smallish but comfortable rooms and a lovely garden. Not far from the Messegelände and the Ku'damm, and a short walk to the nearest U- and S-Bahn station. €€

POTSDAM

Filmhotel & Restaurant "Lili Marlene"
Grossbeerenstrasse 75

Potsdam-Babelsberg
Tel: 0331-743 200
Fax: 0331-743 2018
www.filmhotel.potsdam.de
Movie-inspired decor for the simple, cosy rooms. Park Babelsberg is nearby. €€

Hotel am Luisenplatz
Luisenplatz 5
Tel: 0331-971 900
Fax: 0331-971 9019
www.hotel-luisenplatz.de
Small luxury hotel with individually furnished rooms and apartments, situated in

the city centre and close to the park entrance to Sans Souci. Includes the Luisa restaurant. €€€

NH Voltaire
Friedrich-Ebert-Strasse 88
Tel: 0331-23170
Fax: 0331-231 7100
www.nh-hotels.de
Modern elegant rooms in a former palace. Near the Dutch quarter. €€–€€€

Schlosshotel Cecilienhof
Neuer Garten
Tel: 0331-37050

Fax: 0331-292 498
www.relexa-hotel.de
In this, the former home of the last German emperor's son, designed in English country-house style, Churchill, Stalin, Attlee and Truman met after World War II and signed the Potsdam Agreement. Beautifully located in the Neue Garten. Local specialities feature on the menu. €€€–€€€€

BERLIN TO THE MECKLENBURG LAKES

Chorin

Hotel Haus Chorin
Neue Klosterallee 10
Tel: 033366-500
Fax: 033366-326
www.hotel-haus-chorin.de
A modern building with
comfortable rooms, close
to the Schorfheide-Chorin
nature reserve. Swimming
in the lake. Bikes available
for hire. €€

Güstrow

**GGB Gutshotel Gross
Breesen**
Gross Breesen near Zehna (south
of Güstrow)
Tel: 038458-500
Fax: 038458-50234
www.gutshotel.de
The first bookhotel in
Germany: read to your
heart's content in the library
bursting with 80,000 tomes
(a good number of them in
English). Friendly, well lit
rooms in a huge 19th-
century manor house. €€

Müritz-See

Hotel Altes Gutshaus
Schulstrasse 8, Klink
Tel: 03991-15140
Fax: 03991-151 450
Friendly establishment right
on the lake. €€
Land Fleesensee
17213 Göhren-Lebbin
Tel: 039932-800 101
Fax: 039932-800 102
www.fleesensee.de
A Radisson hotel, an
Iberotel, a Robinson Club,
the Dorfhotel Fleesensee
plus the "Fit for Fun Spa"
form a lakeside holiday
village. Sports aplenty,
including golf. €€–€€€€
Parkhotel Klüschenberg
Klüschenberg 14, Plau am See
Tel: 038735-49210
Fax: 038735-4921 2190
www.klueschenberg.de
Quiet hotel surrounded by
parkland. €–€€
**Schlosshotel Gutshaus
Ludorf**
17207 Ludorf/Müritz
Tel: 039931-8400

Fax: 039931-84620
www.gutshaus-ludorf.de
Beautiful 17th-century
manor surrounded by other
historic buildings and two
national parks, on the west
bank of Müritz lake. €€€

Neuruppin

Up Hus Idyll
Siechenstrasse 4
Tel: 03391-398 844
www.up-hus.de
Well renovated, small hotel
with restaurant. €€

Neustrelitz

Park-Hotel
Karbe-Wagner-Strasse 59
Tel: 03981-48900
Fax: 03981-443 553
www.parkhotel-neustrelitz.de
Close to Fasanenpark. €€

Rheinsberg

**Best Western Premier
Marina Wolfsbruch**
Rheinsberg-Kleinzerlang

Tel: 033921-87
Fax: 033921-88845
www.marina-wolfsbruch.de
Nearly a small village with
hotel, apartments, spa and
its own marina, set amidst
forests and lakes.
€€–€€€
Der Seehof
Seestrasse 18
Tel: 033931-4030
www.seehof-rheinsberg.de
In lovely old buildings.
Good restaurant. €€€
Schloss Hotel Rheinsberg
Seestrasse 13
Tel: 033931-39059
Fax: 033931-39063
www.schlosshotel-rheinsberg.de
Tastefully renovated, with
good restaurant. €€

Waren

Hotel Ecktannen
Fontanestrasse 51, Waren/Müritz
Tel: 03991-6290
Fax: 03991-629 100
www.ecktannen.de
Quiet atmosphere. By the
Ecktannen campsite. €€

BERLIN TO HARZ AND LEIPZIG

Dessau

**Steigenberger Hotel Fürst
Leopold**
Fürst-Leopold Carré, Friedensplatz
Tel: 0340-25150
Fax: 0340-251 5177
www.steigenberger.com
Elegant, contemporary
interior with Bauhaus
touches. €€€

Halle

**Kempinski Hotel &
Congress Centre Rotes
Ross**
Franckestrasse 1
Tel: 0345-233 430
Fax: 0345-2334 3699
www.kempinski-halle.de
Modern luxury facilities
behind historic facade. €€€€
Maritim Halle
Riebeckplatz 4
Tel: 0345-51010
Fax: 0345-510 1777
www.maritim.de
Starkly modern block from
the outside, but
comfortable rooms. €€€

Leipzig

Hotel Fürstenhof
Tröndlinring 8
Tel: 0341-1400
Fax: 0341-140 3700
www.starwoodhotels.com
Opulent palace. €€€€
**Hotel Inter-Continental
Leipzig**
Gerberstrasse 15
Tel: 0341-9880
Fax: 0341-988 1229
http://aktuelles.westin.de/leipzig/
Luxury rooms on 27 floors,
magnificent views. €€€
Ibis
Brühl 69
Tel: 0341-21860
Fax: 0341-218 6222
www.ibishotel.com
A good budget choice. €€
Renaissance Leipzig Hotel
Grosser Brockhaus 3
Tel: 0341-129 2109
Fax: 0341-129 2800
www.marriott.de
Comfortable rooms. Close
to the inner city. €€€
Seaside Parkhotel
Richard-Wagner-Strasse 7

Tel: 0341-98520
Fax: 0341-985 2750
www.park-hotel-leipzig.de
Modern interior behind a
Jugendstil facade. Inside,
some Art Nouveau aspects
remain. All facilities. €€€

Lutherstadt
Wittenberg

Hotel Goldener Adler
Markt 7
Tel: 03491-404 137
Fax: 03491-505 663
www.goldeneradler-wittenberg.de
Modern rooms in a
historic, centrally located
building. €€
**Stadthotel Wittenberg
"Schwarzer Baer"**
Schlossstrasse 2
Tel: 03491-420 4344
Fax: 03491-420 4345
www.stadthotel-wittenberg.de
Traditional and central. €€

Magdeburg

Hotel Herrenkrug
Herrenkrugstrasse 3

Tel: 0391-85080
Fax: 0391-850 8601
www.herrenkrug.de
At the turn of the 20th
century the Herrenkrug, by
the River Elbe, was a
magnificent ballroom. The
hotel rooms are in the new
annexe, which is set in
beautiful grounds. Golf and
horse riding available. €€€

Quedlinburg

Romantik Hotel am Brühl
Billungstrasse 11
Tel: 03946-96180
Fax: 03946-961 8246
www.hotelambruehl.de
Right in centre of the old
town. Smart and very
romantic. €€€
Romantik Hotel Theophano
Markt 13–14
Tel: 03946-96300
Fax: 03946-963 036
www.hoteltheophano.de
Across from the town hall
in a half-timbered building
dating from the 16th-
century. €€–€€€

BERLIN TO DRESDEN

Bad Saarow

Landhaus Alte Eichen
Alte Eichen 21
Tel: 033631-43090
Fax: 033631-430 929
www.landhaus-alte-eichen.de
This friendly hotel with terrace and garden lies on a peninsula in the Scharmützelsee. Individually furnished rooms. €€
Sport & Spa Resort A-ROSA
Scharmützelsee
Tel: 033631-62682
Fax: 033631-62525
www.a-rosa.de
A luxurious place to relax and enjoy outdoor activities at the idyllic Scharmützelsee, 75 km (50 miles) from Berlin. Golf, fitness centre, kids' club, horse riding and more is on offer for residents. €€€€

Burg/Spreewald

Hotel Zur Bleiche Resort & Spa
Bleichestrasse 16
Tel: 035603-620
Fax: 035603-60292
www.hotel-zur-bleiche.de
Surrounded by waterways, the Hotel Zur Bleiche Resort & Spa has luxurious yet cosy country-style rooms and a spa. The restaurant is famous for its regional dishes. €€€€

Cottbus

Hotel Radisson SAS
Vetschauer Strasse 12
Tel: 0355-47610
Fax: 0335-476 1900
www.cottbus.radissonsas.com
Modern premises.
€€

Dresden

art'otel
Ostra-Allee 33
Tel: 0351-49220
Fax: 0351-492 2777
www.artotel.de/dresden/dresden.html
Modern building near Zwinger, recently renovated, displaying more than 600 works of art by A.R. Penck. Californian cuisine.
€€€
Bülow Residenz
Rähnitzgasse 19
Tel: 0351-80030
Fax: 0351-800 3100
www.buelow-residenz.de
Small luxury hotel in the residential Neustadt area. Gourmet dining on the premises.
€€€€
Hilton Dresden
An der Frauenkirche 5
Tel: 0351-86420
Fax: 0351-864 2725
www.hilton.de/dresden
In the heart of the old town, next to the Church of our Lady. Comfortable modern rooms and a sensational choice of 12

bars and restaurants.
€€€–€€€€
Hotel Burgk
Burgkstrasse 15, Dresden (Löbtau)
Tel: 0351-432 510
Fax: 0351-4325 1400
www.hotel-burgk.de
Just to the west of the main station and only five minutes by car from the old town stands this small, friendly hotel. The breakfast buffet is impressive.
€€
Kempinski Hotel Taschenbergpalais
Taschenberg 3
Tel: 0351-49120
Fax: 0351-491 2812
www.kempinski-dresden.de
This is Dresden's number one hotel. Utter luxury lies behind the beautifully restored Baroque facade.
€€€€
NH Hotel Dresden
Hansastrasse 43
Tel: 0351-84240
Fax: 0351-842 4200
www.nh-hotels.com
A very comfortable and well priced modern hotel close to the trendy Neustadt. Great buffet breakfast.
€€–€€€
The Westin Bellevue
Grosse Meissner Strasse 15
Tel: 0351-8050
Fax: 0351-806 1609
www.westin-bellevue.com
Elegant hotel in an old building with a lovely park and view of the historic

skyline across the Elbe River.
€€€€

Frankfurt (Oder)

Zur Alten Oder
Fischerstrasse 32
Tel: 0335-556 220
Fax: 0335-556 2228
www.zuraltenoder.de
In a converted factory building, this hotel has a quiet but central location.
€–€€

Lübbenau/Spreewald

Schlosshotel Lübbenau
Schlossbezirk 6
Tel: 03542-8730
Fax: 03542-87366
www.schloss-luebbenau.de
Elegant rooms with a nostalgic feel, among them a rustic suite available in the tower. Attractive terrace and garden.
€€–€€€

Storkow

Hotel Schloss Hubertushöhe
Robert-Koch-Strasse 1
Tel: 033678-430
Fax: 033678-43100
www.hubertushoehe.de
The elegant old castle in a park at the Storkow lake is renowned for having the atmosphere of a noble hunting lodge. Exquisite restaurant.
€€€€

Strausberg

The Lakeside Burghotel
Gielsdorfer Chaussee 6
Tel: 03341-34690
Fax: 03341-346 915
www.thelakeside.de
An old castle in the English country-house style. By the lake and close to Golfpark Schloss Wilkendorf. €€€
Hotel Neue Spitzmühle
Spitzmühlenweg 2
Tel: 03341-33190
Fax: 03341-331 958
www.spitzmuehle.info
Idyllic place for a quiet holiday. By the lake, with boats for hire and in close proximity to Golfpark Wilkendorf. €€

BELOW: Dresden's crème de la crème, the Kempinski Hotel Taschenbergpalais.

DRESDEN TO WEIMAR

Altenburg

Altenburger Hof
Schmöllnsche Landstrasse 8
Tel: 03447-5840
Fax: 03447-584 499
www.altenburger-hof.de
Modern hotel with sauna/
fitness centre. €

Chemnitz

**Adelsberger Parkhotel
Hoyer**
Wilhelm-Busch-Strasse 61
Tel: 0371-774 200
Fax: 0371-773 377

www.adelsberger-parkhotel.de
The best hotel in town, with
a modern, friendly
atmosphere. Seasonal
regional specialities in the
Alfons restaurant. €€

Freiberg

Hotel Kreller
Fischerstrasse 5
Tel: 03731-35900
Fax: 03731-23219
www.hotel-kreller.de
Full range of modern
facilities in a 300-year-old
building. €

Jena

Best Western Hotel Jena
Rudolfstädter Strasse 82
Tel: 03641-660
Fax: 03641-661 010
www.hotel-jena.bestwestern.de
Big modern hotel in a quiet
area. €€
Schwarzer Bär
Lutherplatz 2
Tel: 03641-4060
Fax: 03641-406 113
www.schwarzer-baer-jena.de
Traditional hotel in the
centre of town. Lovely
period furniture in the

Bismarck room. Breakfast
is served in the Mirror
Salon. €

Zwickau

Zum Uhu
Bahnhofstrasse 51
Tel: 0375-295 044
Fax: 0375-215 715
www.zum-uhu.de
Small *pension* with cosy
rooms, some of them in a
rustic style. The traditional
restaurant with
beergarden dishes up
Saxonian fare. €€

WEIMAR TO WARTBURG

Eisenach

Hotel auf der Wartburg
Wartburg
Tel: 03691-7970
Fax: 03691-797 100
www.wartburghotel.de
In the castle. Modern
comfort has been
combined with aristocratic
style and the rooms have
breathtaking views. €€€
Hotel Glockenhof
Grimmelgasse 4
Tel: 03691-2340
Fax: 03691-234 131
www.glockenhof.de
An old hospice converted
into a friendly hotel with a

modern annexe. Good
restaurant. €€

Erfurt

IBB Hotel Erfurt
Gotthardstrasse 27
Tel: 0361-67400
Fax: 0361-674 0444
www.sorat-hotels.com
Luxurious modern hotel
(part of the Sorat chain)
behind the medieval facade
of the "Old Swan". €€€
Mercure Hotel
Meienbergstrasse 26–28
Tel: 0361-59490
Fax: 0361-594 9100
www.mercure.com

Elegant house in the city
centre. €€€

Gotha

Hotel am Schlosspark
Lindenauallee 20
Tel: 03621-4420
Fax: 03621-442 452
www.hotel-am-schlosspark.de
Deluxe hotel close to
Schloss Friedenstein.
€€€

Weimar

Hotel Elephant
Markt 19
Tel: 03643-8020

www.arabella-sheraton.de
Weimar's top hotel. Elegant
rooms and a beautiful
garden. €€€€
Hotel Liszt
Lisztstrasse 1–2
Tel: 03643-54080
Fax: 03643-540 830
www.hotel-liszt.de
A quiet hotel near the town
centre. €€
Leonardo Weimar
Belvederer Allee 25
Tel: 03643-7220
Fax: 03643-7222 1119
www.leonardo-hotels.com
Pure luxury in a modern
building near Goethe Park.
€€€

MUNICH

Astoria Garni
Nikolaistrasse 9
Tel: 089-3839 630
Fax: 089-3839 6363
www.astoria-hotel-muenchen.de
A comfortable, well-run
hotel in Schwabing close to
the shopping and
entertainment of Leopold-
and Hohenzollernstrasse. €
Bayerischer Hof
Promenadeplatz 2
Tel: 089-21200
Fax: 089-212 0906
www.bayerischerhof.de
A favourite with visiting
celebrities. Swimming pool
on top floor. €€€€
Hotel Königswache
Steinheilstrasse 7
Tel: 089-542 7570

Fax: 089-523 2114
www.koenigswache.de
Only a short walk from the
museums. Chinese
restaurant located on the
ground floor. €€€
Hotel Leopold
Leopoldstrasse 119
Tel: 089-367 061
Fax: 089-3604 3150
www.hotel-leopold-muenchen.de
Situated in northern
Schwabing a short walk
from the Münchner Freiheit
U-Bahn. Comfortable hotel,
conveniently placed, with
its own restaurant. €€€
Platzl
Sparkassenstrasse 10
Tel: 089-237 030
Fax: 089-2370 3800

www.platzl.de
A good mid-range hotel
close to the Hofbräuhaus,
with environmental awards
to its name. Excellent
gastronomy in old vaulted
rooms. €€–€€€
**Splendid-Dollmann im
Lehel**
Thierschstrasse 49
Tel: 089-238 080
www.hotel-splendid-dollmann.de
A comfortable hotel, with
the atmosphere of a small-
town aristocratic
residence. Centrally
located in the residential
district of Lehel, only a
short walk from
Maximilianstrasse.
€€€–€€€€

**Vier Jahreszeiten
Kempinski**
Maximilianstrasse 17
Tel: 089-21250
Fax: 089-2125 2000
www.kempinski-vierjahreszeiten.com
One of Munich's prestige
hotels and long-time
celebrity haunt. €€€€

PRICE CATEGORIES

Prices are for a double
room, including taxes and
breakfast. Hostels and
some smaller/more basic
hotels are priced per person.
€ = less than €50
€€ = €50–110
€€€ = €110–180
€€€€ = more than €180

THE ALPS

Berchtesgaden

Alpenhof
Richard-Voss-Strasse 30
Schönau am Königssee
Tel: 08652-6020
Fax: 08652-64399
www.alpenhof.de
Country hotel offering every facility for the sport-oriented guest. €€€
Alpenhotel Kronprinz
Am Brandholz
Tel: 08652-6070
Fax: 08652-607 120
http://alpenhotel-kronprinz.de
A comfortable hotel with sauna and other fitness facilities, fine restaurant (dinner only) and a great mountain view. €€

Füssen

Altstadthotel Zum Hechten
Ritterstrasse 6
Tel: 08362-91600
Fax: 08362-916 099
www.hotel-hechten.com
In the old city centre, near the river. Pleasant with good restaurant. €€

Garmisch-Partenkirchen

Eibsee Hotel
Grainau-Eibsee
Tel: 08821-98810
Fax: 08821-82585
www.eibsee-hotel.de
A luxurious hotel with a wonderful view. Just the place if you want to splash out. €€€
Grand Hotel Sonnenbichl
Burgstrasse 97
Tel: 08821-7020
Fax: 08821-702131
www.sonnenbichl.de
Traditional, big luxury hotel with all modern facilities; wonderful terrace and a wellness centre. €€€
Reindl's Partenkirchner Hof
Bahnhofstrasse 15
Tel: 08821-943 870
Fax: 08821-9438 7250
www.reindls.de
Complex of three buildings – one almost 100 years old, two of them modern – with that special Bavarian *Gemütlichkeit* (comfort) and great food. Superb suites in country-house style. €€

Mittenwald

Hotel Alpenrose
Obermarkt 1
Tel: 08823-492 700
Fax: 08823-3720
www.hotel-alpenrose-mittenwald.de
Friendly service, good restaurant. Horse-drawn carriage tours can be arranged. €–€€
Post-Hotel
Obermarkt 9
Tel: 08823-938 2333
Fax: 08823-938 2888
www.posthotel-mittenwald.de
Central hotel equipped with sauna, solarium, etc.
€€–€€€

Murnau

Alpenhof Murnau
Ramsachstrasse 8
Tel: 08841-4910
Fax: 08841-491 100
www.alpenhof-murnau.com
Luxury hotel with spacious, individually furnished rooms, with great views of the Alps. Gourmet restaurant. €€€

Schwangau

Hanselewirt
Mitteldorf 13
Tel: 08362-8237
Fax: 08362-81738
www.hanselewirt.de
Traditional inn with reasonable prices. €

Tegernsee

Hotel Bayern
Neureuthstrasse 23
Tel: 08022-1820
Fax: 08022-182 100
www.hotel-bayern.de
The best place in town, with a fine view over the lake and mountains. The core of the complex is an Art Nouveau mansion; a newly designed building contains more stunning rooms. €€–€€€

EASTERN BAVARIA

Bodenmais

Hotel Königshof
Scharebenstrasse 24
Tel: 09924-9530
Fax: 09924-95313
www.hotel-koenigshof.de
Good location with lovely view, good price. €

Grafenau

Hotel Hubertus
Grüb 20
Tel: 08552-964 90
www.hubertus-grafenau.de
Familiy-run hotel with very personal service. Ideal base for exploring the Bayerischer Wald national park: the wellness suite offers post-walk relaxation. €€€€

Landshut

Hotel Goldene Sonne
Neustadt 520
Tel: 0871-92530
Fax: 0871-925 3350
An old-fashioned *Gasthof* (inn) from the 15th century, complete with restaurant and own beer garden. €€
Schloss Schönbrunn
Schönbrunn 1
Tel: 0871-95220
Fax: 0871-952 2222
www.hotel-schoenbrunn.de
Historic atmosphere, restaurant and beer garden. €€

Passau

Wilder Mann
Am Rathamsplatz
Tel: 0851-35071
Fax: 0851-31712
www.wilder-mann.com
Historic hotel right in the centre of town – Empress Sissi stayed here. There is also a museum of glass in the hotel building. €€

Regensburg

Bischofshof
Krauterermarkt 3
Tel: 0941-58460
Fax: 0941-584 6146
www.hotel-bischofshof.de
A great place, very romantic in style, where kings and emperors have stayed overnight. Just behind the cathedral, where there are a number of restaurants offering fine food and rustic Bavarian charm. €€
Hotel Held
Irl 11
Tel: 09401-9420
Fax: 09401-7682
www.hotel-held.de
Quiet establishment. Local dishes served, using meat from their own butcher's. €
Sorat-Insel Hotel
Müllerstrasse 7
Tel: 0941-81040
Fax: 0941-810 4444
www.sorat-hotels.com
Extravagant design hotel in a quiet location overlooking the Danube. The listed building was originally artisan's premises. Great view of the cathedral from some of the rooms and suites. €€€–€€€€

BELOW: stay close to the Danube at the Sorat-Insel Hotel.

ROMANTIC ROAD AND HEIDELBERG

Augsburg

Altstadth Hotel Ulrich
Kapuzinergasse 6
Tel: 0821-34610
Fax: 0821-346 1346
www.hotel-ulrich.de
Just off Maximilianstrasse, within easy reach of the sights and nightlife, but in a quiet street. €€
Dom-Hotel
Frauentorstrasse 8
Tel: 0821-343 930
Fax: 0821-3439 3200
www.domhotel-augsburg.de
Stylish, modern rooms in a historic building in the cathedral quarter. Peaceful garden. €€

Dinkelsbühl

Flair Hotel Weisses Ross
Steingasse 12
Tel: 09851-579 890

Fax: 09851-6770
www.flairhotel.com
A renovated, listed half-timbered barn, with rooms furnished in a modern take on Bavarian style. €€

Heidelberg

Romantik Hotel zum Ritter St Georg
Hauptstrasse 178
Tel: 06221-1350
Fax: 06221-135 230
www.ritter-heidelberg.de
This fantastic building near the marketplace is over 400 years old. €€–€€€
Schönberger Hof
Untere Neckarstrasse 54
Tel: 06221-14060
Fax: 06221-140 639
www.schoenbergerhof.de
In a 200-year-old building close to the city centre and the Neckar. €€–€€€

Nördlingen

Kaiserhof Hotel Sonne
Marktplatz
Tel: 09081-5067
Fax: 09081-23999
www.kaiserhof-hotel-sonne.de
Traditional hotel where royals and nobles used to lodge in medieval times. With restaurant and terrace on the square. €€

Rothenburg ob der Tauber

Burg Hotel
Klostergasse 1–3
Tel: 09861-94890
Fax: 09861-948 940
www.burghotel.eu
You can't beat the romantic atmosphere of this individual, ivy-covered hotel (the smallest in the Old Town). No restaurant. €€€

Eisenhut
Herrengasse 3–7
Tel: 09861-7050
Fax: 09861-70545
www.eisenhut.com
First-class hotel full of history. Rooms in romantic style with great views down over the valley. €€€

BELOW: at the Burg Hotel.

WÜRZBURG AND FRANCONIA

Bamberg

Brudermühle
Schranne 1
Tel: 0951-955 220
Fax: 0951-955 2255
www.brudermuehle.de
A pleasant hotel in the old town. €€
St Nepomuk und Gästehäuser
Obere Mühlbrücke 9
Tel: 0951-98420
Fax: 0951-984 2100
www.hotel-nepomuk.de
This hotel in a romantic setting by the river offers minimalist elegance in the bedrooms (all non-smoking) and gourmet cuisine. €€€
Villa Geyerswörth
Geyerswörther Strasse 15-21a
Tel: 0951-91740
Fax: 0951-917 4500
www.villageyerswoerth.de
A deluxe hotel with a successful blend of modern and historical architecture. €€€

Bayreuth

Goldener Anker
Opernstrasse 6
Tel: 0921-65051
Fax: 0921-65500

www.anker-bayreuth.de
Nice hotel in pedestrian zone, next to Margrave's Opera House. €€€
Zur Lohmühle
Badstrasse 37
Tel: 0921-53060
Fax: 0921-530 6469
www.hotel-lohmuehle.de
Attractive little hotel set in an old mill *(Mühle)*. €€€

Nuremberg

Dürer-Hotel
Neutormauer 32
Tel: 0911-2146 650
Fax: 0911-2146 65555
www.altstadthotels-nuremberg.de
Modern hotel in a great location. €€€–€€€€
Haus am Schönen Brunnen
Hauptmarkt 17
Tel: 0911-224 225
Fax: 0911-225 393
www.hotel-schoener-brunnen.com
Bourgeois comfort by the main square. €€–€€€
Hotel Fackelmann
Essenweinstrasse 10
Tel: 0911-206 840
Fax: 0911-206 8460
www.hotel-fackelmann.de
In a modern district near the railway station, a short walk from the town centre. €€

Le Meridien Grand-Hotel
Bahnhofstrasse 1–3
Tel: 0911-23220
Fax: 0911-232 2444
http://nuernberg.lemeridien.de
All you would expect from a top-class hotel. €€€

Pegnitz

Pflaums Posthotel Pegnitz
Nürnberger Strasse 12–16
Tel: 09241-7250
Fax: 09241-80404
www.ppp.com/de/lowband/german_41.htm
One of the best hotels in Germany. Every room is decorated in a different art style. Top-class food. €€€–€€€€

Würzburg

Best Western Premier Hotel Rebstock
Neubaustrasse 7
Tel: 0931-30930
Fax: 0931-309 3100
www.rebstock.com
Elegant hotel in the town centre, known as a *Gasthaus* since 1408. Reputable restaurant. €€€
Novotel Würzburg
Eichstrasse 2
Tel: 0931-30540

Fax: 0931-305 4423
www.accorhotels.com
Modern building with friendly ambience. Ideally located in the town centre yet very quiet. €€
Schlosshotel Steinburg
Auf dem Steinberg
Tel: 0931-97020
Fax: 0931-97121
www.steinburg.com
Historic atmosphere and dream-like deluxe interior – plus a fine view of the town from the terrace. €€€–€€€€
Zum Winzermännle
Domstrasse 32
Tel: 0931-54156
Fax: 0931-58228
www.winzermaennle.de
Centrally located with a genuine Franconian atmosphere. Newly renovated. €€

PRICE CATEGORIES

Prices are for a double room, including taxes and breakfast. Hostels and some smaller/more basic hotels are priced per person.
€ = less than €50
€€ = €50–110
€€€ = €110–180
€€€€ = more than €180

LAKE CONSTANCE

Constance

Steigenberger Inselhotel
Auf der Insel 1
Tel: 07531-1250
Fax: 07531-26402
www.steigenberger.com
Luxury hotel in a former
monastery. Great location.
Beautiful terrace. €€€

Lindau

**Landgasthof Montfort-
Schlössle**
Streitelsfinger Strasse 38
Tel: 08382-72811
Fax: 08382-73291
www.montfort-schloessle.de
Small hotel outside Lindau
in the middle of verdant

orchards. Fantastic lake
panorama, restaurant with
open fireplace. No credit
cards. Open end March until
beginning of November. €€

Friedrichshafen

Buchhorner Hof
Friedrichstrasse 33

Tel: 07541-2050
Fax: 07541-32663
www.buchhorn.de
Hotel with a long tradition,
set within a former post
house yet with modern
furnishings. The excellent
restaurant keeps the charm
intact.
€€–€€€€

BLACK FOREST

Baden-Baden

**Brenners Parkhotel
& Spa**
Schillerstrasse 4–6
Tel: 07221-9000
Fax: 07221-38772
www.brenners.com
Fabulous luxury hotel (100
rooms) with spa and lush
gardens. €€€€

Baiersbronn

Bareiss
Gärtenbühlweg 14
Tel: 07442-470
Fax: 07442-47320
www.bareiss.com
Modern luxury hotel
offering short-break
packages featuring health
and beauty treatments,
children's activities, spa

and pool complex, sports
and gastronomy. €€€€
Traube-Tonbach
Tonbachstrasse 237
Tel: 07442-4920
Fax: 07442-492 692
www.traube-tonbach.de
Luxury hotel offering similar
facilities to the Bareiss:
sports activities including
hiking, mountain biking and
hot-air ballooning; fitness
centre with pools, spa and
sauna; kids' club and four
restaurants. Herald
Wehlfahrt, one of the most
famous chefs in Europe,
creates haute cuisine in the
restaurant. €€€€

Freiburg

Colombi
Am Rotteckring 16

Tel: 0761-21060
Fax: 0761-31410
www.colombi.de
Luxury hotel with
individually furnished
rooms in a traditional
style; gourmet restaurant.
€€€€
Zum Roten Bären
Oberlinden 12
Tel: 0761-387 870
Fax: 0761-387 8717
www.roter-baeren.de
Said to be the oldest hotel
in Germany (established
1120), its interior is now
a blend of warm colours
and elegant modern
design. €€

Stuttgart

Am Schlossgarten
Schillerstrasse 23

Tel: 0711-20260
Fax: 0711-2026 888
www.hotelschlossgarten.com
Modern building by the
castle park and close to
the city. Cosy interior with
smart country-house
ambience. Fine
restaurants with garden
terrace, wine bar, lovely
café and bar lounge.
€€€

Ulm

Hotel Reblaus am Rathaus
Kronengasse 10
Tel: 0731-986 490
Fax: 0731-986 4949
www.reblausulm.de
Quiet and cosy half-
timbered house in the
centre, with great
breakfasts. €€

FRANKFURT AND SURROUNDINGS

Bad Homburg

Maritim Kurhaus Hotel
Ludwigstrasse 3
Tel: 06172-6600
Fax: 06172-600 100
www.maritim.de
Close to the Taunustherme
(hydro), with sauna,
solarium and pool.
€€€

Frankfurt

**Best Western Imperial
Hotel am Palmengarten**
Sophienstrasse 40
Tel: 069-793 0030
Fax: 069-7930 0388
www.imperial.bestwestern.de
In the University area, near
the Palmengarten.
€€–€€€

Hessischer Hof
Friedrich-Ebert-Anlage 40
Tel: 069-75400
Fax: 069-7540 2924
www.hessischer-hof.de
Former palace belonging to
prince of Hesse. Near the
Messegelände. €€€€
Hotel Am Berg
Grethenweg 23
Tel: 069-660 5370
Fax: 069-615 109
www.hotel-am-berg-ffm.de
Small budget hotel in old
villa close to the *Ebbelwoi*
pubs of Sachsenhausen.
Family-run, with personal,
friendly service. €€
Hotel Miramar
Berliner Strasse 31
Tel: 069-920 3970
Fax: 069-9203 9769
www.miramar-frankfurt.de

Smallish modern rooms,
but great location close
to Paulskirche and
Römerberg. €€
**Ramada Hotel Frankfurt
City**
Weserstrasse 17
Tel: 069-310 810
Fax: 069-3108 1555
www.ramadainternational.com
Period house close to main
station. Excellent Lebanese
restaurant. €€–€€€
**Steigenberger
Frankfurterhof**
Am Kaiserplatz
Tel: 069-21502
Fax: 069-215 900
www.steigenberger.de/frankfurt
Grand hotel with tradition
and old-time elegance.
Thomas Mann was once a
guest here. €€€€

Wiesbaden

Nassauer Hof
Kaiser-Friedrich-Platz 3–4
Tel: 0611-1330
Fax: 0611-133 632
www.nassauer-hof.de
Elegant hotel with modern
amenities near the Kurpark.
Golf and horse-riding. Top
restaurant. €€€€

PRICE CATEGORIES

Prices are for a double
room, including taxes and
breakfast. Hostels and
some smaller/more basic
hotels are priced per person.
€ = less than €50
€€ = €50–110
€€€ = €110–180
€€€€ = more than €180

RHINE AND MOSELLE TO THE RUHR

Aachen

Hesse
Friedlandstrasse 20
Tel: 0241-470 540
Fax: 0241-470 5449
www.hotelhesse.de
Comfortable and quiet, yet in a central location. €€

Bingen

Weinhotel Michel
Mainzer Strasse 74
Tel: 06721-91510
Fax: 06721-915 152
www.weinhotel-michel.de
Reasonable rates. €€

Bochum

Art-Hotel Tucholsky
Viktoriastrasse 73
Tel: 0234-964 360
Fax: 0234-9643 6436
www.art-hotel-tucholsky.de
All rooms tastefully decorated. Tapas bar and very good restaurant. €€

Bonn

Best Western Domicil
Thomas-Mann-Strasse 24–26
Tel: 0228-729 090
Fax: 0228-691 207
www.domicil-bonn.bestwestern.de
Central location, with modern rooms grouped around a courtyard. €€€

Cologne

Chelsea
Jülicher Strasse 1
Tel: 0221-207 150
Fax: 0221-239 137
www.hotel-chelsea.de
Famous among artists and renowned for its artistic displays and extravagant architecture. Good restaurant. €€–€€€
Cristall Hotel
Ursulaplatz 9-11
Tel: 0211-16300
Fax: 0211-163 0333
www.hotelcristall.de
Colourfully designed modern interior. €€–€€€
Dom-Hotel
Domkloster 2a
Tel: 0221-20240
Fax: 0221-204 444
www.domhotel.de
Opposite the cathedral. *Fin-de-siècle* elegance. €€€€

Excelsior Hotel Ernst
Domplatz 1
Tel: 0221-2701
Fax: 0221-135 150
www.excelsiorhotelernst.de
The top city-centre hotel for more than 100 years. €€€€
Hopper Hotel etcetera
Brüsseler Strasse 26
Tel: 0221-924 400
Fax: 0221-924 406
www.hopper.de
Designer hotel with displays of modern art. Popular with artists. Formerly a monastery. €€€
Hotel im Wasserturm
Kaygasse 2
Tel: 0221-20080
Fax: 0221-200 8888
www.hotel-im-wasserturm.de
Luxurious, beautifully designed rooms in an historic water tower. €€€€
Haus Marienburg
Robert-Heuser-Strasse 3
Tel: 0221-937 690
Fax: 0221-9376 9922
www.hotel-marienburg.de
Elegant *fin-de-siècle* villa. €€

Duisburg

Hotel Rheingarten
Königstrasse 78
Tel: 02066-55001
Fax: 02066-55004
www.rheinhotel-rheingarten.de
By the Ruhr river, where the harbour cruises start. €€

Düsseldorf

Orangerie
Bäckergasse 1
Tel: 0211-866 800
Fax: 0211-866 8099
www.hotel-orangerie-mcs.de
At the city's heart, but quiet. Small, friendly, well-designed hotel. €€€

Eltville

Kronenschlösschen
Rheinallee
Tel: 06723-640
Fax: 06723-7663
www.kronenschloesschen.com
A delightful mixture of fairy-tale and elegant country-house style. Beautiful garden, excellent food. €€€
Schloss Reinhartshausen Kempinski
Hauptstrasse 43
Tel: 06123-6760

Fax: 06123-676 400
www.schloss-hotel.de
Quiet castle-hotel with grand interiors in attractive grounds. Relaxing atmosphere. Gourmet cuisine is served on the impressive terrace. €€€€

Essen

Hotel Schloss Hugenpoet
August-Thyssen-Strasse 51
Tel: 02054-12040
Fax: 02054-120 450
www.hugenpoet.de
Luxury in an impressive Baroque castle. Excellent restaurant. €€€€

Koblenz

Diehl's Hotel
Rheinsteigufer 1
Tel: 0261-97070
Fax: 0261-970 7213
www.diehls-hotel.de
Great Rhine views. €€
Hotel Lorenz
Jesuitenplatz 1–3
Tel: 0261-133 360
Fax: 0261-914 3412
www.lorenz-koblenz.de
Small central hotel with modern decor; restaurant with calm street terrace. €€

Münster

Designhotel Mauritzhof
Eisenbahnstrasse 15–17
Tel: 0251-41720
Fax: 0251-46686

www.mauritzhof.de
Modern house in the green zone near the old centre. Designer furniture and the biggest beds in town. €€€
Schloss Wilkinghege
Steinfurter Strasse 374
Tel: 0251-144 270
Fax: 0251-212 898
www.schloss-wilkinghege.de
Old moated castle in lovely grounds. Golf. €€€–€€€€

Rüdesheim

Krone Assmannshausen
Rheinuferstrasse 10
Tel: 06722-4030
Fax: 06722-3049
www.hotel-krone.com
Historic hotel since 1541 with a terrace where poets sought inspiration – from the view and the wine. Highly recommended dining. €€€

St Goar

Schloss-Hotel und Villa Rheinfels
Schlossberg 47
Tel: 06741-8020
Fax: 06741-802 802
www.schloss-rheinfels.de
Magnificent rooms overlooking the Rhine. Gourmet cuisine. €€–€€€

Traben-Trarbach

Hotel Bellevue
Am Moselufer
Tel: 06541-7030

BELOW: Hotel Schloss Hugenpoet, impressive from all angles.

Fax: 06541-703 400
www.bellevue-hotel.de
Luxury Jugendstil hotel.
Bikes for hire. More rooms
and apartments in tastefully
restored buildings close by.
€€–€€€

Trier

Hotel Petrisberg
Sickingenstrasse 11–13
Tel: 0651-4640

Fax: 0651-46450
www.hotel-petrisberg.de
Medium-sized hotel with
views. €€€
Hotel Römischer Kaiser
Am Porta Negra Platz 6
Tel: 0651-97700
Fax: 0651-977 099
www.hotels-trier.de
Hotel with the flair of the
Belle Epoque and with
splendid views of the
Roman Porta Negra. €€€

**Weinhaus Becker &
Becker's Hotel**
Olewiger Strasse 206
Tel: 0651-938 080
Fax: 0651-938 0888
www.beckers-trier.de
One a small rustic hotel,
the other a fine design
hotel. Guests at both
benefit from the excellent
wine cellar and a top-notch
restaurant. Wine-tasting
available. €€

Worms

Dom-Hotel
Obermarkt 10
Tel: 06241-9070
Fax: 06241-23515
www.dom-hotel.de
Located in the centre of
town, near the station, the
Dom-Hotel occupies a
modern building with
furnishings to match.
€€–€€€

FAIRYTALE ROAD

Bremen

**Best Western Wellness
Hotel Zur Post**
Bahnhofsplatz 11
Tel: 0421-30590
Fax: 0421-305 9591
www.zurpost.bestwestern.de
Located in front of Bremen's
main station, the hotel
provides both position and
comfort. Highly regarded
modern French-German
restaurant, L'Orchidée. €€
Park Hotel Bremen
Im Bürgerpark
Tel: 0421-34080
Fax: 0421-340 8602
www.park-hotel-bremen.de
Surrounded by the green
spaces of the Bürgerpark,
this modern hotel affects an
elegant old style. Spa and
fine restaurants. €€€€

Fulda

Maritim am Schlossgarten
Pauluspromenade 2
Tel: 0661-2820
Fax: 0661-282 499
www.maritim.de
Combines modern comforts
with all the splendour of its
Baroque rooms. €€–€€€

Göttingen

Eden
Reinhäuser Landstrasse 22a
Tel: 0551-507 200

ABOVE: the splendid public areas of the Park Hotel Bremen.

Fax: 0551-507 2111
www.eden-hotel.de
Modern hotel, furnished in
traditional style, a few
minutes from the city centre.
Indoor pool, sauna. €€–€€€

Hameln/Hamlin

Hotel Christinenhof
Alte Marktstrasse 18
Tel: 05151-95080
Fax: 05151-43611
www.christinenhof.de
Very warm atmosphere and
modern amenities behind a
half-timbered facade. €€

Hanover

BrainPark Hotel
Büttnerstrasse 19
Tel: 0511-9698 8300
Fax: 0511-9698 8399
Modern family-run hotel
with beer-garden in the

Vahrenwald-Quarter, near
museums, zoos, etc. €–€€
Kastens Hotel Luisenhof
Luisenstrasse 1–3
Tel: 0511-30440
Fax: 0511-304 4807
www.kastens-hotel-luisenhof.de
Right in the city centre.
Stylish hotel steeped in
tradition. €€€–€€€€

Hildesheim

Parkhotel Berghölzchen
Am Berghölzchen 1
Tel: 05121-9790
Fax: 05121-979 400
www.berghoelzchen.de
First-class house in quiet
surroundings in the middle
of a beautiful nature area.
€€–€€€€

Kassel

**Dornröschenschloss
Sababurg**

Hofgeismar-Sababurg
Tel: 05671-8080
Fax: 05671-808 200
www.sababurg.de
The Brothers Grimm
associated the sleeping
beauty with this 14th-
century fairy-tale castle.
Romantic rooms. Zoo,
theatre and concerts. €€€
Schlosshotel Wilhelmshöhe
Schlosspark 8, 34131 Kassel
Tel: 0561-30880
Fax: 0561-308 8428
www.schlosshotel-kassel.de
Quiet rooms in traditional or
modern style. €€

Marburg

Waldecker Hof
Bahnhofstrasse 23
Tel: 06421-60090
Fax: 06421-600 959
www.waldecker-hof-marburg.de
Comfortable and central
hotel dating from 1864. €€

HAMBURG

Alsterhof
Esplanade 12
Tel: 040-350 070
Fax: 040-3500 7514
www.alster-hof.de

Centrally located and a
home from home in noble
traditional style. Exquisite
breakfast buffet.
€€

Hafen Hamburg
Seewartenstrasse 9
Tel: 040-311 130
Fax: 040-3111 3755
www.hotel-hamburg.de

Great harbour view.
Individually designed
rooms. €€–€€€
Hotel Abtei
Abteistrasse 14

Tel: 040-442 905
Fax: 040-449 820
www.abtei-hotel.de
Exclusive hotel (11 rooms)
in an English country-style
villa. Gourmet restaurant.
€€€–€€€€
Kempinski Hotel Atlantic Hamburg
An der Alster 72–9
Tel: 040-28880

www.kempinski.atlantic.de
Vying with the Vier
Jahreszeiten to be
Hamburg's top hotel,
the Atlantic exudes an
atmosphere of style and
luxury. €€€€
Renaissance Hotel Hamburg
Grosse Bleichen, Hamburg

Tel: 040-34180
Fax: 040-3491 8919
www.marriott.de/Renaissance_Hamburg
With its wonderful luxury,
the Renaissance
demonstrates the essence
of style with that great
Hamburg flair for
understated class. Located
right in the shopping area.
€€€€

Vier Jahreszeiten
Neuer Jungfernstieg 9–14
Tel: 040-34940
Fax: 040-3494 2600
www.hvj.de
One of the oldest and
most expensive hotels in
Germany. Great view of
the Binnenalster. Exquisite
Haerlin Restaurant.
€€€€

NORTH SEA COAST

Cuxhaven
Best Western Donner's Hotel
Am Seedeich 2
Tel: 04721-5090
Fax: 04721-509 134
www.donners.bestwestern.de
A modern hotel, whose
Parorama restaurant
offers enjoyable views
over the harbour on top of
the good North German
fare.
€€–€€€

Föhr/Wyk
Duus
Hafenstrasse 40
Tel: 04681-59810
Fax: 04681-598 140
www.duus-hotel.de
Small hotel in old
premises, but with a new
annexe. On the outskirts of
Wyk, close to the beach.
Fine dining in the
Austernfischer (Oyster
Catcher) restaurant.
€€

Sylt/Westerland
Stadt Hamburg
Strandstrasse 2
Tel: 04651-8580
Fax: 04651-858 220
www.hotelstadthamburg.com
Romantic hotel steeped in
tradition. Frisian decor. €€€

Wilhelmshaven
Hotel am Stadtpark
Friedrich-Paffrath-Strasse 116
Tel: 04421-9860

Fax: 04421-986 186
www.hotel-am-stadtpark.de
The best hotel in town, with
wellness centre. €€

Worpswede
Eichenhof
Ostendorfer Strasse 13
Tel: 04792-2676
Fax: 04792-4427
www.eichenhof-worpswede.de
Each room is dedicated to a
different artist. Great place
to relax, good food. €€€

LÜBECK TO FLENSBURG

Flensburg
Romantik Hotel Historischer Krug
Grazer Platz 1, Oeversee
Tel: 04630-9400
Fax: 04630-780
www.historischer-krug.de
The oldest inn in the area
(1519), with the bonus of
modern facilities, including

sauna, beauty treatments,
canoe and bike hire. Great
garden with pond. €€–€€€

Kiel
Parkhotel Kieler Kaufmann
Niemannsweg 102
Tel: 0431-88110
Fax: 0431-881 1135
www.kieler-kaufmann.de

Small hotel in quiet location,
lovingly decorated with
precious textiles and period
furniture. Excellent
restaurant with conservatory
and terrace. €€€

Lübeck
Kaiserhof
Kronsforder Allee 13

Tel: 0451-703 301
Fax: 0451-795 083
www.kaiserhof-luebeck.de
Elegantly decorated
premises within two old
villas on the Elbe-Lübeck
Canal. Green surroundings,
yet only minutes to the city
centre. Gourmet
restaurant.
€€€–€€€€

BALTIC COAST

Heiligendamm
Kempinski Grand Hotel
18209 Heiligendamm
Tel: 038203-740 7676
Fax: 038203-740 7699
www.kempinski-heiligendamm.com
Large hotel with stunning
interiors in Germany's first
seaside resort. The
ultimate in luxury and
relaxation. €€€€

Rügen/Binz
Grand Hotel Binz
Strandpromenade 7

Tel: 038393-150
Fax: 038393-15555
www.grandhotelbinz.de
Modern building in the style
of a traditional grand hotel.
Spacious rooms with great
views. €€€

Schwerin
Haus am Pfaffenteich
Gaussstrasse 19
Tel: 0385-521 950
Fax: 0385-569 613
www.haus-am-pfaffenteich.m-vp.de
Small and comfortable with
a personal touch. €€

Stralsund
Hotel an den Bleichen
An den Bleichen 45
Tel: 03831-390 675
Fax: 03831-392 153
www.hotelandenbleichen.de
Small hotel with the feel of
a family home. A green and
tranquil oasis a short stroll
from the historic centre. €€

Usedom/Ahlbeck
Villa Auguste Viktoria
Bismarckstrasse 1
Tel: 038378-2410

Fax: 038378-24144
www.auguste-viktoria.de
A renovated Art Nouveau
villa dating from 1900.
Elegant yet homely. €€

PRICE CATEGORIES
Prices are for a double
room, including taxes and
breakfast. Hostels and
some smaller/more basic
hotels are priced per person.
€ = less than €50
€€ = €50–110
€€€ = €110–180
€€€€ = more than €180

E ATING OUT

RECOMMENDED RESTAURANTS, CAFES & BARS

Where to Eat

You have no need to worry about going hungry in Germany. In every town you will find a wide range of eateries, ranging from open-air *Imbiss* food stalls to exclusive gourmet restaurants. Portions are generous. For a quick snack, cafés or bistros serve soup, sandwiches, salads and cakes. A *Gasthaus* or *Gasthof* usually offers the specialities of the region. Pubs are popular with those locals who want a snack or a home-made meal to accompany their beer or wine, but drinking is the main activity.

There is no such thing as German cuisine. All regions have their own specialities and these can differ greatly. If you want to sample the local fare, then ask about the *regionale Spezialitäten*. If you prefer Italian, Chinese or Indian food, that will be no problem in the cities, where international restaurants are plentiful. Note, however, that *Internationale Küche* usually means popular dishes from all over the world, such as pasta and Wiener Schnitzel, and unimaginative menus. Vegetarians beware: the emphasis in most restaurants is most definitely on meat, although fish features on many menus.

Traditionally, the main meal of the day in Germany is lunch. It normally consists of a plate of meat and potatoes or some kind of dumpling with vegetables or a salad as a side dish, possibly with a soup starter. Many restaurants have special lunch offers which are better value than dinner.

Families who have eaten their main meal at lunchtime will probably tuck into bread, butter and *Wurst* in the evening. But patterns are changing. Many people now only have a light snack at noon and then cook or go out for dinner in the evening.

Breakfast served in smaller hotels usually consists of bread rolls with jam, honey, cooked meat slices, cheese and a boiled egg. Larger hotels generally offer a sumptuous breakfast buffet including muesli and fruits. It is quite common for breakfast to be included in the room rate.

Cakes and pastries are normally reserved for the afternoon. Going out for *Kaffee und Kuchen* (coffee and cakes) is very popular on a Sunday. Cafés serving *Kaffee und Kuchen* and ice-cream are to be found in all the main tourist spots.

What to Eat

Bavaria

Schweinshax'n: pork knuckle usually served with *Blaukraut* (red cabbage) and *Knödel* (dumpling) is a very popular beer-garden staple.
Saure Lüngerl: lung in vinegar sauce usually served with *Semmelknödel* (bread dumpling).
Krautwickerl: Minced meat rolled into white cabbage leaves, usually eaten with potatoes.
Weisswürste: spiced veal and pork sausages, eaten mainly with sweet mustard *(Weisswurstsenf)*, usually accompany a late-morning beer.
Leberkäs: hot or cold meat loaf.
Semmelknödel: bread dumplings, often served with *Schweinebraten* (roast pork).
Reiberdatschi: thinly grated raw potatoes baked in fat and served with apple sauce. In other regions they are called *Kartoffelpuffer*.
Gugelhupf: cake made out of yeast with raisins, nuts, almonds, etc.
Dampfnudeln: huge yeast dumplings with plums, served hot with vanilla sauce.

Cheeses

The Germans are very fond of their cheeses. *Hartkäse* is hard cheese, such as Emmental, *Schnittkäse* is sliceable cheese like Tilsit, *Edelpilzkäse* is blue cheese like Bergader and *Weichkäse* is soft cheese, like the French varieties Brie and Camembert.

Quark is a type of curd cheese unique to Germany. Made from skimmed milk, it is generally low in fat. Although it comes in many different flavours (such as with garlic, horseradish and chives), it is often served as a fruit-flavoured dessert and is used to make German cheesecakes.

Berlin

Berliner Schlachtplatte: fresh blood and liver sausage, pig's kidney and fresh-boiled pork.
Berliner Weisse mit Schuss: wheaten beer with a shot of raspberry juice or woodruff extract.

Brandenburg

Eberswalder Spritzkuchen: deep-fried ring doughnuts.

Hessen

Handkäs mit Musik: curd cheese served with onions and a drop of light vinegar and oil.
Kasseler Rippchen: smoked pickled loin of pork, named after a Berlin butcher called Kassel.
Zwiebelkuchen: yeast cake (similar to pizza) filled with onions and bacon and usually served with a glass of young wine *(Federweisser)*.
Äppelwoi/Ebbelwoi: apple wine (not cider), a very popular drink.

Lower Saxony

Braunkohl mit Brägenwurst: kale with brain sausage.
Heidschnuckenbraten: roast lamb served with potatoes.
Braunschweiger Mumme: strong dark beer with a high malt content, usually mixed with ordinary beer.

Mecklenburg-Vorpommern

Salzhering in Sahnesosse: pickled herring in sour cream.
Himmel und Erde: boiled potatoes and apples with bacon.

North Germany-Hamburg-Bremen

Kohl mit Pinkel: cabbage with coarse sausage and potatoes.
Labskaus: salted meat, herring and mashed potatoes served with fried egg and beetroot.
Lübecker Schwalbennester: veal filled with hard-boiled eggs.
Lübecker Marzipan: favourite sweet, containing almond paste.
Rote Grütze: pudding made from red berries – mainly raspberries – and served with fresh cream.

Rhineland

Sauerbraten: braised pickled beef with bacon, usually served with potatoes and vegetables.
Hunsrücker Festessen: sauerkraut and peas. *Hunsrücker* pudding is served with potatoes, horseradish and ham.
Halver Hahn: rye bread or roll with cheese and mustard.
Kölsch: light-coloured, surface-fermented beer.
Spekulatius, Muzenmandeln: almond biscuits.

Saxony

Sächsischer Mandelstollen: almond cake.
Leipziger Allerlei: mixed vegetables.
Gallertschüssel: boiled pig's or calf's foot in aspic.
Dresdner Christstollen: Christmas cake.
Grüne Klösse: dumplings made from ground potatoes.
Kirschpfanne: cherry cake made of white bread, eggs, milk and butter.
Pfefferkuchen: gingerbread.
Eierschecke: golden-yellow cake filled with sweet curd.

Saxony-Anhalt

Halberstädter Wurst: sausage.
Salzwedeler Baumkuchen: cake and chocolate in thin layers.

Thuringia

Thüringer Klösse: potato dumplings.
Thüringer Rostbratwurst: grilled sausage with herbs.
Platz: Thuringian yeast cake.

ABOVE: relaxing over a light lunch.

Westphalia

Westfälischer Schinken: delicious ham, best when eaten with Pumpernickel bread.
Mettwurst mit Linsen: pork or beef sausage with lentils.
Westfälischer Reibekuchen: cakes made of grated potatoes and buckwheat flour.

Württemberg/Baden

Flädlesuppe: clear soup with pancake strips.
Spätzle: a kind of pasta made of flour, egg, salt and water, grated and boiled. *Spätzle* are served as a side-dish with meat and vegetables or as a main dish, *Kässpatzu*, when the *Spätzle* are put into a bowl with layers of fried onions and cheese.
Maultaschen: another form of pasta, filled with minced meat and spinach. *Maultaschen* are served either in soup or with salad.

Drinking Notes

If a glass of warm Liebfraumilch is your only experience of German wines, then you're in for a pleasant surprise. First, the Liebfraumilch on offer in Germany is far superior to what is exported. Second, there are many more German whites to sample: from honeyed sweet or rich dry Riesling, to fruity Müller-Thurgau to the spicier, fuller Gewürztraminer.

Although Germany majors on whites, some indigenous reds, such as those produced in Baden, are very palatable *(see page 73).* French red wines are readily available.

Schnapps and Brandy

Schnapps is a collective and colloquial term that describes all colourless *Korn* spirits made from rye, wheat, oats or barley. They have either a

neutral taste or can be flavoured with juniper or caraway. A glass of *schnapps* is usually drunk chilled and neat as an accompaniment to beer. Beware: *schnapps* is very strong. *Weinbrand* is a high-quality brandy, while *Obstbranntwein* is a brandy made from fully fermented fruit such as cherries, plums, apricots, pears, raspberries or blackberries. The best-known of these is *Kirsch* or cherry brandy, and *Williams* or pear brandy.

Sausages

Many varieties of German sausages and hams are well known outside the country, notably the Frankfurter and Westphalian ham, but there are scores of regional products that are equally good but not so familiar. The best place to find a good selection of sausages, cheeses and local delicacies is the weekly market.

There are said to be some 1,500 different varieties of sausages or *Würste*. A *Wurst* is not necessarily the same as a British "banger", although some such as *Bratwürste* are fried or grilled. A few varieties are boiled, such as *Knackwurst, Bockwurst* and, of course, Frankfurters. Many others such as *Bierwurst* (goes well with beer) or *Fleischwurst* are sliced thinly or spread *(Leberwurst)* and eaten with bread.

Preserved sausages *(Rohwürste)* are made from lean pork, bacon and beef, and then smoked or air-dried to give them a long life. These can often be seen, together with the many different hams, hanging behind the counter at market stalls, and delicatessens. The best known are *Pfeffersalami* and *Cervelat*.

BERLIN

Borchardt
Französische Strasse 47
Tel: 030-8188 6262
Elegant old building
integrated into the Neue
Hofgarten near
Gendarmenmarkt. Fine
French cuisine. €€€

Dressler
Kurfürstendamm 207
Tel: 030-883 3530
Unter den Linden 39
Tel: 030-204 4422
There is one of these on
both of Berlin's main
boulevards. A great place
at any time of day or night.
€€–€€€

Facil
In the Mandala Hotel
Potsdamer Strasse 3
Tel: 030-5900 51234
With its glass roof and the
creative Mediterranean
cuisine of Michael Kempf,
this place is a favourite for
business lunches and fine
dining. Closed Sat–Sun. €€€

First Floor
Palace Hotel, Europa-Center
Budapester Strasse 42

Charlottenburg
Tel: 030-2502 1020
Excellent cuisine in elegant
surroundings. Closed Sun
and Mon. €€€

Hackescher Hof
Rosenthaler Strasse 40–1
Tel: 030-283 5293
At the main entrance to the
Hackesche Höfe is this
popular café-restaurant, in
style reminiscent of a 1920s
coffee house. €€–€€€

Hugos
In the Hotel Intercontinental
Budapester Strasse 2
Tel: 030-2602 1263
Exceptional hotel-restaurant
with great food and city
views. Closed Mon. €€€

Lorenz Adlon
Unter den Linden 77
Tel: 030-2261 1960
Gourmet restaurant with a
view of the Brandenburg
Gate. Closed Sun and Mon.
€€€

Lutter & Wegner
Schlüterstrasse 55
Charlottenburg
Tel: 030-881 3440

BELOW: trio of tomato-based starters.

Charlottenstrasse 56
Tel: 030-2029540
Two restaurants/wine bars
with the same name. The
first (€€) has been serving
good food for many years in
the west of the city; the
second (€€€) is in a
modern building on the
Gendarmenmarkt. €€–€€€

Marché
Kurfürstendamm 14/15
Tel: 030-882 7578
Buffet-style "fast-food" with
salads, noodles, meat and
desserts. €–€€

Margaux
Unter den Linden 78
Tel: 030-2265 2611
Their *cuisine avant-garde
classique* combines
classical French delights
with experimental
creations. Evenings only,
closed Sun. €€€

Offenbach Stuben
Stubbenkammerstrasse 8
(Prenzlauer Berg)
Tel: 030-445 8502
Nostalgic atmosphere.
Serves German-Austrian
dishes in enormous
portions. €€

Opernpalais
Unter den Linden 5
Tel: 030-202 683
Complex with a wine cellar,
café and restaurants serving
Berliner and Brandenburg
specialities, including a
selection of cakes. €€–€€€

Refugium
Gendarmenmarkt 5
Tel: 030-229 1661
The interior of this French
dome features beautiful
Baroque vaults whilst
shady trees line the terrace

outside. German cuisine
with seasonal changing
menus. €€

VAU
Jägerstrasse 54–5
Tel: 030-202 9730
An elegant restaurant close
to the Gendarmenmarkt.
Booking well in advance is
recommended. Closed Sun.
€€€

Potsdam

Café Heider
Friedrich-Ebert-Strasse
Coffee house in the Dutch
quarter, offering delicious
cakes and a cosy
atmosphere. €€

Coffee Baum
Kleine Fleischergasse 4
Tel: 0341-961 0061
One of Europe's oldest
cafés, with full meals as
well as good coffee. €

Die Luise
Luisenplatz 6
Tel: 0331-903 663
Friendly restaurant in the
town centre, near the
entrance to Park
Sanssouci. Good food,
good prices. €

Villa Kellermann
Mangerstrasse 34–36
Tel: 0331-291572
In a grand villa in the Neue
Garten with a fine view of
the lake. Quality Italian
dishes and fine wines.
Closed Mon. €€€

Waage
Am Neuen Markt 12
Tel: 0331-270 9675
German, Italian and French
cuisine in this renovated
weigh-house. Closed Mon. €

BERLIN TO THE MECKLENBURG LAKES

Chorin

Alter Klosterschänke Chorin
Am Amt 9
Tel: 033366-433
Traditional *Gasthaus*. Also
a venue for music or
literary events. Popular
brunch on Sundays. €–€€

Rheinsberg

Ratskeller
Markt 1

Tel: 033931-226
Eel and zander, a fish caught
in the Havel, are the
specialities in this traditional
restaurant – which isn't in a
cellar, contrary to what the
name suggests. €€

Ludwigslust

Ambiente
Im Landhotel de Weimar
Schlossstrasse 15
Tel: 03874-4180

Fantastic dining in the
glass-covered courtyard of
this elegant hotel, where
royal hunting guests used
to relax. The food is not
fancy but the top-class chef
uses fresh ingredients of
the highest quality and
locally sourced for the most
part. The right place to
enjoy some culinary
highlights after visiting the
palace and a stroll in the
park.

Waren

Pier 13
Strandstrasse 4
Tel: 03991-664 241
Altes Reusenhus, Schulstrasse 7
Tel: 03991-666 897
Two laidback
establishments under the
same management where
you can make the most of
the lakeside setting – enjoy
fresh or smoked grilled
fish. €€

BERLIN TO HARZ AND LEIPZIG

Brandenburg

Kartoffelkäfer
Steinstrasse 56
Tel: 03381-224 118
Every imaginable potato dish in a historic location. Popular dining area on the terrace. €–€€

Goslar

Das Brusttuch
Hoher Weg 1
Tel: 05321-34600
Regional cooking in an elegant building – also a hotel – with a history going back 480 years. €€€

Leipzig

Auerbachs Keller
Grimmaische Strasse 2
Tel: 0341-216 100
Made famous by Goethe in his version of *Faust*. Beer and wine cellar serving traditional food. €€
Gasthaus Barthels Hof
Hainstrasse 1
Tel: 0341-141 310

Popular restaurant serving dishes with promising names, like "Madame Pompadour's passion". Quiet oasis in the town centre. €€
Goethe Café
Markt 17, Königshaus-Passage
Tel: 0341-211 9810
Traditional coffee house featuring different types of coffee and a large selection of cakes. €
Thüringer Hof
Burgstrasse 19
Tel: 0341-994 4999
Traditional Thuringian food served up in a friendly atmosphere. The building has been a *Gasthof* since 1466. €€

Magdeburg

Sachsen-Anhaltinisches Spezialitätenrestaurant
Rogätzer Strasse 8
The best regional cuisine prepared with ingredients freshly selected from the market. €€€

ABOVE: cold meats feature in a traditional German breakfast.

Quedlinburg

Schlosskrug am Dom
Schlossberg 1
Tel: 03946-2838

Game is the speciality served in this 15th-century building. Nice view over the town from the beer garden. €€

BERLIN TO DRESDEN

Chemnitz

Ratskeller
Markt 1
Tel: 0371-694 9875
Try the good-value set menus, which offer hearty, traditional fare. Great historic vaults with original decoration. €€

Cottbus

Café Altmarkt
Altmarkt 10
Tel: 0355-31036
Cosy café and bar/restaurant in medieval vaults from the 16th century. Elegant dining. €€
Cavalierhaus Branitz
Zum Kavalierhaus
Tel: 0355-715000
Hearty meals in a historic building in the Pückler Park. Early 20th-century decor; outdoor dining area in fine weather. €€

Dresden

Café 100
Alaunstrasse 100
Tel: 0351-801 3957
Popular pub in the Neustadt district, with wine cellar and garden at rear. €
Café and Restaurant Alte Meister
Theaterplatz 1a
Tel: 0351-481 0426
Next to the Old Master's Gallery and an opera house, the chef is inspired by art and good taste. Wonderful terrace. €€
Caroussel
Rähnitzgasse 19
Tel: 0351-80030
In the luxurious Hotel Bülow Residenz. Gourmet cuisine served on Dresden porcelain in an elegant atmosphere. One Michelin star since 1997. €€€
Gasthaus zur Eule
Grundstrasse 100
Tel: 0351-267 8667

Historic restaurant situated above Körnerplatz serving good, solid, Saxony specialities. €€
Hubertusgarten
Bautzner Landstrasse 89
Tel: 0351-460 4700
Specialities are game, fresh trout and carp. Attractive beer garden. €€
Pfunds Molkerei
Bautzner Strasse 79
Tel: 0351-810 5948
"The most beautiful milk-shop in the world" (founded in 1880) has a restaurant upstairs. €
Sophienkeller im Taschenbergpalais
Taschenberg 3
Tel: 0351-497 260
Experience Dresden's famous "funnel drinking" at this place. €
Villa Marie
Fährgässchen 1,
Dresden-Blasewitz, right by the "Blue Wonder" bridge

Tel: 0351-315 440
This attractive Tuscan-style villa dating from the 1860s was saved from ruin and demolition in the 1990s and restored to its former charm. Renowned chef Klaus Karsten Heidsieck now serves up fine Italian dishes with innovative accents, in keeping with the style of the villa itself. Both the joyous river panorama and the quality of the food will easily compensate for the rather high prices. €€€

PRICE CATEGORIES

Restaurants are categorised according to the following approximate prices per head:
€ = less than €10 for a simple one-course meal
€€ = €10–20 for a main course
€€€ = over €20 for a main course

Frankfurt (Oder)

Der Oderspeicher
Hanewald 9
Tel: 0335-535 885
Small brewery serving tasty food. Good atmosphere. €€
Frankfurter Kartoffelhaus
Holzmarkt 7
Tel: 0335-530 747

Rustic-style pub with a charming terrace beside the River Oder. Here you can taste potatoes, prepared the local way and in international dishes. €€

Freiberg

Theaterkeller
Borngasse 3
Tel: 03731-23141
Simple food in medieval vaults. €€

Jena

Roter Hirsch
Holzmarkt 10
Tel: 03641-443 221
Regional meals in a historic setting. €€

Lutherstadt Wittenberg

Ratsschänke
Markt 14
Tel: 03491-405 351
If you're in search of a friendly place serving traditional food, head for the Ratsschänke, located in the town centre. €€

WEIMAR TO WARTBURG

Eisenach

Marktschänke
Markt 19
Tel: 03691-203 461
Reasonable prices, hence its popularity with the locals. €€

Erfurt

Paganini
Fischmarkt 13–16
Tel: 0361-540 1162
Italian cuisine in a magnificent Renaissance building, with a great terrace on the square and a quiet beer garden out in the courtyard. €€€

Gotha

Gaststätte Mönchshof
Salzgitterstrasse 92
Tel: 03621-736 030
Thüringer Klösse served in a rustic atmosphere. €
Pagenhaus
Schloss Friedenstein
Tel: 03621-403 612
Thuringian and international dishes. Garden terrace in summer; cosy interior in the historic Baroque castle complex. €€€

Weimar

Anna Amalia
In the Hotel Elephant, Markt 19
Tel: 03643-8020
The top gourmet restaurant in Thuringia. Menu features Thuringian and Italian cuisine; exclusive atmosphere. €€€
Gasthaus Felsenkeller
Humboldtstrasse 37
Tel: 03643-414 741
Home-brewed beer and Thuringian specialities in the rustic setting of a traditional, popular brewery. Pleasant airy conservatory. €€

Köstritzer Schwarzbierhauses

Scherfgasse 4
Tel: 03643-779 337
Set in a lovely half-timbered house, serving home-made Thuringian food and home-brewed black beer. €
Zum Schwarzen Bären
Markt 20
Tel: 03643-853 847
The oldest restaurant in town, dating from 1540. Plainly typical interior, but the dishes are hearty and seasonal, with local classics such as *Köstritzer Schwarzbiergulasch*. €€

MUNICH

Georgenhof
Friedrichstrasse 1
Tel: 089-393 101
Close to the university quarter. Bavarian dining with a touch of class, in an ambience that manages to be both rustic and slightly elegant. €€

Hofbräuhaus
Platzl 9
Tel: 089-122 1676
Renowned beer hall with an idyllic beer garden. €–€€
Neuhauser Augustiner
Hübnerstrasse 23
Tel: 089-120 2130
Typical old-Munich

atmosphere in a popular *Gasthaus* serving local specialities. Situated between the city centre and Nymphenburg Palace. €–€€
Prinz Myshkin
Hackenstrasse 2
Tel: 089-265 596
Engaging vegetarian

dishes that run the gamut of world cuisine. €€
Spatenhaus
Residenzstrasse 12
Tel: 089-290 7060
Traditional restaurant near the Opera House. Rustic and yet elegant upstairs. €€–€€€
Tantris
Johann-Fichte-Strasse 7
Tel: 089-361 9590
Probably the best and most creative haute cuisine in Munich. €€€
Weisses Bräuhaus
Tal 7
Tel: 089-299 875
A venerable establishment whose Bavarian decor is as authentic as the *Schweinshax'n* and *Knödel* it serves. True Münchners come here at 11am to eat *Weisswurst*, the local sausage. Treat the strong dark *Weissbier* with respect. €–€€

BELOW: Munich is known for its high proportion of gourmet restaurants.

THE ALPS

Berchtesgaden

Hotel-Gasthof Nutzkaser
Am Gseng 10, Ramsau
Tel: 08657-388
A family-run establishment, perched on a steep hillside. Eat your fill of hearty Bavarian fare while admiring the Alpine landscape. €€
Schusterstein
Schönau am Königssee
Tel: 08652-2044
Rural hideaway with great summer terrace and local delicacies. €–€€

Füssen

Zum Schwanen
Brotmarkt 4
Tel: 08362-6174
Located in a 15th-century building and serving elegant, although still

traditional, Bavarian cuisine. Closed Mon. €€€

Garmisch-Partenkirchen

Berggasthof Eckbauer
Eckbauer 1
Tel: 08821-2214
Solid *schmankerl* (delicacies) and a great view – the ideal finish to a stroll around the base of Zugspitze. Access with the Eckbauer-Bahn from the Skistadium. €

Grainau

Eibsee Hotel
On Lake Eibsee
Tel: 08821-98810
Bavarian specialities with a French influence. The lakeside balcony

commands lovely views over the Zugspitze. €€€

Graswang

Gröbl-Alm
On the B23, between Linderhof and Graswang
Tel: 08822-6434
The perfect place for a hearty Bavarian lunch, while enjoying the superb view over the green valley and the Alps. Outdoor terrace. €€

Mittenwald

Alpenrose
Obermarkt 1
Tel: 08823-92700
One of Mittenwald's oldest, and most atmospheric, restaurants. Try something traditional like liver dumpling soup (*Leberknödelsuppe*)

followed by *Schweinebraten mit Blaukraut* (roast pork with red cabbage). €€

Reit im Winkl

Alpengasthof Winklmoosalm
Dürrnbachhornweg 6
Tel: 08640-97440
Typical Bavarian inn, close to where skiing legend Rosi Mittermeier grew up. €

Tegernsee

Leeberghof
Ellingerstrasse 10
Tel: 08022-3966
Excellent cuisine – local catch of the day, venison, and home-grown vegetables and herbs – and a great view from the terrace above the lake. Closed Mon. €€€

EASTERN BAVARIA

Landshut

Isar Klause
Laendgasse 124 (in summer, access from the river)
Tel: 0871-23100
Situated on the Isar, a good place to sample the wine and a *Wurst*, or other dishes, at affordable prices. €€

Passau

Passauer Wolf
Rindermarkt 6–8
Tel: 0851-931 5100
Bavarian fusion food in a traditional ambience. €€
Weisser Hase
Heiliggeistgasse 1
Tel: 0851-92110
Decent local cuisine at modest prices. €€

Regensburg

Historische Wurstküche
Thundorfer Strasse 3, adjacent to the Steinerne Brücke (Stone Bridge)
Tel: 0941-59098
This small kitchen serves tourists and locals alike, either in the tiny interior or outside on the banks of the Danube. €

Restaurant Orphée
Hotel Orphée, Untere Bachgasse 8
Tel: 0941-52977
Located in the centre of the Old Town, the Orphée is in typical French bistro style, original and hardly changed since 1896. Cosy within, on warm days there's also a great atmosphere on the tiny street terrace. Good service. Open daily 8am–1am.

ROMANTIC ROAD AND HEIDELBERG

Augsburg

Fuggerei-Stube
Jakoberstrasse 26
Tel: 0821-30870
Specialities include the likes of *Wurst*, *Rahmchampignons mit Semmelknödel* (creamy mushrooms with dumplings) and Swabian dishes with sauerkraut, *Schupfnudeln* and *Spätzle*. €€
Restaurant Die Ecke (Eckestuben)
Elias Holl-Platz 2
Tel: 0821-510 600
Gourmet cuisine and fine wines are served up in historic surroundings at this restaurant close to the

famous Rathaus. Lovely courtyard, the "Höffe". Mozart and Brecht dined here. €€–€€€

Dinkelsbühl

Weisses Ross
Steingasse 12
Tel: 09851-579 890
This widely acclaimed restaurant offers updated versions of the classics. €€

Heidelberg

Altheidelberger Brauhaus Vetter
Steingasse 9
Tel: 06221-165 850

Local beer and food, with sausages priced according to length. €
Schwarz das Restaurant
Kurfürsten-Anlage 60
Tel: 06221-757 030
Taste culinary perfection in this temple to gourmet cuisine on the 12th floor of the Print Media Academy. Regional delights and French-Italian surprises. €€€

Rothenburg ob der Tauber

Gasthof Zum Greifen
Obere Schmiedgasse 5
Tel: 09861-2281
Traditional Franconian

Gasthaus, popular with the locals. €
Hotel Goldener Hirsch
Untere Schmiedgasse 16–25
Tel: 09861-7080
Food that's a cut above most tourist fare, even if it is a bit pricey. Terrace. €€€

PRICE CATEGORIES

Restaurants are categorised according to the following approximate prices per head:
€ = less than €10 for a simple one-course meal
€€ = €10–20 for a main course
€€€ = over €20 for a main course

TRANSPORT. ACCOMMODATION EATING OUT ACTIVITIES A – Z LANGUAGE

Würzburg and Franconia

Bamberg

Brudermühle
Schranne 1
Tel: 0951-955 220
The restaurant has attracted much attention for its local cuisine and authentic atmosphere. €€€

Schlenkerla
Dominikanerstrasse 6
Tel: 0951-56060
A real institution with a popular beer garden. Try the *Schlenkerla Rauchbier* (beer made with smoked malt). Traditional Franconian cooking. €

Weinhaus Messerschmitt
Lange Strasse 41
Tel: 0951-297 800

Set in a wine merchant's house dating from 1832, this restaurant offers excellent Franconian cuisine and fish from the Main river. Fine wine list. €€

Bayreuth

Zur Lohmühle
Badstrasse 37
Tel: 0921-53060
Franconian fare and fish specialities in a remarkable half-timbered building. €€

Nuremberg

Albrecht Dürer Stube
Albrecht-Dürer-Strasse 6
Tel: 0911-227 209

Half-timbered house ideal for a flavour of local life. €–€€

Bratwurst-Röslein
Rathansplatz 6
Tel: 0911-214 860
The best place in town to sample the delicious *Nürnberger Bratwurst*. €

Goldenes Posthorn
Glöckleinsgasse 2
Tel: 0911-225 153
Germany's oldest wine pub, where the painter Albrecht Dürer was once a regular. Fine Franconian fare, and an ancient wine cellar. €–€€

Würzburg

Bürgerspital Weinstuben
Theaterstrasse 19

Tel: 0931-350 344
Traditional fare similar to the Juliusspital-Weinstuben *(below)*. €€

Juliusspital-Weinstuben
Juliuspromenade 19
Tel: 0931-54080
Here, wines originate in the restaurant's own vineyard; the food is Franconian and international. €€

Zum Stachel
Gressengasse 1
Tel: 0931-52770
The town's oldest wine bar (1413) has an idyllic courtyard and a fine selection of mouthwatering Franconian dishes. Booking is advised for the evening.
€€

Lake Constance

Friedrichshafen

Old City
Schanzstrasse 7
Tel: 07541-7050
Creative regional food in the restaurant of a modern, centrally located hotel. €

Konstanz

Riva
Seestrasse 25
Tel: 07531-363 090
Top-ranking gourmet food in an old villa with new hotel annexe. €€€

Lindau

Landgasthof Köchlin
Kemptener Strasse 41
Tel: 08382-96600
Swabian and Bavarian meals served in 17th-century building. €€

Meersburg

Residenz Am See
Uferpromenade 11
Tel: 07532-80040
Enjoy award-winning, innovative cuisine and lovely views across the lake. €€€

Black Forest

Baden-Baden

Papalangi
Lichtentaler Strasse 13
Tel: 07221-31616
Bistro with attractive courtyard. €€

Zum Alde Gott
Weinstrasse 10, Neuweier
Tel: 07223-5513
Long-standing gourmet restaurant. €€€

Baiersbronn

Traube-Tonbach
Tonbachstrasse 237
Tel: 07442-4920
One of the top gourmet restaurants in Germany. €€€

Breisach

Landgastof Adler
Hochstetter Strasse 11
Tel: 07667-93930
Hotel with excellent cuisine and mainly local wines. €€

Bühl (south of Baden-Baden)

Die Grüne Bettlad
Blumenstrasse 4
Tel: 07223-93130
Set in an antique-strewn 16th-century house, this intimate restaurant offers the very best in Baden cuisine with French influence. Closed Sun and Mon. €€€

Freiburg

Löwen
Herrenstrasse 47
Tel: 0761-33161
Regional cooking served in a cosy atmosphere in the Old Town.
€€

Weber's Weinstube
Hildastrasse 35
Tel: 0761-700 743
Historic cellar serving rustic fare. €

Stuttgart

Alte Kanzlei
Schillerplatz 5
Tel: 0711-294 457
Good regional/international cuisine in contemporary interior. Great terraces. €€

Restaurant Wielandshöhe
Alte Weinsteige 71, Degerloch
Tel: 0711-640 8848
Top cuisine by renowned chef Vincent Klink. €€€

Weinstube Kochenbas
Immenhofer Strasse 33
Tel: 0711-602704
Always crowded. Sample real Swabian fare such as *Maultaschen* (a type of pasta). Closed Mon. €

Tübingen

Café Pfuderer
Kronenstrasse 11
Tel: 07071-22160
Fine view of the town hall; seating outside. €€

Ulm

Schlössle
Schlössleweg 3, Neu-Ulm
Tel: 0731-77390
Traditional meeting point with house brewery and rustic food such as *Kässpätzle* and roast pork in dark beer gravy. Closed Wed Aug–June. €€

Zunfthaus der Fischerleute
Fischergasse 31
Tel: 0731-64411
Swabian cooking in romantic setting. €€

Price Categories

Restaurants are categorised according to the following approximate prices per head:
€ = less than €10 for a simple one-course meal
€€ = €10–20 for a main course
€€€ = over €200 for a main course

FRANKFURT

Café Grössenwahn
Lenaustrasse 97, Nordend
Tel: 069-599 356
A Frankfurt institution. €€
Gargantua
Liebigstrasse 47
Tel: 069-720 717
Exquisite Mediterranean
cuisine in an early 20th-
century villa. A bit pricey.
€€€

Klosterhof
Weissfrauenstrasse 3
Tel: 069-91399 000
Charming wooden interior
with food inspired by
monastic recipes. €–€€
Lagerhaus
Dreieichstrasse 45,
Sachsenhausen
Tel: 069-628 552
Popular inn where the beer

tastes just as good as the
breast of duck. Great
choice of dishes, from
Frankfurt specialities to
Indian and Mexican food.
€–€€
Lorsbacher Tal
Grosse Rittergasse 49
Tel: 069-616 459
Family business in the
heart of Sachsenhausen.

Enjoy *Rippchen* (loin of
pork) and other local
dishes together with a
glass of *Ebbelwoi* (apple
wine). €
Mutter Ernst
Alte Rothofstrasse 12
Tel: 069-283 822
A traditional establishment
catering for bankers and
brokers. €–€€

RHINE AND MOSELLE TO THE RUHR

Bergisch Gladbach

Dieter Müller
(in Schlosshotel Lerbach)
Lerbacher Weg
Tel: 02202-2040
Superb cuisine in
marvellous surroundings
near Cologne. Reservation
recommended. Closed
Mon. €€€

Bernkastel-Kues

Ratskeller
Am Markt 30
Tel: 06531-7474
Inn under the town hall
serving regional cuisine
and local wines. €€

Cochem

Alte Thorschänke
Brückenstrasse 3
Tel: 02671-3931
Wine restaurant housed in
a 14th-century building
specialising in game, trout
and eel dishes. €€–€€€

Cologne

Bieresel
Breite Strasse 114
Tel: 0221-257 6090
Famous for mussels –
prepared in more than 20
different ways. Nice
traditional atmosphere.
€–€€
Bizim
Weidengasse 47–49
Tel: 0221-131 581
Reputedly one of the best
Turkish restaurants in
Germany. Closed Sun and
Mon. €€–€€€
Le Moissonier
Krefelder Strasse 25
Tel: 0221-729 479

French gourmet cuisine by
Eric Menchon in Art
Nouveau ambience. Closed
Sun and Mon. €€€
Päffgen
Friesenstrasse 64–66
Tel: 0221-135 461
Traditional pub and brewery
with down-to-earth food
such as *Himmel und Erde*
(mashed potatoes, apples,
black pudding). €
Peters-Brauhaus
Mühlengasse 1
Tel: 0221-257 3950
Renovated property with a
long tradition. The Zum
Kranz beer hall stood here
in the 16th century. €€

Düsseldorf

Restaurant Im Schiffchen
Kaiserswerther Markt 9
Tel: 0211 401 050
Excellent French cuisine.
Closed Sun and Mon. €€€
Victorian and **Bistro im Victorian**
Königstrasse 3a
Tel: 0211-8655 0222/23
Choose between the
restaurant with grand
cuisine and the not-so-
expensive yet similar
bistro. Restaurant closed
Sun; bistro open daily. €€€

Essen

Dicker Engel
Im Löwental 43, Essen-Werden
Tel: 0201-494 739
Popular spot, with good
wines and tasty Italian
dishes. €–€€

Koblenz

Winninger Weinstuben
Rheinzollstrasse 2

Tel: 0261-387 07
In a former school building
close to the Rhine, the
Weinstuben serves regional
specialities according to
the season. Lovely garden
terrace with river view. Back
in the house, the wine bar
offers a good opportunity
to taste the local wine
before selecting a bottle for
a picnic or to take home.
€–€€

Traben-Trarbach

Die Graifen – Weine, Leben, Essen
Wolfer Weg 11
Tel: 06541-811 075
A great atmosphere
prevails in the famous Dr
Melsheimer wine estate,
where first-class wines
from the local vineyards
and the Moselle area
accompany the market
fresh cuisine. Romantic
conservatory. Organised
events. €€

Trier

Weinstube Palais Kesselstatt
Liebfrauenstrasse 10
Tel: 0651-41178
Old tubs, vats and presses
are the backdrop to simple
but good food, such as
soup, ham and cheese.
€
Zum Domstein
Am Hauptmarkt 5
Tel: 06511-74490
Romantic wine bar in the
cellar, with seating outside.
Many dishes follow Ancient
Roman recipes but there
are Moselle specialities
here too. €€

Worms

Rotisserie Dubs
Kirchstrasse 6
Tel: 06242-2023
Restaurant on the banks of
the Rhine serving excellent
cuisine. Closed Tues and
Sat lunch time. €€€

BELOW: noodle-based *Käsespätzle*, topped with fried onions.

FAIRYTALE ROAD

Bremen

Meierei im Bürgerpark
Tel: 0421-340 8619
Fine European and vegetarian cuisine in 19th-century villa located within Bremen's principal park. Closed Mon. €€–€€€

Fulda

Zum Stiftskämmerer
Kämmerzeller Strasse 10
Tel: 0661-52369
Regional fare served within medieval vault and out on the terrace. Closed Tues. €€

Hanover

Die Insel
Rudolf-von-Bennigsen-Ufer 81
Tel: 0511-831 214
Light and modern food on the banks of the Maschsee. Huge wine list. €€–€€€

Kassel

Osteria Kassel
Jordanstrasse 11
Tel: 0561-773 705
Honest Italian flavours in a compact setting. Gisela Levorato is the fabulous chef. Closed Sun. €€

HAMBURG

Cuneo
Davidstrasse 11
Tel: 040-312 580
The best Italian restaurant in town. Located in St Pauli, with a kitchen that takes orders until 1.30am. Closed Sun. €–€€

Filmhauskneipe
Friedensallee 7, Offensen
Tel: 040-393 467
Decent food in a venue frequented by advertising folk and journalists. €–€€
Landhaus Scherrer
Elbchaussee 130

Tel: 040-880 1325
Gourmet food in a fine, elegant setting right on the river Elbe. Stunning wine list. Closed Sun. €€€
Nil
Neuer Pferdemarkt 5
Tel: 040-439 7823

Excellent meals catering to the smart set in St Pauli. €€
Old Commercial Room
Englische Planke 10
Tel: 040-366 319
Typical Hamburg restaurant serving local specialities. €€

LÜBECK TO FLENSBURG

ABOVE: clever creations in marzipan, a speciality of Lübeck.

Flensburg

Piet Henningsen
Schiffbrücke 20
Tel: 0461-24576
Harbour restaurant with an aptly maritime feel whose fish and seafood menu carries on a tradition begun in 1886. €€

Kiel

Fördeblick
Kanalstrasse 85, Holtenau
Tel: 0431-2376 566
A traditional place right on the waterfront, yet very modern in its nautical

design. It's an atmospheric setting for dining and drinks out on the terraces, and popular with families for weekend lunches. €€

Lübeck

Schiffergesellschaft
Breite Strasse 2
Tel: 0451-76776
Excellent cuisine in the maritime atmosphere of this venerable institution. The building, which used to house the guild of the blue water captains (founded in 1401) was built in 1535. International wine list. €€

BALTIC COAST

Rostock

Zur Kogge
Wokrenter Strasse 27
Tel: 0381-493 4493
Fresh fish is the speciality of this pub crammed full of nautical details.
€€

Rostock-Warnemünde

Seekiste zur Krim
Am Strom 47
Tel: 0381-52114
Small and cosy 140-year-

old restaurant, managed mainly by sea captains until chef Alexander Kadner took over the helm back in 2006.
€€

Rügen/Binz

Villa Salve/Brasserie
Strandpromenade 41
Tel: 038393-2223
Hotel right on the seafront at Binz serving imaginative cuisine with local and Mediterranean influences. Friendly service. €€

Schwerin

Hotel Speicher am Ziegelsee
Speicherstrasse 11
Tel: 0385-500 30
This lakeside warehouse outside the town centre has been restored with great flair. A sea-faring touch and German dishes with a Mediterranean twist. €€

Stralsund

Hansekeller
Mönchstrasse 48

Tel: 03831-703 840
Regional specialities and plenty of fresh fish, in old brick vaults.
€€

PRICE CATEGORIES

Restaurants are categorised according to the following approximate prices per head:
€ = less than €10 for a simple one-course meal
€€ = €10–20 for a main course
€€€ = over €200 for a main course

ACTIVITIES

FESTIVALS, THE ARTS, NIGHTLIFE, SHOPPING, SPORTS AND OUTDOOR ACTIVITIES

THE ARTS

Information

If you wish to synchronise cultural events such as a drama or a music festival with your travel plans, you should contact the local tourist office (or check their website) well in advance to obtain venue details and ticket options.

If you want to know what is going on when you get to your destination, the local daily paper is probably the best source of information. Larger cities publish an events calendar or a *Stadtmagazin* with listings of events, plus reviews of plays, films, and so on.

Buying Tickets

Computer systems such as CTS make it possible to book tickets for major events at your local travel agency before leaving home.

Alternatively, you could enquire at the tourist office in, say, Munich about events in Hamburg some days later.

Saver Cards

Many cities offer their visitors a special discount card. Berlin has the Welcome Card, Hamburg the Hamburg Card, Munich the München Welcome Card, Frankfurt the Frankfurt Card, and Nürnberg the KulTour Ticket. These cards afford free use of public transport and reduced admission prices to many attractions, such as theatres, museums, theme parks and excursions, and sometimes even restaurants.

Late-Night Museums

Twice a year Berlin museums open late-night. The *Lange Nacht der Museen* at the end of January and the end of August attracts tens of thousands of enthusiasts, who enjoy the guided tours, music, poetry, dance and more. The events go on until 2am. Munich and other cities also organise museum extended openings, as well as late nights on other themes. Shuttle buses link the different venues.

In Berlin it is possible to book your hotel room together with a theatre or concert ticket at the tourist office (BTM). Packages with hotel and theatre ticket included are also offered in many smaller towns too. Otherwise, head for the box office yourself and ask what is available. There is a good chance that you will get tickets, if not for the best seats. Berlin has two last-minute box offices, where tickets for the same night are sold with a discount after 2pm. Baby-sitters can also be arranged. Reservations by phone accepted (same day only).

Hekticket
Ticket hotline: 030-230 9930
www.hekticket.de
Karl-Liebknecht-Strasse 12, Mitte (Kiosk opposite Berlin Carree), open Mon–Sat noon–8pm. Hardenbergstrasse 29D, Charlottenburg (in the lobby of the Deutsche Bank), open Mon–Sat 10am–8pm, Sun 2–6pm.

Opera Houses

The traditional German municipal theatre stages drama, opera and dance performances, but for economic reasons some towns have concentrated on just one or two of the above. The season lasts from August/September to June/July (depending on the regional school holidays). The gap in the summer months is usually filled by festivals.

An opera house and its company are still the pride of a city or state – opera usually benefits from a very substantial subsidy. There are more than 120 opera houses in Germany, the oldest of which (dating from 1678) is in Hamburg. The National Theater in Munich and the Semper Opera House in Dresden are architectural gems and worth a visit in their own right. Berlin has three opera houses, Staatsoper Unter den Linden, Deutsche Oper and Komische Oper.

Deutsche Oper Berlin
Richard-Wagner-Strasse 10, 10585 Berlin
Tel: 030-343 840
Fax: 030-3438 4232
Box office: Bismarckstrasse 35, 10627 Berlin, tel: 030-3438 4343.
www.deutscheoperberlin.de
Staatsoper Unter den Linden
Unter den Linden 5–7, 10117 Berlin
Tel: 030-203 540
Box office, tel: 030-2035 4555; fax: 030-2035 4483;
programme information via fax (*spielplanfaxabruf*): 030-2035 4480
http://staatsoper-berlin.de
Komische Oper
Behrenstrasse 55-57, 10117 Berlin
Tel: 030-202 600
Box office, tel: 030-4799 7400; fax: 030-4799 7490
www.komische-oper-berlin.de
Semperoper Dresden
Sächsische Staatsoper, Theaterplatz 2, 01067 Dresden
Tel: 0351-49110
Box office, tel: 0351-491 1705
Guided tours, tel: 0351-491 1496

www.semperoper.de
For guided tours:
www.semperoper-fuehrungen.de
Nationaltheater Bayerische Staatsoper
Max-Joseph-Platz 2, 80539 München
Tel: 089-218 501
Fax: 089-2185 1133
Box office: Marstallplatz 5, tel: 089-2185 1920; fax: 089-2185 1903
Guided tours: Fri 2pm
www.bayerische.staatsoper.de
Hamburgische Staatsoper
Grosse Theaterstrasse 34,
20354 Hamburg
Box office, tel: 040-356 868
www.hamburgische-staatsoper.de
Deutsche Oper am Rhein
Heinrich-Heine-Allee 16a,
40213 Düsseldorf
Tel: 0211-89080
Box office, tel: 0211-892 5211
www.rheinoper.de

Dance

Ballet repertoires generally include both classical ballet and modern choreographies. The choreographer John Neumeier transformed the **Hamburg Ballet** into the country's leading company by giving classical ballet an innovative form.

Among the most famous choreographers are Pina Bausch and her **Wuppertal Dance Theater**, Wuppertal (tel: 0202-569 4444; www.pina-bausch.de). In Berlin, Sasha Waltz presents her choreographic theatre at the **Schaubühne** (tel: 030-890 023; www.schaubuehne.de).

Theatre

There are countless theatres across the German states. As well as all the municipal, state and private theatres, there are numerous unattached, often innovative and experimental, theatre groups. The situation is constantly changing, but a few establishments remain the same:
Deutsches Schauspielhaus und Malersaal
Kirchenallee 39, 20099 Hamburg

Best Concerts

In summertime Berlin's idyllic **Waldbühne** is the place to enjoy concerts, from rock and pop to classics and open-air cinema. This arena has space for 20,000 people, most of whom arrive with picnics and champagne. The concerts given by the Berlin Philharmonic Orchestra are a wonderful experience, attracting audiences from far afield.

Oberammergau Passion Play

Though it takes place only every 10 years, the *Oberammergau Passionsspiele* attracts a worldwide audience and usually hits the headlines with controversies over casting or plot.

The play, a colourful pageant enacting the Passion of Christ, is performed predominantly by locals – of whom up to 200 can be on stage at any one time. It was originally performed to offer thanks to God for delivering the Oberammergau area from plague during the Thirty Years' War in the 1630s, and has become a 10-year tradition ever since. You need to book tickets and accommodation well in advance.

Details of the next performance in 2010 are available from
Verkehrs- und Reisebüro Gemeinde Oberammergau
Tel: 08822-92310
Fax: 08822-923 190
www.passionsspiele2000.de

Box office, tel: 040-248 713
www.schauspielhaus.de
Thalia Theater
Alstertor 1, 20095 Hamburg
Tel: 040-328 140
Box office: 040-3281 4444
www.thalia-theater.de
Münchener Kammerspiele Schauspielhaus
Maximilianstrasse 28,
80539 München
Box office: 089-2339 6600
www.muenchener-kammerspiele.de
Schauspielhaus Bochum
Königsallee 15, Bochum
Tel: 0234-3333 5555
www.schauspielhausbochum.de
Berliner Ensemble
Bertolt-Brecht-Platz 1, Berlin
Tel: 030-284 080
Box office: 030-2840 8155
Fax: 030-2840 8115
www.berliner-ensemble.de
Volksbühne am Rosa-Luxemburg-Platz
Linienstrasse 227
Tel: 030-240 655
Box office: 030-2406 5777
Visitor service: 030-2406 5630
www.volksbuehne-berlin.de
Director Frank Castorf has a radical approach to stagecraft.
Schaubühne am Lehniner Platz
Kurfürstendamm 153, Berlin
Tel: 030-890 023
Famous theatre founded by Peter Stein, today known for contemporary plays.
Deutsches Theater/Kammerspiele
Schumannstrasse 13a, 10117 Berlin
Tel: 030-284 410
Deutsches Theater box office:
030-2844 1225
www.deutschestheater.de
Max Reinhardt's legendary theatre is still a stronghold of classical drama; the adjacent Kammerspiele presents more experimental theatre.

The main theatre festival in Berlin is the **Theatertreffen Berlin** in May. For further information, contact the Berliner Festspiele GmbH, which aims to gather under one roof the full variety of the city's arts and culture:

Berliner Festspiele GmbH
Schaperstrasse 24, Berlin
Tel: 030-2548 9100
Fax: 030-2548 9230
www.berlinerfestspiele.de

Classical Music

The **Berlin Philharmonic Orchestra**, with Sir Simon Rattle as artistic director, and the **Munich Philharmonic Orchestra** with its director, Christian Thielemann, are the leading German orchestras. Concerts by the **Bamberg Symphony Orchestra**, the **Leipzig Gewandhaus**, the **Berliner Staatskapelle** with Daniel Barenboim and one or two others, in particular the **Rundfunkorchester** (radio orchestra) are worth looking out for.

In almost every town there will be a choir and one or more small orchestral groups performing chamber music.

Germany hosts over 100 music festivals, most taking place during the summer, often at historic sites. Tickets for events at the leading festivals sell out rapidly.

Musicals

For a long time Hamburg, Stuttgart Oberhausen, Essen and Bochum have staged musicals such as *Cats* and *The Lion King* (Hamburg), *Tanz der Vampire* (Stuttgart) and *Starlight Express* (Bochum). Tickets can be reserved when you book your hotel room through the tourist office.

Tickets for the shows in Berlin, Hamburg, Bochum, Oberhausen, Essen and Stuttgart can be booked by the **Ticket Online für Stage Entertainment** service, in Hamburg, tel: 0180-54444.

Berlin has two regular performing musical theatres – Musical Theater Berlin on Potsdamer Platz and Theater des Westens.
Theater des Westens
Kantstrasse 12, 10623 Berlin
Tel: 030-319 030 (information) and 0180-54444 (ticket reservation).

For information on the Festspielhaus in Füssen (built for the Ludwig-Musical) contact:
Musiktheater Füssen
Im See 1, 87629 Füssen
Tel: 08362-50770
Fax: 08362-507 7298
www.das-festspielhaus.de

Rock, Pop, Jazz

Major pop concerts are held all over Germany. Most of the larger cities have jazz clubs. Techno, house, hip hop and Latin-American sounds are also very popular. The most spectacular event for ravers is the Love Parade every July, in different cities.

NIGHTLIFE

The larger the city the more choices you have for entertainment at night. Although in many areas early-closing laws hamper night owls, anyone who wants an evening on the town should

not have any problem in cities like Munich, Hamburg, Cologne or Frankfurt. In Berlin, closing restrictions are minimal. There are numerous concert halls and theatres, and classical music lovers will be spoilt for choice. But there are also variety shows, cabaret and late-night revues.

The main cities have English-language magazines/information sheets highlighting what's on and where, for example in Berlin, *Berlin Magazin*; in Munich, *Munich Found*; in Hamburg, *Hamburg Magazin*.

Nightlife in Berlin

Whether you mean to start off your evening at 8pm, when concerts and other cultural events usually begin, or at midnight, it's all possible in Berlin: the city virtually never closes down.

In many areas of the city, locals and tourists often enjoy a late-night stroll and a drink or a meal in one of the many restaurants or bars. In what was once West Berlin, the hotspots are in Charlottenburg around Savigny-

Platz, Wilmersdorf (south of the Ku'damm), Schöneberg (near Winterfeldtplatz) and Goltzstrasse. Kreuzberg has two main meeting points: around Bergmannstrasse and Marheinekeplatz or in Oranienstrasse near Marianneplatz.

In the former East Berlin, the crowds tend to meet in Mitte, mainly along Oranienburger Strasse, around the ruined Tacheles Cultural Centre and the stylishly restored Hackesche Höfe. The social scene in Prenzlauer Berg around Kollwitzplatz is multicultural, and more relaxed.

These are some of Berlin's famous bars:
Bar am Lützowplatz
Lützowplatz 7, Tiergarten
Tel: 030-262 6807
www.baramluetzowplatz.com
Daily 4pm–4am.
Cocktails from all over the world served from a very long bar.
Harry's New York Bar
Gran Hotel Esplanade
Lützowufer 15, Tiergarten
Tel: 030-254 780

Festival Highlights

In the summer Germans love to go out and enjoy the warm weather with beer, wine, food and music.

Many street festivals take a theme such as the wine harvest, the May blossom, summer flowers or the fruit harvest. Others are held just for fun. Some festivals are religious, such as the *Oberammergau Passionsspiele (see page 374)*, others commemorate historical events, like the founding of a city or the successful defence of a city in medieval times. The Munich Oktoberfest draws visitors from all over the world *(see page 376)*. December markets such as Nuremburg Christkindlmarkt attract coachloads of visitors.

Events created as tourist spectacles, such as jousting tournaments and castle or fairy-tale festivals, are also popular.

Music Festivals

These are held in nearly every city – from small chamber music events to the internationally acclaimed Bayreuther Festspiele.
Bayreuth The Bayreuth opera festival (July/August) was founded by Richard Wagner and has been devoted to Wagner operas ever since. Bayreuth's theatre is famous for its acoustics and unpadded wooden seats, which seem to grow harder in the course of a five-hour work like *Parsifal* (www.bayreuther-festspiele.de).

Munich Some of the world's top soloists perform at the Münchner Opernfestspiele in July (www.muenchner-opern-festspiele.de).
Rheinsberg The Kammeroper Schloss Rheinsberg (in July and August) is well known as a springboard for young talent (www.kammeroper-schloss-rheinsberg.de).
Brandenburg *Brandenburgische Sommerkonzerte* take place every weekend in a village church or castle within the state of Brandenburg, round Berlin (www.brandenburgische-sommerkonzerte.de).
Schwetzingen Another beautiful festival is held every spring in the rococo palace of Schwetzingen, summer residence of the Electors of Mannheim, where audiences stroll in the baroque formal gardens during the intermission (www.mozartgesellschaft-schwetzingen.de).
Würzburg The Mozart Festival with its torchlit concerts in the formal gardens of the Residenz is a magnificent occasion (www.mozartfest-wuerzburg.de).
Berlin/Dresden Berlin's Staatsoper has started up a festival in spring (http://staatsoper-berlin.de), Dresden's Semper Oper too (www.semperoper.de).
Schleswig-Holstein The sprawling festival of Schleswig-Holstein, scattered through a number of towns in Germany's northernmost state, presents a wide range of orchestras, soloists, and chamber groups. It has

long been headed by popular pianist Justus Frantz (www.shmf.de).

In addition, many spa towns present festival concerts in their attractive *Kurhäuser*.

Other Festivals

Berlin stages the International Film Festival in February; the biennial MaerzMusic festival in March; the German Theatertreffen in May (the latest productions from the German-speaking world); the Berliner Festwochen (Sept–Oct), with a wide range of concerts and performing arts; and the JazzFest in November, to which famous international artists are invited.
Hamburg The Reeperbahn Festival showcases edgy new bands (Sept)
Munich The Munich Biennale is devoted to new music theatre.
Open-air theatres Many, often in beautiful settings, offer a summer season of light entertainment or serious drama, for instance, the Bad Hersfelder Festspiele, Freilichtbühne Wunsiedel, Bad Segeberg (Karl May Festival) Jagsthausen, Wartburg and others.

The DZT (Deutsche Zentrale für Tourismus) publishes an annual booklet entitled *Events in Germany – Experience Culture*, a detailed calendar listing all the festivals, musicals, exhibitions, sports events and much more.

ABOVE: Berlin is renowned for its cabaret.

www.esplanade.de
Where the rich and beautiful meet.
Newton Bar
Charlottenstrasse 57, Berlin Mitte
Tel: 2029 540
www.newton-bar.de
Elegant bar with large windows facing
the Gendarmenmarkt.
Paris Bar
Kantstrasse 152
Tel: 030-313 8052
www.parisbar.de
Daily noon–2am.
Legendary meeting place for theatre
and film actors; café, restaurant, bar.
Times Bar
Hotel Savoy
Fasanenstrasse 9, Charlottenburg
Tel: 030-442 8076
Pretend you are back home in "olde"
England, and read the English
newspapers with your double scotch.
Trompete
Lützowplatz 9
Tel: 030-2300 4794
www.trompete-berlin.de
After-work parties and live concerts.

Cabaret/Revue/Variety

Friedrichstadtpalast
Friedrichstrasse 107, Mitte
Tel: 030-2326 2326

www.friedrichstadtpalast.de
Everything is vast in this huge revue
theatre. It has space for 2,000
visitors, while the stage – with every
imaginable technical gadget at its
disposal – can put on sumptuous
events. There is a smaller, more
intimate theatre (Kleine Bühne)
adjacent, which is home to the
Comedy Club (shows Thur, Fri, Sat).
Wintergarten – das Varieté
Potsdamer Strasse 96 (Tiergarten)
Tel: 030-2500 8888
www.wintergarten-variete.de
In the nostalgic style of the golden
1920s. The constantly changing
programme is a mixture of variety,
cabaret and music with top artists.
Dinner, or snacks and drinks are
served before the show.
Chamäleon Varieté
Rosenthaler Strasse 40–41, Mitte
(Hackesche Höfe)
Tel: 030-400 0590
www.chamaeleonberlin.de
The younger and rebellious sister of
the Wintergarten. The fabulous
shows include singers and acrobats,
comedians and dancers. Late-night
performances on Fri and Sat.
Ufa Fabrik
Viktoriastrasse 10, Tempelhof
Tel: 030-755 030

www.ufafabrik.de
Diverse programme, including
children's events during the day. One
of the oldest alternative theatre and
variety groups in the city. There is a
school for acrobats.
Bar Jeder Vernunft
Schaperstrasse 24, Wilmersdorf
Tel: 030-883 1582
www.bar-jeder-vernunft.de
Daily shows at 8.30pm; piano bar
11.30pm. The modern "mirror tent"
is the perfect place for intimate
shows, such as music, cabaret,
chansons and comedy.
Tipi – Das Zelt
Grosse Queralle, close to the
Chancellor's office
Tel: 0180-DAS ZELT (327 9358)
www.tipi-das-zelt.de
This sister location of Bar Jeder
Vernunft offers a wide range of comedy
and music shows, especially with
young, lesser known artists. Beer-
garden open Tues–Sat 6pm, Sun 5pm.
Tempodrom
Möckernstrasse 10, near Anhalter
Bahnhof
Tel: 030-6953 3885
www.tempodrom.de
A tent-like roof covers this
multifunctional cultural centre with
its spectacular architecture.
Adjacent is the Liquidrom
(www.liquidrom-berlin.de), which offers
calm and well-being for the body and
soul in warm thermal waters while
listening to soft music.
Estrel Festival Center
Hotel Estrel, Sonnenallee 225,
Neukölln
Tel: 030-6831 6831
www.estrel.de
Wed–Mon 8.30pm; Sat–Sun 5 and/or
7pm. "Stars in concert" is the title of
this Las Vegas-import, with singers
and dancers imitating stars such
as Elvis Presley and Michael Jackson.
BKA
Mehringdamm 32–34, Kreuzberg
Tel: 030-202 2007
www.bka-luftschloss.de
The Berliner Kabarett Anstalt
presents comedy, *chansons*, cabaret,
variety and a lot of trash.
Die Stachelschweine
Europa-Center, Charlottenburg
Tel: 030-261 4795
www.stachelschweine-berlin.de
Classic German *Kabarett*.
Sophisticated humour in a political/-
current affairs vein. Very
entertaining if you understand
enough German.
Die Distel
Friedrichstrasse 101, Mitte
Tel: 030-204 4704
www.distel-berlin.de
The former East Berlin equivalent of
the Stachelschweine.

Munich's Oktoberfest

The Oktoberfest attracts over
seven million visitors every year.
A massive jamboree, it actually
takes place mainly in September,
ending early-October, and is a
thronging fete with processions,
folk music, rides, circus, bands
and much beer drinking.
   The opening ceremony, with
horse-drawn carriages leading a
gigantic procession to the beat of
brass bands, takes place on the
first Saturday. A week later the
brass bands hold a concert. Book
rooms well in advance.
   For information and tickets,
contact the organisers:
Festleitung
Tel: 089-233 3091
www.oktoberfest.de

Casinos

The casino tradition is centuries-old in Germany's spa towns. The first casino (Spielbank) opened in Baden-Baden in 1810, and the town soon became the summer capital for Europe's nobility. Many spent their time and money in the casinos and a good few made their fortunes here.

In 1872, all German casinos were closed by law. They reopened in 1934 and closed again during World War II. But a new chapter in the history of casinos began around 1950, since when they have become places where high society, the nouveaux riche and beautiful people meet. Even if you do not want to try your luck at gambling, they are popular nightspots, with restaurants and bars open until the small hours. Take a jacket; ties can be hired.

The entrance fee is nominal (about €3), and some hotel

packages include a voucher for the casino. General information for all casinos can be found at: www.spielcasino.de.

Some famous casinos are:
● **Spielbank Baden-Baden**
Kaiserallee 1, in the Kurhaus, 76530 Baden-Baden
Tel: 07221-30240
www.casino-baden-baden.de
Open daily from 2pm: slot machines until 2am, Fri–Sat until 3am, restaurants until 2am, Baccara Bar until 5am. This must be the finest casino in Europe.
● **Spielbank Wiesbaden**
Kurhausplatz 1,
65189 Wiesbaden
Tel: 0611-536 100
www.spielbank-wiesbaden.de
Open daily 2.45pm–3am, certain days until 4am. One of the oldest and most elegant casinos in Germany.

● **Spielcasino Aachen**
Monheimsallee 44,
52062 Aachen
Tel: 0241-18080
www.westspiel.de
Famous for its art collection.
● **Spielbank Trier**
Porta-Nigra-Platz,
54292 Trier
Tel: 0651-26075
www.spielbank-trier.de
● **Casino Konstanz**
Seestrasse 21,
78464 Konstanz
Tel: 07531-81570
www.casino-konstanz.de
In an elegant villa by the marina.
● **Bayerische Spielbank Lindau**
Chellesallee 1,
88131 Lindau
Tel: 08382-27740
www.spielbank-lindau.de
Intimate atmosphere and lake views.

Jazz Clubs

A Trane Jazzclub
Bleibtreustrasse 1, Charlottenburg
Tel: 030-313 2550
www.a-trane.de
Daily 9pm–2am, Fri and Sat until late. Modern jazz and avant-garde.
b-flat
Rosenthaler Strasse 13, Mitte
Tel: 030-283 3123
www.b-flat-berlin.de
Cocktail bar open daily 8pm; music starts later. Live jazz in all styles, Tango evenings Sun 9pm.
Quasimodo
Kantstrasse 12a, Charlottenburg.
Tel: 030-312 8086
www.quasimodo.de
Daily 9pm, live music 10pm. Popular jazz cellar (jazz, blues, folk, funk, soul), with regular concerts by international stars as well as a springboard for young talent. Always crowded. Tickets sold in the café, which is open daily from 11am.

The Beatles' Hamburg

SceneBeatles fans can indulge in a bit of nostalgia with a visit to some of the group's old haunts in Hamburg, where John Lennon claimed he grew up. Among venues where they appeared are: Indra strip club (Grosse Feiheit 34), the Kaiserkeller (Grosse Freiheit 38), the Top Ten Club (Reeperbahn 136) and the Star Club (Grosse Freiheit 39).

Nightclubs/Dancing

Berlin is Germany's rave capital. There are hundreds of clubs where you can hear funk, soul, hip-hop, techno, metal or world music. The scene changes rapidly, but there are some venues that have been in existence for quite a few years.

Details of events are usually passed on by flyers distributed outside clubs. Some are only open Thur–Sat, but some hold gigs on Monday too. Berlin also has many traditional nightclubs. The following is just a small selection:
40 seconds
Potsdamer Str. 58, 10178 Berlin
Tel: 030-8906 4241
Fri–Sat, club from 11pm. 40 seconds – the time the elevator takes to reach the fabulous penthouse club where you can dine before either heading for the dance floor or chilling out on one of the roof terraces. Right in the new Potsdamerplatz hotspot.
90 Grad
Dennewitzstrasse 37, Schöneberg
Tel: 030-2300 5954
www.90-grad-berlin.de
Thur–Sat 11pm. One of the "greats" on the club scene and still one of the most popular (disco and house).
Clärchens Ballhaus
Augustsstrasse 24/25, Mitte
Tel: 030-282 9295
www.ballhaus.de
Old Berlin dancing – a popular singles venue, open from 10am; Fri–Sat live music.
Duncker
Dunckerstrasse 64, Prenzlauer Berg
Tel: 030-445 9509

www.dunckerclub.de
Daily 10pm, Fri and Sat 11pm. Gigs and discos.
Kalkscheune
Johannisstrasse 2, Mitte
Tel: 030-5900 4340
www.kalkscheune.de
A popular venue for late-night (post-club) parties, concerts and events.
Knaack
Greifswalder Strasse 224,
Prenzlauer Berg
Tel: 030-442 7060
www.knaack-berlin.de
Mon karaoke, Wed hip-hop at 11pm, Fri and Sat club at 9pm. Live gigs and club nights, plus billiards tables. Fri evenings UNI:BEAT parties, free student entrance with ID card) until 11pm.
Oxymoron
Hackesche Höfe,
Rosenthaler Strasse 40–1, Mitte
Tel: 030-2839 1886
www.oxymoron-berlin.de
A venue for a variety of events ranging from jazz to "pasta operas"; by day a popular café and lunch restaurant. Popular with the beautiful people.
Tresor Club and Globus
Leipziger Strasse 126 A, Mitte
Tel: 030-695 3770
www.tresorberlin.com
Wed, Fri and Sat at 11pm. Techno and hip-hop.
Week-End
Alexanderplatz 5, Berlin Mitte
Tel: 030-2463 1676
www.week-end-berlin.de
Mainly Thur–Sun 11pm, roof open daily in summer from 5 or 6pm, Sun 3pm. Located on the twelfth and fifteenth floors of the former DDR "House of Travel". Fantastic roof terrace views.

Gay & Lesbian Scene

Connection
Fuggerstrasse 33, Schöneberg
Tel: 030-218 1432
www.connection-berlin.de/club.html
Fri and Sat 11pm. Gay club that plays
house and techno.
Hafen and **Tom's Bar**
Both in Motzstrasse 19, Schöneberg.
Hafen daily from 10pm, tel: 211 4118;
Tom's Bar opens 11pm, tel: 030-213
4570.
Traditional meeting places which
always get crowded.
Prinzknecht
Fuggerstrasse 33, Schöneberg
Tel: 030-218 1432
www.prinzknecht.de
Daily 3pm–3am, winter 4pm–3pm.
Bar and café.
SchwuZ
Mehringdamm 61, 10961 Berlin
Tel: 030-6290 880
www.schwuz.de
Fri and Sat 10pm, some gigs Wed and
Thur. A classic gay centre, disco and
venue for live concerts and variety.
Stiller Don
Erich-Weinert-Strasse 67,
Prenzlauer Berg
Tel: 030-283 4392
Open 8pm. Gay pub with a relaxed
atmosphere.

SPORT

Spectator Sports

Try not to choose a Saturday
afternoon or early evening to pay a
visit to a German family, because
this is when the *Bundesliga* football
matches are usually held. Any
serious German football fan will
either be at the match or watching
the game or highlights at home on
the TV.
   The likes of Steffi Graf and Boris
Becker have turned Germany into a
country of tennis watchers (and
players). All the main tournaments
are shown on TV and this once rather
exclusive sport is now very popular.
   Motor racing has become even
more of a national passion following
the success of Formula One star
Michael Schumacher. Hockenheim,
near Heidelberg, which is famous for
the roar of the crowd resounding
round the track, is the venue for the
German Grand Prix and the
Nürburgring is home to the
Luxembourg Grand Prix.
   Other sports that attract
thousands of spectators are hand-
ball, volleyball, basketball, athletics,
gymnastics, cycling and swimming.

Diary of Sporting Events

January 6-Day Cycle Race, Berlin.
April Hamburg Marathon.
April/May BMW International Tennis
Open, Munich
May Jumping and Dressage Derby,
Hamburg.
BMW International Golf Open,
Golfclub Munich Eichenried (north
of the city, in the direction of the
airport).
June Kiel Week sailing.
International Lawn Tennis
Tournament, Halle (Westphalia).
June/July Derby Week,
horse-racing, Hamburg.
July Dressage, Jumping (Rolex
Grand Prix) and Driving Tournament,
Aachen.
MercedesCup, international tennis
tournament Stuttgart Weissenhof.
Travemünder Woche, international
sailing event near Lübeck.

Warnemünder Woche, international
sailing event near Rostock.
German Touring Car Masters,
Nürburgring.
July/August German Grand Prix,
Hockenheim.
August Nacht von Hannover, bicycle
street race event.
Oldtimer Grand Prix, Nürburgring.
August/September Grosse Woche,
international horse-racing event in
Baden-Baden Iffezheim.
September Athletics in Cologne,
Berlin and Koblenz.
Berlin Marathon.
October Köln Marathon.
German Classics riding tournament,
Hanover.
Frankfurt Marathon.
November ATP World
Championships (tennis), Hanover.
6-Day Cycle Race, Munich.

Participant Sports

Most towns have a municipal
leisure centre with the usual sports
facilities, and these are nearly
always busy. Sunday is often the
day for a walk in the park; the more
active will jog, cycle, or head out
into the countryside for a hike.
Some sport clubs give short-stay
visitors temporary membership, or
just pay an hourly fee for the tennis
court or the golf course.
   All tourist information offices
have brochures and information
about local and regional sport
facilities as well as all the main
sporting events. The following
addresses are the national
headquarters for each sport.

Golf

There are numerous golf courses all
over the country, normally in
beautiful settings with luxurious
accommodation nearby.
Deutscher Golf-Verband
Viktoriastrasse 6, 65189 Wiesbaden
Tel: 0611-990 200
Fax: 0611-990 2040
www.golf.de

Horse-riding

Horse-riding is very popular in many
areas. You can take lessons, rent a
horse for a couple of hours or even
enjoy a full riding holiday at a
countryside ranch.
Deutsche Reiterliche Vereinigung
Freiherr-von-Langen-Strasse 13,
48231 Warendorf
Tel: 02581-63620
Fax: 02581-62144
www.pferd-aktuell.de

Outdoor Activities

Hiking and Cycling

These are probably the most popular
outdoor activities. In every part of
Germany you will find well-maintained
and well-signposted paths and tracks
for hiking or cycling. They are usually
looked after by the regional walking
club or *Wanderverein*, who also
publish brochures with maps and
additional information – available at
the local tourist office.
   A list with the addresses of the
local hiking clubs as well as
information about long-distance trails
can be obtained from:
Deutscher Wanderverband
Wilhelmshöher Allee 157–159,
34121 Kassel
Tel: 0561-938 730
Fax: 0561-938 7310
www.deutscher-wanderverband.de
Bund Deutscher Radfahrer
Otto-Fleck-Schneise 4,
60528 Frankfurt/Main
Tel: 069-9678 000
Fax: 069-9678 0080
www.rad-net.de
Kompass-Wanderführer and
Kompass-Radwanderführer are the
best maps for walkers and cyclists.

Climbing

If you are keen on climbing either
as a beginner or as an expert and
wish to book overnight stays in one
of the many mountain cabins,
contact:
Deutsche Alpenverein (DAV)
Von-Kahr-Strasse 2–4, 80997 Munich
Tel: 089-140 030
Fax: 089-140 0311
www.alpenverein.de

The DAV provides tuition and organises accompanied tours. They can also supply experienced guides for private excursions.

Skiing

The best and most demanding areas are Oberbayern and the Allgäu. But the Harz and the Thuringian mountains, the Erzgebirge, the Bayerischer Wald, plus the Taunus, Sauerland and Schwarzwald uplands also have good ski runs.

You can usually rely on the right snow conditions from December through to March. As well as downhill and cross-country skiing, there are also toboggan runs and ice-skating rinks near most winter sports resorts.

The ADAC automobile club has a *Schneetelefon* that gives recorded information about snow conditions: tel: 01805-232 221.

Watersports

There are various watersports available beside the lakes, rivers and sea in the north. Sailing and windsurfing, rowing and canoeing are all very popular. Motorboats and houseboats are available for hire. A licence is required to take the controls of a boat with an output of more than 3.6kW. For more information, contact:

Deutscher Kanu-Verband
Bertaallee 8, 47055 Duisburg
Tel: 0203-997 590
www.kanu.de

Deutscher Ruderverband
Ferdinand-Wilhelm-Fricke-Weg 10, 30169 Hannover
Tel: 0511-980 940
www.rudern.de

Deutscher Motoryachtverband
Vinckeufer 12–14, 47119 Duisburg
Tel: 0203-809 580
www.dmyv.de

Deutscher Seglerverband e.V.
Grindgensstrasse 18, 22309 Hamburg
Tel: 040-632 0090
www.dsv.org

SHOPPING

You will find many unusual and interesting things to bring back home, good quality and bad, at very modest prices or phenomenally expensive.

All cities have shopping centres, mostly with pedestrian zones *(Fussgängerzone)*, where you will find department stores and shops selling clothing, shoes, CDs, books, household goods and so on. Modern shopping malls are likely to be found on the outskirts of towns.

Factory outlets have become quite popular in Germany. The highest

concentration of factory shops can be found in Metzingen (southeast of Stuttgart), originally only a town to shop in for men's fashions by Hugo Boss. For factory outlets check out general websites such as www.factory-outlet-center.biz or the homepage of a given label which might show the address of the *Fabrikverkauf* or the shops in regional outlet centres.

The museum shops are highly recommended for replicas and prints.

If you are an antiques enthusiast, you will find many elegant, well-stocked shops, as well as numerous flea markets, normally held on Saturday.

Regional Specialities

Each region in Germany has something to offer as a souvenir – cuckoo clocks in the Black Forest; *Zwetschgenmännle* (plum cake men) and ginger bread in Nuremberg; Meissen porcelain from the Dresden area; and marzipan from Lübeck. Other possibilities are pottery, hand-made crystal, blown glass or silverware.

Many visitors are tempted by the beer mugs *(Bierkrüge)*. They are available in glass, clay and pewter, brightly painted or plain, with a cap or without. You can usually have your name engraved on the side. Many of them bear the name of famous breweries. In Hessen, you will see the typical *Ebbelwoi* (type of cider) glasses and the quite decorative grey and blue ceramic jugs, *Bembel*, for serving the Ebbelwoi and keeping it cool in summer (they make lovely vases too).

Germany is also known for toys. The Erzgebirge are famous for wooden figures, such as nutcrackers or Christmas trees. Nuremberg makes model railways while Thuringia and northern Franconia are centres of the doll-making industry. Rödental near Coburg is the home of *Hummel-Figuren*, doll-like figures made out of porcelain. In Donauwörth, on the Romantic Road, the very pretty *Käthe Kruse* dolls are produced, named after the woman who started making them more than a century ago. The highest quality teddy bears and other cuddly toys are by Steiff Stofftiere, earmarked with the characteristic button and a red and yellow label. Prices are quite high, but the well-made animals will last for generations.

Violins are made in Mittenwald, Oberbayern, usually in the Italian style, or Markneukirchen in Vogtland (Saxony) following Bohemian methods.

Traditional items of clothing include Bavarian *Loden*, sold in the South, a thick, heavy material that is used for coats, costumes and suits. The classic *Loden* colours are grey, dark green and

ABOVE: invest in some classic *Loden*.

dark brown. Some of the garments are highly decorated, but the plainer ones, like loose-cut jackets, are ideal for walking in the countryside. You'll also find *Walkjacken* (cardigans made of specially treated knitwear), in all colours and sometimes embroidered. Originally part of the traditional Alpine costume for both men and women, they are nowadays produced in a more modern style and suitable for many outdoor activities. In the north, fishermen's attire is often sold as souvenirs, from rubber boots to *Schiffermützen* (caps) and *Seemannspullover* (thick, woollen sweaters). Think twice before getting your wallet out though – will you really wear those fetching *Lederhosen* shorts back home?

Plauener Spitze is filigree lacework made by machines and was invented about 100 years ago in Saxony. This state is also the home of Meissen porcelain. Berlin's KPM (Königliche Porzellanmanufaktur), founded in 1763 by Frederick the Great to rival Meissen porcelain, produces beautiful porcelain in both modern and traditional designs. Meissen's big rival however has always been Nymphenburg porcelain, whose home is the Nymphenburger Porzellanmanufaktur in Munich (with shop downtntown in Theatinerstrasse).

Eastern Germany was, and still is, the traditional centre for the production of porcelain and glass. Two tourist roads, the Porzellanstrasse and the Glasstrasse, run through Oberpfalz and the Bavarian Forest, lined with big names such as Rosenthal for porcelain and Riedel, Schott or Eisch for glass. There are factory shops and small artisans' workshops as well as many museums with good boutiques (www.porzellanstrasse.de; www.dieglasstrasse.de).

A – Z

A HANDY SUMMARY OF PRACTICAL INFORMATION, ARRANGED ALPHABETICALLY

B usiness Hours

Shops The normal closing time for department stores and shopping malls in the big cities is 8pm. In smaller towns and villages, however, shops usually close at 6 or 6.30pm, but may have longer opening hours on Thursday and Friday.

In the morning the hours vary from shop to shop. Some open at 7 or 8am, others at 10am. Bakeries, of course, start selling fresh bread and rolls early on, and at pavement kiosks daily papers go on sale at around 6 or 7am. Some small shops might close for lunch.

On Saturdays small shops normally open 8am–1 or 2pm, and department stores close at 4 or 5pm. For the four Saturdays before Christmas, shops stay open until 6 or 8pm. Sundays are still considered sacrosanct and there is normally no trading, with the exception of bakeries, newsagents, souvenir shops and some others.

Shops at railway stations and airports usually stay open until late.

Petrol stations You can always find a petrol station *(Tankstelle)* open late at night. Many sell not only travel

requirements, but also offer a wide variety of goods from food to cosmetics – but usually at higher prices than supermarkets.

Offices have flexible working hours, usually between 7.30am and 5pm; on Fridays until 2pm only. Business appointments are best made from 9am–noon or 2–4pm.

Banks usually open weekdays 9am–4pm (possibly closed at lunchtime). However they are expanding their services, at least in big cities,

BELOW: keeping in touch is easy.

so these times are no longer rigidly adhered to. Exchange bureaux *(Wechselstuben)* are open until 6pm, sometimes longer, and also on Saturday.

Post offices retain their traditional opening hours: 8am–6pm (5pm in smaller places), and until noon on Saturday. At railway stations and airports you will find post offices open until later, some even opening on Sunday. In villages some shops now double up as "post agencies".

Restaurants and pubs normally close at midnight or 1am. Very often they are closed one or two days a week, and hotel restaurants seldom open Sunday and Monday when business is slack.

Nightclubs and some bars have licences for extended hours. Only in Berlin are there no late-night restrictions, as there is no such thing as *Sperrstunde* (compulsory closing time).

C hildren

Some say that the Germans love dogs more than children, but there is little evidence of that at motorway service stations *(Raststätten)* where, as at airports and stations, there are excellent and plentiful nappy-changing areas (Wickelräume).

Generally, travelling with children is easy. Many restaurants have children's chairs and menus. The German railway company, Deutsche Bahn, makes family compartments available at no extra charge. Well equipped children's playgrounds or Spielplätze are common in urban areas across Germany and there are always lots of interesting things to do with children, such as visits to theme parks, zoos, museums and theatres.

Climate

Germany lies within the continental climate zone, which means it can be very hot in the summer and bitterly cold in the winter. You will, however, experience a slight change in climate when travelling from the northwest to the southeast. In the north around Hamburg and in Schleswig-Holstein and along the Baltic Sea the weather is more oceanic, with milder winters and moderately warm summers. Further south it becomes more continental with greater variations.

The average temperature in the north is 0°C (32°F) in January and 17°C (62°F) in July. In the south, temperature varies from −2°C (28°F) in January to 18–20°C (64–68°F) in July. There can be cold periods in winter with temperatures falling to −10°C (14°F) or even −20°C (-4°F). In summer you may experience "dog days" (Hundstage), a series of hot days in July and August when temperatures can reach between 30°C and 35°C (86–95°F). On the other hand, periods of cold and rain in July and August are not uncommon, with temperatures around 15°C (59°F). So be prepared for any weather and bring along a sweater and an umbrella, as well as clothing for warm sunny days.

There is precipitation all year round, but July is the wettest month, with an average rainfall of 750 mm (30 inches) in the north and 620 mm (26 inches) in the Rhine Valley. The average rainfall in Bavaria, for example, is 1,300 mm (52 inches) with Oberstdorf, where annual rainfall often amounts to 1,750 mm (70 inches), as the wettest place.

The Alps, as well as being the wettest region, also has another climatic phenomenon – the Föhn, a warm, dry wind that blows down from the Alps into Southern Bavaria and Swabia. The Föhn has two effects: it clears the sky so that it is possible to see the Alps even from Munich, but it also tends to cause headaches.

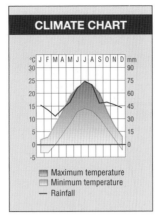

CLIMATE CHART

Maximum temperature
Minimum temperature
— Rainfall

The water temperature of the North and Baltic seas varies significantly between May and September, depending on the weather. But even during the summer months the water temperature doesn't rise above 18°C (64°F).

The best time to travel to Germany is between late May and early October. Skiers will find the best conditions between mid-December and March.

Crime and Safety

Crime exists in Germany, as it does all over the world, but only in larger cities do visitors need to be especially cautious: beware pick-pockets in crowds; do not leave your luggage unaccompanied at any time; and hide any valuables in your car boot. Right-wing extremists have in the past carried out assaults on foreigners, but this is rare. Travelling around Germany is an easy matter whether you go by plane, train, bus or car. Passenger services are frequent and you can rely on the German reputation for punctuality. But also be aware that the smaller the place you want to reach, the fewer the bus or train connections.

Customs Regulations

The following goods may be imported into Germany tax-free:
● 200 cigarettes or 100 cigarillos or 50 cigars or 250g of tobacco
● 1 litre of spirits with an alcohol content exceeding 22 percent by volume; or 2 litres of spirits or liqueurs with an alcohol content not exceeding 22 percent by volume; or 2 litres of sparkling wine and 2 litres of any other wine
● 500g coffee or 200g of concentrated coffee
● 100g of tea or 40g of concentrated tea

● 50g of perfume or 250ml of eau de toilette.

Nationals of EU countries are allowed to import higher quantities of the above-mentioned goods tax-paid but only for their own consumption.

For non-EU residents other goods are tax-free up to the value of around €175.

The tobacco and alcohol allowances apply only to those over 17 years of age, coffee for those over 15.

D isabled Travellers

Germany has installed many facilities to make public areas, public transport and events accessible to disabled people but, of course, older hotels cannot always be redesigned to accommodate wheelchairs. Many websites have a section called Barrierefrei (barrier-free) which explains facilities for disabled travellers.

Travel tips for disabled people and information about facilities in hotels, camp sites, youth hostels and specialised tour operators can be obtained through the following organisation:

Bundesarbeitsgemeinschaft der Clubs Behinderter und ihrer Freunde e.V. (BAG cbf)
Langenmarckweg 2,
51465 Bergisch Gladbach
Tel: 02202-989 9811
E-mail: info@bagcbf.de
www.bagcbf.de

E mbassies

Australia
Wallstrasse 76–79, 10179 Berlin
Tel: 030-8800 880
Fax: 030-8800 88210
Canada
Leipziger Platz 17, 10117 Berlin
Tel: 030-203 120
Fax: 030-2031 2590
Ireland
Friedrichstrasse 200, 10117 Berlin
Tel: 030-220 720
Fax: 030-2207 2299
New Zealand
Friedrichstrasse 60, 10117 Berlin
Tel: 030-206 210
Fax: 030-2062 1114
United Kingdom
Wilhelmstrasse 70, 10117 Berlin
Tel: 030-204 570
Fax: 030-2045 7579
United States
(Consular Section)
Clayallee 170, Dahlem, 14195 Berlin

Electricity

220-volts, two-pin plugs. Visitors from the UK will need an adaptor.

Emergencies

Police 110
Fire brigade 112
Ambulance 112
Operator 0180-200 1033
National directory enquiries
11833
International directory enquiries
11834
All accidents resulting in injury
must be reported to the police.

Tel: 030-832 9233
Fax: 030-831 4926

Entry Requirements

Visas & Passports

Citizens from most western European
countries may travel with just a valid
identity card. Other foreign travellers
must have a full passport. Citizens of
the US, Canada, South America,
Australia, New Zealand, Singapore
and a number of other countries
automatically acquire a three-month
permit on entering Germany. Visitors
from many countries (particularly
Asian countries) need a visa.

Children must have their names
entered in one of their parents'
passports or have their own passport.

Etiquette

Germany is a formal nation. In
business and with acquaintants,
use *Herr* and *Frau* rather than calling
people by their Christian names,
unless they suggest otherwise. Peers
of similar age and standing can also
be on first name terms.

It is customary for people to
shake hands whenever they meet,
and women are often pecked on both
cheeks. If you are invited to
someone's home, always take along
a small gift such as flowers or wine.

G ay and Lesbian Travellers

Germany has become very liberal
and, especially in the bigger towns,
gay clubs (some with a mixed
clientele) have really taken off. City
magazines contain a gay section with
information and listings for bars,
clubs, saunas and events.

Green Germany

Germans are indelibly green. The term
umweltfreundlich readily trips off the
tongue of every citizen and Germany
leads the way with ecological policies.
West Germans recycle 62 per cent of
their waste paper and over 70 percent
of their glass and plastic. Recycling,

refilling cartons and even taking
excess packaging back to its
originator are all second nature.

Even the heavy industry of the east,
which was responsible for serious
pollution, is now being subjected to a
wholescale clean-up, with factories
being closed down or renovated.

H ealth and Medical Care

Healthcare is very good in Germany.
The Federal Republic has a national
health system whereby doctors and
hospital fees are covered by insurance
and only a token fee has to be paid for
medication. Treatment and medication
is also free of charge for EU members
(on presentation of a European Health
Insurance Card) and certain other
nationalities. All other foreign nationals
should have adequate health
insurance before they leave their home
country as, without this, medical fees
can be very high in Germany.

People using special medication
should either bring a sufficient supply
for their holiday or a prescription from
their doctor. If you have to consult a
doctor, contact the nearest consulate
or embassy for a list of English-
speaking doctors *(see page 381)*.

No immunisation is currently
needed for entry into Germany.

Medical Treatment

European citizens who have a
European Health Insurance Card (tel:
0845 606 2030, www.dh.gov.uk, or
obtain an application form from the
post office) are entitled to medical
treatment on the same terms as the
nationals of the country in which they
are travelling. Despite the reciprocal
arrangement afforded by this system,
some form of private medical
insurance is recommended.

People from other countries or
with private insurance will receive
a bill from the doctor or hospital.
Keep this bill and then present it
to your insurance company on your
return home.

In emergencies either go straight
to the nearest hospital's casualty
unit or phone for an ambulance.
For minor ailments, GPs *(Arzt für
Allgemeinmedizin)* usually speak
English and work weekday mornings.
Pharmacies *(Apotheken)* are normally
open 8.30am–6.30pm; they all carry
a list of neighbouring pharmacies
that are open at night and over the
weekend.

I nternet

The internet has become part of
everyday life in Germany. Many
hotels offer wireless internet in the

rooms. Near large railway stations
you will normally find a web café or
internet shop (for instance, easy
Everything) quite easily. Tourist
offices will point you in the right
direction in the smaller towns.

L eft Luggage

There is no reason to hump luggage
around any of Germany's towns. All
main railway stations have banks of
left luggage lockers (the smallest of
which cost about €2 for 24 hours), or
you can leave your cases with station
attendants (about €3 per bag). Most
lockers take a variety of small
change.

M aps

Most tourist offices, bookshops and
newsagents have good local maps of
regional Germany as well as city
plans. The 1:400,000 *Grosse Shell
Atlas* is the best road atlas, with
plans of the major cities. Stanfords
in London offers a mail-order service
for maps (tel: 020-7836 1321;
www.stanfords.co.uk).

Media

Newspapers

The mass media in Germany is very
diverse. Every fair-sized town has at
least one local paper; in Berlin there
are about 10. The main newspapers
available nationwide are: the
Süddeutsche Zeitung (SZ) and
Frankfurter Rundschau (FR), both
liberal; the *Frankfurter Allgemeine
Zeitung (FAZ)* and *Die Welt*, both
conservative; and the leftish/
alternative *Tageszeitung (TAZ)*. *Bild
Zeitung* equates closely with the
British *Sun* or *Daily Mirror* and
reaches the most readers, but all the
main cities have their own tabloid-
style newspaper, such as *BZ* or
Kurier in Berlin, *Express* in Cologne
and *Abendzeitung* in Munich.

For detailed information about
current events (especially cultural),
ask for the local *Stadtmagazin*; there
are two in Berlin, *Tip* and *Zitty*. There
is a free English-language paper, *The
Exberliner*, which offers a large listing
of cultural events.

Die Zeit is a weekly newspaper with
a fairly high-brow readership. The

Lost Property

All bus and rail stations, as well
as town council premises, have
lost property offices. These can
be found in the phone directory
under *Fundbüro*.

ABOVE: the Germans love their press.

famous weekly magazine *Der Spiegel*, with its in-depth analyses, has to compete with *Focus*, also high-brow, and the easy-read *Stern* magazine.

The international press is available at good newsagents, railway stations and the airports.

Television and Radio

German TV is divided into government-controlled television *(öffentlich-rechtliches Fernsehen)* and commercial TV stations, the most popular of which are SAT 1 and RTL. The state-run national TV stations are ZDF and ARD, with the latter providing a regional service. *Landesrundfunkanstalten* provide the so-called "third" programmes as well as a couple of radio stations each. Many households and hotels receive international TV stations such as BBC, NBC and CNN via satellite or cable.

The BBC's World Service is on 90.2FM. English-language news can also be heard on some of the major local radio stations.

Commercial stations provide a regional and local service. Nearly all of them broadcast regular traffic reports. Road-side signposts (blue signs on the motorway, green signs on other roads) show the frequency of the relevant station.

Money

The euro (€) replaced the German Deutsche Mark (DM) in 2002. The euro is available in 500, 200, 100, 50, 20, 10 and 5 euro notes, and 2 euro, 1 euro, 50 cent, 20 cent, 10 cent, 5 cent, 2 cent and 1 cent coins.

Credit & Debit Cards

All major credit cards are accepted in department stores and many high-

quality shops in Germany, plus by hotels, airlines, petrol stations and the majority of restaurants.

However, there are still many occasions, especially in smaller shops and pubs, when credit cards are not accepted, so it is advisable to carry cash, just in case. Note that you cannot use travellers' cheques as payment, as they have to be cashed at a bank beforehand.

Credit and debit cards also give you access to money from cash machines *(Bankomaten)* in Germany. Remember, however, that most banks charge a commission and fee every time you use your credit card abroad; check exact details with your own bank before travelling.

Tax/VAT

VAT *(Mehrwertsteuer)* in Germany is charged at two rates: 19 percent and 7 percent. The reduced rate is applied to food, newspapers, books, theatre tickets and so on. All other goods and services, such as car rental or restaurant meals, are taxed at 19 percent VAT. This is normally included in the final price, but shown as an extra on most bills.

Non-EU residents may get the tax reimbursed provided they fill in a sales form when buying the article from specially designated "tax-free" shops. This then has to be stamped and the article shown at customs before you leave the country for you to receive your refund.

P hotography

If you run out of supplies for your camera or camcorder, you will be able to get everything you need from souvenir shops and so on. Expect to pay much higher prices than in city-centre photography shops or big department stores, though.

Postal Services

Post offices *(Postamt)* are usually open 8am–6pm (Saturday until noon), with smaller branches closing around midday for lunch. In some towns "post agencies" provide all the usual postal services, but also sell other goods.

You can have your mail sent *poste restante* (to a specific main post office), provided the letter is marked *postlagernd*. Look for the *Postlagernde Sendungen* counter.

The yellow local post boxes marked *Briefkasten* are emptied once or twice a day (afternoon/evening, Mon–Fri). Those designated with a red dot are emptied more often and on Saturday and Sunday. Letters usually take two days to the UK, 1–2

weeks to North America and over two weeks to Australia.

Most larger post offices offer fax facilities.

Private carriers such as DHL and Federal Express provide local and international express deliveries. Consult the *Yellow Pages* for the nearest depot.

R eligious Services

Religion About one-third Protestant, one-third Roman Catholic, one-third other religions or agnostic/atheist.

The times of religious services vary from church to church and from town to town. Catholic masses are normally held daily (morning and/or evening), evangelical services are only held on Sundays. Most immigrant communities have services conducted in their own language and denomination. Consult the local telephone books for further details.

S tudent/Budget Travel

As well as reduced fares on airline and train tickets, reduced entry is always available for students to museums, attractions and cultural events like the theatre. Even some of the visitor passes in the larger cities offer students rates. Normally, a valid student ID card has to be shown.

If you are travelling on a low budget, youth hostels or *Jugendhäuser* are the places to stay if you can't find an inexpensive B&B *(Pension)* or guesthouse. In university towns or the bigger cities in particular, you will find a *Mitwohnzentrale*, where you can enquire for a room in a private household. These rooms are normally let on a weekly or monthly basis. *Mitfahrzentralen* are agencies, found

Public Holidays

1 January New Year's Day
March/April Good Friday, Easter Sunday, Easter Monday (variable)
1 May Labour Day
May (Thursday): Ascension Day
May/June Whitsun (Sunday and Monday)
3 October Day of German Unity
25 December Christmas Day
26 December Boxing Day

The following are religious holidays in some areas:
6 January Epiphany
May/June Corpus Christi
15 August Ascension of the Virgin Mary
31 October Reformation Day
1 November All Saints' Day

in most towns and online, which organise inexpensive car-shares, where petrol costs are divided between all the passengers. This is a safe alternative to hitchhiking.

Telecommunications

Most public telephones now only accept telephone cards, which are sold in various denominations at post offices, newspaper stands and some other shops. There are only a few kiosks left that still take coins and most of these carry a small minimum charge.

The privatisation of Deutsche Telekom brought rapid change to the world of telecommunications. Numerous other companies are offering phone calls at cheaper rates, but their systems are not always very convenient for the irregular user. Two such companies are Mobilcom (01019) and Mannesman Arcor (01070): prefix calls you make with their five-digit numbers.

Every town has its own dialling code and these are listed under the local network heading in the telephone directory. Most telephone booths (grey and pink) are not supplied with telephone books, but main post offices usually have a complete up-to-date set for public use. Using directory enquiries can be quite expensive.

Numbers starting with 0800 are free of charge; those starting with 0180 can have quite high charges depending on the number that follows.

Tipping

Restaurant bills always include a 15 percent service charge. However, it is common to reward good service with a gratuity of around 5–10 percent. In taxis it is also usual to add a little extra as a tip.

Toilets

Signposted "Toiletten" or "WC" they are easy to find in public places, city centres and department stores. In the *Raststätten* on the motorway you may need coins to open the door or pay a warden a small fee. Sometimes you may see a small plate close to the entrance containing a few coins, silently asking for a small contribution if you were satisfied with the place.

Time Zone

Central European Time, one hour ahead of Greenwich Mean Time. Summer Time (+ 1 hour) runs from the end of March to the end of October.

Tourist Information Offices

Germany's tourist offices (*Fremdenverkehrsamt*, often shortened to *Verkehrsamt*) are usually extremely helpful, providing everything from glossy brochures to lists of local events and attractions, maps, and hotel and restaurant guides.

Most will also book a room for you, generally for a small fee but sometimes free of charge. And some offer travel tickets and act as booking agents for cultural events. Those in larger towns are open all year, but smaller offices operate limited hours off-season.

Regional Tourist Offices

There are tourist offices all over Germany (look out for the "i" symbol). Write to the office at your destination, or visit their website, for specific information (see *Local Tourist Offices*, page 385). More general information will be supplied by the regional tourist offices listed below.

Berlin
Berlin Tourismus Marketing
Am Karlsbad 11,
10785 Berlin
Tel: 030-250 025
Fax: 030-2500 2424
www.berlin-tourism.de
Bonn
Tourismus & Congress
Region Bonn/Rhein-Sieg/Ahrweiler
Adenauer Allee 131, 53113 Bonn
Tel: 0228-910 410
Fax: 0228-910 4111
www.bonn.de
Bremen
Bremer Touristik Zentrale
Findorffstrasse 105,
28215 Bremen
Tel: 01805-101 030
Fax: 0421-308 0025
www.bremen-tourism.de
Dresden
Dresden Werbung und Tourismus
Ostra-Allee 11,
01067 Dresden
Tel: 0351-4919 2100
Fax: 0351-4919 2116
Room reservations:
Tel: 0351-4919 2222
www.dresden.de

Specialist Holidays

Cycling and walking tours
● Bents, The Blue Cross, Orleton, Ludlow SY8 4HN
Tel: 01568-780800
Fax: 01568-780801
www.bentstours.com
Walking/rambling
● Ramblers Worldwide Holidays, Lemsford Mill, Lemsford Village, Welwyn Garden City AL8 7TR
Tel: 01707-331133
Fax: 01707-333276
E-mail: info@ramblersholidays.co.uk
www.ramblersholidays.co.uk
Walking/skiing
● Waymark Holidays/Exodus (joint enterprises),
Grange Mills, Weir Road,
London SW12 0NE
Tel: 0845-863 9600 (UK),
+44 (0)20-8675 5550 (international)
Fax: 020-8673 0779
www.waymarkholidays.co.uk;
www.exodus.co.uk
Language courses
● Goethe Institut, 50 Princes Gate, Exhibition Road, London SW7 2PH
Tel: 020-7596 4000
Fax: 020-7594 0240
www.goethe.de/london
US/Canada: contact regional institutes or the head office in Berlin:
Department of Communications and Marketing, Neue Schönhauser Strasse 20, 10178 Berlin
Tel: +49-30-2590 6473

Fax: +49-30-2590 6565
E-mail: hauptstadtbuero@goethe.de
www.goethe.de/hauptstadtbuero
Train tours
● Great Rail Journeys, Saviour House, 9 St Saviourgate,
York YO1 8NL
Tel: 01904-521900
Fax: 01904-521905
www.greatrail.com
Festivals/cultural events
● Prospect Cultural Tours,
79 William Street, Herne Bay,
Kent CT6 5NR
Tel: 01227-743307
Fax: 01227-743377
www.prospecttours.com
● Travel for the Arts,
12–15 Hanger Green,
London W5 3EL
Tel: 020-8799 8350
Fax: 020-8998 7965
www.travelforthearts.co.uk
River cruises
● Viking River Cruises, Nelsons House, 83 Wimbledon Park Side, London SW19 5LP
Tel: 020-8780 7900
Fax: 020-8780 7930
www.vikingrivercruises.co.uk
● Peter Deilmann,
First Floor, 19 Margaret Street,
London W1W 8RR
Tel: 020-7436 2931
Fax: 020-7436 2607
www.peter-deilmann-river-cruises.co.uk

Düsseldorf
Düsseldorf Marketing & Tourismus
Der Neue Stahlhof,
Breite Strasse 69,
40213 Düsseldorf
Tel: 0211-172 020
Fax: 0211-161 071
www.duesseldorf.de

Frankfurt
Tourismus & Congress,
Frankfurt/Main, Kaiserstrasse 56,
60329 Frankfurt/Main
Tel: 069-2123 8800
Fax: 069-2123 7880
www.frankfurt.de

Hamburg
Tourismus-Zentrale Hamburg
Steinstrasse 7,
20095 Hamburg
Tel: 040-3005 1300
Fax: 040-3005 1333
www.hamburg-tourism.de

Hanover
Hannover Tourismus
Ernst-August-Platz 8,
30159 Hannover
Tel: 0511-1234 5111
Fax: 0511-1234 5112
www.hannover.de

Heidelberg
Heidelberg Marketing
Ziegelhäuser Landstrasse 3,
69120 Heidelberg
Tel: 06221-14220
Fax: 06221-142 222
www.heidelberg-marketing.de

Cologne
Tourist Information am Hauptbahnhof
Willy-Brandt-Platz 1
Tel: 06221-19433
Fax: 06221-142 254
www.koeln.de

Leipzig
Leipzig Tourismus und Marketing
Richard-Wagner-Strasse 1,
04109 Leipzig
Tel: 0341-710 4265

BELOW: tourist information on tap.

Fax: 0341-710 4271
www.leipzig.de

Munich
Munich Tourist Office
Sendlinger Strasse 1, 80331 München
Tel: 089-2339 6500
Fax: 089-2333 0233
www.munich–tourist.de

Nuremberg
Tourist Information am Hauptmarkt
Hauptmarkt 18, 90403 Nürnberg
Tel: 0911-23360
Fax: 0911-233 6166
http://tourismus.nuernberg.de

Potsdam
PT Potsdam Tourismus
Am Neuen Markt 1, 14467 Potsdam
Tel: 0331-275 580
Fax: 0331-275 5829
www.potsdam.de

Stuttgart
Stuttgart Marketing
Königstrasse 1a, 70173 Stuttgart
Tel: 0711-22280
Fax: 0711-222 8253
www.stuttgart-tourist.de

Weimar
Tourist-Information und Kongress
Service
Markt 10, 99423 Weimar
Tel: 03643-7450
Fax: 03643-240 040
www.weimar.de

Local Tourist Offices

Every state, region and city, and most
towns, have their own very helpful
tourist information offices. Here are
some of the main ones .

Mecklenburg Lakes
● Tourismus-Marketing Brandenburg,
Am Neuen Markt 1, 14467 Potsdam.
Tel: 0331-298 730; fax: 298 7373;
www.reiseland-brandenburg.de
● Tourismusverband Uckermark,
Grabowstrasse 6, 17291 Prenzlau. Tel:
03984-835 884;
www.tourismus-uckermark.de
● Tourismusverband Ruppiner Land,
Fischbänkenstrasse 8, 16816
Neuruppin. Tel: 03391-659 630; fax:
357 907; www.ruppinerreiseland.de
● Fremdenverkehrsverband
Mecklenburgische Seenplatte,
Turnplatz 2, 17207 Röbel/Müritz.
Tel: 039931-51381; fax: 51386.

Harz to Leipzig
● Tourismus-Marketing Sachsen-
Anhalt, Am Alten Theater 6, 39104
Magdeburg. Tel: 0391-567 7080;
www.sachsen-anhalt-tourismus.de
● Saale-Unstrut-Tourismus, Lindenring
34, 06618 Naumburg/Saale. Tel:
03445-233 790;
www.saale-unstrut-tourismus.de
● Harzer Verkehrsverband,
Marktstrasse 45, 38640 Goslar.
Tel: 05321-34040; fax: 340466;
www.harzinfo.de

Tourist Office HQ

The central German Tourist Office
can be contacted at:
Deutsche Zentrale für Tourismus
e.V. (DZT)
Beethovenstrasse 69
Frankfurt am Main
Tel: 069-974 640
Fax: 069-751 903
www.germany-tourism.de

● Tourismusverband Anhalt-Wittenberg,
Albrechtstrasse 127, 06844 Dessau.
Tel: 0340-230 1218; fax: 240 0334;
www.anhalt-wittenberg.de.
● Magdeburger Tourismusverband
Elbe-Börde-Heide, Domplatz 1b, 39104
Magdeburg. Tel: 0391-738 790;
www.regionmagdeburg.de

Berlin to Dresden
● Cottbus Service, Berliner Platz 6,
03040 Cottbus. Tel: 0355-75420; fax:
743 455; www.cmt-cottbus.de
● Tourismus Spreewald, Lindenstrasse
1, 03226 Raddusch. Tel: 035433-
72299; fax: 72228.
● Fremdenverkehrsamt Märkische
Schweiz, Wriezener Strasse 1a, 15377
Buckow. Tel: 033433-57500;
www.kurstadt-buckow.de
● Tourismus Marketing Gesellschaft
Sachsen, Bautzner Strasse 45–7,
01099 Dresden. Tel: 0351-491 700;
fax: 496 9306.
● Tourismusverband Sächsisches
Elbland, Fabrikstrasse 16 , 01662
Meissen. Tel: 03521-76350; fax: 763
540; http://cms.elbland.de
● Marketing-Gesellschaft Oberlausitz-
Niederschlesien, Tourismusverband
Oberlausitz-Niederschlesien,
Tzschirnerstrasse 14a, 02625
Bautzen. Tel: 03591-4877-0; fax:
487748; www.oberlausitz.com

Dresden to Jena
● Thüringer Tourismus,
Willy-Brandt-Platz 1, 99084 Erfurt. Tel:
0361-37420; www.thueringen-tourismus.de
● Gera Tourismus, Heinrichstrasse 35,
07545 Gera. Tel: 0365-830 4480;
www.gera-tourismus.de
● Jena Tourist-Information,
Johannisstrasse 23, 07743 Jena. Tel:
03641-498 050; www.jena.de
● Kyffhäuser Fremdenverkehrs-
verband, Anger 14, 06567 Bad
Frankenhausen. Tel: 034671-71717;
fax: 7I719; www.kyffhaeuser-tourismus.de

Weimar to Wartburg
● Thüringer Tourismus Service-Center,
Weimarische Strasse 45, 99099
Erfurt. Tel: 0361-37420; fax: 374
2388.
● Thüringer Wald. www.thueringer-wald.de
www.thueringer-wald.com;

Munich environs
• Tourismusverband München-Oberbayern, Radolfzellerstrasse 15, 81243 München. Tel: 089-829 2180; fax: 8292 1828; www.oberbayern.de
• Tourismusregion Berchtesgaden-Königssee, Königsseer Strasse 2, 83471 Berchtesgaden. Tel: 08652-9670; www.berchtesgadener-land.info

Alps
• Bayern Tourismus Marketing, Leopoldstrasse 146, 80804 München. Tel: 089-212 3970; fax: 212 39799; www.bayern.by
• FVV des Berchtesgadener Landes, Kur-und Kongresshaus, 83471 Berchtesgaden. Tel: 08652-944 5340; fax: 967 381.
• Kurverwaltung Prien am Chiemsee. Tel: 08051-69050; fax: 690 540.
• Kur- und Tourismusverband Wendelstein, Wilhelm-Leibl-Platz 3, 83043 Bad Aibling. Tel: 08061-90800; fax: 375 156; www.bad-aibling.de
• Fremdenverkehrsgemeinschaft Tegernseer Tal, Hauptstrasse 2, 83684 Tegernsee. Tel: 08022-927 380; fax: 927 3822; www.tegernsee.com
• Kurverwaltung Garmisch-Partenkirchen, R-Strauss-Platz 20, 82467 Garmisch-Partenkirchen. Tel: 08821-180 700; fax: 180 755; www.garmisch-partenkirchen.de

Romantic Road
• www.romantischestrasse.de
• Allgäu Marketing, Allgäuer Strasse 1, 87435 Kempten. Tel: 08 31-5753 730; www.allgaeu.info
• Tourismusverband Allgäu/Bayerisch-Schwaben, Schiessgrabenstrasse 14, 86150 Augsburg. Tel: 0821-450 4010; fax: 4504 0120; www.bayerisch-schwaben.de
• Kultur-Fremdenverkehrsamt, Marktplatz 2, 91541 Rothenburg. Tel: 09861-40492; fax: 86807.

Würzburg and Franconia
• Tourismusverband Franken, Wilhelminen-Strasse 6, 90461 Nürnberg. Tel: 0911-941 510; fax: 941 5110U; www.frankentourismus.de
• Eastern Franconia. http://Oberes-Maintal-Coburger-Land.Bayern-online.de
• Tourist-Information Frankenwald, Adolf-Kolping-Strasse 1, 96317 Kronach. Tel: 01805-366 398; www.frankenwald-tourismus
• Tourismus-Zentrale Fränkische Schweiz, Oberes Tor 1, 91320 Ebermannstadt. Tel: 09194-797 779; fax: 797 776; www.fraenkische-schweiz.com

Eastern Bavaria
• Tourismusverband Ostbayern, Luitpoldstrasse 20, 93047 Regensburg. Tel: 0941-585 390; fax: 585 3939; www.ostbayern-tourismus.de

• Landratsamt Kelheim, Schlossweg 3, 93309 Kelheim. Tel: 09441-207 127; fax: 207 213.
• Landratsamt Regen, Poschetsrieder Strasse 16, 94209 Regen. Tel: 09921-6010; fax: 601 100.
• Verkehrsverein Landshut, Altstadt 315, Landshut. Tel: 0871-922 050; www.landshut.de

Lake Constance (Bodensee)
• Internationale Bodensee Tourismus, Hafenstrasse 6, 78462 Konstanz. Tel: 07531-90940; www.bodensee-tourismus.co

Black Forest to Stuttgart
• Tourismus Marketing Baden-Württemberg, Esslinger Strasse 8, 70182 Stuttgart. Tel: 0711-238 580; fax: 238 5899; www.tourismus-bw.de
• Regionalverband Mittlerer Oberrhein, Baumeisterstrasse 2, 76137 Karlsruhe. Tel: 0721-355 020; www.region-karlsruhe.de
• Schwarzwald Tourismus, Ludwigstrasse 23, 79104 Freiburg. Tel: 0761-296 2271; fax: 292 1581; www.schwarzwald-tourismus.info
• Regio Stuttgart Marketing und Tourismus, Lautenschlager Strasse 3, 70173 Stuttgart. Tel: 0711-222 8240; fax: 222 8253; www.stuttgart-tourist.de

Saarland
• Tourismus Zentrale Saarland, Franz-Josef-Röder-Strasse 9, 66119 Saarbrücken. Tel: 0681-927 200; fax: 927 2040; www.tourismus.saarland.de

Hessen
• Hessen Touristik Service, Abraham-Lincoln-Strasse 38–42, 65189 Wiesbaden. Tel: 0611-774 8091; fax: 774 8040; www.hessen-tourismus.de
• Bad Homburg v.d. Höhe Tourist Info & Service der Kur und Kongress, Kurhaus, Louisenstrasse 58, D-61348 Bad Homburg v.d. Höhe. Tel: 06172-178 110, fax: 178 118; www.bad-homburg.de

Rhine, Moselle and Eifel
• Ahr Rhein Eifel Tourismus & Service, Klosterstrasse 3–5, 53507 Marienthal. Tel: 06551-96560; fax: 96596; www.eifel.info
• Ahr, Rhein Eifel Tourismus, Felix-Rütten-Strasse 2, 53474 Bad Neuenahr-Ahrweiler. Tel: 02641-97730; fax: 977 373; www.wohlsein365.de
• Rheinland-Pfalz Tourismus, Löhrstrasse 103–5, 56068 Koblenz. Tel: 0261-915 200; fax: 915 2040; www.rlp-info.de
• Rhein-Mosel-Eifel-Touristik, Bahnhofstrasse 9, 56068 Koblenz. Tel: 0261-108 419; fax: 300 2797; www.remet.de

• Rheinhessen-Touristik, Wilhelm-Leuschner-Strasse 44, 55218 Ingelheim am Rhein. Tel: 06132-44170; fax: 441 744; www.rheinhessen.de
• Mosellandtouristik. Kordelweg 1, 54470 Bernkastel-Kues. Tel: 06531-97330; www.mosellandtouristik.de

Ruhr
• RTG Ruhrgebiet Tourismus, c/o Regionalverband Ruhr, Gutenbergstrasse 47, 45128 Essen. Tel: 0201-17670, 01805-181 610; www.ruhrgebiettouristik.de

Nordrhein-Westfalen
• Nordrhein-Westfalen-Tourismus, Worringer Strasse 22, 50658 Köln. Tel: 0221-179 450; fax: 179 4517; www.nrw-tourismus.de

Münsterland
• Münsterland-Touristik "Grünes Band", An der Hohen Schule 13, 48565 Steinfurt. Tel: 02551-939 291; toll free in Germany: 0800-9392 919; fax: 939 293; www.muensterland.com

Bergisches Land
• Bergisches Land Touristik, Hauptstrasse 47–51, 51465 Bergisch Gladbach. Tel: 02202-29360; fax: 293 636; www.b-l-t.de

Heidelberg and the Bergstrasse
• Arbeitsgemeinschaft Kurpfalz beim Verkehrsverein Heidelberg, Tourist-Information am Hauptbahnhof, 69115 Heidelberg. Tel: 06221-10821; fax: 167 318.
• Touristikgemeinschaft Odenwald, Scheffelstrasse 1, 74821 Mosbach. Tel: 06261-841 383; fax: 844 750

Fairytale Road to Bremen
• Tourist-Information Spessart-Mainland, Bayernstrasse 18, 63739 Aschaffenburg. Tel: 06021-394 271; fax: 394 258; www.spessart-touristinfo.de
• Deutsche Märchenstrasse, Kurfürstenstrasse 9, 34117 Kassel. Tel: 0561-9204 7910; www.deutsche-maerchenstrasse.com
• TourismusMarketing Niedersachsen, Essener Strasse 1, 30173 Hannover. Tel: 0511-270 4880; www.reiseland-niedersachsen.de.
• Wonderful Nine, die 9 Städte, Prinzenstrasse 6, 30159 Hannover. Tel: 0511-1684 9746; fax: 1684 9709; www.9staedte.de
• Fremdenverkehrsverband Marburg-Biedenkopf, Im Lichtenholz 60, 35043 Marburg. Tel: 06421-4051 345; fax: 4051 509; www.marburg-biedenkopf-tourismus.de
• Tourist-Infozentrum-Rhön, "Haus der schwarzen Berge", Oberbach, Rhönstrasse 97, 97772 Wildflecken.

Tel: 09749-91220.
• Tourismusverband Weserbergland-Mittelweser, Deisterallee 1, 31785 Hameln. Tel: 05151-93000; fax: 930 033; www.weserbergland-tourismus.de

North Sea
• Tourismus-Agentur Schleswig-Holstein, Wall 55, 24103 Kiel. Tel: 01805-600 604; www.sht.de
• Nordsee-Tourismus-Service, Singel 5, 25813 Husum. Tel: 04841-897 575; www.nordseetourismus.de

Lübeck to Flensburg
• Ostsee-Holstein-Tourismus, Strandallee 75a, 23669 Timmendorfer Strand. Tel: 01805-700 708; fax: 700 709; www.ostsee-schleswig-holstein.de

Baltic Coast
• Tourismusverband Mecklenburg-Vorpommern, Platz der Freundschaft 1, 18059 Rostock. Tel: 0381-403 0500; fax: 403 0555; www.auf-nach-mv.de
• Regionaler Fremdenverkehrsverband Vorpommern, Fischstrasse 11, 17489 Hansestadt Greifswald. Tel: 01805-891 189; fax: 891 555; www.vorpommern.de
• Tourismusverband Rügen, Bahnhofstrasse 15, 18528 Bergen. Tel: 03838-80770; fax: 254 440; www.ruegen.de
• Verband Mecklenburgische Ostseebäder, Uferstrasse 2, 19211 Nienhagen. Tel: 038203-77610; fax: 776 120; www.ostseeferien.de
• Tourismusverband Fischland Darss/Zingst, Bartherstrasse 31, 18314 Löbnitz. Tel: 038324-6400; fax: 64034; www.fischland-darss-zingst.de
• Tourismusverband Insel Usedom, Bäderstrasse 5, 17459 Ückeritz. Tel: 038375-23410; fax: 22152; www.insel-usedom.net

Tour Operators

As well as fly-drive packages and short city breaks, travel agents offer numerous "tailormade" holidays in Germany. These include all-inclusive Oktoberfest and "Rhine in Flames" trips, battlefield tours, farmhouse self-catering, wine festival breaks and holidays taking in some of Germany's major sporting or cultural events.
Specialists include:
German Travel Centre Ltd
85 Bridge Street, Pinner HA5 3HZ. Tel: 020-8429 2900; fax: 020-8429 4896; www.german-travel-uk.com
Moswin's Germany
The Birds Building, Fleckney Road, Kibworth Beauchamp, Leicester LE8 0HJ. Tel: 0844-4488 999; fax: 0844-4488 990

Useful Addresses/Websites

Your home country's embassy is one address which you should have to hand in case of emergency. Apart from the embassies listed in this guide *(see page 382)*, you will find a complete list of embassies and consulates on the website of the German Ministry of Foreign Affairs: www.auswaertiges-amt.de.
Local tourist offices will help with room bookings, but the Hotelreservierungs-Service (tel: 0221-2077600; www.hrs.de) will also come in handy if you are after low room rates. To locate top restaurants before you travel, it is certainly worth browsing

Tourist Offices Abroad

German National Tourist Offices are in the following cities:
• **Chicago**
PO Box 59594, Chicago IL, 60659-9594, USA
Tel: 773-539-6303
Fax: 773-539-6378
E-mail: info@gntoch.com
www.cometogermany.com
• **Hong Kong**
3601 Tower One, Lippo Centre, 89 Queensway, Hong Kong
Tel: 852-2526 5481
Fax: 852-2810 6093
E-mail: info@ahk.org.hk
• **London**
PO Box 2695,
London W1A 3TN, UK
Tel: 020-7317 0908
Fax: 020-7495 6129
E-mail: gntolon@d-z-t.com
• **Los Angeles**
1334 Parkview Ave, Suite 300,
Manhattan Beach, CA 90266, USA
Tel: 310-545-1350
Fax: 310-545-1371
E-mail: info@gntolax.com
• **New York**
122 East 42nd St, 52nd Floor,
New York, NY 10168-0072, USA
Tel: 212-6617200
Fax: 212-6617174
E-mail: GermanyInfo@d-z-t.com
• **Toronto**
480 University Ave, Suite 1500,
Toronto, Ontario M5G 1V2, Canada
Tel: 416 968-1685
Fax: 416-968-0562
E-mail: info@gnto.ca
• **Sydney**
c/o German-Australian Chamber of Industry and Commerce,
PO Box 1461, Sydney NSW 2001 Australia
Tel: 00612-8296 0488
Fax: 00612-8296 0487

Weights and Measures

Germany has a metric system:
1 kg = 2 lbs 7 oz
1 km = 0.6 miles

through the German web pages of Gault Millau: www.gaultmillau.de.
For collective information on all national parks, check with EUROPARC Deutschland (Friedrichstrasse 60, 10117 Berlin, tel: 030-2887 8820, fax: 030-2887 88216; www.europarc.org and www.europarc-deutschland.de).
The UNESCO world heritage sites and biosphere reserves are featured on the website of the German UNESCO commission (www.unesco.de) in Bonn.

What to Wear

German weather can be unpredictable. Even if you choose the hottest months (July and August) for your visit you may well encounter cool and rainy days. So bring along clothes for all weathers, such as a waterproof, umbrella, warm sweater and, of course, something light for when the sun shines.
Casual clothes will be suitable for many occasions. For chic restaurants, theatres and concert halls there is not really a dress code, but people tend to dress more smartly than the ultra-casual wear of every day. Unless you are combining business with pleasure, there is no need to pack a suit and tie.
You will need good walking shoes for city sightseeing and if you intend to go walking or hiking in areas such as the Harz, the Black Forest, etc. You will almost certainly need a raincoat and sturdy shoes if you are spending time by the North Sea and the Baltic.

Women Travellers

In Germany, women are socially well respected, equal to men in the world of business and, in general terms, can travel safely. For safety and comfort, women-only parking zones exist in the multi-storey car parks at airports or in the major cities, mostly located close to the exit – the only shame being that they are not really signposted.
It is still usual for men to hold open a door for a woman, but far rarer to offer help with heavy luggage.
If a woman is good-looking or well dressed this will turn heads like anywhere else in the world, but not to the same extent as in Mediterranean countries. Younger men might freely comment upon the looks of a girl or woman and start to flirt, especially at festivals or in pubs and clubs. Some clubs have ladies' nights when women don't pay the entrance fee.

TRANSPORT

ACCOMMODATION

EATING OUT

ACTIVITIES

A – Z

LANGUAGE

LANGUAGE

UNDERSTANDING THE LANGUAGE

German is the native language of about 100 million people, but not all of them live in continental Europe. As well as Germany, Austria, parts of Switzerland, Belgium and some small German enclaves in eastern Europe, there are also German-speaking communities in North America, South America and South Africa.

In terms of language groups, German and English are both part of the West Germanic languages, together with Dutch, Frisian, Flemish and Afrikaans, but while a Dutchman and a German may be able to communicate quite effectively, an Englishman and a German are unlikely to make much progress, despite the many similarities between the two languages. A quick glance at the numbers from one to ten *(see page 393)* will prove that point immediately.

Anyone who learnt Latin at school will be familiar with some of the difficulties that the German language presents to foreigners: nouns have three genders and four cases, verbs are conjugated, pronouns are followed by one of three cases, the word order in sentences is governed by some complicated rules and there are five different ways that you can say "the". The only compensation is that pronunciation is always perfectly consistent with the spelling.

Although many young people speak English throughout Germany and are always keen to try it out on visitors, there are many parts of the country, particularly in the east, where a smattering of German will prove very helpful.

Pronunciation

Most consonants are pronounced as in English with the following exceptions: **g** is always sounded like the g in get; **ch** as in the German composer Bach; **j** is like the y in yes; **k** is pronounced even before an n; **v** is like f; **w** is like the English v; and **z** is pronounced as ts. The *scharfes S* or ß has the same sound as double s, as in sassy.

Vowels and vowels with umlauts (¨) are not so straightforward:
a   as in bad
e   as in hay

i   as in seek
o   as in not
u   as in boot
ä   is a combination of "a" and "e" and pronounced like the "e" in get
ö   combines "o" and "e" like the "er" in Bert
ü   combine "u" and "e" as in mute

Plus there are dipthong sounds:
ai as in tie
au as in sour
ie as in thief
ei as in wine
eu as in boil

The Alphabet

Learning the pronunciation of the German alphabet is a good idea. You will find it helpful to be able to spell your name.
a = ah
b = bay
c = tsay
d = day
e = eh
f = eff
g = gay
h = har
i = ee
j = yot
k = kar
l = ell
m = emm
n = enn
o = oh
p = pay
q = koo
r = air
s = ess
t = tay
u = oo
v = fow
w = vay
x = icks
y = upsilon
z = tset

New Spelling Rules

After years of international negotiations, agreement was reached in 1998 on a series of new spelling rules or *Die Neue Rechtschreibung*. One aim of the new regulations was to make German pronunciation even more consistent with spelling, so, for example, *schneuzen* (to blow your nose) is now spelt *schnäuzen*. Changes have been made to the use of the ß symbol and, when two words such as *Schiff* and *Fahrt* are combined, all three "f"s are written, ie *Schifffahrt*, instead of *Schiffahrt*.

Some standardisation was introduced into the spelling of *Fremdwörter* or loan words, eg, the plural of *Baby* is *Babys* not *Babies*, *Mayonäse* replaces *Mayonnaise* and *Photo* is *Foto*.

Other changes included the deletion of the space between certain word pairs, the use of the upper case with adjectival nouns, and guidance with regard to commas and hyphenation.

WORDS & PHRASES

General

Good morning *Guten Morgen*
Good afternoon *Guten Tag*
Good evening *Guten Abend*
Good night *Gute Nacht*
Goodbye *Auf Wiedersehen*
Goodbye *Tschüs* (informal)
Do you speak English? *Sprechen Sie Englisch?*
I do not understand *Ich verstehe nicht*
Could you please speak more slowly? *Könnten Sie bitte etwas langsamer sprechen?*
Can you help me? *Können Sie mir helfen?*
Yes/No *Ja/Nein*
Please/Thank you *Bitte/Danke*
Sorry *Entschuldigung*
How are you? *Wie geht's?*
Excuse me *Entschuldigen Sie, bitte*
You're welcome *Bitte schön*
It doesn't matter *(Es) macht nichts*
OK *Alles klar*
Pity *Schade*
Thank you for your help *Besten Dank für Ihre Hilfe*
See you later *Bis später*
See you tomorrow *Bis morgen*
What time is it? *Wie spät ist es?*
10 o'clock *zehn Uhr*
Half past ten *halb elf*
This morning *heute morgen*
This afternoon *heute nachmittag*
This evening *heute abend*
Let's go! *Los!*
Leave me alone *Lass mich in Ruhe*
Clear off *Hau ab*
Where are the toilets? *Wo sind die Toiletten?*
large/small *gross/klein*
more/less *mehr/weniger*
now *jetzt*
later *später*
here *hier*
there *dort*

On Arrival

Station *Bahnhof*
Bus station *Busbahnhof*
Bus stop *Bushaltestelle*
Will you tell me when to get off the bus? *Können Sie mir sagen, wann ich aussteigen muss?*
Where can I get the bus to the Adler Hotel? *Wo kann ich den Bus zum Hotel Adler nehmen?*
Does this bus go to the town centre? *Fährt dieser Bus zur Stadtmitte?*
Which street is this? *Welche Strasse ist das?*
How far is the station? *Wie weit ist es zum Bahnhof?*
Do you have a single room? *Haben Sie ein Einzelzimmer?*

Do you have a double room? *Haben Sie ein Doppelzimmer?*
Do you have a room with a private bath? *Haben Sie ein Zimmer mit Bad?*
How much is it? *Wieviel kostet das?*
How much is a room with full board? *Wieviel kostet ein Zimmer mit Vollpension?*
Please show me another room *Bitte zeigen Sie mir ein anderes Zimmer*
We'll (I'll) be staying one night *Wir bleiben (Ich bleibe) eine Nacht*
When is breakfast? *Wann gibt es Frühstück?*
Where is the toilet? *Wo ist die Toilette?*
Where is the bathroom? *Wo ist das Badezimmer?*
Where is the nearest hotel? *Wo ist das nächste Hotel?*

Travelling

Where is the post office? *Wo ist das Postamt?*
Where is the nearest bank? *Wo ist die nächste Bank?*
Where can I change money? *Wo kann ich Geld wechseln?*
Where is the pharmacy? *Wo ist die Apotheke?*
What time do they close? *Wann schliessen sie?*
near/far *nah/weit*
cheap/expensive *billig/teuer*
free (of charge) *kostenlos*
price *Preis*
change *Wechselgeld*
Have you got any change? *Können Sie (mir) das wechseln?*
telephone booth *Telefonzelle*
Is this the way to the station? *Ist das der Weg zum Bahnhof?*
Where is platform one? *Wo ist Gleis eins?*
Where is the airport? *Wo ist der Flughafen?*
Can you call me a taxi? *Können Sie mir ein Taxi rufen?*
Can you take me to the airport? *Können Sie mich zum Flughafen fahren?*
Where do I get a ticket? *Wo kann ich eine Fahrkarte kaufen?*
departure/arrival *Abfahrt/Ankunft*
When is the next flight/train to…? *Wann geht der nächste Flug/Zug nach…?*
to change (flights/trains) *umsteigen*
customs *Zoll*

How to Say "You"

In most cases we have given the polite form for "you", *Sie*. The familiar form, *du*, can sometimes be used if talking to a younger person, but is normally reserved for friends and family.

Have you anything to declare? *Haben Sie etwas zu verzollen?*
entrance *Eingang/Einfahrt*
exit *Ausgang/Ausfahrt*
fee *Gebühr*
height/width/length *Höhe/Breite/Länge*
hospital *Krankenhaus*
picnic area *Rastplatz*
travel agency *Reisebüro*

Shopping

I'd like… *Ich hätte gern…*
How much is this? *Was kostet das?*
Do you take credit cards? *Akzeptieren Sie Kreditkarten?*
I'm just looking *Ich sehe mich nur um*
Do you have…? *Haben Sie…?*
That'll be fine. I'll take it. *In Ordnung. Ich nehme es.*
No, that is too expensive *Nein, das ist zu teuer*
Can I try it on? *Kann ich es anprobieren?*
Do you have anything cheaper? *Haben Sie etwas Billigeres?*
open/closed *geöffnet/geschlossen*

Sightseeing

Where is the tourist office? *Wo ist das Fremdenverkehrsbüro?*
Is there a bus to the centre? *Gibt es einen Bus ins Stadtzentrum?*
Is there a guided sightseeing tour? *Werden geführte Besichtigungstouren durchgeführt?*
When is the museum open? *Wann ist das Museum geöffnet?*
How much does it cost to go in? *Was kostet der Eintritt?*
art gallery *Kunstgalerie*
castle *Schloss*
cathedral *Dom*
church *Kirche*
exhibition *Ausstellung*
memorial *Denkmal*
old part of town *Altstadtviertel*
tower *Turm*
town hall *Rathaus*
open daily *täglich*
swimming pool *Hallenbad* (indoor), *Freibad* (open-air)

Dining Out

A table for one/two/three *Einen Tisch für eine Person/zwei/drei Personen, bitte*
Could we order a meal, please? *Können wir bitte bestellen?*
Can we have the bill, please? *Können wir bitte bezahlen?*
apple juice *Apfelsaft*
beer, wine *Bier/Wein*
bread *Brot*
bread roll *Brötchen*
butter *Butter*
cake *Kuchen*

children's portion *Kinderteller*
coffee *Kaffee*
complain *sich beschweren*
decaffeinated coffee *Haag/*
koffeinfrei
dessert *Nachspeise*
draught [beer] *vom Fass*
dry/sweet *trocken/süss*
egg *Ei*
evening meal *Abendessen*
(hot) chocolate *(heisse) Schokolade*
jam *Konfitüre*
knife/fork/spoon
Messer/Gabel/Löffel
lemonade *Limonade*
lunch *Mittagessen*
main course *Hauptgericht*
menu *Speisekarte*
milk *Milch*
mineral water *Mineralwasser*
mulled wine *Glühwein*
mustard *Senf*
orange juice *Orangensaft*
pay *bezahlen*
potatoes *Kartoffeln*
rice *Reis*
salt/pepper *Salz/Pfeffer*
shandy *ein Radler (Southern*
Germany), Alsterwasser (Hamburg)
snack *Imbiss*
soup/starter *Suppe/Vorspeise*
still/fizzy *ohne/mit Kohlensäure*
sugar *Zucker*
sweet/dry *süss/trocken*
tea *Tee*
tip *Trinkgeld*
tomato sauce *Ketchup*
waiter/waitress *Herr Ober/Fräulein*
wine list *Weinkarte*

Table Talk

I am a vegetarian *Ich bin*
Vegetarier(in)
I am on a special diet *Ich halte Diät*
What do you recommend? *Was*
würden Sie empfehlen?
I am ready to order *Ich möchte*
bestellen
Enjoy your meal *Guten Appetit*
What would you like to drink? *Was*
möchten Sie trinken?
Did you enjoy your meal? *Hat es*
Ihnen geschmeckt?
Cheers *Prost*

Suppen/Soups

Erbsensuppe pea soup
Flädlesuppe consommé **with strips of**
pancake
Gemüsesuppe vegetable soup
Griessnockerlsuppe semolina
dumpling soup
Hühnersuppe chicken soup
Kartoffelsuppe potato soup
Leberknödelsuppe liver dumpling
soup

Vorspeisen/Starters

Austern oysters
Froschschenkel frogs' legs

Gänseleberpastete **foie gras**
Geeiste Melone **iced melon**
Rollmops **rollmop herrings**
Schnecken **snails**
Spargelspitzen **asparagus tips**
Strammer Max **ham and fried egg on**
bread
Wurstplatte **assorted cooked meats**

Fleischgerichte/Meat Courses

Backhuhn **roast chicken**
Blutwurst **black pudding**
Bockwurst **large frankfurter**
Bouletten **meatballs**
Brathuhn **roast chicken**
Bratwurst **fried sausage**
Currywurst **pork sausage with curry**
powder
Deutsches Beefsteak **minced**
beef/hamburger
Eisbein **knuckle of pork**
Ente **duck**
Fasan **pheasant**
Fleischklösschen **meatballs**
Frikadelle **rissole**
Gans **goose**
Gulasch **goulash**
Hackbraten **meatloaf**
Hähnchen/Huhn **chicken**
Hammelbraten **roast mutton**
Hase **hare**
Herzragout **heart stew**
Hühnerfrikassee **chicken fricassee**
Kalbsbries veal **sweetbreads**
Kalbsbrust **breast of veal**
Kalbshaxe **roast knuckle of veal**
Kalbskoteletts **veal cutlets/chops**
Kaninchen **rabbit**
Kasseler Rippchen **smoked pork chop**
Lamm am Spiess **lamb on the spit**
Lammbraten **roast lamb**
Lammkeule **roast leg of lamb**
Leberkäse **processed meat (Bavaria)**
Leberknödel **liver dumplings**
Leberwurst **liver sausage**
Nieren **kidneys**
Ochsenschwanz **oxtail**
Pichelsteinertopf **vegetable stew with**
beef
Pute **turkey**
Rheinischer Sauerbraten **braised beef**
Rind **beef**
Rinderbraten **roast beef**
Rinderfilet **fillet of beef**
Sauerbraten **braised pickled beef**
Schinken **ham**
Schlachtplatte **mixed cold meat**
Schweinebauch **belly of pork**
Schweinebraten **roast pork**
Schweinefilet **loin of pork**
Schweinefleisch **pork**
Serbisches Reisfleisch **diced pork,**
onions, tomatoes and rice
Speck **bacon**
Sülze **brawn**
Wiener Schnitzel **breaded escalope of**
veal
Zigeunerschnitzel **veal with peppers**
and relish
Zunge **tongue**

Fisch/Fish

Aal **eel**
Austern **oysters**
Barbe **mullet**
Bismarckhering **filleted pickled**
herring
Fischfrikadellen **fishcakes**
Flusskrebs **crayfish**
Forelle **trout**
Garnelen **prawns**
Heilbutt **halibut**
Hummer **lobster**
Jakobsmuscheln **scallops**
Kabeljau **cod**
Krabbe **shrimps**
Lachs **salmon**
Makrele **mackerel**
Matjes **young herring**
Muscheln **mussels**
Rotbarsch **red sea bass**
Sardinen **sardines**
Schellfisch **haddock**
Scholle **plaice**
Schwertfisch **swordfish**
Seebarsch **sea bass**
Seezunge **sole**
Steinbutt **turbot**
Thunfisch **tuna**
Tintenfisch **squid**
Zander **pike-perch, zander**

Knödel/Dumplings and Noodles

Leberknödel **liver dumplings**
Kartoffelklösse **potato dumplings**
Klösse **dumplings**
Maultasche **Swabian ravioli**
Nudeln **noodles**
Spätzle **grated pasta**

Eier/Eggs

Bauernomelett **omelette with diced**
bacon and onion
gekochtes Ei **boiled egg**
hartgekochtes Ei **hard-boiled egg**
Rührei **scrambled eggs**
Russische Eier **hard-boiled eggs with**
caviar, capers and mayonnaise
Spiegeleier **fried eggs**
verlorene Eier **poached eggs**

Zubereitung/Preparation

am Spiess **on the spit**
blau **blue (boiled in salt and vinegar)**
gekocht **boiled**
durchgebraten **well-done**
eingelegt **pickled**
flambiert **flambéed**
fritiert **deep-fried**
gebacken **baked**
gebeizt **marinated**
gebraten **fried**
gedämpft/gedünstet **steamed**
gefüllt **stuffed**
gepökelt **salted**
geräuchert **smoked**
geschmort **braised**
Geschnetzeltes **strips of meat in a**
sauce
gratiniert **au gratin**
halbdurch **medium**

Hausgemacht **home-made**
mariniert **marinated**
nach Hausfrauenart **home-made**
nach Jägerart **sautéed with mushrooms**
paniert **breaded**
pikant **spicy**
pochiert **poached**
roh **raw**
rosa **rare to medium**
rot **rare**
süss-sauer **sweet and sour**
überbacken **au gratin**
vom Grill **grilled**

Gemüse/Vegetables

Blumenkohl **cauliflower**
Bohnen **beans**
Brunnenkresse **watercress**
Bratkartoffeln **fried potatoes**
Champignons **mushrooms**
Dicke Bohnen **broad beans**
Erbsen **peas**
Feldsalat **lamb's lettuce**
Fenchel **fennel**
Grüne Bohnen **green beans**
Gurke **cucumber**
Karotten **carrots**
Kartoffeln **potatoes**
Kartoffelpuree **creamed potatoes**
Kartoffelsalat **potato salad**
Knoblauch **garlic**
Kohl **cabbage**
Kopfsalat **lettuce**
Lauch **leek**
Linsen **lentils**
Pellkartoffeln **jacket potatoes**
Maiskolben **sweetcorn**
Meerrettich **horseradish**
Paprika **peppers**
Pommes (frites) **chips/French fries**
Prinzessbohnen **French beans**
Reis **rice**
Rettich **radish**
Risi-Pisi **rice and peas**
Rosenkohl **Brussel sprouts**
Rote Beete **beetroot**
Rotkraut/Rotkohl **red cabbage**
Salat **salad**
Salzkartoffeln **boiled potatoes**
Sauerkraut **pickled cabbage**
Sellerie **celery**
Spargel **asparagus**
Spinat **spinach**
Tomaten **tomatoes**
Weisskohl **cabbage**
Zwiebeln **onions**

Nachspeisen/Desserts

Apfelkuchen **apple cake**
Apfelstrudel **flaky pastry stuffed with apple**
Eis **ice-cream**
Eisbecher **ice-cream with fresh fruit**
Fruchttörtchen **fruit tartlet**
Gebäck **pastries**
Kaiserschmarrn **sugared pancake with raisins**
Käsetorte **cheesecake**
Kompott **stewed fruit**

Krapfen **doughnuts**
Mohnkuchen **poppyseed cake**
Obstkuchen **fruit tart**
Rote Grütze **raspberries or redcurrants cooked with semolina**
Sacher Torte **chocolate cake with jam and chocolate icing**
Schlagsahne **whipped cream**
Schwarzwälder Kirschtorte **Black Forest gâteau**

Früchte/Obst Fruit

Apfel **apple**
Apfelsine **orange**
Aprikose **apricot**
Backpflaumen **prunes**
Banane **bananas**
Birne **pears**
Blaubeere **bilberries/blueberries**
Brombeere **blackberries**
Datteln **dates**
Erdbeere **strawberries**
Himbeere **raspberries**
Kirsche **cherries**
Kiwi **kiwi**
Melone **melon**
Pampelmuse **grapefruit**
Pfirsich **peach**
Pflaumen **plums**
Preiselbeere **cranberries**
Reineclauden **greengages**
Rosine **raisins**
Rote Johannisbeere **redcurrants**
Schwarze Johannisbeere **blackcurrants**
Stachelbeere **gooseberries**
Weintraube **grapes**
Zitrone **lemon**
Zwetschen **plums**

Numbers

0	*null*	80	*achtzig*
1	*eins*	90	*neunzig*
2	*zwei*	100	*hundert*
3	*drei*	200	*zweihundert*
4	*vier*	1,000	*tausend*
5	*fünf*	2,000	*zweitausend*
6	*sechs*	1,000,000	*eine Million*
7	*sieben*		
8	*acht*	1st	*erste(r)*
9	*neun*	2nd	*zweite(r)*
10	*zehn*	3rd	*dritte(r)*
11	*elf*	4th	*vierte(r)*
12	*zwölf*	5th	*fünfte(r)*
13	*dreizehn*	6th	*sechste(r)*
14	*vierzehn*	7th	*siebte(r)*
15	*fünfzehn*	8th	*achte(r)*
16	*sechzehn*	9th	*neunte(r)*
17	*siebzehn*	10th	*zehnte(r)*
18	*achtzehn*	11th	*elfte(r)*
19	*neunzehn*	12th	*zwölfte(r)*
20	*zwanzig*	13th	*dreizehnte(r)*
30	*dreissig*	20th	*zwanzigste(r)*
40	*vierzig*	21st	*einund zwanzigste(r)*
50	*fünfzig*		
60	*sechzig*	100th	*hundertste(r)*
70	*siebzig*	1,000th	*tausendste(r)*

Emergencies

Help *Hilfe!*
Stop *Halt!*
Please call a doctor *Holen Sie einen Arzt*
Please call an ambulance *Rufen Sie einen Krankenwagen*
Please call the fire-brigade *Rufen Sie die Feuerwehr*
Where is the nearest telephone box? *Wo ist die nächste Telefonzelle?*
I am ill *Ich bin krank*
I have lost my wallet/handbag *Ich habe meine Geldtasche/Handtasche verloren*
Where is the nearest hospital? *Wo ist das nächste Krankenhaus?*
Where is the police station? *Wo ist die Polizeiwache?*
Where is the British consulate? *Wo ist das britische Konsulat?*

Days of the Week/Seasons

Monday *Montag*
Tuesday *Dienstag*
Wednesday *Mittwoch*
Thursday *Donnerstag*
Friday *Freitag*
Saturday *Samstag/Sonnabend*
Sunday *Sonntag*
yesterday *gestern*
today/tomorrow *heute/morgen*
last week *letzte Woche*
next week *nächste Woche*
spring *Frühling*
summer *Sommer*
autumn *Herbst*
winter *Winter*

TRANSPORT
ACCOMMODATION
EATING OUT
ACTIVITIES
A – Z
LANGUAGE

FURTHER READING

History and Society

Berlin Interiors by Ingeborg Wiensowski and Angelika Taschen (eds.); Benedikt Taschen Verlag, 2002
Berlin, The Downfall 1945 by Antony Beever; Viking 2002
Bug: The Strange Mutations of the World's Most Famous Automobile by Phil Patton; Simon & Schuster, 2002
A Concise History of Germany by Mary Fulbrook; Cambridge University Press, 2004
A History of Germany 1780–1918: The Long Nineteenth Century by David Blackbourn; Blackwell, 2002
Hitler 1889–1936: Hubris by Ian Kershaw; Penguin, 2001
Living and Working in Germany by Nick Daws; Survival books, 2008
Michael Schumacher: The Ferrari Years by Christopher Hilton; Haynes, 2001
Through Hell for Hitler: A First-hand Account of Fighting on the Eastern Front in World War II by Henry Metelmann; Casemate, 2003
The Wall: The People's Story by Christopher Hilton; Sutton, 2002
The Unification of Germany 1815–1919 by Alan Farmer and Andrina Stiles; Hodder Murray 2007

People and Culture

To understand the German mentality, read any of the classical works by Goethe and Schiller, Heine and Hölderlin, to name but a few. Below is a selection of highly regarded German and English/ American authors:
The Blue Flower by Penelope Fitzgerald
Buddenbrooks by Thomas Mann
Headbirths; The Germans Are Dying Out; The Tin Drum and **The Flounder** by Günter Grass
Germany by Madame de Stael
In A German Pension by Katherine Mansfield
A Tramp Abroad by Mark Twain
The Riddle of the Sands by Erskine Childers
Three Men on a Bummel by Jerome K Jerome

Other Insight Guides

With hundreds of titles in a choice of different formats, *Insight Guides* remain the largest range of visual travel guides on the market.

Insight Smart Guides

Insight Smart Guides packs information into an easily portable and convenient format. Arranged in handy A–Z sections backed up by great photography and full mapping.

Insight FlexiMaps

An instant hit with travellers, *Insight FlexiMaps* have clear cartography complemented by recommendations and photography. These durable maps are laminated so that you can write on them and wipe it off later.

Insight Guides

Famous for their stunning photography, *Insight Guides* are a great appetite-whetter, a practical on-the-spot companion and a superb souvenir.

Send Us Your Thoughts

We do our best to ensure the information in our books is as accurate and up-to-date as possible. The books are updated on a regular basis using local contacts, who painstakingly add, amend and correct as required. However, some details (such as telephone numbers and opening times) are liable to change, and we are ultimately reliant on our readers to put us in the picture.

We welcome your feedback, especially your experience of using the book "on the road". Maybe we recommended a hotel that you liked (or another that you didn't), or you came across a great bar or new attraction we missed.

We will acknowledge all contributions, and we'll offer an Insight Guide to the best letters received.

Please write to us at:
Insight Guides
PO Box 7910
London SE1 1WE
Or email us at:
insight@apaguide.co.uk

ART & PHOTO CREDITS

INDEX

Numbers in italics refer to photographs

A
B
C
D
E
F
G
H
J
a
b
c
d
e
f
g
h
i
k
l

S U Netz B

S
S1	Wannsee ↔ Oranienburg
S2	Blankenfelde ↔ Bernau
S25	Teltow Stadt ↔ Hennigsdorf
S3	Erkner ↔ Ostbahnhof
S3	Erkner ↔ Ostkreuz
S41	Ring ↻ im Uhrzeigersinn
S42	Ring ↺ gegen Uhrzeigersinn
S45	Flughafen Berlin-Schönefeld ↔ Hermannstraße (nur Mo-Fr)
S46	Königs Wusterhausen ↔ Westend
S46	Königs Wusterhausen ↔ Südkreuz
S47	Spindlersfeld ↔ Südkreuz
S47	Spindlersfeld ↔ Bundesplatz (nur Mo-Fr)
	Spindlersfeld ↔ Schöneweide
S5	Strausberg Nord ↔ Westkreuz
S7	Strausberg Nord ↔ Potsdam Hbf
S75	Ahrensfelde ↔ Potsdam Hbf
S8	Ahrensfelde ↔ Lichtenberg
	Wartenberg ↔ Spandau
	(Zeuthen ↔) Grünau ↔ Hohen Neuendorf
	Grünau ↔ Pankow (↔ Hohen Neuendorf)
	(Grünau ↔) Schöneweide ↔ Waidmannslust
S9	Flughafen Berlin-Schönefeld ↔ Spandau
	Flughafen Berlin-Schönefeld ↔ Warschauer Straße

U
U1	Warschauer Straße ↔ Uhlandstraße
U2	Pankow ↔ Ruhleben
U3	Nollendorfplatz ↔ Krumme Lanke
U4	Nollendorfplatz ↔ Innsbrucker Platz
U5	Hönow ↔ Alexanderplatz
U6	Alt-Tegel ↔ Alt-Mariendorf
U7	Rathaus Spandau ↔ Rudow
U8	Wittenau ↔ Hermannstraße
U9	Osloer Straße ↔ Rathaus Steglitz

☾ **U-Bahn-Nachtverkehr**
nur Fr/Sa ca. 0.30–5.00 Uhr
Sa/So und vor Feiertagen
ca. 0.30–6.30 Uhr

S2 **S-Bahn-Nachtverkehr**
nur Fr/Sa ca. 0.30–5.00 Uhr
Sa/So und vor Feiertagen
ca. 0.30–6.30 Uhr